AS TIME GOES BY

As Time Goes By

*From the Industrial Revolutions to the
Information Revolution*

CHRIS FREEMAN AND FRANCISCO LOUÇÃ

OXFORD

UNIVERSITY PRESS

OXFORD
UNIVERSITY PRESS

Great Clarendon Street, Oxford OX2 6DP

Oxford University Press is a department of the University of Oxford.
It furthers the University's objective of excellence in research, scholarship,
and education by publishing worldwide in

Oxford New York

Auckland Bangkok Buenos Aires Cape Town Chennai
Dar es Salaam Delhi Hong Kong Istanbul Karachi Kolkata
Kuala Lumpur Madrid Melbourne Mexico City Mumbai Nairobi
São Paulo Shanghai Taipei Tokyo Toronto

Oxford is a registered trade mark of Oxford University Press
in the UK and in certain other countries

Published in the United States
by Oxford University Press Inc., New York

© C. Freeman and F. Louçã 2001

British Library Cataloguing in Publication Data

Data available

Library of Congress Cataloging in Publication Data

Freeman, Christopher
As times goes by: the information revolution and the industrial revolutions in
historical perspective / Chris Freeman and Francisco Louçã.
p. cm.
Includes bibliographical references and index.
1. Long waves (Economics)—History. 2. Information technology—History.
3. Industrial revolution. I. Louçã, Francisco. II. Title.
HB3729 .F38 2001 338.5'4—dc21 00-049109

ISBN 0-19-924107-4 (hbk)
ISBN 0-19-925105-3 (pbk)

3 5 7 9 10 8 6 4

Typeset by J&L Composition Ltd, Filey, North Yorkshire
Printed in Great Britain
on acid-free paper by
Biddles Ltd, King's Lynn, Norfolk

FOREWORD

Virtually all economic historians are in agreement that the sustained growth of per worker productivity and per capita incomes that has brought a good portion of the world to high living standards is a relatively recent phenomenon. Economic growth in this sense emerged first in the United Kingdom in the last part of the eighteenth century, and then spread to continental Western Europe and the United States, and to other overseas offspring economies of Western European civilization, then to Japan toward the end of the nineteenth century, and still later more broadly. Economic growth, however, has been highly uneven across nations. The disparities in living standards today are particularly dramatic, but they were clearly evident even in the early days of modern economic growth. Quite naturally, understanding economic growth, and cross-national differences, was of central interest to the economic scholars of that era, from Adam Smith to Thomas Malthus, to Friedrich List and Karl Marx.

All of these economists had a broad and deep empirical knowledge of the actual processes and institutions involved in economic growth. Their theoretical explanations of growth reflected their understandings of the complex phenomena involved. And in their analyses, the economic growth of a nation was integrally connected with the economic, social, and political institutions of the nation more generally.

Towards the end of the nineteenth century, economic growth moved from the centre to the periphery of the writings of mainstream economic analysts. While economists like Joseph Schumpeter had a central interest in economic growth, the core interests of most economists of that generation were elsewhere. Understanding the prevailing structure of prices and outputs within a context of general equilibrium theory came to define the agenda of what later came to be called microeconomic analysis. Understanding fluctuations in overall price levels and business cycles more generally came to define what came to be called macroeconomics. Both bodies of theorizing repressed or ignored phenomena associated with long-run economic growth. When in the 1950s economic growth returned as a focal topic, there were three striking differences from the older body of research and theorizing. First, there were many more, and much better, bodies of quantitative data that could be used to study growth. The new gross national product (GNP) statistics were especially important in the new research; indeed, economic growth came virtually to be defined in terms of growth of GNP, or GNP per worker or per person in the population. Second, the new growth theory was lean and abstract, much more so than the growth theories articulated by the great nineteenth-century economists. Third, while there are some exceptions to this proposition, the new study of economic growth and the forces driving it tended to define a body of theorizing and empirical research that was somewhat separate from the work of economists studying economic structures and processes more generally.

The early body of empirical and theoretical research within this new paradigm was virtually unanimous in highlighting the importance of technological advance as a factor in economic growth. Older scholars of economic growth, such as Adam Smith and Karl Marx, would not have been surprised. This theme of course was central in Schumpeter's work. But the new research appeared to place this old conception on a much more solid and rigorous empirical and theoretical basis. One consequence was the birth and flowering of a number of bodies of research by economists that focused explicitly on trying to understand technological advance, and the economic growth processes fuelled by technological advance. As a young scholar participating in this research endeavour, it soon became evident to me that a divide was forming.

The well travelled path was beaten out by economists who had a commitment to characterize economic growth strictly in terms of a set of numbers measuring outputs, inputs, and their changes over time, and who generally also embraced the theoretical orientation of the new neoclassical growth theory, which was very parsimonious regarding the institutions considered as important, and which saw economic growth as a process of moving competitive equilibrium. The economists who began to define the other path increasingly were pulling away from all of these presumptions. On the one hand, while recognizing the value of and making use of the new quantitative measures, this latter group of economists increasingly was proposing that these numbers provided only a partial picture of economic growth and its sources, and therefore needed to be augmented by richer qualitative description of the character of technological change, and the economic growth processes that fed on technological change. Several within this group came to focus on the rich array of institutions bearing on economic growth, to which neoclassical growth theory was blind, and also to argue that, unlike the characterization in neoclassical growth theory, economic growth needed to be understood as an evolutionary process involving disequilibrium in a fundamental way. Of course, this latter point had been argued earlier by Schumpeter.

The group of scholars at the Science Policy Research Unit at the University of Sussex, under the leadership of Christopher Freeman, were prominent pioneers in establishing this second path, which increasingly diverged from the mainstream in economics. A number of distinguished economists have been trained at SPRU, and now are principal articulators of this other point of view. Francisco Louçã is one of the most distinguished of the young scholars who trained there.

Freeman and Louçã long have been concerned with aspects of the history of economic thought outlined above. Freeman has done interesting work reflecting on the Methodenstreit of the early twentieth century which raged between German economists of the 'historical school', who argued that each economic era and each constellation of economic events was, to a considerable extent, unique, and German economists, who stressed the role of general theory and argued that the principal task of economic analysis was specifically to identify laws of economic behaviour that held across eras and particular contingencies. Louçã has done fascinating work studying and analysing the battle among American economic historians that raged half a century later between the Cliometricians, who argued that the principal use of historical analysis in economics was as a testing ground for general economic theory, and the more institutionally oriented economic historians, who stressed the importance of understanding the complexity of the factors that shape important economic developments. In this book, Freeman and Louçã use these two approaches very effectively as a basis for laying out their own perceptions of what a useful theory about economic growth would be like.

The analysis of economic growth developed in this book is organized around the concept of 'long waves'. The long-wave theory espoused by the authors does not argue for any tight regularity of timing and duration. Rather, the central argument is that economic growth as we have experienced it needs to be understood in terms of a sequence of eras. Each era is marked by a cluster of technologies, whose progressive development drives experienced economic growth. The argument is not one of technological determinism. In the long wave theory espoused by the authors, the effective development and implementation of the particular technologies that are central in an era require an appropriate and supportive structure of institutions, a point of view that goes back at least as far as Marx, and was early developed in its present form by Carlota Perez.

The authors see the economic institutions of a country as having an integrity of their own, but also as being intertwined with other major social subsystems and institutions: those concerned with technology, science, politics, and culture more broadly. The authors develop the argument that the central reason why certain countries have been the leaders in different economic eras is that the various subsystems there fit together better to provide a supporting overall structure for the key technologies than was the case of institutions in other countries.

The succession of different economic eras generates 'long waves', the authors argue, because progress based on the core technologies of one era operating under their suited institutions sooner or later runs into diminishing returns, and economic progress based on those technologies inevitably slows down. The resumption of rapid economic growth then requires the emergence of a new set of driving core technologies, and the reformation of institutional structures to suit the new needs. As the authors stress, the change from one era to another very often has been associated with a change in the locus of economic leadership.

The description and analyses of the various economic eras are rich and persuasive. The authors intend this 'reasoned history' as a theory of economic

growth, and certainly their description and analysis sheds light on phenomena of central importance to the economic growth we have experienced that
more standard economic growth theory does not even see. Their analysis of
the particular institutional requirements for the effective advancement and
exploitation of the different core technologies that marked the different eras,
and their discussion of why certain countries were the leaders there, is
especially interesting.

The purpose of a foreword is to whet the reader's appetite, not to summarize the book that lies ahead, and certainly not to pre-empt the authors'
main arguments. Readers of this book have a fascinating adventure in store
for them.

Columbia University   RICHARD R. NELSON
New York City

ACKNOWLEDGEMENTS

We want to express our deep gratitude to the colleagues who participated at different stages of this project, discussing some of the draft chapters, attending and commenting on seminars on these topics, investigating particular subjects, or just submitting the whole idea to a rigorous scrutiny:

Giovanni Dosi, Asli Gok, Eric Hobsbawm, David Landes, M. J. Lewis, Roger Lloyd-Jones, Roy MacLeod, Sandro Mendonça, Richard Nelson, Keith Pavitt, Carlota Pérez, Angelo Reati, Jan Reijnders, Gerald Silverberg, Luc Soete, Nick von Tunzelmann, Andrew Tylecote, and four anonymous referees for the publishers. We would also like to thank the Portuguese Foundation for Science and Technology (FCT) for a grant supporting this research.

Finally, we wish especially to thank Susan Lees in SPRU, without whose patient and thorough work the book could never have been completed.

C.F.
F.L.

CONTENTS

LIST OF FIGURES

LIST OF TABLES

PART I

HISTORY AND ECONOMICS

Introduction: The Fundamental Things Apply

'Quand on a dit que le temps passe, dit l'histoire, on a tout dit.'

Charles Péguy, Clio, 1932; p. 96

Time is as mysterious as life: some thousands of years of efforts by science and philosophy have not been sufficient to unveil its secrets and enable us to understand its nature and motion. But, occasionally, wise men and women have been able to circumvent their perplexities and to accept the challenge of time. Walter Inge, the Dean of St Paul's Cathedral, was one such person. He is supposed to have written as early as 1229 a remarkable narrative of this mystery: 'When our first parents were driven out of Paradise, Adam is believed to have remarked to Eve: "My dear, we live in an age of transition"' (Antonelli 1992: 1). How right he was.

The subject of this book is precisely the age of transition in which we live, although dispensing with some of the intonations of certainty of previous accounts. And there are substantial reasons for prudence. The very notion of transition is a difficult one, particularly in social sciences and in economics: change, instability, mutation, and bifurcation are difficult concepts to measure and to assess, in contrast with permanence, continuity, linearity, and structure—but history is transition, and societies and their economies exist only in time. This is why we prefer to take a clear stance on a crucial topic for the definition of our science: economics is meaningless outside the framework of history, since economies are historical by nature. Economics is a science of transition. Consequently, the acceptance of the impertinent pertinence of evolution is a criterion that distinguishes economics as a tool for understanding from sheer playometrics.

But what exactly is evolution, the modern synonym for transition? When dealing with the subject, some scientists take for granted that, contrary to the plurality of space, time is unitary. Yet, its unity has been understood and explained following at least two contradictory visions. Ancient Greece, as well as the Asian cultures, conceived nature as evolving cyclically. It was a natural interpretation of sensory experience, which imposed the quite natural form of our calendars, arranged in three cycles: the rotation of the Earth about itself established the day; the rotation of the Moon around the Earth defined the month; and the ellipse of the Earth around the Sun set the year. And day, month, and year repeat like the seasons, the harvests, and the monsoon: nature is cyclical. Yet, no day repeats the previous one, and no winter, no harvest, and no year are exactly the same as the previous ones. Nature is cyclical, but the cycle is not the renewal of the same process again and again. And, since change is permanent and irreversible, time repeats never repeating.

Time is movement, therefore: irreversible movement, glory and decay, birth and death, creation and end—and this is the second vision of time. In particular, it gained momentum with the emergence of a new culture and religion, Judaism, then followed by Christianity. The Bible, in particular the book of Revelation, brought about that concept of change in time, but also added a fundamental transcendental myth: that time flows linearly towards a destiny. The concept of time as an arrow is a recent one in the history of civilizations, but it soon dominated imagery and religious reflection: without a supposed end to history, the emptiness of the meaning of daily life would deprive humankind of transcendence.

Yet, it was not because of ancient religion, but rather because of contemporary myths, that the arrow of time associated with the idea of destiny has prevailed up till now. It was science, and the powerful movement of modernization since the Enlightenment, that provided a new departure for the confident assumption of the benefits of the labour of time. This was inaugurated by Leibniz at the end of the seventeenth century, with his notion of progress; simultaneously, Newton confirmed the magnificent possibilities of this new science, which was able to scrutinize everything and to uncover the laws of nature. We now know that Newton was the 'last sorcerer', as Keynes put it (in relation to his alchemy enquiries), as much as he was the first modern scientist. This new wisdom was then reinvented by positivism and so triumphed in the nineteenth century. The triumph was proclaimed by Lord Kelvin at the British Royal Society's end-of-century celebration, when he said that physics had completed the edifice of its knowledge and that only minor refinements would occur in the future. Auguste Comte called it the 'positivist religion', and he knew what he was talking about. Alfred Wallace, the co-author of the theory of evolution, wrote at that time a book in praise of the new inventions of modernity—the trains, telegraphs, telephones, 'the Wonderful Century'—and many shared his confidence. Modern science was built on the conviction that everything can be known, measured, defined, and controlled. General laws, or some equivalents of certainty, have been the legitimate form of expression for this Laplacean dream; given the initial conditions of the system, the whole past can be recalled and the future can be foreseen. Science is domination.

But no more than a couple of years after Kelvin's proclamation, relativity theory and quantum mechanics challenged classical physics and a new science emerged, challenging these positivistic assumptions. It emerged from perplexities about time—always about time—such as from the shock of geological and astronomical depth: by the end of the nineteenth century, scientists understood that the age of the universe had to be measured not by thousands of years but rather by thousands of millions. Humankind had dominated only in the last fractions of this period, and consequently it became clear that creation proceeded through distinctive paths that no rational deterministic history could justify. Evolution was therefore understood as an open process, marked by surprise, change, mutation, bifurcation, feedback, and crises. And, defying the positivist criterion, it is unpredictable. Strict determinism failed in biology, not because the arrow of time was not recognized, but because it became obvious that the arrow could change direction. Evolution evolves but accepts no destiny.

The social framework is even more difficult to encapsulate in the positivist criteria. Because social evolution adds to this first level of complexity—the eventual mutations in the genetic endowment and the process of adaptation to the natural environment—a second level of organizational complexity is imposed by the autocatalytic process of formation of cities, states, technologies, social relations, and conflicts. It shares the same basic characteristics of openness and indeterminacy, but adds a new dimension of intentional choice: societies are livelier than life, since they add some specific structures of change to the permanence of change.

This book is about how societies and economies evolve through time. It argues that their evolution has recognizable patterns, depending on the relations between technological innovation, social structure, economic development, institutional framework, and cultural standards. In particular, it discusses modern industrial capitalist economies—how they change, how they structure their change, and how these patterns of change configure long-term fluctuation, known to economics as long waves or Kondratiev waves.

At the beginning of the twenty-first century, hardly a day passes without some reference to the 'Internet Revolution' or the 'Computer Revolution' and the massive structural changes that are taking place in telecommunications, the media, software business, and so forth. The so-called 'New Economy', as represented by the NASDAQ stock market index, was in a phase of tempestuous growth, producing a dangerous 'bubble' while the 'old' (Dow–Jones) economy languished. Later, this situation was reversed, at least temporarily. Similar phenomena occurred in the past with each great technological revolution—water-powered mechanization, steam-powered mechanization, electrification, and motorization. Part II of this book describes how such new pervasive technologies entered the economic and social system, dominated it for a while, and were finally overtaken by the next new technological regime. We argue that the general equilibrium models, which still dominate mainstream economic theory, are quite incapable of explaining the technological revolutions and social changes of the past two centuries.

But we preface this discussion in the first part of the book with a critique of 'cliometrics', including the attempts of this school to dismiss the Industrial Revolution and to belittle the importance of railways in the nineteenth century. Cliometrics attempted to redefine economic history as a linear process to be studied with the help of mechanical tools, and to relegate the study of institutional and qualitative change to the status of an 'unscientific' and 'old' approach. Like Landes, Mathias, and other 'old' historians, we argue that the fundamentals still apply, as time goes by. The 'new' economic history, as some cliometricians like to regard it, in trying to provide 'counter-factual' accounts of the Industrial Revolution, cannot actually avoid con-firming much of the 'old' interpretation; i.e., there was indeed a profound structural change triggered by a constellation of technical and organizational innovations. Chapters 2–4 present an appreciative critique of the work of some economists who did recognize the historic significance of those peri-odic structural transformations. Chapter 2 deals with the work of one of the most paradoxical of twentieth-century economists, Joseph Schumpeter. Although he stressed the great importance of 'successive industrial revolu-tions' and of 'reasoned history', he never quite escaped from the heritage of Leon Walras. He appreciated the work of Kondratiev on long cycles in eco-nomic growth, which is described in Chapter 3, and, like other leading econo-mists, he supported Kondratiev's membership of the Econometrics Society as a Founding Fellow. However, although he realized some of the limitations of standard econometrics, neither he nor Kondratiev succeeded in present-ing a satisfactory alternative theory of history. Keynes in his debates with Tinbergen pointed out the vital importance of 'semi-autonomous' variables in growth theory, i.e. social and political changes that are not captured in purely quantitative econometric models, but he was almost alone in that. However, all of these economists recognized the great importance of busi-ness cycles for economic theory and for economic history. They all urged that the study of these fluctuations, whether long or short, must be at the heart of economics and not relegated to the fringe.

Some of this tradition was continued by a wide variety of other economists and historians, following the pioneering work of Schumpeter and Kondratiev. Although later repudiated by both mainstream and 'official' Marxist ortho-doxy, at the time they included prominent neoclassical economists as well as a variety of Marxists. Many of the debates were dominated by a discussion of appropriate statistical and econometric techniques, as indeed were Kondratiev's own debates with his colleagues and critics, described in Chapter 3. In Chapter 4 we trace these prolonged controversies and, in the light of this discussion, explain why we ourselves reject the purely economet-ric analysis of fluctuations in the economy and of 'trends' in aggregate GDP. In particular, we reject the various attempts at 'decomposition' of secular trend from cyclical movements. Like Keynes, we believe that some techniques are in danger of embracing a reductionist view of history, which ignores quali-tative changes in politics, in culture, and in technology. It is these changes that are our central concern in Part II of the book, as they were once a crucial concern of both Adam Smith and Karl Marx. From this point of view, we affil-iate to a heterodox tradition in economics, although claiming to return to the fundamentals of our science. Economics was originally, and must continue to be, a historical science, since its subject matter is intelligible only as contextu-alized in history, and since economics and history can illuminate each other. In particular, this book argues that the inquiry into economic fluctuations and structural change must be immersed in time.

In the late 1990s, as in the late 1920s, voices were raised arguing that economies may no longer suffer from oscillations. Events have already falsified such unwise predictions, engendered by irrational stock market exuberance, and they did so *before* 11 September 2001. The major industrial economies had experienced a clear deceleration of their rates of growth for several decades compared with the earlier post-war period. With the bursting of the internet dot.com bubble the United States, as well as Japan and Europe, now confronted further deep problems. As this indicates comparison with the past is an important feature of the discussion of the present: as in previous periods of structural change, it is prosperity that generates depression. Clément Juglar understood this in his first theory of business cycles, and so did Karl Marx, Nikolai Kondratiev, and Joseph Schumpeter. Consequently, in order to study the dynamics of long periods of expansion and depression, we go back to the fundamentals: to the nature of our science, to the purpose of classical political economy, to the mutual fertilization of historical and statistical methods.

Some of those with a very close knowledge of the movements of the American economy in the recent past have been the most sceptical about the attempts to abolish the business cycle. Among many examples is the following answer of Robert Rubin, who was for several years responsible for Clinton's economic policy, to his interviewer from *Newsweek*, on the permanence of economic fluctuations:

Newsweek: As you know, there are people who believe that new technology and globalization have repealed the business cycle.
Robert Rubin: There are people who believe that, and it may turn out that that's true. But there is another possibility, which is that all of human history may turn out to be true instead. And you just have to decide which you think is more likely. (*Newsweek*, Special issue, December 1999–February 2000, p. 61)

Listen to the old song—*you must remember this; the fundamental things apply, as time goes by . . .*

1
Restless Clio: A Story of the Economic Historians' Assessment of History in Economics

1.1 Introduction

This book starts with a thorough discussion of methods in history, in economics, and in the social sciences generally, because this is essential for the theme of the whole book. Our approach to the Industrial Revolution and to the information revolution depends on a distinctive method, which is developed in contradistinction to the prevailing dominant methods in both economics and economic history. The best way to demonstrate this difference is to analyse that curious intellectual movement known as 'cliometrics', which was so important for economic history in the second half of the twentieth century.

Cliometrics erupted into the intellectual arena of economic history at the end of the 1950s, and in a short while became one of the dominant forces in the field. In the economics profession, used to scorning epistemology despite proudly claiming to be united by a specific method, supposed to single it out among the social sciences, cliometricians discussed the philosophy and the consistency of their endeavour and provided new teachings and surprising applications. They generated new rules of investigation, achieved increasing returns for publication, created novelty, and assured conquest, often through the harsh polemics sometimes thought to be necessary for achieving brilliance in academia. In a science balkanized into several schools, cliometrics brought together a heterogeneous group of researchers and disciplined their efforts to the performance of a single major task: to redefine and quantify economic history.

Last but not least, the cliometricians applied cosmopolitan neoclassical economics, invading the resistant small village of history—where Schmoller, and later Schumpeter, Mitchell, and so many others, had taken refuge in order to publish manifestos in an outspoken reformist vein. These refugees had also conducted a great deal of plebeian work in favour of regarding economics as part of the social sciences, as a realist science, and even as a science at all, but the invaders suggested a new and fashionable approach to economic history.

This chapter briefly discusses some of the epistemic foundations of cliometrics, its methods and accomplishments, and the divided legacy of economic history after it had gained primacy. The next section summarizes the history of cliometrics, arguing that the movement itself was split after the first skirmishes with 'old' economic history, while Section 1.3 focuses on the method and on some examples of its application. This provides the opportunity for a general discussion as to which kind of statistical tools are adequate for economic research, which is one of the major purposes of this book. Finally, the conclusion restates the case for history to be included as a part of economics, so that it can deal with its very object: real life economies in evolutionary, irreversible, and complex processes.

1.2 Cliometrics: How Quantification and Economic Theory Conquered Economic History

As the tale goes, cliometrics was born in September 1957, at the National Bureau of Economic Research (NBER) Conference on Income and Wealth, in Williamstown, Massachusetts, and John Meyer and Alfred Conrad were its progenitors (e.g. Fogel 1966: 642; Davis 1966: 658). Within a few years, it had become the epitome for the close integration of economic history into mainstream economics.

Indeed, this conference proved to be a major turning point. Two years earlier, Solomon Fabricant had sent an open invitation to economists and historians to attend a joint meeting; the Economic History Association accepted, and Gerschenkron acted as a co-organizer. During the meeting, two papers constituted the manifesto for the new current, one prepared by John Meyer, himself a director of NBER later on, and one by Alfred Conrad, both authors of which were from Harvard. And their new ideas inflamed the field.

The offensive against 'old' economic history was apparently prepared as a rigorous campaign, as far as one can surmise at the distance of one generation. If the order of authorship reveals their share of the job, Meyer took the lead in epistemology, while Conrad, acting as the first author, delivered a major example of the new approach, conducting a study of the profitability of slavery in the Antebellum South. The final result was a consistent case for the new approach: the papers were simultaneously challenging and daring, powerful and insinuating, concrete and theoretical, exploring new and old hypotheses in a new light.

Twenty years later, Meyer stated, in correspondence with Bob Coats, that they did not intend to revolutionize the *métier*, and that they identified themselves as disciples of the quantitative tradition in American economic history, as represented by Schumpeter, Kuznets, and Gerschenkron (4 October 1977 letter to Coats; quoted in Coats 1980: 187). Reading the material from the conference, however, one cannot avoid feeling a sense of confrontation and scepticism amidst novelty.

Rostow, who presented a paper on 'The Interrelation of Theory and Economic History', rephrased the old resistance of historians to traditional economic theory, arguing that static assumptions and methods were clearly unsuited to the subject-matter of the historian:

For a theorist it is fair enough to say, as Marshall did, that a case of increasing returns is 'deprived of practical interest by the inapplicability of the Statical Method', but this is a curiously chill definition of practical interest for an historian. . . . In short, if the work of the economist is to be relevant, he must work to an important degree outside the theoretical structures that have mainly interested him since, say, J. S. Mill. (Rostow 1957: 515, 517)

Moreover, Rostow identified the nature of the problem as the inappropriate application of the 'Newtonian methods' to economics, conceived as another branch of mechanics, whereas biological metaphors were more appropriate—as Mitchell and Schumpeter had suggested in due time (Rostow 1957: 514, 519). Yet, Rostow did not hide his lack of interest in methodology, a domain of irretrievably personal and subjective choices: 'I do not hold much with ardent debate about method. A historian's method is as individual—and private—a matter as a novelist's style' (p. 509). Following this argument, the whole discussion was a waste of energies.

But Rostow's colleagues did not think this way. The panel of discussants of both Rostow and Meyer–Conrad's papers on method included Martin Bronfenbrenner, Raymond de Roover, Evsey Domar, Douglass North, P. G. Ohlin, and Arthur Smithies. Simon Kuznets performed the task of summarizing, commenting on, and concluding the discussion, and his notes are highly indicative of the interest aroused by the topic and of the intellectual climate of the meeting.

According to Kuznets, one of the putative inspirations of the new movement, the discussants shared some preoccupations, but disagreed on a number of points. Curiously enough, one of their major points of agreement was the fear of an excessive reliance on economic theory, one of the ideas stressed by Meyer and Conrad, since 'the discussants were concerned chiefly with the specific theory to be used, the implication being that there is no single accepted body of economic theory. . . . [Furthermore] in view of the great complexity of the problem faced by economic historians. . . . allowance must be made for various approaches in formulating hypotheses' (Kuznets 1957: 545–6, 547). We will return to this argument against a theoretical bias in the integration of history and economics, but it is important to emphasize now how these economists and historians at this stage devalued the theoretical corpus they were offered and instead stressed pluralism. Following Kuznets's testimony, the participants at the conference did not rate the announced contribution by economic theory very highly:

Traditional economic theory is of little help [for the choice of variables] since it is devoted largely to drawing implications from a sharply defined and correspondingly abstract system of market relations, whereas the economic historian perforce emphasizes the institutional changes that affect the scope and conditions within which the market system operates. . . . It would be dangerously confining to demand that each of these causal sequences be expressible as a mathematical equation with all the variables quantified and with the selected functions simple enough to permit the kind of testing called for in this paper. (Kuznets 1957: 547–8)

Of course, economists engage in such imaginative castle building in the belief that there will be sufficient resemblance to reality for the model to be useful in attempts to deal with explanatory or policy problems. In fact, in the designing of these tools a fair amount of empirical substance is incorporated; and all too often without explicit proof of its validity. (Kuznets 1957: 551)

As a consequence, there were two grounds for suspicion in relation to the new approach. Some economists at the conference—indeed, most of them—rejected with outspoken contempt the applicability of the dominant methods of theorizing and modelling to history: Kuznets indicates that Bronfenbrenner, Smithies, and Domar were 'rather sceptical of the value of greater integration of economic theory and economic history, and particularly of the use of econometric models and statistical tests' (Kuznets 1957: 550). And the historians, at least some of them, feared that the new approach could imply a reductionist vision of history. In spite of this, other historians were more receptive to the new approach. In particular, Douglass North and Gerschenkron welcomed the new development, and the former played a crucial role in it.[1] Kuznets explained this paradoxical fascination in the following terms:

It is easy to exaggerate the impression, but it did seem as if almost all economic theorists participating in the [Williamstown] discussion were doubtful of the value of theory in work on economic history, while at least some economic historians felt that it is needed. And perhaps there is a simple explanation for this somewhat paradoxical situation. Scholars working in the field of economic analysis are all too aware of the limitations of their tools, [while] those working in the field of economic history in which some of these tools have not been widely used, tend to appraise highly the possible returns from such use. (Kuznets 1957: 550)

Although the economists remained sceptical, and some of the historians rather worried, the conference marked the emergence of a constituted body of thought, of a mature methodological approach, supported by some well argued empirical applications. That was all that was needed for inaugurating a school; and a school was indeed inaugurated.

The publication of the volumes of the conference, and the rapid diffusion of the twin manifestos (the slavery paper appeared in the *Journal of Political Economy* in the same year and the methodological one in the *Journal of Economic History* in 1958), paved the way for the 'new economic history', or 'econometric history', as it was called. From 1960 on, the seminars at Purdue

---

[1] Douglass North in 1963 coined, or first used, the term 'new economic history', which became the epitome for the new movement (Fogel 1964: 377). Gerschenkron, on the other hand, never practised cliometrics, while sharing its purpose. Yet he kept a critical attitude, and the 'Harvard wing' of the movement was very sceptical of the excessive reliance on the neoclassical price theory (Sutch 1982: 28).

(with Lance Davis), the Washington group (led by North), the Harvard team (Gerschenkron), and Robert Fogel, as well as other research units at Yale (William Parker), Wisconsin, Pennsylvania, and the Stanford–Berkeley joint Economic History colloquium, were the major poles for the school (Fogel 1966: 643; Coats 1980: 197). According to Lance Davis, Douglass North was by that time its 'chief propagandist and entrepreneur' (Davis 1966: 659).

The counterattack was messy and timorous. The elders were intimidated by the mathematical paraphernalia of the young and did not challenge either their method, which they could barely understand, or their empirical work, which they could scarcely recognize. Indeed, 'many of them withdrew into a kind of internal exile within the profession' (Landes 1978: 5). Furthermore, a controversial editorial decision sparked the confrontation. When a paper by Lance Davis was rejected by the *Journal of Economic History*, the young economic historians summoned their troops in order to claim justice: petitions were circulated, meetings were organized, and the paper was eventually published in 1960. Shortly afterwards, the editors of the journal were replaced. When North and Parker were later appointed as editors of the *Journal of Economic History*, the signal was made quite clear.

Yet, evidence suggests a mild interpretation for the result of the whole process: in spite of some accusations of 'quantomania' and 'numerology' levelled against the new economic historians, they were left free to conquer the intellectual terrain almost without battle. In a matter of a few years, cliometrics had become a powerful new orthodoxy in economic history.[2]

Meyer and Conrad: opening the Pandora's Box of methodology

It is now time to present and discuss the content of Conrad and Meyer's arguments. The paper set as its purpose the discussion of the 'concepts of historical causality and explanation in a stochastic universe and to suggest how the analytical tools of scientific inference can be applied in economic historiography' (Meyer and Conrad 1957: 524). This was by itself quite new. The prevailing wisdom was the opposite vision to that of Samuelson,

---

[2] There was also a political confrontation, mostly ignited by Meyer and Conrad's paper and by Fogel and Engerman's book on slavery: some witness that at the session on 'Slavery as an Obstacle to Economic Growth', organized at the September 1967 annual conference of the Economic History Association, held in Philadelphia, there was an uprising against the authors and their thesis. Fogel and Engerman took pains to argue that the authors of the original work on the topic were either leftists (Conrad) or at least institutionally respectable members of the profession (Meyer was a director of NBER), and that no accusation of a right-wing political bias in their paper was legitimate (Fogel and Engerman 1974: 16). Nick von Tunzelmann, who was present at the 1967 meeting, indicated in private correspondence that the political confrontation was nevertheless contained in the academic standards. Yet, it is true that, very quickly, 'Broad, vague, potentially subversive themes like the history of capitalism, the social consequences and causes of poverty, were eschewed in favour of politically safe exercises deploying positivistic techniques and orthodox neo-classical models' (Coats 1980: 202).

established in his path-breaking 1947 Ph.D. dissertation: causal models and historical models belong to two distinctive and unrelated classes of approach (Samuelson 1983: 272). But the effort to challenge this common assumption and to rebuild economic history in order to model historical processes by stochastic causal systems was shown to be highly profitable.

Based on Hempel (1942), Meyer and Conrad provided a strong version of the positivistic approach: theories should be compared to predictions in order to increase the explanatory value of theoretical assertions through their eventual confirmation (Caldwell 1982: 20, 26–7, 175 ff.). This vindication of logical empiricism was quite exceptional in economics, not because its implicit mode of legitimization was not shared by most, but because the majority of the profession were all too innocent of epistemology.

Denying Popper's distinction between historical disciplines and natural sciences, Meyer and Conrad established an ambitious programme for the integration of economic history into economics—through the assumption and acceptance of the neoclassical framework—and for the corresponding definition of economics as a science, following the Newtonian atomistic mould. Again, this was pure Hempel: all sciences were definable by the Hypothetico-Deductive Model, and therefore all could resort to a causal ordering system. Consequently, science—all sciences—should be able to equate explanation and prediction through the formulation of a general law: 'general laws have quite analogous functions in history and in the natural sciences . . . they even constitute the common basis of various procedures which are often considered as characteristics of the social in contradistinction to the natural sciences' (Hempel 1942: 345, 348).

In particular, the 'irretrievable pastness', or the irreversibility of historical events, would not prevent the use of the proper scientific methods and the definition of causality, provided two conditions were met. The first was the invariant—either sequential or simultaneous—conjunction of two properties, and the second was its asymmetrical character. Now, as the first condition is rather demanding, since it requires no less than the perfect conditions for establishing a covering law, Meyer and Conrad rephrased it in probabilistic terms: all that is required is that we should be able 'to assign some probability to the assertion that the "first" set of conditions will be followed by a "second" . . . and that this process should be irreversible' (Meyer and Conrad 1957: 528). In that case, causal ordering, or the identification of exogenous and endogenous variables, could be established. Of course, identification is relative to a theory: 'in history, no less than in any other branch of empirical inquiry, scientific explanation can be achieved only by means of suitable general hypotheses or by theories, which are bodies of systematically related hypotheses' (Hempel 1942: 352).

But it is not only the reference to the general theory that suggests a difficulty. The crux of the matter is the stochastic element. The structure of the model is deterministic, whereas the random events refer to changes in the course of history:

In formal terms, this implies that while historical explanation does presuppose regularity, it must be assumed that the random elements will dominate the causal system and that the random elements are differently distributed at every moment of historical time. . . . But explanation in a historical system can be interpreted as the estimation of probabilities of transition from one state to a succeeding state, given the initial conditions and a causal law or generalization. In that interpretation the task of the economic historian is to search out the variations in the exogenous variables, that is, to add to the set of empirically realized independent conditions. (Meyer and Conrad 1957: 530–1)

This 'stochastic causal system' should therefore be interpretable following the three main elements: (1) the 'causes', the exogenous variables, (2) the 'effects', the endogenous variables defined by a specific structure, and (3) the random shocks, giving the 'proper meaning of the uniqueness of historical events' (Meyer and Conrad 1957: 532), and the hypothesis should be stated in terms of the equations representing the three classes of variables. It should be emphasized that all three classes must necessarily co-exist in this framework: it is the characteristics of the random element that allows for the probabilistic inference, as it is the exogenous–endogenous dichotomic distinction that allows for meaningful causal assertions in this framework.

At the same time, the hidden assumptions of these methods did not frighten the cliometricians; they even depicted themselves as objects of jealousy in the eyes of their fellow economic historians, who were unable to prevent a general movement towards a positivistic revolution in social sciences. This is how Fogel and his associate Engerman presented the barbaric challenge:

To many humanists this effort to treat man as if he were *an atom* is the ultimate folly. It takes no great effort on their part to ignore such prattle. And that is what many humanists do, except for an occasional snicker in the privacy of their studies when someone mistakenly sends them a reprint of a paper containing a mathematical model of the French Revolution. . . . It was not only the economists who invaded that field in the late 1950s; they were joined by sociologists, political scientists and others. All were armed to the teeth with statistical methods, computer programs, and mathematical models of human behavior. The main body of historians attempted to ignore this incursion, on the assumption that the invaders would flee in retreat when they realized the strength of their opposition, or else, as was true of so many previous barbarian intruders, they would have become assimilated. (Fogel and Engerman 1974: 8–9; emphasis added)

Fogel and Engerman were careful enough to distinguish themselves from previous attempts to mathematize the discipline, arguing that these early efforts were wrongly based on nineteenth-century physics and the presumptions of the First Law of Thermodynamics, asserting the stability of equilibrium as the solution for the system of equations. Apparently, they ignored the fact that neoclassical economics itself was born precisely as the incarnation of energetics in economics, and that its revival in the 1930s under the spell of the probabilistic revolution did not cut such an umbilical cord.

As a consequence, agents were still modelled as atoms, as Fogel and Engerman clearly state. One may, however, ask what kind of behavioural assumptions are possible for these atoms, and how a necessarily limited mathematical model can represent the French Revolution.

It comes as no surprise, therefore, that participants at the Williamstown conference met these claims with great scepticism, particularly in relation to the usefulness of the stochastic approach to economic history.

A major shift in economic history

In spite of such opposition, cliometrics won the day. In retrospect, two reasons may help to explain this outstanding result. For one, it represented the emergence of positivism in economic history, and positivism had been regarded as the hallmark of the scientific character of any discipline since the end of the nineteenth century. Indeed, both in economics and in history, and *a fortiori* in economic history, many had resisted positivism and its overemphasis on measuring and counting for a long time. Adam Smith was an historian as well as a moral or political economist, and it was only afterwards, with Ricardo and Say, that axiomatics took over. But for many years the prevailing view in economic history was that it was designed for the task of counteracting the abstraction and irrelevance of mainstream economics, and Schmoller, Toynbee, and others considered their work as a refuge for realistic economics and as the condition for rehabilitating history. Schumpeter, the most heterodox of the orthodox, proclaimed history as an intrinsic part of the programmatic task of economics and, in his afterthoughts following his first survey of the Methodenstreit, asked for a truce with Schmoller (Louçã 1997: 239 ff. and see also Chapter 2 below).

In general, the allegiance of economic history to realism, and its ambitious concern with the overall reform of a science undercut by reliance on neoclassical behavioural assumptions, led economic historians to take preventive measures to preserve their work from the influence of economics (Schabas 1995: 198). On the other side of the coin, modern economics was defined primarily in opposition to history and its pluralistic tradition: in his 'Plea for the Creation of a Curriculum in Economics', Marshall argued in 1902 for the positivistic criteria of a mathematical science as opposed to the still dominant narrative techniques (Kadish 1989: 200). Consequently, the methodology of economics was taken from physics, and economic history was kept separate, to the benefit of both parties.

This situation was challenged when the epistemic primacy and theoretical corpus of neoclassical economics were well established, after Debreu and Arrow defined the rigorous conditions for general equilibrium. The powerful movement of cliometrics represented that very wave of integration: economics claimed history back into its province.

A second reason for the victory of cliometrics, and not a minor one, was that it challenged young researchers to use new and fancy techniques, and generated increasing returns to the investment in the sophisticated 'new economic history'. They proclaimed the obsolescence of the elders (Landes 1978: 4), and abandoned their programme: history was no longer seen as a form of research into evolution and institutions, but rather as the story of a macro-economic process resulting from the action of innumerable essentially identical and well behaved atoms. This allowed for computation and fancy papers, yet it was soon obvious that the school itself was sharply divided into several undercurrents.

As early as 1965, Fritz Redlich, a retired Harvard professor, wrote a critical assessment of the cliometric school and distinguished its three main undercurrents. First, as he put it, were the 'data processing' scholars, such as Davis, Hughes, and Fishlow, mainly interested in gathering information as the quantitative historians did before, although using more sophisticated statistical tools. Second was the work of North, whose product 'is economic history' and a thorough discussion of hypotheses. Third, there was the 'quasi-history' group: Conrad, Meyer, Fogel—essentially model builders working with figments of imagination, with hypotheses that were neither refutable nor verifiable, and simply required justification (Redlich 1965: 491).

Furthermore, Redlich noted that the latter used two distinctive classes of models: 'models by reduction' (based on empirical material, as the production functions in Section III of the Conrad–Meyer paper), and 'models by construction' (as in the remainder of the Conrad–Meyer paper and in Fogel's work). In both cases, 'a model is never a piece of history, because it is conjectural or subjunctive or, in Max Weber's language used for all ideal types, a distortion of reality' (Redlich 1965: 490).[3] One may therefore wonder (and this was Redlich's line of attack) what clarity can be gained from obviously false assumptions.

This difference widened as time passed. As a consequence, the founders were forced to accept a shared judgement: cliometrics led both to good results and to 'sheer disaster' in its application (Davis 1966: 662) and to 'dull and unimaginative', 'imprecise and fuzzy' research of 'distressing poor quality' (North 1965: 90). These differences eventually led to an internal civil war, under the form of aggressive reviews and other more personal attacks (McCloskey 1978: 23).

These different approaches to cliometrics reveal a great deal about the varied intentions of the respective authors. Originally, Fogel claimed that cliometrics distinguished itself by its being a specific method for the reincorporation of history into economics, subsumed to its general theory, i.e. the basic neoclassical assumptions: 'The methodological hallmarks of the new economic history are its emphasis on measurement and its recognition of the intimate relationship between measurement and theory' (Fogel 1966: 651).

---

[3] According to Weber, an 'ideal-type cannot be found empirically in reality' (Weber 1949: 90, also 42–7, 91–102).

McCloskey was even more conclusive, stating that cliometrics was defined by a 'deep agreement' about the neoclassical equilibrium price theory:

> It is the possession of this method that distinguishes the cliometricians from other economic historians. . . . Not counting but economic theory, especially the theory of price, is the defining skill of cliometricians, as of other economists. A cliometrician is an economist applying economic theory (usually simple) to historical facts (not always quantitative) in the interest of history (not economics). (McCloskey 1978: 15)

This was indeed widely accepted: when a major figure in the econometric movement, Arnold Zellner, proposed the candidature of Fogel as a new Fellow of the Econometric Society, his argument was that 'Fogel is a recognized leader in the movement to introduce econometric methodology in the field of economic history' and 'his work has been an important factor in the encouragement of the use of economic theory in economic history'.[4] Yet, Fogel argued that the impact of the new economic history was 'primarily due to the novelty of its substantial findings' (Fogel 1966: 644), and, implicitly, was not due to its method. Indeed, given both the reasons of the economists at Williamstown and the limited scope and stringent assumptions of the methods in question, one may even wonder how they had succeeded in obfuscating so many bright scholars. From the very first days, the method was accused of inadequacy, even by some who had flirted with it: '[econometric methods in history represent] a form of intellectual tunnel vision. It manifests itself most frequently in a penchant for focussing exclusive attention upon the confrontation between a terribly restricted set of observations and an equally narrowly specified hypothesis concerning some facet of economy behaviour' (David 1971: 464).

But the most important dissidence was that of Douglass North. This was not new. As early as 1965, North had claimed that the 'new economic history falls short of the mark in remedying this situation [the very poor situation in the discipline]' and has been 'generally disappointing' (North 1965: 86, 90).[5] But in 1978, although claiming fidelity to the original purpose of cliometrics, North went much further and criticized his fellow cliometricians for ingenuous belief in the virtue of neoclassical economics:

---

[4] The proposal may be found in the Frisch Archive, Oslo University.

[5] Evsey Domar was a commentator for this paper given by North in 1965, and he had been one of the economists at the Williamstown conference. Although in 1957, as Kuznets told the story, he was quite sceptical of the new approach, in 1965 he readily attacked economic historians for 'their predilection for descriptions and tautologies and their neglect of analytical models' (Domar 1965: 116). Yet, faced with North's outstanding criticism of the current state of cliometrics, Domar decided to refrain from adding to North's 'self-mutilation' (p. 116). It must nevertheless be emphasized that at that time what North was criticizing was the poor quality of the research developed under the flag of cliometrics, not the approach itself. In the same paper, he still considered economic theory to be the most suitable guardian of the temple: 'In summary, it is my conviction that we need to sweep out of the door a good deal of the old economic history, to improve the quality of the new economic history, and it is incumbent upon economists to cast a skeptical eye upon the research produced by their economic history colleagues to see that it lives up to standards which they would expect in other areas of economics' (North 1965: 91).

Emphasis upon the systematic use of theory—particularly price theory—[has been] the most decisive contribution of the new economic history, which is the attempt to develop a more scientific history. The explicit use of theoretical models and the systematic use of statistical inference in testing procedures are the most distinctive contributions of this approach. Where McCloskey and I part company is that I think most of the new economic history simply applies neoclassical economics to the past. That is a contribution, but one that quickly runs into diminishing returns and leaves the economist with the conviction that we are marginal if not dispensable to the profession. (North 1978*a*: 78)

McCloskey challenged this critique: '[North is] a cliometrician who complained (mistakenly) that cliometrics uses economic tools uncritically' (McCloskey 1978: 28). Nevertheless, a different explanation runs as follows. North oriented his research for a long time to 'the central puzzle of human history [which] is to account for the widely divergent paths of historical change' (North 1990: 6), and, in particular, to the study of the formation and evolution of institutions. This vicinity to the old historians' theme forced him to suspect the usefulness of the neoclassical assumptions and finally to conclude that they were the 'fundamental stumbling block preventing an understanding of the existence, formation, and evolution of institutions' (North 1990: 24). Indeed, the consideration of institutions requires the abandonment of the over-simplistic rationality principle and the study of environmental complexity. North did not hesitate in either instance: he replaced perfect information and rational maximizing behaviour with procedural cognition and bounded rationality, and replaced the postulate of simplicity with the discussion of non-deterministic outcomes of social interaction. Consequently, his previous views of institutions as efficient economic units were dropped, as was his representation of institutions through a simple model of transaction costs. As a consequence, North came to be closer to the old historical school[6] than to his fellow cliometricians, and did not hide the impact of his own transformation:

What difference does the explicit incorporation of institutional analysis make to the writing (and for that matter the reading) of economic history and of history in general? . . . A brief answer to the question is that incorporating institutions into history allows us to tell a much better story than we otherwise could. The precliometric history actually was built around institutions, and in the hands of its most accomplished practitioners, it managed to provide us with a picture of continuity and institutional changes, that is, with an evolutionary story. But because it was built on bits and pieces of theory and statistics that had no overall structure, it did not lend itself to generalizations or analysis extending beyond the essentially ad hoc character of individual stories.

---

[6] North had some previous roots closer to the old historical school, since he had been a self-proclaimed Marxist in his youth, although at that time he was already engaged in a 'long term love affair with price theory' (Hughes 1982: 4–5). In the early 1970s his endorsement of some of the critiques of the 'Harvard wing' and the break with the 'neoclassical wing' of the new economic history movement recapitulated crucial arguments of the historical schools. When Fogel and Engerman published *Time on the Cross*, the rupture was already quite evident.

The cliometric contribution was the application of a systematic body of theory—neoclassical theory—to history and the application of sophisticated, quantitative techniques to the specification and testing of historical models.

However, we have paid a big price for the uncritical acceptance of neoclassical theory. Although the systematic application of price theory to economic history was a major contribution, neoclassical theory is concerned with the allocation of resources at a moment of time, a devastatingly limiting feature to historians whose central question is to account for change over time. Moreover, the allocation was assumed to occur in a frictionless world, that is, one in which institutions either did not exist or did not matter. These two conditions gave away what economic history is really all about: to attempt to explain the diverse patterns of growth, stagnation, and decay of societies over time, and to explore the way in which the frictions that are the consequence of human interaction produce widely divergent results. (North 1990: 131–2)

This goes back to the origin of the argument: the specific contribution of cliometrics was the method it implied and used in order to reincorporate history into economics. Let us turn to it now.

1.3. Clio at Work

McCloskey, one of the devotees of the new economic history, and clearly one of the main defenders of its positivistic trend, lauded the novelty of the new approach on two grounds: first, it represented the theorization of economic history; second, it set the pace of quantification. One could not take place without the other, since quantification depended on the 'lunatic' assumption of some functional forms and on the strict capacity to measure them: 'The limits on curiosity about the economic past set by the available facts are few, and cliometricians—bemused by production functions and demand curves and the lunatic belief that they can actually measure them—have led the way in pushing the limits further' (McCloskey 1978: 21).

In comparison with traditional economic history, 'bemused' by complex causal systems determined mostly by qualitative features, namely institutional evolution, this represented a major shift. But at least the early generation of cliometricians was quite aware of the foundations and implication of cliometrics: to put economic history *à la page* with economic theory meant essentially to adopt the general criterion of science as it was conceived of in positivism. As a consequence, history should be indistinguishable from empirical or natural sciences, in the sense that explanation equated the formulation of a general covering law, subsuming every instance under its rule. Carl Hempel (1942) was, for Meyer, Conrad, and Fogel, and eventually for others, the major reference for this reconstruction of history: 'In history as anywhere else in empirical science, the explanation of a phenomenon consists in subsuming it under general empirical laws; and the criterion for its soundness . . . [is] exclusively whether it rests on empirically well confirmed assumptions concerning initial conditions and general laws' (Hempel; quoted in Fogel 1964: 1).

And therefore, 'The fundamental methodological feature of the new economic history is its attempt to cast all explanations of past economic development in the form of valid hypothetico-deductive models' (Fogel 1966: 656).

Although Hempel argued that historical explanation consisted of 'explanation sketches' rather than positivistic conclusions, and that historical models were 'law-like' rather than universal laws (Fogel 1964: 246), he was read as stating the exact conditions for empirical research on a covering law, a set of initial conditions and each particular instance of the events. Those were the 'Hempelian lines' that the cliometricians had sworn to follow (p. 248).

The hypothetico-deductive model was based on a crucial assumption permitting its positivistic formulation (the definition of the rationality of the agents), and was calculable, since all types of event could be represented under the general specifications of the model or of the random shocks allowing for statistical inference. Therefore, it also allowed for predictive and subjunctive conditional statements about non-observed phenomena. These three characteristics will now be discussed in turn.

The acceptance of the rationality principle and of methodological individualism in economic history was a major sign of its espousal of orthodox economic theory. Indeed, most of the previous investigation dealt precisely with exceptions to and refutations of these principles. But conformity with the canon claimed sacrificial victims, and institutional and social history was one of them.

As a consequence, rationality was assumed further and further back in history as a constant in human behaviour, and *Homo economicus* was erected as the intrinsic self of *Homo sapiens sapiens*: 'The tales of the adventures of *Homo economicus* in unlikely places are beginning to accumulate, in nineteenth-century India, for example, or medieval Europe, or declining Rome' (McCloskey 1978: 24).

Yet, this is far from consensual. For decades now, the work of anthropologists and historians has shown that different civilizations organized modes of production, and of social interaction, that were alien to individual profit maximization and were based on co-operative action. From Margaret Mead's research on the Arapesh of New Guinea (Mead 1962: 37) up to much recent work, this thesis was demonstrated time and time again. Contemporary research, namely innovation, firm and institutional theory, emphasizes the very same idea. The notion of a Parmenidean world where all flux is illusory and where *Homo economicus* never evolved over the millennia (Schabas 1995: 198), behaving under the same criteria in Ancient Rome just as he does in the Hong Kong stock market at the beginning of the twentieth-first century, is at least a delightful joke.

But, just like any simple idea, it has a crucial role that can scarcely be distinguished amidst its roughness. It allows for the use of powerful accounting and statistical tools, based on linear or linearized systems, and for the common use of regression analysis as the most frequent device (Fogel 1966: 652). Furthermore, it allows for even more stringent assumptions, such as the choice of Cobb–Douglas production functions and all that they imply—constant returns to scale, marginal productivity factor pricing, unbiased aggregation of supposedly independent factors of production, continuously differentiable production functions (e.g. for the study of British economic growth from 1856 until 1973: Matthews *et al.* 1982: 590).

Some of the technical implications of this mode of investigation and computation, and its adequacy for use in historical series, will be discussed in the next section. But we must add that there is also another powerful implication of this assumption of self-interested and maximizing rationality as the pattern of human and social behaviour, which is its ideological *a priori*. Once again, McCloskey voices this not so hidden assumption: 'Here again economic theory dominates the research, giving it coherence, not conclusions. True, the conclusions have often been variations on the theme, "The Market, God bless it, works"...' (McCloskey 1978: 21).

This ideology is quite obvious in one of the major pieces delivered by the cliometricians: *'Time on the Cross'*, the impressive research by Fogel and Engerman (1974) about the profitability of slave exploitation in the Antebellum South, following Conrad and Meyer. In the book, both planters and slaves are depicted as rationally acting groups—although, at least for one of them, choice was meaningless since they were slaves. The slave owners are presented as 'shrewd capitalistic businessmen', capable of a 'superior management of planters', and the slaves are praised for the 'superior quality of black labor', since they 'competed for [skilled] jobs', 'imbued like their masters with a Protestant ethic', and strove 'to develop and improve themselves in the only way that was open to them' by being 'diligent and efficient workers' (Fogel and Engerman 1974: 73, 150, 201, 203, 210, 231–2, 263). Although the authors claim to try to redeem black history, giving the slaves a rightful central place in the economic development of the American South, the result is meagre if not doubtful.

Since this refers to a much discussed and well known topic in economic theory, and there is nothing novel in its importation by cliometrics, this chapter will not go into the details. Instead, the following section will deal with some specific contributions made by cliometrics.

The Industrial Revolution: random events as the standard mode of variation in history

If the first topic was quite trivial, since cliometrics just adapted orthodox common sense about the rationality postulate without adding anything to it, the second concerns a specific contribution and actually a very important one from the standpoint of this book. It was to be expected: the drive to a 'more scientific economic history'—or econometric history, as it was also dubbed—implied more than the willingness to apply the fancy tools of statistical inference. It required the imposition of some strict conditions, namely the genuinely probabilistic character of history itself.

It is well known how the early statisticians tried to solve the problem of extending their findings and methods to time series. Although some of the first important contributions were made by social scientists, such as Jevons and Edgeworth, these ultimately hesitated to extend their methods to the realm of society and economics. Later on, the same perplexity was stated by one of the founders of econometrics, Ragnar Frisch, who did not follow the probabilistic approach that he had been so instrumental in creating. Nevertheless, the econometricians generalized the concept of randomness, and two of the directions of such a generalization were relevant for the cliometric revolution. The first was the consideration of historical events as random elements impinging upon the basic structure of the regular historical process. The second, as powerful as the previous one, was the statement that historical time series could be thought of as a sample from a large universe of possible realizations of the same process. It would therefore be possible to apply tests of hypotheses following the Neyman–Pearson strategy and to compute the significance of the parameters obtained from fitting the equations of the model to the data. That was the strategy followed by Meyer and Conrad in their papers presented to the 1957 conference: a 'stochastic causal model', precisely defined in terms of endogenous, exogenous, and random variables, was used to determine the minimal conditions for 'causal ordering' (Meyer and Conrad 1957: 532). But it must be added that this crucial point generated the stronger reactions at that conference. Kuznets indicated that a large part of the participants shared the same type of scepticism as Frisch and did not follow Conrad and Meyer or their disciples:

One of the questions raised in the discussion is whether the probability tests permitted by this interpretation of the *e* term are valid for the kind of situation analyzed in economic history. . . . [The] general tenor [of the discussion] suggests a conclusion different from that of the authors. The criterion of the discussion was, I believe, that there are almost *no* cases in which such a 'reasonable approximation' exists . . . [since the] tests would have to be made in terms of a universe of economic trends. (Kuznets 1957: 549–50)

More recently, Crafts discussed this problem in very great detail, and his solution is illuminating. In a paper published in 1977, he accepted that historical events could not be explained under universal covering laws, as necessary and sufficient conditions: 'whenever and only if A, then B' (Crafts 1977: 432). Moreover, the multiple regression would be non-operational, given the severe problems of interpretation, the uniqueness of observations, the multicollinearity of variables, and the insufficient number of degrees of freedom. The suggested alternative, as in the early econometric tradition, was to consider history as an intrinsic process of chance:

All that needs to be maintained is that there are probability distributions of values of Y for given values of any X and that the probability distributions of Y are different for different values of X. . . . [And] the best we can do is to formulate explanatory generalizations with an error term. (Crafts 1977: 433–4)

In order to avoid retrospective inference and the consequential danger of the *post hoc ergo propter hoc* fallacy, Crafts suggested rejecting the concept of chance as ignorance of the true structure of events and alternatively considering chance as the expression of the irreducible randomness in history. Therefore, 'the best we can do is to formulate explanatory generalizations with an error term' (Crafts 1977: 433–4). But that was not a trivial assumption, since it was the decisive step in allowing for regression analysis and other tools of statistical inference. These rapidly became commonly used tools in econometric history and generated a flow of new studies and publications on a wide range of subjects.

The concept was for instance applied to the inquiry into the different motivations behind the distinct performances of Britain and France during the Industrial Revolution and the reason for France lagging behind. In particular, the discussion revolved around the question, why were the spinning jenny of Hargreaves and the water frame of Arkwright invented in Britain?[7] Crafts's answer is that the 'economic development in general and technological progress in particular in eighteenth-century Europe should be regarded as a stochastic process' (Crafts 1977: 431). In other words, it was a 'stroke of genius or luck' (Crafts 1995*b*: 756), or 'strokes of genius, luck or serendipity' that provided decisive macro inventions *ab nihilo* (Crafts 1995*a*: 595)—and that decided the primacy of Britain. Consequently, there is no explanation for the time or location of the decisive inventions in cotton textiles that proved crucial for the acceleration of growth and the Industrial Revolution (p. 596). Then the puzzle becomes: had these inventions occurred in France, could that country have dominated the period of the Industrial Revolution?

The legitimacy and the logical implications of the question itself are doubtful and will be discussed shortly, but they may be ignored for the time being. Two other central aspects of the polemics are more interesting at this juncture: the historical determination of the radical change known as the Industrial Revolution, and the role and measurement of stochastic factors in history.

For a long time now, Crafts has been arguing that the case for the Industrial Revolution had been clearly exaggerated, and that previous computations by Deane and Cole should be revised. Many of his followers went further and

---

[7] Why not also ask why the new process of rolling and puddling, used for the transformation of pig iron into wrought iron (the 'most important single invention during the industrial revolution': Mokyr 1985: 10), was developed by Henry Cort in 1784 in Britain and not by someone else in France? Why did the good fortune of the *anno mirabilis* of 1769, when Watt and Arkwright's patents were registered, not extend to France as well? But the succession of this type of questions provides an answer in itself.

denied the very concept of the Industrial Revolution: it is 'a concept too many' (Coleman 1983: 435 f.), and 'English society before 1832 did not experience an industrial revolution let alone an Industrial Revolution', and '[its] causes have been so difficult to agree on because there was no "Industrial Revolution", historians have been chasing a shadow' (Clark 1986: 39, 66). Someone even added in a pamphleteering vein: 'Was there an industrial revolution? The absurdity of the question is not that it is taken seriously, but that the term is taken seriously ... by scholars who should know better' (Cameron 1990: 563).

There is a quantitative answer to these statements (see Figure 1.1), although the decisive point lies elsewhere. The main facts can be assessed through historical investigation. Table 1.1 was provided by Crafts and compares estimations for the yearly growth in real output for Britain (in percentage terms). Before considering further evidence, it should be stressed that this table—even if one accepts Crafts's more pessimistic estimates uncritically—provides strong evidence for an impressive movement of acceleration in general growth, and in particular in the leading industry, cotton textiles. This is indicated by simple arithmetic. In the same table, we added the indication of the number of years necessary, for each growth rate, to double the level of production for each initial period, and the conclusion is straightforward about the acceleration of the trend of growth. This period is reduced to half or one third in the crucial years of the Industrial Revolution for the economy as a whole, and the textile industry could even double in scarcely more than ten years, when it represented more than 20 per cent of the total output.

Crafts's attack on Rostow and Deane and Cole's view of the Industrial Revolution in favour of 'a more gradualist interpretation' of 'steady growth, rather than a "take-off" or spectacular growth' (Crafts 1989: 65, 67), seems to

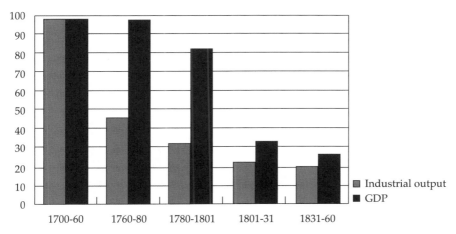

FIG 1.1. Time necessary to double the level of production (number of years), 1700–1860
Source: Crafts (1989).

TABLE 1.1. Growth of real output 1700–1913 (% per year)

	Industrial output				GDP		
	Crafts (1989)	Crafts (1989) (cotton text.)	Deane, Cole,	Hoffman (1965)	Crafts (1989)	Crafts (1995)	Deane, Cole
1700–60	0.7 (99yr)		1.0 (70yr)	0.67 (104yr)	0.7 (99yr)		0.7 (99yr)
1760–80	1.5 (47yr)		0.5 (139yr)	2.45[a] (29yr)	0.7 (99yr)	0.6 (116yr)	0.6 (116yr)
1780–1801	2.1 (33yr)	5.7 (13yr)	3.4 (21yr)		1.3 (84yr)	1.3 (54yr)	2.1 (33yr)
1801–31	3.0 (23yr)	5.6 (13yr)	4.4 (16yr)	2.70 (26yr)	2.0 (35yr)	1.9 (37yr)	3.1 (23yr)
1831–60	3.3 (21yr)		3.0 (23yr)	1.98[b] (35yr)	2.5 (28yr)	2.4 (29yr) (1831–73)	2.0 (35yr)
1873–99						2.1 (33yr)	
1899–1913						1.4 (50yr)	

[a] 1760–1830.
[b] 1830–70.

Source: Crafts (1989: 67); Mokyr (1993: 9). Our computation of the delay, in years for doubling the current values of production is given in parentheses.

be undermined by his own evidence (e.g. Table 1.2). Furthermore, he recognizes that 'within industries were to be found the few sectors where productivity growth was really fast; most notably in textiles, with its radical changes in technology', causing in any case 'enormous changes in the economic structure of Britain between 1760 and 1840', and a 'revolutionary change in the structure of employment', since 'by the second quarter of the nineteenth century the economy had achieved a rate of growth of the total

TABLE 1.2. Labour and output in Britain, 1700–1840 (%)

	1700	1760	1840
Male labour			
Industry	18.5	23.8	47.3
Agriculture	61.2	52.8	28.6
Output			
Industry	20.0	20.0	31.5
Primary sector	37.4	37.5	24.9

Source: see Table 1.1.

factor productivity which would previously have been inconceivable' (pp. 69, 71, 68). This differential growth is the crucial feature of the Industrial Revolution: again according to Crafts, the annual rate of growth of real output of the cotton industry was 1.37 per cent for 1700–60 and 7.57 per cent for 1760–1800, whereas it was just 0.25 and 0.37 per cent for leather and 1.25 and 1.44 per cent for linen for the same periods (Crafts 1985: 23). This dual economy was fuelled by a modern sector of rapid growth, in spite of an ensemble of old sectors moving slowly: cotton, iron, engineering, mining, transport, and some consumer goods (paper, pottery) grew at 1.8 per cent a year for the period 1780–1860, whereas the traditional sectors were responsible for an aggregate growth rate of 0.7 per cent (Mokyr 1985: 4–5).

One may ask then what is the point of the slight differences in estimates and what can possibly be inferred from these differences. Trapped by his own polemics, Crafts is forced to spend pages and pages arguing against the misinterpretations and interpretations, and claiming repeatedly that 'we reaffirm the importance of the industrial revolution as a historical discontinuity' (Crafts and Harley 1992: 721). But the nature of this discontinuity is still to be uncovered, since there is more than a slight difference between explaining the process by historically interconnected causes and explaining it by small and meaningless random perturbations.

Since he adheres to the second explanation, Crafts maintains that the Industrial Revolution was simply a transformation in the existing industries. There is indeed an essential continuity in the economies, since modes of production are transmitted, market traditions and regulations endure, and routine dominates the technical processes. But what also happened, and this is specific to this period, was the superimposition of new techniques, of new procedures, of a new form of best practice, leading to cumulative increases in productivity and to radical changes in the relative position of industries and firms. From this point of view, statistics reveal as much as they hide, since there were different rates of growth between industries but also inside each industry (Mokyr 1993: 9)—and the understanding of the Industrial Revolution is inseparable from the understanding of these different rhythms. As Crafts himself once again pointed out in 1977: '"Industrial Revolution" will be understood as a period of accelerated structural change in the economy, involving a rapid rise in industrial output, in the share of manufacturing in national product, and in factory-based activity (implying a different kind of economy) based on major technological innovation' (Crafts 1977: 431). Figure 1.2 reproduces a graph presented by Crafts himself on the trend growth of industrial production: what better evidence could we have of the discontinuity introduced by the Industrial Revolution?

The question is therefore whether the process was the outcome of one or several random changes in the structure of the economy and, in particular, whether this was the reason for the differences between England and France. Surprisingly enough, one of the opinions invoked by Crafts as corroborating

FIG 1.2. A radical shift: trend growth in industrial production during the Industrial Revolution, 1700–1900
Source: Crafts (1989).

his own view—that of Mokyr[8]—clearly leads to another interpretation: 'the technological definition of the Industrial Revolution is a clustering of macro inventions leading to an acceleration in micro inventions' (Mokyr 1993: 22). Furthermore, Mokyr argued that 'the key to the British technological success was that it had a comparative advantage in micro inventions' (p. 33). Of course, the problem is discovering how and why this comparative advantage was built in.[9] Crafts himself provided relevant information for the answer to this question, pointing out the institutional advantages of Britain over France, namely in the patent system, in prior improvements in trans-

---

[8] Mokyr changed his vision of cliometrics, as far as one can tell from the two versions of his 1985 paper, 'The Industrial Revolution and the New Economic History'. In 1985 he was quite sympathetic to the new approach, despite pointing out its limits: 'The New Economic History has shown itself best qualified to answer questions that it itself poses, often well-defined questions that yield clear, refutable hypotheses. Indeed, the very definiteness of the new methods has confined them to a narrow range of problems' (Mokyr 1985: 2). In his new version of 1993, Mokyr strongly attacked some cliometricians' denial of the Industrial Revolution in Britain.

[9] Apparently, Crafts implies that these macro inventions were random events. Seen from the opposite viewpoint, modern innovation theory argues for a shift in focus, concentrating not on inventions, in relation to which a precise scientific hypothesis can hardly be formulated, but on innovation. In this framework, innovation is the relevant unit for research, being seen as an economic selection process occurring under pervasive uncertainty, bounded opportunities, the influence of technological bottlenecks and trajectories, and experimental and local search behaviour, given the heterogeneity of agents (Freeman 1994). Even if one radically claims that inventions are pure random processes, one must recognize that the selection and canalization of innovation are deeply rooted in the cumulative capabilities of the economy, and are not purely stochastic, but socially defined processes.

portation, in the trade system, and consequently in the ability to diffuse innovation; and, in the opposite direction, the disadvantage of France as far as its 'rent seeking attitude' and the 'ability to resist change' was concerned (Crafts 1995*b*: 759; 1995*a*: 594, 596). North suggested that major organizational innovations accounted for the breakthrough, as much as technological innovations (North 1965: 87–8), and Landes discussed the impact of the new 'factory system' from that same point of view (Landes 1993: 140).

Now, three main approaches have been suggested to interpreting these facts. The first one, much along the same lines as Crafts, suggests that the Industrial Revolution concept is a mere construction of a theoretical artefact: Clapham suggested, as early as 1926 and based on data from the 1851 Census, that the change had been far less radical than the tale tells (Landes 1993: 135). But, arguably, these data are not completely reliable: for example, only in 1861 did the Census include civil engineers along with clergy, medics, and lawyers as 'professionals' (Crafts 1995*b*: 759).[10] Furthermore, the statistical aggregation may smooth over discontinuities and change, and 'drown sectors of innovation and change in a sea of tradition' (Landes 1993: 148). Not only is reliability questionable for statistics, in particular those covering early ages in industrialization, but also 'it is often true that the volume of data available is frequently below the minimum required for standard statistical procedures' (Fogel 1966: 652). Therefore, 'the most that can be done is to make careful "guesstimates" in the light of both the available resources and general economic and statistical reasoning' (Crafts 1989: 66). And, as pointed out before, the evidence of a drastic change in production conditions—as represented by the period necessary for the level of production to double—challenges these 'business as usual' interpretations of the Industrial Revolution.

The second alternative, an elaborate form of the first, is that the Industrial Revolution is accountable by an explanation based on randomness. In that sense, Meyer and Conrad had suggested the formalization of any economic process as a hypothetico-deductive model in the Hempelian mould: a general covering law was represented by a deterministic system expressing all the systematic influences as explanatory variables, whereas the errors of observation, unsystematic influences, and omitted variables were to be represented by the random term (Meyer and Conrad 1957: 535). In this framework, Hargreaves's and Arkwright's inventions would be the expression of a purely chance draw, as Harley put it in 1990: 'The technological breakthrough in industry occurred in Britain in part because of the dynamic character of the economy but Britain probably also benefited from a lucky draw in the random process of invention' (quoted in Landes 1993: 147).

---

[10] This is a clear example of how there is some delay in statistical categories recording the changes in reality and how these same categories may hide its main features for a time. In the same sense, there are multiple examples of new industries that are only accounted for in statistics long after they first emerged.

Crafts's somewhat more sophisticated explanation does not escape from this framework. Arguing in 1977 that Britain's primacy does not prove an *ex ante* larger probability for success, Crafts denied nevertheless that the result was purely fortuitous (Crafts 1977: 441). Yet, some years later, in 1995, he approvingly quoted Crouzet, saying that the mentioned inventions 'could have been fortuitous' (Crafts 1995a: 595). Although the same paper recognized that Landes was right, that the previous growth comparisons which had been the basis for the 1977 argument were false, and that 'it does seem now clear that both France's growth potential and the level of income per head were lower than the equivalent in Britain' (Crafts 1995a: 592), the author did not conclude from this that the stochastic causal approach should be abandoned. Exogenous and random technological shocks and their eventual ramifications continued to account for crucial advantages, even if a larger potential for growth was obvious in British data (Crafts 1995b: 758–9; 1995a: 597).

Landes answered that this potential and the level of prior development were indeed the crucial ingredients for a reasonable explanation:

The possibility of revolutionary accidents has its theoretical interest . . . It is, however, a counsel of despair in the search for understanding and explanation. In other words, it is not the *subsequent* superiority of the British textile industry that tells us about Britain's chances for technological change (Crafts' bugbear of *post hoc ergo propter hoc*), but its *previous* development. (Landes 1995: 600)

This last alternative interpretation simply states that a complex explanation is required for understanding complex reality.[11] In this framework, the formal models, based on the assertion of a covering law and established on the basis of a precise dichotomy between explained variables and explanatory ones added to the largely undefined random variables are nothing but a suspect and limited tool. Instead, our approach recognizes that historical explanation is generally overdetermined and looks for multi-level causation, unlike econometric explanation that is perfectly determined[12] and based on simple correlation or multiple regression. Let then the provisional last word also be with Landes:

Here let me state a golden rule of historical analysis: *big processes call for big causes*. I take this as what economists call a prior. I am convinced that the very complexity of large systemic changes requires complex explanation: multiple causes of shifting

---

[11] This can be recognized by a cliometrician: 'The growth of cities, the increase in population, the rise in national income per head, and the shift from farm to factory happened all at once. Britain could have industrialized without expanding her population or urbanized without enriching herself. Yet in fact, she did all these things together, compounding the effects of one with the effects of the other' (McCloskey 1985: 54).

[12] In his rather critical 1965 assessment of the current state of cliometrics, as previously cited, North wrote that he used to give his students a simple task in order to highlight the limits of 'old economic history' and some of the shortcomings of certain 'new' ones: they should 'make explicit models of [some] articles' (North 1965: 90). This game, of course, is not innocent: it supposes that the logical coherence and explanatory power of a formal mathematical model is the model for explanation in history and, not surprisingly, uncovers its failure.

relative importance, combinative dependency . . . temporal dependency. . . . I would also argue for a kind of reality principle. It is not hard to devise mathematical models for intrinsic inevitability—of small differences that are reinforced over time to produce an ever-widening gulf, of lines of development locked into 'path dependencies'. But any resemblance between such lucubrations and the real world is purely coincidental and highly occasional—fortunately. The real world is made up of actors as well as of people acted upon. People and groups respond to change and challenge, evade constraints, and find other solutions. . . . Let me make a modest proposal. Economic history needs protection against bad numbers. The more artful our econometric techniques, the greater the recourse to quantification, the more protection we need. (Landes 1994: 653–4)

The irresistible logic of counterfactuals

It was previously noted that cliometricians sometimes presented their work as addressing the old problems with new methods,[13] while at other times they argued, quite reasonably, that they were performing a major shift in economic history, both in methods and in the definition of the relevant questions. This 'significant break with the past' has been related to the use of explicit and formal models, to the operational definition of variables as part of a stochastic causal model, and, finally, to the test of 'the model (a logical statement of assumptions and conclusions) against the evidence (the world that did exist) and the counterfactual deduction (the world that did not exist)' (Davis 1966: 657). This use of the model in order to test for a counterfactual hypothesis became a distinctive feature of cliometrics, since it was related to strong claims that the production of positive assertions depended on that test: 'It is only through a comparison of what was with what might have been that we are able to make statements about the nature of events' (p. 658).

The classical example was given by one of the papers Conrad and Meyer presented at the Williamstown conference. The authors suggested that a proper counterfactual test be held on the proposition that 'slavery was not profitable in Antebellum South', as a form of eventually refuting another one— 'if the Civil War had not occurred, the South would have abolished Negro Slavery in an orderly fashion within one generation'—which could not be directly tested.

Addressing these major issues with counterfactual logic is like extinguishing a fire with petrol. Indeed, '[any] logic of causes via counterfactuals can only give us antecedents and consequences in the causal nexus by either an arbitrary decision or by a direct expression of our conceptual grounding' (Climo and Howells 1974: 468).

---

[13] 'Indeed, the new economic historians have not been primarily engaged in launching new counterfactual propositions, but in making explicit and testing the ones they find in traditional theory' (Fogel 1966: 653).

The establishment of causal nexuses via the counterfactual depends either on arbitrary decisions that cannot be logically disciplined or on metaphysical foundations. Consequently, one may argue that the counterfactual cannot provide any substantial inference, since the assumptions are obviously false. This is the traditional problem in logic: *ex falso sequitur quodlibet*; that is, from false assumptions you may conclude either false or true assertions—there is no way to discriminate between valid and invalid inferences. In other words, it is a dead-end. The definition of the counterfactual must be made in terms of a law-like assertion, if it is either a necessary condition or a sufficient and necessary condition, supposing in any case adequacy to the world; but the counterfactual itself is defined as a false statement issued from this model and therefore unrelated to the real world. Trading realism for instrumentalism is a rare craftsmanship indeed.

The previous paragraphs incorporate both a general warning against the widespread use of counterfactuals in economic history, and a discussion of their drastic epistemic limits. But in spite of so many warnings from many different authors, counterfactuals are indeed widely used in economic, statistical and historical reasoning,[14] since it is generally admitted that many claims on causality (more on this later on) may take the form of a counterfactual. It is argued that, since the assertion 'A caused B' can generally be restated under the equivalent form, 'if A did not happen, B would not have occurred', the use of counterfactuals in causal analysis is widespread. This section contradicts that view and discusses the possibilities of an alternative logical development of counterfactuals, following Elster's classical work on the topic (Elster 1978).

The issue of causality is of course the central motivation for the inquiry into counterfactual logic. Consequently, one cannot establish convenient criteria for the validity of a conditional statement, unless a workable notion of causality is defined. It is assumed that the traditional notion of causality, that of Hume, based on spatial contiguity, temporal sequence and constant conjunction, i.e. defining cause as a sufficient condition for an event B, is too restrictive (Elster 1978: 178ff.). Alternatively, we take a broader view of causal implication as a form of weaker determination, abandoning the requirement of permanent conjunction and contiguity, since the complexity and interconnectedness of multiple causes is recognized. But unlike John Stuart Mill, who deduced the rejection of any conditional assertion given the interdependence of causes, Elster suggests that, even in these circumstances, causal links can be discussed in the framework of true conditionals from false antecedents to the true consequent, whereas of course false conditionals from true antecedents to false consequent are useless (Elster 1978: 12).

Rejecting the circular justification of causality through counterfactuals and vice versa, Elster proposes a criterion of legitimacy and another of assertability (and not of truth) in order to establish the validity of the historical counterfactual. The 'dynamic criterion for legitimacy' is simply that 'we

---

[14] Or, more recently, in psychology: Elster argues that counterfactual beliefs are generally present in the formation of emotions (Elster 1999: 49, 265).

must require that a counterfactual antecedent must be capable of insertion in the real past' (Elster 1978: 184). Simple, but not trivial, since it substantially reduces the range of possible assertions and grounds them on concrete history. In that case, the counterfactual would take the form: 'If at time t the configuration had been $A_1...A_{n-k}B_1...B_k$ [instead of the real process, $A_1,...A_n$], then at time $t+t'$ the subset x_{i1}, $x_{i2},...,x_{ip}$ of the variables [the variables exhaustively describing the process] would have assumed the values $C_1...C_p$ [instead of the real event taking place]' (p. 184). This condition of legitimacy presupposes that a theory is provided, enabling the researcher (1) to filter the choice of the antecedent, so that it can be insertable in the real past; sequentially, the second condition, the condition of assertability, requires the theory to be able (2) to establish the inference from the hypothetical antecedent to the hypothetical consequent. In response to Elster, McCloskey argued that sins of vagueness and absurdity could be avoided under the correct specification of a model suitable for testing (McCloskey and Nansen 1987: 702), but this defence is indeed a revelation, since this is just part of the problem. That is why a third condition must be imposed: there must be a minimum distance between the current state and the past branching point permitting the assertable counterfactual. If the actual state is $s_t = [A_1,...,A_n]$ and the hypothetical consequent is $s'_t = [A_1...A_{n-k}B_1...B_k]$, then the distance between s_t and a past state s_{t1} that would permit both trajectories is the distance to be considered, whereas s_{t1+1} would not permit those trajectories. In this framework, 'the counterfactual as a whole is assertable if the consequent holds in the closest world(s) where the antecedent obtains' (McCloskey and Nansen 1987: 191).[15]

These conditions do not necessarily prevent all possible wrong and useless counterfactuals, since their application is not straightforward. But they provide a necessary discipline in the field of historical research and define interpretable criteria for defining legitimacy and assertability in each context.

A major early example was the debate on the effect played by the railroads in the growth of the American economy. Fogel published a seminal work on that topic, assuming stringent counterfactual hypotheses: that no more canals or roads were built after 1890, but that 5,000 miles of canals as well as some roads were improved, that new storehouses would have been built, and that the spatial structure of agricultural production would have been changed to diminish transport costs. In this framework, he computed the social savings from railroads to be around 1.8 per cent of GNP[16] (Fogel 1966: 650).

---

[15] Or, to put it in a different form, 'the possible-worlds account of subjunctive conditionals does, of course, allow some conditionals with false antecedents to be true and some to be false. It will simply depend on whether the closest worlds where the antecedent is true are all worlds where the consequent is true—or, equivalently, whether the corresponding material conditional is true, not just at the actual world, but at every world at least as close as the closest antecedent-worlds' (Jackson 1987: 64–5).

[16] Fogel chose just to compute the effect of the railroads as providers of transportation for four specific goods: wheat, pork, beef, and corn. The effects of the railroads as users of inputs, as transportation for humans or for other goods was ignored. As a generalization, Fogel suggested nevertheless that, if all goods were considered, the total savings would amount to no more than 5% of GNP.

Fogel was careful enough to state that it is 'beyond dispute' that railroads were efficient, although some alternatives were also identified (Fogel 1964: 10). Furthermore, 'the only inference that can safely be drawn from such data is that railways were providing transportation services at a cheaper cost to the buyer than other conveyances' (p. 13). Any economist used to the orthodox argument and finding evidence of a cheaper service and larger profit would stop here and rest their case, since that would supposedly be enough for the acquisition of a cumulative competitive advantage. But Fogel did not, and went for his counterfactual test; and one of his associates in this endeavour stated bluntly: 'The fact that railroads rapidly replaced canals is not evidence of their overwhelming superiority . . . . Their effect of supplying industries was hardly sufficient to justify making the railroads a causal variable, in a theory of growth' (Davis 1966: 661). This could have some truth in it: many examples of lock-in in inferior trajectories are nowadays recognized, although even in these cases there is a causal nexus. But this is not the argument presented by Fogel or Davis: they simply assume that a functional equivalent technique of transportation would have appeared as manna from heaven and produced potentially the same cost reduction as railroads. As a matter of fact, Fogel just looks around for examples of canal transportation firms that adapted adequately to railway competition (Tunzelmann 1990: 296). At any rate, the authors do not state anything else on the matter, and simply argue that the direct effect of railroads was reduced.

The argument is legitimate, since a theory of technological innovation can be provided in order to support this counterfactual. But it is not assertable, following Elster's criteria, since it is based on confusion between atomistic *withdrawal losses* and the systemic effect of *introduction gains* (Elster 1978: 204 ff.): the railroads introduced further flexibility, generalized decisive steps in learning by doing, diffused new production techniques, and trained a layer of professional managers who would be crucial in the managerial revolution of the end of the century (Chandler 1977) (see Chapter 6). Moreover, they generalized a 'cluster of inter-locking, mutually supporting techniques' (David 1969: 510–11); i.e. they stimulated increasing returns. These effects cannot be measured using Fogel and Engerman's techniques, and consequently cannot be transported into the past looking for a suitable bifurcation point.

Although a large discussion has developed around this work, the main counter-arguments are still the original objections. Yes, railroads may have accounted just for 2–5 per cent of the growth of national income, accepting that the available method is accurate enough to measure it. But how much is 2 or 5 per cent? This was Usher's—and Landes's—objection to Fogel's conclusions, as stated in a banquet at Harvard (Landes 1978: 7). It is obvious that the original argument does not stand if one puts logic back on its feet, and looks for a realistic framework for the explanation: growth without the railroads, or a fictitious 97% of actual growth, is strictly meaningless.

The case could not be clearer than with Fogel's argument:

An interesting case in point is the notion that railroads made a unique contribution to the creation of the psychological atmosphere favoring economic growth by building lines across sparsely settled territories. Although the evidence demonstrating that the eruption of a boom psychology followed in the wake of such enterprises is considerable, no evidence has been supplied which demonstrates that the absence of the railroad had deprived the nation of considerable mental disposition. And it is doubtful that such evidence can be supplied. For if the boom psychology was a response to the opportunity to profit from unexpected changes in the value of land and other assets, it was not a unique consequence of railroads. The same favorable mental disposition could have been created by the construction of a new canal or the introduction of any new mode of transportation that unexpectedly and drastically reduced the cost of transportation in a given area. (Fogel 1964: 10–11)

What is really implied, one may argue, is the impossibility of a counterfactual conditional at least in this case: identification of relevant alternatives is not feasible ('the same disposition could have been created . . .'). Furthermore, there are grounds for reasonable scepticism about the whole project ('it is doubtful that such evidence can be supplied . . .').

The example of the exercise by Hawke, who followed Fogel's methodology and studied the global economic impact of railways in Britain, is quite telling. Assuming perfect demand inelasticity, i.e. a powerful and dubious *ceteris paribus*, Hawke concentrates on the passenger traffic; he discusses the cost of alternatives before the creation of railways, using an *ex ante* concept of social savings, and deduces a net effect that is larger than that computed by Fogel: 'Dispensing with the railways in 1865 would have required compensation for between 7 and 11% of the national income' (Hawke 1970: 401). Consequently, a single innovation could have influenced the whole economy in a non-negligible way. But this is just the opposite conclusion to that of Fogel, who tried to deny both the effect of single major innovations and the fact of discontinuities in the evolution of the economy.

The arguments of both authors are obviously dependent on the concrete use of the proposed methodology. The counterfactual is in each case vulnerable to the critique of assertability, based on the impossible insertion in the real past. Our argument is that the historical inquiry could have followed another direction, not abdicating from realism. Indeed, several scholars developed meaningful efforts in that alternative direction. The effect of technical breakthroughs has been addressed both by theories of innovation, which emphasized the importance of technological paths and canalization, and by the institutionalist approach of Alfred Chandler. Chandler showed that railroads provided a major organizational mutation and represented a best-practice frontier for modern firms. In this framework, what Fogel called, in a puzzling way, the 'psychological' impact of railroads can actually be assessed and traced back to the concrete history of firms, of managers, of trade unions, of economic regions and institutions, and so on, not as a bizarre psychological measurement, but as a concrete implication of the development of managerial practices. Indeed, the extensive development of the railroads implied a major change, and it was economically sound: 'By 1840, when the new mode of transportation had only begun to be technologically perfected, its speed and regularity permitted a steam railway the potential to carry annually per mile more than fifty times the freight carried by a canal' (Chandler 1977: 86). Furthermore, 'by the 1840s the railroad construction was the most important single stimulus to industrial growth in Western Europe' (Landes 1969: 153). The preparation of a generation of functional managers, supervising extensive geographical areas and applying rigorous tools of modern accounting, planning, and administration, controlled by intermediate levels of management, was a decisive feature of this process: they were the 'pioneers of modern management' (Chandler 1977: 87). They were the visible hands of this managerial revolution.

After two generations, the change was gigantic. 'Indeed, by 1890, cumulative investment in railroads was greater than that in all non-agricultural industries combined and comprised more than 40% of the non-residential capital formation to date' (Chandler and Hikino 1997: 38). A new transport and communication system was then complete, and that was the setting for the second industrial revolution. The introduction of railways opened a new era of mechanization, of increase in scale of sales and production, generating new modes of functioning of the capital and credit markets and developing new regional patterns in more unified national economies. A new world was taking breath.

We are then back to the problem of historical evolution: is it caused—or explainable—by small, random, independent, isolated and insignificant factors, or is it moved by path-dependent, systemic changes? The question remains. Given the irreversibility of time and the evidence of historical transformation, this puzzle may be translated into another: if random changes occur, but there is no invariant probability distribution over all the state space, i.e. if the asymptotic distribution evolves as part of the history of the system itself and the process is non-ergodic (David 1993: 208), then explanation must be represented by the formulation of a dynamic model considering not only the initial conditions, but also the outcome of the complex process of the interaction of variables throughout the history of the system. That is the work of history, of Clio.

1.4 Conclusions

New economic history represented, and still represents, a major shift in the economic historians' assessment of history and economics. Indeed, there was widespread acceptance that 'the discipline originated largely as a revolt against classical theory' (Fogel 1964: 389), and such abhorrence of the transformation of economics into a branch of mathematics and of social sciences into positivistic sciences was loudly voiced by many. Schmoller had already argued for this independence of quantitative historical economics from economic 'theory', and his argument was part of the original Methodenstreit. The issue of the debate is well known: the 'theoreticians' won the day and the neoclassical revolution was imposed as the epitome for economics. Later, it was revived under the impetus of the second neo-classical revolution, when econometrics emerged in the 1930s and deep-ened the differentiation with economic history. This was why Ashley, when occupying the first chair of economic history at Harvard, asked for a truce based on mutual ignorance and distance between economics and economic history. He was simply ignored by the following generations, and even when Schumpeter joined him and argued, by the turn of the half-century, that history should be part of the education of any economist, their voices did not reach far. But truce there was, not because they asked for it, but simply because no attention was paid any more in the new orthodox eco-nomics to this marginal topic: since axiomatization dominated the efforts of the young generations of neoclassical economists, imposing the rule of sophisticated econometric confirmation and theorization through model-ling, they were not concerned with history, which was too difficult and too different.

But such a situation did not last long. As indicated in the first sections of this chapter, the reincorporation of history into economics became the goal of a new tribe: with the emergence of econometric history, or new economic history, neoclassical economics was back in history and the cliometricians were propelled to the forefront of their profession. Indeed, 'New economic history represents a reunification of economic history with economic theory and then brings to an end the century-old split between these two branches of economics. Economic history emerged as a distinct discipline during the course of the mid- and late nineteenth-century revolt against the deductive theories of classical economics' (Fogel 1965: 94).

Fogel's argument runs as follows: economics was devoted to static models, and therefore history could not be addressed, since historical evo-lution is dynamic by nature.[17] Consequently, the divorce was understand-able as long as dynamic methods were not developed and rigorous quantitative testing was not accessible. Afterwards came the moment for reconciliation, and that was the cliometricians' major contribution to eco-nomics. Yet the old historians reacted as vehemently as they had done on the first occasion: they feared the excess of simplification involved in this excursion. This is why Chandler, more recently, repeated the same plea as

---

[17] By the very same time, Leontief, who could not be accused of anti-neoclassical bias, pleaded for interdisciplinary co-operation and for a pluralistic approach to history (Leontief 1948: 617). He later maintained his criticism of traditional econometrics for requiring dynamic stability as a condition for the legitimacy of a model, whereas the strategy of historical inquiry should be based on the research on the 'developmental process' under a less aggregated form (Leontief 1963: 1–2).

Ashley: 'I see no need to strengthen the union between the two branches and to form a new or special discipline. It seems to me we should encourage an explicit division of labor. Let us each practice our own trade, each stick to our own last, with an awareness of the possibilities and limitations of our own particular fields' (Chandler 1970: 144).

The warning did not work. History, or at least economic history, was thus conquered by neoclassical economics—eventually not all of it, but at least a representative portion of it. As this chapter has argued, several intended and unintended consequences of this fact were the submission of the research on institutions to mere quantitative inquiries and testing, the vindication of instrumentalism against realism, and the primacy of hypothetico-deductive methods with little logical or methodological foundation. Some clarity of measurement was obtained, but at the price of rather obscure and metaphysical hypotheses about what was being measured. New patterns of rigour and exactitude were established, but the techniques designed to go further in the investigation lacked epistemic coherence. The final result of the *Blitzkrieg* was devastation.

A very different earlier attempt to establish rigour and clarity of measurement was that of Wesley Mitchell in his work on business cycles. As the inspirer and first director of the National Bureau of Economic Research (NBER) from 1920 to 1945, he was able to launch a programme of research into the major characteristics of successive business cycles. He decisively rejected general equilibrium theory (Louçã 1997: 155 ff.), while contributing a great deal to economic theory, as well as to quantitative methods. However, as we have seen at the beginning of this chapter, it was at an NBER Conference in 1957, nine years after Mitchell's death, that cliometrics took off. It is all the more encouraging therefore to see in a recent NBER publication (Lamoreaux *et al.* 1999) a rather optimistic (perhaps over-optimistic) view of trends in contemporary economic theory which might facilitate a new *rapprochement* between economics and history. The editors start with a realistic assessment of the depth of the schism:

To the present day, the Business History Conference is dominated by trained historians, whereas the Economic History Association is controlled by trained economists. Despite large areas of common interest, the professional reference groups, not to mention the norms about what constitutes interesting questions, pertinent evidence, and persuasive argument, sometimes seem alarmingly different. Moveover, in the absence of a compelling new interdisciplinary effort, this divergence seems likely to endure. (Lamoreaux *et al.* 1999: 5)

The NBER has been making such an interdisciplinary effort in its own conferences and publications, and claims that '. . . recent developments in economic theory provide a historic opportunity for greater communication and we think that the essays that resulted from these conferences show the new inter-disciplinary approach to be uncommonly promising' (Lamoreaux *et al.* 1999: 5).

Lamoreaux *et al.* contend that the new developments in evolutionary economics mean that the profession is no longer dominated by the old neoclassical thinking of the 1960s and 1970s, and that 'this new thinking has made economic theory much more useful for the writing of business history and vice-versa' (1999: 6). Referring specifically to the ideas of Nelson and Winter and other evolutionary theorists, they describe this as '*the* new economic theory' (emphasis added). We think that this probably exaggerates the extent to which evolutionary economics prevails in the United States or anywhere else, and indeed, they concede that it is not what undergraduates are taught. Nevertheless, we applaud their continuing efforts to resolve the contemporary Methodenstreit.

Lamoreaux *et al.* respond to a necessity: to recombine history and economics. This is a decisive agenda: economics cannot evolve without history. In the historical framework, economic theories, models, and hypotheses must in fact be more precise and effective in understanding and explaining reality. Causality in economics must be assessed as a complex process of determination, not as determinism. Artificial reasoning must be replaced by concrete and detailed research and debate on analysis and on policy making, recuperating economics as a moral science or as political economy, just as it was to Adam Smith and the early classical authors. This argues for Clio, for remarrying economics and history as an alternative strategy to that of cliometrics—indeed, that is what this book is about.

The alternative strategy followed in the remaining chapters of Part I is based on several converging contributions, taking as a common point of departure the verification of distinctive rhythms that constitute the framework for the explanation of crucial historical processes. Hobsbawm identified this 'secular pattern of the world economy' as the recurrence of long periods of expansion and long periods of depression (Hobsbawm 1997: 37, 142, 229, 312), but the idea goes back to the origins of statistical inquiry in economics. Kondratiev, then Schumpeter and some of the early econometricians, were the first to support this conjecture and to take it as the starting point for new theories of capitalist development.

The empirical content and the theoretical coherence of this thesis are discussed in the following chapters. For the moment, let us just conclude, with Temin, that 'It is unlikely that existing economic models can incorporate a deviation from equilibrium that lasts for half a century. If countries are pushed off their growth path for so long, equilibrium theory is hardly relevant' (Temin 1997: 138).

The crucial question, therefore, is how to replace this failing equilibrium theory—and what is required is precisely an alternative to the cliometric strategy of reunification of history and economics. As we will see in the next few chapters, some mathematical economists, and not least the founders of econometrics, shared this new historical heuristics centred on the study of structural changes in the process of capitalist development, i.e. on large impacts of societal innovations and changes. In this framework, the Industrial Revolution cannot be assessed merely from the point of view of the increases in the aggregate volume of investment: it is the creation of the 'new system of machines' (Marx) or the 'factory system' (Landes) that is interesting for our research. And that is why the conjectures on the random effects, historical accidents, and perturbations are marginal—since they could be relevant only in the context of equilibrium theory, for it takes a stable structure to value the explanatory role of shocks.

Accidents are, of course, quite common in history as well as in daily life. In Gettysburg, Colonel Chamberlain was charged to lead the 20th Maine by mistake—it should have been the 2nd—and with his men stubbornly defended Little Round Top, preventing the advance of the Confederates and eventually changing the fate of the battle. In 1930 Hitler miraculously survived a severe car crash, which could have changed the destiny of some millions of human beings in years to come. But the difficult question science can ask and intend to answer is not about the indeterminacy of these events and unexpected mutations in space and time, but rather about their 'long' reasons, the changes they are part of, or that they spark—in other words, the impact and the meaning they acquire in a specific structure.

One example may serve to illustrate this point. In their first encounter in Cajamarca, on 16 November 1532, Emperor Atahuallpa and Pizarro had disparate forces: 80,000 soldiers formed the Inca army, but the Spanish conquerors were just 106 men plus 68 mounted soldiers. Yet they slaughtered and defeated that far larger army and conquered Peru. The behaviour of each soldier certainly counted, but fundamental reasons preparing this outcome include the previous crisis of the Inca Empire, the unknown military impact of horsemen, and the effective and symbolic impact of the new weapons. Retrospectively, one must add the importance of the competitive advantage of Europe in terms of the domestication of animals and plants and, consequently, the increases in population and the control of germs, the creation of industries including the military industry, in determining the outcome of Cajamarca (Diamond 1998: 67–8). To complete the picture, the capacity of the conquerors to manipulate the symbolic languages, associated with the practice of modern institutions of power, also counted and was not at all a minor effect (Todorov 1990).

This is why we do not share McCloskey's too general conclusion about little events that have big consequences (McCloskey 1991: 27). They may do so under certain circumstances—but this is frequently not the case, and it is not what history can *explain*. Furthermore, the use of the metaphor of deterministic chaos is not adequate, since initial conditions refer to a certain structure whose interactions produce complex trajectories, but this structure is still a defined structure once for all, which does not evolve. From this point of view, McCloskey's conclusion is also excessive: according to her view, only narrative methods are available in this chaotic world, and these are not interpretable in a causal sense (McCloskey 1991, and for the debate, Dyke

1990; Roth and Ryckman 1995; Reisch 1991, 1995). From the opposite point of view, Landes emphasizes the intrinsic complexity of economic history: 'Here let me state a golden rule of historical analysis: big processes call for big causes. I take this as what economists call a prior. I am convinced that the very complexity of large systematic changes requires complex explanation: multiple causes of shifting relative importance, combinative dependency . . . temporal dependency' (Landes 1994: 653).

This is certainly not the case in history, since no structure can be postulated to represent the fixed form of a social process; but a structure does indeed exist, although it is evolving. Complexity, in this case, refers not only to the feedback processes, but also and most importantly to the change of the structure itself during the process. This is evolution, and this is why history cannot use either static equilibrium theories or dynamic models based on reversibility, but must resort to processes that have the characteristics of irreversibility, non-ergodicity, and path-dependence (David 1997). The Industrial Revolution, the favourite example for this chapter, proves this point quite well. Small events could have precipitated important alterations in the industrial landscape, but we can understand the landscape itself only if we consider the systemic changes in the logic of the co-ordination processes of the large and interrelated techno-economic or socio-institutional systems. And that calls for reasoned history:

None of these advances [the new mechanical innovations], however, was sufficient in itself to trigger a process of cumulative, self-sustaining change. *For it took a marriage to make the Industrial Revolution.* On the one hand, it required machines which not only replaced hand labour but compelled the concentration of production in factories . . . On the other hand, it required a big industry producing a commodity of wide and elastic demand, such that (1) the mechanization of any one of its processes of manufacture would create serious strains on the others, and (2) the impact of improvements in this country would be felt throughout the economy. (Landes 1969: 81)

Further on in this book, we take on the task of providing an alternative account of the Industrial Revolution (Chapter 5) and of the development and impact of railways (Chapter 6). But we look first to some of the economists who, through the century, contradicted orthodox economic theory, endeavoured to re-establish the role of historical analysis in theory and practice, and tried to unveil the enigma of evolution. We turn first to Schumpeter, since he is often thought of as the founder of evolutionary economics. In fact, this was not as straightforward as it sounds as we hope to explain in Chapter 2. We turn to those efforts to understand and explain economic evolution and its mysteries, which are not simple, as Charles Péguy emphasized so eloquently:

'Rien n'est plus mystérieux, dit-elle, comme ces points de conversions profonds, comme ces bouleversements, comme ces renouvellements, comme ces recommencements profonds. C'est le secret même de l'évènement.' (Charles Péguy, *Clio*, 1932: 269)

2

Schumpeter's Plea for Reasoned History

2.1 Introduction

The econometric revolution of the 1930s and 1940s re-established the dominance of neoclassical economics against the challenge of institutionalism. Paradoxically, one orthodox economist, although a leading figure in the new Econometric Society, which was instrumental in the establishment of the neoclassical dominance, resisted the new orthodoxy. The paradox of Schumpeter's plea for reasoned history is the theme of this second chapter.

As a man and as a scientist, Schumpeter was marked by the difficult times through which he lived: the second industrial revolution, the fall of the Austrian Empire, revolution in Russia and then its extensions to central Europe, the Great Crisis, the victory of Nazism, emigration to America—the first half of the century was a turbulent period indeed. Schumpeter tried to influence these events—in 1919 he was a minister in the new republican government in Vienna, then he was a banker, then he was an abundantly productive writer on economics—but he tried first of all to understand the nature of the changes. This was why his research led directly to the problem we are dealing with in this book: how can economics help to explain history, and how can history help to explain economics?

The origin of Schumpeter's first theoretical sketches can be traced to two fundamental roots. (1) The first was the work of J. B. Clark, who was deeply aware of, but unable to overcome the limits of, the static equilibrium analysis: Schumpeter inherited his research programme and developed it throughout his life, but he too was unable to solve the enigma. (2) The second major influence on Schumpeter's evolution was the Methodenstreit debate, and the growing importance accorded to the historicist arguments. Both of these roots establish a research programme at the margin of the equilibrium paradigm, and this explains the paradoxical attitude of Schumpeter in relation to the economics of his own time: the most Walrasian and orthodox of all neoclassicals, he was also the only mainstream economist to challenge the foundations of the equilibrium paradigm and was therefore the most heterodox.

Consequently, Rosenberg went as far as to argue that Schumpeter was the 'most radical scholar in the discipline of economics in the twentieth century', since 'he urged the rejection of the most central and precious tenets of neoclassical theory' (Rosenberg 1994: 41). Rosenberg is very emphatic: 'Indeed, I want to insist that very little of the complex edifice of neoclassical economics, as it existed in the late 1930s and 1940s, survived the sweep of Schumpeter's devastating assaults' (p. 41). Based essentially on Schumpeter's *Capitalism, Socialism and Democracy* (1942; henceforth *CSD*) and on the preface to the Japanese edition (1937) of *Theory of Economic Development*, Rosenberg identifies the alleged devastating assaults by Schumpeter against the neoclassical paradigm: since change is the decisive feature of capitalism and it means a permanent tendency to disruption, and since equilibrium has no welfare advantage as it means no progress, innovation is alien to rational–equilibrating decision making. In this context, the 'circular flow' described a capitalism deprived of the essential movements of change and one that is therefore merely a simplification; as a consequence, Schumpeter committed himself to the historical analysis of this process of mutation as an alternative to the equilibrium paradigm (Rosenberg 1994: 44–5, 48, 50, 56). Unfortunately, the whole case is based on partial and circumstantial evidence, given the fact that the same Schumpeter denied all these claims at other times, including in posterior writings.

Certainly, one very essential point is clear: Schumpeter was opposed to the neoclassicals in the very definition of the research programme—his *explanandum* was technological and institutional change, and these features are ignored and annihilated in the orthodox view by the *ceteris paribus* conditions (Rosenberg 1994: 50–1). Indeed, the *ceteris paribus* is inoperative in order to study irreversible processes (*CSD*: 95). As a consequence, the real problem for the interpretation of Schumpeter is why did he not break with the neoclassical paradigm he could neither use nor follow. Indeed, he held to the framework of the equilibrium paradigm through all his scientific writings. This paradox, which is not recognized by Rosenberg in his radical remarks, is the essential question or, as Allen puts it in the most complete and authoritative biography of Schumpeter:

Paradox, failure, disaster, and disappointment were the keynotes of Schumpeter's life and work. He lived a paradoxical life and had a paradoxical career. He thought paradoxical ideas and wrote paradoxical books. Time and time again he failed as a scientist, scholar, politician, businessman, and even as a human being. . . . Yet, paradoxically this career of failure was, in its totality, a success. (Allen 1991: i. 4)

This paradox was never clearer than in regard to the grand schema of general equilibrium and its application to the domain of cycles and change, or to history.

2.2 From the Methodenstreit to the Sozialökonomie: The Role of History

The first book by Schumpeter, *Das Wesen* (1908; henceforth *DW*), was actually a large dissertation on the methodological debate opposing Menger and Schmoller, the 'theorists' and the 'historical school'.[1] Schumpeter, who entered Vienna University just after the retirement of Menger and studied under the supervision of his successor, Wieser, supported the 'theoretical' side of the Methodenstreit and praised the importance of the abstract and naturalistic approach in economics: 'From a methodological and epistemological viewpoint, pure economics is a "natural science" and its theorems are laws of nature' (*DW*; quoted in Swedberg 1991: 28), having nothing to learn from biology (p. 27).

Schumpeter was at the time considered a faithful supporter of the Mengerian side, although with strong Walrasian intonations: Hildebrand in 1911 opposed his appointment as teacher in Graz because he did not want the university to be occupied by anti-'historians'. Later on, after the failure of his political career (as Minister of Finance in the republican government of Karl Renner from March to October 1919) as well as of his banking career, the fame of the marginalist 'theorist' would precede him to Germany, the stronghold of the Historical School. Only the influence of his friend Spiethoff, a disciple of Schmoller, assured him a badly needed appointment at Bonn University (Swedberg 1991: 69–70). Schumpeter considered himself a marginalist by that time: in a note in *History of Economic Analysis* (Schumpeter 1954; henceforth *HEA*), he presented his positions as a 'strong partisan of economic theory', just like Wieser (*HEA*: 819 n.). He was also, throughout his life, an extreme positivist, supporting a strong demarcation between positive science and normative intervention. Under the influence of logical positivism, then dominant in Vienna, Schumpeter always defended this form of 'therapeutical nihilism'.

But his balance-sheet of the Methodenstreit changed during the years, and this was already obvious when, three years after the publication of *The Theory of Economic Development* (Schumpeter 1911; henceforth *TED*), Schumpeter again discussed the problem in his *Economic Doctrines and Methods* (Schumpeter 1914; henceforth *EDM*). By that time his position was much more cautious, even though he still supported the marginalist side: the whole debate was considered useless and exaggerated, and he presented 'an explanation for the controversy: it was a struggle between two methods of work, between people of different mental habits, who fought for elbow room or for domination' (*EDM*: 167).[2] It is hard to consider this as a compliment for either side.

---

[1] Schmoller developed a historical method in economics, describing the successive stages of development of societies with a combination of sociological, ethical, and historical insights. His long time perspective was invoked by Marshall when he criticized the Comtian distinction between statics and dynamics: Schmoller's *Grundrisse* was 'an unsurpassed embodiment of wide knowledge and subtle thought' (1907 preface, in Marshall 1890: 48). Nevertheless, Keynes indicated that Marshall had all his life been dissatisfied with the 'learned but half-muddled work of the German Historical School' (Keynes 1972: 210).

[2] Schumpeter maintained this opinion much later: in *HEA* he presented the whole polemic as 'a history of wasted energies' (*HEA*: 814 ff.).

The book was careful to insist on the elements of synthesis, namely on Schmoller's alleged acceptance of the similarity of the causal nexus in social and natural sciences and of the definition of laws as the aim of science (*EDM*: 170). Schumpeter even argued that one of his main previous criticisms of Schmoller's insistence on reform policies could be dropped since the latter had changed his mind (p. 175)—which is not at all evident.

Schumpeter indicated the six major innovative elements of Schmoller's contribution as follows: (1) the relativity of theory, (2) the unity of social life, (3) anti-rationalism, which Schmoller was supposed to have abandoned, (4) evolution and the role of history, i.e. to be compared with Marx, (5) the affirmation of complexity, and (6) the organic conception, as an analogy of society with a body (*EDM*: 175 ff.). The striking fact is that Schumpeter incorporated many of these features into his own research, namely (2), (4), (5), and (6), even if by the time of publishing *EDM* he was still fascinated by the marginalist revolution, a 'purer economics', 'incommensurably more firmly founded', 'more correct', 'simpler', and 'more general' (pp. 181 ff., 189–90).

But the very conception of *EDM* deserves some attention. The essay was prepared for Max Weber's *Grundrisse der Sozialökonomie*, a handbook intended to present a new methodology for a transdisciplinary social science. Weber was strongly opposed to the Methodenstreit itself, which he accused of having led to an artificial polarization of the statistical and theoretical methods against the historical method. The influence of this conception[3] on Schumpeter's thought was a lasting one.

In 1926, after a long period without any theoretical intervention, Schumpeter came back to the discussion of Schmoller's theories in an essay, *Gustav von Schmoller and the Problems of Today*. This represented a major turn, in the sense that it was a very positive assessment of the author and a formal endorsement of the Sozialökonomie, arguing for a fruitful combination of theory, statistics, history, and sociology as the basis for a new economics. And this remained his consistent opinion from then on, with its insistence on the role of history for the understanding of capitalism[4]—this is exactly why Schumpeter is so relevant to the purposes of the argument of this book.

In the opening of *Business Cycles* (Schumpeter 1939; henceforth *BC*) this was clearly stated: history has the 'most important contribution to the

---

[3] This was also another influence of Comte, which Schumpeter registered in *EDM*: the philosopher insisted on the 'altogetherness of social life and the need for an historical method for other problems other than the purely economic ones' (*EDM*: 96). Of course, later Schumpeter developed this programme much further, since historical methods were considered essential to account even for 'purely economic' problems.

[4] One can hypothesize that the rejection of *DW*, the 1908 book on the Methodenstreit, was connected to this important change in Schumpeter's opinion and his later incorporation of essential elements of the Historical School into his own system. Simultaneously, important elements of differentiation with the marginalist school were developed by Schumpeter: unlike Menger, he did not consider that the value theory required any psychological foundation (Bottomore 1992: 19), and he praised Pareto for getting rid of the concept of 'utility' and suggested that maximizing rationality was not a realist feature (*Ten Great Economists* (*TGE*): 179, 192).

understanding of our problem' (*BC*: 13). This book is certainly a major piece of economic historical analysis, and we will come back to it later on. As for his magisterial *History of Economic Analysis*, this is the most complete statement of the programme of Sozialökonomie: the main techniques indicated for research in economics are history ('by far the most important', since 'the subject matter is essentially a unique process in historic time'), then statistics, then theory, and finally economic sociology (*HEA*: 12).

This methodological indication, combined with the definition of economics as the study of irreversible processes of change, plus the organic vision of evolutionary societies, defines the main conclusion of this section: since Schumpeter incorporated some essential traits of the Historical School in a very distinctive framework, and since he invaded the new territory of historical mutation in economies, Schumpeter was indeed not a neoclassical economist, but at the same time, he was not able to cease considering himself to be one, since he did not wholly reject, and even tried to incorporate, the paradigm of equilibrium along with the historical forces of mutation. This is more than the simple restatement of the Paradox, as is obvious in his discussion about the role of the Walrasian system: it is also a programmatic conclusion, since the scientific viability of the modern evolutionary programme depends crucially on the rejection of the Schumpeterian compromise.

This dilemma was obvious on several occasions in Schumpeter's work. The cold reception of *BC* in the scientific community was certainly one of the indications of Schumpeter's increasing difficulty in maintaining his profile as a mainstream economist while developing what was considered as an extravagant or esoteric research. As Kuznets put it, cycles are a quantitative phenomenon and should therefore be dealt with by statistical methods, and not as a qualitative phenomenon as Schumpeter implied. Since Schumpeter had been chairman of the founding meeting of the *Econometric Society* (he was, at the time of the publication of *BC*, its vice-president and was to become its president the following year), he was consequently expected to contribute to quantitative economics and to the mathematical formalism he praised so often. He did not; and in fact, of the whole scientific community, only Frisch received the book with enthusiasm (Swedberg 1991: 271 n.).

Schumpeter acknowledged this contradiction and coped with it dramatically. This was evident at one of the last important scientific meetings attended by him, the 1949 NBER Conference on Business Cycles. At this conference, where 'historians' (the NBER researchers, following Mitchell) and 'statisticians' (the Cowles Commission staff) collided, Schumpeter undertook the task of arguing for the historical method. Furthermore, he had the moral duty to represent Mitchell, the creator and director of the NBER, who had recently died. In his uncomfortable double role as the author of *Business Cycles* and a distinguished member of the Econometric Society, Schumpeter began with a defensive declaration: 'I have no wish to advocate the historical approach to the phenomenon of the business cycle at the expense, still less to the exclusion, of theoretical or statistical work upon it' (Schumpeter 1949: 308). But he then repeated his main definition: 'Economic life is a unique process that goes on in historical time and in a disturbed environment.'

History is needed for the inquiry into exogenous, occasional events, but also and essentially into the very organism of the cycle:

For historical research is not only required in order to elucidate the nature and importance of the non-essentials dealt with so far, but also in order to elucidate the underlying cyclical process itself. . . . But it would not be quite correct to say that historical analysis gives information as regards impulses and dynamic [theoretical] models as regards the mechanism by which the impulses are propagated . . . Very roughly this is so and I should be quite content if my audience accepts the thesis that the role of the econometric model . . . is to implement the results of historical analysis of the phenomenon and to render the indispensable service for describing the mechanics of aggregates. But the econometric models do more than this—they 'explain' situations which in turn 'explain' or help to 'explain' impulses. And the reverse is also true. (Schumpeter 1949: 311–13)

This is a notorious argument, not only by its search for an incisive counter-logic pedagogy—the listeners should be driven to accept the historical method for the precise reason they were opposing it—or by the acceptance of some sort of Frischian formalism of cycles, but also because it indicates how far Schumpeter was engaged in the defence of the role of historical research and qualitative methods. And certainly, the final advice by Schumpeter did surprise his audience: 'To let the murder out and to start my final thesis, what is really required is a large collection of industrial and locational monographs . . . [including the historical change and the "behaviour of leading personnel"]' (Schumpeter 1949: 314).

It is well known that his arguments did not change the course of history, and that the econometric revolution was already well on its way. Although his arguments surprised some of his colleagues— Samuelson,[5] Goodwin ('it was a great shock to me', in Swedberg 1991: 176) and Machlup (1951: 95)— they did not stop the attacks by the econometricians against the historical method (Gordon 1986: 27), nor could they prevent the rise of the new breath of equilibrium economics.[6] Schumpeter could not prevent this, and in fact

---

[5] Samuelson's interpretation of this event is that Schumpeter loved to take the 'unpopular side' of a dispute (Samuelson 1951: 49–50, 50 n.). Faced with the evidence, this is obviously a minor point.

[6] The impact of the Cowles Commission research programme was by then dominant in the profession: the econometric revolution won the day. Friedman, by then a researcher at the NBER, argued at the conference that a final synthesis would be reached between the NBER method and the Cowles approach (Friedman 1951: 114). But Koopmans was so convinced of the superiority of the econometricians' approach that he could recommend, in an internal memorandum to the Cowles group with a balance sheet of the meeting, 'Let's not fight too much' (Epstein 1987: 111).

could not challenge it, since it was too late and too little: he was not ready to break away from the equilibrium paradigm, although he suspected he was 'letting the murder out'. He was right about that.

2.3 Evolution and Evolutionism

Discussing the foundations of economic theory, Schumpeter made a quite bizarre statement at the climax of neoclassicism: without history, our science would not be meaningful. The argument was quite strong: no explanation is legitimate without being contextualized in its proper place in the historical narration. But, then, what is history? Or, more precisely, what do economists need to know about the sequence and temporal structure of events and relations? The answer is simply, yet very demandingly, that they need to understand evolution.

Paradoxical as he was, Schumpeter did not define evolution and his own concept of evolutionism is an entangled mixture of simplifications and confusions. In the first place, evolutionism had no clear status for Schumpeter, in the methodological domain. Indeed, he defined physical science as the authoritative model: 'And so we have reached a stage, perhaps for the first time, where facts and problems are before all of us in a *clear* and in the *same* light, and where analysis and description can cooperate in something like the spirit of physical science' (Schumpeter 1927: 287).

In spite of this rather strong claim, Schumpeter always attempted to deny the incorporation of mechanistic influences into the province of economics, such as the concepts of 'force', 'equilibrium', and so forth. Furthermore, his own theoretical reasoning was dominated by the problem of change—of evolution. The cycle—and the whole 'organic' process of capitalist development[7]—should be explained by another phenomenon rather than equilibrium: by an 'industrial mutation—if I may use the biological term—that incessantly revolutionizes the economic structure from within, incessantly destroying the old one, incessantly creating a new one. This process of Creative Destruction is the essential fact about capitalism' (CSD: 83).

This is indeed a rather exceptional statement,[8] since in general Schumpeter suspected and rejected in the strongest terms any attempt to incorporate an explicit biological metaphor into economics. In 1911, he had written:

Here [in the class of 'metaphysical' tendencies], too, belong all kinds of evolutionary thought that centre in Darwin—at least if this means no more than reasoning by

---

[7] In a letter written in the early 1940s, Schumpeter argued that the organic nature of his thought was responsible for the difficulty of formalization: 'there is nothing in my structures that has not a living piece of reality behind it. This is not an advantage in every respect. It makes, for instance, my theories so refractory to mathematical formulations' (quoted in E. Andersen 1994: 2).

[8] This 'biological term' was used for the first time in 1941, in the Spanish preface to *TED* (Schumpeter 1944: 15).

analogy. . . . But the evolutionary idea is now discredited in our field, especially with historians and ethnologists, for still another reason. To the reproach of unscientific and extra-scientific mysticism that now surrounds the 'evolutionary' ideas, is added that of dilettantism. With all the hasty generalizations in which the word 'evolution' plays a part, many of us lost patience. We must get away from such things. (*TED*: 43)

Almost forty years later, Schumpeter still held the same opinion and expressed it in the same terms. Writing in *HEA* about the 1870–1914 period, he emphatically described biological evolutionism as 'a field infected by ideological bias and by dilettantism to an extent that surpasses anything that even we economists are accustomed to' (*HEA*: 788). In spite of it, Schumpeter considered Darwin's *Origin* as an important scientific achievement, comparable to the definition of the heliocentric system (*HEA*: 445, 445 n.), and Darwin's historical sketch of the previous biological theories as a crucial piece for the sociology of science, but he did not indicate any possible kind of influence of theses texts on social sciences: his sympathetic references were probably due mainly to ceremonial reasons. Nevertheless, it is clear that Schumpeter's purpose was to attack the influential and widespread Spencerian type of evolutionism, which combined 'naive laissez-faire' with a simplified version of Darwinism, leading to conclusions such as the 'silly' suggestion for the abandonment of sanitary regulations or public systems of education and health (*HEA*: 773). Schumpeter also cared to inform the reader, in the introduction to *BC*, that his assumption about the organicity of economic processes did not at all imply his being a supporter of *laissez-faire* (*BC*: vi). Therefore, the concept of 'industrial mutation' was rather exceptional and had been carefully chosen in order to emphasize the non-equilibrium properties of development and evolution. In this, Schumpeter was indeed closer to Marx than to Walras.[9]

In fact, Schumpeter's evolutionism was not based on Darwinism or, in general, on the biological metaphor, which played only a minor role, if any, in his system. But it was nevertheless an evolutionary conception, since it was based upon two central concepts. First, the economy was defined as an 'organic'[10] whole, propelled by a process of development with mutations.

---

[9] Schumpeter's main argument was that the nature of the economic reality was a disequilibrating process, just as Marx conceived it (*HEA*: 77, 774 n.; *CSD*: 83). In the Japanese preface this was indicated when he argued that Marx was, with Walras, the main source of his thought, and that, unlike the latter, he discussed the dynamical processes of change. In *CSD* Schumpeter argued that Marx was the first to abandon the concept of 'crisis' as an accident, and therefore to anticipate Juglar (*CSD*: 41). Elizabeth Schumpeter, in her preface to the 1951 collection of *Essays*, argued that her husband had in common with Marx the vision of capitalism as a dynamical process (Elizabeth Schumpeter, in Schumpeter 1951: 9).

[10] Of course, the 'organic' argument may be a trivial declaration of the self-containedness of a system, and in the previous sections several instances of such a stance were found. In this case, the 'organicity' of the system is fully identified with its mechanistic character, that is, a 'natural' system excludes purposive action. The word is used in this section in a very distinct sense, still indicating the indirect influence of the biological metaphor: an organic system includes complex and indeterminate interactions and feedbacks including with the environment: it is an open system. This is the sense used in connection with the Schumpeterian concept of an organic whole.

Second, this defined a non-mechanistic and historical view of capitalism as one of creation and destruction. Since the concept of 'mutation', the change arising from innovation in the core of the system, has been discussed above, this section will now turn to the concept of the organic system.

Here is how Schumpeter presented the concept, criticizing the biological analogy:

In the first place, we notice the idea that society, being an 'organic' system and not a 'mechanical' one, can be fruitfully analyzed in terms of an analogy with biological organisms such as the human body. . . . But the obvious puerility of this idea must not blind us to the fact that emphasis upon the 'organic nature' of the economic process may be but the means of conveying an eminently sound methodological principle—as it was, for instance, with Ma shall. Theorists—specially of the 'planning' type—often indulge in the deplorable practice of deriving 'practical' results from a few functional relations between a few economic aggregates in utter disregard of the fact that such analytical set-ups are conge..itally incapable of taking account of deeper things, the more subtle relations that cannot be weighted and measured . . . 'Organic' considerations are perhaps the most obvious antidote—though in themselves hardly an adequate one—against such uncivilized procedure. (*HEA*: 788–9)

Besides the polemic bias—that the 'theorists of the planning type' could be easily replaced by the 'theorists of the marginalist type' and the whole paragraph would keep its sense—this is a clear indication of the nature of Schumpeter's thought: organic considerations were supposed to be essential in order to avoid the useless biological analogies and hence to provide an overall method for the economic inquiry: the solution of a system of equations was unable to represent complex or 'more subtle' relations. This explains his approach to causality in economics (*BC*: 7) and to the analysis of its features (Schumpeter 1949: 313). Evolutionism, then, was for Schumpeter simply the consideration of organic evolution in real time, or of historical and irreversible processes of change:

Social phenomena constitute a unique process in historic time, and incessant and irreversible changes are their most obvious characteristic. If by Evolutionism we mean not more than recognition of this fact, then all reasoning about social phenomena must be either evolutionary in itself or else bear upon evolution. Here, however, evolutionism is to mean more than this. One may recognize the fact without making it the pivot of one's thought and the guiding principle of one's method. . . . [James Mill's] various systems were not evolutionary in the sense that his thought in any of those fields turned upon evolution. And it is this that shall be the criterion of evolutionism for us, both as regards philosophy . . . and as regards any 'scientific field'. (*HEA*: 435–6)

It is possible to conclude that Schumpeter defined the social process as an intrinsic dynamic disturbance of equilibrium through the creation of novelty—the innovative mutation—and this was precisely what defined his evolutionary framework. It included stationary processes of equilibrium, the place of Walras, but also forces and processes moving towards disequilibrium, the place of Marx. And it was organic, since both processes were considered to be compatible, and since all the relevant variables were considered to be endogenous to the system, which itself generates movement and change. Moreover, this particular combination was considered to be the very specificity of economics, and so Schumpeter believed that his general and historical approach was the only one able to integrate both the statics of general equilibrium and the dynamics of disequilibrating forces: in a superior synthesis, the unscientific bias of the physical and the biological analogies would be prevented, since those analogies took the part as the whole and thus developed dilettante or simplistic views.

Schumpeter's work on the cycle and the long waves of structural change under capitalism provided one of the more creative examples of his own solution to the difficulties of considering economic processes as part of an evolutionary world.

In 1910, while preparing *TED*, Schumpeter summarized his own views in some short theses:

First, the economic processes divide into two different and also in practice clearly discernible classes: static and dynamic. Second, the latter constitutes the pure economic evolution, that is, those changes in the model of the economy which arise from itself. Third, the economic evolution is essentially a disturbance of the static equilibrium of the economy. Fourth, this disturbance provokes a reaction in the static masses of the economy, namely a movement towards a new state of equilibrium. (Schumpeter, quoted in E. Andersen 1994: 41)

For our present purposes, it is essential to emphasize that Schumpeter distinguished between statics and dynamics, as Mill had previously done, as two real processes, related by the conception that without disturbances the system would be 'static'[11] but that those disturbances arise from inside the system itself. In 1908, Schumpeter argued that the central question for 'pure' economics was statics and equilibrium—which surely deserved the approval of Walras—and considered dynamics as a marginal phenomenon (*DW*, quoted in Bottomore 1992: 171), despite some rhetorical declarations about dynamics as 'the land of the future' (*DW*, quoted in Swedberg 1991: 29–30). But he quickly changed his opinion, as indicated by the 1910 thesis.

It is also certain that *Das Wesen* already presented some clues for the future discussion about the entrepreneur. Schumpeter was influenced by Riedel, an economist of the early nineteenth century, who stressed the role of innovations in economic life; by the previous work on the entrepreneur by Thuenen or Bohm Bawerk; and particularly by his teacher, Wieser, under the ultra-romantic influence so important in Germany at the time: a figure of a 'great

---

[11] In the first edition of *TED* (1911) Schumpeter used the distinction 'circular flow'/'development'; in the second edition (1926) these were replaced by 'statics'/'dynamics'. But since 1934, as indicated in the preface to the English edition of *TED*, 'in deference to Professor Frisch', and also in *BC*, Schumpeter used the distinction between static and dynamic *forms of analysis*, and stationary or development *processes in nature* (*TED* 1934 edn.: 6).

man' and some 'heroic individualism' was defined in economics, just as Spencer did in sociology, Nietzsche in philosophy (Streissler 1994: 19 ff., 34; Allen 1991: 107), and J. B. Clark in economics. Entrepreneurship was interpreted in 1908 as the function of carrying the adventuresome innovation (Allen 1991: 47).

In 1911, in *TED*, Schumpeter presented these conclusions as the distinction between the 'circular flow' and 'development', the main economic processes in action (*TED*: 145). The circular flow, the 'missing link' in economic causality (*EDM*: 43 ff.) supposedly discovered by the physiocrats, described

> how each economic period becomes the basis for the subsequent one, not only in a technical sense but also in the sense that it produces exactly such results as induce and enable the members of the economic community to repeat the same process in the same form in the next economic period; how economic production comes about as a social process, how it determines the consumption of every individual and how the latter in its turn determines further production. (*EDM*: 43)

In other words, this is the stationary process or the condition for equilibrium, which are analytically equivalent (*BC*: 42 n.; also 68). On the other hand, development was defined as a *quantum* jump in the social conditions of the system, 'that kind of change arising from within the system which so displaces its equilibrium point that the new one cannot be reached from the old one by infinitesimal steps' (*TED*: 47 n.; also Schumpeter 1935: 4). The 'static conditions' exclude the cycle but not growth: in fact, 'growth', defined as the combination of the evolution of capital accumulation from savings[12] and of the population, was included in the notion of static equilibrium (Schumpeter 1927: 289 ff.). Equilibrium was thus defined as a 'shifting centre of gravitation' in a system that also generates the internal impulse for change, that is, for the rupture of the equilibrium conditions. While development accounted for the nature of the change (*BC*: 560 n.), equilibrium described the absorption of change (Schumpeter 1937: 159), that is, was defined as the stability property of the system. This topic will be discussed further.

The real economic system cannot be understood without the integration of both processes: in fact, even if Schumpeter sometimes indicated that 'perfect' equilibrium was never really present (*BC*: 52) and that it was a 'methodological fiction' (p. 964), or if he criticized Walras's and Clark's presentation of real prices oscillating around equilibrium (*HEA*: 999, 1000 n.), his general approach was to argue for an integrated account of the development process as including both change and equilibrium. In his 'first approximation' to the

---

[12] Schumpeter's concept of capital was defined as a flexible resource, distinct from the technical structure of the production process (Oakley 1990: 38). It belongs to the circular flow, and is 'that part of the social product of preceding economic periods which maintains the production of the current period' (*EDM*: 54). Thus, there are two sources of accumulation, one being the circular flow and another the development process, which is moved by innovation.

theory of the business cycle, equilibrium existed at the end of the depression and before the prosperity. In the 'second approximation', when the 'secondary wave' was considered and the cycle was described in four phases, equilibrium conditions were met at two of the inflexion points, namely when the recession leads to depression and when the revival leads to prosperity and a new cycle is supposed to begin.

Three main points should be emphasized. First, this schema considered the stationary process or the equilibrium conditions to be a special case of the dynamic movement, specifically, that corresponding to the discrete points where the movement is null (*BC*: 70–1, 963). This quite closely matches the mechanical Mill–Comte definition of the distinction between 'statics' and 'dynamics' and the possibility of conducting a static analysis, the 'bare bones of economic logic', 'clearing the ground for rigorous analysis' (*BC*: 68).

Second, the existence of equilibrium was stated and its stability was defined as the real processes of absorption of change and of disturbance:

The thing that matters to us is nevertheless this tendency [towards equilibrium] considered as an actual force, and not the mere existence of ideal equilibrium points of reference. . . . We wish to distinguish definite periods in which the system embarks upon an excursion away from equilibrium and equally definite periods in which it draws towards equilibrium. (*BC*: 69–70)

Or also, without room for doubt: 'Common sense tells us that this mechanism for establishing or re-establishing equilibrium is not a figment devised as an exercise in the pure logic of economics but actually operative in the reality around us' (*BC*: 47, also 56).

In this sense, the mechanism of equilibration provided the resistance to change in the economic system, namely the defence of established business and institutional traditions: it was the creation of order subsuming the creation of novelty,[13] for example imitation restoring equilibrium after innovation. Equilibrium or order would be the moment of the formation of prices, while development or disorder is the evolutionary process: in Schumpeter's emphatic words, 'fluctuations must be fluctuations around something' (*BC*: 69).

Third, this did not imply that equilibrium was considered the desirable situation. In the first approximation, it was considered the situation where the promises of the boom were fulfilled, that is where the availability of consumption goods increased for the whole community (*TED*: 161). But in the second approximation, this was certainly more complex, since the system was described as in permanent turmoil, and its change—the disequilibrium

---

[13] Rosenberg interprets Schumpeter's position on the circular flow as a theoretical description, as opposed to the real processes of change in capitalism (Rosenberg 1994: 43), and Swedberg interprets it as an ideal-type (Swedberg 1991: 32). But the previous quotations refute this interpretation: for Schumpeter, the circular flow was a real process, *simultaneous* with development, and a complete theory should integrate both dimensions in the same framework.

processes—was the only form of progress. From this point of view, Schumpeter clearly opposed the 'classics' and the general equilibrium paradigm, and even condemned their incapacity to incorporate real economic evolution: as he stressed in *Economic Doctrines and Method*, at the very time when the first modern industrial crises were erupting, the 'classicals' were still arguing for Say's Law and rejecting the theoretical possibility of disequilibrium, against all easily available evidence (*EDM*: 150). The main achievement of Juglar, by contrast, was precisely to define a new agenda for research, indicating the problem, describing it empirically, and presenting an explanation (Schumpeter 1927: 287). In other words, the tendency to novelty that moves the economic system forward depends on the ability of the entrepreneur to challenge equilibrium: 'What a miserable figure he is, this economic subject who is always looking so anxiously for an equilibrium. He has no ambition and no entrepreneurial spirit; in brief, he is without force and life' (*DW*, quoted in Swedberg 1991: 29).

With these qualifications, Schumpeter's theory of the cycle can now be reassessed. The motion of the system was analysed under a steady-state representation; then the possibility of change was introduced as an independent and separable dimension, since both correspond to social processes that can be isolated. In other words, Walras indicated a convenient approach to discussing one of the processes (*BC*: 47), but this was not enough, since evolution should also be explained: for Walras the needs were given, while for Schumpeter the real economic processes created new needs and led to deep transformations. The Schumpeterian research programme consisted of the bold task of providing the dynamic counterpart of the Walrasian schema, in order to create a truly general theory.

This implied that some sort of logical separability was possible between the problems of growth and cycle, since growth was reduced to the monotonic trend of capital accumulation through savings and to population increase, both being added to an equilibrating process. Of course, this did not solve the statistical problem of the assessment of the trend and cycle, since there was no real trend of equilibrium—only a number of discrete equilibrium points, two for each cycle—and since the cyclical process by itself displaces the centre of gravitation upwards.

And, moreover, the three-cycle schema implied that the equilibria of the shorter cycles were defined in the artificial representation of the trend line of the larger cycles, and that the single true equilibrium occurred at the very beginning of a Kondratiev wave, when prosperity was to commence and the equilibria of the three types of cycles coincided. All other points are 'neighbourhoods of equilibrium', therefore unstable for a new, very structural reason: the dynamics of evolution in the larger cycles—the Kondratiev long waves—overdetermined the shorter ones, even when they were in the neighbourhood of equilibrium in their own motion. This was a form of representation of the feedback mechanisms in action in real economies, but it added singular difficulties to the mathematical treatment of the model—and

Schumpeter certainly had these in mind when he accepted that his theories were very hostile to mathematical formalism.[14]

This permanent tendency to the dislocation of the centre of gravity of the system and the complex interaction of the different cycles account for an original form of instability, created by the system itself. Schumpeter's theory was a system of self-generating complexity and instability, where the equilibrium concept really played only a very subsidiary role. But Schumpeter was not prepared to break with the Walrasian half of his theory, for philosophical rather than theoretical economic reasons. The rationale for this refusal can be discovered in his general view of science and the definition of his own place in economic theory, which we will proceed to discuss using the illustration provided by the sharp controversy of Schumpeter against Keynes.

2.4 Schumpeter and Keynes: 'Semi-autonomous Variables' and Reasoned History

Schumpeter and Keynes were born in the same year and, although from distant points, followed the same events, frequented the same theories, and discussed the same topics. But they reacted differently to these times, and formulated quite opposing hypotheses and conjectures. Moreover, there was between them a larger distance than the geographical one: there was misunderstanding and rivalry.

This was mostly true in relation to Schumpeter, who intensely envied the success of his colleague: his review of Keynes's *General Theory*, (Keynes 1936), issued almost immediately after the publication of the book, was a lively and almost incomparable image of bitterness and scientific aggressivity. The short article was full of offensive remarks: Keynes's *General Theory* was based on 'artificial definitions', 'paradoxical-looking tautologies', 'treacherous generality', psychological laws of a 'bygone age'; it was 'Ricardian in spirit and intent', which certainly was not intended to please Keynes (Schumpeter 1936: 792, 793). The final touch is a monument to perversity: challenging Keynes's conceptions of saving and effective demand, Schumpeter gave the example of Louis XV, who was supposed to have called Madame Pompadour in and asked her to spend as much as possible, increasing effective demand in order to avoid depression

---

[14] One of the main reasons for the sense of failure Schumpeter felt in his last years was his incapacity to develop a formal model for his theories. His own diary proves that he worked almost daily and helplessly with systems of equations, at least since 1934 when preparing *BC* and afterwards, looking for a general equilibrium model accounting for the time path of the variables (Allen 1991: ii. 8, 142, 177, 190, 227). But his colleagues, such as Goodwin, witnessed his difficulties with mathematics. In spite of that, he suspected that the available differential and difference equations were unsuited to define an evolutionary system including social relations and complex behaviours.

and thereby guarantee the well-being of the people—of course, concluded Schumpeter, if it all finished in a blood-bath, this was a mere coincidence.

But still, this review indicated two important themes. The first was the critique of the short-term view ('a theory of another world'), which did not make possible any change in the production functions, since 'reasoning on the assumption that variations in output are uniquely related to variations in employment imposes the further assumption that all the production functions remain invariant. Now the outstanding feature of capitalism is that they do not but that, on the contrary, they are being incessantly revolutionized.' (Schumpeter 1936: 793). Consequently, a theory of short-term movements would 'exclude the salient features of capitalist reality', as Schumpeter maintained later on (*HEA*: 1144).

The second theme was the critique, on the same grounds, of the three *dei ex machina* of the *General Theory* ('there is a whole Olympus of them', wrote Schumpeter (*HEA*: 794)): expectations, the psychological law of consumption, and the schedule of the liquidity preference—all three could not be part of an economic explanation, according to Schumpeter. These two main critiques are discussed in the following pages, in order to provide a brief comparison between the research programmes of Keynes and Schumpeter and their assessment of evolution.

In the 1936 review, Schumpeter rejected the use of expectations and of all psychological laws (such as Keynes's explanation of consumption and of liquidity preference), which were introduced as exogenous factors and as ultimate causes for the economic behaviour. Those explanations were considered to be tautological,[15] like any purely exogenously driven form of causality.

The exact nature of expectations in Keynes's system is a matter of controversy. Mini considers that they are not independent variables, since they are part of the nature of economic agents (Mini 1991: 179). But this is not completely convincing, since economics is not necessarily a global explanation of all the features of real-life agents. O'Donnell, on the other hand, considers that long-term expectations—those concerned with decisions to invest and hence with transformations of the economic system—are typically independent variables, while short-term expectations, concerned with decisions to use the existing capital equipment, are endogenous (O'Donnell 1989: 241, 236). In this interpretation, long-term economic expectations determine the short-term expectations in the specific sector of capital goods, and thus the employment in this sector, while short-term expectations determine the employment in the sector of consumption goods.

---

[15] 'But expectations are not linked by Mr Keynes to the cyclical situations that give rise to them and hence become independent variables and ultimate determinants of economic action. . . . An expectation acquires explanatory value if we are made to understand why people expect what they expect. Otherwise expectation is a mere *deus ex machina* that conceals problems instead of solving them' (Schumpeter 1936: 792 n.). Of course, this would be the relevant form of causality if Schumpeter still accepted his previous account in *TED*, where the cause was considered to be the first relevant exogenous factor for the system (*TED*: 10).

Keynes's treatment of expectations was once again deeply rooted in his philosophy. From the first drafts of what would become the *Treatise on Probability*, (Keynes 1921; henceforth *TP*), Keynes insisted that logic should include uncertainty and not only deductive relations, which are certain or true if logically correct. This general logic implied the passage 'from the logic of implication and the categories of truth and falsehood to the logic of probability and the categories of knowledge, ignorance and rational belief' (*TP*: 62).

In this theory of rational belief, uncertainty can arise from three different sources: from the probability of an event (the measure of the degree of certainty), from the weight of the argument (namely, the nature of the available evidence), and finally from the unknown probabilities of events. But the traditional approach to mathematical expectations assumes the numeric and measurable nature of all variables and events, and thus ignores the weight of the argument and risk.[16]

In other words, uncertainty was to Keynes the reflection of a world where there are measurable and non-measurable qualities, or quantitative and qualitative phenomena. O'Donnell suggests that Keynes's interpretation of reality distinguished between those features of a quality that could be described by a degree and those that could not, including in this first category those objects or properties describable as the sum of its parts (weight), those for which the degree of the whole equates the degree of the parts (colour), and finally those for which the whole is independent of the parts (beauty) (O'Donnell 1989: 62). In this framework, 'colour' and 'beauty' are the examples of organic units, while 'weight' is a non-organic one. Expectation is typically one of such variables that can only be represented as an organic system, and therefore are non-calculable and impossible to represent in the Cartesian world of purely deductive logic. This corresponds to the notion of *semi-autonomous variables*, which are to be represented as endogenous or exogenous depending on the scope of the model,[17] since they represent the crucial connection between distinct levels of abstraction in the context of non-contained models. The relevance of these variables flows from the fact that they are not compatible with the deterministic view of causality, and that they represent the organic synthesis of network causality and complexity.

Rejecting this whole approach to expectation from his very first writings,[18] Schumpeter tried several times to formulate an alternative one. He failed to

---

[16] Risk was defined by Keynes as the mathematical expectation times the probability of failure (Keynes 1921: 348)—this was written approximately one decade before the seminal book by Knight.

[17] In the *General Theory* (*GT*) these variables (propensity to consume, marginal efficiency of capital, rate of interest) were formulated as independent, although Keynes recognized that it was an impure solution since they were influenced by other variables (expectations, etc.). The designation of the semi-autonomous variables as exogenous is the *testemonium paupertatis* of modelling.

[18] In *TED*, before the publication of any of Keynes's writings, Schumpeter had already stated that he was firmly opposed to the 'psychological prejudice which consists in seeing more in

do so. In *Business Cycles,* dealing with Knight's concept of expectations, Schumpeter went back to the stationary state in order to indicate that, even without omniscience, expectations are based on experience, and perfect foresight is possible and indeed trivial in that case (*BC*: 52). But if disturbances affect the system, expectations consequently change: they may either preserve or prevent disequilibria (p. 53). The drastic solution was to treat expectations as equilibrating features, and this was postulated in a very uncomfortable way, which is distinctively dogmatic and neoclassical:

> But although they [the disruptive effects of 'certain types of expectations'] may often temporarily counteract it, they do not in themselves disprove the existence of an equilibrium tendency or the proposition that at times it prevails in such a way as actually to draw the system toward equilibrium. The real trouble to the theorist comes from the fact that introducing expected values in his variables—we will now, on the one hand, assume that they are expected with certainty and, on the other hand, also include past values—changes the whole character of his problem and makes it technically so difficult to handle that he may easily find himself unable to prove an equilibrium tendency which, nevertheless, may exist, or even the existence and stability of the equilibrium position itself. (*BC*: 54)

In such a framework, expectations can then be treated either as endogenous variables contributing to the equilibrating tendencies, or as exogenous variables fully known; but both solutions are unsatisfactory. Schumpeter clearly preferred the first solution,[19] arguing that otherwise expectations would constitute a theoretical blank to fill another blank (*HEA*: 312). But even in that case, he argued there is no explanation for these variables *ad hoc* defined as endogenous: the only available interpretation for expectations is to ignore them, since they are so difficult to handle (*BC*: 55).

In our view, the only solution for this difficulty is that represented by the concept of semi-autonomous variables, those not wholly endogenously explainable by the system and whose behaviour is not autonomously determined by exogenous events in its full extent. In fact, they are not parameters, but the theoretical counterparts of the organic and complex realities; that is, they indicate the building nonlinearities of the system. Now, what is striking is that Schumpeter in some way touched this exact problem when he left the domain of stationarity—where he discussed Knight's concepts of uncertainty and risk—and considered the notion of development.

In *Business Cycles,* Schumpeter argued that there are three different types of variable: (1) *theoretical,* that is, those related to a law and, consequently,

---

'motives and acts of volition than a reflex of the social process' (*TED*: 43). But in *TGE,* Schumpeter credited Keynes with the dynamic feature of the concept of expectations (*TGE*: 381), even if this aspect was never developed in Schumpeter's work. As a matter of fact, Schumpeter was generally opposed to the Keynesian concept of expectations.

[19] 'Unless we know why people expect what they expect, any argument is completely valueless which appeals to them as *causa efficients.* Such appeals enter into the class of pseudo-explanations which already amused Molière' (*BC*: 140).

invariant in their behaviour; (2) *random*; and (3) *historical*, defined as 'hybrid variables', since they represent the 'theoretical law in a process of change' (*BC*: 194–5). 'Hence we may . . . define a historical variable as a variable, the stochastic normal of which changes owing to a change of its theoretical normal' (p. 196). And since 'the very concept of historical sequence implies the occurrence of irreversible changes in the economic structure which must be expected to affect the law of any given quantity' (*CSD*: 72 n.), it implies that very peculiar sort of variables, the kind that cannot be defined as endogenous and cannot be simplified as exogenous (in the Schumpeterian sense of purely stochastic variables, or otherwise as identified factors that are exterior to the scope of the theory). In other words, the morphogenetic process of mutation and evolution cannot be encapsulated in the strict formalism of the mathematical models of simultaneous and linear equations under the current qualifications—since these are not organic representations—and requires the inclusion of a new type of explanation, historical by nature.

Innovation, the key concept of Schumpeter, cannot be fully understood unless in that framework, and it is easily verifiable that all of Schumpeter's arguments against the Keynesian concept of expectation are directly extensible to innovation. Its source (invention) is exogenous and therefore not explained. Its diffusion is endogenous, but it is simultaneously a source of disruption in the system. Nowhere is it fully explained nor is it completely explainable by the system, since it cannot be represented by the postulated relations, as it depends on singular decisions. Innovation is endogenous to the system, but it is finally determined by the entrepreneurial function, that unique capacity to make new combinations, which is clearly outside the domain of the model. And, of course, this boundary between endogenous and exogenous variables can change according to the purposes of each inquiry, as Schumpeter was aware, and is therefore irrelevant as a classification criterion.[20]

In a much more prudent and realist way, Keynes introduced three main expectations-dependent variables: propensity to consume, marginal efficiency of capital, and liquidity preference. He was right to do so and to stress

---

[20] 'What precisely is looked upon as inherent [endogenous] in it [the system] will, of course, depend on how we delimit it and which facts and relations we decide to treat as data, and which are variable' (*BC*: 7 n.). Just at the end of the book, he indicated that variables such as 'mentality' could be considered as exogenous, as usually, or as endogenous, according to the researcher and to the research—*BC* is said to take normally a 'narrow sense' (p. 1050 n.). Of course, this created the greatest confusion among the historians of economic thought.

Hansen considered the exogeneity or endogeneity of Schumpeter's theory a 'perennial and inexhaustible subject for discussion', not clarified by the author himself. Here is Hansen's own interpretation, a Salomonic solution: 'It is exogenous in the respect that it places primary emphasis upon changes in the data. Yet it is also an endogenous theory in the respect that it runs in terms of an internal, self-perpetuating system . . . whose impelling force, innovation, cycle after cycle renews the wave-like the movement. . . . [The business cycle] is an endogenous process determined by the inner nature of a dynamic economy, but it is exogenous in the sense that innovation is a change in the basic data' (Hansen 1951: 80).

the irreducible uncertainty in organic systems.[21] The reason he could do so, without being entangled like Schumpeter in a self-contradictory net of explanations, was because Keynes's philosophy suggested the notion of organicity and therefore liberated him from the stringency of the concept of equilibrium, although he was not able to incorporate these notions in a dynamic approach.[22]

This is not the end of the story, for in the Schumpeterian explanatory system there is a further complication: he postulated the existence of a tendency to equilibrium, which was offset for some periods by a counter-tendency propelled by innovation, and insisted on the actual existence of some equilibrium points in every cycle. This suggests the application of the traditional statistical methods of analysis of the trend as the *loci* of those equilibria, and of the cycle as the deviations, as in the mainstream tradition. But Schumpeter did not accept that scheme, in spite of some rhetorics supporting Wicksell's and Frisch's rocking horse metaphor, since his own impulses were defined as endogenous and therefore equilibrium was supposed to be by nature unstable: instability was structural, the disturbances changed the system, and that was the condition for the progress of capitalism. As a consequence, econometricians reacted with great hostility to his formulations, which could not be reduced to a domesticated system of equations.

Tinbergen sharply criticized *Business Cycles*, considering that the book was 'alien to econometrics', since for Schumpeter the relevant variables were the shocks, and he 'belittles the importance of the mechanism', which for econometricians 'deserves the main attention'. Tinbergen could not accept Schumpeter's theory of the impulses being endogenous to the system, since this was not compatible with the traditional cycle model and econometric schemata (Tinbergen 1951: 59, 60). Schumpeter implicitly answered this criticism, commenting that Tinbergen's model 'describes repercussions and propagations without saying anything about the forces or causes that put them into motion' (Schumpeter 1937: 162).

In fact, Schumpeter tried to save his allegiance to orthodoxy, stating that the impulses could be of two kinds, both compatible with equilibrium:

Now, what causes economic fluctuations may either be individual shocks which impinge on the system from outside, or a distinct process of change generated by the system itself, but in both cases the theory of equilibrium supplies us with the simplest code of rules according to which the system will respond. This is what we mean by saying that the theory of equilibrium is a description of an apparatus of response. (*BC*: 68)

---

[21] In his *GT* Keynes clearly stated that a mathematical model could not represent expectations (Keynes 1936: 162–3).

[22] Because of its statistical framework, in *GT* expectations were modelled as exogenous variables and the explanation was abstracted from uncertainty, except in chap. 22, in which expectations were introduced in order to understand fluctuations. For what matters for this book, cycles and irregular growth cannot be explained unless in a dynamical context.

Later on in the same book, Schumpeter compared the impulses with a water flow (*BC*: 179), which is close to Frisch's analogy in his 1933 paper. Nevertheless, there remain some remarkable differences: Frisch supposed a damping propagation mechanism, which is the most coherent way to reintroduce the notion of stability of equilibrium, while Schumpeter described a specific oscillator, representing a cyclical and unstable form of growth. And this is why Schumpeter could never accept Frisch's metaphor of the rocking horse as a convenient representation for the process of cycles (Louçã 1997).

In the *History of Economic Analysis*, there is another metaphor for the explanation of this particular system—and, eventually, for the failure of the current statistical methods—when Schumpeter indicates that the economic system is a resonator for the impulses, just like a violin: the impulse and propagation autonomous systems are clearly stated, but neither the wooden box nor the movements of the fingers of the musician may fully explain the aesthetical pleasure of a concert (*HEA*: 1167).

Furthermore, the propagation and cyclical mechanisms in Frisch's model may explain the cycle, but they do not explain the trend–cycle behaviour. This is, of course, a major difference with Schumpeter's theory, which was instead concerned with the creative responses of the economic system to whatever impulses may exist (*BC*: 72). Indeed, when developing his theory, Schumpeter discussed this problem in detail. The propagation mechanism was traditionally considered as the equilibrating Walrasian feature of the modelled economy, but the theory did not indicate when those equilibrium conditions are fulfilled. Schumpeter argued that the equilibrium force really existed, but he stressed that actual equilibria were attainable only at discrete and rare points, to be immediately abandoned by the motion of the system. Therefore, the equilibrium line indicated in the statistics was only an artificial representation:

They [the neighbourhoods of equilibrium] are the most relevant items of a series . . . A line or curve through those points, or a band or narrow zone through those neighbourhoods, supplies a trend that really has economic significance. . . . We know . . . that this trend does not describe a phenomenon distinct from the cycle. On the contrary, since evolution is essentially a process that moves in cycles, the trend is nothing but the result of the cyclical process or a property of it. . . . Moreover, we also know that it carries realistic meaning only in discrete points or intervals. If we connect them by straight lines . . . it must be borne in mind that the stretches between the neighbourhoods are nothing but a visual help, and devoid of realistic meaning. No fact corresponds to them. Real is only the cycle itself. (*BC*: 206–7)

Or else, criticizing the statistical methods: 'if trend-analysis is to have any meaning, it can derive it only from previous theoretical considerations, which must not only guide us in interpreting results, but also in choosing the method. Failing this, a trend is no more than a descriptive device summing up past history with which nothing can be done. It is, in fact, merely formal' (Schumpeter 1930: 166).

Schumpeter acknowledged the efforts by Mitchell to solve the same problem of the relation between the trend and cycle through the 'reference cycles', 'a judicious compromise between eliminating trend and leaving it in' (Schumpeter 1952: 339), and he even defined the formal trend as those sub-intervals where the mean value is monotonically increasing or decreasing (Schumpeter 1935: 3). But the economic meaning of the trend and the applicability of the 'statistical method' (of least squares) were supposed to depend on the interpretation of an economic mechanism explaining the monotonic variation. The only mechanism of that type is growth (savings and population), which constitutes the 'real trend' (*BC*: 201 ff.); but, as previously indicated, this was considered to be a minor influence in the overall behaviour of the system.[23]

In short, Schumpeter claimed that there was a real trend of growth that was a secondary feature of the model, that there were discrete points where the tendency towards equilibrium was achieved, and that there was a causal process inseparably explaining both cycle and evolution. Thus, the meaningful trend, the 'trend-result' describing evolution and the cycle, synthesized one and the same process, and therefore no multiple regression could be successfully applied to it, according to Schumpeter, since it implied the decomposability of this process. But, according to the theory, there was no meaningful separation of the variables of impulse (innovation) and its propagation mechanism, since both are endogenous, and every decomposition would be arbitrary: 'It follows that barring the elements of growth the trends of our times series are not due to influences distinct from those that create the cyclical fluctuations but simply embody the results of the latter. To these "result-trends" . . . it is entirely unwarranted to apply formal methods of the type of least squares' (Schumpeter 1935: 6).

The same argument was given in other works (Schumpeter 1930: 167; *BC*: 198). This was a substantial reason for the rejection of the Slutsky effect of the impact of random shocks on the propagation mechanism (*BC*: 180–1). Here is the heart of Schumpeter's model: equilibrium was the reference to the trend, but this was without implication in the choice of method of analysis, since it could not in any case be meaningfully separated from the cycle itself. Furthermore, to add to the analytical difficulty, the theory provided an explanation for the automatic disturbance of equilibrium and indicated the relevant process to be the disequilibrating and innovative process of creative destruction, the central feature of capitalism—and the very reason for its survival and adaptation.

This was in fact the consequence of the centrality of 'hybrid variables', whose 'theoretical norm' changes following the irreversible process of mutation (*BC*: 196, 198): the historical approach is therefore necessary to a general theory of the cycle, since the cycle is always a 'historical individual'

---

[23] For reasons of criticism of the correlation methods, Keynes shared such suspicion about decomposition and the concepts of 'trend' and 'residuals' (Keynes 1921: xiv. 319).

(Schumpeter 1935: 2). The trend exists, but in our analytical mind: it is the 'gravitational axis of the smoothed curve' in our own representation (*BC*: 210). Equilibrium exists, but it is exiled to the domain of the secondary and artificial representations.[24] The cycle is the only persistent and meaningful reality: it is the name of progress.

And with the cycle we are back to the concept of evolution, or history: 'The essential point to grasp is that in dealing with capitalism we are dealing with an evolutionary process' (*CSD*: 82).

2.5 Conclusions

Schumpeter's ambition was immense: he intended to do no less than for-mulate a theory sufficiently general to encompass the determinateness of general equilibrium and the indeterminateness of general disequilibrium. 'I was trying to construct a theoretical model of the process of economic change in time, or perhaps more clearly, to answer the question how the economic system generates the force which incessantly transforms it' (Schumpeter 1951: 158–9). This revolutionizing force, the *alma mater* of capi-talism, was innovation, and Schumpeter had been after it since 1911–12 (Schumpeter 1927: 292).

But innovation is historical by nature, and can be understood only as a historical process: its clustering and non-random distribution (*BC*: 75), and its relation to the changes in organizational and institutional structure, are part of the organic functioning of modern capitalism. This is why reasoned history should be used in economics as part of the core function of theo-rizing, in a triple sense. First, theory itself can be understood, according to Schumpeter, in two different senses: either as a *corpus* of explanatory hypotheses, or as a body of conceptual tools (Schumpeter 1952: 326–7), and his preference for the former interpretation was based on a consideration of the nature of economics itself as an evolutionary process, resistant to the simplistic tools of applied mechanics. Second, the theory of changes could itself be self-defeating, based as it was on occasional disturbances—the analytical form to introduce explanatory events, abandoning any hope to explain them—but it could also choose an alternative strategy, and study the movements of disequilibrium: 'the cycles are the form of capitalist evo-lution' (Schumpeter 1952: 333, or 1927: 295), and this is why reasoned history is the ultimate complete theory (1927: 298). Third, and because of the previous arguments, the formal methods, based on the rigour of statis-tics, could fail us just when they are most needed to prove a theory: rea-soned history is required since the subject matter of this research, i.e.

---

[24] In realist accounts, the problem is further complicated by the abandonment of the hypo-thesis of perfect competition: under oligopolistic situations equilibrium becomes indeterminate (*CSD*: 79–80), and the same happens under monopolistic competition (*BC*: 57).

change and evolution, is by nature historical—the cycles 'carry historical meaning which . . . is much more important than fulfilment of any formal criterion' (Schumpeter 1935: 7).

Following these assumptions and intuitions, Schumpeter pleaded for the 'coalition', or combination, of different types of economists in his introductory paper to *Econometrica* (Schumpeter 1933: 7): rigour and proof depended, he claimed, on this articulation of knowledge, essential for the explanation of real economies.

In all this inquiry, one forerunner, who was also a contemporary, played a major role in the definition of Schumpeter's vision: that was Kondratiev, a Russian economist widely known at the time for his hypothesis on long cycles. Schumpeter endorsed this theory and indeed became its major proponent: it completed his own vision of the evolutionary process of capitalist development, providing the historical framework for the process of structural change provoked by major innovations. Kondratiev provided the bridge to Marx: accumulation explained the inherently disequilibrating and catastrophic process (*HEA*: 749).

Unlike Kondratiev, Schumpeter did not use large statistical evidence to corroborate his theory: historical theory, abstract models, and description of the evolution of real series and events were the dominant methods in *Business Cycles*. For one reason, he was not convinced about the qualities of the available statistical devices, and he rejected the methods of least squares and polynomial fitting, given that they require uniform variance and normal distribution of the residuals, which could not be taken for granted (*BC*: 201). For another reason, he believed that the entangled cycles could be approximately decomposed, since he presented the cycles as perfect multiples of one another and argued that the level of the nth cycle is the equilibrium level for the trend of the $(n+1)$th cycle; but he also accepted that the results could not be unambiguous, since he simultaneously suspected that nonlinear phenomena ('mutations') could occur and could dominate historical–economic evolution. The lack of regularity in the real cycles accentuated this suspicion (Fellner 1956: 44–5). In this sense, both Schumpeter and Mitchell accepted that the best fit could lie.

On the other hand, Schumpeter presented the trend as the result of the cycles, and defined it as a line passing through certain neighbourhoods of equilibria—and a line with the property of being economically meaningful only at those discrete points. He therefore had substantial reasons for rejecting the principle of decomposition, since no available technique could deliver those results without a shadow of a doubt. But Schumpeter did not develop a new theory of statics and dynamics and accepted the dominant views. He was bounded by the ideology of equilibrium and considered that the irreversible processes were representable by a moving equilibrium frontier, as Kondratiev did.

Schumpeter knew that the reversible movements are actions without change and thus fictitious entities: reversibility does not exist in economics.

Last but not least, it is irrelevant to explain cycles as fluctuations over a trend if the basic historical process, which generates the trend and the cycle itself, is unexplained. This had been the *vexatio questio* of Kondratiev's whole academic life and work.

3
Nikolai Kondratiev: A New Approach to History and Statistics

3.1 Introduction

As we saw in the previous chapter, when he needed an inspiration for his life-long attempts to recombine history and economics, Schumpeter looked to Kondratiev for applied research on reasoned history and statistics. This chapter presents and discusses what he could have learnt, and what we can use nowadays from that inheritance.*

Nikolai Kondratiev (1892–1938) was one of the, if not the most, influential of the talented young Russian economists working in the first third of the century, and certainly the best known internationally at that time. His decisive contribution was the presentation of the hypothesis of long waves in capitalist development—named by Schumpeter and known thereafter as 'Kondratiev waves'—which for some time represented an important topic in the research agenda of economics. Nevertheless, the contemporary dominance of equilibrium economics exiled this research to the fringes of economic history, which is still considered to be a secondary, and not entirely scientific, distant relative of the discipline.

Yet, at least for a few decades, there was widespread agreement about (a) the relevance of the long-term movements identified by Kondratiev, since the existence of long periods with impressively distinctive patterns of development was widely recognized, and (b) the relevance of the newly developed statistical methods for checking the existence of the long waves. Such a consensus did not, however, extend to the precise explanation of the causes of these long phases or cycles.

This chapter presents an inquiry into the disputes, the syntheses available during the first half of the last century, and the problems emerging from this research, which are still crucial for any inquiry into the dynamics of capitalism, as Kondratiev suggested a challenging agenda for the recombination of history and economics. Section 3.2 indicates the direct inheritance of Kondratiev's research. Then the predecessors, the key features of Kondratiev's analysis, and the elements of the consensus and dissension it generated among contempo-

* Part of this chapter is based on previous work of one of us published in *History of Political Economy* (Louçã 1999). We thank the editors of that journal for the due authorization to use that material.

rary authors are in turn discussed in Sections 3.3 and 3.4. Section 3.5 deals with the decomposition problem. Finally, Section 3.6 considers the impact of his work at the time, and Section 3.7 presents some conclusions.

3.2 Kondratiev's Life and Work

Nikolai Dimitrievich Kondratiev was born on 4 March 1892 in the province of Kostroma, north of Moscow, into a peasant family. He studied at the University of St Petersburg, following courses given by Tugan-Baranowsky and other economists, epistemologists, and historians. A member of the Revolutionary Socialist Party, his initial professional work was in the area of agricultural economics and statistics and the important problem of food supplies. On 5 October 1917, at the age of 25, he was appointed Minister of Supply of the last Kerensky government, which however only lasted for a few days.

After the revolution he dedicated his attention to academic research. In 1919 he was appointed to a teaching post at the Agricultural Academy of Peter the Great, and in October 1920 he founded the Institute of Conjuncture, in Moscow. As its first director, he managed to develop the Institute, from a small body boasting just a couple of scientists into a large and respected centre with fifty-one researchers in 1923.

In 1923 Kondratiev intervened in the debate about the 'scissors crisis' (the growing divergence between prices of agricultural and industrial products), adopting the line taken by most of his colleagues. In 1923–5 he worked on a five-year plan for the development of Soviet agriculture. In 1924, after publishing a book in 1922 presenting the first tentative version of his theory of the major cycles (see Table 3.1), Kondratiev travelled to England, Germany, Canada, and the United States, and visited several universities before returning to Russia. As a supporter of the 'New Economic Policy' (NEP), he favoured the strategic option for the primacy of agriculture and the industrial production of consumer goods over the development of heavy industry.

Kondratiev's influence on Russian economic policy lasted until 1925, declined in 1926, and was over by 1927 (V. Barnett 1995: 431). By that time, the NEP had been abandoned after a political shift in the leadership of the CPSU. Kondratiev was removed from the directorship of the Institute in 1928 and arrested in July 1930, accused of being a member of an illegal but probably non-existent 'Peasants' Labour Party'. As early as August of that year, Stalin wrote a letter to Molotov asking for his execution (V. Barnett 1995: 437).

Condemned to eight years in prison, Kondratiev served his sentence, from February 1932 onwards, at Souzdal, near Moscow. Although his health deteriorated and the conditions were bad, he still managed to continue his research and had even decided to prepare new books. Some of these texts were indeed completed and were published in Russian in the early 1990s and later abroad (Kondratiev 1998). While in prison, Kondratiev sent his wife the plan for a five-volume work that would include discussions on statistics, methods for social sciences, long waves, and other matters. He would never conclude that work.

His last letter was to his daughter, Elena Kondratieva, on 31 August 1938. Shortly afterwards, on 17 September, he was subjected to a second trial, condemned, and executed by firing squad. Kondratiev was 46 at the time of his murder and was rehabilitated only after almost forty years, on 16 July 1987.

During his short and tragic life, Kondratiev gained the respect of academics all over the world. He was a member of several international scientific associations and his papers were translated and published abroad. Political leaders commented on his work, his interpretation of the history of capitalism proved to be a powerful and challenging vision, and he contributed to the early spread, application, and discussion of new statistical methods and concepts. Consequently, when the inaugural list of Fellows of the Econometric Society was to be drawn up, his name was immediately proposed: Frisch wrote to Schumpeter on 7 October 1932 suggesting two Russians, Kondratiev and Slutsky.[1] Subsequently, Kondratiev—who was already in prison—became the sole Russian among the twenty-nine founding Fellows of the Econometric Society elected in August 1933,[2] along with Frisch, Mitchell, Schumpeter, Keynes, Divisia, Bowley, Amoroso, Fisher, Moore, Schultz, Gini, Haberler, Hotelling, and other eminent economists.

Table 3.1 lists Kondratiev's major works dealing with the problem of long cycles. (Some early work on epistemology is not mentioned and has not yet been translated into non-Russian languages.[3]) Note the early translations into German and English of some parts of his crucial papers.

Kondratiev's papers had an immediate and major impact when they were published, and the rapidity with which parts of his papers were translated and published helps to explain his fame and election to the Econometric Society. Moreover, some of the most influential economists, statisticians, and

[1] Slutsky, who had also been involved with the Institute of Conjuncture, did not become a member of the Econometric Society (ES). He was a friend and a regular correspondent with Frisch, the driving force behind the new association, and his 1927 paper (later published in *Econometrica* in 1937, under the auspices of Frisch) was widely circulated and attracted much attention. When invited to participate in the new association, Slutsky declined, arguing that he was a statistician more than an economist, although one can speculate that his fear of the political consequences of being associated with a foreign institution was decisive. At any rate, Slutsky survived the Stalinist purges. On the other hand, the inclusion of Kondratiev is also an enigma, since he was at that time in gaol. Either he accepted via his wife, or the founders of the Society took his participation for granted from previous contacts with him.

[2] The difficulty or impossibility of corresponding with Kondratiev nevertheless implied that his name was sometimes referred to (September 1934 list of the Fellows) and sometimes omitted (October 1933 list), while at times there was a reference to the fact that he was a member 'if living' (lists included in the Schumpeter Archive, Harvard University).

[3] Kondratiev's first works discuss the methodology of historical research (1915). In 1918 he published a critique of Bolshevik economic policy; several papers on agricultural economics and planning were also published in the 1920s.

TABLE 3.1. Main works by Kondratiev

Date	Book/paper	Notes[a]
1922	*The World Economy and its Conjunctures During and After the War*	State edition, Vologda, 258 pp.; P&C
1923	'Some Controversial Questions Concerning the World Economy and Crisis (Answer to Our Critiques)'	Originally in *Socialititcheskoie Khoziaistvo*, 4–5: 50–80; LF
1924	'On the Notion of Economic Statics, Dynamics and Fluctuations'	Originally in *Socialititcheskoie Khoziaistvo*; a section published in *QJE*, 29, 1925: 575–83, under the title 'The Static and Dynamic Views of Economics'; LF
1925	'The Major Economic Cycles'	In *Voprosy Konjunktury*, 1(1): 28–79; German trans. in *Archiv für Sozialwissenschaft und Sozialpolitik*, 56 (1926): 573–609; partial trans. into English in *Review of Economic Statistics*, 18 (1935): 105–15; complete trans. into English (1979 and 1984), and French (1981)
1926*a*	'About the Question of the Major Cycles of the Conjuncture'	In *Planovoe Khoziaistvo*, 8: 167–81
1926*b*	'Problems of Forecasting'	In *Voprosy Konjunktury*, 2(1): 1–42; German version in *Annalen der Betriebswirtschaft*, 1, 2 (1927): 41–64 and 221–52; LF; P&C
1928*a*	*The Major Cycles of the Conjuncture*	Originally published in Russian with the 1926 papers and debate with Oparin (*Economitcheskaia Jizn*, 288 pp.); LF; P&C
1928*b*	'Dynamics of Industrial and Agricultural Prices (Contribution to the Theory of Relative Dynamics and Conjuncture)'	*Voprosy Konjunktury*, 4(1): 1–85; German abridged version in *Archiv für Sozialwissenschaft und Sozialpolitik*, 60 (1928): 1–85; LF
1934	'Main Problems of Economic Statics and Dynamics'	Russian edn. 1992 (Moscow: Nauka); P&C

[a] LF: Fontvieille's edition of Kondratiev's works (Paris: Economica, 1992); P&C: Warren Samuels *et al.*, edition of Kondratiev's Works for Pickering and Chatto.

mathematicians of his time wholeheartedly supported this type of explanation, or at least considered it to be a meaningful and pertinent hypothesis—this was the case with Frisch, Tinbergen, Spiethoff, Kuznets, Mitchell, Schumpeter, Lange, Hansen, and many others.

Yet what they read was not the whole text, and in some cases was indeed a misrepresentation of Kondratiev's ideas. With the single exceptions of Kuznets and Garvy, who could read Russian and who knew the original contributions, the others read just the German or the American translation of parts of the 1925 paper, and missed out on both the 1926 paper and the debate that took place that same year, not to mention other texts by Kondratiev on central methodological issues. Furthermore, they read inexact translations: as Escudier has shown, 'long cycles' were uniformly translated into German as 'long waves', whereas Kondratiev preferred to use the concept of waves for the analysis of variables, and to use the concept of long cycles for his interpretation of global movement (Escudier 1990: 128). Moreover, these terminological and conceptual mistakes were later reproduced in the derived translations, such as the American one. This version of Kondratiev's 1925 paper, which for a long time was the most widely accepted, appeared in 1935 in a major journal, the *Review of Economic Statistics*, but was itself translated from the second-hand German translation, did not include the theoretical part, and was limited to the presentation of the statistical method and empirical laws (Kondratiev 1935; Stolper 1984: 1647). Last but not least, not only were the essential texts not translated at the time, but they were ignored until the 1980s or 1990s, not to mention the papers written by Kondratiev while in gaol and made available in Russian only in the 1990s.

As a consequence, 'Kondratiev waves' have long since been discussed by authors who did not know the most important aspects of Kondratiev's texts. In general, until the 1990s non-Russian-speaking authors knew only the first translations of the 1920s. In fact, a complete English edition of his 1922 paper was published only in 1979, and his 1925 paper was published only in 1984. As a consequence of this ignorance of the original texts, each interpreter could attribute to Kondratiev their own version of part of his work. Only in 1992 was a collection of the main papers of the 1926 debate at the Institute of Conjuncture published in French, and in 1998 published in English.

In spite of this, what may be considered surprising is the resilience of the research programme on long waves, or long cycles as Kondratiev called them. Not only did this research attract various scientists in the 1930s and 1940s, despite their different approaches to economics, but also it was reactivated later on, just before and just after the '30 Golden Years' of postwar expansion in the industrial economies. And more recently, in the entirely new framework of complexity theory, some authors have suggested that the 'long wave' could be thought of as the representation of specific modes of entrainment of oscillations, emerging from the complex nature of economic processes (Mandelbrot 1987: 126; Lo 1991: 1308). The nature of the early consensus generated by Kondratiev in the 1920s and 1930s is the theme of the next section.

3.3 Predecessors: The Early Consensus

The first part of this section briefly presents the contribution made by some of Kondratiev's distinguished predecessors, both in those cases where he was aware of their arguments and built on them and in those where he was ignorant of or completely ignored their writings. The second part of the section presents the 'Kondratiev hypothesis', in keeping with its original formulation and the ensuing debate.

The first wave of predecessors included Hyde Clarke, W. S. Jevons, Karl Marx, and Friedrich Engels. One of these was completely ignored by Kondratiev: this was Hyde Clarke, who in 1847 published a paper in *The British Railway Register* and a short pamphlet (included in Louçã and Reijnders 1999; see also Black and Collison 1992), but who owed his fame mostly to the fact that Jevons pointed to him as the creator of the hypothesis of a long cycle in economic activity (Jevons 1884: 129), and not to his own original contribution, which still remains largely ignored. Indeed, Clarke argued that the crisis of scarcity in 1847 was part of a repetitive phenomenon, and that the approximately ten-year cycles were part of a fifty-four-year movement of the whole economy, mostly motivated by harvest conditions and eventually by the impact of weather conditions. He was inspired by the previous research on time series carried out by Mackenzie (J. Klein 1997: 113–15). Jevons accepted these ideas.

Marx and Engels did not discuss cycles in very much detail, and when they did comment on the topic they essentially referred to industrial, business cycles. While engaged in writing *Das Kapital*, Marx suggested in a letter dated March 1858 that a thirteen-year cycle, obtained from the empirical evidence provided by Engels's experience as a manager, was the convenient unit for his theory explaining the timetable of the crisis by the renewal of fixed capital.

But in the second volume of *Das Kapital* Marx acknowledged Engels's comments on the shortening of the period of the business cycle, while also considering other longer periods. He quoted Scrope at some length; after describing the five to ten-year period for the construction of productive tools and fixed capital, Scrope wrote: 'The capital spent on buildings, e.g. factories, shops . . . seems not to circulate. But, in reality, these premises . . . are used up while in operation and the owner must reproduce them in order to continue his operation. . . . This invested capital follows a 20 or 50 year rotation' (Scrope, quoted in Marx 1885: ii. 163; our translation).

Marx commented approvingly on this passage, stating that it presented an organic view. So Marx was aware that the reproduction of capital followed different rhythms, underlying its 'permanent disharmony', as he frequently pointed out in the third volume of *Das Kapital* and in *Theories of Surplus Value*.

Schumpeter, who singled out Marx and mainly Engels as the predecessors of the long wave research, argued that Engels's 1894 editorial notes to the third volume of *Das Kapital* constitute an anticipation of Kondratiev (Schumpeter 1990: 420 n.; see also Chapter 2 above). In fact, Engels simply discussed changes in the rhythms of business cycles in the preceding decades and indicated the possible reason for this—the changes in the world market as a result of the expansion of transport and communication systems—concluding that the alteration in the industrial cycle might explain the increase in the duration of upswings and downswings (Engels, in Marx 1894: iii. 489 n.). In this sense, his intuition was that the 1870s and 1880s were periods of structural change, but there was no further theoretical explanation for this phenomenon. Nevertheless, this early prefiguration of the changes in regimes of accumulation influenced some of his followers.

In an appendix to the 1886 US edition of his early book on the British working class, Engels went so far as to describe different historical periods— 1825–42, 1842–68, 1868– . . . —that fitted in fairly well with the long wave chronology. Of course, both Marx and Engels were aware of the major changes caused by industrial and technical revolutions, and Marx discussed these processes clearly, outlining a theory of long fluctuations in employment and volumes of production, combined with major technological revolutions. This is indeed the closest indication of any inkling of long waves to be found in Marx's writings:

There are intervals during which technical revolutions are less notable and accumulation appears to be, above all, a movement of quantitative expansion upon the new technical base already achieved. What begins to operate to a greater or lesser extent in such a case, whatever the actual structure of capital, is a law whereby the demand for labour rises in the same proportion as capital does. But just when the number of workers attracted by capital reaches its peak, the product becomes so plentiful that the social mechanism seems to have come to a standstill in case of the slightest obstacle arising in the way of their sale; it is the process of alienating labour by capital in great proportions and in the most violent way that comes into operation at once; the very disruption of production makes it imperative for capitalists to strain every nerve to save labour. Detailed improvements building up little by little are concentrated under that high pressure so to speak; they find themselves embodied in the technological modifications which revolutionize the structure of capital throughout the entire periphery of major areas of production. (Marx, *Complete Works*, Russian edn., v. 49: 220–1, as quoted in Menshikov 1987: 69)

Nevertheless, this passage is mainly a descriptive account, and it is well known that this long rhythm was not discussed when Marx formulated his law of the tendency of the rate of profit to fall, or the counter-tendencies to this trend. One possible interpretation for this is that Marx did not consider that these shifts from one period to another affected the outcome of the process of striving for the realization of profit. And although some of the counter-tendencies explicitly dealt with technical change (changes either in the value of the constant capital or in the process of extraction of relative surplus), Marx did not give technological revolutions a prominent role in his theory. Furthermore, he did not explain or define these successive long periods—indeed, it would have been difficult for him to do so, since he was writing in the years of the second wave, the first one to have a really international character. From this point of view, Marx and Engels cannot be considered direct predecessors of the long wave research, even if their concept of the reproduction cycles of fixed capital influenced most of the forerunners in this research.

Yet, Clarke, Jevons, Marx, and Engels all emphasize the same point: all witnessed periods of unrest, economic turbulence, and great famines in the midst of overproduction and plenty. And they noticed the regularity of these ups and downs, as well as the great structural changes that accompanied capitalist development. Other authors, writing in the following years, repeatedly arrived at the same conclusion: John Bates Clark detected a period of forty-five years in the maturation of new methods of production (Clark 1899: 429); and Parvus (1901), Tugan-Baranowsky (1901: 52–3), Wicksell, and Pareto used the same calendar for describing the long periods. Thus, the first essential element of the early consensus was the recognition of what may be called the 'Kondratiev problem' as well as the dating of the evolutionary processes in the development of nineteenth-century capitalism. The recurrence of long periods marked by expansion as well as long periods marked by depression was believed to be indisputable, although their explanation was not. Several authors followed Marx's insights and endeavoured to explain these processes of change.

Parvus was not an economist by training:[4] his 1901 paper was just a short text about the new conditions created by the turning point in the 1896 crisis. Considering the years of prosperity marked by the development or expansion of cities, the increased capital accumulation, and the spread of new inventions (he referred specifically to electricity, typewriters, and bicycles), Parvus argued that there are periods when there are 'jumps' in capitalist production, long periods of '*Sturm und Drang*', i.e. of capital expansion (Parvus 1901: 12, 16, 19, 20, 26), followed by contractions. The undulatory movement of capital accumulation corresponds to the irregular development of the world market, to the 'laws of capitalist oscillation' (p. 27).

Parvus acknowledged that Marx and Engels had dealt only with the shorter industrial cycle and had not explained the longer periods of accelerated and retarded development, namely the possibility of these *Sturm und Drang* periods (p. 27). Yet he used and generalized their theory to explain crises by overproduction, the organic consequence of the enlarged reproduction of capital. Social and political factors were also considered: he pointed out, for instance, that the textile unions' fight for a reduction in working hours had been a major contributory factor in the 1896 crisis. His

---

[4] 'Parvus' was indeed the alias of Alexandre Helphand, an active member of the Social Democratic International in the beginning of the century. As he always signed his papers with his pseudonym, we follow the same procedure and take 'Parvus' as the reference of the author of the texts.

contribution was, however, superficial and mainly descriptive. He intu-
itively noted the possibility of periods of general expansion that were longer
than the business cycle upswing, but presented no theory or general historical vision to account for this. As a consequence, Duijn's claim that long
waves should be called 'Parvus cycles' (Duijn 1983: 61) is clearly exaggerated. Like the early authors who noted the change of tide from the dominance of expansion to the dominance of depression in the long fluctuations,
Parvus noticed the striking differences in the transition from one phase to
another and registered some of the relevant differences, but he provided no
explanation for this.

The next authors to deal with this matter were much more concerned with
rigorous proof and statistical identification of the long movements. Van
Gelderen's 1913 article was the single most important contribution to the
research before Kondratiev's work.[5] He acknowledged Parvus's insights,
namely the distinction of the *hausse* years, the *Sturm und Drang* of capital
considered to occur because of the capitalist mode of production—unlike
Sombart, who noticed the periods of expansion and contraction but considered that these were simple coincidences (van Gelderen 1913: 45, 46). He
then analysed price movements as symptoms of the division of productive
forces between sectors of production and detected a longer movement than
the industrial cycle: 'Apart from the on-average ten-yearly fluctuations in
the general price level, the price-curves also show a longer wave movement,
which in the course of its up and downward movement comprises several
decades' (p. 14).

As a consequence, an expansion period from 1850 until 1873, a depression
from 1873 until 1895 and an expansion after 1896 were detected. The 'spring
tide' and the 'ebb periods' of expansion and contraction were explained by
concrete factors such as the changes in transport costs deriving from the construction of railroads, the consequent increase in the demand for metals, and
the emigration to America as far as the expansion of 1850–1873 was concerned (van Gelderen 1913: 15, 22). But this analysis was not limited to the
factors influencing price movements, since van Gelderen pointed out the
impact of major structural changes in industrial production, namely the
development of the electricity sector and the increase in gold production (p.
20).

Van Gelderen then undertook a systematic study of four types of causal
factor, whose presence was discussed in several time series (pp. 22 ff.):

1. the acceleration of production, from the 'sudden emergence of a pro-
   duction-branch, which, in a more powerful way than before, satisfies a

---

[5] Mandel argued that neither Kondratiev nor Schumpeter nor Dupriez matched the depth
and scope of van Gelderen's theory of long-term fluctuations (Mandel 1975: 52). This is an over-
statement, since Kondratiev developed a larger body of empirical work and more sophisticated
theoretical explanations, although one might comment that he did not use the most suitable
methods or provide general explanations.

certain human need (automobile and electricity industries)' (p. 40); the emergence of 'electrical engineering' was particularly stressed;

2. the expansion of transport systems, especially to colonies;
3. the evolution of the trade turnover through the expansion of the capitalist system to new areas, such as the industrialization of the USA, Russia, and the East Asia regions;
4. the interest rate movements, in connection with the changes taking place in the monetary system, especially the increase in gold production.

The necessary condition for the 'spring tide' was considered to be the expansion in aggregate demand caused by the increase in production. The faster rate of growth of production and the cost increase provoked by the inflationary pressures in raw materials were then supposed to create the conditions for a crisis and for the subsequent downswing.

Since it not only considered nominal and real variables, but also explained the evolution of the economic system in a concrete historical context, van Gelderen's paper was in fact the first building block for long wave research. The tragic fate of his work (ignored by most of the writers to follow, and translated into English only in 1996) and of the author himself (he committed suicide in 1940 when the Nazi invasion of the Netherlands was imminent: Reijnders 1990: 54 n.) cries out for justice to be done in this regard. The recent publication of his essay (in Freeman 1996), as well as the publication of Clarke's, de Wolff's, and Parvus's works (Louçã and Reijnders 1999), is a step in the direction of highlighting the importance of the contribution of these forerunners.

Working at the same time as van Gelderen, yet ignoring his contribution, some other authors investigating the relation between economic movements and political and institutional conditions produced valuable arguments in support of the long wave hypothesis. Alfonso Pietri-Tonelli, claiming to apply the 'scientific procedures' of physics (Pietri-Tonelli 1911: 220), described the economic system as a pendulum; its dynamics was consequently studied as a form of energy propagation accounting for the waves, which were generated by exogenous factors (p. 222). Pietri-Tonelli considered the interplay of economic and political factors in an attempt to explain the major turning points and, like Pareto, used simple statistical methods (a first-degree polynomial to account for the trend). In 1921, he conducted an extensive investigation into the symptoms of the long fluctuations, namely the time series of prices, theatre tickets, marriages, and criminal activity: his dating scheme included an expansion from 1852 until 1873, a contraction from 1873 until 1897 and a new expansion from 1897 until 1913.

Bresciani-Turroni wrote an article in 1913 identifying long waves in prices (with a trough around 1850, a peak around 1870 and a new trough around 1895), which he explained through Cassel's theory of the impact of the volume of gold. But in a later paper, he instead considered the fluctuations of profits—including certain factors such as the costs of production, technical advancement, the discovery and exploitation of new territories—as the central cause for the observed long fluctuations (Bresciani-Turroni 1917: 9).

In 1913 Pareto wrote a paper explaining the long waves in an economy by the social conflict inside the elite, i.e. the ruling class, between entrepreneurs (speculators) and *rentiers* (traditional capitalists): their alternating domination explained the successive periods of daring expansion and timid contraction. He developed the same theme in his subsequent work (Pareto 1916). At the same time, Aftalion (1913: 1–7), Lenoir (1913: 148–9), and Lescure (1912: 452–90) detected and discussed these long movements. Aftalion followed the Marxian tradition in his 1913 book, explaining the cyclical fluctuations by the long periods required for the reproduction of fixed capital, influencing the formation of expectations and creating 'wave movements of wide amplitude' which caused the 'fairly long cyclical variations' (Aftalion 1927: 165). Kondratiev developed this approach later on.

In spite of the diversity and importance of these insights, a large part of this debate was lost, since most of these papers were not widely publicized, partly because of the language barrier. As an illustration, when the Institute of Conjuncture organized a debate about Kondratiev's 1926 paper, Spektator referred to Parvus, and Falkner criticized Kondratiev for not acknowledging the works of de Wolff, Bresciani-Turroni, and Pietri-Tonelli. In his reply, Kondratiev indicated that, after the preparation of the 1926 draft, he had read Bresciani-Turroni (Kondratiev 1992: 244, 250, 289), but not the others. No one yet referred to van Gelderen. Later Kondratiev at least read de Wolff (and became acquainted with van Gelderen's arguments through de Wolff's) and Pietri-Tonelli, so that only in 1928 could he consider and classify all these contributions according to the nature of their explanations.

The main exception is the work of van Gelderen, since his paper was partially accessible abroad through the reference made by his friend Sam de Wolff (1924, appearing for the first time in English in Louçã and Reijnders 1999). De Wolff was a Dutch social democrat who published an account of van Gelderen's theory on long waves in a book that was widely known, since it was the Festschrift for Karl Kautsky. De Wolff adopted the same dating (1825–49, ebb tide; 1850–73, spring tide; 1873–95, ebb tide; 1895 and afterwards, spring tide or *Sturm und Drang*) and used sophisticated descriptive statistical methods following van Gelderen.

These authors are important forerunners: they indicate a broad consensus on the calendar of the long waves, showing that price oscillations and (at least for some authors) the impact of new industrial branches were so noticeable that they accounted for them by each reaching the same conclusions independently. Such initial consensus established the main agenda for future research, including topics such as the place of social and political factors, particularly for the explanation of the turning points (as the Italians argued for), the historical role of innovation and structural change (van Gelderen), the relationship between price and production series, single (Cassel's monetary theory) or multi-causal explanations, and the statistical treatment of the series in order to detect and demonstrate regularity and recurrence.

3.4 Kondratiev: An Organic Approach

In spite of the importance of the previous writers, it was Kondratiev who established the foundations of the research, since his works were more complete and general—having been developed independently—than those of van Gelderen. Kondratiev's ideas had a greater impact, since some of them were soon translated and frequently discussed in broader scientific circles. But his theoretical argument could not be studied in detail, as it was not translated and the Russian debate was almost completely ignored. For a long time Garvy's 1943 paper was the most precise and complete source of reference in this debate—and a still rare reference in English, together with Day's (1981) and V. Barnett's (1998) books and a few other contributions—but it is a somewhat biased summary of the arguments. In short, not only was Kondratiev condemned by the Stalinist courts for crimes he did not commit, but his work has been discussed for at least five or six decades on the basis of incomplete and incoherent versions of his original writings. This section provides a short review of that work, briefly outlining the main theses, while some of the analytical contributions will be examined in the following section.

In 1922, Kondratiev published a book formulating in passing the long cycle hypothesis based on his inspection of some statistical series. His conclusion was very tentative and amounted to his claiming that there were long periods of upswing and downswing in historical data. In the paper prepared the following year as an answer to his critics, Kondratiev emphasized that the 'major cycles of the conjuncture were only considered as probable' (Kondratiev 1923: 524). This was interpreted by some as implying a simple mechanical recurrence so that, after the First World War and the severe depression of the subsequent postwar years, a longer period of recovery would necessarily occur.

On the basis of his previous work on epistemology and the analytical representation of history, Kondratiev argued that irreversible and reversible processes coexisted,[6] although 'the evolution of the economy as a whole is an irreversible process' (1923: 496), comparable to that of an organism. Although declaring not to be a Marxist, Kondratiev insisted that he was precisely following Marx's understanding of the genetic process of capitalism, in keeping with the analysis of major cycles by Lescure, Aftalion, Trotsky, Panekoek, and Kautsky. Apparently Kondratiev just wanted to claim to be part of a much larger research into reversible processes (such as those encapsulated in the

---

[6] The French translation of Kondratiev's works, edited by Fontvieille, is followed here.

concepts of the transformation of the commodity, the reproduction of fixed capital and the crises) and irreversible processes (such as those accounting for technological and social change). Furthermore, he argued that the major cycles could be organically explained by the action of internal factors of change further affected by secondary environmental circumstances.

Trotsky reacted in June 1923 and published an article criticizing Kondratiev's hypothesis. This text introduced a rather important debate, since it marked out the boundaries and implications of the controversies, which have frequently been misunderstood, in later interpretations. Trotsky referred to two concepts of equilibrium: (1) the 'secular equilibrium', i.e. the general trend of development encapsulated in the 'curve of capitalist development', and (2) the 'cyclical equilibrium', imposed after the restoration of the system following the elimination of the crises of disproportion (Trotsky 1923: 7 ff.). Equilibrium, in this sense, was an epitome for the general cumulative process of capital transformation and circulation, considered to be inherently unstable although very resistant.[7] In particular, the long-term trend of development could be changed by political events: for Trotsky, long fluctuations were trend variations and not cycles, as they were exogenously generated. The essential difference is that cycles were supposed to be driven by the internal contradictions of the economic system—i.e. determined by the clock of capital reproduction and accumulation—whereas the shifts in the curve of capitalist development were supposed to be brought about by major external events. These major changes were dated according to the general consensus of the time, 1781–1851, 1851–73, 1873–94, 1894–1913, 1913– . . . (pp. 7 ff.). In order to illustrate his argument, Trotsky used a table published in January 1923 by *The Times*, describing political, ideological, and economic evolution over more than one hundred years.

This distinction had a political intention, namely to preserve the possibility of ruptures imposed by anti-systemic forces, by conscious social decisions. In this framework, exogeneity once more emphasized the creative role of strategy and social design. As Day notes, Kondratiev's efforts to 'endogenize' Trotsky's factors of change were contradictory to the very nature of his world vision:

[presenting] a continuous curve generated by a single equation instead of a segmented trend-line, Kondratiev made manifest the ideological assumption implicit in the concept of moving equilibrium: the lack of unevenness in the historical developments of capitalism. By 'internalizing' Trotsky's external conditions, he produced an ultra-deterministic theory of history that few Marxists could contemplate. (Day 1981: 89)

---

[7] In his report to the June–July 1921 Third Conference of the Comintern, Trotsky wrote: 'Capitalism thus possesses a dynamic equilibrium, one that is always in the process of either disruption or restoration. But at the same time this equilibrium has a great power of resistance' (Trotsky 1921: 226).

The contradistinction was very sharp, since Kondratiev instead considered an 'irreversible' movement, one that could not be changed by any sort of event and was indeed wholly ignored in the analysis, and political and social factors that were endogenously determined by the very nature of the 'reversible' processes. Furthermore, the relevant features were the reversible oscillations around a moving equilibrium. Trotsky rejected this concept and concluded that the moving equilibrium concept implied some sort of harmonization process.

This criticism quite surprized Kondratiev. Indeed, in his 1923 reply he quite candidly quoted Varga's position and Trotsky's speech at the Third Conference of the Comintern, in which they acknowledged the decisive change in the international conjuncture (Kondratiev 1923: 521–2). In these remarks about the change of the conjuncture Kondratiev saw something else, a more general statement about the possible evolution of a new long-term expansionary wave immediately after the depression years which would not require a new change in political conditions. Furthermore, by 1923 the setting was already completely different and the economic situation had once more deteriorated.

Eventually, because of the political implications of the argument about the nature of equilibrium, Kondratiev preferred not to develop this matter any further. In fact, the 1926 internal debate at the Institute of Conjuncture was more important from the statistical and methodological point of view, although it merely redefined the earlier questions about broader interpretation issues.

The controversy involved at least four important topics: (1) the legitimacy of the formal analogy, in both methods and theory, between the (Juglar) business cycles and the longer movements, which was implicitly supported by Kondratiev and explicitly criticized by Trotsky; (2) the evaluation of the conjuncture, in order to know if a new long-term revival was emerging in the early 1920s or if the conjuncture was still dominated by a general downturn; (3) the nature of the causes of the 'reversible' movements, and thus of equilibrium and of endogenous and exogenous factors; and their links to (4) the nature of the 'irreversible' movement.

Refining his argument, Kondratiev maintained later that the 'essence' described by static equilibrium was supposed to be the core of the identity and invariance of phenomena, while dynamics was supposed to describe change and difference, under the concept of 'dynamic equilibrium' (Kondratiev 1924). But, according to Kondratiev, change presupposes the ontological identity of the object, and that is why dynamics was considered to include statics. In that sense, he argued that dynamic processes comprise two types of movement: (1) irreversible processes, which have a fixed direction, e.g. the growth of population and the volume of production, the models of enlarged reproduction (p. 17); and (2) reversible processes, which may change direction, e.g. interest rate, prices, employment (p. 12). The long cycle, or the 'curve of the conjuncture', belongs naturally to the second type,

if one disregards certain irreversible processes. As Kondratiev acknow-
ledged, he was using a metaphor drawn from physics, the concept of *sub-stratum*, although he recognized that this did not have a convenient analogue
in economics (pp. 14–15).

In 1925 and 1926 Kondratiev again elaborated his theoretical approach.
The thesis has three main theoretical characteristics. First, Kondratiev
argued that crises are 'organically' a part of the capitalist mode of production, as Marx and Juglar considered (Kondratiev 1928a: 111). This was an
important argument in favour of rejecting simple exogenous causality, but it
also had a precise holistic consequence: the organic concept of 'totality'
implies that there is something more than the simple sum of the components, that there is 'something new' in the whole (Kondratiev 1926b: 63), and
Kondratiev was fully aware of this implication. If this is so, no purely atomistic concept is useful or acceptable for the analysis of reality. Consequently,
all cycles are part of the same economic process, as he stressed in a debate
with Pervushin (V. Barnett 1996: 1021).

Second, Kondratiev considered that this organic, holistic, and non-atom-
istic epistemology was the necessary counterpart of the reality of social
processes, in which the rationality of 'human interventions' implies the creation of a greater diversity than in the case studied in natural sciences
(Kondratiev 1926b: 83). In other words, unlike the neoclassicists, for whom
rationality is typically associated with the pattern of a representative agent,
Kondratiev defined economics as a research into the creation of variation.

Third, for Kondratiev such variation was still compatible with equilibrium. The system always tends towards a moving equilibrium: 'So the long
cycles of the conjuncture represent a deviation in the real level of the elements of the capitalist system in relation to this same system's equilibrium
... a process in which the level of equilibrium itself changes' (1928a: 159).

So impulses were conceived of as disequilibrium processes, caused by
'radical changes in the conditions of production' through infrastructural
investment in essential capital goods (1928a: 158, 160). Kondratiev did not
discuss in any detail this equilibrium around which the reversible processes
were supposed to be organized. He just implied that equilibrium represented the most probable state of the system, and did not deal with the
changes in the system itself.

Overall, this was a contradictory and incomplete vision. The holistic and
organic view that Kondratiev endorsed does in fact preclude the decomposition procedure or absolute distinction between different types of dynamic
movement, as if they were atomistic and unrelated phenomena. Equilibrium
was assumed, but one of its empirical counterparts, the irreversible process
or the trend line in which it was supposed to be located, was absent from the
inquiry. Furthermore, the concept did not explain the change of structure
from one long cycle to the next; Kondratiev was forced by the logic of his
argument to assume a strict separability between irreversible and reversible
movements, and to ignore the effect of cycles on the trend and vice versa.

This implies a major contradiction, since some of the structural factors that were supposed to influence the longer-term evolution of productive forces were then defined as mere endogenous consequences of the cycle itself.

Many authors centred their criticism of Kondratiev on the imprecision and vagueness of his causal explanation for the long cycle, which was based on two essential factors that could account for the revival: Tugan-Baranowsky's theory of 'free loanable funds', and Marx's theory of the echo-cycle of fixed capital reproduction. Our argument is that this debate was indeed relevant, yet it was of secondary importance: the main limitations of Kondratiev's theory were not the rather fascinating explanatory hypotheses he created, but the very concepts of statics and dynamics, of irreversible and reversible movements, and, as a consequence, of equilibrium. These formed the basis for his trend-decomposition procedures, a contradictory and puzzling technique with dubious epistemological foundations.

On the other hand, Kondratiev detected long-term fluctuations that could not be explained by general equilibrium macroeconomics; he described such fluctuations as specific phenomena in distinct epochs in the history of capitalism. This led him to carry out an impressive and detailed inductive research, presented in his 1926 paper, and producing vast amounts of evidence and statistical as well as graphical information.[8]

In this study, just as van Gelderen had done fifteen years earlier, Kondratiev identified some major transformations in productive forces, such as the new industrial revolution that was driving the transition from the II to the III long wave, based on the chemical, electrical, and motor industries (Kondratiev 1928a: 140). He established the first rigorous dating scheme for the long wave: the upswing of the first long wave from the end of the 1780s or the beginning of the 1790s until 1810–17, and the downswing from 1810–17 until 1844–51; the upswing of the next wave from 1844–51 until 1870–5, and the downswing from then until 1890–5; the upswing of the third wave from 1891–6 until 1914–20, and the downswing from 1914–20 onwards. (See the comparison between Kondratiev's dating scheme and those of his forerunners and contemporaries in Table 3.2.) Furthermore, Kondratiev made a valuable contribution to the research when he decided to include in his explanatory model different technological, economic, social, and political factors: as in the case of the previous authors, from van Gelderen to Pareto, this interconnection became an important part of research.

---

[8] Kondratiev identified four empirical laws. (1) Some years before the beginning of a new long cycle, important changes occur in technological innovation, monetary circulation, the role played by new countries (1928a: 138); these changes could occur as much as 20 years before (p. 141). (2) The class struggle, including wars and revolutions, is more intense in the upswings. (3) Agricultural depressions are more intense in the downswings. (4) The downswings of the shorter cycles are more intense in the downswings of the long cycle, and the reverse is also true (pp. 140 ff.). Van Gelderen had already formulated this last 'empirical law' (van Gelderen 1913: 49—see Table 8.13 below).

TABLE 3.2. Dating of long waves

Author/period	First LW		Second LW		Third LW	
	Upswing	Downswing	Upswing	Downswing	Upswing	Downswing
Engels		1825–42	1842–68	1868–...		
Pietri-Tonelli			1852–73	1873–97	1897–1913	
Bresciani-Turroni			1852–73	1873–97	1897–1913	
Van Gelderen			1850–70	1870–95	1895–...	
De Wolff		1825–49	1850–73	1873–95	1895–...	
Trotsky	1781–1851		1851–73	1873–94	1894–1913	1913–...
Kondratiev	1780/90–1810/17	1810/17–1844/5	1844/5–1870/5	1870/5–1891/6	1891/6–1914/20	1920–...

Note: As the table shows, Kondratiev prudently indicated his periodization with large intervals for the starting and ending periods.

The crucial discussion of these ideas was centred upon the paper presented by Kondratiev on 6 February 1926 at a seminar of the Institute of Economics of the Association of Social Science Research Institutes. One week later, assisted by a large staff, Oparin presented his own counter-report, and in 1928 a pamphlet was published including both Kondratiev's and Oparin's contributions and the minutes of the seminars. Kondratiev's confrontation with Oparin was mainly about statistical methodology, since Oparin supported an alternative theory—Cassel's monetary theory—but was not very emphatic about it, and Kondratiev very easily showed that such a theory of equilibrium produced the same type of statistical problems, if not worse. Many of Oparin's points were, however, fully justified, such as the lack of theoretical justification and the arbitrariness of the choice of the detrending functions, producing some sort of 'perspectivistic distortion'. This topic will be discussed in more detail in the next section.

Eventov and Bogdanov, who unlike Oparin did not have to formulate alternatives, presented interesting arguments against detrending, namely that the trend (the growth of the economy) and the cycles (the acceleration and deceleration of growth) are quite simply the same phenomenon (Kondratiev 1992: 246 ff.; Garvy 1943: 210), therefore implying that decomposition was not justified. Sukhanov endorsed Kondratiev's argument about the organic nature of social systems in order to argue, on the basis of a life-cycle concept, that no further explanation of the long-term changes was necessary: 'The physiology of an organism in evolution is different in the successive stages of its evolution. Capitalist evolution is an organic process with definite different stages: youth, maturity, decline . . . and even death' (quoted in Garvy 1943: 214).

As the next section will indicate, this debate was important, although not conclusive: it detected some of the most important mistakes in Kondratiev's statistical techniques, but could not solve them.

3.5 The Decomposition Problem

Kondratiev dealt at length with the decomposition problem, as a consequence of his early works on statics and dynamics. In 1923, answering to the critiques of his first and very rough sketch of a long wave theory, Kondratiev stated that the economy is an irreversible and dynamic process, comparable to an organism with cyclical functions (blood circulation, nutrition) and irreversible processes (Kondratiev 1923: 496). This vision was compared to that of Marx, who was supposed to have indicated irreversible processes (accumulation of capital, concentration) and their reversible counterparts (crises, metamorphosis of the commodity). The conclusion was that two different domains were open for study: those of the irreversible phenomena (theory of the stages of development) and those of reversible processes (theory of the cycles: 1923: 496–8). Kondratiev recognized that the distinction is not always self-evident: 'Of course, in practice, in the inquiry it is very difficult to establish perfect limits between both objects' (p. 497).

But, unlike Schumpeter—and J. B. Clark, who inspired Schumpeter in this particular theme—Kondratiev did not consider that statics described real phenomena; in fact he explicitly criticized Schumpeter on this matter in his 1924 paper (Kondratiev 1924: 7–8, 10–11), stating that only dynamic movements were real: 'One must not forget that in reality we have one only dynamic process in economic life, and that it is just for the sake of scientific analysis that we may decompose it in irreversible tendencies [the trend] and reversible oscillatory movements' (1924: 29; also 1923: 496; 1925: 575–6).

The argument was that economic dynamics represented the totality of the social process and therefore the very nature of historical evolution—and that an understanding of its internal mechanism was decisive for the development of a convenient and pertinent explanation. As a consequence, Kondratiev invoked the dogma of endogeneity as the locus of the epistemic legitimacy for a scientific explanation:

These episodic and external causes are also included in the overall process of the socio-economic dynamics and for that reason cannot be considered as external factors causing the cycles. From our point of view, the explanation of the long cycles and in particular of the price movements must be sought in the character of the mechanism and in the internal laws of the general process of socio-economic development. (Kondratiev 1928b: 425)

A pertinent causal claim was consequently described as the set of necessary conditions for an event in a simple and mechanistic framework. Everything was then ready for the use and abuse of the early standard mathematical procedures to decompose the series, to interpret its elements, and to attribute the value of proof to the conclusions emerging from a surgically precise analysis of a split world.

Kondratiev accepted and argued for such a decomposition, although recognizing that the reversible processes always include some irreversible elements, so that decomposition is somewhat artificial (1924: 13), given that no real independence exists between both types of movement: the distinction was merely made 'for the purpose of the scientific analysis' (p. 14). From this point of view, the decomposition was a subsidiary problem to that of the distinction between statics and dynamics (to be represented, for instance, by the tendency of the profit rate to fall or by the increase in the organic composition of capital), and statics was a specific dimension of dynamics: 'if one abstracts from the dynamic processes, we may discover the statical regularities. . . . In this sense, statics is a moment of dynamics and the formula of statical regularity is that of dynamical regularity to which the time element is subtracted or reduced to zero' (p. 69).

In the 1926 paper Kondratiev again took up the same issues. He began saying that there is no independence of the reversible processes in relation to the irreversible ones, and that the whole is the real process: 'Indeed, I think that the real process of dynamics is unique' (1926*b*: 102–3). At the same time, he argued that the decomposition was acceptable just for purposes of study:

Economic evolution as a whole must without doubt be considered as a single and indivisible process, since only by taking it into account is one able to understand completely the characteristics of economic dynamics. Though economic evolution as a whole must doubtless be considered as a single and indivisible process, the acceptance of the classification of economic processes and elements here suggested is absolutely necessary for the purpose of scientific analysis of economic realities. (Kondratiev 1925: 583)

In order to avoid an arbitrary fitting procedure, namely in the choice of the function, Kondratiev argued that he favoured 'collective work'; in fact, he trusted the least squares method to give him precise guidance (1928*a*: 115). But he recognized that some arbitrariness was unavoidable: 'I do not affirm at any moment that the theoretical curves I found represent the real curve of evolution. On the contrary, I do affirm that we do not have for the moment the methods to exactly determine those curves' (p. 163).

However, Kondratiev trusted his method to detect both the underlying irreversible movement and the long cycles of the reversible conjuncture:[9]

I suppose that to this curve, theoretical by construction, may correspond the real tendencies of the evolution. But we cannot affirm that the theoretical curves we found correspond exactly to those tendencies . . . We may only say that the theoretical curve exactly represents the tendency of the given empirical curve . . . It is evident that the task is then to determine if there exist long cycles in the deviations of the series in relation to the theoretical series. (Kondratiev 1928*a*: 116)

According to Garvy's interpretation of Kondratiev's argument, decomposition was always artificial: the distinction between reversible and irreversible movements was technically necessary in order to legitimate the decomposition and to look for long waves in the detrended series, but since the trend indicated some average rate of growth of the system and the long cycles indicate the acceleration or retardation of that growth, both were supposedly created by the same set of factors and indistinguishable in reality. As a consequence, decomposition was 'purely artificial' (Garvy 1943: 210).

---

[9] Nevertheless, Kondratiev was fully aware of the arbitrariness of detrending. He said so in 1925: 'The term "evolutionary," or non-reversible process applies to those changes which, in the absence of extraneous (non-economic) disturbing causes, develop a certain definite direction and therefore are not subject to repetition or reversion. As an example, one may point to the permanent tendency of population to grow, of the total volume of production to increase, and the like. It is clear that this conception of non-reversible processes is similar to that of a secular trend. Yet I am of the opinion that the current conception of secular trend is only technical and statistical; it is not economic. A certain secular trend, represented, for instance, by a straight line, will fit a certain period of production. But if we consider the same period only as part of a greater one, another secular trend may appear, represented, say, in the form of a parabola. This indicates that the conception of secular trend does not always give to economists an exact idea of the character of the economic dynamic process. And for that reason it is not used in the present article' (Kondratiev, 1925: 579–80). Nevertheless, he widely used it in the articles that followed.

Of course, it is impossible to accept simultaneously both arguments: either the real process is singular and non-decomposable, and then any procedure of decomposition may create spurious results—and Kondratiev did not indicate any protection against this danger—or the real process is decomposable, and there are real distinct entities which can be meaningfully addressed by separate theoretical explanations and by some precise functions. Although Kondratiev paid lip service to the first interpretation, it is obvious that the second one dominated his work, which would otherwise be unjustifiable and irrelevant. Several distinct functions were used by him in order to extract the trend, and the choice of functions did not obey any uniform criterion, being dictated by mathematical convenience; in no case was an interpretation indicated for those functions or for the values obtained for the parameters. In spite of his concern, Kondratiev was one of the authors who used the decomposition method most intensively: his debate with Trotsky and Bogdanov was precisely about these relations between trends and cycles as unitary processes or as separable sets of factors. In spite of the sophistication of the current techniques, the decomposition problem is still with us, and it will be further discussed in the next chapter.

3.6 The Contemporary Impact of Kondratiev's Writings

Given the subsequent history, the impact of Kondratiev's few articles published in English and German was not only very effective but also quite surprising. A large part of the economists involved at the core of the project for developing the new approach of econometrics (including Frisch, Tinbergen, and Schumpeter), and simultaneously some of the more distinguished economists involved in quantitative and historical research (Mitchell, Kuznets), took notice of Kondratiev's work and fully endorsed it or referred to it with varying degrees of enthusiasm.

Frisch visited the United States in the spring of 1927, and in April prepared a long manuscript, 'The Analysis of Statistical Time Series', which was widely circulated among American economists with the precious help of Mitchell, although it was never published. From the first pages, Frisch subscribed to Kondratiev's hypothesis of 30 to 50 years of 'long time movements around which the business cycle is fluctuating', forming a 'major cycle' (Frisch 1927: 4). The source of the reference was the 1926 German translation, but Frisch had also borrowed a manuscript by Kuznets (the book to be published in 1930), which included not only an account of the Russian debate but also statistical information giving credit to Kondratiev's theory. It is quite obvious that Schumpeter—later on a close friend of Frisch, and who also shared this idea—developed his approach autonomously from Frisch: the correspondence between them first began in August 1927, after the dissemination of the time series paper. It did not mention Kondratiev, whose hypothesis had already been publicly accepted

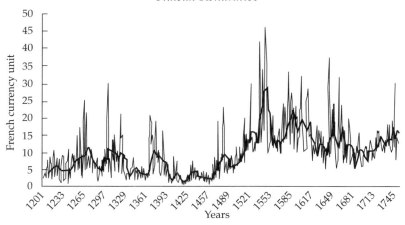

FIG 3.1. D'Avenel's series for the price of wheat in France, 1200–1800, as represented by Frisch (1927)

by Schumpeter. Indeed, their adherence to the long wave hypothesis was simultaneous but independent.

Schumpeter became the main Western defender of the theory of long cycles, and dedicated a large part of Business Cycles (1939) to it, although it is also obvious that he had read the 1926 German translation and had accepted its main idea since then. As this is quite well known, Schumpeter's arguments in favour of Kondratiev will not be discussed in this chapter. But it is worth emphasizing Frisch's engagement in the same camp; although he did not discuss the hypothesis in detail in his scientific and mathematical texts, he did try to show that some of his models of cycles could generate long waves for certain ranges of parameters, and considered this to be an indication of the likelihood of the models. Moreover, Frisch insisted again and again on his interpretation of the depression of the 1930s and the dangers of war by means of the long wave argument, and in 1932 he gave a series of radio lectures in which the question was discussed. Later, in the pamphlet including these lectures and dedicated to the discussion of the conjuncture, Frisch illustrated his argument with a long series of wheat prices for 1201–1800 from a nineteenth-century book by D'Avenel (Figure 3.1).

Frisch looked at the years 1300–1800 in particular; he used a ten-year moving average, much as Kondratiev did, and detected large persistent movements, which he interpreted as indicating long cycles of prices for the whole history as described by the graph.[10] Since this explanation was very effective for understanding the great ravages of the 1930s, at least as far as Frisch was concerned, he maintained it throughout his life.

---

[10] There are some severe shortcomings in this story, since D'Avenel's series is merely an average of eclectic local observations and the meaning and coherence of the series itself is at best doubtful. But this did not prevent Frisch's acceptance and profound belief in this interpretation.

Tinbergen very soon, and also independently, defended the same hypothesis for quite similar reasons, since he had read de Wolff's book and reviewed it in 1929, noticing that a parallel line of investigation was being carried out in Russia: 'Research on long waves is still in an initial stage, and it is mainly in Moscow that valuable work has been done on this subject' (Tinbergen 1929: 29). Like Frisch, Tinbergen maintained the same interest all his life and continued to participate in conferences on this topic well into the 1980s. In 1987 he wrote a rather favourable preface to Kleinknecht's book on the issue (Kleinknecht 1987b).

In Wesley Mitchell's important book, first published in 1927, he acknowledged the work by van Gelderen, de Wolff, and Kondratiev (once again based on Kondratiev's 1926 German translation—Mitchell 1956: 227 ff.) and commented on their contributions, although the theme of the book was the (Juglar) business cycle. In a later work, Burns and Mitchell again discussed 'the most celebrated of the long cycle theories', 'the daring hypothesis that long waves in the wholesale prices are an organic part of a long cycle characteristic of capitalism' (Burns and Mitchell 1946: 431–40).

As far as immediate reactions are concerned, Kuznets was the other important young researcher interested in Kondratiev's works at the time. As he was able to read Russian, Kuznets was the first to study Kondratiev's work in depth, namely his 1922 book, his 1925 paper (plus the German translation), and the Kondratiev–Oparin controversy (Kuznets 1930: 259 ff.). Furthermore, Kuznets was familiar with Trotsky, van Gelderen, and de Wolff's arguments, and included a synthesis of their contributions in his own book. His important 1940 survey of Schumpeter's *Business Cycles* indicated a much more critical attitude towards the long wave hypothesis, and it is well known that he developed an alternative account of long-term historical evolution. (For a more recent reappraisal, Solomou 1987.)

During the late 1930s interest in Kondratiev's work apparently began to fade, and no new contributions were added to the research, with the major exception of Schumpeter's *Business Cycles* (1939). At the same time, other researchers into business cycles, such as Haberler, distanced themselves from any claim about long waves. In spite of this, and basing himself on Spiethoff and Schumpeter, Haberler accepted that each long cycle had a historical physiognomy of its own and that a general theory was admissible, although he doubted if anyone could show the existence of regular factors generating the fluctuations (Haberler 1937: 308).

Another distinguished researcher, Alvin Hansen, acknowledged and quoted from the 1935 US translation of the 1926 German translation, and compared Kondratiev's arguments to those of Spiethoff, Schumpeter, Mitchell, and von Wantrup. He found that the regularity of the three long waves was comparable to that of the shorter business cycles: 'as high a degree of periodicity has prevailed for these three waves as any which we find for the major business cycles' (Hansen 1941: 29). It should be added that later Hansen took a much more 'agnostic and even very sceptical position' on the same issue (Hansen 1951: 56).

It is obvious that by that time—the end of the 1930s and the beginning of the 1940s—Schumpeter had become the main proponent of the thesis, or at least the person most involved in its defence, since both Frisch and Tinbergen were isolated in Europe and surrounded by war, and in any case had decided not to devote their professional attention to this issue.[11] In 1942 Frickey published a book that included an important argument against trend decomposition and suggested a not entirely specified alternative genetic method. Frickey argued that the secular trend should be assessed as 'a problem in historical description', not as 'a problem in mathematical curve fitting', and he demonstrated that the fit of different functions could imply arbitrarily created cycles and therefore spurious conclusions (Frickey 1942: 8). His conclusions from US data were presented as compatible with Kondratiev's hypothesis (pp. 231 n., 232, 340).

The long paper by George Garvy (1943) presented Kondratiev's main theoretical arguments, methods, and statistical evidence, and compared these with those of his opponents, concluding with Garvy's own view. Garvy's main criticism concerned the lack of explanation, in Kondratiev's assessment, for the lower turning point, and therefore the lack of any theoretical basis for the claim that there is a 'rhythmical movement of long duration of the economic system as a whole' (Garvy 1943: 208). Furthermore, he argued that there was no explanation for the trend—insisting that Kondratiev recognized his inability to show that the trend corresponded to the real economic evolution—and that the acceptance of Cournot's distinction between supposedly independent entities as trends and cycles forced Kondratiev to look upon 'the economic processes as a sum of the actions of independent forces' (Garvy 1943: 210). Discarding the long waves hypothesis, Garvy nevertheless argued that the enigma was relevant, since successive stages with differential growth rates could be detected in economic history, and actual dynamics should account for them (pp. 219–20).[12]

In the 1940s, another researcher taught the Kondratiev thesis at the London School of Economics: W. W. Rostow (1948: 9, 29, 45) based his lectures on Schumpeter and in particular on the 1935 translation of Kondratiev's paper. Others, such as the very young Richard Goodwin, learnt the thesis from Schumpeter and later spread it to others. At the same time, Fellner took a somewhat more sceptical position. In 1949 he had prepared a manuscript, which was discussed with Schumpeter, entitled 'On the Waves

---

[11] Frederick Mills was one of the economists Schumpeter took pains to convince: in a letter dated 12 April 1940, Mills kindly thanked Schumpeter for an evening spent discussing the hypothesis, 'certainly an intriguing one and a useful one' (Box HUG(FP) 4.21, Schumpeter Archive, Harvard University); but he did not seem to be convinced.

[12] This is quite comparable with Maddison's position on the same subject (Maddison 1991: 95 f., 105 ff.).

of Different Lengths with Particular Reference to the Long Waves' (letter from Fellner to Schumpeter, 26 March 1949, Harvard University). Fellner was probably under the spell of Schumpeter's argument, but his own contribution exhibits some doubts about the nature of the interrelation between the 'process' and the 'external factors', suggesting for instance that in the future the innovations accounting for a next Kondratiev wave could be exclusively or predominantly generated in the military sector, therefore being 'external'. Later, Fellner took up the issue again, presenting Kondratiev's statistical methods (Fellner 1956: 38) and inspecting a certain number of empirical series (pp. 40–1); his conclusions indicated the acceptance of long rhythms, but as irregular features of development. As a consequence, 'we prefer not to assert the existence of long cycles of fifty years' (p. 42), since 'the so-called long cycles in general economic activity are merely alternations between intermediate trends of greater and of lesser steepness' (p. 49).

This impressive list of scientists, including some of the major figures from several decisive research traditions in the first third of the century—neoclassical economics, econometrics, quantitative economics, heterodox approaches, evolutionary economics—clearly proves that Kondratiev was not alone in recognizing major structural changes and patterns of evolution in the history of industrial capitalism. The approximate dating of these processes was generally agreed upon by these researchers, although they disagreed as to the explanation and the epistemological and analytical solution to the difficulties felt by Kondratiev. And this is probably why there was such an impressive early consensus about the Kondratiev hypothesis, as will be further discussed in Chapter 4. There had been major economic and social changes, and Kondratiev provided a framework with which to date, interpret, and discuss these changes.

Nevertheless, there was no agreement on the causes or even on the nature of these periods of change. Indeed, these same difficulties are still felt by our contemporaries, since the puzzle these scientists tried to solve is still on the agenda, and important methodological insights can be gained from these earlier controversies.

3.7 Conclusions: Evolving Economics

Kondratiev's research was one of the first major quantified inquiries into economic history. It established a general consensus on the approximate dating of the initial long-term economic movements, and for a certain time it became a paradigm of the explanation of changes in capitalist development. It was one of the first applied statistical researches in economics, and it endured as a reference point for future research, although the controversy surrounding this effort illuminated some of its shortcomings and incoherences. Two conclusions are therefore in order.

The first concerns the importance, depth, and scope of Kondratiev's endeavours. His work—in spite of its naivety and simplicity—should be read by economic historians, macroeconomists, and statisticians, since it clearly presents part of the conundrum of the application of mechanical statistical methods to real, concrete, and live history. Indeed, Kondratiev's paper on forecasting (1926b) is one of the masterpieces in the early literature on statistics and history. It is a powerful survey of the contemporary authors in economics, mathematics, physics, and philosophy,[13] and deals in detail with the problem of the relation between reversible and irreversible processes.

Kondratiev adopted a cautious stance on recurrence and causality: there is no more than a slight chance of repetition of exactly the same causal environment, so *ceteris paribus* conditions are not met in economic history—each event is unique. But, according to Kondratiev, there is also a stable causal structure, which accounts for a certain regularity of phenomena. Of course, this implied that the explanation of the complex whole is a priority for any inquiry in social sciences: 'We must emphasize in particular that each given whole is not the simple summation of its components and cannot be understood from the peculiarities of these elements as such. Each totality represents something new, something peculiar, which cannot be reduced to the elementary phenomena unless by default' (1926b: 63).

Although Kondratiev dismissed the possibility of a precise forecast, since the initial conditions are not known, and the causal structure and its regularity are only approximately understood, induction was presented as the sole method capable of increasing the level of understanding of historical data. 'Historico-comparative' and 'statistical' methods were therefore the two available forms of induction, and both were to be used in that quest (1926b: 74). Moreover, they should be combined, since no definitive conclusion is possible from statistics itself:

The statistical method is no other than the method of knowledge acquisition [induction], which meets a series of difficulties whenever it is applied, that prevent it from strictly and exactly revealing the real relations and regularities. The difficulties do not just arise from the complexity of reality, but also from the quality of materials, the impossibility of disposing of the quantity of necessary elementary events and, finally, of our subjective errors. (Kondratiev 1926b: 77)

The combination of methods is therefore one of the central inheritances of Kondratiev's research, even if he clearly preferred the certainties that derived from quite arbitrary statistical demonstrations. Our argument is that this feature was part of the reason for the success of his writings, since at the time it was generally admitted not only that capitalism was characterized by

---

[13] The text included references to, and quotations from, not only Clark, Bowley, Babson, Jevons, Tugan-Baranowsky, Beveridge, Denis, Schmoller, Cournot, List, Marshall, Mill, Kautsky, Engels, Marx, and Pareto, but also Person, Strouvé, Durkheim, Mach, Poincaré, Meyerson, Comte, Simmel, Laplace, Boltzmann, Planck, and the Portuguese Teófilo Braga.

different patterns of growth, but also that history and statistics were each blind without the other.

Kondratiev assessed economic history as part of societal evolution, used the available analytical and statistical tools, and discussed their epistemological foundations. The original consensus obtained among his contemporaries demonstrated that long periods with distinctive characteristics were an imposing feature of industrial capitalism for so many of them, and the disagreements about his own explanation highlighted some of the limits of the methods and theories being used at that time. This was indeed Kondratiev's decisive contribution, and what makes him worthy of our attention: he convincingly argued that history is part of economics, and economic methods are necessarily analytical and historical.

4

The Strange Attraction of Tides and Waves

4.1 A Broken Consensus

As we have seen, in the first part of the twentieth century there was wide-spread acceptance in the economics profession of the cyclical nature of capitalist development, including long periods of expansion and contraction. There were sound reasons for this periodization: the evidence from price statistics was strong, and the existence of a previous long period of expansion under relatively stable political and institutional conditions (British domination and the gold standard) was followed by the violent changes created by the technological revolution of electricity and steel. These changes had been witnessed by some of the early researchers and were still matters of recent memory. As a consequence, the evidence of each period of restructuring of social relations, of institutional settings, and of international relations was naturally theorized as a new regime of accumulation, in a longer perspective than that of the Juglar cycles.

These reasons were still valid for the following generations of researchers: the trough in the 1880s and early 1890s, known at that time as the 'Great Depression', was followed by a stormy period of expansion marked by the culture of the 'Belle Epoque' and then by the First World War and another Great Crisis in 1929–33; the thirty 'golden years' after the Second World War once more nourished confidence in long-term growth, and again the institutional arrangements were stable (US domination and the Bretton Woods order). After the international crisis of 1974–5, the cyclical depressions became deeper, and we are obviously now experiencing a technological and economic transition. In spite of that, much economic theory and most of the statistical methods failed to reflect these larger patterns, as identified by history.

The present chapter briefly surveys the research on the dynamics of modern capitalism following Kondratiev and Schumpeter. Although the problem of long-period fluctuations continued to interest many historians and economists, it is clear that the early consensus on the importance of these longer-term changes no longer held. The reason for this was partially given in the previous chapter. After the econometric revolution and the victory of the mainstream synthesis in eliminating the major alternatives to neoclassical economics, and in the framework of the postwar years of a seemingly indefinite exponential expansion, any claim about a long cyclical pattern of intense structural changes appeared to be theoretically unjustifiable and practically nonsensical. New statistical and econometric studies appeared to disprove the previous existence of systematic long-term fluctuations in aggregate GDP. The long waves research programme was quickly considered obsolete and was abandoned; the dominance of mechanistic theories and models erased any concern about these mysteries of evolution.

The revival of the programme occurred only as a consequence of individual work in the framework of heterodox paradigms: Mandel (1964) was the first to reassess the question, followed by Hobsbawm (1968), both rightly announcing the coming end of the long expansion, and then by Boccara in the early 1970s, by Mensch (1975), Freeman (1977), and Duijn (1983), as well as by Forrester and his collaborators. In the 1980s, after the major economic turn of the previous decade, the research gathered momentum with major contributions by Pérez, Kleinknecht, Shaikh, Gordon, and Reijnders, among others, as well as with some new statistical (Maddison) and historical (Braudel, Wallerstein) work. The debate included the Social Structures of Accumulation (SSA) school, the Regulationist schools, some neo-Schumpeterians, some Marxists. In the 1990s, Tylecote, Bosserelle, and Fayolle among others contributed with major new developments.

This research on historical mutation in the economies has been criticized mainly from three perspectives. The first is the orthodox view, which ignores structural change and views the economies as cumulative and simple processes, driven by unexplained technological change and under artificial conditions (maximizing rationality, free competition, full availability of perfect information, etc.). In this framework, realism and the definition of distinctive periods of history are considered to be irrelevant or illogical. Of course, the long waves research programme strongly challenges these critiques, since it establishes an alternative evolutionary approach in which the abstraction of the representative agent is completely ignored, where diversity and the creation of novelty are considered the main factors in economic change, and where time matters and morphogenetic processes are identified to describe the real economies.

The second view is that of some critics who study the *historical* processes of change but doubt the adequacy of, or simply reject, the available long wave models. Kuznets was, of course, the best known, since he was the first to criticize Schumpeter's concept of cycles driven by clusters of investment in major innovations. Kuznets's, or Lange's, or Rosenberg's criticisms are in fact addressed mainly to the general methodological conditions for the scientific demonstration of long waves rather than to some specific model, although they base their remarks on the Schumpeterian and some neo-Schumpeterian models and, as it will be argued, their main arguments only stand up against the most obvious weaknesses of such models.

Some researchers, such as Maddison or authors of the SSA or Regulation schools, take a third view. These authors recognize that there were different historical periods—and in fact concentrate most of their research on the study of the precise definition, the nature of the changes, and the evolution of those sequences—but suspect adequacy of concepts like cycles or waves. However, given that they do not share the ancient and trivial account of history as a simple sequence of successive events, their debate about the rationale of social evolution is indeed close to our own research programme, since some of them explicitly wrote in such a context (Gordon and the initial SSA work) and others discuss the long-term fluctuations of capitalist economies, classified as 'stages' (Regulation schools) or 'phases' (Maddison). Boyer, among other leading French economists, contributed a great deal to the theory, with the concepts of regimes of accumulation and regulation, which include the institutional framework in economic research. If the new consensus is to emerge—and this book is a plea for it—it must synthesize various contributions on the historical evolution of the economies. Co-evolution, mutation and structural crises, and selective and adaptive behaviour should be the main conceptual references for that brand of economics brought back to life by evolutionary economics, in its constituent pluralism. In this perspective, a clarification of the past and present misunderstandings is needed.

In the sections that follow, three distinct groups of models, of proof, and of theorization will be briefly considered: (1) traditional statistical methods, (2) historical narratives, and (3) pure simulation from formal models. Although they are not completely alternative, these methods suggest different approaches to the analysis of long-term fluctuations and change in economic series (Table 4.1).

Long wave analysis began in the last decade of the nineteenth century and the first few decades of the twentieth century as an interpretation of crucial changes in the capitalist mode of production (van Gelderen, Parvus, Kondratiev) and as a tool for the integration of the socio-political determinations in long-term economic analysis (Bresciani-Turroni, Pietri-Tonelli, Pareto). In both cases, the research programme was defined as historical by nature. Nevertheless, the first methods to be used by these founding authors were limited either to a description of some indices or to the uncritical utilization of inappropriate tools taken from mainstream economics, itself under the influence of the analogy of the mechanics and thermodynamics of conservative systems. The obvious inadequacy of these procedures to demonstrate this scheme of historical succession of periods with distinctive social, political, and economic features consequently created strong doubts about the justification for the research itself.

The dominant methods in this analysis of long-term fluctuations can be traced back to the time of Kondratiev. By the time he began his systematic inquiry, the two current demonstrative methods were the historical and narrative account of oscillations and the early econometric techniques, and he used both. In its initial version, historical description is the method that includes the visual inspection of time series of data of aggregate production, consumption, prices, and trade, as well as the analysis of political events and social processes (including major ruptures such as wars and revolutions), of the role and evolution of institutions, and of the history and geography of the expansion of the world system. This method was important for the first Marxian authors, but was then relegated to oblivion by the dominance of econometric techniques until its resurrection in the 1970s, 1980s, and 1990s by Tylecote, by Perez, by new Marxist approaches, and by some of the Regulationist and neo-Schumpeterian work.

Unlike these descriptive and conceptual methods, the statistical methods originated some of the most intense early disputes about long waves. In the statistical and econometric methods, three main groups of techniques can be distinguished. First, there is the moving-average smoothing techniques and the trend-deviation computation (typically by Kondratiev, Oparin, Kuznets, Imbert, Zwan, Duijn, Nakicenovic, Sipos, Menshikov, Chizov, Craig and Watt, Glismann, Taylor, etc.). In this approach, if the average growth rate over a long period was computed as being above or below the long-term trend, this was taken as evidence for long wave fluctuations. The second group of techniques relates to the growth rate transformation and the analysis of long fluctuations from the behaviour of shorter ones (Mandel, Gordon, Kleinknecht, Duijn, Dupriez, Hartman, Ewijk, etc.), and the third, to spectral analysis (Ewijk, Metz, Kuczynski, Reijnders, etc.). Although the utility of each of these techniques is disputed, they were widely used, either as a complementary device in relation to the historical method or else, and essentially, as an attempt to demonstrate the existence of a cyclical structure by analogy with the accepted business cycle models, so that the inquiry might be legitimized by the comparison.

The general failure of such methods to provide absolutely conclusive evidence stimulated some researchers to look for new alternatives. The third set of methods to be considered in this chapter was born in the 1970s under the influence of Jay Forrester, from MIT. The use of pure simulation, unlike the previous two families of methods, does not present any direct claim for the interpretation of time series, given that it is simply based on a mathematical model with no direct empirical claim and, unlike traditional econometrics, its parameters are tuned according to the requirement of the demonstration but ignoring the available evidence on the real fluctuations. The model is considered to be explanatory simply if the simulation is able to mimic some of the features of the aggregate economic series. The closeness of the resemblance is therefore the desired proof for the causal implications represented by the abstract model.

These three large families of methods are summarized in Table 4.1. The listed authors are relevant examples and the list is not exhaustive; nor is it strictly chronological, since in some cases the theoretical vicinity is privileged. As the criterion for classification is the main method used by each author, the table simplifies some cases of use of a multiplicity of methodologies. Finally, not all the authors here considered identify themselves as part of the programme: this is certainly not the case of Kuznets, or of Maddison and the Regulationists. But it is legitimate to consider their work in this

TABLE 4.1. The main constellations of methodologies in the research programme

Model analysis	Statistical and econometric analysis		Historical analysis
	Kondratiev		Trotsky
	Oparin		
	Kuznets		
	Imbert		
	Dupriez		
	Duijn	Mandel	Maddison
Forrester	Kleinknecht	SSA	
Sterman	Menshikov	Gordon	Regulation schools
Mosekilde	Hartman	Aglietta	
	Metz	Boyer	Freeman
Mensch	Reijnders		Pérez
	Ewijk	Reati	Tylecote
	Zwan	Kuczynski	Fayolle
Silverberg		Shaikh	Bosserelle
		Entov	
		Poletayev	
		Moseley	
	(others: Sipos, Chizov, Craig/Watt, Glismann, Taylor, Nakicenovic, Marchetti)		(others: Braudel, Wallerstein, Modelski)

context, since they are important parts of the debate and/or contributed in some significant way to the research.

Some intermediary cases are indicated between the three main and well identified constellations of methods, whenever it is impossible simply to classify the author according to a single criterion. The authors suggesting a specific theoretical problem are included in Table 4.1 in the shaded box, in a transition area between statistical analysis and pure historical description. They include Mandel, Gordon, Shaikh, Boyer, and others, who used some of the statistical and econometric methodology but were concerned mainly with the evolution of the rate of profit and therefore with concrete historical analysis. In the following pages these various methods and problems will be described and briefly discussed.

It will be argued that some of the dividing lines in past controversies are in fact avoidable consequences of the use and abuse of the wrong and mechanistic statistical methods that pervaded the research, under the influence of mainstream concepts. In particular, the methods defined by analogy to those applied to traditional business cycle and growth analysis, i.e. the standard decomposition procedures as applied to 'trends' and 'cycles', are criticized and rejected in the sections that follow. Sections 4.2–4.6 contain some unavoidable technical detail in the discussion of the statistical problems. Readers who do not wish to follow this in depth may proceed to Section 4.7; that section sums up the conclusions of the technical discussion on methods in Sections 4.2–4.6 and is followed by proposals for a new type of research agenda in Sections 4.8 and 4.9.

4.2 Trend Deviation and Smoothing Techniques

The problems of decomposition of trend and cycle that confronted Kondratiev have already been discussed in Chapter 3. Many authors used the same type of detrending and smoothing procedure as Persons and Kondratiev.[1] Kuznets, in a book written during the same years as the main work by Kondratiev (1925–7), used the term 'trend-deviation analysis' to account for the distinction between 'primary' (trend) and 'secondary' movements (around 22 years) in the secular evolution of the economies (Kuznets 1930: 325). A moving-averages filter eliminated the primary movements, and logistic or other curves were fitted in some minor cases. (Kuznets did not use extensively the least-squares procedure, 1930: 61.) Not surprisingly, in a final note to the volume, he acknowledged that Kondratiev used what he called the 'modern methods of statistical analysis' (p. 263).

During the first revival of long wave research, after the Second World War, Imbert followed similar procedures: the trend was eliminated with logistic, parabola, or hyperbola curves, and Imbert fully endorsed Kondratiev's methodology, which was only criticized for not using logarithmic transformations (Imbert 1959: 20, 92 f.). This procedure was frequently followed, although, accepting the sensitivity of the results to the choice of the detrending function, van Duijn suggested a log-linear trend transformation of the index of industrial production, and tested the comparison between growth rates of successive Juglars (Duijn 1980: 224 ff.). Menshikov and Klimenko were also aware of the effects of the trend-deviation procedure, but they still used an exponential trend, and then a trigonometric regression, in order to eliminate fluctuations in the residuals if these were larger than fifty years and, finally, a nine-year moving-average filter on the residuals, although they argue that the use of a moving average is legitimate only when the fluctuations are systematic and quite deterministic (Menshikov and Klimenko 1985: 76, 77).

---

[1] Persons's method of detrending through curve fitting and moving averages became the standard form of decomposition: 'His [Persons'] methods (or closely related ones) for detrending data, for removing seasonal variations and for smoothing out erratic fluctuations are now such a standard part of data-preparation for econometric work that they are barely given a thought' (Morgan 1990: 63).

The three essential methodological problems were not solved by any of these procedures: detrending supposes an economic distinctive reality for the trend and consequently implies its strict separability from the cycle; the choice of a specific curve for detrending is equivalent to the previous definition of a certain hypothesis about the economic behaviour of the long-term series; the smoothing techniques may create artefacts. No alternative was found to these problems, either in the domain of detrending or in that of linear filtering techniques.

Yet these methods have been repeatedly used, and uncritically abused. There are two substantial reasons for this and for recourse to the current detrending procedures. The first one is meta-theoretical: the trend is supposed to embody the equilibrium conditions and those should be identifiable; orthodox economics consequently favoured this assumption. But the second one is technical: the simpler available statistical methods require the data to be stationary, that is time-independent on average and on variance, and detrending is the simplest way to get a series of stationary residuals.

One of these stationarity transformations that has a somewhat intuitive theoretical justification is the computation of growth rates: it corresponds to common measures, to reference points in the usual analysis of economic conjunctures, and to standard descriptions of time series. Moreover, it is interpretable as an economic entity by itself: growth rates information configures the expectations and contributes to government's, firms', and individuals' decisions. Several authors, some of them well aware of the difficulties of the detrending procedure, used the growth rate transformation in order to proceed to different statistical tests. Yet, the transformation acts as a 'high pass filter', biasing the spectral properties towards higher frequencies or shorter cycles (Reijnders 1990: 219 f.; Fayolle 1994: 136), for instance biasing the results in the sense of indicating the presence of Kuznets cycles wherever Kondratiev waves eventually existed (Bieshaar and Kleinknecht 1986: 190–1).

In spite of this, the growth rate transformation has been widely used in statistics: Burns used ten-year periods and computed their growth rates at five-year intervals, in order to define the trend, and Abramovitz evaluated the annual growth rate from peak to peak and from trough to trough of predefined cycles, analysing the trend from these oscillations.

In the analysis of long waves, the methods led to contradictory results. Ewijk followed Imbert's criterion of comparison of growth rates of different Juglars, and did not find general evidence in favour of the long wave hypothesis: a longer secular cycle is detected in Great Britain (expanding from 1780 to 1860 and contracting from 1860 until 1920), but some evidence for Kondratiev waves is found in French industrial production and in German data (investment and imports) for 1830–1913; no such trace appears in US data (Ewijk 1981: 340, 355 f.). Ewijk acknowledges one of the crucial criticisms of this method, namely its dependence on the definition of the turning points, and suggests the computation of a 'normal' growth rate for the whole period (p. 347). Van Duijn follows the same approach, defining a statistical test whose null is the hypothesized relationship between the growth rates of successive Juglars; but, contrary to Ewijk, he accepts the existence of long waves (Duijn 1980: 226; 1983: 149 f.).

Bieshaar and Kleinknecht defined a one-sided *t*-test for differences in the slopes of log-linear trend curves between predefined turning points (Bieshaar and Kleinknecht 1984: 282). Kleinknecht tested the differences of growth rates in the upswing and downswing of the long-term movements (Kleinknecht 1987*b*: 15 f.), and obtained some evidence for long waves after 1890, except for Britain, where a very long 'hegemonic life cycle' is defined (Kleinknecht 1987*a*: 219 f.).

Since the method introduces obvious bias, all these results are subject to caution. The growth rate transformation suffers from the same problems as the general methods to obtain stationarity, but has a somewhat better control system, since it may use preliminary historical knowledge of the turning points in the business cycle and the pre-definition of the periods—that is an advantage and not a limitation of this procedure, given that it openly presents the historical hypotheses followed by the modeller. In other words, the assumptions of the model are arguable and the choice of turning points may determine the conclusion of the test, but at least they are clearly stated and controllable, unlike the hidden but theoretically relevant assumptions of the choices of other techniques of curve fitting.

4.3 The Enigma of the Sphinx: The Decomposition Problem Reassessed

The previous section discussed some of the problems generated by the use of standard statistical techniques. Here we continue to pursue this question, considering the impact of such an analysis of historical periods on capitalist evolution. In traditional statistical analysis, if decomposition is accepted, then the identification and theoretical characterization of the various elements becomes crucial. One of the simplest ways to proceed is to assume an additive (or log-additive) relation between trend, cycle, seasonal variation, and random shocks. This simplifies the issue to the extreme, since any other type of interdependence is excluded. Each of the elements can then be described in a specific causal context; they can be separately analysed; and it is accepted that the series is the result of their summation. This atomistic hypothesis is coherent with mainstream statistics, and, since stationarity is needed to proceed to the typical tests, researchers are pressed to abandon their objections and to use the decomposition in order to achieve some publishable results quickly enough. But this implies that time and history are consequently put into parentheses, and the inquiry is centred on a new statistical entity, deprived of historical tendencies but hopefully gifted with equilibrium properties. Keynes already had warned of these dangers.

In spite of the investment of treasuries of imagination and of skilful technique in this paradigm, the adoption by so many of the long wave researchers of this perspective was highly damaging, given that the programme was directed to study long-term evolution of the economies and could not therefore dispense with history as an inseparable part of the object to be studied.

In this framework, four types of solution to the problem of decomposition have been put forward: (1) some of the researchers fully endorse the decomposition procedure and use it without any restriction; (2) some indicate that utilization is 'purely artificial' and merely argumentative; (3) others oppose the standard methods but try to find alternative procedures of decomposition; and (4) finally, some reject any solution of this kind. These alternative views will be briefly described.

The first group consists of some researchers who are apparently unaware of the difficulties and biases of decomposition procedures, namely its critical issues: the theoretical assumptions implicit in the choice of function to represent the trend; acceptance of the structural stability of that representation; and the postulated additive (or log-additive) relationship between trend and cycle, that is, a strong but unrealistic assumption that there is no interdependence between the trend and the cycle. A particular form of the decomposition procedure, widely used in past works on the topic, is the 'binary split' method, which uses price series to fix the dating scheme and then proceeds to tests on volume series in order to check the explanatory power of those periods. But this technique requires the price and volume series to be closely cointegrated, otherwise the tests are irrelevant—either the proof is already implicit, or no further clue is provided by the experiment.

The second stance was favoured by several researchers who discuss the pitfalls of decomposition procedures, but nevertheless use them for illustration or for some 'purely artificial' purpose, as Garvy put it (Garvy 1943: 210).

The third group of researchers criticized the decomposition methods, tried to find some alternative, but still used them in some very particular ways. Unlike the previous group of scientists, who were also aware of and commented on some of the pitfalls of the method, this category of researchers generally tried to avoid the procedure. That was the case of Kuznets, who in his 1930 major work asserted that no detrending procedure was atheoretical and technically objective as claimed, and none could distinguish between alleged independent processes:

Secular movements are continuous, irreversible changes that underlie the cyclical fluctuations of a time series. . . . The precision of our knowledge of these movements depends to a large extent upon the definiteness of our conception of cyclical variations. Nor is this dependence [of secular movements and business cycles] dissolved by any refined mathematical methods of curve fitting or smoothing. (Kuznets 1930: 60)

Kuznets's alternative was to incorporate some clear theoretical assumptions into the choice of the detrending curve: 'And if a hypothesis is to be verified, the secular movements should be described by a curve that incorporates the assumptions to be tested' (1930: 61). Of course, he assumed that there are always elements of arbitrariness in this choice of the function, and that 'we must bear in mind the essential uncertainty of the whole process of separation, or we shall be unduly influenced by the mechanical methods of fitting' (pp. 62, 67). And finally: 'They [the fitted curves] are not the only mathematical expressions possible, but tentative equations to be used in attempting a uniform, analytic description of secular movements' (p. 68).

Least-square methods were presented as the paradigm of those 'mechanical methods' to be avoided, and researchers were advised to look elsewhere for new methods. But, as no concrete alternatives were available, the main recommendation was still to consider carefully the theoretical assumptions and to accept that the results of 'mechanical' fitting were not conclusive tests for those hypotheses. In fact, Kuznets used logistic or Gompertz curves to detrend his series, and furthermore used moving averages to compute his 'secondary movements'. Like Kondratiev, he used different functions according to the structure of each series. Yet his criticism influenced younger researchers.[2]

The fourth group of researchers includes some more radical opponents of any decomposition procedure. These include early opinions such as that of Dupriez, who stated that long waves cannot be meaningfully represented as trend deviations, since arbitrariness in the choice of the trend curve could not be avoided (Dupriez 1959: 243), or Fellner, who argued that the long fluctuations were merely intermediate trends of more or less steepness (Fellner 1956: 49), or later views such as that of Silverberg, who rightly points out that the assumption about nonlinearity abolishes any possibility of decomposition, since both cycle and trend are generated by the same constellation of processes, or interact in crucial forms (Silverberg 1985: 274).

A recent debate in the *Journal of Monetary Economics* (41: 1998) discussed some of these questions. Fabio Canova compared different methods of detrending and concluded rather sceptically that they were unable to discriminate robust stylized facts, independent of the theoretical definition of the cycle. Although Craig Burnside answered that the complex form of historical series is imposed by the superimposition of frequencies of distinct cycles, but that we can establish adequate filters and analyse this process in the frequency domain, the debate is open. Anyway, the definition of a broad

---

[2] Some years after Kuznets, Frickey strongly criticized Warren Persons's decomposition methods, which had inspired Kondratiev and so many others: 'we expressly reject the notion of commencing the investigation by application of the conventional procedures for trend–cycle separation—fitting secular trends and computing cyclical deviations therefrom . . .' (Frickey 1942: 9). In particular, Frickey discussed the arbitrariness of curve fitting choice. Considering a long series of pig iron production, Frickey fitted 29 different curves for the secular trend, obtaining cycles in the residuals that varied from 2–3 years up to 40–45 years (p. 10). As a consequence, he rejected the mechanistic method and suggested a search for an alternative 'genetic' method, based on theory and history and using some statistical devices (e.g. checking the patterns of dispersion of various series, in order to make comparisons: pp. 9–10). Nevertheless, Frickey used the log-linear trend and the inspection of its residuals as a 'first approximation' for the detection of long movements (pp. 21, 250, 260 f.); he claimed that his results were consistent with the long wave hypothesis (pp. 231 n., 232 n., 255 n., 340).

range of frequencies corresponding to each theoretical cycle does not satis-
factorily explain historical mutation and therefore maintains the difficulty of
the decomposition, since it indeed tries to address a moving target.

The decomposition enigma can be solved only if three interrelated problems are satisfactorily addressed. The first is the assumption of structural
stability of the trend, which reintroduces the concept of equilibrium, and
the series is supposed to be generated by the same function with the same
parameters over a long period of time. Some authors explicitly accept this
assumption, although most of them only consider it implicitly. However,
whatever technical sophistication is invested in it, the assumption is not
convincing, given that it amounts to the extraordinary claims that the trend
is structurally the same for an era, but there are distinct structures for several
of the subperiods considered. Moreover, it is obvious that this subvariety is
defined according to the particular interests of the researcher, some looking
for fifty-year cycles, others for twenty-two-year cycles, and still others merely
for ten-, seven-, or four-year cycles, those periods defining the alleged
changes of substructures. This leads to a paradox: the scheme is incoherent,
since the equilibrating structure of the decomposition between cycles and
shocks is part of the disturbances of the previous decomposition between
trend and cycle—in this case, equilibrium must have both the face of Mr
Hyde and that of Dr Jekyll.

The second problem is the definition of a criterion for the choice of the
function representing the trend. This was discussed by most of the authors
mentioned above, and no shared conclusion was reached. But if there is no
criterion to discipline the research, then there is no room for a demonstrative
logic and proof is reduced to a tautology: the researcher is merely supposed
to verify what they already know, since the evidence was created by their
own convenient method of verification. If this is the case, any hope of
solving the first problem must be abandoned.

The third problem is the assumption of the strict independence of the
trend and the cycle and of the connected assumption about the linearity
of the generating system, so that the series can be defined as a summation of
both processes. Some of the authors also discussed this problem, but most of
them accepted that the assumed independence was merely a stratagem in
order to make the statistical work possible.

In other words, the answers to all three questions indicate that the decomposition problem cannot be solved within this framework. The decomposition problem is in fact tailored by the availability of methods: as an
econometric analysis is considered to be the authoritative element for the
demonstration of a theory, and as stationarity is currently required for that
analysis, detrending becomes a strategic issue. But, given that all its assumptions—equilibrium, linearity, decomposability, independence of the components—are unacceptable in historical analysis, the conclusion that follows is
that their lasting influence in the discipline simply proves that the right solutions were found for the wrong problems.

4.4 Simulation Models

All the methods discussed so far have an implicit method of proof, which is based on the analysis of real time series: the statistical test and its ability to confirm the hypotheses to establish the legitimacy of the demonstration. But the deficiencies of the decomposition methods and the danger of inconclusive or spurious results led some researchers to look for alternatives. Forrester and his collaborators, in particular, rejected the econometric procedures and supported a different system of proof, considering that, if a model can generate data comparable to the historical series, that is a relevant test and provides sufficient proof. This method is designated a 'structural change approach' as an alternative to the 'episodic events approach' and the 'coherent wave approach' (Mosekilde *et al.* 1987: 257–8), and it is supposed to make possible historical analysis, unlike the traditional statistical method, which cannot be applied to long wave analysis (Forrester *et al.* 1985*a*: 224). On the other hand, these authors argue that, since some a priori theory is needed to develop any empirical research, and no statistical test proves a causal assertion, a theory encapsulated in a model, based on acceptable behavioural assumptions, and generating data similar to reality is necessary for overcoming the limitations of the inconclusive econometric analysis (p. 236).

The National Model established by Forrester and his collaborators represented a major effort in that direction, and had a large impact in the early 1980s following the discussion about the 'Limits to Growth'. It generates three types of cycle from various causes: (1) business cycles are created by inventory and employment interactions; (2) Kuznets cycles are created by the evolution of capital and labour; and (3) Kondratiev cycles are created by five distinct mechanisms: (*a*) self-ordering of capital, that is, the positive feedback from the fact that capital is an input for itself; (*b*) the evolution of real interest rates and prices, another positive feedback loop; (*c*) the inflation spiral; (*d*) the introduction of innovations, namely a fifty-year cycle in basic innovation and the bunching process induced by the model; and (*e*) the effect of political and social values (Forrester *et al.* 1985*b*: 204 f.).

As far as the shorter cycles are concerned, they require the presence of exogenous random impulses; in contrast, the long wave is a 'self-generating process' in the model (Forrester *et al.* 1985*b*: 209; Sterman 1987: 132). The main factors are the positive feedback loops, particularly the capital self-ordering ones, although capital and labour interactions or real interest rate dynamics are also considered (Mosekilde *et al.* 1992: 198); in that case, technology is a secondary and even dispensable factor for the longer oscillations: 'The National Model has demonstrated that the long wave can arise even when the level of technology is constant and the rate of innovation is zero' (Forrester *et al.* 1985*b*: 208). One of the stated causes for the long waves process, technological evolution, and change, is exogenous to the model, unlike the main cause (capital self-ordering) and like the evolution of population, government activity, and the small random shocks (Sterman 1987: 130 f.; Mosekilde *et al.* 1992: 192). This creates a particular contradiction between the functioning of the model and its ability to describe reality—and, according to the selected criterion of the proof, this is a major problem— since it is accepted that each long wave is really related to a specific techno- logical pattern: 'Although innovation is not necessary to explain the long wave, there is little doubt that each long wave is built around a particular ensemble of basic technologies. . . . These ensembles evolve synergistically and, like species in an eco-system, compete against other candidates for a limited number of available niches' (Sterman 1987: 152).

Now, this points to one severe difficulty in the logic of the demonstration, since the status of the difference between the model and reality itself is not clear: the authors first define the model (which dispenses with innovation) but then acknowledge that in real economic processes the long wave is generated by the impact of systemic innovations and its 'echo' effect. In fact, if Sterman and his colleagues are correct about the importance of technologi- cal innovation, then the model is only able to generate a simulation whose proximity to real time series is more apparent than real, given that each 'par- ticular ensemble of basic technologies' is ignored in the model. The example shows that this proof by similitude is not a satisfactory criterion and may be as arbitrary as the econometric procedures it is intended to reject.

Later, Forrester's collaborators provided a new generation of models. They pointed out that socio-economic systems must be described with positive feedback reactions (Mosekilde *et al.* 1992: 212), which imply auto-catalytic (Sterman 1988: 395, Rasmussen *et al.* 1989: 281) and mode- or frequency- locking processes, that is, the coherent entrainment of distinct oscillations (Sterman 1988; Mosekilde and Sterman n.d.: 1, 8), generated by the coupling of different modes of periodic behaviour, a quite general phenomenon in nonlinear systems. These important insights were obtained by persistent work on models; they do not prove that reality is identical to the model simu- lations, but nevertheless suggest important new conjectures. In other words, this work confirmed the role and importance of metaphorical innovation in science, although it does not make possible new direct evidence about the existence of long waves. The creation of conjectures, although decisive for the development of new knowledge, is nothing but the first step in science.

But there is also a second order of reasons to impose some discipline on the use of purely abstract simulation from models in the research about long processes in economic history, since models themselves have a history of their own. In fact, in economics much more than conjectures have been demanded of the models prevailing in our science, and this is why an uncriti- cal use of simulation is not welcome. Furthermore, the recent generation of the dominant models in economics is by itself a tentative solution to the para- doxical failure of the macroeconometric models supporting the neoclassical synthesis of the 1950s and 1960s, as the current discussion on their value is highlighting. Indeed, given the difficulty of structural estimation, the new

Real Business Cycle models presented an alternative that questioned the cognitive value of statistical inference. Consequently, Lucas championed a sceptical critique of the previous experience and suggested the use of 'toy-models', based on artificial economies, whose behaviour should mimic the real series. In that sense, calibration replaced estimation, and the neo-classical school implicitly recognized the intrinsic limits of its investigation: instead of producing assertions on the real economies, an economic theory should just map the construction of a metaphorical entity, a purely 'mechanical imitation' (Lucas 1980: 697).

This absolute confidence in the heuristic value of the mechanical life of the artefact emphasizes how wise Ragnar Frisch was when he attacked, in his speech at the ceremony of the award of his Nobel Prize—the first to be given for economics, shared with Jan Tinbergen—the danger and practice of 'playometrics'. And this is also a good reason to refine the methods of historical inquiry in economics.

4.5 Endogeneity: The Dispute over the Adequacy of Models

Yet, none of these methods means the end of trouble. A complementary question concerns the obvious contradiction between a century-old proclamation in favour of unified societal theories and the profound difficulty of economics in considering concrete history. This section develops the argument that long wave theories are useful to address the critical issue of a general economic vision of historical processes, and that the ignorance of these insights results from the pressure originated by the reverence for neo-classical standards.

Kuznets's review of Schumpeter's *Business Cycles* took up the issue in 1940. According to Kuznets, there are two conditions necessary to establish the credibility of the research programme: it must prove (1) that the oscillations are general, and (2) that there are external factors or internal peculiarities of the economic system that create the recurrence (Kuznets 1940: 267). Otherwise no satisfactory proof exists, and in that regard Schumpeter provided a theory that was not even 'tolerably valid' (p. 269).

Now, recurrence is conceptually a very imprecise requirement. In a literal sense, it simply implies that upswings must follow downswings and, conversely, that there is an always repeated order of phases of the cycle, without any necessary constraint about the timing or nature of the causality. In other words, the cycle is the consequence of the previous sequence—this may be called the *weak version* of the recurrence requirement, which we endorse and exemplify in Part II, especially in the Conclusions to that Part, where we argue that this type of recurrence is to be theoretically explained by a defined causal system. A stronger version, the one that is in fact implied by Kuznets and most of the above authors, means that recurrence must conform to further definitions: it must be a time variation in certain precise limits and with well defined and stable causal relations, to be repeated over and over again. In short, the requirement for the *strong* version of the recurrence turns out to be that the analysis must closely follow the analogy with the business cycles traditionally analysed as the summation of irregular impulses generating regular cycles.

In a clear-cut way, Kuznets asked the research on Kondratiev waves to conform to this stronger version: recurrence could be legitimately explained only by either the impulse (exogenously) or the propagation mechanism (endogenously). As no linear model with strong and exogenous shocks can generate such a cyclicity without implying some sort of historical supranatural design, the burden of proof lies in the characteristics of the endogenous mechanism and an assumption about the distribution of the shocks. These requirements were presented as the scientific condition for the demonstration.

Oskar Lange reviewed the same book by Schumpeter in 1941 and, although denying the Kuznets cycles and accepting that the Kondratiev waves were 'better established empirically', doubted that they could be called 'cycles', since they were exogenously driven by 'historical "accidents" due to discoveries in technologies [rather] than regular fluctuations in the rate of innovation connected with fluctuations in the risk of failure' (Lange 1941: 192). Criticizing the Schumpeterian, 'rather mechanic' extension from the business cycle analysis to the longer movements, Lange dismissed the cyclical nature since recurrence could not be proved and the exogenous factors dominated. Nevertheless, the alternative solution—recurrence based on a cyclical explanation of endogenous factors—became the favourite strategy.

These two possible implications—recurrence requiring the causality to reside in the propagation and equilibrating mechanism and dominance of exogenous factors implying the possibility of no recurrence in the strong version—dominated the debate on the question for some decades.

It is well known, after Frisch's model of cycles, that no linear deterministic system can by itself generate sustained fluctuations—without exploding or damping away—except under a very precise and unchangeable choice of parameter values, and such a structural and parametric rigidity is not acceptable. That is why the following step in the development of cycle theory was the incorporation of random shocks. But these introduce a new set of problems: originally defined as residuals, that is as measures of ignorance, and thus as depending on the modelling devices and not being sufficient to explain the origin of the fluctuation, the shocks came to be integrated in the models as a new concept of causality. This type of determination was introduced either because the theory implies a strong influence of some non-economic factor, or simply because a large part of the economic factors cannot be modelled as endogenous variables since they are not known or hypothesized, or finally, just because the model is restricted to a limited and manageable dimension.

Of course, none of these motivations justifies the causal attributions of the shocks. This did not stop some authors from considering a purely exogenous causality. Such was the case of the pendulum analogy initially used by Frisch to represent Schumpeterian innovations. But the model indicates the nature of the difficulties in obtaining an unequivocal definition of the variables, given that Frisch defined innovation as exogenous, while Schumpeter fiercely resisted and argued that the impulses had an endogenous character (Louçã 2000). As Goodwin put it, his formulation of the fountain metaphor—which is equivalent to Frisch's pendulum—'means accepting the idea that the exogenous (to economics, narrowly formulated) events of social history play an essential role' (Goodwin 1987: 28; also 1985: 12).[3]

It is difficult to define recurrence on the basis of pure exogenous causality. This is why Kleinknecht, among many others, emphatically argued for the alternative strategy and claimed that that credible theory depends on a causal endogenous explanation: 'The question whether or not such fluctuations are true cycles depends on whether theoretical explanations can convincingly demonstrate their endogenous character' (Kleinknecht 1992: 5; also 1987a: 222; 1987b: 13, 33). So did Poletayev (1992: 166), Ewijk (1981: 325), Metz (1992: 82) and others.[4]

This definition creates great methodological difficulties, since the formalization of the model, by analogy to business cycle analysis, imposes a strict and exhaustive definition of the nature of the variables, which is rather incompatible with an inquiry into real historical processes. In fact, it makes possible exogenous causality, which may prevent or create regularity or even recurrence, requiring some heroic assumptions or, alternatively, some endogenous transformation when the system is submitted to exogenous shocks and propagates them according to an internally defined mechanism. As a consequence, the linear impulse propagation system defines two precise families of extreme causal assertions: either a strong version of complete exogeneity, or a strong version of complete endogeneity (requiring the impulses to be random, small, and economically non-significant, although being decisive for the maintenance of the oscillation). In the latter case, non-correlated random shocks create correlated fluctuations, and simplicity and order emerge from complexity.

Some of the researchers went so far as to identify a completely endogenous explanation as the condition for a demarcation between scientific and

---

[3] In a more general way, Reijnders formally endorses the rocking-horse analogy of the equilibrium apparatus moved by exogenous shocks: 'Like in the impulse and propagation theory of the "familiar" business cycle, the long run movements are interpreted here as a particular manifestation of the working of a mechanism through which the economy counterbalances and absorbs the shocks to which it is subjected' (Reijnders 1990: 52).

[4] In the same direction, Escudier defined endogeneity as the scientific condition for the success of the programme (Escudier 1990: 128) and Glismann called for an 'endogenous theory' (Glismann 1985b: 221), as did Kuczynski (1992: 264), Delbeke (1985: 11), and Duijn (1983: 129). Altvater argued that factors that are exogenous from the strict economic point of view could be considered endogenous to the dynamics of capitalist crisis (Altvater 1983: 13); so did Frank and Fuentes (1992: 1, 5) and Rosier and Dockès (1983: 125, 183), for whom the class struggle is endogenous since generated by capitalism. Recently, Bosserelle argued that recurrence and endogeneity were the conditions for the success of the investigation on long-term fluctuations (Bosserelle 1994: 47).

non-scientific propositions. Of course, such completeness is purely rhetorical, since the object cannot be the whole world. One of the most relevant examples was that of Kondratiev, to whom endogeneity meant that all the relevant variables could be defined as having been generated by the economic system itself:

> This just means that these episodic and external causes ['in particular the variations in the extraction of gold'] are themselves included in the whole process of the socio-economic dynamics and for that reason cannot be considered as external causes accounting for the cycles. From our point of view, the explanation of the long cycles and in particular of those of prices must be looked for in the character of the mechanism and the internal laws of the general process of socio-economic development. (Kondratiev 1928*b*: 425)

Consequently, these very general laws should account simultaneously for the discovery of gold in California and Australia, for the two world wars, for the decline of the British Empire, and for the electricity revolution at the end of the nineteenth century: they should explain the co-variation of all these variables and do so from the standpoint of a non-defined 'general process of socio-economic development'. But the claim is obviously excessive, and in some places Kondratiev indicated that he understood this; while repeating that the generally considered exogenous causes were really consequences of the economic system, and therefore of endogenously determined factors, he still accepted that there was in society 'an element of creation' (Kondratiev 1928*b* : 149, 150–1). He furthermore wrote that the cycles corresponded to an 'internal logic', which was a sequence of cumulative causal effects, but that new historical conditions could precipitate the cyclical fluctuations (p. 164).

Kondratiev's tradition amounts to (1) that only 'endogenous models' are valid, and (2) that all relevant factors of all kinds must therefore be modelled as endogenous variables. As a consequence, the scope of the model is defined in such a way that it must include all social, economic, political, and institutional realities. Paradoxically, most of the authors referred to above suggested models that cannot, of course, correspond to this theoretical requirement of universality, since they are limited to a small number of variables and are by this sole fact forced to ignore most of the relevant factors, which are finally condensed under the form of some exogenous residual random term.

Clearly, the very definition of endogeneity depends on the scope of the operational model that is used. Of course, the problem is also one of terminology, and several authors use the concept in a rather loose way. Endogeneity can be rigorously addressed only in the framework of a formal model, since it is non-definable in the context of a general social theory, in which it refers to any possible ingredient of the explanation. It is obvious that there is a dramatic trade-off between on the one hand simple and formal models, which can be tested against empirical evidence and whose definition of exogenous and endogenous variables is exhaustive, and on the other hand broader theoretical frameworks, where that definition is not so precise. Whoever opts for formal and testable models must accept their standard limitations, such as a small number of dimensions, generally a linear configuration, and decomposability. Alternatively, the other option implies the acceptance of the notion that the boundaries of the economic sphere are not objectively defined and that it is not possible to endogenize artificially such factors as state intervention, social institutions, or cultural features, which are obviously so relevant for economics since a formal model cannot completely determine these variables. In other words, either the models are testable but do not explain reality, or they explain reality but are not necessarily operational. Consequently, the useful role of simple formal models is not in the precise explanation of socially complex processes, but in the creation of conjectures for their study—it is unwise to ask metaphors to deliver what they do not know.

On the other hand, complete endogeneity refers to an ideal, all-comprehensive model that is unreachable. It should represent the whole universe, and then the distinction between the endogenous and exogenous variables becomes useless since everything is endogenous by definition in that case. But this cosmic vision, useful as it may be, does not provide the foundations for an operational model and is essentially a literary device to bridge over contradictions between general theories and concrete modelling.

Alternatively, one may define capitalism as a concrete historical process, some of whose contradictions may be captured by the concrete economic analysis of production and distribution, while others remain outside the scope of each model. As the economic subsystem is partially and conceptually autonomous from the other social and political spheres, where independent processes may develop, the theory must address both their relative autonomy and their interconnections.

If researchers on long series take this interpretation, then they must consider not only the economic forces, but also the social and institutional environment and the historical events—each wave is one 'historical individual', wrote Schumpeter—in order to formulate a theory.

So it is not just the extreme versions of exogenous and endogenous determination that are at stake: it is the very purpose of the antinomy that is rejected. In fact, the standard distinction between endogenous and exogenous variables implies no less than: (1) the linear and additive representation of the trend and the cycle; (2) the fact that therefore decomposition is possible and meaningful; (3) that the relevant object of the study is the cycle and not the trend; (4) that the cycle is the reversible process to be explained by the endogenous mechanism; and finally (5) that the trend represents equilibrium and that the reversible movement is organized around equilibrium. But this paradigm defines models with no time, with no change, and with equilibrium properties that are the more absurd if extended to a period of history covering nearly two hundred years, and indeed are clearly contradictory with the observable reality of contemporaneous capitalism.

Moreover, no theory about history can ignore the evolution of the socio-economic environment and of historical contingent events; neither can it fully integrate those factors as mere consequences of the economic endeavour. In fact, in the historical perspective a strict endogeneity is either trivial or wrong, and merely constitutes a self-confident *vue d'esprit*. This is why Mandel defined an asymmetric and integrated explanation for the long wave (Mandel 1979: 14–15), just as Reati did ('Comment' in Poletayev 1992: 169), or Shaikh (1992: 175), or Pérez (1985: 453).

The final question concerns the nature of the difference between endogenous and exogenous variables. This identification is somewhat arbitrary, even within the dominant paradigm which favours that formalism: investment may be modelled either as 'autonomous' (exogenous) or as induced by the evolution of the system (for instance, by the aggregate product), or as both simultaneously, and then causality may not be unequivocally determined. On the other hand, the candid belief that economies can be exhaustively represented by a formal model with a finite and normally very reduced number of variables whose legitimate relations are calculable, which is the rationale for the instrumentalist epistemology, is incompatible with the analysis of real evolutionary processes.[5] That was the sense of Schumpeter's and Keynes's arguments about 'hybrid variables'.

Given that most research on long-term economic movements stuck to the first generation of mechanistic models, it is understandable that the postulated legitimacy or intelligibility of the theory has been associated with endogeneity. Thus, the acceptance of Kuznets's or Lange's requirements amounted to an open invitation to search for the Grail: a perfectly all-comprehensive endogenous model capable of generating the cycles, or a Laplacean demon knowing everything.[6]

---

[5] More recently, these constitutional dogmas of decomposition have been challenged by the abandonment of the assumption of linearity. Some nonlinear dissipative models, such as Goodwin's 1990 model, require a forcing factor to mimic reality. This is not a random shock procedure, since it is economically defined and parameterized. It represents simultaneously endogenous and exogenous causality in a model whose nonlinear functioning generates evolution and change, structure and intrinsic randomness, so that the changes in basic technologies impact on the economy, which acts as a 'frequency converter' (Goodwin 1985: 271–2), changing both the dynamics and the structure of the society. As a consequence, the strict separability between endogenous and exogenous variables is dissolved: as far as this model is concerned, the forcing factor is both endogenously determined and influenced by the initial conditions, and then is exogenously reparameterized every half century. And, second, the endogenous variables create oscillations that are deterministically irregular although apparently random (Goodwin 1990).

[6] This quest for the Grail tradition is indeed responsible for the most extravagant characteristics of some work, both in the desired scope for the research (it should include series on criminality, suicides, divorces, school attendance, and strikes, according to Imbert 1959: 151 f.; on the adoption and diffusion of stamps, the book printing industry since 1470, England's war fleet since 1485, US murder rates and even killing techniques, or the building of the first Metro line in major cities, according to Marchetti 1993: 6, 10; 1986: 377, 383; on women's clothing fashion, Arizona's trees growth or advertising strategies, following Beckman, Shearlock, or Lorenz; quoted by Marshall 1987: 3) and in its predictive capacity. (Marchetti predicted, in the same vein

The whole quest amounted to a tremendous and self-defeating loss of energies. The Grail cannot be found, simply because it does not exist: a complete endogenous explanation whose scope is the complete universe itself is either a literary device and an aesthetic vindication leading to resignation, or a meaningless methodological criterion, since causality is not self-sufficient except in theology.

Split between these two contradictory requirements—the standard formalism necessary in order to legitimate the inquiry in relation to the discipline as a whole, and the inclusion of the whole universe in the operational model—the modelling procedures in the long wave programme have been generally inconclusive.

4.6 Spectral Analysis as an Example of the Decomposition Procedures

The critique of the traditional econometric methods for cycle analysis led to the defence of non-parametric methods for the statistical inspection of time series, and of historical methods to establish the hypotheses for that inquiry. Spectral analysis, one of the most powerful statistical alternative methods, corresponds to the first requirement, although not necessarily to the second one. Its applications in long-term economic analysis are reviewed in this section.

Spectral analysis, which is based on the decomposition of the total variance of a series into the contributions of individual frequencies, has been commonly presented as a 'theoretically free' device, allegedly independent from any theory about the nature of the trend. It is, but although this quality is certainly adequate for experiences and for laboratory replications, it is not necessarily so for the analysis of social evolution in the long term, given the irreversibility of historical mutations.

The first applications of spectral analysis for the study of long-term fluctuations, before revival of the long wave programme, were naturally concerned with long swings, as suggested by Kuznets. Adelman, in 1965, reconsidered a previous experiment with a randomly shocked Klein–Golderberger model, which could generate long swings and mimic real series quite well. Adelman used a log-linear trend and least squares to stationarize the series and compute the residuals. The conclusion was that the Kuznets swings 'are due in part to the introduction of spurious long cycles by the smoothing process, and in part to the necessity for averaging over a statistically small number of random shocks' (Adelman 1965: 459). In 1968

as Mensch, that a major innovation wave was to be expected in 1984–2002, (Marchetti 1988: 2); Hall and Preston that the IV Kondratiev would end by 2000 or 2003 (Hall and Preston 1988: 21); and Islam that 1990–2000 will constitute the recovery period (Islam 1985: 66).) In the same vein, and in a bold generalization of Jevons's position, Abalkin suggests that the future of the long-wave research may be connected to the understanding of cosmic processes (Abalkin 1992: 14).

Howrey came to the same conclusion: he used a growth rate transformation in order to make possible the spectral analysis, and concluded that no evidence could be found of the presence of long swings in the US 1869–1955 and 1860–1961 series of GNP, population, GNP per capita, industrial production, and others (Howrey 1968: 250).

The applications of spectral analysis to the inquiry into Kondratiev waves came much later: Ewijk claims to be the first to have applied the method to data from the United States, Britain, France, and West Germany. He introduced two different transformations for stationarity—first differences and first differences in logs—and confirmed evidence of long waves in the price series but not in the production series, except for France, after the interpolation for the Second World War years (Ewijk 1982: 478, 486, 489). Other authors followed.[7]

In this framework, three main methodological problems persist in spectral analysis. The first one is common to other econometric procedures: conclusive results require longer series than the available ones. As early as 1965, Adelman commented that the seven Kuznets periods available were not enough for a conclusive test (Adelman 1965: 451), and Duijn justified the need to look for qualitative data, given the insufficiencies of the statistical information for spectral analysis (Duijn 1977: 567). There was general lack of agreement on the number of cycles necessary to test the long wave hypothesis—10 cycles (Ewijk 1981: 336–7), 8–10 cycles (Beenstock 1983: 139), 7–10 cycles (Duijn 1983: 169), 7 cycles (Solomou 1988: 16), and longer series (Bieshaar and Kleinknecht 1984: 281; Glismann 1985a: 231). This disagreement is rather general, and not easy to solve, at least in the short term.

The second major problem is the sensitivity to the decomposition procedure, for the trend elimination. Bieshaar and Kleinknecht note the problem (1984: 281), and several authors address the core issue of stationarization: Duijn argues that the process can affect the turning points (Duijn 1983: 169), and is supported by Metz (1987: 392); Gerster notes that the trend-decomposition assumption implies that the series under scrutiny must be free from any evolutionary movement (Gerster 1992: 124). Indeed, the series must be conceived as a realization of a purely random, a stationary Gaussian process (Gerster 1992: 128; Howrey 1968: 229; Adelman 1965: 448).

The third problem is that the results can be affected if the amplitude and period of the cycles change abruptly (Glismann 1985a: 231; Chizov 1987: 5;

---

[7] At the same time, Haustein and Neuwirth used the same type of procedure to compute the spectrum of deviations from a long-term exponential growth in world industrial production. Other series, such as energy consumption, inventions, innovations, and patents, were treated in the same way, and the authors found evidence for 50–year cycles, but also for 40-, 32-, 20-, 13-, and 7-year cycles (Haustein and Neuwirth 1982: 53, 66, 69 ff.). These cycles were interpreted as lag cycles and not as life cycles; no dominant auto-correlation cycle was found, and as a consequence the hypothesis could not be supported. Beenstock differenced the data and concluded from very long price series (Beveridge series on European wheat prices from 1500 to 1869 and Phelps-Brown and Hopkins historical series of prices) that there was some evidence for 157-, 40-, 27-, and 14-year cycles, and still no support for the Kondratiev hypothesis (Beenstock 1983: 139 ff.).

Taylor 1988: 427), that is, if the assumption about structural stability is challenged. The trend representation is essential and it is essential that it captures the whole process generating the series for a very long period without any possible interruption: this is implicitly assumed by many of the statisticians.

One of the efforts to address these problems was developed by Jan Reijnders, who attempted to incorporate spectral analysis in the framework of long wave research and to avoid the purely mechanistic procedure of trend decomposition. His choice is to make explicit the assumptions about the economic description of the trend: he develops a very sophisticated discussion about previous methods in econometric analysis, and suggests a new technique, considering the trend as the summation of a 'standard trend' and 'systematic deviations'. The standard trend is computed from the average growth rates for a very long period, given that Reijnders points out the danger of the 'perspectivistic distortion' whenever the size of the window is not enough to account for complete cycles (Reijnders 1990: 190, 133, 135 f.). The standardization procedure thus adopted—or the elimination of the standard trend—is based on the values of the longest available series, the 690–year long Phelps-Brown and Hopkins index for a set of prices. The spectral analysis on residuals from the trend (conceived as underlying all the series) is the test for the presence of long waves (Reijnders 1990: 218), and Reijnders concludes that there is positive evidence in price series after 1700, and in production series, provided that the war years are interpolated (pp. 227, 230).

In this case some of the major problems with spectral analysis are avoided, namely the purely atheoretical application which is correctly rejected. Reijnders also provides a powerful critique of the dominant techniques: he shows that the growth rate transformation implies predetermined windows and an increased danger of the 'perspectivistic distortion' (1992: 25); that is, it hides the longest waves. Finally, he argues that the problems of heteroscedasticity and auto-correlation, which are obviously to be expected in historical series, can be only partially and tentatively solved (1990: 155–6).

But this effort is still neither conclusive nor complete. For the sake of the available data, Reijnders assumes heroically that there is an implicit economic trend influence for the last 690 years in all his British series, which can be represented by the evolution of the prices of a basket of consumables in the southern part of Britain for seven centuries. (The original series is 1264–1954.) He further assumes that this trend, embodied in an increasing monotonic function, an exponential function, can be meaningfully separated from the cyclical influences in all other series (Reijnders 1990: 132). As a consequence of both options, he obtains non-explained results, such as very long cycles of 376 and 242 years, which are not supported by any theory.

The difficulty seems to be insurmountable: spectral analysis still assumes the superimposition of frequencies as a specific form of the trend–cycle relation, and consequently is submitted to the general critique of decomposition.

But this is not all. Precisely because they opted for econometric procedures requiring the stationarization of the series in order to test the hypotheses, many of these researchers were confronted with the concrete difficulty of dealing with the most extreme economic situations, such as the war periods with their extraordinary economic turbulence. In general, the application of these statistical methods required the a priori elimination of the impact of those war periods on the mean and variance of the series, in order to make a proper analysis possible.

Without exception, and this is hardly surprising, those engaged in this type of statistical inquiry accepted the necessity for those punitive methods.[8] According to Metz, only a linear interpolation for the war periods may rehabilitate the Kondratiev hypothesis; otherwise the test indicates the sole presence of Kuznets swings in the twentieth century (Metz 1992: 89). Metz goes as far as saying: 'From a statistical point of view, most of the World War values can be regarded as outliers which disturb the "normal" structure of the time series' (p. 110, also p. 89).

Kleinknecht strongly supports that view. He gives three reasons for this: (1) war impacts are very severe and thus distort the data; (2) the statistics may otherwise give implausible results (namely, a Kuznets downswing in the 1950s); and (3) there is no theoretical explanation for the Kuznets cycles, which would survive if no elimination of the 'outliers' were decided (Kleinknecht 1992: 4). Of course, it is difficult to see the relevance of the first reason for a realist epistemology, and the second and third are merely a restatement of the correction of the theory, in spite of, and in contradistinction to, the statistical results. The paradox is that the fascination for these methods was based on their capacity to challenge a priori interpretations and to reveal new evidence. But in this case, and contrary to what has been proclaimed, the evidence is tailored to the existing theory in a very frank and open way, and no independent test is accepted: if the evidence does not obey the theory, the evidence is changed by the statistician. The epistemology of confirmation never went so far, and never was so little confirmatory.

---

[8] Ewijk was able to find some evidence for long waves in French industrial production, provided the Second World War years are linearly interpolated (Ewijk 1982: 486). Bieshaar and Kleinknecht also used the GLS technique in order to smooth the differences in variance resulting from the presence of war impacts (Bieshaar and Kleinknecht 1986: 185). Klimenko and Menshikov simply suggest excluding the war years and their presumable influence in the period 1933–57 (Klimenko and Menshikov 1987: 351). Solomou, in his research on British data, uses dummy variables and linear interpolation for war years, and finds no evidence of Kuznets long swings in the period after 1913 (Solomou 1987: 25, 34–5). Rasmussen and his colleagues justify the elimination of war influences through interpolation, since those periods can account for most of the variance of series and since wars are supposed not to be 'directly involved in the basic mechanisms of the economic long wave' (Rasmussen *et al.* 1989: 288).

There is no possible causal implication from this kind of test. If a series that excludes the war time periods is tested and confirms the existence of long waves or of long swings, this statement may be interesting, but surely is completely irrelevant to describe or analyse reality, given that history stubbornly but unfortunately did include those hidden wars. Erasing parts of history is not a method to study history: the creation and manipulation of an historical artefact does not allow for any reasonable claim about real evolution, unless one could proclaim the absolute separability of international militarism in relation to the economic movements.

4.7 Problems and Perspectives

Two main families of methods have been reviewed in the last sections: what could seem to be a technical detour from the essential theoretical problems was instrumental in addressing some of the current limits of a research pervaded by *ad hoc* concepts, mechanistic models, and equilibrium theories. A summary of these families of methods is now in order, so that new alternatives can be explored.

The first constellation of methods, the standard statistical and econometric approach, did not solve the decomposition problem. This was to be expected, since the simple transposition of the dominant methods in business cycle analysis, where the assumption of no major economic change holds, to the study of long-term processes of growth and change, where it is obviously inconsistent, ought to fail. Indeed, the metaphor is incoherent, given the implausibility of structural constancy for fifty or one hundred years or longer. It is worth remembering that Keynes's discussion with Tinbergen was motivated by his opposition to correlations established for *ten* years. The presumption of causal stability, the exact same causes acting in exactly the same fashion in such different periods, furthermore added to the requirement of endogeneity, i.e. the same causes explaining the whole time process are not compatible with real history.

Finally, in order to preserve the method, some supplementary assumptions were made, such as the declaration of irrelevance of the inconvenient part of history (wars and major economic crises) which should not be considered in order to make possible the study of the relevant part. But this amounts to a confession of failure, since structural changes in economic history cannot be explained in ignorance of the concrete historic ruptures.

Otherwise, the standard econometric methods could not solve the decomposition enigma, since it is probably not possible to solve it. Some promising avenues were presented, namely non-parametric methods such as spectral analysis, but, given the irreducible irregularity of historical series, the wisest use of those new types of method is to establish conjectures rather than to claim to have the last word in the testing of hypotheses. Indeed, the most sophisticated statistics require the most developed theoretical and historical explanations.

The second constellation of methods is the model approach. This creates a much larger degree of freedom in the search for causal systems, and may even contribute to overcome another major limitation of the dominant traditional econometric methods, which is the presumption of linearity. In fact, nonlinear systems and models question the traditional definition of endogenous and exogenous variables, differentiate the impact of external perturbations according to the state of the system, produce mode-locking behaviours, model structural instability and dynamic stability in the same context, and interpret complexity. But models alone cannot sustain a demonstrative logic or an adequate interpretation of reality, since simulation is not demonstrative proof. In this sense, models are useful metaphors for the creation of hypotheses in order to analyse reality, but they are not the reality itself, nor can they reproduce it.

A third constellation, the approach based on the complexity of reasoned history, has to be developed in the intersection between the historical, analytical, and descriptive statistical methods for hypothesizing causal relations and the modern and infant methods of nonlinear quantitative and qualitative research. This agenda includes:

1. the rejection of the claim for a complete quantitative description of the universe, as made by classical positivism and empiricism;
2. priority for the 'reverse problem' in quantitative analysis, i.e. for identification of features of the real time series, instead of the fabrication and simulation from an abstract model;
3. the acceptance of complex determination and the importance of social, institutional, and political factors, represented by semi-autonomous or 'hybrid' variables. Those factors are part of social and economic coordination, that is, of the cohesive processes such as those defining the rules of social conflict, economic determination, and political decisions contributing to the reproduction of the mode of production. They underlie the evolution of institutions and explain the economic behaviour dubbed as 'equilibrium', i.e. the dynamic local stability of the system, in spite of, and together with, its constant drive to change.

For these reasons, the reasoned history approach denies the extreme assumption about self-contained models and methods, and looks for integrated theories that will be incomplete and not definitive, explanatory and not predictive, historical rather than simply economicist, and evolutionary rather than mechanistic. A long time ago, Kuznets himself argued for such an interdisciplinary approach, although this plea had little effect on the profession:

If we are to deal adequately with processes of economic growth, processes of long term change in which the very technological, demographic, and social frameworks are also changing—and in ways that decidedly affect the operation of economic forces proper—it is inevitable that we venture into fields beyond ... economics proper.... It is imperative that we become familiar with findings in those related social disciplines that can help us understand population growth patterns, the nature and forces in technological changes, the factors that determine the characteristics and trends in political institutions ... (Kuznets 1955: 28)

As Chapters 2 and 3 have tried to show, Kondratiev and Schumpeter also argued for this, even though inconsistently. Our own approach takes up this challenge and ventures into those fields where economics is to be reconstructed as a social science.

4.8 A New Research Agenda

Is the metaphor of the wave the most appropriate to describe the long-term evolution of structures of accumulation, of employment, of production or trade? It is certainly reminiscent of the equilibrium paradigm, since waves and tides alter the level of the water, but there is still a reference situation that would occur if no attraction of the moon, no winds, and no disturbances existed around which the real levels gravitate. Indeed, Walras, argued for the unimportance of crises and the primacy of the static analysis based on the metaphor of the surface of the lake being agitated by transient waves. Consequently, one can ask if this new metaphor does help to master the nature of irregular growth and to create some pertinent conjectures for its discussion.

The metaphor of the wave is deficient—and it will be used here only because it is the established reference—since in real economic series non-stationarity and time dependence do matter, and indeed are the central features to be explained by the theory: the economic variables really do evolve and, with the absolute exceptions of entropic death of societies, they do not stabilize around some imaginary permanent level or constant rate of growth. In other words, persistent processes with long memory typically drive the macroeconomic variables. But still, this metaphor implies that only intermittent equilibrium exists, under the form of two attractors (the maximum and the minimum levels of the tide). Of course, even in these conditions, the analogy is limited—society is not constrained by this type of permanent boundary, given the persistence of material development.

Moreover, evolution is nothing more than the creation of variety and novelty, and *a fortiori* no fixed attractor or strictly unchangeable mechanism can represent that process. Irregular waves do exist, and they cannot be studied under the diktat of the *ceteris paribus* conditions: time is turbulence. The theories of cycles tried to encapsulate these phenomena under deterministic equilibrating representations, and then some exogenous noise was added for the sake of the quality of the simulation; naturally, they failed to produce either logical explanations or coherent descriptions.

Alternatively, we suggest that nonlinear complex models are necessary to address the duality of dynamic stability (around the attractors, in a region bounded by the availability of material resources, labour, or technological capacities) of systems that are nevertheless structurally unstable (inducing switches of regime from changes in the structure). These evolutionary models must address the central features of real economies: capitalism is unstable and contradictory, but it controls its process of accumulation and reproduction. Even more, critical instability generates new developments and new phases of dynamic stability: this morphogenetic feature is the peculiar strength of capitalism that fascinated Schumpeter and was so vividly described in Marx's and Engels's Communist Manifesto as the programme of modernization, 'all that is solid melts into air . . .'.

In long wave research, some authors addressed these criteria. The SSA and Regulationist schools discussed historical determinations, and so did the historians of the economic stages and several Marxists or neo-Schumpeterians. Some of their models explored nonlinear relations and established new hypotheses, and many authors claimed, and rightly so, that the general equilibrium paradigm was inappropriate.

But the state of the art in this research, as argued before, clearly indicates the difficulties and contradictions that dominated so far, the pervasiveness of inadequate methods, and the dependence on mainstream epistemological requirements for the construction of theories and the definition of models. Neoclassical doctrines were frequently rejected, but the general recourse to linear econometric methods reintroduced the equilibrium concept and imposed drastic restrictions on the historical nature of the series. Positivist standards were often rejected, but many authors accepted the atomistic and deterministic implication of the decomposition of time processes. The implication was self-defeat.

A new agenda implies a return to the organic and evolutionary metaphor; in particular, it requires the incorporation of two concepts: those of morphogenesis, or the study of structural crises in economic history, and those of co-evolution.

Morphogenesis implies two essential features: change and control, or rupture and continuity. Both coexist and are interdependent and inseparable: the one-sidedness of the analysis of a single term of the social process is indeed responsible for most of the relativist trends in economics, the extreme examples of theories of continuity being those defined by an assumption of perfect rationality and the general equilibrium paradigm.[9]

---

[9] See this new example of the contradictions of the assumption of rationality: 'Why is it that human subjects in the laboratory violate the canons of rational choice when tested as isolated individuals, but in the social context of exchange institutions serve up decisions that are consistent (as though by magic) with predictive models based on individual rationality?' (V. Smith 1991: 894). Vernon Smith, one of the founders of the programme of experimental economics designed to repair the averages of the rationality postulate, is right to call for the spell of magic to save the general equilibrium. A somewhat more secular explanation would indicate that institutional or social processes operate in order to coordinate decisions and to avoid extreme tensions and ruptures in the social process.

Coordination is the appropriate concept by which to interpret and analyse control systems and cohesive functions in historical development. Co-ordination, as a social process subjected to complex interactions—and not equilibrium, which is a state—explains the existence of attractors in growth patterns, the weight of social institutions, and the relation between the economic system and other parts of society. It establishes, from that point of view, the condition for the viability of morphogenesis, originally defined at the organismic level but then metaphorized to the general evolutionary process of society. In other words, coordination explains why disequilibrium processes exist but are constrained, why different rhythms are mode-locked, and why structural instability persists but does not drive the system towards explosion.

Turing, celebrated as a forerunner of computer science but frequently ignored as one of the first discoverers of complexity, modelled morphogenesis with a very simple chemical system of two components diffusing at different rates under random shocks: the system attained the 'onset of instability', given its auto-catalytic properties. In the case of that model, the emergence of a pattern of organization shows that it is instability that entails the development of the structure (Turing 1952: 37). This is order emerging out of complexity, and we may conjecture that this provides the example of a general case.

Of course, there are major differences between those simple chemical and organic systems and the social ones. The balance of positive and negative feedbacks in ecological niches, the channelization [in other literature, the term used is 'canalization'] of development, the selection of the spaces of viability and of stability are mainly driven by naturally coordinated processes, while in economies and in societies there is a combination of natural processes and of conscious choice and purposeful action. In this sense, social coordination may be defined as the working of two related sets of variables: (1) the technological, scientific, economic, political, institutional and cultural subsystems, and (2) the semi-autonomous variables connecting those subsystems. So far, an important part of the discussion on long wave movements in economic history was concerned with precisely these distinct sets of variables. Nevertheless, it has been limited through the assumption of strictly independent, separable, and additive subsystems and of a narrow atomistic hypothesis to interpret each of them. A new research agenda requires emancipation from such constraints.

4.9 Conclusions: Evolution and Mutation, the Epitomes for a New Consensus

In his reference to the Kondratiev cycles, Mandelbrot suggested that the superimposition of different orders of cycles should be assessed by hierarchical descriptions (Mandelbrot 1987: 126). Such is the approach of this book: emergence, complexity, and open systems are central features of the evolutionary theory as applied to social historical processes. In that sense, the basic hypotheses can thus be stated under the following form. (1) The social subsystems (science, technology, economy, politics, culture) generate a large number of irregular fluctuations, namely cyclical and wave-like movements with different approximate periodicities, caused either by specific subsystem cycles (political business cycles, technological trajectories, cultural movements, life-cycles of products or industries, etc.) or by the lags and feedbacks in the inter-subsystem connections. (2) Those streams are combined in some bands of fluctuation by specific coordination processes emerging after structural crises. These coordination processes are therefore the crucial causal determination for the business cycles and the long wave movements in real historical development, and that is the focus of Part II of this book.

In various ways, several authors anticipated these hypotheses. Van Gelderen was the first author in long wave research to have formulated a related interpretation, when he indicated that periodicity was connected not simply to the technological subsystem but also to the working of the capitalist system as a whole, that is to the construction of social order (van Gelderen 1913: 45). Of course, fifty years earlier Marx had anticipated the importance of the coordination process of 'capitalism as a whole', and had explained it as the outcome of profound tendencies and counter-tendencies, i.e. of conflict. For both Marx and van Gelderen, coordination was the rationale of the organic metaphor, and they were followed by modern evolutionary economists.

Some of the main consequences of this approach are no other than the previously stated epistemological conclusions: given that each subsystem is defined as the heuristics for some social relation, their interrelations cannot be deterministically discriminated by an exhaustive account of a simple model or by endogeneity or exogeneity of variables. On the other hand, semi-autonomy therefore means that the variable most relevant to the understanding of historical dynamics is the coordination process itself. In summary, the hierarchical explanation considers the specificity of each of the five subsystems and of their types of determination, as well as their organic totality.

This five-subsystems approach has three central innovative features. (1) It is a description based on the overlapping of subsystems, since their relationship is more adequate to explain reality than the artificially isolated description of each of the subsystems. (2) It analyses the crises and phase transitions from the viewpoint of the lack of synchronicity and maladjustment between subsystems, which defines the time band of major fluctuations. (3) The social conflicts of all types are generated and articulated by the coordination process, that is by power under all its forms, from the production of legitimacy to strict coercion. This coordination process proceeds at several simultaneous levels. The first level is that of the actions embodied in the social working of the economic system, the tension to integrate the conflicts, the conventions, and the institutions, and the second level is that of power, strategy, and domination.

In this sense, the fact that there is coordination does not imply that there is harmony or equilibrium, either in the ideological sense of a general feature of the capitalist economies or in the precise sense of a permanent dynamic stability property prevailing in the markets—which would require some hyper-centralized architecture of decision. In other words, complexity and structural change can be explained only as historical developments, as co-evolutionary processes. This is a building block for a new consensus: as we have shown in previous chapters, several economists—from heterodox traditions, from the original econometric movement, from the NBER—have been arguing for an effective change of paradigm. The Nobel prizewinner in physics, Philip Andersen, one of the founders of the Santa Fe Institute, put it in this way: 'Theoretical economics will have virtually abandoned classical equilibrium theory in the next decade; the metaphor in the short term future will be evolution, not equilibrium' (*Science*, 17 March 1995: 1617).

Conclusions to Part I: A Theory of Reasoned History

'Time present and time past
Are both perhaps present in time future
And time future contained in time past'

T. S. Eliot, 'Four Quartets'

1 Introduction

In this first part of the book, we have argued a case for reasoned history: for an approach to economic history including technological innovations, structural changes, and the co-evolution of economic and social movements within the framework of institutional settings and modes of regulation. In Part II we shall present an account of the development of modern capitalist societies over the past two centuries, based on a model of the diffusion of successive technological revolutions through the economic system. This concluding chapter sums up the argument of Part I: the fundamentals still apply as time goes by, even though each period has its own unique characteristics.

We have argued that both cliometrics and standard econometrics have failed to capture the most important features of institutional and technical change. Nevertheless, as methods for ordering concepts and testing ideas, they can be a useful complement to historical research. The problem with history is the almost infinite multitude of events, all of which have to be classified, described, and analysed. A simplifying theoretical framework is essential and inevitable.

Having presented the idea of the co-evolution of five semi-autonomous subsystems of society, in Section 4.9 we tentatively developed this simplifying classificatory framework. We argued that five historical processes or subsystems of society have been shown by historical research to be relatively autonomous but interacting major influences on the process of economic growth. We fully accept the points made by Keynes on econometrics and discussed in Chapter 2—the fundamental importance of *qualitative* change and the role of semi-autonomous variables. The five overlapping subsystems, which we shall very briefly discuss in Section 2 below, are science, technology, economy, politics, and general culture. In addition, humans share with other animals the natural environment, and this too can powerfully and reciprocally influence economic growth. Whereas the five historical processes each have their own partly autonomous 'selection environment' and are uniquely human, which is one reason why biological evolutionary analogies have limited value, the *natural* environment is common to both humans and other animals; but that is where the similarity ends. It is essential to understand the distinct human selection environments within the various subsystems. For example, the accumulation of scientific knowledge and of technological knowledge and artefacts are uniquely human processes, even though they may have originated, as with other animals, in the search for food and shelter and the communication associated with this search. In the case of technology, there are birds and mammals that make use of 'tools' in the sense of twigs, branches, or stones, but the systematic design and improvement of tools and other artefacts are uniquely *purposeful* human activities, with their own partly autonomous selection environment.

Economists often use a biological analogy to analyse the competitive behaviour of firms in a capitalist economy and the survival of the supposedly 'fittest' firms. This entails the borrowing back of an analogy that Darwinian theory originally took over from economics. But again, the selection environment that confronts firms in their competitive struggle is actually very different from the natural environment confronting animals and plants, and this economic environment is itself rapidly changing in ways that are unique. Finally, the political system and the cultural milieu are again uniquely human and they powerfully influence the evolution of the economy, as they also, reciprocally, influence the evolution of science and technology. Evolutionary theories that deal only with the survival of *firms* (Alchian 1951), or only with the survival of artefacts or of nations, are inadequate for the study of economic growth (Freeman 1991). We have no alternative but to confront the unique features of human history.

Although each of the five subsystems has its own distinctive features and relative autonomy, it is their interdependence and interaction that provide major insights into the processes of 'forging ahead', 'catching up', and 'falling behind' in economic growth. Positive congruence and interaction between them provides the most fertile soil for growth, while lack of congruence may prevent growth altogether, or slow it down.

2 A Theoretical Framework for Reasoned History

The theory put forward here resembles many earlier explanations of economic growth. For example, Marx's materialist conception of history stressed the tensions between 'forces of production', 'relations of production', and 'superstructure' as a source of social and political change or of stagnation in economic growth. Many other historians and economists (e.g. Veblen, Mokyr, von Tunzelmann, Galbraith, Perez) have stressed in particular the interaction between technical change and organizational change within firms, as well as political and institutional change at other levels in society. Our approach differs from most of them in two respects. First, it attaches greater importance to science and to general culture. In this, it resembles the theories of scientists such as Needham and Bernal and some historians, such as Margaret Jacob, Maxine Berg, and Kristine Bruland. Second, it does not attempt to assign primacy in causal relationships to any one of the five spheres at this level of analysis, whereas most other theories assign primacy to technology or to the economy, or to both. It emphasizes rather the relative autonomy of each of the five spheres, based on the division of labour and, most important, each with its own selection environment. It is this co-evolution that generates the possibility of mismatch between them and, periodically, of radical institutional innovations, which attempt to restore better coordinated development. Such coordination in new regimes of regulation, however, is not necessarily favourable to economic growth, which is not the only objective pursued by human beings. 'Congruence' that is favourable to economic growth must be distinguished from other types of congruence, for example to achieve and maintain military conquest.

However, our analysis here is concerned primarily with economic growth and with those societies in which this objective has been of major importance. A theoretical framework for the history of economic growth should satisfy four main requirements. First, it should provide a plausible explanation and illumination of the stylized facts, which summarize the main features of the growth of the world economy, especially over the last two centuries, but ideally for a much longer period. Second, it should do this for the three main categories identified by Abramovitz (1986): forging ahead, catching up, and falling behind. Third, it should identify the major recurrent phenomena in each category to pave the way for generalizations, which should of course be constantly tested against new historical evidence, as well as newly unfolding events. Finally, it should provide a framework for analysing and reconciling the research data, case studies, and generalizations emerging from the various subdisciplines of history: the history of science and of technology, economic history, political history, and cultural history.

As a first step in an inevitably ambitious and hazardous undertaking, the following definitions are tentatively proposed for the subject matter that is of interest, and from which the evidence is drawn for explanations of economic growth.

1. *The history of science* is the history of those institutions and subsystems of society that are primarily concerned with the advancement of knowledge about the natural world and the ideas of those individuals (whether working in specialized institutions or not) whose activity is directed towards this objective.

2. *The history of technology* is the history of artefacts and techniques and of the activities of those individuals, groups, institutions, and subsystems of society that are primarily concerned with their design, development, and improvement, and with the recording and dissemination of the knowledge used for these activities.

3. *Economic history* is the history of those institutions and subsystems of society that are primarily concerned with the production, distribution, and consumption of goods and services and of those individuals and institutions concerned with the organization of these activities.

4. *Political history* is the history of those individuals, institutions, and subsystems of society that are primarily concerned with the governance (legal and political regulation by central, local, or international authorities) of society, including its military affairs.

5. *Cultural history* is the history of those ideas, values, artistic creations, traditions, religions, and customs that influence the behavioural norms of society and of those individuals and institutions that promote them.

Finally, human beings share with other animals the *natural environment*, and this too has its own history and largely independent evolution. Although this is not usually studied by historians, but is left to geologists, ecologists, astronomers, meteorologists, physicists, and others, it is nevertheless an important influence on human history and is certainly reciprocally influenced by industrialization and economic growth. Moreover, it is now possible that ecological factors may predominate in determining the rate and direction of economic growth during the course of the twenty-first century. However, in view of the special factors involved in this discussion, this aspect of economic growth is not further developed here.

On the basis of these conclusions, we will now attempt briefly to justify the use of these five subdivisions for conceptual and analytical purposes while accepting of course that people make only one history, and recognizing that in real life the five streams overlap and intermingle. However, the use of subdivisions is not simply a matter of convenience in handling an extremely complicated topic, nor is it just a question of following the academic departmentalization and specializations, that have emerged in the twentieth century. These two factors do play some part, and the academic specialization does provide some indication of the importance of the independent consideration of each sphere. Moreover, the establishment of separate subdisciplines reflects the sense of dissatisfaction felt especially by scientists, technologists, and economists that their special interests were being neglected within the wider rubric in which they were contained. 'History' was often felt to be mainly the story of kings, queens, emperors, empresses, presidents, constitutions, parliaments, generals, ministers, and other agents of the state (i.e. 'political history' in terms of the above definitions) or, at most, political and cultural history. The editor of the *Encyclopaedia of the History of Technology* was certainly not alone in protesting at the neglect of technology in this approach (McNeil 1990).

However, these five subdivisions are proposed here for far more fundamental reasons. In the first place, they are proposed because each one has been shown to have some semi-autonomous, and certainly not insignificant, influence on the process of economic growth, varying in different periods and different parts of the world. Finally, and most important of all, it is precisely the *relative* autonomy of each of these five processes that can give rise to problems of lack of synchronicity and harmony or, alternatively, of harmonious integration and virtuous circle effects on economic growth. It is thus essential to study both the relatively independent development of each stream of history and their interdependencies, their loss of integration, and their reintegration.

The study of 'out-of-synch' phenomena and of the positive or negative interaction between these five different streams is as essential for the understanding of Abramovitz's (1979, 1994) distinction between 'potential' for growth and realized growth as it is for Leibenstein's (1957) 'X' inefficiency.

Anyone who has debated with historians of *science* brought up in the Lakatos tradition must have been impressed by their strong attachment to the 'internalist' view of their subject and their resistance to 'externalist' ideas about the influence of the economy or of political events on the development of science. For them, the 'selection environment' that operates for novel scientific hypotheses and theorems consists purely of the criteria and methods of the scientific community itself. They are wrong to ignore the 'external' influences, but so too are those historians who belittle or ignore the 'internal' selection environment of the scientific community.

Similarly, with the history of *technology*, studies of the evolution of the ship, of the hammer, of flints for tools and weapons, of the harnessing of the horse, and of the steam engine or the plough emphasize alike the relative autonomy of the improvements that were made over the centuries to these artefacts, so essential for human civilization. The same point emerges from the recent impressive volume on *Technological Innovation as an Evolutionary Process* (Ziman 2000). The selection environment, which interests, inspires, and constrains engineers, designers, inventors, and mechanics and many historians of technology is primarily the technical environment, the criteria of technical efficiency and reliability and of compatibility with existing or future conceivable technology systems.

The reciprocal influence of science and technology upon each other has been demonstrated in numerous studies and is indeed obvious in such fields as computer technology and biotechnology today as well as in earlier developments, such as thermodynamics and the steam engine. Technology has to take account of the laws of nature and hence of science. Nevertheless, Derek Price (1984), Nathan Rosenberg (1969, 1974, 1976, 1982), Keith Pavitt (1995), and many others have produced cogent arguments for recognizing the special features of each subsystem precisely in order to understand the nature of their interaction. Nor does this refer only to recent history, as the massive contributions of Needham (1954) to the history of Chinese science and technology clearly illustrate.

Historians of technology, such as Gille (1978) and Hughes (1982), have amply demonstrated the *systemic* nature of technologies and analysed the interdependencies between different elements in technology systems. Both they and Rosenberg (1969, 1982) have also shown that the technological imperatives derived from these systemic features may serve as focusing devices for new inventive efforts. Such efforts are of course also often powerfully influenced by economic advantages and rewards. Finally, in their seminal paper 'In Search of Useful Theory of Innovation', Nelson and Winter (1977) drew attention to the role of *technological trajectories*, both those specific to particular products or industries and general trajectories, such as electrification or mechanization affecting a vast number of processes and industries. They rightly identified the combination of such trajectories with scaling up in production and markets as one of the most powerful influences on economic growth, as we hope to show in every chapter of Part II. These ideas were further developed by Dosi (1982) in his work on technological trajectories and technological paradigms, in which he pointed to the relative autonomy of some patterns of technological development by analogy with Kuhn's paradigms in science. Despite the obvious close interdependence between technology and the economy or technology and science, it is essential to take into account these relatively autonomous features in the history of technology.

A satisfactory theory of economic growth and development must take account of these reciprocal interdependencies, but it should also recognize that the *relative* autonomy of evolutionary developments in science and technology justifies some independent consideration. In terms of growth models, there is a strong justification for the procedures adopted by Irma Adelman (1963: 9) in separating S_t from U_t in her production function ($Y_t = f(K_tN_tL_tS_tU_t)$) where K_t denotes the services of the capital stock at time t, N_t stands for the rate of use of natural resources, L_t represents the employment of the labour force, S_t represents society's fund of applied knowledge, and U_t represents the socio-cultural milieu within which the economy operates.

An essentially similar argument applies to *economic* change. No one can seriously doubt the importance of capital accumulation, profits, changes in company organization, and the behaviour of firms and banks for the evolution of industrial societies over the past two centuries. Economic institutions too have some relative autonomy in the cycles of their development. We may fully accept Supple's critique of the treatment of capital accumulation in growth models, but still pay attention to such variables as the share of investment in GDP, business cycles, the trend of the capital–labour ratio, the capital–output ratio, and so forth. This also applies to the growth of the labour force, levels of employment and demographic trends, and the availability of land and natural resources, although all of these are also influenced by cultural and political trends as well as by technology. Explanations of economic growth must pay especially close attention to the interdependencies between economic history and technological history. This has inspired much of our account in Part II. It is precisely the need to understand the changing nature of this interdependency that leads us to study 'out-of-synch' phases of development, when, for example, changes in technology may outstrip the institutional forms of the production and market system, which may be slow to change or impervious to change for relatively long periods. The reverse may also occur, providing impetus to new technological developments, as with the assembly line or factory production.

Some of these out-of-phase synchronicity problems may be on such a scale that they affect the entire *political* and *legal* organization of society. An obvious example was the institution of serfdom in mediaeval Europe. Most historians and economists would argue that mobility of labour was one of the essential preconditions for the emergence of capitalist industry. It would appear on almost all lists of 'stylized facts' about the Industrial Revolution. In his six 'major characteristics' of modern economic growth, Simon Kuznets (1971) points to the rapid shift from agricultural to non-agricultural occupations, and most historians agree that the exceptionally early relaxation of the obligations of serfdom in mediaeval Britain was one of the main factors contributing to Britain's later 'forging ahead' in the Industrial Revolution. By the same token, the tightening up of the 'Second Serfdom' in Eastern Europe and other institutional constraints on the mobility of labour are often advanced as one of the main reasons for the retarded economic growth in Russia and some other East European countries (Dobb 1947), although there is continuing debate on the sequence of events that led to this retardation. These points apply even more to the institution of slavery. Even though, as shown in Chapter 1, we disagree profoundly with the a-historical approach adopted by the cliometricians to slavery in the United States, we would certainly accept the necessity to study this institution in order to understand the development of the American economy.

Finally, *cultural* change is generally accepted as an important influence on economic growth and has recently been justifiably re-emphasized by Berg and Bruland and their collaborators. At the most elementary level, literacy and the quality of general education (as well as purely technical education) are assigned a crucial role in much of the 'new growth theory' and in the World Bank (1992) Development Report. Over the longer term, the classic works of Max Weber (1930) and of R. H. Tawney (1926) on 'Religion and the Rise of Capitalism', although still controversial (see Kitch 1967 and Castells 1998), demonstrated that a change in attitudes towards usury, the rate of interest, work, consumption, and accumulation was important for the rise of acquisitive entrepreneurial behaviour in mediaeval Europe. The fact that these changes were made by Catholic as well as Protestant theologians does not diminish their importance. Some historians might be inclined to treat religious activities as part of the ideological 'superstructure' of society, but the relative autonomy of many religious orders and traditions, as well as the conflicts between Church and State and the role of religion in establishing cultural norms, mean that it cannot be regarded simply as a part of the political system.

Nor, even more obviously, can politics be denied some independent role, as indeed Engels (1890: 477) himself recognized. Throughout Part II, and certainly in the final chapter, we shall emphasize the role of the 'regime of regulation' and of political power in dealing with social conflicts arising with each successive technological regime.

Clearly, there are important points of resemblance as well as difference between a simplistic Marxist scheme and that which is tentatively proposed here. It tries to avoid some of the rigidities and classification problems of that scheme while recognizing its major original contribution to historiography.

This first part of the book has attempted to outline a theoretical framework for the study of economic growth and to provide tentative definitions of five historical processes, which are believed to be of the greatest importance for the explanation and understanding of growth. It suggests that each one of these should be studied, both in its own autonomous development within each society and in its reciprocal interactions with the other elements, with a view to identifying and analysing retardation or acceleration phenomena. However, an historical approach to economic growth is unlikely to be acceptable, unless it not only tells a story using this type of theoretical framework, but is also capable of identifying and explaining *recurrent* phenomena, as well as special cases. As Werner Sombart (1929) put it, 'all history and particularly economic history has to deal not only or mainly with the special case, but with events and situations which recur, and, recurring, exhibit some similarity of feature—instances which can be grouped together, given a collective label and treated as a whole' (Sombart 1929: 18).

3 Recurrent Phenomena

In Part II we shall identify some recurrent phenomena, but we should re-emphasize here our belief that this recurrence is limited in scope and content. Each technological revolution and each phase of economic growth has its own unique features.

This does not mean, however, that we cannot learn a great deal from even this limited recurrence as well as from unique events. Both meteorology and seismology are natural sciences, which have difficulty with long-term prediction but provide probabilistic forecasts useful for policy-making. In fact, since the entire universe is evolving, even those long-term predictions in which we have great confidence, such as the date of the next eclipse, are really no more than conditional probabilistic forecasts with a very high degree of probability attached.

It is in this context that Sidney Winter's recollection of the Heraclitean standpoint that 'we cannot bathe in the same river twice' is so thought-provoking. There is no doubt that Heraclites (and Sidney Winter) were right that, whatever river we may choose to bathe in tomorrow, it will not be the same as the one we bathed in yesterday or today, even though it may have the same name and look the same to all outward appearances. This is also true of the entire physical universe. It is indeed evolving all the time, and no part of it is exactly the same today as it was yesterday. Nevertheless, there are sufficient relatively stable characteristics of most rivers for a sufficiently long time (centuries if not millennia) that we can use the knowledge of these characteristics, and of recurrent patterns of change, to navigate some and to use them or others for irrigation. Useful generalizations can be made about rivers, even though they will certainly not be valid for all time. For example, one of the earliest great human civilizations was based on such scientific observations and identification of recurrent patterns in the behaviour of the Nile and the use of this knowledge for large-scale irrigation of agriculture. Models can be made of the silting of estuaries or of the influence of rainfall on the rate of flow, which may be useful both for the advance of science and for technology. Of course, it would be foolish to ignore processes of change, such as climatic change, erosion, or pollution, which may affect the behaviour of those who might wish to drink the water or bathe in it, but the regularity of recurrence has been sufficient for many practical human purposes. This is still true despite the recent occurrence of some catastrophic flooding in various parts of the world and despite the fact that problems of access to water supply have assumed an alarming new importance in many areas.

Thus, despite the validity of Heraclites' statement, we can nevertheless agree with Popper that we can make limited conditional generalizations, both about the recurrent behaviour of rivers and about the human institutions that make use of this knowledge. However, the latter statement is subject to greater qualifications. The questions for historical research are: how much similarity persists and over what periods, what brings an end to the identifiable recurrent patterns, and how do new patterns emerge?

These are indeed the questions that have preoccupied economists in the study of *business cycles*, whether these are inventory cycles (Kitchin cycles), the (now 'traditional') business cycles (Juglars), or long (Kondratiev and Kuznets) cycles. Analysis of economic growth must certainly be concerned with repetitive behaviour, whether in modern capitalist economies or older civilizations. Although there have been many irregularities, there has also been sufficient recurrence, at least in recent times, to provide some useful indications for generalization and for policy-making. The work of Carlota Perez (1983, 1985, 1988) on long waves has shown that, even if *identical* behaviour is ruled out, as it must be, there may still be striking similarities or dissimilarities and some hidden ones too, which are helpful in understanding the phenomena and even in making probabilistic forecasts and indications for policy. In the Conclusions to Part II we shall discuss some recurrent phenomena which we believe to be helpful to an understanding of economic history over the last two centuries.

There are also some fundamental characteristics of the evolution of human societies that have endured for millennia, although their manifestations may have varied very much. Such characteristics would be those that primarily distinguish human behaviour from animal behaviour. These have been enduring characteristics of all human societies from a very early period of differentiation of humans from higher apes, and they depend on *learning* in various ways, so that the analysis of changes in the modes of learning should be a central feature in the study of economic growth.

In earliest times, the learning of humans probably closely resembled that of the foraging animals from which we are descended. It was essentially a search and observation process, based on trial and error and the accumulation of knowledge about edible and poisonous, potential and actual, sources of food. With the domestication of other animals, the use of fire, and above all with settled agriculture, the learning and dissemination became far more complex, but it was still based essentially on search, experiment, language, communication, and of course serendipity. Contrary to many theories of history, it would therefore be possible to date the origins of science not in the Middle Ages but in Palaeolithic times or even earlier. What has changed is not the search, observation, and learning, but the modes of conducting and organizing search, re-search, learning, accumulating, recording, validating, and disseminating knowledge about the natural world (science) and about ways of producing, using, and improving tools and artefacts (technology). As the division of labour proceeded within families and tribes and in varying different geographical environments, learning about production and exchange systems (economics) became increasingly important. As some knowledge became routinized in customs and traditions (culture) and in forms of regulating social behaviour (politics, war, slavery), so the separate streams of knowledge became increasingly important as well as their intermingling in general culture.

Every human economy has been a 'knowledge economy' and not only the contemporary one, which we, in our arrogance, proclaim today. Consequently, the distinction we have made at the outset between the various historical processes is not something that emerged only in very recent times, or in the Middle Ages, but has been a feature of human history for millennia. What have been changing are the ways of learning and accumulating knowledge and passing it on, interacting with changing ways of organizing production, and of regulating economic activities and social behaviour. Learning by doing, even if it was once mainly learning by gathering and eating, has always been with us. Learning by producing and using have been with us since the early use of tools of various kinds. Learning by interacting has always been with us. These are persistent human activities across all civilizations. What have changed are the modes of learning, of recording and disseminating what has been learnt, and the ways in which different modes of learning interact with each other.

Another unique but related feature of human evolution is the extent and nature of the division of labour in human societies at least for several millennia. It is true that some animal species, such as ants and bees, also exhibit a fairly complex pattern of social organization. In the study of these animal societies, too, it is essential to pay close attention to the patterns of communication and control, as well as to hierarchical patterns of organization (Fabre 1885; Marais 1975). The division of labour in human societies, however, is unique, both because of its complexity and because of the speed of emergence of new specializations, associated with the rate of knowledge accumulation, the rate and direction of change in techniques, and the associated changes in the patterns of communication and hierarchical organization. The behavioural routines of colonies of ants and bees have, of course, evolved over biological time, but they are so stable that relatively firm predictions can be made, which may be useful to bee-keepers. The behavioural routines, which also affect human behaviour, are less predictable and stable.

Nevertheless, here too there are some deep and very persistent rivers, even though modes of navigation may appear to change beyond recognition. We have argued that the search for new knowledge, inventive behaviour in relation to techniques, innovation, and routine behaviour in relation to economic and political organizations are relatively autonomous, but persistent, streams or historical processes. Analogies with the behaviour of bees or ants break down, above all, because of the role of imagination and changing purpose in these activities. As Marx so cogently pointed out, what distinguishes the worst of architects from the best of bees is that the architect first of all constructs a building in the imagination.

As we have already emphasized in Chapter 4, the role of imaginative, conscious, purposeful activity is important in all spheres of social life and is undoubtedly one of the most important distinctive features of the evolution of human societies. There are, of course, some scientists and theologians who believe that there is a purposeful element in the evolution of the universe in general, or of this planet or of a chosen nation in particular (for example, Gaia theories). Still others believe that the mode of evolution is itself sufficient to impart the appearance of purpose without its actual presence ('blind watchmakers', some versions of chaos theory, etc.). Whatever may be the truth in any of these theories, the element of purpose is overtly present in human history in the conscious activities of human beings in a way that is manifestly not the case either in the evolution of other animal species or geological evolution.

Of course, there are some similarities with the animals from which we have evolved, even in the purposeful use of tools on a very small scale, or in language, communication, and forms of social organization. But at least for the last five thousand years, the differences have become so great that it would be absurd simply to follow biology (or any other natural science) as a model for a theory of human history.

It is for this reason that we cannot accept Popper's restrictive approach to the purposeful action of social groups, as well as individuals. Popper tends to dismiss the effectiveness of purposive action by groups of people, maintaining that 'groups, nations, classes, societies, civilizations, etc.' are 'very largely postulates of popular social theories rather than empirical objects' (Popper 1963: 341). He emphasizes that 'the best laid schemes of mice and men gang oft agley' and lead to pain and tears rather than to promised joys. He is very wary of 'conspiracy theories', that attribute social purpose to entities that can have no such collective purpose, and formulates 'the main task of theoretical social sciences' as the disclosure of the unintended social repercussions of intentional human actions' (p. 342). This type of analysis has certainly played an important part in economic theory, especially Keynesian theory, and it is obviously important in considering the unintended environmental consequences of the widespread application of some new technologies. However, sometimes groups do achieve at least some of the objectives they set out to achieve, just as individuals do, even if they are involved in conflicts and failures. Therefore, historical analysis cannot restrict itself to analysis of 'unintended consequences', but should also take account of 'intended consequences'. The possibility for individuals to imagine a desirable future and to associate with other individuals to achieve a variety of collective purposes, such as catching up in standards of living or improving the environment, is surely an important difference between human beings and other animals, and an essential part of the study of economic growth. Certainly, this study should include unintended as well as intended consequences; for example, falling behind rather than catching up may be the actual outcome of some policies designed to accelerate economic growth. But, in spite of Popper's well justified aversion to conspiracy theory, we cannot rule out the study of purposeful actions, both by individuals and by groups, as well as both their intended and their unintended consequences. In this study, comparisons between success and failure in achieving intended objectives may be especially fruitful. Even though human beings often may not attain the ends that they seek or may even court disaster by persisting with conflicting or irreconcilable objectives, or because the outcome of many different purposes may be quite different from each taken separately, nevertheless, the role of purposeful activity cannot be ignored.

4 Conclusion

Precisely because of the role of purposeful activity and of conflicts, we are not attempting to predict the outcome of the various attempts now being made to shape the institutions of the unfolding 'information society'. In Chapter 9 we shall touch on some of the problems for a future regime of regulation, such as information overload and monopolistic efforts to control the content and the flow of information and entertainment. We do, however, share the view of Manuel Castells that the culture of the 'network society' may be very different from earlier periods in history and may reciprocally have a powerful influence on the ways in which the whole of society evolves.

Castells (1996, 1997, 1998) is well aware of these new possibilities. Not the least of the many virtues of his analysis of the fundamental trends in the information society is his open-mindedness and avoidance of the pitfalls of single-factor determinism, whether cultural, economic, political, scientific, or technological determinism. Like Weber and Keynes, he recognizes that the complexity of the interactions between the various subsystems of society is such that, at different times, one or other of these subsystems may exert a temporarily predominating influence. Like Gomulka in his critique of neoclassical economic growth theory, Castells is inclined to believe that, in the early stages of the evolution of the information society, the impulses derived from the rapid changes in technology were the primary source of dynamism for the economy and for the system as a whole. Like Weber, however, he recognizes that cultural 'petrification' or political sterilization may ensue, as apparently at one time in mediaeval China. Like Laski (1944) in his much neglected work on the decline of the Roman Empire (*Faith, Reason and Civilization*), Castells recognizes also that the ethical poverty of the 'spirit of informationalism' and the deepening inequality in the global economy may render informational capitalism as incapable as ancient Rome in withstanding the assault of other creeds (which are the subject of his second volume on *The Power of Identity*: Castells 1997).

PART II

SUCCESSIVE INDUSTRIAL
REVOLUTIONS

Introduction: Technical Change and Long Waves in Economic Development

In Chapter 1 of the book we have attempted to justify some strong criticism of cliometrics as a method and theory of history. We also criticized some long wave theories, including those of Kondratiev in Chapters 3 and 4, for their attempts to use standard econometrics, rather than a deeper analysis of qualitative change, in their interpretation of long-term fluctuations in the economy. Finally, in Chapter 2 we made some criticisms of Schumpeter for his lack of a consistent approach to the use of history in economics, despite his frequently declared enthusiasm for the subject. Nevertheless, we argued that both Kondratiev and Schumpeter made outstanding contributions to economic history with their long wave theories. In particular, we agree with Schumpeter that any satisfactory explanation of the evolution of capitalist economies must place innovations, their profitability, and their diffusion at the centre of analysis. Such a view is by no means confined to Schumpeter and his followers or to so-called 'evolutionary' economists. Historians and other social scientists have generally accepted a view of technical change as one of the major sources of the qualitative transformation of the economic system. A particularly notable recent example of this recognition of the fundamental importance of innovation in the evolution of social systems is the volume edited by Ziman (2000) on *Technological Innovation as an Evolutionary Process*. Differences emerge not in the recognition of the importance of technical innovations, but in the ways in which they are classified, measured, and analysed and how their relationship with other social and economic phenomena is interpreted.

Some economists take the view that technical change has been and is still today always a slow and gradual process. While accepting the importance of such gradual incremental improvements in many products and processes as those described by Gilfillan (1935) in relation to the ship, or by Hollander (1965) in relation to rayon plants, or by Hughes (1982) for electric power generation and distribution, we share Schumpeter's (1939) view that the appearance and diffusion of innovations is inherently a very uneven process and is sometimes explosive, sometimes very gradual. Furthermore, the clustering of innovations may give rise to phenomena best described as 'technological revolutions'. Consequently, it is essential to take into account discontinuities as well as continuity, both for individual innovations and for whole families of innovations that are interdependent. The Canadian economist Keirstead (1948) in his book on Schumpeter's economics described these changing configurations as 'constellations' of innovations, and we shall adopt this expression in our own analysis.

There is some resistance to such an approach. Many economists who appreciate the importance of innovations nevertheless concentrate their attention on specific innovative projects, rather than tackle the huge complexity of attempting to generalize about the entire process. Still others argue that since history, including technological history, is a unique process, and since innovations are so varied, our project is in principle unsound. In particular, some historians and economists reject the concept of 'technological revolutions' to describe some of the major changes, such as electrification or computerization.

As we have seen in Chapter 1, some historians even reject the concept of the industrial 'revolution' itself. Such attitudes have become rather less common since the widespread application of information technology in every branch of the economy. This led many people to accept some such description of events as the 'microelectronic revolution' or the 'information revolution'. It is hardly possible to pick up a newspaper or a magazine today without some reference to the 'Internet Revolution' or the 'Computer Revolution'. However, there is a serious point behind the objection to the expression 'revolution', which it is important to address. Are the major processes of technical change an infinite series of marginal improvements to already established techniques, or are there significant discontinuities which are better described as 'radical innovations' or, in the case of combinations of such innovations, as 'technological revolutions'?

We take the latter view, and, following Schumpeter, we believe that the changes that have occurred in the last two and a half centuries are well described as 'successive industrial revolutions'. We shall attempt to justify this view in this second part of the book by assembling the evidence for such pervasive and profound changes in industrial structure and technology. These changes, we shall attempt to show, appeared to contemporaries, as well as to ourselves and to competent historians since, to represent major discontinuities and to merit our designation of technological revolutions.

We shall quote at some length the comments of contemporary observers, including novelists and artists, to illustrate the point that these clusters of innovations had a dramatic impact at the time, even though, as time goes by, their novelty is blurred and they may become just part of the landscape. In Table 1, for each great technological revolution we cite a few contemporary events that were especially conspicuous and that clearly demonstrated not only the technical feasibility of major new products or processes, but also their huge potential profitability. Andrew Tylecote (1992) originally used this method, and we follow him in believing that such dramatic 'demonstration effects' were extremely important in establishing for a wide public the likelihood and the dawning reality of a technological 'revolution'. Many people began to jump on the Schumpeterian bandwagon after these events. In part, whether or not the expression 'revolution' is used to describe them is simply

TABLE II.1. Condensed summary of the Kondratiev waves

Constellation of technical and organizational innovations (1)	Examples of highly visible, technically successful, and profitable innovations (2)	'Carrier' branch and other leading branches of the economy (3)	Core input and other key inputs (4)	Transport and communication infrastructure (5)	Managerial and organizational changes (6)	Approx. timing of the 'upswing' (boom) / 'downswing' (crisis of adjustment) (7)
1. Water-powered mechanization of industry	Arkwright's Cromford mill (1771) Henry Cort's 'puddling' process (1784)	Cotton spinning Iron products Water wheels Bleach	Iron Raw cotton Coal	Canals Turnpike roads Sailing ships	Factory systems Entrepreneurs Partnerships	1780s–1815 1815–1848
2. Steam-powered mechanization of industry and transport	Liverpool–Manchester Railway (1831) Brunel's 'Great Western' Atlantic steamship (1838)	Railways and railway equipment Steam engines Machine tools Alkali industry	Iron Coal	Railways Telegraph Steam ships	Joint stock companies Subcontracting to responsible craft workers	1848–1873 1873–1895
3. Electrification of industry, transport, and the home	Carnegie's Bessemer steel rail plant (1875) Edison's Pearl St. New York Electric Power Station (1882)	Electrical equipment Heavy engineering Heavy chemicals Steel products	Steel Copper Metal alloys	Steel railways Steel ships Telephone	Specialized professional management systems 'Taylorism' Giant firms	1895–1918 1918–1940
4. Motorization of transport, civil economy, and war	Ford's Highland Park assembly line (1913) Burton process for cracking heavy oil (1913)	Automobiles Trucks Tractors, tanks Diesel engines Aircraft Refineries	Oil Gas Synthetic materials	Radio Motorways Airports Airlines	Mass production and consumption 'Fordism' Hierarchies	1941–1973 1973–
5. Computerization of entire economy	IBM 1401 and 360 series (1960s) Intel microprocessor (1972)	Computers Software Telecommunication equipment Biotechnology	'Chips' (integrated circuits)	'Information Highways' (Internet)	Networks; internal, local, and global	??

a question of semantics. Whereas meteorologists can reach agreement about which wind force should be designated as a 'storm', a 'gale', or a 'hurricane', it has proved more difficult for historians and economists to agree on what constitutes a 'revolution'. Some observers regard the diffusion of electronic computers as the gradual extension of the use of other calculating and measuring devices, such as slide rules, tabulating machines, and the abacus; others find no problem in regarding the events of the late twentieth century as the 'computer revolution'.

It was, of course, true that some of those industries, which later became most characteristic of the Industrial Revolution, were already growing in the sixteenth or seventeenth or even earlier centuries—many innovations in textile machinery, for example, were being made in the Middle Ages, and some of the major social and cultural changes that are often regarded as part of the climate of the Industrial Revolution began much earlier. Nevertheless, we would maintain that the acceleration of the rate of growth of several key industries in the late eighteenth century, the wave of inventions and innovations that made such acceleration possible, and the shift from domestic to factory production did constitute a set of events which legitimate the use of the expression 'revolution'. We shall attempt to justify this view with supporting evidence in Chapter 5.

Even though the critics rightly insist that the new products and industrial techniques were initially confined to a few sectors, they nevertheless comprised new modes of developing, producing, transporting, and distributing a widening range of goods and services. Such discontinuities have long been familiar to archaeologists with their taxonomies of 'Stone Age', 'Bronze Age', 'Iron Age', etc. We shall argue that there is a justification for a similar approach to the far more rapidly changing and complex technologies of industrial societies. In this second part of the book we hope to provide convincing evidence to justify this approach.

It has been common parlance for a long time among historians to use such expressions as 'the age of steam' or the 'age of electricity', even if only for convenient descriptive periodization. As we have argued in Part I, this type of taxonomy is needed not just for convenience, but because it enables us to develop a better understanding of the successive patterns of change in technology, in industrial structure, and, indeed, in the wider economic and social system. Most historians of technology have recognized and emphasized the importance of the *systemic* features of technology (Gille 1978; Hughes 1982). The innovation and diffusion of new products and new processes are not isolated events, but are always and necessarily related to the availability of materials, energy supply, components, skills, infrastructure, and so forth. Very often, again as Schumpeter observed, innovations appear in clusters and are rarely, if ever, evenly distributed over time or in space. There are obvious reasons why this should be so, such as scientific discoveries which open the gates to whole families of new products, as for example, with biotechnology or macro-molecular chemistry. A new or rapidly growing source of energy or materials may have similar effects, as with oil and electricity. Rikard Stankiewicz (2000) has described this as the opening up of new 'design space' for engineers and entrepreneurs, while Bresnahan and Trajtenberg (1995) coined the expression 'General Purpose Technologies' (GPTs) to describe those changes that have very pervasive effects. Much earlier, Nelson and Winter (1977) used the expression 'generalized natural trajectories' to describe this phenomenon.

While recognizing that scientific discoveries may have a major influence on the development of general purpose technologies, this does not of course mean that we subscribe to the much-abused 'linear model of innovation'. The relationship between science and technology is an interactive one and, as we hope to show in the following chapters, new constellations of innovations depend on advances in both.

This second part of the book is about how such new constellations emerge, spread, and ultimately come to dominate an industrial society for a few decades before giving way, after a period of several decades of great turbulence, to the next such combination. We suggest that these phenomena underlie the 'long waves' of capitalist development that have been identified and studied by many economists as shown in Chapters 2–4. The denial of the existence of these long waves is based mainly on the formal use of simplistic econometric techniques for the measurement of 'trends' in aggregates such as GDP, industrial production, and so forth. But, as Schumpeter already insisted, such aggregates conceal as much as they reveal, since they ignore those structural and qualitative changes in the economy that are at the heart of the process of economic growth. In Part I we argued that it is not just the *aggregate* growth of the GDP that is important, but the emergence of new industries and the adoption of those new technologies, which make growth possible. Louçã (1997) has written a critique of the purely econometric approach to business cycles, and the first part of this book has further developed this critique. Part II has an additional purpose: to analyse in some depth those processes of technological, structural, and social change that give rise to long waves of development. The next chapter attempts such an analysis for the first Kondratiev wave, while the following chapters (6, 7, 8, and 9) attempt it for the later waves.

Schumpeter was, of course, the principal economist to build his theory of cycles primarily on innovations and their diffusion, and our approach owes much to his pioneering work. However, as Chapter 2 has shown, it differs from his in some important respects. He exhorted later writers to amend his work in the light of new evidence and ideas, and we have followed his advice.

Kuznets, Rosenberg, and other critics of Schumpeter have argued that:

1. no innovations are big enough to give rise to major cyclical fluctuations in profitability, investment, employment, and growth throughout the economy;

2. even if innovations combine together, no one has shown how such combinations could form and develop together to give rise to such fluctuations over periods of roughly half a century.

In the 1980s and 1990s an answer to these critics began to emerge. Schumpeter's notion of the clustering of innovations is now well established among historians and theorists of innovation. Many economists have explored this concept, and in the long wave debate it was developed especially by Freeman *et al.* (1982) and by Perez (1983). They used the expression 'New Technology Systems' to analyse these constellations, taking in particular the examples of electronics and synthetic materials to demonstrate the pervasive nature of some processes of technical change, the discontinuities that they entailed, the structural changes in the economic system, and patterns of employment and the long time scales involved in these processes of *system* diffusion.

Such concepts as the *systemic* nature of innovation and the range of *pervasive* applications have found very general acceptance. This applies also to some economic theorists who have not been directly involved in the long wave debate at all. For example, Helpman (1998) and his colleagues adopted the expression 'General Purpose Technologies' from Bresnahan and Trajtenberg's paper in the *Journal of Econometrics* (1995). Helpman accepts the important distinction between incremental innovations and those that he describes as 'drastic' or major innovations. In his model it is the drastic innovations that drive the GPTs because of their 'innovational complementarities' and their 'generality of purpose': 'When these effects are particularly strong, as for example, in the case of electricity, they lead to monumental changes in economic organizations. Sometimes they also affect the organization of society through working hours, constraints in family life, social stratification and the like'(Helpman 1998: 4).

The use of the expression 'monumental' and the inclusion of organizational and social changes are particularly notable and bring this analysis in the 'new growth theory' closer to the work of those economists who have been studying innovation systems and participating in the long wave debate, especially the work of Carlota Perez (1983). She was particularly notable for her emphasis on institutional as well as on technical changes. As she has consistently argued, *system* changes cannot take place except through a combination of profound social and organizational, as well as technical, innovations, and this necessarily takes a long time.

As already noted in Chapter 3, at the end of the nineteenth century one of the founders of the American Economics Association, John Bateson Clark, detected a period of forty-five years for the maturation of new methods of production, based on his empirical observations in Germany and the United States (Clark 1899: 429). The type of systemic changes that we discuss in this part of the book took even longer. Indeed, it is for this very reason that the irregular periodization we are postulating is a matter of 'half-centuries' rather than the five to thirteen years of the 'ordinary' (Juglar) business cycle. As we have seen in Chapters 3 and 4, many long wave theorists, including Kondratiev himself, explained the long waves partly in terms of the long life of infrastructural investments and their 'echo' replacement every half-century or so. We rejected this explanation, but we certainly do accept that the emergence, crystallization, and diffusion of new technology systems is a matter of decades, not just years. These new constellations *do* include new infrastructures, as well as new industries, new services, and management systems, but it is not the 'echo' replacement of the older infrastructures that leads to the long wave. It is the prolonged process of emergence and diffusion of the new technology through the economy. Many empirical studies of innovation have concentrated on individual products or processes and have found market saturation occurring more quickly, for example after ten or twenty years; the diffusion of an entire technology *system* is a different matter. Indeed, as Carlota Perez (2000) has pointed out, the rate of diffusion of individual products will often depend on the maturity (or otherwise) of a related system. Obviously, new electrical products could diffuse much more rapidly when a new infrastructure was in place, when the appropriate skills of electricians and engineers were generally available, and when consumer attitudes and the legislative environment were more favourable to the new technology. In the early days of a new constellation, all these things may present barriers and cause delays to diffusion, if indeed the new products can be imagined or designed at all.

Some historians who, like ourselves, fully endorse the importance of periodization and of the role of technology (for example von Tunzelmann, Chandler) nevertheless prefer a classificatory scheme that brings together the first and second Kondratiev waves as the 'First Industrial Revolution'. In their scheme, the third and fourth waves become a 'Second Industrial Revolution' and the present change a 'Third'. This second part of the book will make clear why we prefer the 'Kondratiev' wave classification, even though we are not entirely happy with the 'wave' metaphor for reasons explained in Chapter 4.

The *entire* life cycle of a technology system will usually be much more than a century. Railway systems originating in the middle of the nineteenth century are still very important today. Electrical technology is the essential foundation for electronic systems and the automobile has certainly not disappeared. But the entire life of a technology system goes through several phases. In the very earliest days it may still be mainly or entirely a laboratory phenomenon and apparently unconnected scientific discoveries may be the most important events. Only after successful demonstration of technical and commercial feasibility can large-scale diffusion begin.

The selection environment in capitalist economies means that the most profitable innovations will probably experience a phase of explosive growth, following the first successful applications. As the technology finds an increasing range of applications, the macroeconomic effects may be very substantial, as is obvious today from the example of the Internet and information technology. However, exponential growth cannot continue indefinitely, so that a mature stage ensues when profitability is eroded and growth slows down. More new technologies compete for a place in the sun but the erstwhile dominant technologies do not disappear but co-exist in a multi-technology world.

Thus, in a simplified and schematic way, the following phases in the life cycle of a technology system may be distinguished:

1. the laboratory-invention phase, with early prototypes, patents, small-scale demonstrations and early applications;
2. decisive demonstrations of technical and commercial feasibility, with widespread potential applications;
3. explosive take-off and growth during a turbulent phase of structural crisis in the economy and a political crisis of coordination as a new regime of regulation is established;
4. continued high growth, with the system now accepted as common sense and as the dominant technological regime in the leading countries of the world economy; application in a still wider range of industries and services;
5. slow-down and erosion of profitability as the system matures and is challenged by newer technologies, leading to a new crisis of structural adjustment;
6. maturity, with some 'renaissance' effects possible from fruitful co-existence with newer technologies, but also the possibility of slow disappearance.

In this part of the book we shall try to show that it is phases 2–5 that are associated with those wavelike movements in the economic and social system that have been designated since Schumpeter as 'Kondratiev waves' or cycles. In phase 6 the system no longer has the huge effects on the economy that we are postulating for phases 2–5. In phase 1, the *economic* effects are scarcely perceptible although this phase may last a very long time.

The prolonged gestation and diffusion periods are obvious today from the example of information technology and the Internet. As Chapter 9 will attempt to show, the origins of this technology go back for much more than half a century in terms of science and invention, but in terms of the *macro-economic* effects of diffusion these were felt especially in the final quarter of the twentieth century. They may be even greater in the first quarter of the twenty-first century, when the world-wide diffusion of information and communications technology (ICT) affects all countries and all sectors of the economy. The rate of diffusion may slow a little below the tempestuous early days, but the weight of the new technology systems in the aggregate economy is now far greater, so that the macroeconomic effects are enormous. We shall attempt to show in the chapters that follow that each successive industrial revolution showed this kind of pattern, although each had its own unique features too.

It was Carlota Perez (1983) who first suggested that some technology systems, such as ICT, were so pervasive that they dominated the behaviour of the whole economy for several decades in this way and reciprocally influenced major social and political changes. She proposed several crucial original ideas which we have used in the analysis that follows.

1. For each long wave, Perez suggested that one or more 'key factors' (iron, coal, steel, oil, electronic chips) became so cheap and universally available that they gave rise to a potentially vast array of new factor combinations (what Stankiewicz later called a vast new 'design space'). The producers of key factors she called 'motive branches'; these became major industries with each successive wave. In this book we use the expression 'core inputs' rather than 'key factors' because the word 'factor' is used in so many different senses and the word 'input' conveys more precisely what we have in mind.

2. Perez suggested further that new products based on the availability of these core inputs and some complementary inputs could stimulate the rise of other new industries, whose rapid growth and great market potential ('carrier branches') would give a major impetus to the growth of the entire economy (cotton textiles, steam engines, railways, electrical products, automobiles, computers, etc.). A new infrastructure would serve the needs of the new industries and would reciprocally both stimulate and facilitate the rapid growth of both carrier and motive branches (Table 1). Perez's concept resembles that of historians such as Rostow (1963), who used the expression 'leading sectors' to describe these new fast-growing industries. We also use the expression 'leading sectors' to embrace 'carrier branches', 'motive branches', and new infrastructures. Still other branches of the economy follow in the wake of the leading sectors ('induced branches'), for example service stations, repair shops, garages, and distributors in the case of automobiles, and the later development of mass tourism and 'fast food' restaurants.

3. The structural transformation arising from these new industries, services, products, and technologies is inevitably associated with the combination of organizational innovations needed to design, use, produce, and distribute them. Gradually new 'common-sense' rules of managing and organizing the new technology emerge through trial and error, which could prove effective in older industries as well as the new ones. Factory-based production could be used for other textiles as well as cottons; mass and flow production techniques could be applied in the food industry and the catering industry as well as in automobiles and oil; computer systems could be used in almost any industry or service. This new approach to management and organization Perez described variously as a 'new technological style' and a 'new techno-economic paradigm'. Once it had emerged and demonstrated its effectiveness, she suggested that it had a wider influence in society, affecting government and the general culture as well as business firms.

4. Such a widespread process of structural and organizational change could hardly take place in a smooth and gradual way. The new 'techno-economic paradigm' would not be easily and universally accepted despite its evident superiority and profitability in many applications, because there would be strong vested interests associated with the previous dominant paradigm and the regulatory regime and cultural norms associated with that older paradigm. Thus, what had often been described as the 'downswing' of the long wave would be a period of great turbulence characterized by the rapid growth and high profitability of some newer firms and industries, side by side with slower growth, declining trends, or stagnation in others, and by political conflict over the appropriate regulatory regime. Monetary disorder, relatively high levels of unemployment, and tariff disputes would be typical phenomena of these transitional periods of structural adjustment. The 'mismatch' between the old institutional framework and the new constellation of technologies could be resolved in various ways in different countries and different industries.

There has been in the past, and will continue to be, a wide variety of institutional changes in response to the pervasive effects of the new technologies. Autonomous and semi-autonomous processes of social and institutional change in various countries will influence the diffusion process. The spread of the new paradigm will be very uneven by firms and by industries as well as by countries. Some will be deeply and immediately affected, others affected only after a long time-lag, still others hardly at all. The Perez concept of paradigm change certainly did not mean that all firms in all countries could adopt the same organizational model, only that such processes as electrification or computerization would have a world-wide influence on the evolution of the behaviour of firms, albeit mediated through great local variety of adaptation, experiment, and previous local historical experience. Following a turbulent period of structural change and the general acceptance of the new paradigm, a period of greater stability would ensue, corresponding roughly to the 'boom' or upswing phase of the long wave.

These ideas have aroused considerable interest and some acceptance (see e.g. Tylecote 1992; Lloyd-Jones and Lewis 1998, and the three volumes containing selections of key papers on the history of the long wave debate edited respectively by Freeman 1996 and by Louçã and Reijnders 1999). In this second part of the book we shall attempt to test and clarify them more systematically. This will require:

1. assembling and analysing the empirical and historical data for each wave to see whether they do indeed support or refute the above propositions; this will involve both quantitative and qualitative analysis at the level of firms, industries, technologies, and countries;
2. developing an 'appreciative' historical description which takes account of the unique features of each wave and demonstrates how each new 'constellation' of innovations was developed and was promoted (or

hindered) by the technological, scientific, economic, political, and cultural environment through its rise to dominance and its maturity. Such historical narrative will be based on our conclusions about reasoned history in Chapter 4. It is necessary both for plausibility and to avoid those teleological interpretations that assume the pre-existence of a paradigm and portray its diffusion in idealistic rather than evolutionary terms. It recognizes that each new paradigm may have a very different combination of favourable influences and that its diffusion is an untidy and uncertain historical process.

The analysis begins with the British Industrial Revolution, and most of the next chapter is concerned with the British case. This is because the 'catch-up' process of industrialization did not begin in earnest until the second half of the nineteenth century so that the necessary data for the first Kondratiev wave are available only for Britain. In the second Kondratiev wave, the United States and Germany were catching up in many industries and technologies and were beginning to draw ahead in some. Therefore, while continuing to concentrate on the British case, we also analyse some other countries, particularly the United States. Later chapters (7, 8, and 9) take up the story of the third and fourth Kondratiev waves in several countries and the emerging characteristics of a fifth Kondratiev wave based on information and communications technologies. We recognize that it is a weakness of our book that we deal with only a few leading countries. Although we do believe that their role has been exceptionally important, we would certainly accept that the relationship with the rest of the world is and always was important, as Tylecote rightly insisted. We hope that future work will overcome this shortcoming of our book.

It will be useful also at this stage to indicate two of the ways in which our approach differs from Schumpeter's. In particular, we place far more emphasis on the diffusion of innovation than he did. In our view, the earlier inventions and innovations have very little perceptible effect on macroeconomic behaviour, essential though they are for technological development (phase 1 of the system evolution outlined above). The big surges of investment, output, and trade depend on diffusion and scale economies. Thus, whereas Schumpeter classifies the steel industry in the upswing of the *second* Kondratiev wave, we classify it to the third wave (Chapter 7) when the Bessemer and other new steel manufacturing processes became widely diffused. Small quantities of steel were of course used long before either the second or the third wave, but in our view it was the huge expansion of the steel industry in the third Kondratiev wave that was the important phenomenon from a *macro*economic perspective. The upswing of the economy during the Industrial Revolution itself was based mainly on iron, not steel. Second, whereas Schumpeter constantly stressed the role of the 'heroic' entrepreneur (thus inviting Kuznets's jibe: did they get tired every fifty years?), we stress rather the changes in management systems that accompanied each technological revolution (column (6), Table 1).

We would maintain that the evidence of rapid growth of the 'motive branches' producing the core inputs, and of the 'carrier branches', acting as exemplars for an entire historical period, is quite strong and indeed is supported by most historians. So, too, we believe is the evidence of falling relative prices, multiple applications, and universal availability of the core inputs. On the role of physical infrastructures, the evidence is also, in our view rather compelling and has been well marshalled and presented by Nakicenovic and Grübler (1991).

Of course, every technological revolution is uneven in its effects, whether we are talking about information technology or the earlier pervasive technologies. For this reason, we postulate an irregular periodization of the long waves (only *approximately* half a century). For this reason, too, we believe that the wave metaphor itself is not the most suitable, as explained in the concluding part of Chapter 4. The wave metaphor may give an impression of a smoothness and regularity that is certainly not characteristic of the turbulent processes we are describing. Some key industries and services are undoubtedly profoundly affected, others only to a small extent, and the speed with which these changes occur will also vary considerably. Some products and industries will begin to be affected soon after the first emergence and crystallization of a new constellation, others only decades later. In Table 1, as already indicated, column (2) gives a more precise indication of a few decisive events, which first clearly demonstrated to a very wide public both the technical *and* the economic advantages and potential of a new system. In his book, Tylecote (1992) gives a similar presentation of this point, showing a period of several years which he describes as a period of 'crystallization' during which a new paradigm demonstrates 'clear-cut superiority'.

The speed with which a new technological style becomes dominant after it first demonstrates clear-cut superiority and widespread (international) potential (Tylecote 1992: 68) depends to a considerable extent on the new infrastructures that are needed for its diffusion. These infrastructures are of two kinds. On the one hand are the physical infrastructures for communication and transport, as shown in Table 1; but there are also other very important infrastructures, which are needed for training and educating people in the new skills and for designing and developing a new range of products and services (the science–technology infrastructure). Investment in both types of infrastructure always requires political initiatives and changes in the regulatory regime, and these are normally the subject of intense political debate and conflict. Here the fourth point in the Perez model outlined above is highly relevant, and here too she has made an important original contribution with her suggestion that in the 'downswing' periods the growth of the new constellation may be retarded in various ways by the old institutional and social framework, which is more resistant to change than the technology itself. It is also plausible that a period of political, social, and cultural change may lead to the development of a framework that offers greater scope and support to the new constellation—a new 'regime of regulation'. These ideas are reminiscent of Marx's notion of tension between the 'productive forces' and 'relations of production', but, whereas Marx applied his theory to capitalist social relations in general, and to earlier social formations, the Perez theory was developed in relation to successive changes within the framework of a predominantly capitalist economy.

It is an extraordinarily difficult and challenging task to disentangle the interplay of technical and organizational changes within the economy with wider political, cultural, and social changes in a variety of different countries. However, we have been encouraged by the pioneering work of Tylecote (1992) and by the recent work of Lloyd-Jones and Lewis (1998), and have attempted in the chapters that follow to address some of these fundamental problems, albeit only briefly. We agree with Helpman (1998) that the diffusion of major new technologies does indeed lead to 'monumental' organizational and institutional changes, which co-evolve with the technology. The expression 'structural crisis of adjustment' has been very widely used recently to characterize some of these problems that arise in the turbulent periods of transition from an old technological regime to a new one. While the account that follows concentrates on the change in technology and in the structure of the economy, the concluding sections in each chapter do introduce some of these wider social problems, which, as we have insisted in Chapter 4, are an essential part of the historical narrative (Hodgson 1999). Some of these issues are further developed in the Conclusions to Part II.

In these conclusions we shall discuss some of the *recurrent* features of each Kondratiev wave, which we believe justify the use of the expression 'Kondratiev waves', rather than a simple scheme of periodization. We fully accept that each wave has unique characteristics and, despite the limitations of space, we try to describe some of the unique features of each wave in the chapters that follow. Nevertheless, there are also recurrent features to which we return; they include the phenomenon of pervasive and interdependent constellations of innovations, and the role of core inputs, of carrier branches and new infrastructures, and of new management styles. Finally, profound structural changes can come about only through a crisis of adjustment in each wave, which necessitates many changes in the institutional and social framework. The political system of a country and its local culture have their own dynamic also. The theory that we are advancing does indeed lay great stress on technical change and on changes in the structure of the economy, but this does not mean that it can be fairly classified as 'technological determinism'. Technical change is itself partly the outcome of social, political, and cultural influences. In the concluding chapter, we return to these fundamental questions of co-evolution, which face and perplex all historians and which we have introduced in Chapter 4 and the Conclusions to Part I.

5

The British Industrial Revolution:
The Age of Cotton, Iron, and Water Power

5.1 Introduction: Acceleration of Growth from 1770s

Historians[1] differ in their interpretation of the main features of the British Industrial Revolution. Some put the main emphasis on entrepreneurship, some on inventions and innovations, some on culture and science, some on transport, communications, and trade, and some on the growth and composition of market demand. However, almost all agree that single-factor explanations are inadequate, and almost all mention most or all of these together with the changes in agriculture and, of course, the accumulation of capital and mobility of labour.

Our interpretation of the picture that emerges from the major studies of the Industrial Revolution, and most notably from the eleven-volume history of *The Industrial Revolutions*, published by the Economic History Society (Church and Wrigley 1994), is summarized in Sections 5.1–5.8, followed by concluding sections on the transition from the first to the second Kondratiev (Sections 5.9 and 5.10).

Economic historians mostly agree that there was a fairly sharp acceleration of British industrial output, investment, and trade in the last few decades of the eighteenth century. In one of the early estimates, Hoffmann calculated the rate of growth of British industrial output from 1700 to 1780 as between 0.5 and 1 per cent per annum, but from 1780 to 1870 at more than 3 per cent. More recent estimates (Crafts 1994) have reduced the estimated growth rates for the later period but do not change the fundamental picture (Table 5.1; Figure 1.2). As Chapter 1 has shown, and as Landes has consistently argued, the 'revisionist' historians, although sometimes setting out to destroy what they thought of as the 'myth' of accelerated growth, actually confirmed it. Supple (1963: 35) summed up the consensus as follows: 'economic change did not experience a steady acceleration, rather there was a more or less precise point (which most historians place in the 1780s) after which innovation, investment, output, trade and so forth all seemed to leap forward'.

---

[1] e.g. Ashton (1948); Supple (1963); Deane (1965); Hobsbawm (1968); Habbakuk (1963); Floud and McCloskey (1981, 1994); Rostow (1960); Mathias (1969); Landes (1969); von Tunzelmann (1978, 1995*a*); Paulinyi (1989); Mokyr (1994*b*); Hoppit and Wrigley (1994); Berg (1994); Lloyd-Jones and Lewis (1998), Berg and Bruland (1998).

Although it was the surge of growth in *industry* in the late eighteenth century that was the principal component of the acceleration in British economic growth, Deane and Cole (1962) estimated that the rate of growth in national income as a whole over the period from 1800 to 1860 was twice as high as the rate from 1740 to 1800. Estimates by Crafts (1994: 196) show somewhat slower growth for the period 1780–1800 than some of the earlier calculations: he estimates national income growth at 0.7 per cent per annum from 1760 to 1780, 1.32 per cent from 1780 to 1800, and 1.97 per cent from 1801 to 1834. This is nevertheless a very substantial change, and it marked a transition to a sustained rate of economic growth over a long period greater than any that had ever been previously achieved.

Historians also agree that the surge of growth in British industry was emphatically not simply 'balanced reproduction' ('balanced' growth of all industries simultaneously), but was characterized by the exceptionally rapid growth of a few leading sectors, above all the cotton industry and the iron industry (Table 5.1). The share of cotton in total value added of industry grew from 2.6 per cent in 1770 to 17 per cent in 1801. This was an extraordinarily rapid change of industrial structure; as Supple noted, 'in the initial decades of the British Industrial Revolution it was the cotton textile industry which experienced the most spectacular expansion. Subsequently, after 1840 railroad investment and the spread of a transportation network seemed to dominate the economy and in the third quarter of the century, the steel industry and steamship construction leapt ahead' (Supple 1963: 37).

The backward and forward linkages to other industries were of course also important, but the exceptional role of the cotton textile industry has generally been acknowledged both by contemporaries and by historians ever since. Imports of raw cotton grew from an average of 16 million pounds per annum in 1783–7 to 29 million pounds in 1787–92 and 56 million pounds in 1800 as the main source changed from the West Indies to the US slave plantations. The rate of increase in imports was described by a nineteenth-

TABLE 5.1. Sectoral growth of real industrial output in Britain, 1700–1760 to 1811–1821 (% per year)

Years	Cotton	Iron	Building	Industrial output (weighted average)[a]
1700–1760	1.37	0.60	0.74'	0.71
1770–1780	6.20	4.47	4.24	1.79
1780–1790	12.76	3.79	3.22	1.60
1790–1801	6.73	6.48	2.01	2.49
1801–1811	4.49	7.45	2.05	2.70
1811–1821	5.59	−0.28	3.61	2.42 ·

[a] Including other industries: 1700–90 based on 1770 weights; 1790–1821 based on 1801 weights.
Source: Crafts (1994).

century historian (Baines 1835) as 'rapid and steady far beyond all precedent in any other manufacture'. The invention of the cotton gin by Eli Whitney in the United States in 1793 ensured continuous rapid expansion of the supply of raw cotton. Baines attributed the extraordinary rise in the 1770s and 1780s directly to the effects of technical inventions and their diffusion: 'from 1771 to 1781, owing to the invention of the jenny and the water-frame, a rapid increase took place; in the ten years from 1781 to 1791, being those which immediately followed the invention of the mule and the expiration of Arkwright's patent, the rate of advancement was prodigiously accelerated.'

It was on the basis of a whole series of inventions and improvements (Chapman 1972; Hills 1994; Mann 1958; von Tunzelmann 1995*b*) that big increases in productivity became possible, based increasingly on their exploitation in the new system of factory (mill) based production (Table 5.2(*a*)). These improvements in process technology in the cotton industry made possible the rapidly falling prices, which in turn provided the competitive strength for British exports to undercut Indian and other Asian textiles and indeed all other producers. Exports of cotton textiles reached 60 per cent of output by 1820 and became the biggest single commodity in nineteenth-century trade, accounting for over 30 per cent of British exports of manufactures in 1899, when Britain was still by far the biggest exporter.

The fall in the price of Lancashire cotton yarn was remarkable, occurring as it did in the inflationary period of the Napoleonic Wars. The price of No. 100 Cotton Yarn fell from 38/- in 1786 to 6/9*d* in 1807. Landes (1965: 109) estimates that by 1837 the price of cotton yarn had fallen to one-twentieth of its level in 1760. This cannot be mainly attributed to a fall in the price of the raw material, but must be ascribed to innovations in the processing of cotton yarn and the organization of production (Table 5.2(*b*)).

However, extraordinarily important though it undoubtedly was for the leading sectors of the British Industrial Revolution, cotton yarn hardly corresponds to the Perez definition of a 'core input' or 'key factor', since it did not have a potentially wide range of applications but concerned only the cotton industry itself. The role of 'core input' and 'motive branch' belongs rather to the other fast-growing industry of the Industrial Revolution: the iron industry

TABLE 5.2(*a*). Labour productivity in cotton: operative hours to process (OHP) 100 pounds of cotton

	OHP
Indian hand spinners (18th century)	50,000
Crompton's mule (1780)	2,000
100-spindle mule (*c*.1790)	1,000
Power-assisted mules (*c*.1795)	300
Roberts's automatic mule (*c*.1825)	135
Most efficient machines today (1990)	40

Source: Jenkins (1994: xix).

TABLE 5.2(*b*). Technical changes in cotton spinning, 1780–1830[a]

| | Spinning costs per 100 lb of cotton | | Working hours for spinning 100 lb of cotton |
	£	Index	Index
1780	2.10	100	100
1790	1.07	49	—
1795	0.57	23	15
1810	0.21	5	—
1830	0.13	4	7

[a] All data for English Cotton number 80.
Source: Paulinyi (1989: 66).

(Table 5.1). This section, therefore, after briefly discussing the cluster of innovations in the cotton industry, goes on to consider the key innovations in the iron industry, followed by the innovations in water power and in transport, the infrastructure of the first British Industrial Revolution.

5.2 Invention and Innovation in the Cotton Industry

The cotton industry may be more properly regarded as a 'carrier branch' in the Perez sense, or as a 'leading sector' in Rostow's terminology. As we shall see, many of the organizational as well as technical innovations in cotton were followed later by other branches of the textile industry and by manufacturing more generally.

Virtually all accounts, whether contemporary or otherwise, agree on the importance of inventions, both in the cotton industry and in other industries, for the spurt in economic growth. Indeed, they were often given pride of place in the older textbooks on English history. Like Adam Smith (1776), recent studies stress the continuous improvement of processes in the factory or workplace, as well as the original major inventions. They also sometimes stress the speed with which inventions became innovations and were then rapidly diffused, as we have seen in the case of Baines. The number of patents sealed had been about 80 per year in the 1740–9 period but increased to nearly 300 in 1770–9 and to over 600 in 1790–9 (Table 5.3). Patents are an imperfect indicator, but there were no changes in this period that might invalidate the series (Eversley 1994). A high and growing proportion of this number were in capital goods related to the cotton industry and other leading sectors of the Industrial Revolution (Table 5.3).

There is some disagreement on the nature of the major inventions of the eighteenth century. Some authors argue that they were typically very simple; they 'leave the impression that the inventions were the work of obscure mill-wrights, carpenters or clock-makers, untutored in principles, who stumbled by chance on some device' (Ashton 1948). Ashton argued that 'these accounts

TABLE 5.3. Patents for various capital goods in eighteenth-century Britain

Patent classes	1770–79	1780–89	1790–99
Power sources (prime movers and pumps	17	47	74
Textile machinery	19	23	53
Metallurgical equipment	6	11	19
Canals and road building	1	2	24
Subtotal	48	90	170
(% of all patents)	(16)	(19)	(28)
All capital goods patents	92	168	294
(% of all patents)	(31)	(34)	(45)
All patents	298	477	604

Source: C. MacLeod (1988).

have done harm by obscuring the fact that systematic thought lay behind most of the innovations in industrial practice' and overstressed the part played by chance. Further, 'Many involve two or more previously independent ideas or processes, which brought together in the mind of the inventor issue in a more or less complex and efficient mechanism. In this way, for example, the principle of the jenny was united by Crompton with that of spinning by rollers to produce the mule . . . ' (Ashton 1963: 154).

Landes also stresses the high skills of the mechanics, smiths, millwrights, and tool-cutters of the Industrial Revolution:

Even more striking is the theoretical knowledge of these men. They were not on the whole, the unlettered tinkers of historical mythology. Even the ordinary millwright, as Fairbairn notes, was usually a fair arithmetician, knew something of geometry, levelling and mensuration, and in some cases possessed a very competent knowledge of practical mathematics. He could also calculate the velocities, strength and power of machines, could draw in plan and section. (Landes 1965: 296)

At the opposite extreme, some accounts give the impression that the inventions were the result of individual genius or scientific brilliance, rather than the outcome of a continuous social process. In part, these differences of interpretation arise from the fact that (as still today) there is a very wide spectrum of inventions and innovations. The vast majority, then and now, were incremental improvements to existing processes and products and, as Adam Smith observed, were often made by workers who used machines in different types of workplace.[2] They were facilitated by specialization based on division of

[2] Hills (1994: 112), basing his comments on experience of actually running spinning machines in the North Western Museum of Science and Industry, stresses the trajectory of *improvement* exploited by Hargreaves and Arkwright: many of the inventions were based on adapting the old techniques of cottage industry to the new conditions of factory production.

labour, but again, as Adam Smith observed, still other inventions resulted from the work of scientists whose skill was to observe dissimilar processes.

Von Tunzelmann (1995*b*) provides evidence that the main inducement for innovators was *time*-saving, and that the savings in fixed and working capital, in labour, and in land were the indirect result of this time-saving objective, pursued within a general paradigm of relatively straightforward mechanization. He also brings out the role of focusing devices and *co-ordination* in the whole production system. Baines stated: 'Replication of the particular components which represented the most constrictive bottlenecks was often carried out in addition to speeding them up. The cylinder for block printing could thus be replicated by up to five times' (Baines 1835: 236), and 'The same innovation strategy underlay the jenny, which multiplied the traditional spinning wheel initially to 8 and eventually to sometimes 120 within the one machine' (p. 15).

Nevertheless, the combined effect of the inventions of Hargreaves, Arkwright, Crompton, and their predecessors and successors was revolutionary rather than gradual (Table 5.2(*a*)). The leap in labour productivity at the end of the eighteenth century reduced the number of operative hours to process (OHP) 100 pounds of cotton by much more than an order of magnitude. Table 5.2(*b*) also shows Paulinyi's (1989) estimate of the similar order-of-magnitude reduction in the *cost* of spinning 100 pounds of cotton between 1780 and 1810. The power required to operate the later innovations meant that machinery had to be installed in purpose-built premises (factories). Arkwright limited his licences to machines of a thousand spindles, but human muscle and horse power were succeeded by water power and later by steam (Jenkins 1994). He made his own fortune from his factories and not from licensing his invention. By 1788 there were over 200 Arkwright-type mills in Britain, mostly constructed in the 1780s after the first successful challenge to Arkwright's patents. Typically these mills were three or four storeys high, with about a thousand spindles and a 10 HP water wheel (Chapman 1992: 27). The dramatic impression made by this wave of factory construction can be seen from William Blake's poem 'Jerusalem' (1804), which became almost a second national anthem in Britain and described the new factories as 'dark satanic mills' in 'England's green and pleasant land'.

The example of Arkwright, who became an extremely wealthy man, although often an unpopular one, made a deep impression on other industrialists and the cotton industry began to influence other sectors too. In his excellent monograph, Chapman cites:

[much] undisputed evidence of the wide-ranging contribution of cotton to the growth of the British economy between 1770 and mid-nineteenth century. Arkwright's techniques were not difficult to apply to worsted spinning and worsted mills modelled on his cotton mills were soon being built in the hosiery districts of the Midlands and in parts of Lancashire, the West Riding, and Scotland. . . . In the linen industry John Marshall of Leeds inaugurated the factory system by adopting Arkwright's techniques and factory organization. (Chapman 1992: 57–8)

Chapman goes on to describe the direct and indirect imitation of cotton industry techniques in other branches of the textile industry and the influence of cotton on the birth of new activities in other sectors of the economy, including the construction of multi-storey iron-framed buildings lit by gas, and the design and construction of specialized cotton machinery and components, using iron as well as wood. Roberts developed the standardized production of mules and looms in his Manchester factory in the 1820s, and these techniques were applied later to the manufacture of locomotives (Musson 1980: 91).

5.3 Water Power and the Rapid Growth and Multiple Applications of Iron

The smelting of iron ore with coke instead of charcoal and Cort's process for the conversion of pig iron into malleable (wrought) iron by 'puddling' were the two decisive innovations for the metalworking industries in the eighteenth century. Together they made possible the huge increase in the supply of relatively cheap iron which took place between 1780 and 1840 (from about 60,000 tons per annum to about 2 million tons per annum) (Figure 5.1). Many

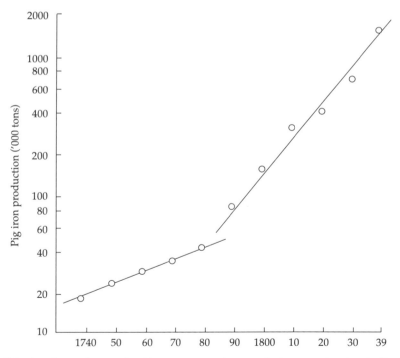

FIG 5.1. Accelerated growth of iron as a core input: pig iron production in England, 1740–1839

Source: Oxford History (1958: iv. 107).

other incremental innovations in blast furnace technology were made locally to adapt output to local supplies of coal, coke, iron ore, and water, but Cort's innovation and the use of coke for smelting were the two decisive innovations which gave the British iron industry a clear lead in Europe by the end of the eighteenth century.

It was as early as 1709 that Abraham Darby first used coke in a blast furnace to smelt iron ore, but further inventions were needed before the output reached a reasonably high quality. One of the important additional innovations was introduced by Joseph Smeaton in 1762. This was the use of water-driven bellows to raise the temperature in the blast furnaces.

Even with the improvements in blast furnace technology, *pig iron* remained a rather brittle material, unsuited for many applications, and its conversion to *wrought iron* by repeated heating and hammering was expensive and labour-intensive. Consequently, the next great innovations in the iron industry—the 'puddling' and rolling processes invented by Henry Cort (who was originally an outfitter for the Navy)[3]—were at least equally important. Patented in 1783 and in 1784 and subsequently improved, these processes made possible both a huge increase of supply in wrought iron (500 per cent between 1788 and 1815) and a fall in price, from £22 per ton to £13 per ton from 1801 to 1815. This fall was especially remarkable taking into account the huge rise in military demand for iron during the Napoleonic Wars as well as the simultaneous increase in civil demand for the numerous applications of the Industrial Revolution. The fall in price of iron continued for the next few decades, so that iron was a core input not only for the first but also for the second Kondratiev wave (Figure 5.2). It was not until after the Napoleonic Wars that Cort's puddling and rolling innovations diffused to the European continent, so that throughout the wars British manufacturers had a decisive advantage in the cost and quantity of iron, which was available for both military and civil applications. In the 1820s, the technique was diffused by the migration of skilled Welsh craftsmen to France and Germany.[4] In this later period the use of steam engines helped to reduce

---

[3] Cort himself was not a foundry man, but as an outfitter for the Navy he had a good knowledge of the price and quality of British iron products in the 1770s, which at that time made the Navy reluctant to use iron. However, in 1775 he acquired a small foundry from a business partner in settlement of a debt. At this foundry in Fontley, near Portsmouth, he was able to conduct various experiments in the production of iron, and when he received a big order from the Navy in 1780 he enlarged his works, so that he had both a forge and a rolling mill. Instead of the usual Swedish iron, he innovated in local production, leading to his key patents in 1783 and 1784. He and his skilled craftsmen then helped to design six puddling and rolling works in South Wales and Shropshire. His technique became the most important in the iron industry for nearly a century (Paulinyi 1989: 125–8; Mott 1983). The grooved rollers were as important as the puddling itself, although both patents had been anticipated by predecessors in Sweden and England (Schubert 1958: 106).

[4] After the defeat of Napoleon, British puddlers went to Belgium, France, and Germany to teach their craft. The first puddling and rolling works in France were installed in 1818–19 and in Germany in 1824–5. In all of these the British puddlers who were employed came from South Wales (Schubert 1958: 107).

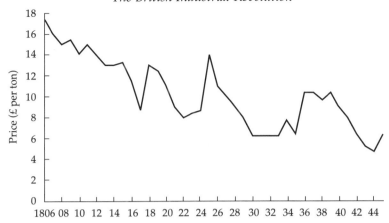

FIG 5.2. Price of iron: English merchant bar at Liverpool, 1806–1845
Source: Mitchell (1988).

prices further, but the early innovations of the eighteenth century in the iron industry were based on the use of water-power in the iron foundries.

As the *Oxford History of Technology* (Oxford History 1958: iv. 200) observed, as early as the sixteenth century 'the water wheel was by far the most important source of power in Europe. It was the basis of mining and metallurgy and hammers and bellows driven by the water wheel were essential for the manufacture of wrought and cast iron. The hoisting, crushing and stamping of ore, the drilling of gun barrels and the drawing of wire were carried out with the aid of water wheels. Water power had also been adopted in the mining of copper and silver.' Eventually, the improved design and efficiency of steam engines led to the replacement of water wheels by steam engines in forges, rolling mills, and blast furnaces; but for most of the eighteenth century water power predominated.

Joseph Smeaton (1724–92) decided at the age of 27 to investigate 'how the design and efficiency of water wheels could be improved. Having been apprenticed to a mathematical instrument-maker, he made a really good model with his own hands and tested it accurately' (Oxford History 1958: iv. 203). On 3 and 24 May 1759 Smeaton presented two papers to the Royal Society entitled 'Experimental Enquiry into the Natural Powers of Wind and Water to turn Mills'. As a consulting engineer, he designed numerous mills all over Britain. His experiments showed that the best effect was obtained when the velocity of the wheel's circumference was a little more than 3 ft/sec. It became a general rule to design overshot water wheels at their circumference of 210 feet per minute.

Smeaton was consulting engineer to the Carron Ironworks, by far the largest producer of cast iron in Europe, and was able therefore to experiment with and develop the use of cast iron parts for machinery, one of his greatest contributions to mechanical engineering. His first cast iron water wheel axle was made in 1769 for the Carron No. 1 furnace blowing engine. Cast iron gearing was used for Brook Mill, Deptford in 1778 and frequently afterwards.

Smeaton's designs mark the end of an era of wooden water wheel construction which had lasted for eighteen centuries. His numerous improvements enabled him to reach the limit of power that could be generated and transmitted by wooden wheels ... After his death, revolutionary developments in design took place, the most important being all-metal construction. (Oxford History 1958: iv. 209)

What Tylecote (1992: 42) designates as 'the Smeaton Revolution' must have reduced the cost per unit of available energy for a best practice wheel around 1780 to about 20 or 30 per cent of what it had been in 1750. This reduction was due to a combination of the effects of the falling price of iron, the increased efficiency and size of wheels, and their reduced maintenance costs.

The life and work of Joseph Smeaton demonstrate very well the fruitful interplay between design, consultancy, and entrepreneurship which was a feature of the newly industrializing sectors of the British economy. It shows too that the divide between 'science' and 'technology' was not of great significance at that time in Britain for either scientists or technologists, and that they moved easily between factory, construction site, and laboratory. The award of the Royal Society Medal for his two scientific papers complemented his numerous practical innovations.

The use of iron in water wheels was of course only one of innumerable new applications of this versatile material in the eighteenth and nineteenth centuries. It may truly be regarded as the typical core input for the Industrial Revolution since it had so many applications in so many industries. As Mokyr points out, 'It is possible to imagine an industrial revolution based on water power and linen or wool. In fact in many places that is precisely what happened. There was no substitute for iron, however, in thousands of uses, from nails to engines. As its price fell, iron invaded terrains traditionally dominated by timber, such as bridges, ships and eventually buildings' (in Floud and McCloskey 1994: 29).

Iron became the essential material for new applications of both water power and steam power. It was only when Boulton and Watt entered into an arrangement with the iron-master, John Wilkinson, that their new enterprise could build engines suitable for applications other than pumping. Wilkinson, who was both an inventor and an entrepreneur, had taken out a patent in 1775 for a cylinder-boring machine. Although originally designed for boring cannons, it proved equally effective for boring the cylinders of Boulton and Watt engines to a much higher degree of accuracy. Some of the first engines were actually made by Wilkinson himself for use in his own blast furnaces. He also introduced the first steam-hammer in 1782. He was such an enthusiast for iron that he was known as 'iron-mad' Wilkinson and even made an iron coffin for his own burial. (In the event, by the time he died in 1808, he was too fat to fit in this coffin.) He also made the first wrought-iron boat in 1787 and was associated with the initiative for the first famous 'Ironbridge', although he did not build it himself.

As metal components and machines were increasingly substituted for wooden ones, the cotton industry itself, as well as the other textile industries, became increasingly dependent on the metalworking industries and the skills of the toolmakers.

Among the numerous other applications of iron were the following:

Rails for mines	Winding gear for mines
Gears and other components for water wheels	Pumps for mines Blowing cylinders
First cast iron cog wheels from Carron foundry 1760	Cutlery Clocks and instruments
Complete water wheels	Bridges
Ships' anchors and chains	Grates and stoves
Munitions and weapons	Machinery for locks on canals
Vessels and pipes for the chemical industry	Rollers for various industries Textile machinery
Hammers and other tools for the metallurgical and construction industry	Iron frames for multi-story cotton mills and warehouses from 1795
Shovels and picks for the mines and construction	Cast iron water pipes and tanks Cooking utensils
Nails	Furniture
Iron ploughs and other farm implements	Ornamental objects
Steam engines of various types	

While iron had been used for centuries, the scale of use for old applications was greatly expanded while the range of new applications widened enormously. Maxine Berg (1998) has pointed out that there was an important interaction between design and invention for consumer products, including ornamental and fashion-driven metal products and the design of capital goods. Military applications were of course especially important during the Napoleonic Wars, and it was no wonder that the victor of Waterloo, the Duke of Wellington, was nicknamed the 'Iron Duke'. As Prussia in subsequent decades began to catch up with industrialization, the young Otto von Bismarck convinced his fellow Junkers that Germany would be unified not by parliamentary majorities but by 'blood and iron'.

The rapidly falling price of iron in the late eighteenth and early nineteenth centuries satisfied the third criterion proposed by Carlota Perez for the core inputs of a long wave, as well as the criteria of universal availability and multiple applications. The falling price was due mainly to technical innovations but also in some parts of the country to falling transport costs following the construction of a network of canals between 1750 and 1800. It is to these transport innovations that we now turn. They facilitated a reduction in costs of all kinds of commodities but especially of the bulkiest and heaviest materials.

5.4 The Transport Infrastructure: Canals and Roads

The Industrial Revolution is often associated with railways as well as with steam engines, but their widespread use outside coal mines came only in the 1830s and 1840s. The first wave of industrialization depended upon water power, canals, and much better roads known as turnpike roads. These networks were the focus of what was in those days a heavy investment (Figure 5.3). From 1700 to 1750 Parliament had been passing Turnpike Acts at the rate of eight a year, but in the 1760s and 1770s this increased to a rate of forty per annum.

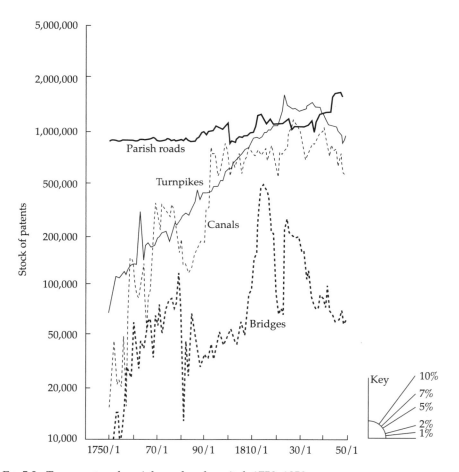

FIG 5.3. Transport and social overhead capital, 1750–1850

Note: Expenditure on creating, improving, and maintaining canals and roads, etc. 1750–1850 (current prices).

Source: Hawke and Higgins (1981: 230).

TABLE 5.4. Investments in canals and railways in the eighteenth and nineteenth centuries (% of nominal capital invested)

	Canals 1755–1815 (1)	Railways 1820–1844 (2)	Canals 1755–1780 (3)	Railways 'early years' (4)	Canals 1780–1815 (5)	Railways 'later years' (6)
1. Peers, gentry, 'gentlemen', etc.	22	28	41	22	22	37
2. Land: farmers, graziers, etc.	2	—	1	—	2	—
3. Commerce: merchants, traders, tradesmen, etc.	39	45	27	52	40	38
4. Manufacturers	15	11	8	15	15	7
5. Professions, including clergymen	16	9	16	8	16	10
6. Women	6	5	8	2	6	8
	100	100	100	100	100	100

Source: Hawke and Higgins (1981).

Transport infrastructure is surprisingly neglected in many studies of the Industrial Revolution, including the otherwise comprehensive Volumes 2 and 3 of the Economic History Society set of papers (Hoppit and Wrigley 1994). However, in his chapter on the supply of raw materials, Wrigley (1994) refers to the supply of coal, iron, and other minerals as being the main driving force for canal building in the late eighteenth century. This view is supported by information on the role of landlords as investors (Table 5.4) as well as statistics of the value of freight carried and the geographical pattern of canal construction.

The sea transport of coal from Newcastle to London was established long before the Industrial Revolution, but the wave of canal and turnpike road construction from the 1760s onwards reduced the cost of transporting coal to many areas of Britain by about 50 per cent.[5] One of the earliest canals—the Duke of Bridgewater's Canal from Worsley to Manchester—was already demonstrating this cheapening of coal prices in the 1760s. It became famous because at the Worsley end it went underground almost to the coal face, while it crossed the River Irwell on an aqueduct. The canal was designed and built by James Brindley, one of the early millwrights, who engineered both waterwheels and canals.

These improvements benefited all industries and services by widening markets as well as improving supplies. Hobsbawm (1968) points out that the

---

[5] Canals linked the North and Irish Seas with the navigable reaches of the major rivers—the Mersey, the Ouse, the Severn, the Thames, the Trent, the Clyde, and the Forth—and the growing centres of population in the Midlands, the North, and Scotland in the second half of the 18th cent.

'wide scattering' of British industry through the countryside, based on the putting out system, the coal-mining regions, the new industrial textile regions, the 'village industries', and London as a huge centre of population, trade, and services (the largest in Europe), had two major consequences. First,

[it] gave the politically decisive class of landlords a direct interest in the mines which happened to lie under their lands, (and from which, unlike the Continent, they, rather than the King, drew royalties) and the manufactures in their villages. The very marked interest of the local nobility and gentry in such investments as canals and turnpike roads was due not merely to the hope of opening wider markets to local agricultural produce, but to the anticipated advantages of better and cheaper transport for local mines and manufactures. (Hobsbawm 1968: 16)

The second consequence was that manufacturing interests could often determine government policy, unlike other European countries and even the Netherlands, where merchant and landed interests were still dominant. The oligarchy of landed aristocrats in England was unlike the feudal hierarchies of other European countries in several ways. They were a 'bourgeois' aristocracy, with an interest in profitable investments. Their contribution to investment in the new transport infrastructure was remarkable (Table 5.4), but the contribution of merchants was as great or even greater. Both landlords and merchants appreciated the value of canals, and they were able to take advantage of a fairly well developed capital market. This had already developed on a significant scale in the seventeenth and early eighteenth centuries, mainly on the basis of accumulation from trade and government debt. As Mathias pointed out:

Investment in an inland transport system, shipping and ports is one of the prerequisites for industrial growth; yet to create such a system, there must be extensive prior mobilization of capital and the agencies to effect it . . . Financing canals and turnpikes showed how plentiful capital was in eighteenth century England and how favourable the social context was for investment. (1969: 105–7)

This 'prior mobilization' of capital was described by Adam Smith as 'previous' accumulation and more graphically by Marx (1867a/1938) as 'primitive accumulation'. In the final chapter of his first volume of *Kapital* he has a vivid indictment of its nature: 'The discovery of gold and silver in America, the extirpation, enslavement and entombment in mines of the aboriginal population, the beginning of the conquest and looting of the East Indies, the turning of Africa into a warren for the commercial hunting of black skins, signalised the rosy dawn of the era of capitalist production' (p. 775).

Using the records of the East India Company, the trial of Warren Hastings, and many other official and first-hand accounts of the looting and corruption that accompanied eighteenth-century colonialism of the British and other European powers, Marx showed how the proceeds of this 'primitive accumulation' flowed back to the mother countries. Thackeray's *Vanity Fair*

shows from a novelist's perspective how the 'Nabobs' of the East India
Company and their new-found wealth had affected English society by the
time of the Napoleonic Wars. The Nabobs derived their wealth and power
from the monopoly contracts awarded to the employees of the East India
Company for salt, opium, betel, and other commodities, and from their
monopoly of the China trade. As Marx sarcastically remarked, they 'received
contracts under conditions whereby they, cleverer than the alchemists, make
gold out of nothing. Great fortunes sprang up like mushrooms in a day;
primitive accumulation went on without the advance of a shilling. The trial
of Warren Hastings swarms with such cases' (Marx 1867*a*/1938: 777).

Equally important, in both Marx's account and those of other historians,
was the establishment of the Bank of England in 1694 and the rise of the
National Debt in Britain with the regular trade in government bonds. The
availability of substantial private capital seeking profitable investment was
demonstrated by the South Sea 'Bubble' of 1720, which attracted speculation
from poets such as Alexander Pope, as well as aristocrats and shopkeepers.
It was the existence of this well developed capital market that made possible
the finance of infrastructural investment, and not the contribution of industrialists, which was relatively small. The cotton industry itself was not the
main source of funds for investment in the new infrastructure, for reasons
that Wrigley makes clear:

The movement of cotton presented no great difficulties to the methods of goods
transport which had been in use for centuries. The movement of raw cotton was
measured by the million pounds rather than the million tons and bore a far higher
value per unit weight than, say, coal . . . The fact that many early mills were built in
quite remote Pennine valleys close to a head of water, underlines this point. (Wrigley
1994: 103)

At this time the landed aristocracy and merchants were still by far the
wealthiest part of the community so that their active involvement in the new
infrastructural investment was a major factor. The new textile industrialists
were struggling to raise sufficient capital for their own investments in
machinery and mills, small though these investments still were. However,
the fact that manufacturers made a much smaller contribution to infrastructural investment than either landed gentry or merchants (Table 5.4) does not
mean that they were unaffected or that they did not perceive its immense
importance. On the contrary, an industrialist such as Josiah Wedgwood was
enthusiastic in his promotion of canals and roads in the Midlands, for he
realized very well that his ambitions to export his pottery all over the world
depended upon this new investment.

However, infrastructural investment, especially in canals, differed from
the industrial investment of those times in its scale and its 'lumpiness'. As
Peter Mathias (1969: 105) pointed out, 'A large transport project needs to be
complete before its benefits accrue to the economy or before any income can
be created', and it therefore required extensive prior mobilization of capital.

The rewards could be very great, as the Duke of Bridgewater's canal from Worsley to Manchester showed in 1761. Hobsbawm (1968: 30) estimated that canals cut the cost per ton between Liverpool and Manchester or Birmingham by 80 per cent in the eighteenth century; but there could also be failures. The fluctuations in expectations led to the typical phenomena of euphoria and 'mania', as in the canal boom of the 1790s, alternating with periods of pessimism. These bandwagon and bubble phenomena were to become typical of the very fast-growing sectors in each successive Kondratiev wave, indicating the co-existence of very great perceived opportunities for profit with a high level of uncertainty for the individual project and a cyclical pattern of growth.

5.5 The Entrepreneurs of the First Kondratiev Wave and the New Techno-economic Paradigm of Industrialization

Sections 5.1–5.4 above have outlined in a very condensed form some of the main features of a constellation of fast-growing sections of the British economy from the 1770s to the 1820s. The cotton, iron, and construction industries, as a result of this high growth, accounted for about half of all value added in industry by 1831, compared with about one-fifth of the total in 1770. It is true that agriculture still accounted for about a quarter of total employment and output, but industry and construction had already overtaken agriculture by 1810. In our view, this fully justifies the use of the expression 'Industrial Revolution'.

This Industrial Revolution was a question not just of changes in the share of output, but also of social, organizational, and cultural changes in industry and in the economy as a whole. This is not the place to consider it, but agriculture itself was becoming an industry organized on capitalist lines with tenant farmers employing hired labour and producing for the market. The cotton industry outgrew all other branches of industry, but they were also changing. Whereas from 1770 to 1801 the cotton industry and the iron industry were growing at several times the rate of all industry, by 1831 their growth rate had slowed a little and other industries were growing faster (Table 5.5).

Some other industries, such as the pottery industry, had grown almost as fast as the leading sectors from the 1760s onwards, taking full advantage of the new infrastructure for the transport of their heavy materials and their final products. No one expressed better than Josiah Wedgwood, the leading entrepreneur in the pottery industry, the aspirations and ideals of the new group of entrepreneurs who were reorganizing production on a factory basis and marketing their products world-wide. In his letters to his partner, Thomas Bentley, and in other writings and speeches, he articulated the main principles of the new techno-economic paradigm of industrialization. At this stage it was the individual entrepreneurs themselves who organized and managed most aspects of the business.

TABLE 5.5. Structural changes in the first Kondratiev (annual % growth rates)

Sector	Pre-industrial	Industrial Revolution	
	1700–60	1770–1801	1801–31
Cotton	1.4	9.0	6.0
Iron	0.6	5.0	4.5
Construction	0.7	3.2	2.9
of which, canals	1.0	6.0	3.0
Total, all industries	1.0	2.0	2.8

Source: Crafts (1994), except canals (authors' estimates).

Wedgwood was responsible not only for numerous design and process innovations, but also for many organizational innovations. He was motivated by ideals of political and social change as well as technical change and capital accumulation. He was very active in promoting the construction of canals and turnpike roads in his own native county of Staffordshire, and he had a vision of the reforming, even revolutionary, role of himself and his fellow industrial entrepeneurs. He wrote to Thomas Bentley as early as 1766:

Many of my experiments turn out to my wishes and convince me more and more of the extreme capability of our manufacture for further improvement. It is at present (comparatively) in a rude uncultivated state, and may easily be polished, and brought to much greater perfection. Such a revolution, I believe, is at hand, and you must assist in and profit by it. (quoted in Jacob 1988: 136)

Among the many interesting features of this letter are his emphasis on 'experiments' and his description of his innovations as a 'revolution'. In another letter to Bentley he outlined his principle of factory organization and division of labour: 'to make such machines of the Men as cannot err'. This often quoted phrase sums up the efforts of many entrepreneurs of that age to rationalize the sequence of operations in the new factories and overcome human error, whether arising from ignorance, incompetence, laziness, drunkenness, boredom, or fatigue. It was a project that is today by no means exhausted, as the experience of Taylorism and many current tendencies in computerization and robotics amply testify; and it was an objective that was seized upon by the critics of industrial capitalism, from Marxists to romantic poets and artists, to denounce the dehumanizing tendencies of industrialism, which made men and women mere appendages of machines, and where, as Werner Sombart put it, 'the soul should be left in the cloakroom on entry'. Wedgwood also introduced an elaborate system of fines and penalties to maintain discipline and correct hours of work in his factories.

However, it would be a profound mistake to portray Josiah Wedgwood as an inhuman slave-driving boss. True it was that he and other entrepreneurs were very much concerned with the pace of work and the coordination of the various operations of the new machines in their new factories. Wedgwood's friend Erasmus Darwin (grandfather of Charles Darwin) was the founder and leading spirit of the Derby Philosophical Society, which brought together scientists, inventors, and entrepreneurs to discuss such topics as the ideal factory with a central observation point from which all workshops and workers could be seen. But they also discussed town lighting, central heating, indoor toilets, and even the French Revolution and republicanism (Jacob 1988: 167).

These men saw themselves as idealistic but practical reformers, harnessing science, capital, and machinery to usher in a new age of material improvement which would benefit everyone (Briggs 1960). Wedgwood's imaginative vision of the future of his industry extended to almost all aspects of his enterprise, and his skills and innovations as a potter, a designer, an engineer, and a factory manager are often and rightly cited as a part of his success story. He was himself the thirteenth son of a poor potter, and many historians (e.g. Ashton 1948, 1963; C. Wilson 1955) stress that social mobility was much greater in Britain than in other countries at that time. The entrepreneurs came from very diverse backgrounds, and the role of 'dissenters' (Quakers and adherents of other unorthodox religious denominations) is frequently mentioned. Ashton states that it is not easy to distinguish inventors, 'contrivers', industrialists, and entrepreneurs and that they came from every social class and from all parts of the country.[6]

One reason why Dissenters were so prominent in entrepreneurship may well have been their nonconformist outlook and often their rationalism. However, Ashton also points out that the exclusion of Dissenters from the universities and from office in government forced many to make their careers in industry. Moreover, the non-conformist zeal for education led them to establish their own schools, and the non-conformists 'constituted the better educated section of the middle classes'. Presbyterian Scotland provided an unusually high proportion of the leading inventors (Watt and most of his assistants, Sinclair, Telford, Macadam, Neilson, and many others) at a time when Scotland had by far the best primary education system in Europe and some of the best universities. 'It was not from Oxford or Cambridge, where the torch burnt dim, but from Glasgow and Edinburgh, that the impulse to scientific enquiry and its practical application came' (Ashton 1963: 157). The Dissenters' academies, established in English towns such as Bristol, Manchester, Warrington, Northampton, etc., did for England much of what the universities did for Scotland.

---

[6] They included aristocrats like Coke of Holkham Hall, who innovated in agriculture, or the Duke of Bridgewater in canals. Clergymen and parsons, such as Cartwright and Dawson innovated new ways of weaving cloth and smelting iron. Doctors of medicine, such as John Roebuck and James Keir, took to chemical research and became industrialists. 'Lawyers, soldiers, public servants and men of humbler station than these found in manufacturing possibilities of advancement far greater than those offered in their original callings. A barber, Richard Arkwright, became the wealthiest and most influential of the cotton-spinners; an inn-keeper, Peter Stubbs, built up a highly esteemed concern in the tile trade; a schoolmaster, Samuel Walker, became the leading figure in the North of England iron industry' (Ashton 1963: 156).

5.6 The New Proletariat and Hours of Work

The rise of the new industrial proletariat was not simply a question of land-less agricultural labour being obliged to seek work in towns, but was a more complex process. The removal of constraints on mobility from very early times was certainly a unique and important feature of English industrializa-tion, as was the early rise of wage labour relationships in rural areas as well as in towns. In addition, the special features of the demographic revolution must be taken into account as well as immigration. The demographic changes were also very important in the growth of the home market in the late eighteenth century, as per capita incomes apparently did not increase by much between 1780 and 1820.

The increased supply of labour for the Industrial Revolution was not just a question of men, women, and children going to work in factories, but also of course of hours of work, work organization, and discipline. Indeed, some theorists (notably Marglin 1974) explain the rise of factory work mainly in terms of the maintenance of labour discipline rather than economic or tech-nical factors. The techno-economic explanation of Landes still appears far more plausible, but whatever the explanation, once the factory system was established, it had its own dynamic in terms of the shift in investment from working capital to fixed capital, the coordination of many operations, and the organization of shifts and division of labour (von Tunzelmann 1995b). Circulating capital continued to be very important, even after new invest-ment in machinery. The time spent in transporting materials, holding stocks, and getting wares to market meant that the reduction of working capital was among the main motives for infrastructural investment. (See Javary (1999) for an original analysis of the theory of time, power, and capital accumulation.)

The importance of *time* in the context of work discipline has been brilliantly illustrated by Edward Thompson (1994). He starts his paper with a quote from the nineteenth century novel of Thomas Hardy, *Tess of the D'Urbervilles*: 'Tess . . . started on her way up the dark and crooked lane or street not made for hasty progress; a street laid out before inches of land had value and when one-handed clocks sufficiently sub-divided the day' (p. 448).

The metaphor of 'one-handed clocks' (sun-dials) serves to introduce a beautiful account of the way in which notions of time changed over the centuries and how older concepts of time based on the seasons, the sun, the cockerel, and even the direction of the wind gave way to the tyrannical two-handed clock, the waker-up (knocker-up), and later the alarm clock, the second hand, the stop-watch, time and motion study, 'clocking on' (and later still the micro-seconds of contemporary computer technology). Thompson observes: 'the irregularity of the working day and week were framed, until the first decades of the nineteenth century within the larger irregularity of

the working year, punctuated by its traditional holidays and fairs'
(E. P. Thompson 1994: 468).

In view of the prevalence of these 'pre-industrial' attitudes towards time,[7]
it is hardly surprising that the growth of factory industry was accompanied
by an enormous cultural and organizational change and acute social conflicts about working hours. In the eighteenth century complaints about the
licentiousness, drunkenness, laziness, ill-discipline, and debauchery of the
English 'lower class' were commonplace, and schools were seen as one of
the main ways of inculcating time discipline, in addition to factory penalties
of the kind implemented even by paternalistic employers, such as Josiah
Wedgwood.

The pressures to increase working hours were strong in the first period of
industrialization, and early in the nineteenth century gas lighting was one of
the technical inventions that facilitated the use of longer hours and shift
work in factories, but the resistance of the new factory proletariat was also
strong and led to the prolonged efforts of the unions to reduce working
hours. These efforts at reform were resisted by Senior and other classical
economists on the grounds that profit depended on the 'last hour' of the
working day. John Stuart Mill, however, supported the advocates of a ten-
hour day for women and children on 'higher than commercial grounds'.

However, it was not only the new trade unions and reformers, such as
Lord Shaftesbury, who were appalled by the long hours of work, but also
more enlightened industrialists such as Robert Owen, Josiah Wedgwood,
and Samuel Whitbread. These entrepreneurs, who were among the most
successful, argued that technical and organizational innovations, together
with improved education and training, and paternalistic reforms in the
enterprise would raise productivity more than the crude lengthening of the
working day. Trade unions were already common in the second half of
the eighteenth century, although records are very incomplete, because they
suffered from legal penalties and intolerance and were sometimes short-
lived (Laybourn 1992). The more successful unions were those of the most
skilled craft workers, whose bargaining position was relatively stronger and
who were able to reach a working understanding with their employers.
Robert Owen's sympathies with the workers went much deeper than this
and he promoted a 'Grand National Consolidated Trade Union' (GNCTU) in
the 1830s, which aspired to organize all workers, including the unskilled, in
one big union. It had only very limited success, but nevertheless the experience of this and other short-lived unions, as well as the more durable and
stable craft unions and friendly societies, served to create a sense of solidarity
and a working class culture, which also found expression in the very strong
support for the 'People's Charter' in the 1830s and 1840s. This marked the

---

[7] 'In seventeenth-century Chile time was often measured in 'credos'; an earthquake was
described in 1647 as lasting for the period of two credos; while the cooking time of an egg could
be judged by an 'Ave Maria said aloud' (Thompson 1994: 450).

recognition that universal suffrage and other political objectives offered the best hope for amelioration of the often lamentable suffering of the new urban working class. Some limitations on working hours for women and children were indeed achieved by legislation promoted by Lord Shaftesbury and other reformers, as well as by the struggles of the unions themselves. In his study of *The Factory Question and Industrial England 1830–1860*, Robert Gray (1996) attributes the main credit for the 1847 legislation, reducing working hours for young people and women to ten hours per day, to the influence of Chartism itself.

These movements and the numerous conflicts over factory discipline serve to remind us that the Industrial Revolution was by no means a conflict-free consensual transition. The resistance of those who suffered most reached a peak in 1842–3, when numerous riots, the first General Strike, and actual insurrections in several towns in England and Wales brought Britain quite close to social revolution.

A profound cultural and social change in attitudes towards time was an essential feature of the Industrial Revolution. The combination of von Tunzelmann's work on time-saving technical change with Thompson's work on attitudes towards time in pre-industrial and industrial societies brings out one of its most crucial features. E. P. Thompson concludes:

Mature industrial societies of all varieties are marked by time-thrift and by a clear demarcation between 'work' and 'life' . . . The point at issue is not that of the 'standard of living'. If the theorists of growth wish us to say so, then we may agree that the older popular culture was in many ways otiose, intellectually vacant, devoid of quickening and plain bloody poor. Without time-discipline we could not have the insistent energies of industrial man; and whether this discipline comes in the form of Methodism, or of Stalinism, or of nationalism, it will come to the developing world. What needs to be said is not that one way of life is better than the other, but that this is a place of the most far-reaching conflict; that the historical record is not a single one of neutral and inevitable technological change, but is also one of exploitation and of resistance to exploitation; and that values stand to be lost as well as gained. (Thompson 1967: 93–4)

Finally, it is necessary to keep in mind that, although factory production became the norm for the most rapidly growing leading sectors of the economy, such as cotton, these still accounted for a relatively small minority of *total* employment until well into the nineteenth century.

The growth of the British economy in the 1770s and 1780s, although certainly significant, was still very narrowly based in a few leading sectors. From the 1790s to the 1820s industrialization affected a growing number of industries, notably cotton weaving as well as spinning and other branches of the textile industry, such as wool and linen. The great majority of cotton mills were still using water power in 1800 but steam engines were slowly diffusing in this and a few other industries. As von Tunzelmann (1978) showed, the really widespread diffusion of the steam engine and the mechanization of many other industries depended on greatly improved high pressure steam engines, which became available in the 1830s and 1840s (see Section 6.4 below).

Despite the narrow base of the first Kondratiev wave, we cannot improve on the successive endorsements of Landes's summary:

numbers merely describe the surface of the society and even then in terms that define away change by using categories of unchanging nomenclature. Beneath the surface, the vital organs were transformed; and although they weighed but a fraction of the total—whether measured by people or wealth—it was they that determined the metabolism of the system. (1965: 20; see also Lloyd-Jones and Lewis 1998: 20)

The social innovation of factory production was one of the most fundamental changes of 'metabolism' in the Industrial Revolution. Landes (1965) stresses that neither the workers nor the older class of merchant capitalists, who organized cottage production systems, welcomed this change. It was a radical leap, made possible by an exceptional combination of favourable circumstances in eighteenth and early nineteenth-century England, sufficient to overcome the inertia and active resistance of older institutions and attitudes. Landes maintains that the adoption of the factory system of production was driven not only by its much greater profitability, but also by a crisis of the cottage-based system.

Recent work by economic historians has increasingly recognized the role of cultural and political change, as well as the more traditional emphasis on technical change and more narrowly economic factors. Particularly notable in this connection is the work of Berg and Bruland (1998) and the earlier work of Edward Thompson (1963) on *The Making of the English Working Class*. Thompson argued that 'collective self-consciousness' of the working class was indeed the 'great spiritual gain of the Industrial Revolution', and that this was

perhaps, the most distinguished popular culture England has known. It contained the massive diversity of skills, of the workers in metal, wood, textile and ceramics, without whose inherited 'mysteries' and superb ingenuity with primitive tools the inventions of the Industrial Revolution could scarcely have got further than the drawing board. From this culture of craftsmen and the self-taught there came scores of inventors, organizers, journalists and political theorists of impressive quality. It is easy enough to say that this culture was backward-looking or conservative. True enough, one direction of the great agitations of the artisans and outworkers, continued over fifty years, was to resist being turned into a proletariat. When they knew that this cause was lost, yet they reached out again, in the Thirties and Forties, and sought to achieve new and only imagined forms of social control. (Thompson 1963: 831)

5.7 Changing Patterns of Demand

The emphasis in this chapter so far has been on the 'supply' side—on product innovations, process innovations, and organizational innovations. This does not mean, of course, that changes in demand, in consumer habits, and in tastes played no part. An influential piece of work on this topic was that of Elizabeth Gilboy, first published in 1932 and reprinted in three other independently edited collections of papers since (Church and Wrigley 1994). She argued that the role of demand had been neglected and pointed to contemporary accounts of the role of fashion, imitation, and changing tastes in stimulating demand for new goods, as well as old ones. As Marx had also suggested, these might at first be described as 'luxuries' but would come to be accepted later as 'necessities'. She summed up her position in these words:

> Theoretically, then, it is possible to conclude that far-reaching and widespread industrial changes cannot occur except in a society in which demand and consumption standards are undergoing swift and radical readjustment. Such a society is characterised by mobility between classes, the introduction of new commodities leading to the development of new wants, and a rise in real income of the people as a whole. (Gilboy, in Church and Wrigley 1994: 361)

Her argument about the role of 'keeping up with the Joneses' has been generally accepted by many authors since, notably Eversley (1994) and Landes (1969). (For other references to the reiteration of her theory, see Mokyr 1994*a*.) However, it has been very heavily criticized by Mokyr (1994*a*) in rather the same manner that Mowery and Rosenberg criticized the exaggerated claims for *demand*-led innovation in the 1960s.

It should be noted that Elizabeth Gilboy's own argument for stressing the role of demand was modestly presented and did not deny the Schumpeterian view that in the early stages of radical innovation entrepreneurs must create their own market demand, since consumers can have no prior knowledge of the product. She did not attempt to use statistical sources to justify her position with empirical evidence; but Eversley (1994) did so, stressing especially the expansion of *home* market demand in the period from 1750 to 1780, based on rising population and rising living standards. He gave various examples of contemporary descriptions of changing tastes and evidence of a more varied pattern of consumption, facilitated by big developments in the infrastructure, especially canals:

> we can cite a mass of contemporary sources alleging the prevalence of 'luxurious habits' amongst the 'poor'; a complaint shorn of its moralising overtones, means nothing more than that some labourers liked tea with sugar even when both were heavily taxed; that women decked themselves out in clothes considered too good for them; and that in some cottages you might find a bit of carpet or even a piano. What seems necessary for growth is that the very exceptional expenditure should become

a little less so, that articles described by Nassau Senior as 'decencies', half-way between luxuries and necessities, should spread through some more of the 'middling sorts of people' and that some labourers should take it into their heads (according to their betters) as to go short of food and put themselves into debt for a looking glass or a pair of gilt buckles for their Sunday shoes. (Eversley 1994: 294)

As an example of the kind of goods he is talking about, Eversley quotes the example of the inventory of goods for the cottage of Richard Wainwright, a nailer who as early as August 1739 possessed: a fire shovel, a coal hammer, a toasting iron, bellows, a copper can, wooden furniture, scissors, a warming pan, two iron pots, a brass kettle, a pail, two barrels, two bedsteads, a sieve, candlesticks, a rug, a blanket, a kneading tub, a brass skimmer and basting spoon, linen, glass bottles, and various other kitchen utensils (Eversley 1994: 319). This inventory of modest household possessions shows that it is not accurate to regard 'consumerism' simply as the product of the twentieth century. It is this changing composition that matters.

Eversley believed that the construction of the Midlands canal network and the Lancashire canals in the third quarter of the eighteenth century brought down the price of food as well as coal and other commodities in many towns, especially Birmingham. The improvements in regularity and speed of mail and passenger travel on the coaches in the 1770s also facilitated the creation of larger regional markets for new goods, especially simple metal products. The first regular stage coach services from London to and from other cities were launched in the 1780s.

More recently, Maxine Berg (1998: 153) has argued that industries such as decorative metal products and furniture have been neglected not only from the demand side but also from the supply side. She recalls that Adam Smith already pointed to the importance of 'fashion and fancy products' for the metal industries of Birmingham and Sheffield and argues that product innovation in such industries merits much greater consideration by historians along with the traditional emphasis on process innovations in machinery. She analyses patent statistics from 1627 to 1825 to show that patents for ornamenting, engraving, painting, and printing, as well as for buckles and fastenings, were of considerable importance among the inventions of the Industrial Revolution. Even more importantly, she points to the interactions between those firms and trades designing and producing ornamental and decorative products and those producing machines and instruments. In particular, she points to the strong mutual influence between Boulton and Wedgwood.

Many authors, including of course Adam Smith, on the basis of his extensive travels in Europe, maintained that standards of living in eighteenth-century Britain were well above those in other European countries. In particular, this was held to be true for a larger and wealthier middle class. Habbakuk (1963: 115) advances this as one of the main explanations of the British Industrial Revolution: 'average per capita incomes were higher than on the Continent. There were larger numbers of people with a reasonable margin of subsistence for the consumption of manufactured goods. The inducement to expand an individual industry was not therefore impeded by the very inelastic demand which faces an industry in the poorer countries of the modern world.'

5.8 Congruence of Culture, Politics, Economy, Science, and Technology

Despite this acknowledgement of the points made by Elizabeth Gilboy and Maxine Berg, and the earlier emphasis on cultural and political changes, the account given in this chapter may appear to some as 'technological determination' or as 'techno-economic determinism', but we would stress that the innovations could be made, financed, and diffused only in a hospitable cultural and political climate. It was the *congruence* of favourable developments in all the main subsystems of British society and their positive mutual interaction that made it possible for this fast growth constellation to emerge and diffuse. This point about congruence confirms the analysis of Part I.

Supple provides an admirably terse summary of this favourable congruence of economic, technological, scientific, political, and cultural characteristics in Britain:

Britain's economic, social and political experience before the late 18th Century explains with relatively little difficulty why she should have been an industrial pioneer. For better than any of her contemporaries Great Britain exemplified a combination of potentially growth-inducing characteristics. The development of enterprise, her access to rich sources of supply and large overseas markets within the framework of a dominant trading system, the accumulation of capital, the core of industrial techniques, her geographical position and the relative ease of transportation in an island economy with abundant rivers, a scientific and pragmatic heritage, a stable political and relatively flexible social system, an ideology favourable to business and innovation—all bore witness to the historical trends of two hundred years and more, and provided much easier access to economic change in Britain than in any other European country. (Supple 1963: 14)

Adam Smith's book *The Wealth of Nations*, appearing as it did in 1776, exemplified the political and cultural foundations of the British Industrial Revolution, just as it provided an extremely influential economic ideology. This doctrine was so powerful that it persuaded the British prime minister (William Pitt) to declare to Adam Smith: 'We are all your pupils now.' Smith's extraordinary influence was due to the fact that he provided an almost perfect rationalization for the profit-seeking activities of the new industrialists and merchants. They could believe that what they were doing was serving the community through the pursuit of their own self-interest.

The very title and main theme of his book shifted the focus of economic inquiry from trade to growth and from agriculture to productive industry. It meant that the pursuit of growth, capital accumulation, and national prosperity became to some extent the shared objective of the State, the industrialists, the aristocracy, and the merchants. Thus it was that, despite the fact that the landlords were still by far the most wealthy and politically influential class, economic policies were followed that promoted the interests of the rapidly growing but still small new industries. The reduction of the power of local monopolies and of restrictions on trade, advocated so eloquently by Adam Smith, was by no means a conflict-free process and only reached its denouement in the 1840s with the repeal of the Corn Laws. In the late eighteenth century, a non-interventionist *laissez-faire* policy reducing state involvement with industry and trade was welcome to many landlords as well as industrialists. Small-firm competition became a reality in late eighteenth-century Britain, and the opening of domestic and foreign markets did indeed promote technical and organizational change and productive investment in the way that Smith advocated. His language was not far removed from the general culture of society and was intelligible to a broad readership, which is unfortunately often no longer the case with economics today.

The broad social consensus exemplified by Smith's *Wealth of Nations* did not of course amount to unanimity. It expressed a rationalization above all of the interests of the industrialists and merchants. However, the rent income of landlords was justified by Smith in a way it certainly never was forty years later by Ricardo. Smith attacked monopoly 'conspiracies' against the public interests, whether by unions to raise wages or by merchants to raise prices, yet he was very much concerned with the improvement of the living standards of the poor. In his day, *laissez-faire* doctrine did not yet carry the uncaring stigma that it acquired as a result of a half-century of intensive urbanization and industrialization, the social critique of two generations of poets and novelists, and the resistance of many workers to inhuman conditions of work. The 'collective intentionality' that emerged in eighteenth-century Britain was a consensus that did not embrace the still illiterate and poor majority, but their acquiescence could be obtained with a relatively limited amount of violent repression, despite the fact that living standards for many of them improved little, if at all. The Combination Acts of 1799 and other earlier Acts were used to limit the powers of trade unions, and more severe penalties were used against the Luddites.

The consensus necessary to harmonize many differing individual purposes was of course not exclusively dependent on the widespread acceptance of a particular type of economic theory or rationalization. It was far more broadly based on the general culture of the time. The Renaissance, the Scientific Revolution and the Reformation of the sixteenth and seventeenth centuries all contributed directly or indirectly to the prevalence of a pragmatic, individualistic, empiricism that is hard to measure, but is widely recognized as characteristic of eighteenth-century Britain. Moreover, although the English Civil War of the 1640s ended with the Restoration of the Monarchy and no other monarch suffered the fate of Charles I, the eighteenth century monarchy was very different from that of the sixteenth century or the absolutist monarchies still strongly entrenched on the Continent of Europe. *De facto* parliamentary sovereignty without a written constitution was firmly established from 1688 onwards. The tradition of parliamentary government, with the give and take of political debate and the toleration extended to organized opposition, set the example for many other institutions, high and low. Trial by jury, the common law, the establishment of national news-papers, the philosophic tradition of Bacon, Locke, and Hume, the 'Dissenting Academies', and the non-Conformist sects were among the many insti-tutions, that if not entirely unique to England, were in combination impressive evidence of a democratic culture providing a fertile soil for the flowering of local initiatives in all parts of the country.

This general culture both contributed to and was strongly influenced by the Scientific Revolution of the seventeenth and eighteenth centuries. The influence of science is underestimated by many historians in much the same way as economists today still often underestimate the contribution of science to contemporary innovation. Some Marxist historians have been inclined to overstate the contribution of technology to economic growth by comparison with science, although others, such as Needham and Marx himself, have not been. Eighteenth-century science was, of course, very different from twentieth-century science. Nevertheless, even though the expression 'scientist' had not been coined in his time, and even though men of science or natural philo-sophers were very few in number, Adam Smith was well aware of their great importance and emphasized it in the opening pages of *The Wealth of Nations*.

Ashton (1948), Musson and Robinson (1969) are among the historians who have done most to demonstrate both the direct (especially Musson) and the indirect (especially Ashton) contribution of science to technology and the general culture of English and Scottish society. While von Tunzelmann (1981) may be right in emphasising that French science was ahead of British science in some respects, this does not undermine the basic argument that an experimental, enquiring, rational spirit and approach was a necessary con-dition for the work of scientists and inventors alike. In fact, von Tunzelmann points out that 'the scientific revolution, dated either at the foundation of the Royal Society in 1660 or earlier in the century (Webster 1975), *preceded* the financial revolution, the commercial revolution, the transport revolution and the Industrial Revolution, as these overlapping changes are conveniently dated' (von Tunzelmann 1981: 148). Furthermore, he also stresses the positive influence of science on the general climate of ideas, within which inventors worked. Ashton insists that:

The stream of English scientific thought, issuing from the teaching of Francis Bacon, and enlarged by the genius of Boyle and Newton, was one of the main tributaries of the Industrial Revolution. Newton indeed was too good a philosopher and scholar to care whether or not the ideas he gave to the world were immediately 'useful', but the belief in the possibility of achieving industrial progress by the method of observation and experiment came to the eighteenth century largely through him. (Ashton 1948: 155)

Like Musson and Robinson, Ashton gives numerous examples of the ways in which the leading physicists, chemists, and geologists of the day were in intimate contact with the leading figures in British industry. A good example of this was the chemist, Joseph Priestley, discoverer of oxygen and inventor of soda-water, whose brother-in-law was the iron-master, John Wilkinson, and who was a scientific adviser to Wedgwood. As we have seen in the case of Smeaton, men like him or James Watt, William Reynolds, and James Keir were as at home in the factory as in the laboratory. The various scientific societies of the day, including especially those in Manchester and Birmingham, but also the Royal Society in London, were another forum for contact between scientists and inventors. As Ashton points out, even taking into account the growth of scientific specialization that Adam Smith observed, the language of science had not yet become so esoteric as to preclude contact with the language, culture, and practice of ordinary people. Thus, despite the fact that science had its own institutions, procedures, and publications, it certainly influenced both technology and the general culture of society in ways highly favourable to technical change and innovation.

It is often said today that United States culture has been especially favourable to innovation, and a contrast is frequently made between this intellectual and business environment and that of contemporary Britain, supposedly now far more conservative and unreceptive to innovation. While these attitudes are extraordinarily hard to measure, it should be noted that many eighteenth-century observers believed that British society was at that time exceptionally favourable to innovation. With typical caustic wit, Dr Johnson gave the bizarre example of techniques of hanging to illustrate this point: 'The age is running mad after innovation . . . all the business of the world is to be done in a new way; men are to be hanged in a new way. Tyburn [the site at which executions were held] itself is not safe from the fury of innovation . . .'

A later American equivalent of Dr Johnson could have cited the electric chair as an equally gruesome example of the spirit of innovation that pervaded the United States, as it became the next major example of a country leading the world in technical innovation in the late ninteenth century and twentieth century (see Chapter 7).

This chapter has attempted to show that the surge of economic growth and structural change in the British economy in the late eighteenth century was propelled by a constellation of innovations, both radical and incremental, based primarily on iron as a core input, on water wheels providing power, on canals providing cheap transport for heavy materials, on turnpike roads facilitating movement of people and lighter commodities, and on the new factory style of organization with a series of mechanizing innovations in the leading fast-growth cotton industry. This constellation of innovations could be introduced and could flourish as nowhere else because of an exceptionally favourable congruence of political and cultural changes in Britain—

changes that were to prove even more important in the second phase of the Industrial Revolution.

5.9 The British Transition from the First to the Second Kondratiev

There is very broad agreement about the acceleration of British economic growth in the late eighteenth and early nineteenth century but there is rather less agreement about the period from 1815 to 1845. This was a period of falling prices and, following Jevons, was taken by most of the earlier writers on long cycles as the 'downturn' of the first long cycle (see Chapter 3). However, later research on output showed that there was little evidence of a serious down-swing in the growth rate of *production* in this period, so authors such as Solomou used these data to argue that they demonstrated the non-existence of Kondratiev waves, at least in the first half of the nineteenth century.[8]

However, in our approach the problems of precision in GDP measurement in this period are not so acute, since we are concerned primarily with *structural* and *qualitative* changes. What this concluding section of the chapter will seek to show is that the period was characterized in the first place by the rapid growth of a new constellation of fast-growing industries, services, and technologies and, in the second, by social turmoil and heavy unemployment as a result of the structural changes engendered by these developments. It may well be the case that the aggregate growth of British GDP did not slow significantly, if at all.

The main features of the new fast growth constellation were a new infra-structure (railways), a new source of power (steam engines), and new machine tools and other machinery which had the effect of spreading the Industrial Revolution to new areas of the country and to industries hitherto less affected by the first Kondratiev wave, as well as improving the productivity of some that had already been industrialized. In some ways, therefore, the first two Kondratiev waves may be seen in Britain as two successive phases of the Industrial Revolution, the first based primarily on water-powered mechanization and the second on steam-powered mechanization, but both sharing the core inputs of iron and coal. In countries other than Britain, especially in continental Europe, it was the second Kondratiev wave that brought industrialization and structural transformation. The catch-up process combined features of the first and second waves.

---

[8] It should be noted that there are great difficulties in the precise measurement of output in Britain before 1850. Retrospective estimates of GDP are notoriously difficult to calculate, whether from the income side, the expenditure side, or the physical output side. Crafts commented that estimates of GDP before 1850 can be little more than 'controlled conjectures'. One of the leading early scholars who worked on these statistics, Phyllis Deane (1948), commented on the serious weaknesses of the income estimates which had led her and other researchers to concentrate on estimates from the expenditure side, although the methodological problems in this area were almost as great as from the output side.

The evaluation of the effects of the Napoleonic Wars on the growth of the British economy and on continental Europe is a complex problem and still a matter of controversy among historians. However, despite difficulties in some areas of British trade with the European Continent over relatively short periods, there is little doubt that the British economy emerged from these wars in much better shape than its main continental rivals, including, of course, France. In his book on *The Rise and Fall of the Great Powers*, Paul Kennedy sums up the British gains at the expense of France:

the seizure of Santo Domingo—which had been responsible for a remarkable three quarters of France's colonial trade before the Revolution—was by the late 1790s, a valuable market for *British* goods and a great source of *British* re-exports. In addition, not only were these overseas markets in North America, the West Indies, Latin America, India and the Orient growing faster than those in Europe, but long-haul trades were usually more profitable and a greater stimulus to the shipping, commodity-dealing, marine insurance, bill-clearing, and banking activities which so enhanced London's position as the new financial centre of the world. (Kennedy 1988: 179)

Despite some disruption, total British exports increased from £21.7 million in 1794–6 to £44.4 million in 1814–16 and the key sectors of the economy (especially iron and cotton) continued to grow rapidly throughout this period. The period from the 1780s to 1815 should therefore certainly be classified as one of *upswing* and boom. Paradoxically, this was confirmed by the difficulties experienced when the Napoleonic Wars ended and the exceptional demand for such products as iron fell sharply. Social distress was widespread as the economy moved to a new pattern of peacetime output. Nevertheless, the impetus from the Industrial Revolution was sufficient for the aggregate growth of the economy to continue to outpace all other European countries (Tables 5.6 and 5.7).

In the chapter of his book entitled 'Continental Emulation', Landes emphasized how far other European countries lagged behind Britain:

At mid-century then, continental Europe was still about a generation behind Britain in industrial development. Whereas in 1851 about half of the people of England and Wales lived in towns, in France and Germany the proportion was about a quarter. . . . The occupational distribution tells a similar story. At mid-century, only a quarter of the British male working force (twenty years and older) was engaged in agriculture. For Belgium, the most industrialised nation in the Continent, the figure was about 50 per cent. Germany took another 25 years to reach this point; indeed, as late as 1895, there were more people engaged in agriculture than in industry. (Landes 1969: 187–8)

For this reason, our account continues to concentrate on technological and industrial developments in Britain as the leading country, at least down to the 1870s, when the United States began to emerge as the new technological leader (Chapter 7). This should certainly not be taken as an underestimation of the importance of new developments in technology and science in a number of other European countries, especially France, Sweden, the

TABLE 5.6. Relative shares of world manufacturing output, 1750–1900 (%)

	1750	1800	1830	1860	1880	1900
Europe as a whole	23.2	28.1	34.2	53.2	61.3	62.0
United Kingdom	1.9	4.3	9.5	19.9	22.9	18.5
Hapsburg Empire	2.9	3.2	3.2	4.2	4.4	4.7
France	4.0	4.2	5.2	7.9	7.8	6.8
German states/Germany	2.9	3.5	3.5	4.9	8.5	13.2
Italian states/Italy	2.4	2.5	2.3	2.5	2.5	2.5
Russia	5.0	5.6	5.6	7.0	7.6	8.8
United States	0.1	0.8	2.4	7.2	14.7	23.6
Japan	3.8	3.5	2.8	2.6	2.4	2.4
Third World	73.0	67.7	60.5	36.6	20.9	11.0
China	32.8	33.3	29.8	19.7	12.5	6.2
India/Pakistan	24.5	19.7	17.6	8.6	2.8	1.7

Source: Kennedy (1988: 190); Bairoch (1982: 294).

TABLE 5.7. Per capita levels of industrialization, 1750–1900 (relative to UK in 1900 = 100)

	1750	1800	1830	1860	1880	1900
Europe as a whole	8	8	11	16	24	35
United Kingdom	10	16	25	64	87	[100]
Hapsburg Empire	7	7	8	11	15	23
France	9	9	12	20	28	39
German states/Germany	8	8	9	15	25	52
Italian states/Italy	8	8	8	10	12	17
Russia	6	6	7	8	10	15
United States	4	9	14	21	38	69
Japan	7	7	7	7	9	12
Third World	7	6	6	4	3	2
China	8	6	6	4	4	3
India	7	6	6	3	2	1

Source: Kennedy (1988: 190); Bairoch (1982: 294).

Netherlands, and various German and Italian states before the unification of those countries. Despite the fact that the main changes in industry during the Industrial Revolution took place in the North and in Scotland, London also played a key role in bringing knowledge of Continental inventions and technologies into Britain. For example, the earliest water-powered silk mills in Britain were built at Derby in 1705–7 by Thomas Cotchett, a London silk reeler, based on Dutch technology. Another Londoner and silk merchant, Thomas Lombe, improved and extended these mills with technology from Leghorn, where silk-reeling mills were well established. Lombe succeeded in making the mills profitable because of his knowledge of up-to-date Italian technology and because of his management of the 300 employees. The Derby mills and their work organization were copied in ten other mills in the North of England between 1732 and 1769 (Chapman 1972/1992: 14). According to Chapman's account, these influenced the early development of the factory system in the British cotton industry because Arkwright's partner in Derby, Jebediah Strutt, copied the organization of the silk mills and the Stockport and Sheffield silk mills were converted to cotton production (p. 15). Other similar examples could be quoted, and Chapman comments: 'London also played an important role in technical innovation in the cotton industry, acting as a nursery for techniques brought from the Continent or from India, until they were ready for transplanting to the provinces. . . .' (p. 12).

There were 1,500 Dutch looms in use in large workshops in Manchester by 1750, and this could reasonably be regarded as the first step in the transition to the factory system (Wadsworth and Mann 1931). All of these examples show that technologies from countries outside Britain were important in the Industrial Revolution, and it is certainly not our intention to belittle these contributions or the influence of foreign markets and the experience of foreign trade. We concentrate our account on Britain, and later on other leading countries, because we contend that it was the capacity to innovate at home, and to combine this with the input of foreign technology, that distinguished the technological leaders and the congruence of political, cultural, and economic circumstances that enabled them to do this.

5.10 The Structural Crisis of Adjustment

In Britain the process of industrialization proceeded in two distinct phases, and the birth-pangs of the second phase were in some respects more painful than those of the first, especially with respect to unemployment in the severe recessions of the 1830s and early 1840s. The GDP estimates tell us little about unemployment and the harsh treatment of the unemployed following the introduction of the 'New Poor Law' in the 1830s. Yet we do know from several sources that these social problems were much more severe in the 1830s and 1840s than in the earlier period of industrialization from the 1780s to the 1820s.

A major feature of the structural crisis of adjustment in the 1830s was the increasing unemployment in rural as well as urban areas. The increase in population was not immediately accompanied by rural depopulation, and according to Mathias (1969: 238), 'Rural pauperism proved to be the greatest single scourge of the 1820s and 1830s'. Poor rates rose to a peak in the early 1830s, and the 1834 Poor Law Act was particularly designed to combat the evils of rural destitution by encouraging, if necessary in a brutal way, migration away from areas where employment did not offer a living minimal wage for a family.

This harsh new Poor Law, offering to the destitute and unemployed relief only in institutions known as 'workhouses' (although often no work was done there) replaced the 'Speenhamland' system introduced in 1795 and so-called because it was started by the justices in the county of Berkshire meeting in Speenhamland at the Pelican Inn. These justices decided to subsidize the wages of labourers through a system of 'outdoor relief' in accordance with a scale dependent upon the price of bread. The system became general during the Napoleonic Wars and persisted after the end of the war. It became increasingly expensive as the population grew and farmers paid lower wages in the expectation of supplementary relief in times of high food prices. These were kept high by the Corn Laws restricting imports of grain. The thorny problem of the repeal of the Corn Laws was not confronted by Parliament until the 1840s, but the solution attempted in the New Poor Law was at the expense of the poorest part of the population. It led to increases in unemployment and in emigration and, again according to Mathias (1969: 238), it 'assumed a quite false diagnosis of the ills of industrial society, for unemployment in cyclical depressions or from technological and structural change was involuntary rather than a deliberately chosen option'.

While there are no national statistics of unemployment comparable to those available in the twentieth century, there were local statistics of the numbers of 'paupers' in the main industrial areas. As Hobsbawm (1994) has shown, in the main industrial districts of Lancashire and Yorkshire (the heartland of the Industrial Revolution) unemployment rates as high as 20–30 per cent of the adult male population were by no means rare in the worst recession years. The new 'cyclical' unemployment of modern industry related to fluctuations in investment and trade, and especially to the fluctuations in railway investment in the 1830s and 1840s, and to the ruin of the handloom weavers.

Even more revealing than retrospective estimates of unemployment, based on the Poor Law statistics and local records, are the accounts of contemporary novelists and historians. Novels such as Dickens's *Hard Times* or Mrs. Gaskell's *North and South* are in many ways more impressive than these statistics. In particular, Elizabeth Gaskell's heroine from a comfortable home in the South confronting the realities of the industrial North for the first time leaves an indelible impression. Perhaps most vivid of all contemporary accounts is that of Thomas Carlyle in 1843, confronting the paradox of large-scale cyclical unemployment in an industrial society for the first time:

England is full of wealth, of multifarious produce, supply for human want in every kind . . . with unabated bounty the land of England blooms and grows; waving with yellow harvests; thick-studded with workshops, industrial implements, with fifteen millions of workers . . . Of these successful skilful workers some two millions, it is now counted, sit in Workhouses, Poor Law prisons; or have 'outdoor relief' . . . the Workhouse Bastille being filled to bursting . . . They sit there these many months now; their hope of deliverance as yet small. In Workhouses, pleasantly so-named because work cannot be done in them. Twelve hundred thousand workers in

England alone . . . sit there, pent up, as in a kind of horrid enchantment; glad to be imprisoned and enchanted that they may not perish starved. (Carlyle 1843: 1–2)

Following an account of the expressions on the faces of men who would like to work but are condemned to idleness, even in the so-called 'work' houses, Carlyle goes on to describe the poverty in Scotland, then without a Poor Law, where 'there are scenes of woe and destitution and desolation, such as, one may hope, the sun never saw before in the most barbarous regions where men dwelt'. He concludes: 'Things, if it be not mere cotton and iron, things, are growing disobedient to man. . . . We have more riches than any Nation ever had before; we have less good of them than any Nation ever had before. Our successful industry is hitherto unsuccessful; a strange success if we stop here! In the midst of plethoric plenty, the people perish . . .' (Carlyle 1843: 5).

The spectacle of mass unemployment (estimated by Carlyle apparently at nearly 15 per cent of the total labour force) in what was then the wealthiest and most prosperous country in the world clearly struck him as an extraordinary paradox, and it is difficult not to feel that this was a period of turbulent transition rather than one of steady prosperous growth, conveyed by some of the adherents of smoothed trends in reconstructed estimates of GDP growth. Particularly interesting is Carlyle's brief suggestion that, whereas 'cotton and iron' may be 'obedient to man', the rest of the economy is not so 'obedient'. Here again is the impression of a period of turbulent structural change rather than one of smooth progression.

Finally, there is the evidence of the social and political turmoil of the 1830s and 1840s. This was the only period in the nineteenth century when Britain came close to a social revolution. Armed rebellions did actually take place in several towns and general strikes in many. The demonstrations of hundreds of thousands of workers in the northern towns in support of the Chartist demands for universal suffrage were greater than any seen before or since, while trade union organization and activity also reached its highest point in the century in the 1830s, despite the legal inhibitions. All of this followed the wave of Luddite machine-breaking during and soon after the Napoleonic Wars. Working people no longer saw a halt to industrialization as a realistic possibility but sought, as an alternative, redress by new forms of regulation through political pressure and legislative reforms.

This impression of the period that culminated in the repeal of the Corn Laws in 1846 as one of great turbulence and structural change is further confirmed by the most recent work of Lloyd-Jones and Lewis (1998: chapter 3). They describe the period as one that illustrated 'both an enthusiasm for and a resistance to the degree of change at the structural level of the economy' (p. 33). The structural crisis of the 1830s and 1840s led to a new political mode of coordination in the concessions made by the landlord class to the now stronger class of industrialists and merchants. The conflict of interests had now become acute between the landlords, who wanted to maintain protection of agriculture, and the industrialists, who wanted repeal of the Corn Laws in order to lower the cost of food, put downward pressure on wages, and alleviate discontent in the industrial towns. Whereas Adam Smith had smoothed over this conflict, Ricardo had placed it at the centre of his analysis, and his view was reinforced by Malthusian pessimism about the growth of population and the availability of fertile land for agriculture. Economics, which in Smith's day had been relatively optimistic in tone, now became the 'dismal science'. The free traders had the bit between their teeth and succeeded in enlisting widespread popular support for the repeal of the Corn Laws, so that ultimately the Tory Party itself was split and its leader, Robert Peel, acquired a parliamentary majority for repeal.

British industry could now derive great benefits from its leadership in many branches of production and its domination of the world shipping industry. So strong was this position that Britain not only could gain many advantages from this spread of free trade practices around the world, but also could safely repeal the Navigation Acts in 1849, which had restricted the carriage of goods to British vessels. A political *modus vivendi* was achieved for the mid-Victorian boom.

We turn now in Chapter 6 to the main features of the fast growth constellation which was at first less 'obedient to man' than cotton and iron, but ultimately led to the prolonged period of Victorian prosperity in the 1850s and 1860s.

6

The Second Kondratiev Wave:
The Age of Iron Railways, Steam Power,
and Mechanization

6.1 The Fast Growth Constellation
of the Second Kondratiev Wave in Britain

Some features of the second Kondratiev wave in Britain were essentially based on changes already introduced in the earlier phase of industrialization. For example, iron as a core input was already well established between 1780 and 1840 (Figure 5.1). What was new about the iron industry in the second Kondratiev wave was mainly the large-scale use of iron for railways and for new kinds of machinery.

The new industries and technologies that characterized the upswing of the second Kondratiev wave, and had already come together in an interdependent constellation in the 1820s and 1830s, were first and foremost these iron railways, both as infrastructure and as the fastest growing services for freight and for passengers from 1831 to the 1890s (Figures 6.1, 6.2, and 6.3). Intimately linked with the growth of railway services was of course the industry constructing steam locomotives and other rolling stock and railway equipment. The steam engines that powered the railway locomotives comprised a large fraction of the total output of steam engines. Many technical innovations in the design, power output, safety, and fuel consumption of steam engines were made following the use of Newcomen engines in British coal mines and of Watt engines in textiles and iron in the eighteenth century (Table 6.1). It was the new, vastly improved high pressure steam engines that made it possible to use steam power, not only on railways, but in many sectors of industry and even in agriculture. The building of such steam engines was at the heart of a rapidly growing engineering industry, making machines and machine tools of all kinds on the basis of technologies developed in the 1820s and 1830s. The locomotives could only be built by the use of these new machine tools. Machines for making machines were essential for the mechanization of other industries. Finally, all of these sectors used the core inputs of coal and iron (Table 6.2). Mathias summed up these interdependent advantages of what we are describing as the new constellation:

Steam power was pioneered through the demand for draining mines; the increasing demand for coal and iron ore was the greatest stimulus for applying steam power to transport. By 1850 the railways were the biggest single market for the iron industry

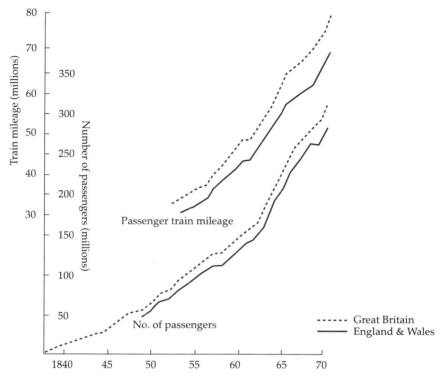

FIG 6.1. Passenger traffic in Britain, 1840–1870
Source: G. R. Hawke (1970: 54).

and through that for coal. It was exactly in this combination of accessible coal and iron ore—the strategic new materials—that Britain's natural resource position was ideal. It was exactly in the skills associated with the strategic new industries of iron and engineering that her lead over other countries was most marked. (Mathias 1969/1983: 129)

6.2 Railways

The role of railways as a new transport infrastructure is obvious and has been one of the main foci of analysis in the cliometrics debate (see especially Fogel 1964; G. R. Hawke 1970; and Chapter 1 above). However, their role as an exemplar for organizational and management innovation was no less important, although it has been relatively neglected in the cliometrics literature.

The railways conformed to most of the characteristics of a 'carrier branch' summarized in the Introduction to Part II. They gave an impetus to qualitative and structural change throughout the economic system. It is these aspects of the railway industry that have been most strongly emphasized by Chandler

FIG 6.2. Railway revenue from various types of passenger traffic in Britain, 1842–1870

Source: G. R. Hawke (1970: 55).

(1965, 1977, 1990) in the United States and by Mathias (1969/1983) in Britain, and which we too will stress in the following sections.

The infrastructural developments have been amply documented in standard histories of the Industrial Revolution and the essential facts are clear. The main railway network was already constructed in Britain in the 1840s, following an initial burst of investment in the 1830s. Other countries, especially Germany and the United States, were also embarking on railway construction in the 1840s (Table 6.3); but, taking geographical factors into account, the British lead was still substantial, and this was illustrated by the British role in railway investment, design, and construction in many parts of the world, as well as by the export of railway equipment and iron rails. The investment in British railways in the 1830s and 1840s was by far the largest ever undertaken, and the two waves of investment in 1834–7 and 1844–7

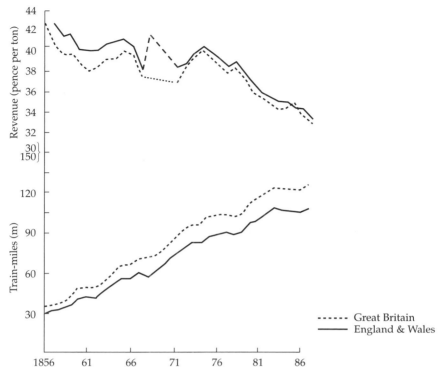

FIG 6.3. Revenue per ton and million train miles of freight carried in Britain,
1856–1886

Source: G. R. Hawke (1970: 58)

have generally been described, both at the time and since, as outbursts of
'railway mania' comparable to, but much larger than, the canal mania of the
1790s. A feature of the railway mania, as of the earlier canal mania or
the contemporary Internet bubble, was the exaggerated expectation of the
profits to be made. The actual profits were indeed quite high in some of the
early railways (e.g. the Liverpool–Manchester Railway) and this, together
with the euphoria of press speculation, was sufficient to induce the type of
'bandwagon' effects analysed by Schumpeter. The rush to build railways all
over the country without much regard for the national network and
involving much duplication meant inevitably that many lines and
companies would turn out to be unprofitable in the end, or even quite early
on, while many projected lines were never actually built. As Mathias pointed
out, in this respect the British railways were similar to the earlier canals and
turnpike roads:

The economic potential of these transport media was therefore never fully realized.
The turnpikes were piecemeal with many gaps and their management bedevilled by
corruption . . . the canals came into existence without a national strategy, with different

TABLE 6.1. Major events in the development of steam power, 1642–1845

Year	Event	Country
1642	Torricelli demonstrates a vacuum	Italy
1654	Von Guericke makes an air pump	Germany
1690	Papin's piston-in-cylinder model	France
1698	Savery's pumping engine	Britain
1712	Newcomen's atmospheric engine	Britain
1725	Hammered iron plates and deadweight safety valve on boilers	Britain
1761	Watt's first experiments with steam	Britain
1765	Watt's first patent for separate condenser, air pump, closed cylinder top, and steam jacket	Britain
1769	Cugnot's steam carriage	France
1774	Smeaton's improved Newcomen engine attains duty[a] of 10.3 million	Britain
1775	Boulton and Watt partnership	Britain
1776	Watt's first pumping engine	Britain
1783	Watt's double-acting rotative engine	Britain
1792	Watt's engine attains duty[a] of 32.8 million	Britain
1800	Watt's restrictive patent expires	Britain
1801	Trevithick's high-pressure self-moving engine (Cornwall)	Britain
1802	Trevithick's London carriage and portable engine	Britain
1803	Oliver Evans's high-pressure engine	USA
1803	Trevithick's Coalbrookdale locomotive	Britain
1804	Trevithick's Pen-y-Darren locomotive hauls trains effectively	Britain
1807	Fulton's *Clermont*, first commercial steamer	USA
1812	Bell's *Comet*, first European commercial steamer	Britain
1814	G. Stephenson's first locomotive, *Blücher*	Britain
1819	PS *Savannah*, first Atlantic crossing with steam assistance	USA
1825	Stockton and Darlington railway	Britain
1827	Maudslay's improved oscillating cylinder	Britain
1829	Seguin's multi-firetube boiler for locomotives	France
1829	Rainhill Locomotive trials	Britain
1831	Liverpool–Manchester Railway	Britain
1835	Otis's steam excavator	USA
1835	West's Cornish engine attains duty[a] of 125 million	Britain
1836	Iron screw propellor, Ericsson	Sweden
1836	Iron screw propellor, Smith	Britain
1838	*Sirius* and *Great Western* cross Atlantic entirely under steam	Britain
1839	SS *Propeller,* later *Archimedes,* demonstrates effectiveness of screw propulsion	Britain
1841	Stephenson's long boiler locomotive	Britain
1843	Brunel's *Great Britain,* iron screw steamer	Britain
1845	Admiralty trials of screw propellors	Britain

[a] Measure of the comparative efficiency of a pumping engine and its boilers: number of lbs. of water lifted 1 ft high by 94 lbs. of coal.

Source: Van Riemsdijk and Brown (1980).

TABLE 6.2. Fast growth constellation: annual percentage growth of output and exports, 1837–1846 to 1866–1874

Sector	Production	Exports
Core inputs		
Coal	4.0	8.3
Iron and steel	5.4	4.8
Carrier branch		
Machinery	5.1	5.1
Carrier branch and infrastructure		
Rail transport		
Freight	12.5	—
Passengers	8.9	—
Earlier leading sector		
Cotton	3.9	4.3
All industries	(2.8)[a]	(4.6)[a]

[a] Authors' own estimates.

Source: Coppock (1963: 223).

TABLE 6.3. Railway building in the early industrializers, 1830–1850 (cumulative kilometres opened)

Km of line opened by end	Britain[a]	France	Germany	USA	Belgium
1830	157	31	—	37	—
1831	225	31	—	153	—
1832	267	52	—	369	—
1833	335	73	—	612	—
1834	480	141	—	1,019	—
1835	544	141	6	1,767	20
1836	649	141	6	2,049	44
1837	870	159	21	2,410	142
1838	1,196	159	140	3,079	258
1839	1,562	224	240	3,705	312
1840	2,390	410	469	4,535	334
1841	2,858	548	683	5,689	379
1842	3,122	645	931	6,479	439
1843	3,291	743	1,311	6,735	558
1844	3,500	822	1,752	7,044	577
1845	3,931	875	2,143	7,456	577
1846	4,889	1,049	3,281	7,934	594
1847	6,352	1,511	4,306	9,009	691
1848	8,022	2,004	4,989	9,650	780
1849	8,918	2,467	5,443	11,853	796
1850	9,797	2,915	5,856	14,518	854

[a] Ireland is included in the British figures for 1831–9 and 1841–7.

Source: Tylecote (1992: 201).

widths and depths and much inefficient routing, which caused considerable delays and trans-shipment. All this was to be duplicated on an even larger scale with the railways, including the liability of over-investment when capital was cheap and the expectations of potential shareholders uncritically optimistic. (Mathias 1969/1983: 105)

The supersession of one transport or energy infrastructure by another can by its nature never be an overnight event (Grübler 1990). What happens, rather, is that the limitations of one network become increasingly apparent and the demand for new facilities accumulates until the feasibility of an alternative and/or additional network becomes apparent. The Liverpool–Manchester Railway was the event that fired the public imagination and the entrepreneurial spirit on the necessary scale for new investment. In the 1820s, Huskisson promoted the Liverpool–Manchester Railway Bill through Parliament on the grounds that the canals held the merchants and manufacturers to ransom and that cotton took longer to get from Liverpool to Manchester than from New Orleans to Liverpool. Canal tolls were cut from 15/- per ton to 10/- per ton as soon as the railway opened in 1830 (Mathias 1969/1983: 252). Higher speed, greater regularity, and greater reliability were among the major advantages of railways for much commerce, while canals and roads were affected adversely by frost and other hazards of the weather.

The advantages for passenger traffic were even greater, and the big surprise of the 1830s and 1840s was that passenger traffic initially grew faster than freight. Fares were much lower than by mail-coach and 400,000 people travelled on the Liverpool–Manchester line in its first year of operation. It was not only the comfort of travellers and the big saving in fares that led to this change, but also the needs of commerce. Wedgwood had already introduced a code of practice for his travelling salesmen in the eighteenth century, and by the 1830s many industries depended on the efforts and speed of their commercial travellers and executives. These competitive pressures and requirements of business are omitted from the calculations of cliometrics but were of great economic and social significance, just as airlines are today.

Of course, as has often been shown, the early railways were far from being an 'optimal' investment and suffered from many shortcomings. Moreover, the number of horses in use on British roads in the nineteenth century continued to increase since they were needed more than ever for the journeys beyond the railway stations. Canals continued to be more convenient for some freight transport because of the failure of the new rail networks to connect some important transport nodes. Only much later were other serious deficiencies of the early British railway investment to be fully revealed, such as the selection of a narrow gauge for most railways instead of Brunel's broad gauge. As Landes (1969) pointed out, this also affected the efficiency of industries such as iron and steel because of the small capacity of the freight-wagons compared with the German or American railways.

As Chapter 1 has shown, some cliometricians have belittled the contribution of railways to British (or American) economic development and have sought to erect a fantasy quantitative 'counterfactual' based on the notion that if railways had not come into existence canals and roads could have done the job with relatively small losses to GDP. Following Fogel's work on US railways, G. R. Hawke (1970) calculated the 'social savings' from British railways (i.e. the gains from carrying passengers and freight on the railways compared with the extra costs that would have been borne by moving the same traffic by canal and road) as 4.1 per cent of GNP for freight, and either 2.6 per cent or 7.1 per cent of GNP for passenger traffic, depending on how 'comfort' is costed.

Mathias (1969/1983: 257) dismisses such calculations out of hand, arguing that it is 'impossible to quantify the total gains which railways brought to the British economy' and that 'the importance of the coming of the railways as a service for the economy as a whole lies in the fact that they enabled economic activity in all other sectors of the economy to expand'. This standpoint is fully consistent with our notion of a carrier branch at the heart of a constellation of fast-growing industries and a 'veritable incarnation of a technological revolution'.

The extraordinarily strong impact of the railways on the social and economic development of the country is apparent not only from economic statistics, but also from art and literature. Turner's famous painting 'Rain, Steam and Speed' is only the best-known of a large number of examples of railway art inspired by the sight of the new locomotives. A woman who observed Turner on the railway journey that inspired the painting has described how he jumped up to open the window, 'craning his head out and finally calling to her to come and observe a curious effect of light. A train was coming in their direction, through the blackness, over one of Brunel's bridges, and the effect of the locomotive, lit by the crimson flame and seen through driving rain and whirling tempest, gave a peculiar impression of power, speed and stress' (Faith 1990: 52).

Wordsworth is, of course, equally well known for his dislike of railways, although this too illustrates their dramatic impact on social life. Other poets were inspired by railway journeys and some even attributed erotic imagery to the locomotives.[1] Later on, Conan Doyle was to give railway journeys a central and regular place in many of his Sherlock Holmes stories. By that time, railways were simply an accepted part of everyday life.

While it is true that canals and roads continued to carry much traffic, after the 1840s almost the whole of the increase in traffic was carried by the railways, both in Europe and in North America. Patrick O'Brien (1994: 259), in his paper on 'Transport and Economic Development in Europe 1789–1914', writes: 'networks of lines across Europe rising from nearly 3,000 kms of track in 1840 to 362,000 kms by 1913 placed railway companies in a

---

[1] Much later, Freud himself was to insist on the 'exquisite sexual symbolism' of railway travel and to attribute the widespread desire of boys to be engine drivers to the pleasurable sensations of movement in rail travel (Faith 1990: 48). A more common interpretation was in terms of the relatively high wages, secure employment, and social status of drivers at that time.

position to provide nearly all the additional passenger-kilometres sold to consumers of travel . . . They also met the demand for an extremely high proportion of the extra ton-kilometres supplied for the transport of freight.'

Not only did the railways carry almost the whole of the increase in transport services all over Europe for this long period, but transport services as a whole were rapidly increasing as a share of GDP. O'Brien estimates that this share more than doubled between 1840 and 1913 and attributes this to the high passenger income elasticity of demand, together with the fact that both internal and foreign trade increased more rapidly than output of goods.

All the beneficial effects of widening markets identified by Adam Smith for scale economies and specialization were realized more rapidly with railways than with the earlier canal networks: 'it is certainly evident that real costs per passenger-kilometre and per ton-kilometre of transport services fell sharply with the diffusion of railways and steam locomotives' (O'Brien 1994: 256).

O'Brien points not only to these direct benefits to all sectors of the economy from the construction of railway networks, but also to many of the indirect benefits, often omitted from the calculations made by cliometricians, but crucial for our analysis. For example, he highlights the role of the railways (and also of the canals at one time) in training many kinds of labour—engineers, foremen, and managers 'whose skills (initially acquired in transportation) contributed to the development of other industries'. Chandler (1965; Chandler and Hikino 1977) takes this point much further, arguing that the American railways provided the first example for the whole of the American business community of how to manage and run very large organizations, with attention to long-term costing, maintenance, and depreciation, as well as to the recruitment, training, and deployment of personnel. The railways were also important in establishing workshops for the repair, maintenance, and manufacture of components and equipment (Usselman 1999; Atack 1999). These were often the equivalent of quite large engineering firms and in some ways amounted to an internalized R&D department, even though they did not bear that name and research was not their main activity. As we shall see in Chapter 7, Andrew Carnegie, the most successful entrepreneur in the American steel industry in the third Kondratiev wave, attributed his success to the experience he had in management as a young man working on the American railways.

The first great British railway promoter—George Hudson—who epitomized 'the very archetype of the vulgar swaggering adventurer bred world-wide by the railways' (Faith 1990)—set out to build an enormous empire based on numerous amalgamations, and on fraudulent transactions in land, railways, docks, and finance. He was the focus of great attention from the media at the time of the 1840s railway boom and survived the crash of 1847 only to fall two years later. Although he controlled nearly a third of the 5,000 miles of British railways, he did not control some of the key lines and his fraud was ultimately discovered and exposed.

The huge scale and intensity of the railway mania of 1844–5 has been well described by P. J. G. Ransom:

The bubble of financial speculation that was called the Railway mania was inflating wildly. It was much helped by the activities of men such as George Hudson . . . For a railway company promoter, a judiciously spread rumour that Hudson 'The Railway King' was interested could send the price of shares soaring. Railway promotion, originally a matter for routes where the need was evident and the engineering practicable, had spread first to routes where demand was doubtful and the engineering full of problems . . . But then promotion had spread still further. . . . With the public clamouring for railway shares, companies now were being formed solely so that promoters might in due course unload their shares at a premium, leaving others to hold their unlikely babies. (Ransom 1990: 86)

It was this type of promotion that led to the low esteem of the public for railway entrepreneurs and promoters and to the special role of railway shares in Lewis Carroll's poem 'The Hunting of the Snark'. However, the genuine railways, as they came into existence, were certainly popular, and it was the railway engineers and engineer-entrepreneurs who were national heroes. Men like Brunel and Stephenson embodied the spirit of creative enterprise to a far greater extent than promoters like Hudson. Stephenson's funeral in 1848 was attended by over 100,000 people, a tribute to an engineer never witnessed before or since in Britain. Thus, the contribution of the railways to a new model of large-scale business activity, although tarnished by promoters like Hudson, was by no means extinguished. Employment on the railways was much sought after and, for the time, relatively well rewarded. They were the model of progressive business.

Despite its excesses, the mania for railway shares led in the end to the construction of a national network, which in 1846–8 accounted for about half of total investment in Britain and a labour force of 250,000 people working on construction. This was of course at the peak of the boom, but the numbers in regular employment on the railway system itself continued to grow fast. Mathias (1969/1983: 259) estimated investment in fixed capital in railways in the 1860s boom as a quarter of the total and still over 10 per cent in the 1870s. Railway investment on any method of calculation imparted a tremendous stimulus to the growth of the national economy. (See Gourvish (1980) for various slightly differing estimates.) Hawke's estimates for the growth of traffic (Figures 6.1, 6.2, and 6.3) are somewhat lower than those of Coppock (1963) (Table 6.2), especially for freight, but are nevertheless very impressive.

Among the characteristics of an efficient business enterprise that were fostered and diffused by the railways, and which today we take for granted, were such elementary practices as a high level of punctuality, forward planning of services, regular maintenance, control of competent specialists for subcontracting, and speed of delivery for both goods and travellers. The railways also developed methods, which were so important for the large-scale enterprises of the late nineteenth century, of controlling operations at many different locations from a single centre. All of these were facilitated by another major technical and organizational innovation—the electric telegraph, invented by Wheatstone, a professor at King's College London in 1837 and diffused extremely rapidly alongside the new railway tracks in the 1840s. Numerous other innovations, in signalling equipment, in rolling stock, and in civil engineering for tunnels and embankments, were made by or for the railway companies and their numerous suppliers all over the country. With what E. P. Thompson called the 'enormous condescension of posterity', it is easy to over-look these achievements, often now so obvious that they are hardly noticed.

O'Brien notes other indirect effects of railway investment:

Accelerated rates of capital formation which took place in transport sectors throughout Europe in the nineteenth century also gave rise to a range of externalities, or spin-offs, which are not captured either in the declining real prices of transport services, or changes in the structure of relative prices. For example . . . canals and later railways made voracious demands for capital over relatively short periods of time which prompted the expansion and improvement of financial intermediaries for the mobilization of domestic and foreign savings. Once established, such institutions continued to meet the needs of other sectors of the economy. (O'Brien 1994: 254)

The more direct backward linkages of the railways to the coal, iron, and engineering industries are more easily assessed and are reviewed in the following subsections. Again, the *qualitative* changes in the ways of organizing production were more important than the simple *quantities* of coal or iron transported or consumed by the railways. It was the railways that made it possible to diffuse a new technological style based on coal, iron, and the steam engine throughout the Victorian economy. They may deservedly be viewed in every sense as the 'carrier branch' of the second Kondratiev. This applies *a fortiori* to the American railways, which will be discussed in Section 6.6.

6.3 Core Inputs: Coal and Iron

Some accounts of railway development stress that the steam locomotives of the railway boom themselves consumed only a relatively small proportion of total coal consumption—probably less than 2 per cent. However, this way of looking at the 'backward linkage' ignores two main features of the link between coal and railways. First, it neglects the demonstration effect—the fact that all over the country people could see the power of the steam engine fuelled by coal in a spectacular form. Second, and even more importantly, the railways made coal universally available to all kinds of other users and at a lower price than hitherto. In fact, as we shall see, steam locomotives and iron rails were developed between 1800 and 1830 mainly to haul coal.

Coal was not one of those inputs with a steeply falling price based on technical innovations. Steam engines were used in the mines for pumping from early in the eighteenth century (Newcomen engines) and, although coal mining remained one of the major markets for steam engines, technical change in coal mining itself was relatively slow. The price of coal did fall in many areas in the early nineteenth century, but this was due far more to improvements in transport, including the railways, than to innovations in mining (Table 6.4). Geological conditions imposed a constant tendency for costs to increase in many coalfields.

The case of iron was very different. As already shown in Chaper 5 (Figure 5.2), the price of iron fell substantially both during and after the Napoleonic Wars as a result primarily of technical innovations (coke smelting and Cort's puddling and rolling process). Both of these innovations depended on the availability of plentiful coal supplies. The reduction in transport costs certainly benefited iron production and facilitated the continuing fall in the price of iron, especially of heavy duty wrought iron for the manufacture of iron rails, first demonstrated in 1821 by Birkinshaw (Tylecote 1992). The use of better steam engines for blowing in blast furnaces, and for steam hammers in forges, also contributed to the falling cost of iron products.

Whereas for coal the direct consumption by the railways was less than 2 per cent of total output, for the iron industry it was a far higher proportion—about a quarter of domestic sales in 1840 and nearly half of total consumption at the peak of the railway construction boom in 1848. After 1850, the share of railway consumption in domestic sales of iron fell to about 10 per cent or just over. But this was largely offset by a big rise in railway exports. These were separately measured only from 1856, but the combined home and export sales of iron to railways accounted for over 20 per cent of total sales from 1856 to 1870. These exports were not included in G. R. Hawke's (1970) estimate of 'social savings' (Riden 1980). After 1870, *steel* rails became a core input for the third Kondratiev, and, as will be shown in Chapter 7, the falling price and universal availability of steel was a major feature of that new constellation of fast-growing industries.

What the railways did was to make coal and iron (and later steel) available as cheap inputs in all the industrializing areas of Britain, and only a little

TABLE 6.4. Coal prices in Britain by region, 1800–1850 (shillings per ton)

	London	Birmingham		Manchester	
1800	46	9		16	
1810	38	12		13	(1813)
1820	31	13		10	(1823)
1830	26	6	(1832)	10	(1833)
1840	22	8		7	(1841)
1850	16	5		6	

Source: von Tunzelmann (1978: 96).

later now in other European countries. Even outside the industrial areas, coal and/or coal gas became the preferred fuels for domestic heating as the distribution networks extended their range. The fact that coal and iron became available almost everywhere meant that the engineering industry could develop in new centres, for example around London, Berlin, and Paris. As Tylecote (1992: 46) puts it, 'steam-powered machinery was liberated in its location; coal could be hauled reasonably cheaply to any railhead, to provide power for factories of any size. Thus the spread of steam on wheels assisted the spread of stationary steam.'

Cotton retained its extraordinary lead in British exports right down to the 1920s (Table 6.5 and Figure 6.5), but between 1830 and 1860 the *share* of iron increased while that of cotton was falling. Exports of machinery and of coal also grew rapidly in the second half of the nineteenth century, but their importance for the domestic economy was far greater. While coal could be regarded as a second 'core input' after iron, the engineering industry, to which we now turn, was in some respects another carrier branch of the second Kondratiev wave, together with the railways.

6.4 Steam Engines, Machine Tools, and the Engineering Industry

In assessing the contribution of the steam engine to the Industrial Revolution, David Landes wrote: 'The development of mechanized industry concentrated in large units of production would have been impossible without a source of power greater than what human and animal strength could provide and independent of the vagaries of nature . . . Coal and steam did not make the Industrial Revolution, but they permitted its extraordinary development and diffusion' (Landes 1969: 41).

The relatively slow diffusion of the steam engine, including the Watt engine, in the early period of the first Kondratiev wave appears to have been due mainly both to the technical limitations and to the high costs of these engines. The Watt patents, which were extended by Parliament for a very long period, also constrained inventive and innovative activity, so that at the turn of the century the number of applications was still relatively small. It was between 1800 and 1850 that the major technical advances were made which reduced the cost and improved the performance of the steam engine to the point where it could be very widely applied both for transport and for stationary engines. It was the sequence of innovations in the machine tool industry in this period, but especially between 1800 and 1830, that made it possible to construct high pressure engines which were both safer and far more efficient. The reduction in coal consumption (in pounds of coal per hour per HP) is shown in Table 6.6. Von Tunzelmann (1978) estimated that still less than a quarter of cotton output came from steam-powered mills in 1800 and that the costs of water power and steam were about the same in that year. Several of the leading cotton

TABLE 6.5. Exports from the United Kingdom, 1830–1938[a] (current prices)[b]

	Textiles (total)		Cottons		Iron and steel, etc.		Machinery		Coal		Vehicles, etc.		Total
	(£m)	(%)	(£m)	(%)	(£m)	(%)	(£m)	(%)	(£m)	(%)	(£m)	(%)	(£m)
1830–9	31.7	72	20.9	48	5.0	11	0.3	1	0.3	1	—		43.9
1840–9	38.2	69	24.6	44	8.2	15	0.8	1	0.9	2	—		55.4
1850–9	59.9	60	35.6	36	17.9	18	2.4	2	2.3	2	—		100.1
1860–9	98.5	62	57.6	36	24.0	15	4.6	3	4.5	3	—		159.7
1870–9	118.6	54	71.5	33	35.0	16	7.7	4	8.8	4	—		218.1
1880–9	113.8	49	73.0	32	35.3	15	11.8	5	10.5	5	—		230.3
1890–9	104.3	44	67.2	28	32.5	14	16.1	7	17.5	7	1.1	0	237.1
1900–9	126.2	38	86.4	26	45.7	14	23.8	7	32.9	10	8.4	3	333.3
1910–19	200.2	40	135.0	27	62.9	12	27.0	5	50.0	10	9.4	2	504.6
1920–9	288.9	37	192.7	24	96.5	12	58.1	7	65.2	8	29.4	4	791.4
1930–9	106.0	24	62.8	14	54.1	12	41.8	10	37.7	9	24.8	6	438.8

[a] Annual averages per decade.
[b] Groupings for categories listed: Textiles (total): cotton, woollens, linen, silk, hats, haberdashery, apparel, etc.; Iron and steel: iron and steel, hardware, cutlery, non-ferrous metals and manufactures; Vehicles etc: vehicles, aircraft, new ships and boats.

Source: Mitchell and Deane (1962: 282–4, 302–6); Mathias (1983: 432).

entrepreneurs, including Arkwright himself, the Peels, and Major Cartwright, were involved in costly failures with early steam mills, while others complained of maintenance and running costs far in excess of water wheels (Chapman 1972/1992: 19). The big fall in costs of steam power and the big rise in the use of steam engines, especially in weaving, came after 1835, and in von Tunzelmann's view it was the use of high-pressure engines that had the greatest effect. These were originally developed in the Cornish tin mining industry by Trevithick and others (Table 6.1).

Some users of water power had built their mills on particularly favourable sites and disliked the intrusive competition of steam power. For them this was not simply a question of economic or technical advantages; such considerations were reinforced by cultural and political factors. Indeed, in some cases resistance to the adoption of steam power persisted in spite of the clear possibility of making larger profits by adoption of the new technology. Sejerstedt (1998) has provided a particularly good example of this in the case of the Norwegian sawmill industry in the 1840s and 1850s. At that time this was the main export industry in Norway, and the mills that were licensed for export of timber enjoyed a special privileged position dating back to the eighteenth century or even earlier. The system of regulation came under attack from liberals and advocates of steam power from early in the nineteenth century, but, despite a succession of inquiries by various commissions and committees, was not finally abolished until 1860. Sejerstedt points to the example of one sawmill owner called Christopher Tostrup, who was a leading opponent of deregulation but who, after the political battle was lost, built a large new steam-powered mill which became one of the most profitable enterprises:

Tostrup identified himself with the old production system, or with the privileged group of sawmill owners. We must understand his motives as a businessman within this social

TABLE 6.6. Coal consumption in various types of steam engine in manufacturing applications

Type of steam engine	Pounds of coal per hour per HP
Savery engine (18th century)	30
Newcomen engine (mines) (1700–50)	20–30
Newcomen engine (1790)	17
Watt low-pressure engines (1800–40)	10–15
High-pressure engines (1850)	5

Source: von Tunzelmann (1978: 68–70).

and cultural framework. Within the system he pursued the maximization of profit in competition with the other mills. However, when faced with a more fundamental threat against the system which gave him his success, he put aside the consideration of profit maximization and replaced it with the aim of preserving the system. In short, this is a beautiful example of how rationality somehow has to be bounded. (Sejerstedt 1998: 238)

Furthermore, the deregulation, when it came, was pushed through by the Norwegian state against the opposition of the owners in the name of modernization and technical progress.

Problems of regulation were also involved when it came to the construction of railways in Britain, since each new railway required a special parliamentary bill. This procedure was attended by an enormous amount of lobbying by landowners and other special interests. Parliament had passed 23 bills authorizing public railways before the Stockton–Darlington railway was promoted in 1823. Most of these were short horse tramways with a length of 15 miles or less, and almost all were to haul coal. Half a dozen engineers were striving to adapt the steam engine to haul locomotives, and it was George Stephenson who was the most successful of these. 'By throwing the exhaust steam up the boiler-fire chimney the power of the fire and steam-raising capacity were much increased. This did for the locomotive what Watt's separate condenser had done for the steam engine in the 1770s' (Mathias 1969/1983: 255).

Mathias concluded that 'successful innovation came after a ferment of experimenting in different parts of the country'. Almost all the experiments were inspired by the desire to improve the haulage of coal and were conducted in colliery areas, often by mining engineers. George Stephenson himself was completely self-taught and worked as a boy with his father, who was the fireman tending a pumping engine at a Newcastle colliery. Inspired by the ideal of building a steam locomotive, he started a factory in Newcastle for this purpose in 1823, with his own son, Robert.

However, it was Trevithick, a former wrestler, who designed the first steam locomotives between 1802 and 1805 (Table 6.1), and who almost certainly inspired Stephenson's later superior design. Stephenson took a leading part in both track and locomotive design for the Stockton–Darlington railway, and when the Liverpool–Manchester Railway was due to open his 'Rocket' locomotive won the competition organized for the best locomotive design at the Rainhill trials. Before this, the gradients were too steep for the earlier designs of locomotive to compete and short railways used stationary engines and/or horses for these stretches. The Stockton–Darlington Railway in 1825 also used horses and winding gear as well as Stephenson's engine (called 'Locomotion'). In 1826, Stephenson had already asked one of his engineers to make detailed comparisons of the costs per ton-mile of fixed engines, locomotives, and horses. The 1829 Rainhill trials and the first year of operation on the Liverpool–Manchester Railway were the decisive events that demonstrated to the public at large, as well as to engineers and railway companies, that steam locomotives were the power of the future. The combination of technical and cost advantages had become decisive by that time (see Table 1 in the Introduction to Part II).

It had become possible to design and make far better steam engines, not because later engineers were more brilliant than James Watt, but in large part because of advances in machine tool technology and in the precision of engineering. In particular, the boring of cylinders to precise dimensions was essential for the high-pressure engines that powered locomotives. As already described in Section 5.3 above, John Wilkinson's boring machine, patented in 1775, played a crucial role in the improvement of the performance of the Boulton and Watt steam engine. Wilkinson's machine was only the first of a whole series of machine tool innovations which were already the object of design and development work by engineers in the late eighteenth century, but it was the establishment of a specialized machine tool industry led by Henry Maudslay (1771–1831) that was decisive for making high-performance machines powered by steam generally available. Between 1800 and 1830, Maudslay's factory became a Mecca for most of the best engineers in the country, including Roberts, Nasmyth, and Whitworth, each of whom was responsible for major innovations.

Iron firms often went into the manufacture of boilers, engines, and machines, and according to Musson (1980), this close association continued right down to 1870. However, as Musson points out, it was the emergence of *specialist* machine tool firms that led to the widespread diffusion of the 'machines to make machines'. It was this technology that Paulinyi (1989) has described as the 'Alpha and Omega' of the Industrial Revolution. Maudslay pioneered vital measurement instruments and techniques essential for high-precision work, including gauges, true-planes, and screw-making tackle, and in the 1820s, Roberts was already selling standard gear-wheels and screws together with machine tools from his Manchester factory. He 'developed standardized production of mules and looms using templates and gauges, and later applied the same technique to locomotive manufacture' (Musson 1980: 91).

N. Rosenberg (1963) is justly well known for his account of specialization in the American machine tool industry and its crucial role in American industrialization. However, Musson claims that it was in fact the British machine tool industry that pioneered 'mass production', and that Rosenberg was mistaken in attributing priority to the 'American system of manufactures' for small arms production.

Most famous of all was Whitworth, with his machine tools and precision engineering, the supreme practitioner and propagandist of standard measurements, gauges and screwthreads, mass production and interchangeability, from the late 1830s right on throughout the third quarter of the century. By the late 1850s he was able to claim, and it was generally recognized, that these methods had been widely, indeed almost universally, adopted in heavy engineering. (Musson 1980: 92)

Musson maintains that the American pre-eminence was in *light* engineering, whereas the British lead was clear-cut in interchangeable parts and mass production for heavy engineering, going right back to block-making for the Navy. Maudslay constructed all the block-making machines designed by Brunel for the Admiralty plant in Portsmouth between 1802 and 1809. In 1810 this plant was making 100,000 blocks per annum and was the first large-scale plant employing machine tools for mass production. With these machines, ten unskilled men could do the work of 110 skilled block-workers. Apart from two large sawing machines, all the others were of metal and precise in operation to allow the assembly of component parts (Corry 1990).

Thus, by 1820 the development of true-planing of metal surfaces and of slotting and shaping machines had already eliminated much costly filing, chiselling, and hand grinding. In Musson's view the British development of 'mass production' was not 'precocious', but simply reflected the fact that 'mechanical engineering, particularly the development of machine tools, originated earlier and spread more extensively in Britain than in the USA, during the late eighteenth and first half of the nineteenth century. This is indeed what one would expect, since the Industrial Revolution occurred first in Britain' (Musson 1980: 91). Chapter 8 will review the concept of Fordist mass production and discuss this in relation to such earlier systems as the British engineering industry and what is often known as 'the American system of production'.

By 1870 the official statistics (Returns of Factory Employment) showed that 167,000 people were engaged in the 'manufacture of machinery'. They were employed in 2,000 factories with steam engines deploying 42,000 horsepower. Both the railways and the cotton industry employed more people than this, but the role of the machine-building industry in providing engines and machinery for mechanizing these and other sectors gave it a unique importance.

6.5 Steam Ships, Iron Ships, and Shipping

In the 1830s and 1840s, the British ship-building industry had lost out in competition with American shipyards, which were designing and building longer and deeper sailing ships. According to Mathias (1969/1983: 286) American ships had smaller crews, but sailed faster and carried more cargo. He estimates that British ships were twenty years behind American ones in design in this period, and American ships carried three-quarters of the Anglo-American trade.

It was the iron steamship that restored the British competitive position and made ship-building and shipping two of the most successful British industries in the closing decades of the nineteenth century. Brunel was not only a great railway engineer and bridge builder: he also designed some of the first steamships, including the Great Western (1837) which established the transatlantic steam service to New York, and the Great Eastern (1858), of 19,000 tons, which had both a screw propeller and paddle wheels to provide extra power. The iron screw propeller was invented simultaneously in 1836 by Francis Smith in England and John Ericsson in Sweden. Admiralty trials in the 1840s established the clear superiority of the screw propeller and led to the dominance of steam and iron. The establishment of a global network of coaling stations and huge improvements in engine design consolidated the British lead in iron steamships. By 1890 Britain had more registered tonnage than the rest of the world put together, and between 1892 and 1896 nearly 80 per cent of merchant tonnage launched came from British yards. However, it had taken a fairly long time for the steamship to defeat competition from the sailing ship, which also began to use iron hulls. The competitive innovations in sailing ships are sometimes described to this day as the 'sailing ship effect', to indicate this possibility in technological competition for a threatened industry. It was actually only in the 1870s that the steam tonnage exceeded the sailing ship tonnage launched from British yards (Figure 6.4). The basic innovations in iron steamships were British and were ultimately successful in driving the sailing ship out of world competition for all heavy cargoes. Out of 138 steamships of over 4,000 tons launched in 1883, 128 were British, and in 1887 Lyon Playfair wrote of the effects of the British innovation, the triple expansion engine:

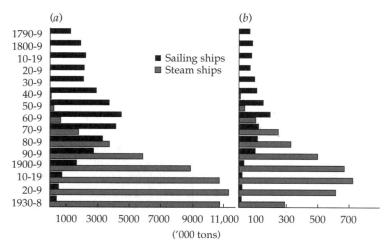

FIG 6.4. Steam ships and sailing ships: tonnage registered in Britain, 1790–1938

Notes

(a) Shipping tonnage registered in the United Kingdom.

(b) Ships built and first registered in Britain.

Source: Mathias (1969: 288).

Not long since a steamer of 3,000 tons going on a long voyage might require 2,200 tons of coal and carry only a limited cargo of 800 tons. Now a modern steamer will make the same voyage with 800 tons of coal and carry a freight of 2,200 tons. While coal has been economized, human labour has been lessened. In 1870, it required 47 hands on board our steamships for every 1,000 tons' capacity. Now only 28 are necessary. (Court 1965: 165)

While other British industries suffered in world competition in the 1880s and 1890s (Figure 6.5), ship-building did well right down to the First World War, but the main benefit to the British economy came from the effect of this industry on shipping. Where trade was carried in British ships, the revenue from many other financial and commercial services benefited the British balance of payments and the City of London. The repeal of the Navigation Acts in 1849 did not have catastrophic effects on British shipping, mainly because of the iron steamship. In 1910 over 40 per cent of all tonnage entered and cleared in world trade was still British, and British ships remained the carriers of the world down to the serious losses of tonnage in the submarine warfare of the First World War. The British government's support for the establishment of four subsequently famous shipping companies in 1839 and 1840 proved a highly successful policy, reinforced by the rapid growth of foreign trade in the 1850s and 1860s (Figure 6.5).

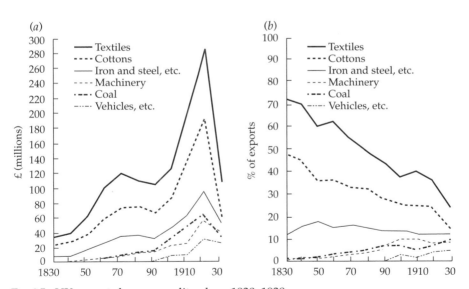

FIG 6.5. UK exports by commodity class, 1830–1938

Notes

(*a*) Exports.

(*b*) Percentage of total exports.

Source: Mathias (1969: 285).

6.6 The Railroads and Catch-up by the United States

The account given in Chapter 5 concentrated on the British case, since it was only in Britain that we can speak of a 'first Kondratiev wave' and Britain was also the leading country in the second wave (Tables 5.7 and 5.8). However, by 1870 British supremacy was coming to an end. Between 1870 and 1913, the United States overtook Britain and forged ahead in terms of productivity and rate of growth of the economy (Table 6.7). This section, therefore, no longer concentrates primarily on Britain but shifts the focus to the United States.

In the first half of the nineteenth century, despite a rich endowment of natural resources and many favourable institutions, growth in the United States was still retarded by the lack of an appropriate transport infrastructure to take advantage of the natural endowment and size of the country and its market. The advent of railways and the new technologies of the late nineteenth century enabled it to forge far ahead of the rest of the world. At first, the United States imported much of this technology, as well as much capital and labour, from Europe, but from the very beginning American inventors modified and reshaped these technologies to suit American circumstances. By the end of the century, American engineers and scientists were developing new processes and products in most industries that were more productive than those in Britain.

As argued in Chapter 5, among those institutions most favourable to economic growth in eighteenth-century Britain were the scientific spirit, which was influential in the national culture, and the support for technical invention. These features were readily transferred to the United States, and respect for science and technology has been an enduring feature of American society from Benjamin Franklin onwards. As de Tocqueville observed in his classic on *Democracy in America* (1836: 315), 'In America the purely practical part of science is admirably understood and careful attention is paid to the theoretical position which is immediately requisite to application. On this head the Americans always display a free, original and inventive power of mind.'

The relative abundance of land, the westward moving frontier, the destruction of the native civilizations or their confinement to a relatively

TABLE 6.7. Relative productivity levels, various countries, 1870–1950 (US GDP per hour = 100)

	1870	1913	1950
UK	104	78	57
France	56	48	40
Germany	50	50	30
15 countries	51	33	36

Source: Abramovitz and David (1994: 9).

small part of the territory—all favoured a purely capitalist form of economic development. The big exception to these generalizations was of course the slave economy of the South.

It is difficult to assess the degree to which the economic growth of the South in particular and of the Union in general was retarded by the prevalence of this slave economy,[2] but it was in the period that followed the victory of the North in the Civil War that the United States achieved rates of growth well above any previously achieved by Britain. Even after its abolition, slavery left an enduring legacy of social and economic problems, some of which persist to this day, but the maintenance of the Union meant that the predominantly modern capitalist path of development in the North and West prevailed throughout the country. In these circumstances, an entrepreneurial culture could flourish as nowhere else. The United States overtook Britain and all other industrial countries in share of world manufacturing output between 1860 and 1900 (Table 5.7).

In their analysis of the sources of economic growth, Abramovitz and David argue that the higher relative price of labour in North America induced substitution of capital and natural resource inputs for skilled labour. This stimulated, as early as the first half of the nineteenth century, the development of a specific American labour-saving, capital-intensive technological trajectory of mechanization and standardized production. As the nineteenth century advanced, 'the engineering techniques of large-scale production and high throughput rates became more fully explored and more widely diffused. American managers became experienced in the organization, finance and operation of large enterprises geared to creating and exploiting mass markets' (Abramowitz and David 1994: 10).

The extent to which this specific American trajectory of capital-intensive technology diverged from that of Europe (and Japan) can be clearly seen from Table 6.8. Until the 1880s, Great Britain still had an overall capital–labour ratio higher than that of the United States, but by 1938, like all other countries, the ratio had fallen to less than half of the US ratio. The large cost reductions and productivity gains associated with this North American technological trajectory can be illustrated from numerous industrial sectors. The extraordinary productivity gains in mining and mineral processing are emphasized in particular by Abramovitz and David (1994). Gavin Wright (1999) has shown that the education and professional standards of mining engineers and other engineers were one of the main factors in sustaining the high rate of technical change in these industries. They were especially important in the design and scaling up of large plants for steel, non-ferrous

---

[2] That it *was* retarded was recognized even by those cliometricians who took the slavery example as one of the main illustrations for their theory. They argued that both slaves and slave-owners were motivated by essentially similar motives to those of the workers and entrepreneurs of industrial capitalism. But Fogel (1966: 646) nevertheless conceded that, 'although slavery was a viable economic system, it could nevertheless have thwarted economic growth in the South by reducing the saving rate or by stifling entrepreneurship'.

TABLE 6.8. Comparative levels of capital–labour ratios, various countries, 1870–1950 (USA=100)

	Germany	Italy	UK	Avg. of 13 European countries	Japan
1870	73	—	117	—	—
1880	73	26	106	68	12
1913	60	24	59	48	10
1938	42	32	43	39	13
1950	46	31	46	39	13

Source: Abramovitz and David (1994: 8).

metals, oil, and chemicals. Steel, copper, and electricity are the main focus of the account that follows in Chapter 7, because they were the key elements in the new constellation of fast-growing industries and technologies at the heart of the third Kondratiev wave.

Whereas in the early period of railway construction Britain was the source of much of the capital invested in the American railways and of the iron rails themselves, as well as most of the major inventions, as the American railway network expanded the role of American capital, entrepreneurship, innovations, and equipment became predominant. Cornelius Vanderbilt was rather more successful than George Hudson had been in Britain as a railway magnate. Before his death in 1877 he amassed a fortune of over $100 million from his operations in shipping and railways, which he passed on to his son, William Henry Vanderbilt, who doubled this fortune from railways, leading the fight against government regulation. Alfred Chandler's (1965) study of *The Railroads: The Nation's First Big Business* shows how important their development was for American management methods, and Chapter 7 illustrates this point with the example of Andrew Carnegie, the leading entrepreneur in the steel industry. The huge scale of American railway construction and traffic provided opportunities for many other industries supplying rails, engineering products, brass, felt, timber, and components throughout the second half of the nineteenth century. About 2,000 miles of track were added each year on average to the US rail network in the 1850s and the 1860s, despite the Civil War, and this rose to over 5,000 miles of new track each year in the early 1870s. This huge expansion of track mileage continued right up to the First World War, albeit at a slower rate. Chandler (1965: 22) estimates that by the 1860s the railways were using half the iron rolled in the United States and, by 1880, three-quarters of all the steel produced there.

The complementarities between the growth of railways and the coal and iron industries were even greater in the United States than they had been in Britain because of the huge trans-continental scale of American railway construction and operation. Nor did Germany, France, and Belgium differ very substantially with respect to the role of railways, coal, and iron in the third quarter of the nineteenth century. This constellation was characteristic of all those industrializing countries that made substantial progress with 'catch-up' in the nineteenth century. In Belgium in particular, these three industries dominated economic development and the complementarities between the three were extremely close (Boschma 1999).

While Fogel (1964) has contested the views of Chandler and other historians on the importance of the railways in the growth of the American economy, he nevertheless admits that 'the idea of a crucial nexus between the railroad and the forward surge of the American economy following 1840 appears to be supported by an avalanche of factual evidence' (Fogel 1962: 164). He cites Savage's comment in his *Economic History of Transport* (Savage 1959) that the 'influence of the railroad can hardly be over-estimated', and Rostow's (1960) view that the 'railroad was historically the most powerful single initiator of take-offs' and that it led to the rapid development of the coal, iron, and engineering industries. In disputing these widely held views, Fogel argues that association does not prove causality and that his 'social savings' technique demonstrates the possibility of a 'counterfactual' account based on the continued predominance of canals and water transport. While it is true that canals, lakes, and rivers continued to be more important in the United States than in most European countries throughout the nineteenth century, it is hardly possible to deny that railways, together with the telegraph, brought great competitive advantages to many sectors of American industry and agriculture, notably in speed and reliability of transport and communication.

Chandler also stresses the complementarities between the railway and the telegraph in spreading simultaneously across the Continent and permitting control of rail operations *within* the network as well as huge externalities to third party users. He summarizes the combined effects of the railroad, the steamship, and the telegraph:

[They] made transportation and communication faster, cheaper and more certain than it had ever been before. The telegraph provided almost instantaneous communication to nearly every part of the nation, while the railroad and steamship permitted a fast and regular movement of mail . . .

Of still more significance was the impact these new firms had on the movement of goods and passengers. Speed and volume increased immediately. The rail-road reduced the time required for a trip from New York to Chicago from more than three weeks to less than three days. In the winter when the canals and rivers were frozen, the passage west by stage coach had taken even longer. For freight the shipping time had been greater than for passengers, and in the winter months only the lightest and most valuable types of freight could be moved at all. (Chandler 1965: 7)

It was the new regularity and volume of transportation and the greater certainty and accuracy of communication that made possible the growth of the factory system of production throughout the United States as well as the huge growth of wholesale and retail business in the cities. Fogel failed to take fully into account the critical importance of railways for the *stocks* of materials and components in industry and commerce and the reduction in costs of circulating capital.

Finally, Chandler argues that the most significant contribution of the railroads to the growth of the American (and indirectly the world) economy was in the sphere of institutional change, i.e. new patterns of finance, labour relations, management, competition, and government regulation: 'Railroad promoters and managers pioneered in all these areas not because they were a particularly intelligent or perceptive breed of entrepreneurs but because they had to. Their capitalization, their plant and equipment, their running expenses and labor force were much larger than those of any other business of that day' (Chandler 1965: 9).

Thus, there are ample reasons for regarding the railways in the United States, as in Britain and other European countries, as the carrier branch of the second Kondratiev wave, in the most literal sense as well as in many other senses. Marx concluded from his own analysis and experience of this period that 'it was only during the decade preceding 1866 that the construction of railways and ocean steamers on a stupendous scale called into existence the cyclopean machines now employed in the construction of prime movers' (Marx 1867: 41). Once established, the railway network also provided an infrastructure for the next great wave of structural change in the American economy.

6.7 The Structural Crisis of Adjustment in the 1870s, 1880s, and early 1890s

Some economists have interpreted the rapid growth of the American economy in the years after the Civil War of 1861–5 as evidence that there was no Kondratiev downswing at the close of the second Kondratiev wave, nor indeed any Kondratiev upswing from 1895 to 1913 (e.g. Solomou 1987). These arguments, based on the trends in aggregate GNP, ignore the structural crisis of adjustment experienced by the United States in the 1870s, 1880s, and early 1890s as in several West European countries. Major qualitative changes were taking place in these decades, and the recessions of the 1880s and 1894 were more severe than any experienced before. Moreover, unemployment first appeared as a serious phenomenon in the US economy during this period, and contemporaries had no hesitation in characterizing the period as one of 'depression'.

For example, David Wells in his fascinating book *Recent Economic Changes*, published in 1890, starts straight away with the following sentences:

The existence of a most curious and in many ways unprecedented disturbance and depression of trade, commerce and industry, which, first manifesting itself to a marked degree in 1873, has prevailed with fluctuations of intensity up to the present time [1889] is an economic and social phenomenon that has been everywhere recognized. Its most noteworthy peculiarity has been its universality . . . (D. A. Wells 1890: 1)

He goes on to consider the causes of these 'disturbances' and again has no hesitation in placing the main emphasis on technical and structural changes. He attributes the falling prices of the 1880s to the world-wide improvement in transportation, brought about by the railway, the steamship, and the telegraph and such huge projects as the Suez Canal (1869). He gives special emphasis to the advent of the Bessemer steel rail and what he calls 'the epoch of efficient machinery production', which has made possible the phenomenon of 'over-production' and excess capacity. Citing the example of copper, he mentions that

When in 1885 the United States produced and put on to the market seventy-four thousand tons as against forty thousand tons in 1882, the world's prices of copper greatly declined. A large number of the smaller producers were compelled to suspend operations or were entirely crushed; but the great Spanish and other important mines endeavoured 'to offset the diminution of profit on the unit of quantity' by increasing their production and thus the price of copper continued to decline until it reached a lower figure than ever before known in history. (D. A. Wells 1890: 74)

Wells concludes from the example of copper and other evidence that 'under such circumstances *industrial overproduction*—manifesting itself in excessive competition to effect sales and a reduction of prices below the cost of production—may become chronic and there appears to be no other means of avoiding such results than that the great producers should come to some understanding among themselves as to the prices they will ask; which in turn naturally implies arguments as to the extent which they will produce . . . ' (p. 74)

The copper industry was only one of a constellation of new industries experiencing rapid growth and technical change. So impressive were these changes that many observers, both at the time and since (e.g. Chandler), described them as a '*Second* Industrial Revolution'.[3]

Wells attributes the general instability, 'economic disturbances', and prevalence of unemployment in the 1880s to a combination of the achievements of a previous wave of technical change (railways, mechanization, steamships, etc.) and the rise of the new technologies and industries affecting the world economy—Bessemer steel, oil, electricity, copper smelting, and so forth. He argues that 'all investigators substantially agree that the depression of industry in recent years has been experienced with the greatest severity in those countries where machinery has been most extensively adopted' (D. A. Wells 1890: 68).

We have argued in the Introduction to Part II and in Chapter 5 that each crisis of structural adjustment in the economy is based on the conjuncture of the rapid rise from small beginnings of a constellation of new products, processes, and services and the slowing down of the impetus from a previous wave of

---

[3] This is not unreasonable, because, as we have argued earlier, the first and second Kondratiev waves were not really distinguishable outside Britain and would be regarded simply as the first Industrial Revolution. However, this nomenclature is sometimes a source of confusion since we, like other writers on long waves, describe the rise of electrification, steel, and copper as the 'third Kondratiev' wave.

technical change. In the period from the 1840s to the 1870s, both the United States and many European countries had experienced a boom based on railways, iron, steam power and mechanization. In the case of the United States, this was of course disrupted by the Civil War of 1861–5, but Wells was able to observe the exceptionally large productivity gains coming through in the postwar period, based on the huge improvements in the transport infrastructure and the technical changes introduced in many industries by capital-intensive mechanization. At the same time, he could see the employment displacing effects of this mechanization before the employment-creation effects of the new constellation had achieved a sufficient magnitude. The situation was analogous to the British crisis of structural adjustment in the 1830s and 1840s.

The new wave of technical advance and structural change from the 1870s onwards was driven not only by a new constellation of inventions and innovations but also by the declining profitability, intensified competition, and diminishing opportunities for new profitable investment in the now mature older industrial sectors, as can be clearly seen from the example of the railway industry itself, both in the United States and in Britain. Chandler comments on this change:

The change in the railroad world from expansion to competition in the 1870s affected nearly all the ways of doing business. Intensified competition brought the associations and consolidations that in turn led to the demand for government regulation. The rise of the great consolidated systems raised new problems of finance and increased the role of the investment banking house in American railroading. The management of the huge new systems became immensely more complex. Finally, depression, competition, and the resulting reduction in pay and lay-offs of personnel helped to transform the railroad brotherhoods from fraternal and mutual-aid societies into instruments of economic power. Their members began to use the union to improve their wages, hours and conditions of work through collective bargaining supported by the threat of a strike. (Chandler 1965: 15)

By the 1890s the American railroad network was almost complete. By then, the Interstate Commerce Commission was already involved in rate-making and regulation and the rising new industries were beginning to adopt and modify the practices initially developed by the railroads. As in the case of the United States, economists preoccupied with aggregate trends in GDP in Britain have argued that there was no downswing or depression in the 1870s and 1880s (e.g. Solomou 1987; Saul 1969). However, the evidence of a structural crisis of adjustment was very strong, both at the time and since, as was the evidence of a decline in British competitiveness in world export markets and rate of export growth. Indeed, it would otherwise be almost impossible to explain why so many people at the time described the period as 'the Great Depression'.

S. B. Saul (1969), in his monograph on the *Myth of the Great Depression 1873–1896*, does not deny that 'the last quarter or so of the nineteenth century was a watershed for Britain as competition developed overseas and the rate of growth markedly slackened' (p. 54). He also accepts that 'during the last quarter of the nineteenth century, Britain and several countries overseas went through unusual and worrying economic experiences, which sometimes they characterized at the time as "a great depression"'.

Mathias recalls that when Alfred Marshall, already a famous Cambridge economist in 1886, was interviewed by the Royal Commission inquiring into the depressed state of the British economy, he acknowledged a 'depression of prices, a depression of interest' and 'a depression of profits' but not any other considerable depression. Mathias (1969/1983: 365) points out that the appointment of the Royal Commission itself was not without significance, and he maintains that, 'despite Marshall's opinion, recent calculations have revealed some more deep-seated weaknesses in the pattern of events'. In particular, he stresses the drastic change in the pattern of British exports and the balance of payments. The export *values* of the 1870s were not surpassed again until the second half of the 1890s. Since imports continued to grow, there was an increasing deficit in the balance of trade. Part of the fall in value of exports was of course due to falling prices, but the *volume* of exports fell from an average rate of increase of 5 per cent per annum from 1840 to 1870 to a rate of 2 per cent per annum from 1870 to 1890 and 1 per cent from 1890 to 1900. The fall was especially marked in the older industries, such as cotton goods, where the export values of 1872 were not reached again until 1904 (Figure 6.5). Mathias points out that the depressed prices and profits inevitably had repercussions on the rate of investment and growth in domestic industries.

A more general description of the relative decline of productivity gains in the older industries in Britain is given by Landes:

such calculations as we have of her rates of industrial growth and increase in productivity—and they are confirmed by the major industrial time series—show a distinct falling-off after the mid-century decades of high prosperity. *They do not turn up again until after 1900. From 1870 on, with the exception of a branch like steel, which was transformed by a series of fundamental advances in technique, British industry had exhausted the gains implicit in the original cluster of innovations that had constituted the Industrial Revolution. More precisely, it had exhausted the big gains.* The established industries did not stand still. Change was built into the system, and innovation was if anything, more frequent than ever. But the marginal product of improvements diminished as the cost of equipment went up and the physical advantage over existing techniques fell. (Landes 1969: 125; emphasis added)

6.8 Organizational, Managerial, and Institutional Change

The first industrial revolution was the work of very small firms. In Adam Smith's day hardly any firms employed more than a hundred people, and even by the 1840s only a very few firms, mainly in the cotton and iron industries, employed over a thousand. During the next few decades this number steadily increased, including, of course, some large railway companies and engineering firms. In other European countries too, the more successful firms were growing rapidly in size and market power. The railways and the telegraph were for the most part publicly owned as they were widely believed to be essential for strategic commercial as well as military reasons. Friedrich List is well-known in Britain and America as an advocate of protection for 'infant industries', which indeed he was. However, he was often better known in Germany as an advocate of a national railway network, which was an essential infrastructure for industrialization and for a customs union (*Zollverein*) of the various German states. The achievement of both these objectives enabled German firms greatly to expand their markets and their scale of operations. The firm of Krupp, for example, which employed only just over 100 employees in 1848, already employed over 1,000 by 1857 and 8,000 by 1865; by 1873 this had doubled to 16,000, which was of course largely due to the exceptional advertisement for Krupp armaments in the Franco-Prussian War of 1870–1 (Menne 1937). However, other German, French, Italian, and British firms were also growing rapidly and numbering their employees in the thousands rather than the hundreds by the 1870s and 1880s.

Even at the more typical level of several hundred employees, the entrepreneurs of the mid-nineteenth century found increasing difficulties in the management of their enterprises. Few could behave as Josiah Wedgwood did in the eighteenth century and look after all aspects of their business. The solution most commonly adopted, which evolved naturally from the increasing variety of machines and skills, was to devolve responsibility to the skilled craftworkers or foremen, who would be given responsibility, often in the form of a subcontract, for a whole group of workers and machines. So far did this devolution go in some English firms that the skilled workers identified with management to a considerable extent and it was not unknown for some to arrive at work wearing top hats. Although this solution worked fairly well in many industries for many decades, it came under increasing strain towards the end of the century. Its success over a long period in the cotton industry has been very well described by Mass and Lazonick (1990). They attribute the prolonged commercial success of the British cotton industry over a long period in the nineteenth century largely to the accumulation of specialized skills, the cooperative attitude of the skilled craft unions, and the devolution of responsibility to the skilled workers. However, in common with other historians, Lazonick (1990) also points to the decline of this shopfloor management system in Britain and the rise of the American professional managerial bureaucracy in the late nineteenth and early twentieth centuries. This change in the American managerial organization and the parallel changes in Germany are described in some detail in Chapter 7.

The craft- and shopfloor-based management system came under pressure both from structural change and from technical change. The newer industries, such as electrical equipment, oil, and chemicals, needed a hierarchy of professionally qualified managers as well as skilled craftworkers. Taylorist management philosophers and consultants favoured the shift of power away from the shopfloor to the office and laboratory. At the same time, the unskilled and semi-skilled workers who were left out of the sometimes cosy relationship between managers and craft unions began increasingly to assert themselves in the years of the depression in the 1880s and 1890s. There had been sporadic attempts to organize 'general' unions and industrial unions before, but these became more persistent and successful in the late nineteenth century. The 'new unionism' was not only often overtly hostile to capitalism as such, but was also less than friendly to the old craft unions whose members it also sometimes sought to enrol.

Following the defeat of the 1848 revolutions all over Europe, governments generally embraced the philosophy of liberal *laissez-faire* and of free trade. Business interests were now dominant in most European countries, and the landowning aristocracy was generally obliged to share power, if not to surrender it. Only in eastern Europe and in parts of Russia did the old institution of serfdom and aristocratic privilege linger on, as in many countries in Asia and Latin America. Nor did the new urban working class yet represent a major challenge to the hegemony of the bourgeoisie from 1848 to 1870. It was indeed the 'Age of Capital' but as Hobsbawm (1975: 356) pointed out in his book of that title, in the fourth quarter of the century all of this changed dramatically: 'Politically, the end of the liberal era meant literally what the words imply . . . [the Liberals] . . . were undermined not only by the defeat of their ideology of free trade and cheap (i.e. relatively inactive) government, but by the democratization of electoral politics . . . which destroyed the illusion that their policy represented the masses.'

Hobsbawm argued that it was the depression of the 1870s and 1880s that undermined free trade and greatly strengthened protectionist pressures from both industry and agriculture: 'The trend towards freer trade was reversed in Russia in 1874–5, in Spain in 1877, in Germany in 1879 and practically everywhere else except Britain—and even here free trade was under pressure from the 1880s.' (p. 356)

As we have seen, the growth of industrial production was both more broadly based and more rapid in the second Kondratiev wave than in the first. The boom that followed the 1848 revolutions and the sharp recession of 1847–8 was remarkable in several ways. British exports expanded more rapidly than ever before, and so too did the exports of several other European countries. The Great International Exhibition organized in the new 'Crystal Palace' in London in 1851 was a massive and triumphant display of self-confident industrial and technological progress. Numerous industries showed off their latest designs, but perhaps none was more impressive or symbolic than the largest piece of *coal* ever displayed. The Crystal Palace Exhibition was visited by over 6 million people between May and October, with an average attendance of about 43,000 per day. In Turgenev's novel *Smoke* (1867:1914), he describes the impression made on a Russian visitor by the Crystal Palace; he was depressed by the fact that Russian inventions played no part in 'a sort of exhibition of everything that has been devised by the ingenuity of man' (p. 154). The Philadelphia Exhibition in 1876 attracted even more visitors—over 10 million. Similar exhibitions in several major

European cities played a very important role in stimulating public awareness of the vast range of new products becoming available on world markets and promoting world-wide business contacts. The huge expansion of production and exports was facilitated by the new transport infrastructure of shipping and railways and by the victory of international free trade. The institutional and social framework all over the industrializing countries was changing to adapt to the free market, not only in matters of trade but in many other respects too, as in company legislation and labour market legislation.

According to data presented by Hobsbawm (1975: 55), total world steam power rose from 4 million HP in 1850 to 18.5 million in 1870, world iron output quadrupled, and world industrial production more than doubled. A calculation made in 1880 showed that world tonnage of steamships increased from 264,000 tons in 1851 to nearly 2 million tons in 1871. Not surprisingly, these prodigious increases induced a sense of euphoria, especially in Germany after the Prussian victory in the Franco-Prussian War of 1870–1, the unification of the Reich under the Prussian Emperor, and the founding of numerous new companies. 'Never was economic euphoria among businessmen higher than in the early 1870s' (Hobsbawm 1975: 62).

Although the trade cycle was by then a well recognized phenomenon and had been thoroughly analysed in the 1850s by the French doctor Clement Juglar, whose name was given to it, the severity of the 1870s depression nevertheless came as a shock. German share prices fell by 60 per cent between peak and trough and the iron industry suffered a drastic cut in output with many blast furnaces shutting down. Commodity prices fell continuously through the 1870s and 1880s. Several German commentators emphasized the persistence of crisis phenomena, as did David Wells (1890) in the United States. The structural crisis of adjustment was *felt* as a period of depression, even though aggregate production was rising.

It was also a period when the discontent of the growing class of industrial workers found increasingly radical expression. The Paris Commune of 1871 was a unique explosion but it caused great alarm and stimulated socialist movements all over Europe. The shortcomings of what Lassalle called 'the night-watchman state' were increasingly criticized. Bismarck and other right-wing nationalists not only attacked the Social Democrats with legal persecution (the Anti-Socialist Laws of 1879), but also endeavoured to steal their thunder by passing social legislation, creating an embryonic welfare state as well as educational reforms (Rosenberg 1976). In his thorough analysis of the Great Depression of 1873–96, Hans Rosenberg deals with cultural and political phenomena, as well as economic and technological transformation. He uses the expressions '*Klima-Unschlag*' and '*Gesinnungs-, Glaubens und Idee-enverlagerung*' to describe these cultural and political transformations (van Roon 1984).

Hobsbawm ascribes the emergence of three new tendencies in European politics in reaction to the effects of the economic depression, which led everywhere to social agitation and discontent:

1. the rise of socialist and often Marxist parties;

2. the rise of demagogic nationalist anti-liberal parties and organizations, such as the Pan-German Union;

3. the shift within the larger parties from identification with liberal ideology towards nationalism.

Even in Britain, the stronghold of liberal *laissez-faire* politics, these tendencies were manifest in the 1880s and 1890s and led to a new type of politics down to the First World War, as described by Lloyd-Jones and Lewis (1998) in their analysis of the tariff reform movement. The new configuration of European politics and the accompanying institutional changes meant that the era of liberal triumph, which commenced with the defeat of the 1848 revolution and the apparent certainties of *laissez-faire* economics, ended in some disillusion and confusion and with the emergence of new international and social conflicts.

7

The Third Kondratiev Wave: The Age of Steel, Heavy Engineering, and Electrification

7.1 The Fast Growth Constellation of the Third Kondratiev Wave

In Chapter 6 we argued that the depression of the 1880s was the outcome of the conjuncture of diminishing returns in the older and now established industries of the Industrial Revolution—coal, iron, and railways—and, on the other hand, the rapid rise of new industries and technologies with new skill requirements and new patterns of location. Among these new industries, electricity and steel were outstanding, both having innumerable applications throughout the economic system. The surging demand for electricity led to the construction of a vast new infrastructure—a network of power stations generating electricity and of transmission systems distributing it—ultimately to almost every factory, office, and home in the industrialized countries. New industries also grew up manufacturing plant and equipment for this network, designing and making new machines, appliances, instruments, and tools for every other branch of industry and for households. This vast wave of electrification is analysed in Section 7.2.

No less dramatic was the rise of the steel industry from the 1870s to the 1890s, described in Section 7.3. Steel was, of course, a well-established industry long before this, but the development of several new processes, and especially the Bessemer process, between the 1850s and 1880s brought about an immense change. It was now possible to supply cheap, high quality steel on a vast scale so that, for example, the railway network switched over from iron rails to steel rails and the ship-building industry from iron plates to steel plates in a relatively short period. At this time too, new alloys for steel with non-ferrous metals and new processes for these metals and their alloys vastly widened the range of applications, including, of course, the new electrical plant and equipment itself, from pylons to electric motors.

The new electrical industry was also a voracious consumer of copper (Section 7.4) for cables, wire, and a variety of other applications. Reciprocally, the copper industry was itself revolutionized by electrolytic processes, as were several other industries producing nonferrous metals, and the heavy chemical industry. The expansion in consumption of copper and other metal ores was made possible by an improved transport infrastructure world-wide and by new sources of supply, including the colonization of Africa in the last quarter of the nineteenth century. The development of global shipping lines,[1] based increasingly on steel steamships, has already been described in Chapter 6 and these could now make use of the Suez Canal, completed in 1869, and the Panama Canal by the end of the century, as well as connecting increasingly with transcontinental railways.

International trade could now outstrip the expanding volume of industrial production, even though this was increasing more rapidly than in any previous period. However, as the final section of Chapter 6 has already described, international free trade was increasingly eroded at the end of the century by protectionist measures and by the growth of nationalism and imperialism world-wide. Trade actually grew a little more slowly than production between 1899 and 1913 and much more slowly between 1920 and 1940 (Maizels 1963: 81).

In the new industries, giant firms grew up in the final quarter of the nineteenth century. US steel was worth $1 billion in 1901, whereas the large *ante bellum* US textile firms did not surpass $1 million (Porter 1973: 9, 64). The new giant electrical firms concluded international agreements for the division and re-division of world markets and made monopolistic arrangements for the protection of their own domestic markets as well. The leading firms that emerged in the world electrical industry pioneered new management techniques to control their vast global operations based on the professionalization of such functions as design, R&D, accountancy, marketing, and personnel. The rise of these new giant firms in electricity and steel is analysed in Section 7.5 and their organizational and managerial innovations in Section 7.6.

Finally, although the new industries expanded rapidly between 1895 and 1914 in almost all the industrialized countries, the pattern of growth was very uneven. In particular, it was much slower in Britain than in Germany and the United States. The institutional and social framework which had been so favourable to British industrial growth from the 1780s to the 1870s now proved less favourable for the new industries and technologies of the late nineteenth century. Section 7.7 discusses these changes and argues that, so far from invalidating the model outlined in the Introduction to Part II, they actually serve to confirm it.

The gap in growth rate and per capita incomes between rich and poor countries now became very wide, and the division of the world between industrialized (rich) countries and 'underdeveloped' poor countries emerged as a legacy for the twentieth-century global economy.

---

[1] These developments in global shipping were especially important for North–South trade between Latin America, Australia, and South Africa and the European countries and North America. The invention of refrigerated cargo ships and refrigerated warehouses in the leading ports greatly accelerated the growth of meat exports from Argentina, New Zealand, and Australia in particular. But trade with the Southern Hemisphere in general benefited enormously from the improvements in global transport systems.

7.2 Electricity as the Carrier Branch (Leading Sector) of the Third Kondratiev Wave

As we have seen in Chapter 5, scientific attitudes and experiments were certainly important in the development of the new technologies of the Industrial Revolution, but the electrical industry was much more directly science-related than either textiles or steam engines. In the eighteenth century scientists in several European countries and in the United States had already investigated the electrical properties of materials, and electro-chemistry was developed in laboratory experiments. Benjamin Franklin undertook various experiments with electricity in thunderstorms in the 1740s and was fortunate to escape the fate of his German contemporary, Georg Richman, who was killed attempting similar experiments in 1753. However, Franklin's experiments led him to suggest the invention of the lightning conductor. With the invention of the primary battery by Volta in 1800 it became possible to extend the uses of electricity outside the laboratory, and Cruickshank's battery was already widely used early in the nineteenth century (Table 7.1).

However, although they were certainly important, these early low-power applications were largely confined to communications. It was not until the 1850s and 1860s that the development of magnetos and dynamos reached a point where they could be used on a commercial scale for illumination. The first major application for magneto-powered arc lighting was in British lighthouses. Following the 1858 experiments for lighthouse illumination at South Foreland, Faraday was invited to report on the trials for the lighthouse authorities (Trinity House) and was very impressed: 'The light produced is powerful beyond any other that I have yet seen so applied and in principle may be accumulated to any degree; its regularity in the lantern is great, its management easy and its care can therefore be confided to attentive keepers of the ordinary degree of intellect and knowledge' (Dunsheath 1962: 106).

Even though specialized applications were spreading in the 1860s, it was only with the development of a further series of inventions and innovations (armatures, alternators, rotors, etc.) in the 1860s and 1870s that dynamo technology ('self-excited generators') reached the point where the large-scale generation and transmission of electric power could be successfully achieved in the leading industrial countries.

Rathenau, who became one of the outstanding industrialists associated with electrical engineering and the founder of AEG, spent a period in the 1870s uncertain in which direction to employ his inventive and entrepreneurial skills. He had already been very successful in the mechanical engineering industry but felt that it no longer offered anything exciting and new. After some years he turned to electrical technology as the wave of the future. This sense of excitement associated with electricity and steel also emerges from accounts of the other major German electrical 'dynasty'—the Siemens

TABLE 7.1. Science and technology in the evolution of electric power and its main applications, 1800–1910

Years	Science and invention	Innovation, technology, and applications
1800–30	Measurement, analysis and theory of electricity by laboratory scientists (Volta, Arago, Faraday, etc.) First primary battery, 1800 (Voltaic Pile)	Cruickshank's primary battery (1800) widely sold Daniel two-fluid cell (1830) later used extensively for electric telegraph
1830–50	Electro-magnetic induction demonstrated by Faraday (1831) Magneto by Pixii (1832), Paris Electric telegraph by Wheatstone (1837) and Morse First patents for electroplating (early 1840s) Arc lamps by Staite (1840s)	Commercial development of early generators by Clarke (1834) (London); Stoehrer (Leipzig) (1840–43) Rapid commercialization of electric telegraph alongside railways Multi-core cables Gutta–Percha insulation
1850–70	Hjorth patent for 'magneto-electric battery' (1855) Siemens armature (1856) Swan's early research on carbon filament lamps Reis demonstrates first electric telephone in Frankfurt (1861) 'Self-exciting generators' (Wilde, 1863; Siemens, Varley 1866) Maxwell's theory of radiation (1864) First patent for electrolysis (1865) (Elkington) Leclanché cell (1868)	First submarine telegraph (1851) 4,500 miles of telegraph in use in Britain by 1855 Manufacture of generators on small scale Holmes demonstrates use of generators for lighthouses (1857) Trans-Atlantic cable (1858) First large cable factory (1859) First telegraph New York to San Francisco (1861) Use of rubber insulation spreads First electrolytic copper refinery, South Wales (1869)

TABLE 7.1. (cont.)

1870–90	Gramme armature and first reliable dynamos	Illumination of some public buildings, fairgrounds, streets, etc. with arc lighting.
	Bell telephone patents (1876)	Formation of Edison Electric Light Co. (1878) and first power as a commodity (early 1880s)
	Brush invents open coil dynamo (1878)	Swan and Edison lamps go into high volume manufacture and domestic use
	Edison electric light bulb (1878–9)	
	Helmholtz fundamental theory of telephony and radio	First telephone exchanges in Britain (1878–9)
	Establishment of Physikalische und Technische Reichsanstalt (1886)	Bell manufactures 67,000 telephone sets (1880)
	Hertz demonstrates electro-magnetic radiation (1887)	Edison's Pearl St (New York) generating station (DC) (1883)
	Parsons turbine (late 1880s)	Electric tramways and urban railways (1880s)
		Electroplating widely used for canning
		Electrolytic process for aluminium (1887) and for chlorine (1888)
		Westinghouse introduce AC (1886)
1890–1910	National Physical Laboratory established (1891)	'Battle of the Systems' (AC v. DC) (1887–92)
	Braun's cathode ray tube (1897)	Westinghouse high-voltage transmission, Niagara (1893)
	Many radio inventions and patents (1890s–1900s)	AC power for numerous industrial applications
	J. J. Thomson discovers electron (1897)	AEG and Oerlikon manufacture electric motors (1891)
	Marconi demonstrates radio communications in various experiments	Formation of General Electric Co. (1892)
	Fleming's thermionic valve (1904)	Acetylene from calcium carbide in electric furnaces (1892)
	Cathode ray oscillograph (1901)	First large-scale electrolytic copper refining, USA (1893)
	Electrocardiograph (1909)	High speed tool alloys and power tools (1895)
		Marconi Wireless Telegraph Co. (1897)

family—who made an enormous contribution both to steel and to electrical invention and entrepreneurship, and whose firm was built on the combination of electric telegraph, steel, and electrical engineering (Siemens 1957). As early as 1866, in a paper to the Berlin Physical Society on the significance of his new dynamo, Werner Siemens described it as the pivot of a great technical revolution 'which would make cheap and convenient electrical power available to industry everywhere' (Hall and Preston 1988: 126). A further spurt of innovations in the 1880s included the carbon filament lamp, which meant that the new power stations could find markets in household domestic lighting as well as in public illumination. In 1889, the replacement of electric light bulbs was already one of the many types of work studied and timed by Frederick Taylor with his new 'science' of time and motion studies.

Many applications of electric power were opened up on a small scale in the 1870s. Electricity was used for the illumination of the Gare du Nord in Paris in 1876, of The Times printing works and the Gaiety Theatre in London in 1878, and of the Kaiser arcade in Berlin. In that year also, 30,000 people in Sheffield witnessed the first ever football match played under electric lighting. Show grounds and public fairs were also illuminated by the new source of power.

One of the earliest and most important uses of electric power generation was for tramways and urban electric railways, sometimes underground. Some of the early electric power companies, especially in Japan, were set up specifically for this purpose. Following the first demonstrations of the electric railway by Siemens and Halske in Germany in 1879–81, the first British electric railway was installed at Brighton by Volk, mainly for recreational purposes, in 1883. Much more important were the 'tube' railways, which followed in London from 1887 to 1900, again illustrating the new constellation of steel, electricity, and heavy engineering technologies. It was a sign of the times that the electrical equipment was supplied by US firms. In one of the earliest writings on long waves, Parvus (1901) pointed to the extremely rapid spread of electric tramways in German cities: from only two cities in 1891 to ninety-nine in 1900 and twenty-eight more under construction. He concluded that this example showed that 'electricity will have a greater revolutionary effect on our century than steam had on the nineteenth century' (Louçã and Reijnders 1999).

Chandler (1977) also emphasized the speed of this change in the United States at the turn of the century. By 1890 15 per cent of urban transit lines were already using electric-powered street cars, and by 1904 this had risen to 94 per cent. In fact, the suburban sprawl and the long journey to work often attributed to the automobile were first made possible by electric tramways and railways; it was not until later that the automobile took over as a major mode of travel to and from work and as an accelerator of urban sprawl. In this industry, as in so many others, the new technology brought with it a revolution in management style since it involved expensive equipment, advanced technology, complex maintenance and repair, sophisticated accounting and statistics, and new forms of coordination and political arrangements. The new full-time salaried managers replaced the old owner-operators or municipal managers of horse-drawn systems.

Even more important in the long run than domestic lighting systems or transport systems were the new industrial applications of electricity. The first of these were mainly in electro-metallurgy and electro-chemistry. The electrolysis of copper, first introduced on a small scale in South Wales in the 1870s but on a much larger scale in the 1890s, was particularly important for the subsequent growth of the electrical industry itself (see Section 7.4). The aluminium industry also depended on electricity almost from the outset. Hall's process in the United States and Heroult's in France were invented almost simultaneously in 1887. The electrolysis of chlorine followed in 1888; this transformed the heavy chemical industry and led to many new applications of chlorine. In the 1880s too the electric furnace was first used for producing acetylene from calcium carbide, and this was followed in the 1890s by the production of synthetic silicon carbide (carborundum).

The convergence of heavy and electrical engineering technology with chemistry was most clearly evident in the rapidly growing German chemical industry. In his study of *Science and Industry in the 19th Century*, Bernal (1953) distinguished electricity and chemistry as the two areas where scientific research began to be directly and intimately related to industrial development. It was in the German dyestuffs industry that the 'in-house' R&D laboratory was invented in the 1870s. As the scaling up problems for a wide range of new and old products were encountered in the 1880s and 1890s, the cooperation of engineers and chemists in large-scale process design became the hallmark of the German industry. This culminated in the Haber–Bosch process for synthetic ammonia in the years leading up to the First World War. Not just in chlorine production or in electrolysis, but in many other processes, electrical technology played a central part in the extraordinary rapid growth of the German industry. Particularly notable was the German lead in acetylene chemistry,[2] which played a big part in organic chemicals (J. Fabre 1983).

Arora and Rosenberg argue that electro-chemistry was no less important (or perhaps even more important) for the US chemical industry:

---

[2] Electrical furnaces were used for the production of acetylene from calcium carbide in 1892, but the main applications were in metallurgy. The first electric furnaces were invented by Siemens in 1878 and Stevens in 1879, but the large-scale use of iron and steel scrap as an input in much larger types of electric furnace came only during and after the First World War. In the early period, the applications of the electric furnace were for nonferrous metals and a new range of special steels and alloys. Originally these were produced in non-electric crucible furnaces, but the electric furnace gradually took over, especially in Germany and the USA. The new electric furnace permitted control of temperature between 5°C and 15,000°C, which was unattainable with combustible fuel (Fabre 1983). The new steels proved vastly superior both for high-speed machinery and for abrasion resistance.

The production of electro-chemicals, the most prominent of which were chlorine and chlorine-based compounds such as bleach, by its nature required cheap electrical power. The United States was abundantly endowed with sources of cheap hydro-electric power. In turn, the commercial exploitation of these natural resources presumed a certain level of technological sophistication and large-scale production to offset the large fixed cost of hydro-electric power. Process technology was sometimes European in origin but adapted to US conditions, most importantly to allow for production on a much larger scale than had originally been envisaged. (Arora and Rosenberg 1998: 77)

They stress especially this scaling up of electro-chemistry in the growth of the Dow Chemical company and of Union Carbide, which became two of the largest US chemical firms.

Most important of all in the long term, although not clearly envisaged in the early days of electricity, were the applications in every industrial sector opened up by the electric motor. The *Oxford History of Technology* puts it well:

The conspicuous attribute of electrical energy is mobility. It can be taken to any point along a pair of wires. Other methods of converting energy from a central plant to smaller consumers were tried, but none was as convenient or efficient as the electrical method, by which the heat energy of a boiler-furnace, or the kinetic energy of falling water, is converted into electrical energy and then again transformed into mechanical energy by the consumer's electric motors. Technologically this is by far the most important role of electricity. Electrical energy as a source of light and more recently of heat, as a means of communicating information, and as an agent in chemical processes, has clearly transformed industrial practices; but its chief significance has been to place power, great or small, in the workman's hands or at his elbow. (Oxford History 1958: v. 231)

Very soon electric motors were to be produced in their tens of thousands as the advantages of a flexible, robust, and reliable source of energy were recognized. As we have seen, Werner Siemens had anticipated the widespread use of electric motors as early as 1866, when he suggested that electricity could bring about a renaissance of small firm production and even of household domestic industry.

A specific example illustrates this point well. Delbeke (1982) investigated the development of the stock of engines of all types in Antwerp. The structure of industry in this region was varied, but food, furniture, metals, and diamonds were the major industries and there were many small firms in these industries. The dramatic change from steam to electricity is illustrated in Figure 7.1, which shows that the share of electricity by number of engines rose from nil in 1895 to over 90 per cent by 1915. For a short time, gasoline engines had an advantage in the late nineteenth century, but in the twentieth century electricity displaced both steam and gasoline except for the largest engines. Most of the new electric motors were not however direct substitutes for steam or gasoline, but simply new installations for small firms able to afford this cheap, new, robust, and flexible source of energy to aid their mechanization.

Successive Industrial Revolutions

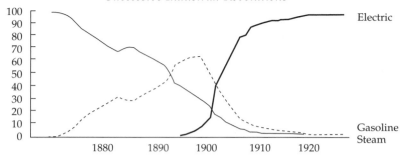

FIG 7.1. The share of different types of energy engines in the annual installed total number of energy engines (9-yearly moving averages) in Antwerp, 1870–1930
Source: Delbeke (1982).

This example brings out the point that electrification was an *electro-mechanical* revolution. Schumpeter's 'creative destruction' did not mean that mechanical technology disappeared: it continued to be extremely important, but in new ways. The mechanical engineering industry was not destroyed, but transformed.

To round off this picture, we must add that the combination of the electric telephone and 'transmissible power' transformed the location and operation of many services as well as manufacturing industries. Hall and Preston (1988) rightly point out that the early office applications of electricity used very little power and the electric typewriter was very late on the scene. Nevertheless, the telephone greatly facilitated the administration of large organizations with dispersed branches of operations, as well as giving new flexibility to many small firms. By 1890, 228,000 telephones were in use in United States, and by 1900, nearly one and a half million. The telephone and the typewriter together began the process of office mechanization which characterized the emergence of 'bureaucracy' in large firms and in central and regional governments. The steel filing cabinet also played a humble but essential role.

Thus, after half a century of innovations in communications, illumination, transport, generation and transmission, and new industrial applications, by the late 1880s or early 1890s, electricity had reached the point where a myriad of new investment opportunities were opening up on all sides. All the conditions were satisfied for an explosive upsurge of new investment based on cheap steel and electric power. The full exploitation of these opportunities, however, required an enormous new infrastructure. Hitherto generators had usually been installed for each specific application, but in the 1880s Edison and others realized that electricity could be generated and transmitted both to households and industrial consumers as a publicly available 'utility' or 'commodity'. Edison launched his first generating station (using DC) in New York in 1882. Granovetter and MacGuire (1998) have presented interesting evidence of the way in which a group of like-minded engineers and executives pushed the direction of the development of electric power to the advantage of the 'utility' companies and the disadvantage of the local decentralized 'in-house' generators of electric power. In their account, it was the 'social construction' of a technological system through the manipulation by the Edison 'mafia', rather than any general technical or economic advantages of a system of generation and distribution by large utilities, that determined the main thrust of development. Edison's legal lieutenant, Samuel Insull, and his supporters succeeded in dominating the relevant trade associations and in pushing through the crucial decisions in favour of the centralized Edison utilities. But, whether through utilities or in-house generating facilities, a huge upsurge of investment occurred everywhere.

In some countries the state and municipalities played a much greater role than private firms in the development of the industry. Hughes (1982) has contrasted the patterns of development in Berlin, Chicago, and London, showing in particular the weaknesses of the British pattern of legislation and standards. Whatever the particular national and local institutional framework, the growth of the new electricity infrastructure required a new regulatory framework, new legislation, new standards, and massive private and public investment. The 1880s were thus a period of intense public debate, which led to a range of different policies at municipal, regional, and national levels. This debate was not confined to the terms under which the new infrastructure should develop, but extended to the whole wide range of electrical applications as the new technology diffused. Engineers argued vehemently not only about the relative merits of AC and DC (see David 1987; Tell 2000), but even more about work organization, the implications of electric power for factory layout, machine design, location of industry, management structure, and scale of enterprise. In other words, the combination of cheap steel and electric power brought with it not merely a new source of energy and materials, but a transformation of the whole productive system and socioeconomic structure.

Figure 7.2 shows how (in the USA) the vast majority of factories and households were supplied with electricity over the half-century of the third Kondratiev wave. Figure 7.3 shows that by 1920 over half the power for industry in the USA came from electricity and by 1930, over three-quarters. Because of classification problems and the inadequacies of the relevant industrial statistics, it is hard to give precise figures, but Hall and Preston (1988) report estimates by German economists that the electrical industry accounted for between 30 and 40 per cent of the growth of industrial production in the period leading up to the First World War.

As this vast wave of electrification got under way, new constellations of interrelated innovations emerged and consolidated, linking together steel and the new industrial materials with their wide new range of properties and applications and the new flexible source of energy. First and foremost, this affected factory design and layout in almost all sectors of manufacturing,

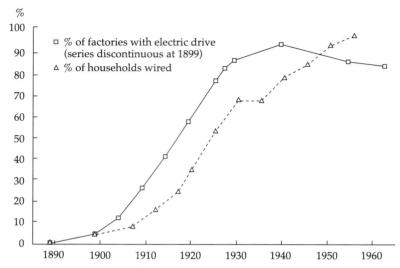

FIG 7.2. Electrification in the United States, 1890–1960
Source: *Historical Statistics of the United States*; Ayres (1989).

with new machinery and power tools replacing the old steam-powered machinery. Under the old system all the shafts and countershafts rotated continuously no matter how many machines were actually in use; a break-down involved the whole factory (Devine 1983).

Attempts were made in the 1880s and 1890s to overcome the inflexibility of the old system by using several steam engines, but once electricity became generally available it proved far superior. Although the new potential of electric power was recognized as early as in the 1880s, it was not until after 1900 that manufacturers generally began to realize that the indirect benefits of using unit electric drives were far greater than the direct energy-saving benefits. Unit drive gave greater flexibility in factory layout, since machines were no longer placed in line with shafts, making possible big capital savings in floor space. For example, the US Government Printing Office was able to add forty presses in the same floor space. Unit drive meant that trolleys and overhead cranes could be used on a large scale unobstructed by shafts, counter-shafts and belts. Portable power tools increased even further the flexibility and adaptability of production systems. Factories could be made much cleaner and lighter, which was very important in industries such as textiles and printing, both for productivity and for product quality. Production capacity could be expanded much more easily.

The full expansionary benefits of electric power on the economy depended, therefore, not only on a few key innovations in the 1880s, but on the development of a new 'paradigm', 'style', or production and design philosophy. This involved the re-design of machine tools, handling equipment, and much other production equipment. It also involved the relocation of many plants and

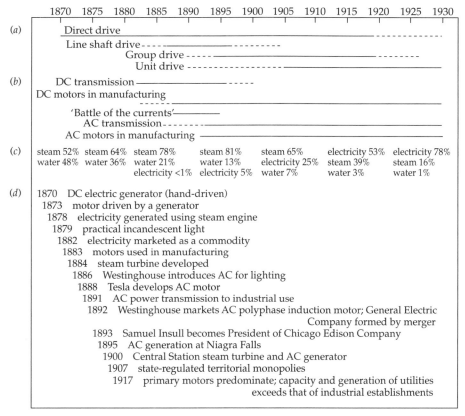

FIG 7.3. Chronology of the electrification of industry

Notes

(a) Methods of driving machinery.

(b) Rise of alternating current.

(c) Share of power for mechanical drive provided by steam, water, and electricity.

(d) Key technical and entrepreneurial developments.

Source: Devine (1983).

industries, based on the new freedom conferred by electric power transmission and local generating capacity. The change of paradigm was comparable to the present change of paradigm based on the Internet and information technology or to the earlier mechanization of industry based on steam power.

Not surprisingly, each of these paradigm changes involved a structural crisis of adjustment over a fairly extended period before the new technologies and new ideas were generally accepted as 'common sense' and the metaphors of the new technology were incorporated into everyday speech as commonplace expressions, such as 'she's a live wire' or 'he's on a short fuse'.

As in the earlier case of steam power, art and literature were strongly influenced by the dramatic upsurge of electric power. In one of his early (1895) short stories, entitled 'The Lord of the Dynamos', the young H. G. Wells even describes a human sacrifice to a dynamo in Camberwell power station in South London. More prosaically, Theodore Dreiser makes his most self-possessed and intellectual character in his novel *Sister Carrie*, an electrical engineer. His other characters regard electrification as 'an exciting and alluring aspect of the new city' (Nye 1990: 146).

David Nye recalls that Edison himself made many Utopian predictions about electrification that were more characteristic of the popular fiction accounts. At one time, he planned also to co-author a novel about a life transformed by science: 'He predicted that electrification of the home would eliminate the distinction between night and day and speed up women's mental development, making them the intellectual equals of men [*sic*]. Constant light might lead to the elimination of sleep. In later years, he even hinted that he was experimenting with electrical ways to communicate with the dead' (Nye 1990: 147).

According to Nye, more than 160 Utopian books appeared in the United States in a twelve-year period at the turn of the century. Electricity was one of the three most commonly mentioned marvels of the future. In the most famous *Utopia: Looking Backward* by Edward Bellamy (1888), which sold several million copies, it was assumed that there had already been a prodigious impulse to labour-saving productivity and in the year 2000 electricity takes the place of all fires and lighting. However, Bellamy's main purpose was to design a more equal and just society by eliminating wasteful competition. The links between progressive social ideals and electrification were a common feature of this popular literature, but of course, some of the negative threats and fears were also featured, as in Mark Twain's *A Connecticut Yankee in King Arthur's Court*.

The exaggerated hopes and fears, the Utopias and the Dystopias—all reflected the immense intellectual disturbance, as well as the economic effects of the revolutionary new technology system. While Nye's (1990) comprehensive study on *Electrifying America* contrasts the theorizing and speculation of the intellectuals with the down-to-earth assessment of the benefits by ordinary American workers, it nevertheless portrays the profound effects of electrification throughout American society. It was indeed a revolutionary technology.

7.3 Steel as the Core Input of the Third Kondratiev Wave

Steel had, of course, been produced in small quantities long before the Industrial Revolution, but it was expensive to make and quality control was difficult. Iron was used far more extensively (Figure 7.4). In the first half of the nineteenth century the United States still depended on imported British steel because of these quality problems, and several Sheffield steel works actually had American names because of their dependence on

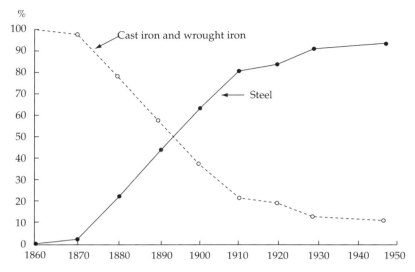

FIG 7.4. Penetration of steel, USA, 1860–1950 (percentage of all iron and steel products)
Source: Ayres (1989).

exports to the United States. Many of the saws, axes, and other tools that moved the American frontier westwards were also made in Sheffield. Geoffrey Tweedale, in his study of *Sheffield Steel and America* (1987), speaks of a 'century of commercial and technological interdependence', but it was in the first half of this period that the dependence on Sheffield was at its peak.

As late as 1880, US steel output was only just over a million tons and iron output was more than three times as large, but by 1913 US steel output had climbed to 31 million tons. This prodigious increase (even faster than the growth of cotton in Britain from 1780 to 1810) was made possible by a number of radical process innovations between the 1850s and the 1880s, notably the Bessemer process, the Siemens process, and the Gilchrist–Thomas process. These innovations did not originate in the United States, but priority for the inventions is still disputed, and American inventors were not far behind their British, French, and German counterparts in the early development of these and other process innovations. In the pig iron industry, 'hard driving' of blast furnaces was an American innovation which contributed to the much higher profitability of the US iron and steel industry (Berck 1994). Over the same period (1880–1913) British steel production rose from 1.3 to 7.7 million tons, while German output rose from 0.7 million to 18.9 million tons. The relative acceleration of German and US production is obvious from these statistics.

When Carnegie built his first Bessemer plant for steel rails in 1875, it was on the basis of the technology he observed during his visit to Britain, but the scaling up of production was far more rapid and led to numerous incremental innovations by US steel firms. As a result of these innovations, costs and

TABLE 7.2. Price of steel rails in the
United States, 1870–1930

	Steel rails ($ per ton)	Consumer price index
1870	107	38
1875	69	33
1880	68	29
1885	29	27
1890	32	27
1893	28	27
1895	24	25
1898	18	25
1900	32	25
1905	28	27
1910	28	28
1915	30	30
1920	54	60
1925	43	53
1930	43	50

Source: *US Historical Statistics.*

prices fell almost as dramatically as in the earlier case of cotton in Lancashire. By far the main application in this period was in steel rails (Table 7.2).

Landes (1969) estimated that the reduction in cost of crude steel was between 80 and 90 per cent from the early 1860s to the mid-1890s. According to the *Encyclopaedia Britannica* (1898), the price of steel rails fell from $165 per ton in 1865 to $18 per ton in 1898, while that of iron rails moved from $99 to $46 per ton. Steel rails lasted five or six times as long as iron rails. All prices were inflated during the American Civil War so the 1865 price was high. But Figure 7.4 shows clearly that steel was becoming both cheap and abundant in the 1880s and 1890s. This certainly suggests that steel satisfied the Perez criteria of a 'core input', even though after the low point of 1898 the new steel cartel succeeded in stabilizing and raising the price of steel rails in a period of general price inflation.

Another major application of steel was in ship-building. The first steel ships were made in the 1850s, but these were for specialized purposes. Designers were still distrustful of steel, even in the 1870s, as can be seen from a paper to the Institution of Naval Architects by Barnaby, chief naval architect to the British Admiralty in 1875:

No doubt excellent steel is produced in small quantities by the converter and the bath at a much cheaper rate than it could be produced ten years ago; and where the management is strict and careful considerable quantities may be delivered of trustworthy materials. Nevertheless, our distrust of it is so great that the material may be said to be altogether unused by private shipbuilders, except for boats and very small vessels, and masts and yards ... The question we have to put to the steel makers is: what are our prospects of obtaining a material which we can use without such delicate manipulation and such fear and trembling? (Robb 1958: 373)

However, the launching of the steel warship, HMS *Iris*, in 1877 showed conclusively that these doubts had been overcome. Down to the end of the 1870s, steel still accounted for only a tiny proportion (less than 10 per cent) of the ships built on the Clyde, but by 1890 it was well over 90 per cent. This rapid switch indicates that the major problems of quality, availability, and cost raised by Barnaby were largely resolved. The thickness of plates could be significantly reduced, and this was true of many other applications in the construction and engineering industries, so that the cost saving was much greater than that indicated by a simple comparison of relative price per ton. As already described in Chapter 6, steel ships were the basis of the ship-building boom in Britain and Germany before the First World War, culminating in the naval arms race. Although these countries were the world leaders in both civil and naval ship-building, the role of steel was similar in the United States (Heinrich 1997).

The US steel industry led not only in large-scale production, but, together with the German and British industries, in the development of *special* steels, and with US engineering firms in numerous new applications of steel. The advantages of steel were not simply in comparative cost, although this was a decisive incentive in the redesign of many products and processes. Steel also made possible many new products, tools, and processes, in machinery, engineering, and construction. In 1868 Mushet had already discovered that by adding vanadium and tungsten to steel a much harder tool steel could be made in his small Gloucestershire works. This was followed by the development of other new alloys containing nonferrous metals, with much harder cutting edges in a wide range of machinery and much greater precision in the production of many engineering components. Before he became a management consultant, Frederick Taylor worked for Midvale Steel from 1878 to 1889, when he was developing his theories of 'scientific management', and later at Bethlehem Steel, where he made a major invention in high-speed tool steel and a series of machinery and metallurgical inventions related to the use of tool steels.

The new heat treatment invented by Taylor and White in 1895 at the Bethlehem Steel Company produced alloy steel, which could cut five times faster than the carbon steels previously used for machine tools, and this was soon trebled again by the newer alloys. The Sheffield firm of Hadfield's produced manganese steel in the 1890s, which had very high abrasion resistance and found world-wide applications in construction and engineering (and of course armaments); one example was the teeth of the shovels that dug the Panama Canal. Hadfield's also developed silicon steel, which was at one time called 'electrical steel' and was an essential component for electrical transformers and generators because of its excellent magnetic properties and high electrical resistance (and hence low energy loss)

(Pearl 1978). The interdependence of developments in steel and electrification is again evident from these examples.

The properties of stainless steel were investigated between 1903 and 1910 by the inventor of vanadium steel, L. Guillet in France, but it was Strauss and Maurer in Germany and Harry Brearley in Sheffield who first realized the commercial possibilities. Brearley made his discovery of the extraordinary corrosion resistance of stainless steel while testing the suitability of high-chromium steels for rifle barrels. The armaments race between Britain and Germany leading up to the First World War was an important stimulus to the development of new steel alloys with exceptional properties and the development of heavy engineering generally. Both Midvale and Bethlehem Steel worked on US naval contracts for armour plate, and Taylor was also an active consultant to US arsenals and naval yards after 1906.

It was not only in heavy engineering, machinery, and armaments that steel found a wide range of new applications. There were many consumer industries that owed either their existence or their rapid growth primarily to the availability of cheap and plentiful steel. This was the case, for example, with the canning industry, which was growing rapidly in the United States since the American Civil War, and later in Europe. The substitution of steel strip for iron in the cans and the introduction of electro-plating for the tin deposition process revolutionized the industry. Steel now accounted for 98 per cent and tin for only 2 per cent of the metal used in a 'tin' can, and the industry could become a truly mass production industry. By the First World War many households were using dozens of tin cans every year for food and many other consumer goods, and the armies depended on tinned food for their rations. Stainless steel found its main applications ultimately in the cutlery, food, and chemical industries. Another consumer product that owed its rapid growth in the 1890s partly to cheap good quality steel was the bicycle. The techniques used for its manufacture before the 1920s were not yet 'Fordist' mass production techniques, but they were certainly high volume production, taking advantage of the new potential of steel-intensive products.

Yet another constellation of innovations that illustrates the interdependence and complementarities of technical and economic developments in the steel, heavy engineering, and electrical industries was in the construction of large buildings. Before the 1880s, to support the weight of a lofty building on walls of brickwork, the walls had to be immensely thick in the lower stories. 'Even with the weight of the interior carried by cast iron columns, a thick very lofty external wall capable of carrying its own weight could spare only a limited area for window openings' (Hamilton 1958: 478).

In 1883, when William Jenney was commissioned by the US Home Insurance Company to build a ten-storey block which would be fireproof and let plenty of natural light into every room, he used cast iron columns and wrought iron beams for the six lower floors, but above that level he used steel beams. The Rand–McNally Building in Chicago in 1890 used a completely steel frame. With a complete steel skeleton, it was possible to build walls at several levels independently and simultaneously. Soon external walls became 'weather screens' in the panels between columns and beams, and the age of the 'skyscraper' had arrived. But of course, the spread of sky-scrapers would have been impossible without the electric lift (1889) (and indeed, the electric telephone); hydraulic lifts were slow, not always safe, and difficult to use above five storeys. Chicago and New York rivalled each other for the tallest and most spectacular building.

The rolling of steel beams for large structures (power stations, bridges, fac-tories, skyscrapers) began at Dorman Long in 1885 and at other steel works in Britain, Germany, and United States later in the 1880s. In addition to large office blocks, the new types of factory using electric power and overhead cranes, as well as the power stations themselves, made extensive use of new steel girders and other steel products.

Steel was at the heart of a whole wave of innovations affecting every branch of industry and services. It became 'common-sense' to design big projects and new products large and small, using steel and/or steel alloys, as the following (non-comprehensive) list indicates:

ammunition	hand tools	rail wagons
artillery	instruments	railway stations
automobiles	locomotives	refrigerators
barbed wire	machine tools	ships
bicycles	machinery of many	skyscrapers
boilers	kinds	tanks
bridges	motors	tin cans
chemical plant	oil refineries	transformers
cranes	piping	turbines
cutlery	power tools	warehouses
factories	pressure vessels	warships
filing cabinets	pylons	wire
generators	rails	

Schumpeter discussed steel mainly in terms of *steam-powered machinery*. One reason for this somewhat arbitrary cut-off is that Schumpeter associated steel primarily with the second Kondratiev wave, which he described as a revo-lution 'wrought by railroads, steel and steam' (1939: 397). But, as we have seen, while the major process innovations in the steel industry did indeed originate in the 1850s and 1860s, they could not be regarded as a driving force of the upswing of the second Kondratiev. It was the *iron* horse, the *iron* rail, and the *iron* machine that were the basis of the first big wave of steam power and 'railroadization'. The consumption of steel remained relatively small right into the downswing of the 1870s and 1880s. It was only in the 1880s and 1890s that the diffusion of the new processes permitted the large-scale use of cheap steel in a thousand-and-one new applications and products first intro-duced experimentally over previous decades. In general, our emphasis is on *diffusion*, while Schumpeter was preoccupied with the dates of first original innovation, possibly because of his theory of entrepreneurship.

Moreover, the complementarities between electrical machinery and processes and the uses of steel, although relatively neglected by Schumpeter, were even more important than the complementarities with steam-powered mechanical equipment. Not only did much electrical equipment use steel, alloys, copper, and other nonferrous metals from the outset, but the applications of electricity in many other industries, such as machine tools, were strongly associated with the use of steel and its alloys. To us, therefore, it appears more justifiable to describe the third Kondratiev as an 'age of steel' and the first and second as an 'age of iron'.

Andrew Carnegie, architect of the giant American steel firm that was later to become United Steel and the embodiment of American entrepreneurship, brought with him a model of management derived almost entirely from his railway experience. Carnegie had himself worked on the railways from the age of 18 as a clerk and as a telegraph operator. In 1856, at the age of 24, he became a departmental head and familiar with cost-accounting systems. During the American Civil War, with financial help from friends, he set up companies to make iron rails, locomotives, and bridges. He was also heavily involved in various forms of financial manipulation and speculation with Union Pacific and other railroad companies. One of his biographers (Mackay 1997: 144) describes his 'conversion from speculation to manufacturing': 'Hitherto he had concentrated on speculation, playing the stock market, manipulating shares and selling short on the exchange. Henceforward, he would spurn such doubtful and dubious practices. Instead he would concentrate on heavy engineering and the manufacture of steel.'

Following a visit to Britain in 1872, Carnegie became convinced that the Bessemer steel process would revolutionize the world iron and steel industry, and his experience in financial services helped him when it came to raising the large sums needed for steel manufacturing. He was able to survive the financial crash of 1873 and to launch the production of steel rails on 1 September 1875. Carnegie and his subordinates with railway experience introduced rigorous statistical cost systems, which were one of the earliest and most important achievements of the new management style: 'These cost sheets were Carnegie's primary instrument of control. Costs were Carnegie's obsession. One of his favourite dicta was: "Watch the costs and the profits will take care of themselves"' (Chandler 1990: 167). By 1880 Carnegie's cost data were more detailed and accurate than those of almost any other enterprise in the United States. They were used to control departments and foremen and to check the quality and mix of raw materials. They were also used to make improvements in processes and products, so that technical advance and cost-cutting moved together hand in hand.

By 1880 Carnegie was already a millionaire. The son of a Chartist weaver who emigrated from Scotland in the 1840s because of the poverty, he became one of the richest men in the world by 1900. His firm continued to make profits in the years of depression when many firms were making losses. However, when the workers in his Homestead plant in Pennsylvania went on strike in 1892 in a wages dispute, the strike was suppressed with considerable brutality and the support of the Pinkerton Detective Agency. This delayed the unionization of the steel industry until the 1930s (see the Conclusions to Part II). This paradoxical character was depicted by some writers, such as the novelist John dos Passos, simply as a slave-driving boss, whereas others argued that he was also a philanthropist, who endowed hundreds of public libraries.

Chandler describes the contribution made by Carnegie to the tempestuous growth of the US steel industry as follows:

The history of the American steel industry illustrates effectively how technological innovation, intensified use of energy, plant design, and overall management procedures permitted a great increase in the volume and speed of throughput and with it a comparable expansion in the productivity of operation. Carnegie's pre-eminence in the industry came from his commitment to technological change and from his imaginative transferral to manufacturing of administrative methods and controls developed on the railroads.

Technological and organizational innovation paid off. Carnegie's prices were lower and his profits higher than any producer in the industry. As soon as the E.T. Works was opened in 1875 it recorded profits of $9.50 a ton. In 1878 Carnegie's steel rail mill recorded a profit of $401,000 or 31 per cent on equity. It rose in the next two years to $2.0 million. As the business grew, so did its profits. At the end of the 1890s Carnegie's larger and more diversified enterprise had profits of $20 million. For the year 1900 they stood at $40 million. By becoming a pioneer in the methods of high volume production in steel, Carnegie quickly accumulated, as John D. Rockefeller had done in petroleum, one of the largest fortunes the world had ever seen. (Chandler 1990: 169)

This admirably sums up not only Carnegie's entrepreneurial qualities but also the interdependence of scale economies, technical and organizational innovation, productivity, and profitability.

7.4 Copper as an Additional Essential Input

Copper was used as an industrial material as early as 8000 BC, as a substitute for stone, from deposits in the free natural state. The melting and casting of copper marked the beginning of metallurgy. By 5000 BC copper weapons and implements were interred with the dead in Egyptian graves, and bronze was widely employed by the third millennium BC. As an alloy of copper and tin, it was harder than either, and down to the present day copper has a greater variety of alloys than any other metal. When the 'Bronze Age' was followed by the 'Iron Age', copper became still more widely used for household objects, for pipes, and for coinage.

All of these applications have continued to the present time, together with many others, but they have been outstripped by the applications of copper in the electrical industry, which have amounted to more than half the total consumption of the metal since the end of the nineteenth century. It was only in the 1960s that aluminium displaced copper as the second most important

TABLE 7.3. World production of nonferrous
metals, 1850–1900 ('000 metric tons)

Metal	1850	1875	1900
Copper	55	130	525
Lead	130	320	850
Zinc	65	165	480
Nickel	—[a]	1	8
Aluminium	—[a]	—[a]	7

[a] Negligible.

Source: Oxford History (1958: v. 73).

metal after iron. The exceptionally rapid growth of the production and consumption of both copper and aluminium in the twentieth century was intimately related to the rise of the electrical industry.

In the fourth quarter of the nineteenth century, copper was the fastest
growing of the major non-ferrous metals (Table 7.3) and this was due primarily to its role in the electrical industry. At the beginning of the century
world copper production was only about 9,000 tons, and three-quarters of
this output was smelted in South Wales, which was still the main base of
production in 1850. But by 1870 new centres of production had come to the
fore, and at the end of the century US production accounted for over half of
the total world output. The United States owed its new leadership on the one
hand to resource abundance and engineering capability, and on the other
hand to the rapid growth of its electrical industry. Michigan, Arizona, and
Montana all became centres of copper mining and smelting, with Chile and
Spain as major additional sources of supply. The new enterprises enjoyed the
advantage over the Swansea (South Wales) industry of being able to integrate mining, smelting, and refining on a much larger scale than the firms in
South Wales where more than 600 small furnaces were in use for smelting
very small quantities of copper. By 1900 Arizona and Montana were producing 200,000 tons of copper a year, while the Welsh firms were producing
only a small fraction of this total and ceased operations altogether in 1921.

Many improvements were made in the furnace design of smelters in the
1870s and 1880s, varying with the local ores and impurities, but by far the
most important development in copper technology was the introduction of
electrolytic refining. The first patent for this process was taken out in 1865 by
J. B. Elkington in South Wales, and his basic technique of suspending copper
plates in parallel rows in an electrolytic cell remained the fundamental
design principle in later industrial operations. Even the recovery of gold,
silver, antimony, and tin impurities was mentioned in the original patent
application. The first electrolytic refining was executed in 1869 near Swansea
in the copper smelting plant of Mason and Elkington, but it was not until
1892 that the first American electrolytic refinery was built (Chadwick 1958).

The importance of electrolytic refining lay in the removal of impurities from the metal for electrical applications. As early as 1850 the deleterious effect of even small impurities on electrical conductivity was realized, but very few of the commercial grades of copper reached the desirable standard of purity. For most of the non-electrical applications this did not matter, but for electrical applications it mattered very much. The strong interdependence of the growth of the electrical industry and of the copper industry was summarized by Chadwick:

Although Lake Superior ores were capable of producing high-grade copper by normal fire-refining methods, in general high-conductivity copper could be produced solely by electrolytic refining, and this became commercially feasible only with the advent of cheap electric power, while conversely, efficient power generation called for electrolytically refined metal for dynamo windings and bus-bars. (Chadwick 1958: 84)

In the early period of expansion of electrical applications, this reciprocal feedback relationship was sustained by the huge reserves of copper ore in North and South America and the advances in mining, smelting, and refining techniques, which made it possible for copper supply to keep pace with the extraordinary growth of demand. From about 1873 to 1890 copper experienced a falling price trend, but, according to Herfindahl (1959) in his major study of copper prices, after 1900 the price was stabilized as also occurred with steel. Like most commodities in the nineteenth century, the price did fluctuate from day to day, month to month, and year to year. Nevertheless, as Figure 7.5 shows, after a clear downward trend from the 1860s to the 1890s, apart from a short sharp rise in the early 1870s, a price of about 10¢ per lb generally prevailed. However, the growth of demand early in the

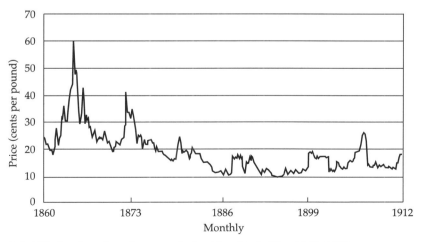

FIG 7.5. Wholesale price of copper, Lake, New York City, 1860–1912
Source: Herfindahl (1959).

twentieth century, resulting from the world-wide expansion of the electrical industry, led to some temporary shortages, and copper rose in price from 1899 to 1913 and, of course, more steeply during the First World War.

We have described copper as an additional 'essential input', but it differed in important respects from steel. The range of applications, although wide, was far less than for steel. Moreover, the huge increase in demand was due almost entirely to electrification. It was an essential input for electrification, as is demonstrated so clearly by the case of electrolytic processes, whether for copper itself, for other nonferrous metals, or for the chemical industry. Consumption rose because of its special properties of conductivity and corrosion resistance, rather than simply because of low price and abundant supply.

Copper supply was able to catch up with demand, not only because of the huge expansion of North American and Latin American mining, smelting and refining, but because of European colonization of Africa, often influenced by the presence of mineral resources, especially copper. Cecil Rhodes, who led the conquest of those African territories that became known as Rhodesia and who dreamt of a Cape-to-Cairo railway, was himself heavily involved in business ventures in mineral production, primarily gold and diamonds, and was certainly not unmindful of the copper resources of the territories that later became one of the major world producers. The role of copper in stimulating imperialist adventures and European exploitation of mining was even more prominent in the case of the Congo, where Katanga became a major world producer in the years before the First World War. The availability of global shipping was essential for all these developments of world trade in copper and other metal ores and minerals.

7.5 The Rise of the Giant Firm and Cartels

The managerial and organizational innovations that accompanied, followed, or preceded the technical innovations mostly facilitated a larger scale of operation by the leading firms. A revolution was brought about in offices and in services—indeed, in all business organizations—and in the conduct of government and of war, by the electric telephone and telegraph. These new media of communications (supplemented at a later stage by radio) greatly facilitated the development of large corporations with more complex management structures controlling plants in various locations and the production and delivery of materials, components, and machinery from distant lands. With the new infrastructure of world shipping and railways already established in the second Kondratiev and the division of the world between the great powers, this meant that competition for the world market became more intense and the export of capital was greatly facilitated.

One example of the new type of company was the rise of the house of Krupp in Essen, Germany, which was by 1903 the largest private industrial undertaking on the European Continent (Menne 1937), comprising iron mines in Spain as well as coal mines in Germany, steel mills and armaments works in Essen, and the Germania shipyard in Kiel, that was to be the birthplace of the modern submarine, soon to prove so effective in the First World War. The sheer scale of these firms, whether in steel, electricity, or heavy engineering itself, required a new management structure. This developed along somewhat different lines in Germany and the United States, but in both countries it involved a more substantial role for professional managers and especially for cost accountants and professional engineers. Although an individual 'heroic' inventor–entrepreneur, such as Rathenau, Edison, or Siemens, was often involved in the early rapid growth of these firms, the management problems soon outstripped the managerial capacity of the single entrepreneur, as Schumpeter himself recognized.

The 'new model' of management organization in large firms, although first developed during the second Kondratiev in the railway companies, was a major departure from the management system, which predominated in the United States and Europe during that period. In most manufacturing firms, the old system involved subcontracting or delegating responsibility for shopfloor management to senior foremen or 'overseers', who were often experienced craft workers. The new system was based on departmental structures controlled by professional managers.

In the electrical industry, before the First World War the main American firms, General Electric and Westinghouse, and the dominant German firms, AEG and Siemens, had already grown very rapidly to become giants which were among the largest firms in the world at that time (Table 7.4). Both GE and AEG grew partly as a result of mergers, which involved the participation of strong financial interests. From fairly early on the electrical firms, like the railways before them, needed very large amounts of capital, as they were involved in the development of a large, physical network. From 1878 Thomas Edison was getting help from Drexel, Morgan & Company, while Elihu Thomson soon had the backing of Boston capitalists, who were also involved in the financing of railroads, the telegraph, and the telephone.

TABLE 7.4. Sales of major German and American electrical companies, 1893–1913 (£'000, exchange rate equivalent)

	USA			Germany	
	Westinghouse	General Electric		Siemens	AEG
		Thomson Houston	Edison		
1893	1,000	2,060	2,180	800	550
1899	2,400	4,480		3,300	n.a.
1906	4,820	12,020		n.a.	8,750
1913	8,000	17,840		23,600	22,650

Source: Byatt (1979).

General Electric was a merger of two of the three large electrical equipment manufacturers in 1892, which were themselves the result of mergers. Henry Villard, an eminent railroad financier who had helped to finance some of Edison's early developmental work, engineered the merger. Villard had recently returned to the United States after a three-year stay in Germany, where he had become closely associated with the powerful Deutsche Bank of Berlin and with Siemens–Halske, the leading German electrical manufacturers who were already beginning to sell in the American market. He planned, according to Edison's biographer Matthew Josephson, to create a 'world cartel' (Chandler 1977: 427).

The idea of a 'world cartel' was not such a distant dream. This was a period marked by a strong trend towards cartelization in many industries. The electrical engineering industry was one in which international patent agreements between the dominant firms played a major role, at least down to the Second World War. Market sharing agreements were also far from uncommon, and monopolistic purchasing policies characterized the relationships between the big utilities and their 'national' heavy equipment suppliers. General Electric and Westinghouse were notorious for their duopolistic practices, and in the international market GE and the German AEG systematically divided up the world. Lenin commented that this division of the world between two powerful firms did not remove the possibility of *re-division* as a result of uneven development or war. Such a 're-division' did in fact take place when, in 1922, the agreement was renegotiated, following the German defeat in the First World War. The terms were more favourable to GE, which had acquired 25 per cent of the newly issued stock of AEG in 1920.

The rapid growth of concentration in the electrical equipment industry was stronger than in most others, but there were similar trends throughout the economic system. The establishment of a world-wide transport and communications network meant that firms could now operate on a global scale, not only in terms of exports, but also in terms of vertical integration with raw material suppliers, the control of manufacturing facilities and sales agencies in many countries, and the finance to organize such operations. Whereas the Lancashire textile firms in the late nineteenth century enjoyed few plant economies of scale and benefited from extensive external economies, the new American industries internalized many functions that were external to the small and medium-sized enterprises (SME's). Plant-level economies of scale, which were important in oil, metals, and chemicals, could now be exploited in many other industries and over much larger markets. But economies of scale in finance for new investment, in the procurement of materials, in the establishment of marketing networks, and in research, design, and development now became of equal or greater importance. The cumulative advantages of a highly skilled and trained labour force now extended to several echelons of professional managers in these functions.

In heavy electrical equipment they were certainly important, but, although the main trend in the electrical industry itself was towards the development of very large firms, this was offset by the consequences of electrification for many other industries and services. The new technology and the new source of energy gave opportunities for thousands of SMEs to flourish in such diverse industries as lumber (saw mills), instruments, power tools, and other mechanical products. The flexibility of the power source, as the whole country became electrified, permitted the development of entirely new industrial districts, the decentralization of some industries, the rise of other entirely new industries, and the transformation of still others.

The example of small firms in the Antwerp area has already been cited. At the same time that electrification gave new impetus to the growth of some established areas of heavy industry, previously based on coal and iron (Sheffield, Tyneside, the Ruhr, the Middle West, Southern Belgium, etc.), it also facilitated the emergence of entirely new areas of industrial concentration. The entry of new countries such as Sweden and Switzerland was an important feature of third Kondratiev industrialization. The suburbs of capital cities such as Berlin, Tokyo, London, Paris, and Stockholm now themselves became much more attractive as industrial sites, because of electrified transport, cheap fares, and good communications. Berlin was described as 'Electropolis' and accounted for 50 per cent of all electrical employment in Germany (Hall and Preston 1988), which increased at an extraordinary rate after 1895 (Table 7.5).

7.6 Managerial and Organizational Innovations: The Rise of Bureaucracy and Taylorism

The rise of a professional manager class in the United States was stimulated not only by changes in the structure and administration of large firms and changes in technology, but also by developments within the management class itself and in the education system. The real significance of 'Taylorism' was not that it introduced 'scientific management' but that, together with other similar schemes and models, it provided a rationale for a whole set of organizational innovations. These displaced the old model and substituted a

TABLE 7.5. Employment in the German electrical industry, 1895 and 1925

	All industries	Electrical industry	
			(as %)
1895	6,647,000	24,000	0.4
1925	11,108,000	449,000	4.0

Source: Hall and Preston (1988: 103).

management-intensive style based on the professionalization and specialization of the various functions of management—above all, cost accounting,
production engineering, sales management, and in some cases also design
and development, personnel, public relations and intelligence, and market
research (as in the case of General Electric). The management 'bureaucracy'
was the main organizational innovation of the third Kondratiev.

Daniel Nelson's (1980) biography of Taylor makes clear that, in common
with other mechanical engineers with industrial experience, Taylor saw
himself as a 'professional'—as a 'scientist'—who could see the need for a
radical change in the old 'contractor' system to take advantage of the new
technologies. The rise in fixed costs, associated with rising capital intensity,
put pressure to sustain or improve profitability by using physical capacity
more fully and to control the flow of materials and components. At the
same time, engineers were needed in sales to give technical service to customers. Selling too had to become an organized professional function of the
firm. When the financier Villard reorganized General Electric, a sales force
was established with seven regional offices, each headed by a district
manager who controlled the work of the salesmen and engineers responsible for installation, service, and sales. The transition from the second to the
third Kondratiev was thus characterized by new forms of management
organization and firm structure in large firms, which were no less important than the new technologies and accompanied their diffusion, interacting
with them. Weber was characteristic of German sociologists in seeing the
progressive positive side of 'bureaucratic' administration, as well as some
negative features.

In placing the rise of 'Taylorism' in a historical context, Daniel Nelson
explained the immense difficulties in reorganizing the old production
system, based as it was on subcontracting within the firm and devolving
many managerial functions to foremen:

By the 1880s the benefits and costs of the first factory system had sparked widespread
debate among managers and workers . . . In an age of short-lived, intensely competitive manufacturing firms, it was in many respects an ideal arrangement. Yet there
were also flaws. Technological innovation could place enormous strains on the
decentralised management system. In some heat-using industries a shift from large
batch to genuine flow production produced demands for better scheduling and
coordination and, inevitably, for a larger managerial staff. The growing size of the
plant had a similar effect. No matter how the manufacturer sought to insulate himself
from day-to-day affairs, his role in the factory, particularly in labour–management
relations, inevitably increased. The obvious response was to recruit a corps of specialists . . . In the following decades the factory revolution obliterated most features
of the nineteenth century manufacturing plant (1980: 10).

However, although Taylor's ideas were influential from the 1890s in the
United States and later world-wide, no firm actually adopted his full ideal of
'power to the planning department' and extreme specialization. Most took
over only some of his ideas. The diffusion of these managerial and organi-

zational innovations interacted with the diffusion of the technical innovations and systems characteristic of the third Kondratiev: electric power, telecommunications, precision machinery, and steel-intensive products, processes, and structures. Firms such as General Electric were a new type of capitalist enterprise especially suited to the conditions prevailing in the United States. They enabled the US economy to continue its fast growth when the erstwhile leader, Britain, was slowing down.

For the period 1870–1950, the two examples we have given of the steel industry and the electrical industry both demonstrate the rise of a new type of giant US corporation, using professional managers and a fairly complex administrative structure. Both took advantage of the special features of the US economy at that time—the relatively cheap and abundant supply of coal, iron, copper, and other minerals, which became available after the railways were built, and the huge scale economies of the American market.

Developments in the management of the large German enterprises, although bearing some resemblance to those in the United States, were marked by specific national features derived from German history. The chancellor of Imperial Germany in the early years of the twentieth century, Prince Bernhard von Bülow, although showing full awareness of the new industries and technologies, was rather amusingly concerned to draw a parallel between the outstanding German industrialists and the royal line, calling them 'princely merchants' and recalling earlier periods of German strength:

The perfected means of communication opened for us, in a very different manner from what was possible before, the markets of even the remotest countries . . . the incomparable progress in mechanical and electrical engineering placed at our disposal new industrial machinery . . . When employers and princely merchants like Stumm and Krupp, Ballin and Rathenau, Kirdorf and Borsig, Gwinner and Siemens were found to take advantage of these favourable conditions . . . the nation turned more and more towards the new prospects opening before it. The lower classes deserted the land and flowed in a stream into industrial undertakings. The middle and upper classes of the commonalty provided a large number of capable industrial officials. The industrialization which had given signs of growth in the middle of the nineteenth century was accomplished in Germany after the founding of the Empire, and especially after the end of the eighties, with a vehemence which had only been equalled in the United States. (von Bülow 1914: 207–8)

Weber's (1922) many contributions to economics and sociology reflected the exceptionally important role of bureaucracy in Germany. In his comments on *Capitalism and Bureaucracy in German Industrialization before 1914* (O'Brien 1994), Jürgen Kocka makes it clear, however, that Weber was well aware of some of the contradictions between capitalist and bureaucratic modes of management. He makes the important point that state bureaucracies in Prussia and other German states were well developed long before the bureaucratization of large German firms, and on a much larger scale than in either the United States or Britain (Kocka 1994). This imparted a specific thrust to the institutional changes in the German economy in the late nineteenth and early twentieth centuries. The state played a much bigger role in attempting to orchestrate the 'catch-up' of the German economy. The bureaucracies, which developed in such firms as Siemens, were strongly influenced by the procedures of the state bureaucracy in such questions as salary scales, recruitment, administrative procedures, and qualifications. Siemens–Halske was established in 1847 and employed 4,000 people by 1895 and 57,000 by 1912, of whom a high proportion were '*Angestellten*'—salaried employees who expected a career with the firm. Many of these were professional engineers or had other specific professional or craft qualifications and skills. The Verein Deutscher Ingenieure (VDI) was founded in 1856 and clearly excluded manual and craft workers, who were often described as 'engineers' in the United States and Britain. The VDI stressed theoretical background as well as practical knowledge and this became a strong characteristic of the German engineering profession.

The founder of the firm, Werner Siemens, had received part of his training in a technical military school in Berlin and had spent fifteen years in a military career before establishing his own business. Doubtless this influenced management style, although Kocka stresses that the owner–entrepreneur at Siemens always retained the capability to break with traditional hierarchical procedures and practices if business needs required it. From an early stage, written rules and instructions and fixed lines of communication prescribed norms of behaviour, and the 'influence of bureaucratic patterns from outside the firm was also evident in the status and self-image of the early salaried employees' (Kocka 1994: 8).[3]

7.7 Forging Ahead, Catching Up, and Falling Behind in the World Economy

While the displacement of Britain as the leading industrial power and the emergence of the United States as world leader was a dominant feature of the global economy at the close of the nineteenth century (Table 7.6), other changes were of greater long-term significance, although they are largely beyond the scope of this book. In particular, the gap between the leading

---

[3] In describing the changes at Siemens during the period of tempestuous growth after 1890, Kocka stresses the role of 'detailed centrally issued regulations' in sales departments and field offices: 'They were organized like public administrations and most of the activities performed in them were highly specialized and routinized. By 1910 Siemens and Halske introduced a revised shop organization. The planning and control of the factory work now took place in new planning offices in advance, clearly separated from the operations on the shop floor. Production and operations were increasingly standardized: A painstaking system of written prescriptions and controls, using forms and cards of different colours to an unprecedented extent, was introduced to rationalize the production process. It seems that Siemens, like other large German enterprises, adopted elements of 'Taylorism'—without using the name—even before these American principles of industrial organization were propagated in Germany in the last years before World War I' (Kocka 1994: 9; Homburg 1978).

TABLE 7.6. Relative shares of world manufacturing output, 1880–1938 (%)

Country	1880	1900	1913	1928	1938
Britain	22.9	18.5	13.6	9.9	10.7
United States	14.7	23.6	32.0	39.3	31.4
Germany	8.5	13.2	14.8	11.6	12.7
France	7.8	6.8	6.1	6.0	4.4
Russia	7.6	8.8	8.2	5.3	9.0
Austria-Hungary	4.4	4.7	4.4	—	—
Italy	2.5	2.4	2.4	2.7	2.8

Source: Bairoch (1982: 296); quoted in Kennedy (1988: 259).

industrialized countries and the less developed economies now became an impressive and disturbing feature of the world system. China, India, and many other countries in Asia, Africa, and Latin America now lagged far behind in industrialization and economic growth rates. Moreover, the leading ideologists of the industrialized countries were for a long while ready to accept this division as a 'natural' and enduring feature of the world system, finding its expression in the colonial subjugation of large parts of the world to European powers. Even the proponents of free trade, although often opposed to colonialism, did not really expect the division to be overcome. For example, Richard Cobden, who led the Free Trade ideology in mid-nineteenth century Britain, declared, when Egypt attempted to industrialize in the 1830s: 'All this waste is going on with the best raw cotton, which ought to be sold to us. . . . This is not all the mischief, for the very hands that are driven into such manufactures are torn from the cultivation of the soil.'

Hobsbawm, who quotes this passage from Morley's biography of Cobden, comments on the forcible imposition of free trade on Egypt in 1839–41:

Not for the first or last time in the nineteenth century the gunboats of the West 'opened' a country to trade, i.e. to the superior competition of the industrialized sector of the world. Who, looking at Egypt in the time of the British protectorate at the end of the century, would have recognized the country which had fifty years earlier—and to the disgust of Richard Cobden—been the first non-white state to seek the modern way out of economic backwardness? Of all the economic consequences of the age, this division between the 'advanced' and the 'underdeveloped' countries proved to be the most profound and the most lasting. (Hobsbawm 1977: 221)

While many countries in Africa, Asia, and Latin America, whether they were colonized or nominally independent, lagged further and further behind the leading countries, a few, especially in Europe, began to make serious progress in catching up. These were mainly countries that recognized the importance of the new technologies in industrialization and set out to acquire the necessary skills and capital (Berg and Bruland 1998). 'Catch-up' became increasingly an organized process orchestrated by the state, and not just a spontaneous reaction to the market. This was particularly true in

Imperial Germany, after the Prussian victories in the Austro-Prussian War of 1866 and the Franco-Prussian War of 1870–1.

When Friedrich List wrote his *National System of Political Economy* (1841), he had considerable doubts that Germany would ever succeed in overtaking Britain, so great did the British lead appear to contemporaries in technology, in productivity, in skills, in exports, in investment, and in wealth in the mid-nineteenth century. There was also, of course, the problem of unification of the various German states, even though one of them, Prussia, was already much stronger than the rest. But by 1913 Germany had closed this gap in many respects and was challenging Britain for commercial and naval supremacy. The United States had overtaken Britain and drawn well ahead in productivity and per capita income. The third Kondratiev wave was therefore a period of dramatic change in global economic strength and market shares and of intense international rivalry leading to the First World War. Historians are generally agreed that this 'catching-up' process by Germany and the United States was the major feature of world economic development in the last decades of the nineteenth century, although the first signs that the British lead was slipping became evident somewhat earlier.

Landes (1969: 187) argues that at mid-century continental Europe was still 'about a generation behind Britain in industrial development', and that 'when the gap between leader and follower is not too large to begin with, that is, when it does not give rise to self-reinforcing poverty, the advantage lies with the late-comer. And this is the more so because the effort of catching up calls forth entrepreneurial and institutional responses.' Prince von Bülow, as we have seen, emphasized this same point.

'Catching-up', however, is not just a question of continuing along an established technological trajectory on a fixed track; at times of paradigm change, it involves running in new directions (Perez and Soete 1988). W. A. Lewis, in his analysis of this period, points to the variation by sector and by technology, as well as by country:

When we talk about productivity we must distinguish between the old industries of the industrial revolution, including coal, pig iron, textiles and steam power, and the new industries which grew up after 1880, especially electricity, steel, organic chemicals and the internal combustion engine.

British productivity was much higher than German productivity in the old industries around 1880. Therefore, it was easy for German productivity to keep rising. In Britain, however, the old technology had been extended about as far as it could. In the cotton textile industry, and again in the utilization of coke for making pig iron, productivity moved on to a plateau in the 1880s. Even so, German productivity was still lagging, and had not fully caught up with the British even in 1913. (Lewis 1978: 121)

In the case of electricity, German firms forged well ahead of British, even though many of the original inventions and innovations had come from Britain. Contributions to the understanding of electricity in the eighteenth and nineteenth centuries were made by scientists from almost every

European country including Denmark, Sweden, Belgium, Holland, Austria, Hungary, Croatia, Serbia, as well as all the larger countries. But there is little doubt that the discoveries and inventions of Faraday, Swan, Holmes, Maxwell, Wheatstone, and Fleming were among the most important. An interesting point to note is that they made a particularly big contribution not just to scientific theories, but to very practical types of invention and innovation (Wheatstone's telegraph, his dynamo, and his use of perforated paper for operating automatic machines; Holmes's magneto and lighthouse illumination; Parsons's steam turbine, Swan's carbon filament lamp and his Newcastle factory; Fleming's thermonic valve). It might have been supposed therefore that Britain was as well placed to lead in this new pervasive technology as in the case of steam power. That it did not do so must be attributed primarily to institutional factors and particularly to inertia and rigidity in the social system.

In his Inaugural Lecture at the London School of Economics, Leslie Hannah pointed out that:

By 1914 the largest German electrical giant, Siemens–Schuckertwerke, employed as many as 80,000 men and Allgemeine Elektrizitats Gesellschaft was not far behind; and this at a time when no British electrical manufacturer employed more than 10,000. Even these small electrical firms in Britain were, moreover, not led by native entrepreneurs seeking out the new opportunities. Two of the largest—British Westinghouse and British Thomson–Houston—were subsidiaries of the American multinationals, Westinghouse and General Electric. A third, Siemens Brothers, was an offshoot of the German Siemens. Only one of the top four, GEC—no relation to GE of America—seems at first sight to have had a Briton in charge: Lord Hirst of Witton, a prominent propagandist of Empire, Conservative supporter of Joe Chamberlain, and member of the House of Lords, certainly appears English, but on close investigation this founder of GEC, though a naturalised Englishman, emerges as born Hirsch, a Jewish refugee from Prussian militarism, who came to Britain at the age of 16 in 1880. (Hannah 1983: 27)

All of this provides strong supporting evidence for Schumpeter's thesis of a lag in entrepreneurship in Britain, in comparison with Germany and the United States. However, this lag must be seen in the much wider context of social, political, cultural, and institutional changes in the three countries. On the one hand, the British educational system was not supplying sufficient people with the necessary skills for management and technical development in the new industries. On the other hand, British financial institutions (and British entrepreneurs) were directing their efforts increasingly in the 1880s and 1890s to a different type of investment (earning a higher short-term rate of return) outside Britain, especially in the Empire. Many other institutional factors contributed to the British lag.

The lack of sufficient qualified professional engineers in Britain and the smaller size of firm clearly retarded the professionalization of management, which had occurred in the United States. It also prevented the emergence of the engineering management culture, which became (and remained) such an important feature of the German (and later Japanese) style of management. Subcontracting systems and the delegation of responsibility to established craft skills remained characteristic of British industry for a long time (Lazonick 1986, 1990). Taylorism became a big influence in Britain and France only in the interwar period. A lag in the diffusion of managerial and organizational innovations was a major feature of the change in techno-economic leadership which marked the closing decades of the nineteenth century.

In both Germany and the United States, new institutions of higher education were set up in the 1870s, 1880s, and 1890s (the *Technische Hochschulen* in Germany and the institutes of technology in the USA), which greatly increased the number and improved the quality of the engineers entering the economy. In these countries, too, financial institutions adapted their structure and their policies to the needs of financing the new technological developments on a large scale. As a result, as we have seen in Section 7.5, much larger firms developed in the steel and electrical industries in both Germany and the United States, and such firms were the focus of new types of management system and new types of entrepreneurship. The new 'professionalization' of management, which was characteristic of both Germany and the United States (although in very different forms), hardly touched the higher levels of most British firms until later. In Germany in particular, highly qualified professional engineers (and chemists in the chemical industry) came to dominate management culture and to influence long-term product development and investment strategy in a way that made '*Fortschritt durch Technik*' a real phenomenon in the leading sectors of German industry.

If anything, even more serious was the failure in Britain to develop systematic education and training for middle and lower-level technical and craft skills. The British tradition of part-time training and education 'on the job' may have been appropriate for the techniques based on mechanical ingenuity and learning by doing in the early stages of the Industrial Revolution, but they were increasingly inappropriate for the skills associated with the new technologies. This was the single biggest difference between Britain and most other European countries. There was no shortage of warnings from educationists, industrialists, and indeed from official government inquiries and commissions (C. Barnett 1986), so that the failure to take effective action must be attributed to socio-political choices and priorities and to inertia in British institutions. R. M. Macleod (1977) gives a particularly thorough account of the failures in educational reform in nineteenth-century Britain.

The wave of electrification and heavy engineering required considerable investment, but comparisons of capital formation in Britain and other countries show that a much higher proportion of national product was being invested in Germany, the USA and some 'newly industrializing countries' such as Italy and Sweden from the 1880s onwards (Table 7.7).

TABLE 7.7. Capital formation as a percentage of national product

	UK[1]	USA[2]	Germany[3]	Italy[4]	Sweden[5]
1825–1836	3.8[a]				
1836–1845	5.4				
1845–1857	7.0		8.9[b]		
1857–1866	7.1		10.8	9.1[c]	
1866–1873	6.8		12.8[d]	8.9	
1873–1883	7.8		11.1[e]	8.4[f]	10.8[g]
1883–1890	5.5	22.0[h]	11.5[i]	10.8[i]	9.1[j]
1890–1903	7.7	17.9[k]	12.9	9.3	12.0[l]
1903–1913	6.5	17.2	15.3	14.8	12.1
1913–1920	4.4	11.6		5.9	12.1
1920–1929	8.4	14.6	11.9[m]	15.2	13.0
1929–1937	9.1	6.1	5.3	15.5	15.1
1937–1948	7.1	7.7		15.3	18.8
1948–1957	14.0	16.3	14.7[n]	18.0	21.4
1957–1966	16.8	15.3	19.6	19.5	23.8
1966–1973	18.5	15.5	17.2	18.2	23.3
1973–1979	18.4	15.1	12.3		21.4
1845–1873	7.0		10.7[o]	9.0[p]	
1873–1890	6.8		11.3[q]	9.6	9.9[r]
1890–1913	7.2	17.5[s]	13.9	11.7	12.1[t]
1920–1929	8.4	14.6	11.9[m]	15.2	13.0
1929–1948	7.9	7.0		15.3	17.3
1948–1973	16.3	15.7	17.4[u]	18.6	22.8

Notes

Percentages are arithmetic averages of annual rates.
[1] Gross capital formation, excl. stocks, as % of GNP.
[2] Gross private domestic investment, excl. stocks, as % of GNP.
[3] Net capital formation, incl. stocks, as % of NNP.
[4] Gross capital formation, incl. stocks, as % of GNP.
[5] Gross capital formation, excl. stocks, as % of GDP.

[a] 1830–6 [b] 1850–7 [c] 1861–6 [d] 1866–72 [e] 1872–82 [f] 1873–82 [g] 1870–81 [h] 1890–5 [i] 1882–90 [j] 1881–94 [k] 1895–1903 [l] 1894–1903 [m] 1925–9 [n] 1950–7 [o] 1850–72 [p] 1861–73 [q] 1872–90 [r] 1870–94 [s] 1895–1913 [t] 1894–1913 [u] 1950–73.

Sources: USA: Kendrick (1961) for 1890–1948; *Economic Report of the President*, 1980, for 1948–79; all other countries: Mitchell (1981); van Duijn (1983: 159).

Table 7.8 shows that from 1905 to 1914 foreign investment amounted to more than 50 per cent of British net capital formation. Obviously, therefore one explanation of why Britain was overtaken by Germany and the United States was the UK's failure to invest enough in the domestic economy to diffuse the new technologies and expand the scale of production. Since there were major economies of scale in electricity, as well as in steel and in many other growth industries, such as chemicals, this could account for part of the British lag. Only in some industries based on world-wide

TABLE 7.8. German and UK foreign investment as a
percentage of total net capital formation (at current prices)

Germany		United Kingdom	
1851/5–1861/5	2.2	1855–64	29.1
1861/5–1871/5	12.9	1865–74	40.1
1871/5–1881/5	14.1	1875–84	28.9
1881/5–1891/5	19.9	1885–94	51.2
1891/5–1901/5	9.7	1895–1904	20.7
1901/5–1911/13	5.7	1905–14	52.9

Source: Lewis (1978).

networks of mining (RTZ), plantations, oil extraction and refining (Shell), tobacco, and such services as insurance did large British firms do relatively well and retain a position in the population of the world's largest firms (Hannah 1997).

The tendency for British firms to seek a higher rate of profit in overseas investment was already described by Hobson (1902) and by Lenin (1915) in their studies of 'imperialism'. British colonial possessions and spheres of influence at that time offered opportunities for profitable investment, in plantation and mining activities supplying raw materials, in 'railroadization', and in other types of infrastructural investment. In terms of markets, too, the Empire offered well established and relatively secure and sheltered channels of shipment, distribution, finance, and communications. Whereas financial services in Germany and the United States were geared predominantly to the rapidly expanding capital requirements of domestic industry, this was not the case in Britain. At the same time, the enormous strength of the City of London in financial services meant that 'finance capital' and overseas portfolio investment increasingly dominated in economic policymaking, rather than manufacturing. The social and cultural changes described by Hobson and, more recently, by Hobsbawm (1968) meant that the impetus to bring about a different type of institutional change, more conducive to the renovation of the British industrial and technological structure, was greatly weakened.

The failure of the British economy to keep up with the growth of Germany and the United States after the depression of the 1870s and 1880s is often cited as evidence to 'disprove' the hypothesis of long waves in the world economy. In a macroeconomic statistical sense, there was indeed little or no third Kondratiev upswing in Britain (Table 7.9). Schumpeter (1939: 430), after observing that 'the London money market concerned itself in fact mainly with foreign and colonial issues to an extent never equalled in England or in any other country', and that 'at home entrepreneurial activity in the fundamental lines distinctly stayed behind America and Germany', commented that in Britain 'electricity affords one of the few cases in which performance of the private entrepreneur was so inadequate

TABLE 7.9. Long wave upswing and downswing growth rates and industrial production, USA and Europe

	United Kingdom		United States		Germany[a]	
2nd Kondratiev						
Upswing	1845–1873	3.0	(1864–1873	6.2)	(1850–1872	4.3)
Downswing	1873–1890	1.7	1873–1895	4.7	1872–1890	2.9
3rd Kondratiev						
Upswing	1890–1913	2.0	1895–1913	5.3	1890–1913	4.1
Downswing	1920–1929	2.8	1920–1929	4.8	1920–1929	—
	1929–1948	2.1	1929–1948	3.1	1929–1948	—
4th Kondratiev						
Upswing	1948–1973	3.2	1948–1973	4.7	1948–1973	9.1
	France		Italy		Sweden	
2nd Kondratiev						
Upswing	1847–1872	1.7				
Downswing	1872–1890	1.3	1873–1890	0.9	1870–1894	3.1
3rd Kondratiev						
Upswing	1890–1913	2.5	1890–1913	3.0	1894–1913	3.5
Downswing	1920–1929	8.1	1920–1929	4.8	1920–1929	4.6
	1929–1948	−0.9	1929–1948	0.5	1929–1948	4.4
4th Kondratiev						
Upswing	1948–1973	6.1	1948–1973	7.9	1948–1973	4.7

[a] 1948–73: West Germany.

Sources: UK: W. G. Hoffmann (1955) for 2nd Kondratiev (GB data); Feinstein (1976) for 3rd and 4th Kondratiev; Germany, France, Italy, and Sweden: B. R. Mitchell (1981); Van Duijn (1983: 156).

as to invite, on the obvious merits of the case acknowledged by all parties, government initiative and public planning' (p. 432). Nevertheless, his conclusion from this comparison between Germany, the USA, and Britain was: 'Our sketch suffices to show that in England's case economic history from 1897 to 1913 cannot, owing to the comparative weakness of the evolution (in our sense) of her domestic industries, be written in terms of our model—the only case of this kind within the epoch covered by our material' (p. 435).

So far from the 'English case' not conforming to 'our model', it is the English case that most powerfully demonstrates the validity of the model, as we have outlined in the Conclusions to Part I. We emphasized there the necessity to take full account of the 'semi-autonomous' developments in the political and cultural subsystems, as well as in technology and the economy. As we have seen, Schumpeter does in fact touch on some of the institutional lags and negative features that retarded and frustrated the growth of the new technological systems in Britain, but, characteristically, he tends to attribute the difference mainly to a lag in 'entrepreneurship activity'. His model does not permit him to give any prominence to the institutional and social framework as constraining or stimulating both entrepreneurship and the technological transformation of the economy. Consequently, he has to treat England as an exception. In terms of our model advanced in the Conclusions to Part I and the Introduction to Part II, however, it is precisely this English 'exception' that 'proves the rule'.

Despite the great German successes in overtaking Britain in the period before 1914, both Germany and Britain suffered a relative decline by comparison with the USA. As described by von Bülow (1914) in his book on *Imperial Germany*, leading circles in German industry felt disadvantaged by the size of the British colonial empire and world-wide British access to sources of raw materials and markets. The world-wide intensification of export competition led to increasingly strained international relations and to the Anglo-German naval arms race in the years before 1914.

Von Bülow (1914) recalled that 'to build a sufficient fleet was the foremost and greatest task of German policy after Bismarck's retirement: a task with which I also was immediately confronted, when on June 28th 1897, I was entrusted by his Majesty the Emperor with the conduct of foreign affairs'. He had no doubt that the naval arms race was directly related to commercial competition following successful German industrialization: 'Today German industry has its customers even in the remotest corners of the earth. The German merchant flag is a familiar sight in foreign ports and knows that it is protected by the German navy' (p. 206). He was also well aware that the successful German 'catch-up' had created serious internal as well as external strains:

We have reason to be proud of our mighty industrial success, and the satisfaction of the German patriot is justified, if he points out in what an extraordinary short space of time we Germans in our economic development have covered the ground which half a century ago separated us from nations that we have now outstripped. Such success is only possible due to the exuberant vitality of a nation thoroughly sound, strong of will and full of ambition. But we must not conceal from ourselves the fact that the almost furious speed of our industrial ascent often hindered calm organic development and created discords which demanded adjustment. (von Bülow 1914: 206)

Extraordinary though it may seem today, the 'threat' of the German navy was taken so seriously in the upper echelons of the British government that a pre-emptive strike to 'take out' the embryonic German fleet was seriously contemplated. The defeat of Germany in the First World War and the reparations imposed after the war seriously damaged the German 'catch-up', but the US economy emerged even stronger than its European competitors. This led to a very sharp contrast between the United States and Europe in the 1920s and to a world-wide structural crisis of adjustment in the 1920s and 1930s, which is analysed in the next chapter.

8

The Fourth Kondratiev Wave: The Great Depression and the Age of Oil, Automobiles, Motorization, and Mass Production

8.1 From the Third to the Fourth Kondratiev Wave

In previous chapters, we have explained why we did not accept a standard econometric view of long waves based simply on changes in the trend growth rate of GDP. For us, the 'downswing' of a long wave is not just a slower rate of growth in aggregate production, although this may well occur: it is a period of structural adjustment to the very rapid rise of a new constellation of technologies. It is the sharp contrast between the surging growth of the new industries and the slow-down, stagnation, or even contraction of the old ones, that is the main feature of the 'downswing', not the combined aggregate of all industries.

At the end of Chapter 5 we described the turbulent period following the Napoleonic Wars and the previous upsurge of the Industrial Revolution. Total production continued to grow in Britain in the 1820s, 1830s, and 1840s, but it was a period of great structural change, with some old industries, such as handloom weaving, in deep decline and some new ones, such as railways and steam engines, enjoying rapid growth, even to the extent of 'bubble' phenomena. Periods of heavy unemployment in some areas accompanied this change, which gave rise to acute political and social conflicts and to major institutional changes.

In Chapter 6 we attempted to show that, with the new institutional framework of free trade and *laissez-faire* social and industrial policy, a period of prosperous and more even growth ensued, based on the new railway infrastructure, steam ships, and the mechanization of many industries through steam power. However, as the final section of that chapter showed, this period of mid-Victorian prosperity also ended with a structural crisis of adjustment, not only in Britain, but also in the newly industrializing countries, especially Germany and the United States. Turbulent political and institutional changes were other outcomes of this structural crisis, with the rise of protectionism, nationalism, and imperialism, as well as socialist parties, new industrial unions, and strike waves.

In Chapter 7 we again traced the rise of a pervasive new technology—electrification—and a new core input—steel and its alloys—until they came to dominate the world economy from the 1890s to 1914. This upswing phase of the third Kondratiev wave was once more followed by a crisis of structural adjustment in the downswing of the 1920s and 1930s. But, for several reasons, we shall treat this downswing and the ensuing crisis in the first sections of this chapter rather than in the final section of Chapter 7.

In the first place, the final phase of the crisis of structural adjustment, known ever since as the 'Great Depression', was deeper and had more profound social consequences than any previous crisis. Second, this crisis followed the first *world* war, fought on a scale and with an intensity never previously equalled. (For this reason, it has been known as the 'Great War', depressing though it may be to contemplate these events as the landmarks of the twentieth century.) The Great Depression led to an even more destructive *second* world war. It was indeed, as Hobsbawm (1994) designated it, an 'Age of Extremes', and it was also marked by the first major attempt to establish an entirely different type of economy—the Russian Revolution of 1917 and the Five-Year Plans of the 1920s and 1930s. It was thus an extraordinary period of political and social change.

These international conflicts and sharp political struggles within countries were closely intertwined with the rise of a new constellation of technologies based on oil, aircraft, and tanks, as well as the automobile and consumer durables. We have therefore chosen to start our account of this new constellation with the downswing of the third Kondratiev wave, which was in part the result of, and in part the reason for, the very uneven development of the world economy (Section 8.2). The unevenness was aggravated by the persistence of conflicts over reparations in the 1920s, following the exhausting battles of the First World War. As Keynes (1920) had so accurately predicted, the reparations required from Germany created such a heavy burden of international indebtedness that they gave rise to great economic instability, to *revanchisme* in Germany, and to a new war in 1939 (Section 8.3). It is true that other political and social factors influenced this outcome, but this economic disturbance was certainly a major factor.

The very rapid rise of the automobile industry in the United States aggravated still further the uneven development of the world economy and the internal structural problems within the United States itself. Sections 8.4– 8.8 analyse the new constellation based on the automobile and mass production (8.4), on oil as the core input (8.5), and on a network of motor highways as the new transport infrastructure. Section 8.6 considers the influence of automobiles and oil on many other industries, and Sections 8.7 and 8.8 describe the triumph of the mass consumption paradigm and of mass culture in the prolonged period of prosperous growth following the Second World War. Section 8.9 briefly describes the new regimes of regulation that emerged as a result of the Allied victory in the Second World War and the outbreak of the Cold War. These gave a far greater role to state coordination both in the military and in the welfare fields. Finally, Section 8.10 brings the wheel full circle with an account of the new crisis of structural adjustment from the 1970s to the 1990s.

8.2 The Great Depression in the United States

Economists may disagree about some of the variations in GDP growth rates in the earlier Kondratiev waves, but there is very little such disagreement about the downswing of the third (*c.* 1918–40) or about the subsequent boom after the Second World War and the downswing that followed from the 1970s to the 1990s. This disagreement centres not on the decline in growth rates in the Great Depression of the 1930s and the heavy unemployment that accompanied this decline, but on the causes of the Great Depression. Our own emphasis is on the instability engendered by the tempestuous growth of new industries, the euphoria attending this growth, and the uneven development of the global economy, aggravated by international conflicts over reparations, arms, and trade.

In his review of alternative explanations, Aldcroft (1977) distinguishes numerous possibilities but puts the main emphasis on two types of explanation: 'monetary' and 'real'. Milton Friedman is renowned for his explanation based almost entirely on failures in monetary policy (Friedman and Schwartz 1963), but this is contested by many other economists (see, e.g. Temin 1976). Most recently, Christopher Dow (1998), in his *magnus opus* on the *Major Recessions* from 1920 to 1995, made a detailed critique of the Friedman–Schwartz theory (Dow 1998: chap. 6 and Appendix). Aldcroft too mainly favours the 'real' explanations of the turning point in 1929, mentioning in particular those by T. Wilson (1948), R. A. Gordon (1951), Hansen (1951), and Rostow (1971), with their emphasis on the exhaustion of investment opportunities in the US boom in the 1920s; but he accepts the importance of monetary factors in the prolongation of the recession (Aldcroft 1977: 282), as we would ourselves.

The general view of the US economy in the late 1920s was highly optimistic. The Report of the National Bureau of Economic Research on *Recent Economic Changes* (the Hoover Report) spoke of 'the unprecedented utilisation of power and its wide dispersion by automobile and tractor, in which this country leads the way . . . the great development of corporate enterprize has gone on to new heights. It may be creating, as some think, a new type of social organization' (Hoover Report 1929: 6–7).

It seems that euphoric ideas about a 'new economy' have a rebirth with each great technological revolution. Academic economists argued that stocks were not overvalued, and even Irving Fisher, regarded by many as the greatest American economist, spoke of stocks 'on a permanently high plateau' (Galbraith 1954: 95). At the end of his life, however, Fisher broke away from monetary theories of the business cycle and developed an original theory of the depression, summarized in the first volume of *Econometrica* in 1932. In this theory, debt-financed Schumpeterian innovations fuel a boom, which is followed by a recession, which can turn into a depression via an unstable interaction between excessive real debt burdens and deflation (Tobin 1987:

375). Our own interpretation continues this emphasis on technical and structural change.

This chapter concentrates on the structural changes in the American economy in the first place, because the United States continued to be the leading power in the world economy after the First World War. In 1914 US manufacturing accounted for 56 per cent of world manufacturing output, Germany for 16 per cent, and Britain for 14 per cent. This disparity was even greater by 1918. Moreover, the United States was the technological leader in the cluster of innovations that predominated in the fourth Kondratiev, as it was in the third. Despite the fact that many of the original inventions for the internal combustion engine were made in Europe before the end of the nineteenth century, it was in the US automobile industry that mass production took off before the First World War, and the United States completely dominated the industry in the 1920s, accounting with Canada for nearly 90 per cent of the world output of trucks, cars, and tractors (Figure 8.1).

Although most economists agree that internal factors in the US economy were among the most important influences in the explanation of the depression, several have pointed to international factors as equally important, such as the transformation of the United States from a major debtor country to the leading creditor country. In particular, the problems of Germany as a debtor country and the contraction of US foreign lending to Europe and elsewhere have been seen as major contributing factors to the instability of the 1930s (e.g. Landes 1969). We therefore also devote considerable attention to Germany as well as the United States (Section 8.3). The role of Britain in the world economy was by now greatly reduced, but the adoption of protectionism in what was then the 'British Empire' was still a notable event in the 1930s.

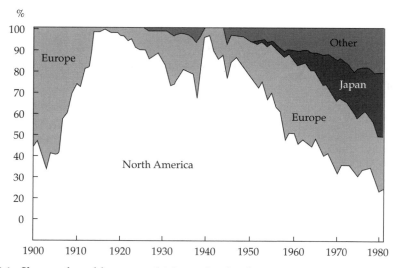

FIG 8.1. Shares of world motor-vehicle production by region, 1900–1980
Source: Altshuler *et al.* (1995).

Dow (1998: 171) distinguishes between those events that started the 1929 recession and those that made it the deepest and most prolonged recession in history, especially in the United States. In the first category, he identifies five factors that, in his view, imparted 'a perceptible exogenous shock' in 1929:

1. the Wall Street Crash;
2. the end of the housing boom;
3. the rise in interest rates;
4. the contraction of the exports of the primary producing countries;
5. the beginnings of the 'slightly earlier and largely independent recession in Germany'.

He considers, however, that the effect of each one of these five was relatively small and that, even together, they could not explain the depth of the 1930 downturn, which he therefore attributes to 'a swing in consumer and business confidence' in reaction to the preceding boom. The main factor that prolonged the depression in the United States was, in his view, the structure of the banking system and the resulting bank failures. The 1920s boom was driven more by the indirect effects of the expansion of the automobile industry than by the auto industry itself:

Especially in the years up to 1926, there was a very rapid expansion of the automobile industry. Investment in producing cars, though rising rapidly, was itself much less important than the investment stimulated by their greater use—in roads, service and supply centres, and oil refining and the new urban and suburban building that occurred as households moved out of cities once they had cars. This was indeed to some large extent a once-for-all stimulus. The same is true of the post-1921 investment boom in electric power, other public utilities and the telephone system. (Dow 1998: 167)

J. K. Galbraith, in his classic and highly entertaining book on *The Great Crash* (1954), had no hesitation in asserting that '[t]he polar role of the stock market in American life in the summer of 1929 is beyond doubt' (p. 109) and in assigning to the stock market crash in October 1929 a crucial role in triggering the depression. He stressed that, as with earlier financial bubbles, in the final stage of a boom 'all aspects of property ownership become irrelevant except the prospect for an early rise in price' (p. 46).

Dow also does not hesitate to describe the US stock market in 1929 as a 'bubble situation', and he too stresses its special position in the American economy. However, he does not follow the events in 1929 in so much detail as Galbraith, nor does he discuss the financial manipulation which sustained the bubble for so long. Galbraith gives a more vivid picture of the psychology of euphoria and of panic, which both he and Dow agree were important in the Great Depression, and which coincides with the popular understanding of that event.

Galbraith emphasizes that, contrary to a view widely held in the United States in the 1920s the so-called 'fundamentals' of the economy were not 'sound'. While it was true that production and employment were high and rising, the distribution of income was increasingly unequal, agriculture (which still accounted for over a quarter of total employment in the 1920s) was very depressed, and the fragility of the real estate bubble had already been exposed in 1925–6. In Galbraith's view, the stock market crash had such a devastating effect because 'business in 1929 was *not* sound; on the contrary, it was exceedingly fragile. It was vulnerable to the kind of blow it received from Wall St. . . . . Yet when a greenhouse succumbs to a hailstorm, something more than a purely passive role is normally attributed to the storm. One must accord a similar significance to the typhoon which blew out of lower Manhattan in October 1929' (Galbraith 1954: 204).

One indication of the crisis of structural adjustment in the 1920s in the United States was the inability of either the old transport infrastructure (the railways) or the new infrastructure (the roads) to cope with the Florida real estate boom:

Throughout 1925 the pursuit of effortless riches brought people to Florida in satis-factorily increasing numbers. More land was sub-divided each week. What was loosely called seashore became five, ten or fifteen miles from the nearest brine. Suburbs became an astonishing distance from town . . . . The congestion of traffic into the state became so severe that in the autumn of 1925, the railroads were forced to proclaim an embargo on less essential freight which included building materials for developing the subdivisions. Values rose wonderfully. (Galbraith 1954: 34)

Even in the early 1920s, there were demonstrations of protest in American cities about the inadequacy of the road network, and the young Eisenhower, later to become commander-in-chief and US president, was one of those who took part.

A more serious cause of instability was the emergence of over-capacity in several industries, especially automobiles. Automobile production had reached over 4 million vehicles by 1926, and the rest of the economy had problems in adjusting to this headlong rate of expansion. Galbraith puts considerable emphasis on the tendency for the growth of productive ca-pacity in the automobile and other durable goods industries to outstrip the growth of the domestic market. In his view, the limits of the market and the over-capacity were in turn related to the unequal distribution of income, and to restrictions on imports from the United States in Europe and elsewhere (Table 8.1).

As has been the case with other very rapidly growing industries (the semi-conductor industry is a good contemporary example), the advance of the automobile industry was not smooth, occurring rather in short rapid spurts alternating with years of slower growth or actual decline. Thus, production fell sharply in 1918, in the 1921 recession, in 1924, and again in 1927 (Fearon 1987). One reason for this last fall was that Henry Ford discontinued pro-duction of the Model T car in 1927, closing his plants and laying off

TABLE 8.1. Tariffs on passenger cars, 1913–1983 (% of customs value)

	USA	Japan	France	Germany	Italy	UK
1913	45.0	n.d.	9–14	3	4–6	0
1924	25–50[a]	n.d.	45–180	13	6–11	33.3
1929	10.0[b]	50	45	20	6–11	33.3
1932	10.0	n.d.	45–70	25	18–123	33.3
1937	10.0	70[c]	47–74	40	101–11	33.3
1950	10.0	40	35	35	35	33.3
1960	8.5	35–40	30	13–16	31.5–40.5	30.0
1968	5.5	30	0/17.6	0/17.6	0/17.6	17.6
1973	3.0	6.4	0/10.9	0/10.9	0/10.9	10.9
1978	3.0	0	0/10.9	0/10.9	0/10.9	0/10.9
1983	2.8	0	0/10.5	0/10.5	0/10.5	0/10.5

Notes
Ranges in this table indicate that tariffs varied by type of vehicle or reciprocally with foreign tariffs. For example, in the 1920s the US tariff varied from 25 to 50 per cent, being adjusted within that range to equal the auto tariff in the country of origin. The 'slashes' in the entries for the European countries after 1968 (1978 in the case of the UK) indicate the elimination of tariffs within the EEC and a common external tariff.

[a] 1922; [b] 1930; [c] 1940; n.d. = no relevant data available.

Sources: Altshuler *et al.* (1985).

thousands of workers. General Motors now became the dominant firm in the US and world industry, and Mariana Mazzucato (1998) has shown that instability in market shares and in stock exchange valuations remained a feature of the US industry right down to the 1940s (Figure 8.2).

Auto production in the United States increased sharply again in 1928 by 28 per cent and by 23 per cent in 1929, but despite this upsurge total output of vehicles was only a little higher than in 1926. However, these fluctuations in output were dwarfed by the fall from 4.8 million in 1929 to 2.8 million vehicles in 1930 and 1.1 million in 1932. Exports fell even more catastrophically, from over 600,000 in 1929 to 65,492 in 1932. This colossal fluctuation in the output and export of automobiles and other durable goods was one of the most notable features of the Great Depression.

As we have seen, Christopher Dow emphasized the induced growth of road-building, service stations, and supply centres in the 1920s boom in the USA, but in addition there were many other areas of induced growth, notably the rubber industry, the steel industry, the glass industry (see Table 8.2), and numerous suppliers of engineering components and machine tools. Dow also mentions oil refineries; their output of petrol (gasoline) was growing even faster than that of the automobile industry, as indeed it had to, to keep pace with the demands of car and truck drivers. This growth was only made possible thanks to a series of innovations in the cracking of petroleum, described in Section 8.4. All of these industries and services were affected by any downturn in automobile sales, as much as by their tempestuous growth. Thus,

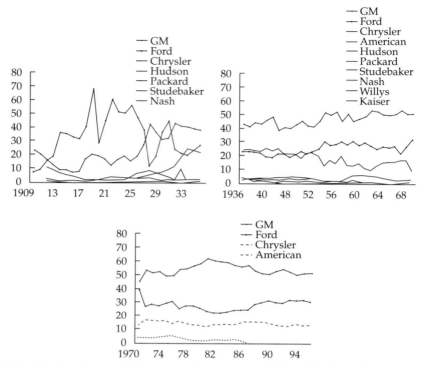

Fig 8.2. Market shares of US automobile producers, 1909–1995 (% of US production only)

Source: Mazzucato (1998).

rapid structural change contributed to the instability of the US economy in the 1920s and to the collapse in the 1930s.[1]

Unemployment fell as low as 1.8 per cent of the civilian labour force in the United States in 1926 and varied between this level and 5 per cent during most of the 1920s after the severe recession of 1921. But, although this might be regarded as close to full employment, Fearon (1987) and others have stressed several features of the employment situation which made for a widespread feeling of insecurity in employment. Two of the industries that experienced considerable growth—construction and automobiles—were subject to major seasonal fluctuations and temporary layoffs without pay.

---

[1] A Hungarian economist working in Moscow (Varga 1939) in the 1930s gave an interesting contemporary estimate of the contrast between what he called 'new' and 'old' industries in the 'capitalist world' in the period 1905–36 (Table 8.3). Pointing to the very rapid growth of some 'new' industries even during the depression of the 1930s, he commented: 'all these data show clearly that there can be no talk of stagnation or even of a crippling of the productive forces of the capitalist world economy in the period of general crisis. The development of productive forces goes on even if the rate is slowed down, even if it is extremely unequal both according to countries and branches of industry, and although it is seriously deflected by war preparations' (Varga 1939: 34).

TABLE 8.2. Share of automotive consumption in total consumption of selected products USA, 1929 and 1938 (%)

	1929	1938
Strip steel	60	51
Bar steel	29	34
Sheet steel	29	41
Alloy steel	—	54
Steel, all forms	18	17
Malleable iron	52	53
Plate glass	73	69
Rubber	84	80
Aluminium	37	11
Copper	16	12
Tin	24	9
Lead	31	35
Zinc	6	10
Nickel	26	29

Source: Landes (1969: 443).

Several of the older industries, such as ship-building, cotton, coal, and railways, were relatively depressed. Fearon reports several studies that revealed widespread anxiety about technical change and structural change in the work-force. He also points out that the separation rate for workers in 1923–9 was three times as high as in 1899–1914. Consequently, despite the boom in the economy, it seems legitimate to regard the 1920s as a period of considerable turbulence, instability, and insecurity. This was, of course, even more true of conditions in Europe, where unemployment was typically higher, growth slower, and civil strife widely prevalent, with revolutions in several countries following the Russian Revolution of 1917.

8.3 The Great Depression in Germany

As in the period from 1873 to the 1890s, described in the final section of Chapter 6, the higher levels of unemployment and insecurity gave rise to extreme nationalist movements in Europe, as well as to the rise of socialism and communism. Fascist and militarist regimes were established in several European countries, most notably Italy and Germany.

The triumph of Hitler in 1933 was, of course, directly related to the depth of the crisis in Germany. It is quite often said that the rise of the Nazis was due to the hyperinflation of 1923, and no doubt the social damage inflicted by this extraordinary inflation was one of the contributory causes. However, the attempt by Hitler and Ludendorff to launch a *putsch* in 1923 in Bavaria was an abject failure, and the vote for the Nazi Party never amounted to

TABLE 8.3. 'Old' and 'new' production of the capitalist world, 1905/13–1933/6

	'Old' branches of industry				
	Coal and brown coal (m tons)	Iron (m tons)	Steel (m tons)	Shipbuilding (m registered tons)	Consumption of cotton (m centners)
1905–1913	1,133	63	57	2.5	14
1914–1918	1,252	66	73	2.9	12
1919–1923	1,228	56	64	4.4	41
1924–1929	1,398	80	95	2.2	51
1930–1932	1,186	57	66	1.7	45
1933–1936	1,149	55	80	1.2	46
	Index (1913 = 100)				
1905–1913	85	80	75	75	89
1914–1918	96	83	96	87	85
1919–1923	92	71	84	132	83
1924–1929	104	101	124	69	104
1930–1932	89	72	86	51	92
1933–1936	86	72	104	36	94

	'New' branches of industry				
	Petrol (m tons)	Aluminium ('000 tons)	Nitrogen ('000 tons)	Artificial Silk ('000 tons)	Automobiles ('000)
1905–1913	40.2	35	178	16	263
1914–1918	64	96	459	—	1,241
1919–1923	104	114	566	32	2,534
1924–1929	162	210	1,090	123	4,957
1930–1932	169	211	1,555	218	3,037
1933–1936	201	213	—	381	4,302
	Index (1913 = 100)				
1905–1913	78	56	51.5	100	46
1914–1918	123	151	133	—	214
1919–1923	202	180	163.5	196	438
1924–1929	314	332	315	759	858
1930–1932	328	334	315	1,348	858
1933–1936	390	338	—	2,351	743

Source: Varga (1939: 43–4)

more than about 3 million votes (out of an electorate of over 30 million) before 1930. It was only after the steep rise of unemployment in 1930–2 that the vote for Hitler's party climbed, first to 6 million in 1930 and then to 13 million in 1932. By that time there were about 6 million unemployed workers in Germany, and they provided a fertile recruiting ground for the paramilitary formations of the Nazi Party (the SA and SS) as well as giving rise to immense general discontent and a big vote also for the German Communist Party in 1932.

It was mainly in the 1930s that important sections of German industry began to look to the Nazi Party to find a way out of the Depression and to crush the Communists. Sohn-Rethel (1978) provided a fascinating account of this evolving relationship, which he was able to observe at first hand while working as an editorial assistant on the *Führerbriefe*, an exclusive newsletter serving the top echelons of big business. According to his account, some of the largest firms, such as the chemical giant IG Farben and Siemens, stood somewhat aloof from the Nazi Party until after Hitler took power. The sections of German industry that had the closest embrace with the Nazis were the 'old' branches rather than the 'new' ones. The steel industry, and particularly Krupp, were the strongest supporters of the 'Harzburg Front', an alliance of the Nazis and other nationalist groups, seeking to restore some of their past glories.

Sohn-Rethel attributed the dominant influence of Krupp to the financial independence and strength of the concern even in the 1930s, and to its very intimate relationship with the army High Command. As the leading firm in the steel industry, Krupp spoke for those sections that had been, to some degree, disadvantaged after the First World War and during the structural crisis of the German economy:

The iron and steel industry had lost the independent competitive role it had played before the 1914–18 war. It had attained its powerful position by building railways, ships and armaments in which it had held the initiative to sub-contract to other branches of industry. But now this relationship was to a large extent reversed . . . by the end of the 1920s the leading role had fallen to the so-called new industries . . . while the iron and steel magnates had slipped into the subordinate position. This was hardly to their liking and one need only visualize the domineering role they were to play in the first three years of the Hitler regime to understand the goals which the lords of the *Stahlhof* had in mind for the Harzburg Front. Only a determined policy of rearmament could realize their aims and free the full productive potential of their plant from the restricting shackles of the market system, opening up the sluice gates for an all-out resumption of activity. (Sohn-Rethel 1978: 46)

The above account of the relationship between the structural changes in the economy and the political changes has concentrated on the German example because it was to prove the most fateful for the future of the entire world, but the Great Depression stimulated a search for new solutions everywhere, and some of these were very different from the Nazi solution. Progressive social reforms were attempted in several countries in Europe, especially in Spain and in Scandinavia, both in the sphere of social policies and in that of economic policy. The 'New Deal' following Roosevelt's election in 1932 and his triumphant re-election in 1936 were the most obvious manifestation of new attempts to bring about institutional changes that might return the economy to the pre-Depression levels of prosperity. However, it was the militaristic and nationalist solutions in Germany and Japan that initially proved more successful in restoring growth and employment in the short term. The Japanese economy was the first to recover, stimulated by the invasion of Manchuria in 1931 and the subsequent war on China. The United States did not again reach the 1929 level of aggregate output until 1937, and then only briefly. It was the Second World War, with its growth in world-wide demand for goods and services, that restored prosperity to the American economy. The fast growth constellation of the fourth Kondratiev became the dominant force in the war economy with its huge production of military vehicles, tanks, aircraft, petrol, aviation fuel, machine tools, armaments, and synthetic rubber.

Neither Dow nor Galbraith gives much emphasis to international factors in the Great Depression. Indeed, Dow argues explicitly that it was overwhelmingly an American phenomenon, and that other countries were far less seriously affected (Tables 8.4 and 8.5). 'It has become fashionable to say that the Great Depression of the 1930s was not just a US but a world depression. That is less than half true. Quantitatively, much the greater part of the depression was in the United States and (it will be argued) the causes of both its origin and its amplification lay mostly there also' (Dow 1998: 158).

However, he does concede that the recession severely affected the less developed countries which supplied primary commodities and which had to reduce dramatically their imports of manufactures from both the USA and Europe. Dow estimates that Europe's exports to primary producers fell from about 5 per cent of GDP at its peak to 2 per cent in 1932. 'This immediately provides an explanation for a good part of the recession in countries outside the United States' (p. 159).

Moreover, even though he assigns the primary role to the internal factors in the United States, he does maintain, in his critique of Friedman's explanation of the Great Depression—exclusively in terms of monetary policy— that other countries were profoundly influenced by the United States:

there is an international dimension which Friedman and Schwartz do not face up to, which creates a similar difficulty for their argument. Depression in the United States was so deep that it must, I think, be held to have largely determined the coincident depressions in other countries, and in the transmission process *non-monetary* channels (international trade) must have been important. (Dow 1998: 216)

TABLE 8.4. Unemployment levels as a percentage of the labour force, 1929–1935

	1929	1931	1933	1935
Belgium	0.8	6.8	10.5	11.1
Denmark	8.0	9.0	14.5	10.0
Germany	5.9	13.9	14.8	6.5
Italy	1.7	4.5	5.9	n.a.
Netherlands	1.7	4.3	9.7	11.5
UK	7.2	14.3	13.9	10.8
USA	3.1	15.2	20.5	14.2

Source: Freeman *et al.* (1982: 2).

TABLE 8.5. Effects of the Great Depression: movement of industrial output in the 1930s (%)

	1929–32	1932–37	1929–37
Group I			
Japan	−2	74.4	71
Greece	1	49.5	51
Finland	−17	79.5	49
Sweden	−11	67.4	49
Hungary	−23	77.9	37
Denmark	−9	47.2	34
Rumania	−11	48.3	32
Norway	−7	37.6	28
UK	−17	49.3	24
Group II			
Germany	−42	100.0	16
Austria	−39	73.7	6
Group III			
Canada*	−42	72.4	00
Italy	−33	49.2	—
Czechoslovakia	−36	50.0	−4
Belgium	−31	36.2	−6
United States	−46	70.3	−8
Netherlands	−38	46.7	−9
Group IV			
Poland	−46	57.4	−15
France	−31	4.3	−28

*Including construction and electric power.

Source: Landes (1969: 391).

Most historians (e.g. Kindleberger 1973; Arndt 1944) and most commentators at the time assign rather more importance to the reciprocal influences of events in Europe, the United States, and the primary producers. In particular, the recession in Germany, which was more severe than in most other European countries, began *before* the US recession (as Dow himself recognizes: 1998: 168) and was strongly affected by the pressures for external debt repayments going back to the First World War. As we have already observed, in his brilliant critique of the Versailles Treaty, Keynes (1920) had argued that it would be impossible for Germany to pay the reparations demanded and that the attempts to enforce repayment would lead to a second world war. Both predictions proved accurate, and even though the war debts were successively scaled down under the Dawes Plan and the Young Plan, German external payments remained a major source of instability throughout the 1920s.

In common with most other European countries, Germany imposed increasingly severe tariffs on imported automobiles (Table 8.1), and behind this protective wall the German automobile industry recovered in the 1920s, although it remained far smaller than that of the United States. European production of motor vehicles grew from less than 5 per cent of total world production in 1920 to over 20 per cent in 1930 (Figure 8.1), with Germany and the UK leading the European expansion.

The German recovery from the depth of the depression in 1932 was far more rapid than that of any other European country. Covert rearmament had already begun before Hitler came to power in January 1933, but with his accession it became the major driving force in the German economy. On 17 March Schacht was reappointed as president of the Reichsbank and one of his first decisions was to pledge a Reichsbank loan of 600 million marks for the construction of a network of super-highways—the so-called *Autobahnen* (Weitz 1997). A few days earlier he had endorsed a government-subsidized programme for urban renewal and factory construction. Road-building was quite a widely used technique for creating employment in the 1930s and plans had actually already been prepared. It was this type of programme that earned him a (somewhat undeserved) reputation as the 'first Keynesian'—he was an ingenious, pragmatic banker, not a theoretical economist.

Schacht embodied the combination of financial skills and a strong conviction about the importance of massive German rearmament, which guided macroeconomic policies firmly in the direction of a managed war economy from 1933 onwards. True enough, as Landes (1969: 414) points out, Schacht was still in some respects a 'fiscal conservative'. Like most bankers, he was still preoccupied with the dangers of inflation, and some of the Nazi leaders, such as Goering, were impatient with what seemed to them in 1936 and 1937 the slow pace of rearmament. Nevertheless, arms production grew with extraordinary speed and the use of raw materials and skilled labour was controlled by a series of decrees in the 1930s. By 1938 permits were required for all construction projects using more than 2 tons of steel.

The motivation for the Autobahn network was not merely employment creation and infrastructural investment for the new economy, but was also for troop movements and war preparation. In his biography of Schacht (*Hitler's Banker*), Weitz (1997) shows that, despite his minor disagreements with the Nazi leaders, Schacht was always a firm believer in a strong rearmament policy and immediately set about large-scale rearmament. He set up a small corporation misleadingly called the Metallurgische Forschung GmbH (Mefo), or Metallurgical Research Corporation. In fact, its purpose was to finance large-scale government contracts for armaments. Weitz estimates that there were 21 billion marks in orders.

Payment was guaranteed by the Reichsbank . . . All sub-contractors were also paid in Mefo bonds, which were really IOUs. They would then present their bills to the Mefo Corporation, which took them to the Reichsbank. . . . At the same time manufacturers earned a 4 per cent interest on the bonds for as long as they held them . . . Because payment was guaranteed by the Reichsbank corporate capital reserves . . . came out of hiding. (Weitz 1997: 157)

The project began with four large owners of Mefo—Krupp, Siemens, Rheinstahl, and Gutehoffnungshütte—but was now joined by others, and the value of bonds grew from the original 1 million marks to 12 billion, half of which could be traded on the open bond market.

The participation of Siemens was interesting, as Sohn-Rethel (1978) had noted that this firm stood rather aloof from the Nazi Party before Hitler took power and even supported representations made by Max Planck to Hitler on behalf of the Kaiser Wilhelm Society. They had fears for the weakening of German science by the Nazi treatment of leading Jewish physicists, but Hitler replied: 'Yes, well, what does it matter if Germany, for one generation, has no leading physicists? The racial purity of the German people is much closer to my heart' (Sohn-Rethel 1978: 40).

The despair of Siemens in the early years of the Hitler regime about the fate of German science and the loss of the company's export markets was compensated by the rise of new markets in rearmament. The great mass of financially weak German firms welcomed Hitler's rearmament policy because 'they could escape the more or less acute danger of bankruptcy' (Sohn-Rethel 1978: 39).

Weitz summarized the Mefo project: 'Schacht called it an inventive way of priming industrial production and wiping out unemployment. Many others considered it a well-camouflaged ruse for cranking up armaments production without much visible accountancy or unduly alarming the outside world' (Weitz 1997: 156).

Overy (1975) argues that the motor industry was even more important than rearmament in the German recovery in the 1933–6 period. Certainly, both Schacht and Hitler demonstrated their awareness of the key role of automobiles and roads for the German economy as well as for its war machine by their joint appearance at the opening ceremony of the first Autobahn (Frankfurt–Darmstadt) and by their support for the mass production of the 'People's Car' (Volkswagen) established as a state enterprise.

The Second World War was above all a *motorized* war. While it was true that the German army began the war with more divisions using horse transport than motorized vehicles, it was the *Panzer* divisions and the motorized infantry divisions that ended the trench warfare stalemate of the First World War and advanced to the Channel coast so rapidly in 1940 and to the outskirts of Moscow in December 1941. Military historians appear to agree that the decisive battle of the war was the massive tank battle at Kursk in the summer of 1943, when the Red Army was able for the first time to deploy a large enough number of tanks of a quality sufficient to inflict a major defeat on the German tank divisions. They also agree that in the final stages of the war in Western Europe it was the overwhelming

Anglo-American superiority in aircraft, tanks, and motorized equipment that was decisive. Finally, the extraordinary strategic importance of oil and rubber was demonstrated by the massive German effort to develop and produce synthetic oil and rubber in very large quantities, as well as by the Japanese and American strategy in the Far East in 1940–1 and the creation of the vast American synthetic rubber industry during the war.

This section has already introduced the new fast growth constellation of the fourth Kondratiev wave, based mainly on the automobile and oil industries, and has described the period of turbulent structural change that attended its rapid growth in the 1920s and 1930s. The more settled period of prosperity, high growth, and full employment that followed the Second World War in many countries rested mainly on the Keynesian techniques of demand management adopted by many governments and by international organizations and on the induced growth of many other industries and services, which are described in Sections 8.6 and 8.7. It was also based on many organizational and managerial changes at micro level, which are described in the following section.

8.4 The Automobile Industry and Mass Production

Following Carnot's theoretical enquiries, the internal combustion engine was originally developed mainly by French and German inventors and engineers in the 1860s and 1870s. Nikolaus Otto built his first gasoline-powered engine in 1861, but the first four-stroke engine was patented by a French engineer, Beau de Rochas, in 1862. Otto continued to develop improved engines, and in 1876 designed and built a very successful four-stroke engine. However, in 1886 his patent was revoked in the light of Rochas's earlier patent. A still more efficient internal combustion engine was patented by Rudolf Diesel in 1892. Diesel was a product of the new Munich Technische Hochschule, where he had a brilliant academic record. Through the 1890s he worked hard at the firm of Linde, with the support of Krupp and the Augsburg Machine Works, to design and produce a series of prototypes. Finally, in 1897, he demonstrated a 25 HP four-stroke engine operating on his principle of compression without spark ignition. It was immediately a great commercial success, and provides a good example of the inventor making a fortune from the royalties. However, the diesel engine's success was limited to the 'heavy' applications for marine engines (including submarines) and stationary industrial power, tractors, and heavy trucks. This range was greatly extended in the 1930s with the development of the diesel-electric locomotive at the R&D laboratories of General Motors. A major advantage of the diesel was that it could use low-grade fractions of oil. However, with the development of distillation techniques in oil refining and the availability of cheap gasoline (Section 8.5), the lighter internal combustion engines retained their advantage for the great majority of cars.

By 1905, however, hundreds of small companies were producing automobiles in the United States as well as the main European countries. They all used craft techniques and general purpose machine tools scattered in small machine shops. The craft workers were highly skilled and coordinated by the assembly entrepreneur. A few firms today still make a small number of cars by craft techniques, but they are very expensive and account for only a tiny proportion of total output. Most of the small firms have long since gone bankrupt or been taken over as the industry made the transition to mass production. It was Henry Ford, more than anyone else, who was responsible for this transition.

Section 8.2 has already demonstrated the crucial role of the United States automobile industry following Ford's introduction of mass production techniques before the First World War. However, it is essential to distinguish Ford's technology from numerous earlier attempts to introduce mass production in various industries.

In the late nineteenth century, the use of interchangeable parts had already spread from its first innovative application in the US Ordnance Department's Springfield Armory to other American industries and the even earlier applications in British machine tools and block-making for the Admiralty described in Chapter 5. In the early twentieth century, many new applications were being found, but none of these, not even the Armory itself, had been able to dispense with skilled craft workers to file and fit at least some, and usually quite a high proportion, of the components. What existed in the so-called 'American system of production' before Ford was, in fact, a hybrid or 'late craft system', in which some interchangeable parts co-existed with many craft-shaped parts in the final product. This was the situation in such industries as sewing machines, small arms, agricultural machinery, and bicycles (Hounshell 1984).

The first true application of mass production techniques was by Henry Ford in his Highland Park Plant at Detroit. Between 1908 and 1914, Ford gradually eliminated craft-made components in the manufacture of the Model T, and this process culminated with the introduction of the moving assembly line in 1913. As the MIT book on the 'International Motor Vehicle Project' (IMVP) emphasizes (Womack *et al.* 1990), the assembly line itself was made possible only by Ford's introduction of machines and presses, which could cut, shape, or stamp out each one of the components. Technical innovations accompanied the organizational and managerial changes, but in this section we shall discuss mainly the organizational innovations in the automobile and related industries. We concentrate on organizational and social change because the 'mass production paradigm', or more simply the 'Fordist paradigm', dominated management philosophy for more than half a century and only late in the twentieth century began to give way to a new style of management thinking and organization.

The IMVP authors (Womack *et al.* 1990) provide a beautiful illustration of what it meant to change from craft to mass production. When a wealthy

English MP, Ellis, went to buy a car in 1894, he did not go to a dealer, as none existed: he went to the French machine tool manufacturer, Panhard et Levassor (P and L), and 'commissioned' an automobile. He wanted the transmission, brake, and engine controls moved from their usual place. The IMVP authors point out that 'for today's mass producer, this would require years—and hundreds of millions of dollars to engineer', but for the craft producers of that time such a request was quite normal.

B. H. Klein showed that in 1900, steam[2] and electric vehicles accounted for about three-quarters 'of the four thousand automobiles estimated to have been produced by 57 American firms' (Klein 1977: 91). However, by 1917 about three and a half million automobiles had been registered in the United States, of which less than 50,000 were electric. Steam vehicles were disappearing; the last major steam manufacturer, the Stanley Motor Carriage Company, produced 730 steam vehicles in 1917—fewer than Ford produced in one day before lunch (Volti 1990: 43). The simple explanation of the decline of steam and electric vehicles seems to be, with the benefit of hindsight, that the internal combustion (gasoline) engine was 'better' or even 'optimal'. However, in his fascinating article 'Why Internal Combustion?' Rudi Volti shows that things were by no means so simple. In the very early days both steam and electric cars had many technical advantages, and the IC automobile had some severe disadvantages, notably the sliding gear transmission invented by Emile Levassor (the 'L' in 'P and L') in 1891. His own description of his invention became famous: 'C'est brutal mais ça marche!' The electric car was simpler to start and to drive, having no clutch or transmission; moreover, it was quiet, reliable, and odourless. Yet by the 1920s the internal combustion engine completely dominated the car market, leaving the steamers and electrics to very specialized niche markets or museums.

A longer operating range was undoubtedly one of the decisive advantages of the IC engine, but this was not purely a technical matter. The chain of re-fuelling stations and repair and maintenance facilities could conceivably have been organized on a different basis, given different strategies and policies of the utilities, manufacturers, and regulators. Indeed, in the 1990s policies were being developed to cope with battery recharging services for electric cars in California and elsewhere, because of the pollution problems caused by millions of IC engines. However, the 'lock-in' to the IC engine makes any such change to an alternative system a truly massive undertaking. There were over 500 million automobiles in use in the world by the mid-1990s. The availability of cheap low-cost petrol (gasoline) was a decisive advantage of the IC engine (Section 8.4), and compounded by this vast lock-in to the internal combustion engine was the success of Ford's assembly line, which reduced the cost and price of the Model T dramatically. The price of a Model

---

[2] The first steam car was actually built in 1801 by R. Trevithick, but no one would buy it and so it was scrapped and the engine sold to a mill. The lack of any suitable infrastructure was the basic problem (Cowan and Hulten 1994).

T fell from $850 in 1908 to $600 in 1913 and to $360 in 1916, because of a combination of organizational, technical, and social innovations. The price of electric cars in 1913 was $2,800. Not surprisingly, the sales of the Model T increased fifty times over and market share increased from 10 per cent in 1909 to 60 per cent in 1921. Profits on net worth were sometimes as high as 300 per cent per annum, and the USA attained a dominant position in world export markets. This was indeed 'fast history', analogous to the tempestuous growth of the semiconductor industry half a century later or the cotton industry a century earlier, with its similar drastic price reductions, rapid changes in market shares, sudden profits for innovating firms, and world export hegemony for the leading country until imitators caught up. In the end, the Model T sold 15 million units before it was discontinued in 1927.

At first, in 1908, when Ford had achieved a high degree of interchangeability of parts, it was the workers who moved from car to car around the assembly hall, and already the division of labour into specialized tasks had achieved big increases in productivity. Womack *et al.* believe that these increases were greater than those achieved by the moving assembly line itself, when it was introduced in 1913. But the moving line was a highly visible change, and therefore attracted more attention. Table 8.6 shows a contemporary calculation of the productivity gains made between 1913 and 1914 by the introduction of the moving assembly line at the Highland Park plant in Detroit. The designation of the 1913 system as 'late craft' is questionable, as by then the filing and fitting of each inaccurate part had been virtually eliminated. In fact, the Ford production system differed already from all the earlier efforts to develop interchangeability of parts, as Hounshell (1984) showed in his classic work, *From the American System to Mass Production*.

Ford himself, in his own accounts of the triumph of mass production, emphasized on the one hand the resemblance to flow production in flour milling and to the dis-assembly line of the Chicago meat packers, and on the

TABLE 8.6. Craft production versus mass production in the assembly hall, 1913 and 1914: minutes of effort to assemble various products and % reduction in effort[a]

	Late craft production, fall 1913[b]	Mass production, spring 1914	% reduction in effort
Engine	594	226.0	62
Magneto	20	5.0	75
Axle	150	26.5	83
Major components into a complete vehicle	750	93.0	88

[a] Calculated by the authors from data given in Hounshell (1984: 248, 254–6). Hounshell's data are based on the observations of the journalists Horace Arnold and Fay Faurote (1915).
[b] 'Late craft production' already contained many of the elements of mass production, in particular, consistently interchangeable parts and a minute division of labour. The big change from 1913 to 1914 was the transition from stationary to moving assembly.
Source: Womack *et al.* (1990: 29).

other hand the *mass consumption* arising from the cheapness of large-scale production. Singer, McCormick, and Pope, who have sometimes been described as pioneers of mass production, all sold their products at high prices; like Wedgwood for a part of his range (see Chapter 5), their prices were the highest in their respective industries (Hounshell 1984: 9). Ford, on the other hand, insisted that the Model T was truly designed as a car for the masses. The reduction of prices was an essential part of his doctrine, and Peter Drucker (1946) maintained that his demonstration of falling costs and prices with the increasing scale constituted a revolution in economics as well as in management techniques. Moreover, unlike many other early IC engine cars, the Ford T was deliberately designed for ease of maintenance and ease of operation. It was also designed as a very robust car, which could be used on rough roads. The sixty-four-page owner's manual was intended to help the owner to solve many of the common problems that might arise. Ford assumed, however, that many of his early customers would be farmers, with experience of farm machinery and some tools to hand (Womack *et al.* 1990). Geographical and social characteristics of the US market and his attention to them also contributed to Ford's success. Personal mobility at low cost was the decisive advantage of the internal combustion engine to the consumer.

The radical change in the production system was not an easy one for the work-force:

the assembler on Ford's mass production line had only one task—to put two nuts on two bolts or perhaps to attach one wheel to each car. He didn't order parts, procure his tools, repair his equipment, inspect for quality, or even understand what the workers on either side of him were doing. Rather he kept his head down and thought about other things. The fact that he might not even speak the same language as his fellow assemblers or the foreman was irrelevant . . . the assembler required only a few minutes training. (Womack *et al.* 1990: 31)

The machining of parts was also reduced to a few simple operations by the redesign of the tools and presses to carry out one simple repetitive task each. New machine tools were a very important part of the Fordist revolution (B. H. Klein 1977: 97). In this way, the need for skilled workers was reduced to a minimum and the plant was controlled and coordinated by the new profession of industrial (production) engineers and an army of foremen and indirect workers responding to their orders. Ford took advantage of a situation where Taylor's ideas were already widely diffused (see Chapter 7), but he developed the doctrine much further. Discipline was strict and unions were banned. Ford tried hard to implement Wedgwood's principle (Chapter 5): 'to make such machines of men as cannot err'. He failed in this objective. Poor industrial relations were a major problem for Ford after the Model T, and GM took advantage of this in overtaking Ford in the 1920s (Lazonick 1990). In the 1930s, despite bitter opposition, the new industrial union, United Automobile Workers, and industrial unions in the other mass production industries succeeded in unionizing the major plants. Roosevelt's

New Deal legislation facilitated this major change in American industrial relations (see Conclusions to Part II).

With respect to wages, the new system did not work out quite as Ford (or Babbage, even earlier) had imagined. The speed of the line, the boring nature of the work, and other unpleasant features of employment, such as the work discipline, led to an extremely high turnover of labour during the first year of operation. In 1913 it reached nearly 400 per cent, so that Ford was obliged on 5 January 1914 to introduce the '5–Dollar Day', which meant in effect that the wages of Ford workers were doubled. 'With highly mechanized production, moving line assembly, high wages and low prices on products, "Fordism" was born' (Hounshell 1984: 11). The much higher productivity of the new system meant that these high wages could easily be paid and Ford could still remain by far the most profitable automobile company in the United States and in the world. For the workers, there was a trade-off between higher wages and the unpleasant conditions of employment on the assembly line. Immigrant workers were important in the automobile industry in the United States and Europe partly for this reason.

Detroit in the early 1920s became a place of what can only be described as a pilgrimage of top industrialists, engineers, and celebrities from Europe. Indeed, Ford's plants in Detroit retained their competitive advantage in costs right through the interwar period, even over their own new plants established in Europe (Womack *et al.* 1990: 18).

At an early stage, Ford and his collaborators had to accept the obvious fact that some defective parts were an inevitable feature of his system. The solution adopted was not to improve the skills or responsibilities of the production line workers, but to have an inspection and 're-work' department at the end of the line. Even so, of course, some defective cars would get through this procedure too, so that customer complaints always accompanied mass production. One of the main objectives of the Japanese producers who challenged the Fordist system after the Second World War was to make a drastic reduction in the number of defective parts or subsystems. They had some success in achieving this objective, but for half a century American and European producers simply accepted defects and rejects as a cost of mass production which they believed was greatly outweighed by the benefits of a vast output of cheap and fairly efficient machines.

Ford's immense success obliged other American firms to introduce the assembly line, to become small niche producers, or to go to the wall. A few of them were combined in a new company, General Motors (GM), which offered a successful challenge to Ford in the 1920s by modifying some of his more eccentric and autocratic ideas. Alfred Sloan, the chief architect of this giant corporation, introduced a more sophisticated strategy, with various divisions taking responsibility for specific market segments, a greater range of models, more frequent model changes, and steady incremental improvements, coming partly from production engineers, but also from a large R&D activity. Many of Ford's key personnel left him and joined GM (Lazonick 1990: 240).

The IMVP authors point out that GM's research laboratory[3] 'proved vital to the welfare of the entire world auto industry when its scientists and engineers—on very short notice—perfected the exhaust catalyst technology, now used by every car company in the world to produce automobiles that meet emission standards' (Womack *et al.* 1990: 129). However, they also offer some interesting comments on why GM failed to introduce radical innovations in the manufacture of the automobile itself: 'Unfortunately, in the absence of a crisis—a situation in which the future of the company was at stake and normal organizational barriers to the flow of information were suspended—new ideas percolated from the research centre to the market very slowly.' They list the Corvair Project (1950s), the Vega Project (1960s), the X-Car Project (1970s), and the high-tech factories for the GM-10 products in the late 1980s among GM's failures: 'In each case, innovative ideas for new products and factories foundered when implementation could not live up to the original technical targets' (p. 129).

Womack *et al.* offer another particularly interesting explanation of why GM was not more innovative in automobiles in the interwar and postwar years. They point out that, although Sloan was an MIT graduate in electrical engineering, he maintained that 'it was not necessary to lead in technical design or run the risk of untried experiments [provided that] our cars were at least equal in design to the best of our competitors in a grade' (Sloan 1963).

The MIT authors appear to suggest that it was the existence of a tight oligopoly of only three large producers with GM as the dominant firm (see Figure 8.2 and Mazzucato 1998), that restrained radical innovation:

when GM had sewn up half the North American auto market, any truly epochal innovation—say a turbine-powered truck or a car with a plastic body—could have bankrupted Ford and Chrysler. The auto makers' plight would certainly have attracted the attention of a US government intent on preventing monopoly in its largest industry. So caution made sense. GM hardly wanted to innovate its way to corporate dismemberment. (Womack *et al.* 1990: 128)

Utterback (1993) has shown that the pattern of evolution displayed in the twentieth century by the US automobile industry was characteristic of several other industries, both before and since, such as typewriters, bicycles, sewing machines, televisions, and semi-conductors. An early radical product innovation leads to many new entrants and to several competing designs. Process innovations and the scaling up of production then lead to

---

[3] GM has had a highly successful R&D activity, although paradoxically some of its most important inventions and innovations have been made outside the automobile industry—in diesel–electric locomotives and in chemicals. Kettering persuaded GM in 1930 to purchase two companies already quite advanced in the development of diesel–electric technology. 'The combination of the diesel-engine and electric traction equipment was not new, but General Motors, by acquiring two small pioneering firms, by placing the large resources of their research organization to the task, and by taking advantage of a large potential domestic market, finally established the great commercial advantage of the system' (Jewkes *et al.* 1958/1969: 251).

the emergence of a dominant robust design, the erosion of profit margins, and a process of mergers and bankruptcies, ending with an oligopolistic structure of a few firms. Incremental innovations then tend to prevail in both product and process; 'lock-in' to a dominant paradigm is regarded simply as 'common sense'.

Among both European consumers and European managers and engineers, there remained a certain arrogant contempt for mass-produced goods, which contrasted with American cultural traditions and probably also was a retarding factor in diffusion. However, this fairly rapidly diminished once per capita incomes began to rise in the postwar world and the masses actually had the opportunity to purchase cars and other consumer durables. Most of Western Europe caught up in per capita incomes between 1950 and 1975, and the pattern of ownership of durables came to resemble that of the United States fairly closely. West European car output surpassed that of the United States in the 1960s (Table 8.7).

This catch-up process was mainly based on the now successful diffusion of American industrial technology and management techniques. The Marshall Plan, the European Recovery Agency, and its successor the OEEC (later OECD) all laid great stress on this transfer, and many industrial missions went to study US productivity in American firms in the early postwar years. US companies and especially Ford and General Motors had long established production plants in several European countries, and this too facilitated the absorption of American techniques. However, European

TABLE 8.7. World automobile production and exports, 1929–1980 (million units)[a]

	1929	1938	1950	1960	1970	1980
Production						
North America	4.8	2.1	7.0	7.0	7.5	7.2
Western Europe	0.6	0.9	1.1	5.1	10.4	10.4
Japan	—	—	—	0.2	3.2	7.0
Centrally planned	—	0.1	0.1	0.3	0.7	2.1
Rest of world	—	—	—	0.4	1.0	1.8
Total production	5.4	3.1	8.2	13.0	22.8	28.6
Exports						
Intra-North America	0.1	—	—	—	0.9	1.1
Exports from North America	0.4	0.2	0.1	0.1	0.1	0.1
Intra-Western Europe	—	0.1	0.2	1.0	2.7	3.7
Exports from Western Europe	0.1	0.1	0.4	1.2	1.8	1.3
Japanese exports	—	—	—	—	0.7	3.9
Other exports	—	—	—	—	0.2	0.8
Total exports	0.6	0.4	0.7	2.3	6.4	10.9

[a] Not available or negligible.

Source: D. T. Jones (1985: 136).

manufacturers were not purely passive recipients of American technology or simply imitators. They were active innovators themselves, and were especially innovative in design (see Womack et al. 1990: 46–7). They had a big export success with small cars, sports cars, and some luxury cars.

Among the important innovations of West European producers in the 1960s and 1970s were front-wheel drive, disc brakes, fuel injection, unitized bodies, five-speed transmissions, and high power-to-weight ratios. American firms had led with 'comfort' innovations, such as power steering, air conditioning, stereos, and automatic transmission. The rise in oil prices in the 1970s gave some advantages to the Europeans, especially in small fuel-efficient cars, and they took this opportunity to expand their exports to the United States. From being the dominant producer and exporter of cars for half a century, the United States became a net importer.

However, the main reason for the loss of American dominance in the world market was not so much European competition as the meteoric rise of Japan. As with Ford in 1913, this rapid rise was based on a radical redesign of the entire production system. Since the Meiji Restoration of 1868 in Japan, there had been great emphasis on the improvement of imported technology by process innovation. The method of assimilating and improving upon imported technology was mainly some form of 'reverse engineering' (Pavitt 1985; Tamura 1986; Freeman 1987). The widespread use of reverse engineering in the 1950s and 1960s had several major consequences for the Japanese system of innovation, affecting especially the characteristic R&D strategy of the major Japanese companies. Japanese management, engineers, and workers grew accustomed to thinking of the entire production process as a system and of thinking in an integrated way about product design and process design. This capability to redesign an entire production system has been identified as one of the major sources of Japanese competitive success in industries as diverse as ship-building, automobiles, and colour television (Peck and Goto 1981). Whereas Japanese firms made few original radical product innovations, they did redesign many processes and make many incremental innovations to improve productivity and raise quality. The automobile industry is probably the most spectacular example (Altshuler et al. 1985; D. T. Jones 1985; Womack et al. 1990; Graves 1991).

By 1989 Japan was producing more cars (over 9 million) than the United States (just under 8 million). The International Motor Vehicle Project (IMVP) was organized with the support of most of the main automobile producers world-wide, because of their recognition of the importance of Japanese techniques in process technology and management organization. The American producers were successful in imitating some key features of the Japanese system, and by the late 1990s the US industry had regained world leadership. Japanese firms also invested in their own plants in North America. The industry was now a mature oligopoly, with US and Japanese producers taking over some of the few remaining small and medium-sized European producers.

8.5 Oil as the Core Input of the Fourth Kondratiev

It was the combination of the mass production of automobiles and the availability of cheap and abundant petroleum that made possible the motorization of the world economy in the twentieth century.

However, one of the products of oil (kerosene/paraffin) had been used as an illuminant long before the product now known as gasoline or petrol began to be used on a large scale as a fuel for the internal combustion engine. The oil industry was developed, first of all, as a source of kerosene for lighting and of heavy fuel oil for heating. It took a series of inventions and innovations before gasoline could be separated in sufficiently large quantities of good enough quality and at low enough cost to provide it on the scale needed for the mass use of automobiles. John D. Rockefeller made his vast fortune from the Standard Oil Company, which he founded, not from automobile-derived demand, but from the transport and sale of oil to refineries and to market by rail for use in lighting and heating.

By 1860 there were already fifteen refineries distilling crude oil for kerosene. Production rose to 3 million barrels in 1862 and hundreds of new oil companies were floated. The first bubble burst in 1866–7, but this was only the beginning. In these early days the output of oil was counted in millions of barrels, but when it became the core input for the dominant mass production style of manufacture it was counted in billions of barrels (Table 8.8). As this table suggests, by 1939 it had satisfied the criterion of universal availability, and in fact, between 1910 and 1939 production increased so rapidly that the industry grew much faster than world industrial production (Table 8.3). The price of oil, relative to other commodities, was falling from the high levels of the 1860s down to very low levels in the 1960s (Figure 8.3). Its production thus satisfied the twin criteria of universal availability and descending price. Tankers, containers, wagons, and refineries were scaled up accordingly for global distribution.

Even before its large-scale use as the preferred fuel for automobiles, oil was the object of an intense competitive struggle for control both within

TABLE 8.8. World crude oil production, 1939–1991

	Oil produced (bn barrels)
1939	2.1
1950	3.8
1960	7.7
1973	20.4
1991	22.6

Source: authors' own estimates.

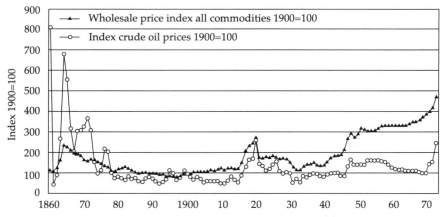

FIG 8.3.(*a*) Variation of oil price index in relation to the wholesale price index, USA, 1860–1973

Source: Data from US Department of Commerce, *Oil Economists Handbook*, 5th edn., and authors' own calculations.

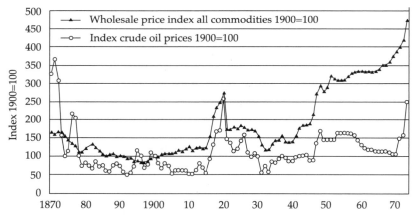

FIG 8.3.(*b*) Variation of oil price index in relation to the wholesale price index, USA, 1870–1973

nations and between nations. Once it became the fuel for trucks, cars, aircraft, and many types of ship, its strategic importance made it the object of world-wide military diplomacy. This became particularly obvious during the so-called 'OPEC' crises of 1973 and 1979, when the temporarily successful efforts of some of the main producing countries to raise the price precipitated both economic and political crises in many countries. But the Middle Eastern oilfields had already become the objects of intense great power interest even before the First World War. In 1911 Churchill became convinced that war with Germany was inevitable and decided as First Lord of the

Admiralty that the Royal Navy had to convert to oil from coal (Yergin 1991: 11). Diesel oil was also the chosen fuel for the new German submarines.

None of this vast development of the oil industry would have been possible without the numerous process innovations in the refineries, which began with the Standard Oil Company's first efforts to establish a regular research activity. These process innovations have been particularly well documented by Enos (1962), whose book shows in detail how the combination of successive innovations and scale economies reduced the cost of gasoline by almost an order of magnitude between 1910 and 1960 (Table 8.9).

The man who introduced the first really successful commercial cracking process was William Burton, who took a Ph.D. in chemistry at Johns Hopkins University in 1889. Perhaps the most significant fact about his first industrial employment is that he was deliberately recruited and appointed by Standard Oil to run a laboratory at the Whiting refinery in the Indiana subsidiary. Although the laboratory was in an old farmhouse and he had to make many of his own instruments, Burton was able to make a number of improvements in the refinery methods. As a result, he was rapidly promoted to be superintendent of the refinery and two other Ph.D.s were appointed to the laboratory. As refinery manager, Burton was able to command the resources necessary for pilot plant experimental development in 1909 and 1910. He and his colleagues were able systematically to test out the results of cracking at various temperatures and pressures on different fractions of oil and to develop a satisfactory thermal cracking process.

Enos estimates that the development cost of $236,000 was paid back ten times over in the first year of operation, 1913. Subsequently, the royalty income alone amounted to over $20 million. The patent position, on both the original invention and the improvement inventions, was strong, and Standard Oil of Indiana charged 25 per cent of the profits for using the process. Altogether, nineteen companies were licensed by 1921, but they were restricted to selling in certain areas under the terms of the agreements.

TABLE 8.9. Comparison of the productivity of the Burton and fluid cracking processes

Input	Consumption of inputs (per 100 gallons of gasoline)		
	Burton process	Fluid process, original installation	Fluid process, present installations
Raw material (gallons)	396.00	238.00	170.00
Capital (1939 $)	3.6	0.82	0.52
Process labour (man-hours)	1.61	0.09	0.02
Energy (m BTUs)	8.4	3.2	1.1

Source: Enos (1962: 224).

Moreover, they acquired the patent rights only, with no accompanying technical know-how. These circumstances provided a significant stimulus to the development of alternative processes as well as leading to the collapse of many small refineries. In 1920 four, and in 1921 five, more new cracking processes were introduced, which gives some idea of the intensity of the inventive effort that followed the extremely profitable Burton process.

The high profits made by some innovators in the oil industry paralleled the extraordinary profits made by Ford in the mass production of automobiles (Section 8.4) and assured the success of the new paradigm already by the 1920s. However, the world depression of the 1930s brought about a drastic change for a short period. Harold Ickes, the US Secretary for the interior, after receiving a telegram from the governor of Texas about the catastrophic fall in oil prices, introduced a new regime of regulation under Roosevelt's 'New Deal'. Ickes was fully aware of the vast importance of oil for the future of the US economy. 'There is no doubt about our absolute and complete dependence on oil. We have passed from the Stone Age, to Bronze, to Iron, to the Industrial Age, and now to an Age of Oil. Without oil, American civilization as we know it could not exist' (quoted in Yergin 1991: 254). From 1935 to 1940, the price of oil was stabilized at about $1 per barrel.

Technical progress in cracking methods continued rapidly in the 1920s and 1930s and efforts were concentrated on catalytic techniques for cracking after a French engineer–inventor, Eugene Houdry, began his experiments in 1925. The successful introduction of a catalytic cracking process by Houdry's Corporation working with Sun Oil and Socony Vacuum was a powerful stimulus to the parallel work of Standard Oil of New Jersey. Licensing negotiations indicated that the Houdry Process Corporation expected to get about $50 million if the Houdry process was adopted as its standard cracking process. This very tough attitude led New Jersey to reject this possibility and to concentrate instead on developing its own process. It was inclined to do this in any case, because of the limitations of the fixed-bed Houdry process, Standard Oil's own R&D capability, and the know-how it had acquired from IG Farben, the giant German chemical firm, on hydrogenation at high pressure. Standard Oil was convinced that world-wide demand for gasoline would continue to expand for a long time to come, so that long-term strategy required a strong technical effort in this field. The organization was in a good position to challenge the Houdry process by 'leapfrogging' to a better one. From the outset, it was recognized that a fully continuous flow process would be far better than the semi-continuous Houdry fixed-bed catalyst system. Another major aim was to establish a process that could be used for a wide variety of crude stocks and not limited to higher grades.

In pursuing these aims, Standard Oil of New Jersey made common cause with other oil companies and process companies that felt themselves threatened by the Houdry process. In 1938 a group was formed, known as Catalytic Research Associates, consisting originally of Kellogg, IG Farben,

Indiana Standard, and New Jersey Standard, and soon joined by Shell, Anglo-Iranian (BP), Texaco, and UOP. Interestingly, it was Kellogg, a process design and construction company, that took the initiative in convening the first meeting in London which led to the joint research programme. The group (without IG) commanded the resources of R&D facilities employing about 1,000 people (400 in Standard Development), and the work demanded the cooperation of specialists in many different fields.

The collaborative R&D, which was carried out from 1938 to 1942 to develop the fluid catalytic cracking process, was one of the largest single programmes ever set up before the atom bomb. Although the total costs of R&D were ultimately over $30 million, the process was extremely profitable. New Jersey Standard had received over $30 million in royalties alone by 1956. By this time the process accounted for over half of total world cracking capacity and had prevented the Houdry process from ever achieving more than a 10 per cent share. The original fixed-bed process declined rapidly after 1943, but improved versions (TCC and Houdriflow) continued to compete. The fluid process was a triumph for the big battalions and demonstrated that oil had indeed become the core input for the entire economy, both for civil and for military applications. The new processes provided very good high-grade aviation fuel.

Thus, during the Second World War, as a result of intensive and large-scale R&D in some of the strongest companies in the world at that time, technology had reached a point where supplies of gasoline, diesel fuel, and aviation fuel could meet the vast increase in military demand. In Germany and the rest of continental Europe too, despite the Allied blockade, the innovations of IG Farben assured a supply of synthetic oil from coal, albeit at higher cost. Only Japan still felt severely disadvantaged, which was one of the main factors precipitating the war in the Far East and the occupation of Indonesia and other parts of East Asia. The Second World War could be fought with motorized weapons and oil and the basis was laid for the decades of prosperity that followed.

8.6 Other Fast Growth Industries: Aircraft, Tractors, Consumer Durables, and Synthetic Materials

It is not possible here to do justice to the full range of industries and services of the fourth Kondratiev constellation and to their technical and economic interdependencies. Some grew as rapidly as the oil and automobile industries, because their products and services were directly needed by these leading sectors. Such was the case, for example, with the numerous distributors of these products and the service stations required for repair and maintenance. Others supplied components, such as tyres and brakes for automobiles, or tankers, pumps, valves, and compressors for the oil refineries. Still others, while not directly serving the automobile industry, grew up using similar production techniques and often similar materials. Such was the case with consumer durables like refrigerators and washing machines.

The importance of the tractor industry should certainly not be overlooked. Based on an essentially similar technology to the automobile industry and the manufacture of heavy trucks and tanks, it made possible the mechanization and motorization of American agriculture and later of world agriculture. By 1930, despite the relatively depressed state of American agriculture, there were already nearly a million tractors in use on American farms. The transfer of US tractor technology to the Soviet Union in the 1920s and 1930s was a critical element in Stalin's plans for the collectivization of Soviet agriculture, which were based on a network of machine and tractor stations (MTSs) serving the new collective farms. Some automobile producers, such as Ford, also entered tractor production, but most of the heavier models were made by specialist firms, such as Massey Ferguson. Light commercial vehicles (trucks) were normally made by the automobile firms, but the heavier products usually became the business of specialists, who also often made buses and coaches.

Then there were those industries such as the aircraft industry, certainly one of the most important of the twentieth century, that took advantage of the experiences of engine and component manufacturers for the automobile industry and of the technical change in the oil refining industry. Scale economies were not so great in the aircraft industry as in automobiles. Nevertheless, an engineer in the Curtis–Wright aircraft company, T. P. Wright, attempted in the 1930s to demonstrate the cumulative advantages of a large volume of production, inspired by the example of the automobile industry. The notion of the 'learning curve' embracing dynamic economies of scale was widely applied. Although the aircraft industry could not strictly be described as a mass production industry, the impetus from the two world wars, and especially the Second World War, vastly expanded the scale of production for military aircraft. Even before the war broke out, production was increasing very rapidly in the 1930s (Table 8.10); during the war itself, the United States, Germany, the UK, and Japan accelerated production even

TABLE 8.10. Aircraft production in the 1930s, by country

Country	1933	1936	1939
France	(600)	890	3,163
Germany	368	5,112	8,295
Italy	(500)	(1,000)	(2,000)
Japan	766	1,181	4,467
UK	633	1,677	7,940
USA	466	1,141	2,195
USSR	2,595	3,578	10,382

Source: Kennedy (1988: 419).

more as one of the top military priorities. Above all, in the United States an enormous effort was made to increase the scale and speed of the production of bombers and, in particular, the 'Flying Fortress'. The story of this aircraft, manufactured at the Boeing No. 2 Plant in Seattle, has often been told, but the study by a Japanese engineer (Mishina 1999) is of outstanding interest.

Mishina argues that the increase from just five aircraft delivered in September 1941 to over 360 delivered in August 1944 was made possible only by an 'early pre-figuration' of the 'just-in-time' strategy later made famous in the Japanese automobile industry. According to his account, it was not so much the learning skill of the operatives, or the increase in their number, that brought about this remarkable result, but the production planning and control, which drastically reduced the waste of time and stocks of materials and components during manufacture. This illustrates the point that, although the moving assembly line had become the archetypal Fordist innovation for mass production industries, the influence of the automobile scaling-up of production extended much more widely than this single innovation, to the style of management and control of production systems generally.

The Korean War and the 'Cold War' that followed the Second World War meant that the military aircraft and missile industry continued to be of the greatest importance in the United States, the Soviet Union, Britain, and France in the decades that followed. In Germany and Japan, however, restrictions were imposed on its growth. Nevertheless, the scale and intensity of research and development for military products, together with very rapid growth of the civil industry in the 1950s and 1960s, made aircraft one of the key industries in the postwar upswing of the fourth Kondratiev.

In some cases the moving assembly line approach could be directly imitated, as in the consumer durables industry or in such diverse cases as egg production with battery chickens or fast food catering. In many others the influence was less direct and affected mainly the standardization of components, the flow of materials, the subdivision of work tasks, and the empowerment of production planning and control staff. Of course, there were still many industries where customized small batch and 'one-off' production remained the predominant method and craft skills remained an essential asset. Finally, there were those industries in which the flow production techniques of the oil and chemical industries had a greater relevance than the assembly line. Some engineers regard the assembly line simply as a specialized application of flow production.

In its early days the automobile industry used mainly metal components, although it was also a big user of glass, rubber, leather, and other materials for upholstery (Table 8.2); but at a later stage, as advances in macromolecular chemistry led to a whole range of new synthetic materials, these were increasingly substituted for metals and for leather, rubber, and textile materials. The transition in the chemical industry from coal-based to oil-based synthetic materials, the increased use of continuous flow-based production techniques, and the abundance of cheap feedstocks from refinery byproducts all facilitated the extraordinarily rapid growth of the various synthetic material industries. In the first place, this was driven by the German war economy, with its imperative need for substitutes for those natural materials whose supply might be cut off by wartime blockade; the same motive inspired the US government to create a vast synthetic rubber industry in the 1940s. Later, however, synthetic materials continued to expand at a very high rate in the civilian economy, based on their technical and economic advantages as substitutes for natural materials and metals in the manufacture of consumer durables, in construction, in engineering, and in textiles. This was in itself a secondary 'constellation', since it also led to the development of a machine-building industry for injection moulding, extrusion, etc., as well as for a variety of specialist chemical firms. The growth of this constellation is described in more detail in Freeman *et al.* (1982) and, in the case of synthetic rubber, in Solo (1980).

Section 8.2 reported the view of Christopher Dow (1998) that the effects of the automobile on the growth of the US economy in the 1920s were even greater in the service and construction industries than in manufacturing itself. Peter Fearon (1987), in his account of the pervasive influence of the automobile in the 1920s, also stresses the immense importance of these 'induced' effects. After pointing to the huge demand for steel, rubber, glass, and oil from the motor industry and to the changes in the technology of these and many other industries, he emphasizes the highway construction boom, the showrooms, the service stations and repair shops, the tourist business, the suburban real estate boom, the shopping plazas on the fringes of cities, and, particularly important, the hire purchase business:

In 1919, General Motors, with the foundation of its Acceptance Corporation, pioneered the development of modern consumer credit. By the mid-1920s, over 70 per cent of motor car sales were financed by hire purchase, which was vital, as they were relatively expensive. There seemed to be scarcely any part of the economy which was not influenced by the car, the truck, the bus or the tractor. (Fearon 1987: 56).

8.7 Mass Consumption and the Triumph of Mass Production

Consumer credit innovations were especially important for the whole family of consumer durables, whose ownership also became widespread in the United States in the 1920s and 1930s along with automobiles. A survey of one hundred Ford families with an income of $1,700 or more in 1930 found that 47 per cent owned an automobile, 36 per cent a radio, 19 per cent an electric vacuum cleaner, and 5 per cent an electric sewing machine. Nearly 60 per cent of these families had outstanding hire purchase commitments (Fearon 1987: 57).

By 1935 over half of *all* American families owned an automobile, and by 1989, 84 per cent did so (86 per cent of white families and 69 per cent of black families). The purchase of refrigerators, washing machines, and other household appliances followed soon after (Table 8.11). In European countries it was only in the 1950s and 1960s that ownership of these appliances began to catch up with the American levels (Table 8.12). The huge scale of this diffusion depended, of course, on the availability of electricity to every household and often required the adaptation of the kitchen and other rooms to meet this need (Lebergott 1990). Most American farmers did not yet have electricity in the 1920s and 1930s, although they would often have an automobile and sometimes a tractor.

Still other electrical appliances followed the refrigerators and washing machines, including microwave ovens, dishwashers, freezers, electric carving knives, and garden tools. By the 1990s the majority of American households owned many of these appliances and European and Japanese households were not far behind. In his brilliant little book on *The Pursuit of Happiness*, Lebergott relates these changes in household expenditure to the experience of women in the home and their hours of work, poking fun at those sociologists, like the Lynds, who tried to find something noble or uplifting in the heavy work of washing, cleaning, and cooking in the nineteenth century:

When the Lynds warned Americans against hypnosis by the 'gorged stream of new things to buy' in 1937, three in every four housewives had already bought electrical equipment for the house. Why had these housewives yielded to the hypnotic pull of the automatic refrigerator? Most, surely, could have sawed ice in frozen ponds and hauled it home ... After all, 80 per cent of French housewives managed without refrigerators as late as 1957, and 87 per cent of British housewives. (Lebergott 1990: 112)

Of course, there were cultural and political changes, such as women's liberation movements and consumerism, which interacted with changes in household incomes, the availability of electric power, and the marketing of many improved and new products. But Lebergott's book gives a salutary

TABLE 8.11. US families owning various appliances, 1900–1970 (% of all families)

	Electric light	Mechanical refrigerator	Washing machine	Vacuum cleaner
1900	3	nil	n.a.	nil
1920	35	1	8	9
1940	79	44	n.a.	n.a.
1960	96	90	73	73
1970	99	99	70	92

Source: Lebergott (1993: 113).

TABLE 8.12. Households possessing specified conveniences, by country, 1960 (%)

	USA	UK	Netherlands	Luxemburg	France	West Germany	Belgium	Italy	Soviet Union
All households	100	100	100	100	100	100	100	100	100
With hot running water	93	77	67	57	41	34	25	24	n.a.
With washing machine	55	45	69	74	32	36	52	8	15
With refrigeration (electric or gas)	96	30	23	57	41	52	21	30	5
With sewing machine electric	45	12	24	15	14	10	13	5	n.a.
hand/foot powered	(*)	34	55	47	42	50	34	51	n.a.
With stove (coal or wood)	n.a.	7	2	67	54	50	45	44	n.a.
With automobile	77	35	26	48	40	26	30	20	n.a.

* Less than 1%.
Source: Lebergott (1993: 111).

common-sense corrective to the purely cultural interpretations by pointing to the sheer drudgery of much housework before the days of mass consumption and mass production. Henry Ford was surely right to emphasize mass consumption via the cheapening of durable consumer goods as a major feature of his Fordist style in the economy.

Previous waves of technical change had led to a new and widening range of consumer goods in every case. Cheap cotton underwear and garments, kitchen utensils and iron bedsteads from the iron foundries and potteries of the Industrial Revolution, cheap railway excursions and tours, new ways of heating and lighting the home, postal services, telecommunications, and a vastly wider variety of imported goods and foodstuffs—all these seemed important to contemporaries. Nevertheless, there was a real difference between the changing patterns of consumer behaviour associated with Fordist mass production and the earlier changes. First of all, the increase in purchasing power of very large numbers of people was actually greater than in any of these previous episodes. The 'golden age' of growth in the quarter-century after the Second World War saw the biggest increase in GDP and in per capita consumption ever recorded in the history of industrial capitalism. Second, the nature of the purchases marked a break with previous patterns of consumption in several ways. Automobiles and consumer durables had some of the characteristics of capital goods, and, indeed, most of these were sold as capital goods to manufacturing and service industries, as well as to households (trucks, vans, laundry equipment, cold stores, etc.). Third, these characteristics had such a marked effect on the pattern of demand that they offered entirely new possibilities for techniques of Keynesian demand management. For all these reasons, the claim of Henry Ford that his techniques had ushered in an age of mass consumption deserves to be taken seriously.

It is important to note that even in the 1920s radio sets had become a very widely distributed 'consumer durable', and that in the period after the Second World War both radio and television were diffused to over 90 per cent of American, European, and Japanese households. These goods shared many of the characteristics of other durables, but they were also the forerunners of the electronic revolution and the new constellation of goods and services based on information and communication technology, which would follow the age of oil, automobiles, and mass consumption (Chapter 9).

We have emphasized mass consumption and mass production in this chapter, because these were the key ideas in the techno-economic paradigm of the fourth Kondratiev wave. They affected not only industry, but services and government activities as well. As we have seen, the concept of 'mass consumption' took root first of all in the United States and was indeed one of the central tenets of Henry Ford's own philosophy. It is therefore not surprising that it was in the United States that the idea of 'mass services' was first propounded. As early as 1929, a report known since as the 'Hoover Report' (*Report of the Committee on Recent Economic Changes*) was submitted to the President by a group of NBER economists. It drew attention to the growing problem of 'technological unemployment' between 1922 and 1929 and to the continuing threat of cyclical unemployment, but on the whole the tone of the comments on employment was relatively optimistic. This was because it identified in the service industries a major source of new employment which would save the country from a severe crisis of unemployment (Hoover Report 1929: pp. xvi, 12).

This report was published on the eve of the worst unemployment the United States had ever experienced, and with the benefit of hindsight, it is easy to ridicule some errors of judgement in it, such as its comments on the 'strength and stability of our financial structures, both government and commercial'. However, the Hoover Report also contained much interesting analysis which has stood the test of time. Although the growth of the service industries and American financial structures did not save the country from the Great Depression, the growth of service employment between 1922 and 1929, including employment in financial services, was nevertheless an important phenomenon and one that proved to be even more important in the second half of the twentieth century. The Hoover Report mentioned the 'accelerated growth' of travel, entertainment, education, insurance, communications, the facilities of hotels, restaurants, delicatessen stores, steam laundries, and public libraries and described this as 'an evolution which has been going on for centuries' (Hoover Report 1929: p. xvi). It then went on to say that:

We now apply to many kinds of services the philosophy of large-scale production. We integrated these services and organized them and we have developed *the new philosophy* to such a degree in recent years that we now have what might be termed 'mass services'. These have helped to create a new standard of comfortable living in the United States and have afforded employment for millions of workers crowded out of agriculture and the extractive and fabricating industries. (Hoover Report 1929: p. xvi; emphasis added)

These 'mass services' also grew very rapidly in most European countries and later in Japan in the long boom after the Second World War, and the growth of service employment has been one of the most notable changes in the OECD structure of employment. Two of the most conspicuous examples are mass entertainment and mass tourism. The latter was the subject of an excellent study by Auliana Poon (1993), describing the ways in which technical innovations, especially in the aircraft industry, interacted with social innovations, such as paid holidays for the masses, and with business innovations in the tourism industry, to create mass tourism in the postwar world. In the prewar days it was almost unheard of for families of industrial workers in northern Europe to have one, two or even three weeks' holiday in Spain, Greece, or Italy, but it became commonplace in the 1960s and 1970s, thanks to this combination of innovations. It was the standardization on Fordist principles of the 'packaged holiday' that brought down the cost of travel and accommodation to a point where all this became possible.

The Hoover Report spoke of 'delicatessen stores', but it could as well have taken almost the whole of retail distribution as one of the main arenas of the growth of mass services. Starting with the innovation of self-service in fairly small grocery stores, a series of organizational innovations and a few technical innovations revolutionized the retail business. 'Supermarkets' and 'hypermarkets' are names that themselves tell the tale of growing concentration, giant firms and huge units of distribution for standardized packaged products. All these are examples of the dominant influence of the 'new philosophy', as the Hoover Report called it, or the 'new paradigm', as we have called it.

8.8 Mass Culture

Of all the subsystems of society that we discuss in this book, culture is the most complex. The production of works of art has a logic and time of its own—quite often, it anticipates the future or constructs alternative worlds. Yet the producers live in concrete societies, and their horizon is largely defined by the potentialities of their epoch. In the same sense, the creation of a specific culture, in the general sense of the coherence of forms of communication, be this in fashion, food, literature, architecture, music, the evolution of languages, or other social artefacts, is largely bound by its particular epoch. The technological framework, the social structure, and the historical process of the formation of knowledge defines the setting for the work of art and for the overall construction of social cultures. The advent of mass production, mass consumption, and mass culture is perhaps the clearest example of this relationship.

There are however considerable lags between causally connected events and trends; moreover, there is a large margin of autonomy between technological transformations, allowing for new methods of diffusion and permitting new experiences of the process of modernization, and their cultural counterparts. Yet the creation of new technological means sets the pace for the transformation. The undisputed example is the creation of the 'Gutenberg Galaxy' in the fifteenth century: this allowed for the development 'of a system essentially dominated by the typographic mind and the phonetic alphabet order' (Castells 1996: i. 331). As the alphabet was the dominant 'conceptual technology' since 700 BC Greece, it had established itself as the privileged infrastructure for the codification of cumulative knowledge. But it became a dominant mode of communication just when the industrial capacity established the printed word as the direct form of expression. Consequently, for a long period sounds and images were outside the scope of written discourse and were relegated to the domain of the separate and slightly esoteric artistic production.

A new epoch was opened when Fordist production spread to the whole social fabric and extended to the mechanical reproduction of works of art.

Radio and film—the first distinctively media art form—became the then dominant modes of communication. The cinema was truly mass entertainment, and it probably did more to diffuse the ideas of mass production and consumption world-wide than any other cultural medium from the 1930s to the 1950s, when it was overtaken by television—which however continued many of the traditions and techniques of the cinema and also harnessed the resources of the film studios. The car chase has been a feature of the cinema ever since the 'Keystone Cops', Buster Keaton, and the early days of silent films. At one time it became almost an obligatory episode in any adventure or crime film, culminating in the hyper-exotic technology car chases of the Bond films.

Generally, the cinema and television have been media that publicized and often glamourized mass consumption goods and services, but there have also been a minority of films and TV productions that satirized them. Charlie Chaplin's *Modern Times* is probably still the best example of a profound, yet extremely funny, critique of mass production, while Fassbinder's *Marriage of Maria Braun* and some of his other films are a devastating commentary on some of the unforeseen and adverse consequences of consumerism.

Many intellectuals were deeply pessimistic about the 'dumbing down' associated with mass culture. One of the most pessimistic and influential was Adorno (1991), a leading member of the Frankfurt School of sociology, who coined the expression 'the Culture Industry' to describe the influence of the mass production paradigm on works of art. His deep pessimism was partly the result of the triumph of the mass propaganda of German fascism and the ways in which the German culture industries were used to spread and implant reactionary ideas about race, war, and violence. However, his analysis was already developed in the 1920s, and he saw the mass culture regime as leaving people with hardly any escape from the saturating and suffocating images and sterotypes of the mass media, even without political repression.

An interesting parallel economic analysis of mass consumption and mass culture was that of Scitovsky (1976) in his book on the *Joyless Economy*. Scitovsky tried to explain why it was that a huge increase in the sheer quantity of goods produced and consumed did not lead to an equivalent increase in satisfaction. His explanation was mainly in terms of the loss of that satisfaction, which was associated with the decline of customized craft production. Only the very rich could still afford this type of consumption, although of course Scitovsky recognized that this was also the case for most people even before the advent of mass production. It was a Russian novelist (Dudintsev) who recalled an older and simpler explanation in the title of his book, *Not by Bread Alone*.

8.9 The Regime of Regulation

Both the mass production industries and the mass services contributed to the longest and greatest boom the world economy had yet experienced in the quarter-century after the Second World War. Changes in the institutional framework during and after the war facilitated the boom, especially Keynesian methods of managing the economy. The contrast with the years following the First World War was very sharp. At that time, Keynes had resigned from the government and had failed to influence the Versailles Treaty. In 1944–5 he was the architect of international as well as national economic policies. Whereas the Juglar cycles in the interwar period had been fairly deep, in the long postwar boom they were relatively shallow and did not lead to large-scale unemployment (Table 8.13). It was for this reason that Dow described the 1950–72 period as a long interval without major recessions.

Corporatism had already made advances during the First World War and the interwar period, but it now became a firmly established mode of coordination for the crucial economic and industrial policies. Like Schacht, Keynes had already warned in 1937–8 about the inflationary dangers of rearmament, and this warning was reinforced in his 1940 Cambridge lectures. When he moved into a policy-making role, with the aid of Richard Stone and other colleagues he was able to develop the necessary statistical basis for macro-economic management, which later became an essential tool for the peacetime 'Keynesian' management of the civil economy, and for national income and expenditure statistics generally. In his view, this meant counteracting excessive inflationary as well as deflationary dangers.

Although the role of government control and coordination was less pronounced in the United States than in wartime and postwar Europe, nevertheless, the combination of Roosevelt's New Deal with the wartime mobilization of industry left a legacy of macroeconomic coordination there, too, which endured after the war. American industry had frequently resisted New Deal legislation, sometimes with the support of the Supreme Court, but during the war the necessary coordination was far more easily achieved, and the 'military–industrial complex' about which President Eisenhower warned in the 1950s was remarkable not so much for its opposition to government

TABLE 8.13. Short (Juglar) business cycles in long (Kondratiev) waves

Output trend and deviations	Long wave upswing (1950–72)		Long wave downswings (1920–38 and 1972–93)	
	4 'fast' phases	5 'slow' phases	4 'fast' phases	5 major recessions
% deviation of output from previous trend	3.0	−2.9	5.6	−10.9
Length of period (years)	2.0	2¾	2¾	2½
% of output deviation reflected in unemployment	10.0	21	66	55

Source: derived from Dow (1998).

intervention and expenditure, as for its insistence on a grander scale of this expenditure.

Politically and culturally, therefore, the stage was set in the 1940s for the long postwar boom and the transition from a war economy to the Keynesian managed civil economy of the 1950s and 1960s. Unlike the 1920s, this was of course a transition to a 'Cold War' economy, rather than to a peacetime economy. Government expenditures remained at a fairly high level, especially for R&D and sophisticated weapon systems, and this had become politically acceptable. A relatively stable institutional framework had evolved for the mass production and mass consumption paradigm.

In most European countries, and even to some extent in the United States, this framework included a greatly enlarged 'welfare state' with mass provision of a variety of social benefits and public services. Public ownership of many industries, especially in the fields of energy and transport infrastructure, and heavy public investment in roads and airports were also typical of this period. Primary education was already established on a 'mass' (i.e. universal, compulsory) basis at the beginning of the century, but mass secondary education now became an accepted goal of state policy in many countries, and mass tertiary education appeared on the horizon.

The dominance of the mass production paradigm did not, of course, mean that *every* industry and service used Fordist production techniques. Only a minority did so. Craft production methods and small batch production continued to prevail in many sectors of the economy. Nor did mass consumption mean that all consumer products could be described in these terms. Many bespoke and customized products continued to be sold. Nevertheless, in our view, the impulses given to the economy by the fast-growing leading sectors of automobiles, oil, and consumer durables, and the induced effects of these industries on many other industries and services, were so great that they justify the description of this period as an age of mass production and consumption. It generated the biggest boom in the history of the world economy, although the productivity growth in the United States was not greater than that achieved in previous periods of high growth of output and labour productivity (Tables 8.14 and 8.15; Figure 8.4).

It was the *qualitative* transformation of the economy that was the most important feature of the period. A significant part of the more rapid growth in Europe and even more in Japan must be attributed to 'catch-up' with the more advanced technologies long since deployed in the United States. These were now diffused through a combination of overseas investment by American corporations, autonomous innovations, and the import of technology and management methods by European and Japanese firms. Whereas after the First World War this transfer was impeded by the postwar indebtedness and many other obstacles, this time it was facilitated and accelerated by the Marshall Plan and other measures of cooperation and coordination adopted by the United States and the West European countries. Eastern Europe was out in the cold, but was nevertheless also

TABLE 8.14. Average annual growth rates of gross domestic product, 1870–1980 (%)

	1870–1913	1913–50	1950–60	1960–70	1970–80	1973–80
France	1.7	1.0	4.7	5.6	3.5	2.8
Germany[a]	2.8	1.3	8.1	4.8	2.8	2.4
Italy	1.5	1.4	5.1	5.3	3.1	2.8
Japan	2.5	1.8	8.6	10.3	4.7	3.2
UK	1.9	1.3	2.7	2.7	1.8	1.0
USA	4.1	2.8	3.2	3.2	2.9	2.1

[a] Federal Republic 1950–80.

Sources: Maddison (1980); OECD (1981).

TABLE 8.15. Average annual growth rates of labour productivity, 1870–1980 (GDP per man-hour)

	1870–1913	1913–50	1950–60	1960–70	1970–80	1973–80
France	1.8	1.7	4.3	5.1	3.8	3.7
Germany[a]	1.9	1.2	6.6	5.2	3.6	3.2
Italy	1.2	1.8	4.3	6.3	2.5	1.7
Japan	1.8	1.4	5.7	9.6	4.3	2.6
UK	1.1	1.5	2.3	3.2	2.4	1.6
USA	2.1	2.5	2.4	2.4	1.5	0.8

[a] Federal Republic 1950–80.

Sources: Maddison (1980).

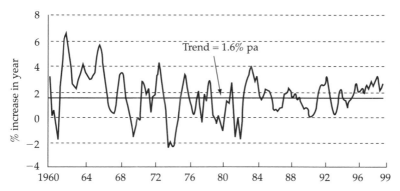

FIG 8.4. US productivity growth, whole economy, 1960–1999
Source: Lloyds TSB *Economics Bulletin*, December 1999.

able to achieve fairly high growth rates in the 1950s and 1960s through a combination of Soviet-style planning and imported mass production techniques. Even some of the less developed countries were able to achieve some periods of high growth and 'catch-up'. At first, some Latin American countries were classified as 'Newly Industrializing' and later the much more successful East Asian countries were referred to as 'Tigers'.

The automobile industry, the diesel engine and tractor industries, the aircraft industry and airlines and all their component suppliers, the oil, petrochemical, and synthetic materials industries, the highway and airport infrastructure, the supporting repair, maintenance, and distribution services, the various mass services dependent on motorization—together these constituted a huge proportion of total national output in the leading countries by the 1960s, perhaps as much as a third of the total. Yet these industries and services had barely existed before 1900. This represented a fundamental structural transformation as well as a technological revolution and a massive cultural change. The shock was all the greater when the very survival of this mass production regime appeared to be threatened by the loss of its core input—oil.

8.10 The Structural Crisis of Adjustment of the Fourth Kondratiev

The 'OPEC' oil crises of 1973 and 1979 were major shocks to the industrialized countries of the OECD because of these countries' very heavy dependence on this core input. In the end, the oil shortages turned out to be not quite as serious as they first appeared in the 1970s, and even the huge price increases were eroded in the 1990s when more non-OPEC oil became available and the growth rate of oil consumption had declined. Nor was the oil price increase the only cause of inflation or of the slow-down in the world economy after 1973 (Table 8.14). Nevertheless, the immediate shock was severe and was significant because it marked a general recognition that fossil fuel supplies were indeed a diminishing asset, even if oil reserves were much greater than they had first appeared and coal reserves more abundant still. The MIT models on *Limits to Growth* (Forrester 1971; Meadows *et al.* 1972) had already presented a more general argument that growth must slow down, and this had impressed a very large audience world-wide. The pollution effects of an industrial structure based on burning fossil fuels and on non-renewable resources began to figure prominently in the political debate on environmental issues. The mass production paradigm began to appear somewhat tattered and was increasingly questioned. It was also challenged by a new strike wave and rebellious student demonstrations in the late 1960s.

Opposition to the war in Vietnam was another contributory factor to the wave of discontent that was evident before the OPEC crisis of 1973. Dissatisfaction with the working conditions and management style in the automobile industry was particularly clear in the strike wave of the late 1960s. The uneasy peace purchased by Ford in 1914 with his '5-Dollar Day' was always somewhat fragile, and in Europe it was often only immigrant workers who could be persuaded to accept the mass production work regime.

Even in the United States, the heartland of the mass production paradigm, the Fordist philosophy of industrial management was increasingly challenged, culminating in a book entitled *Made in America* (Dertouzos *et al.* 1989), produced by a highly respected group of engineers and economists from MIT. This book was remarkable for its forthright criticism of management techniques in many sectors of US industry, coming as it did from an institution that was at the forefront of new technology and closely involved with many industrial firms. The self-confidence of the 1960s had gone, to return only in the 1990s on the basis of a new paradigm, described in Chapter 9.

However, the first official reaction of economists and policy-makers close to OECD governments was to treat the OPEC crisis of 1973 as a temporary 'blip' which would soon go away. This was clearly evident in the OECD's 'McCracken Report' (1977), prepared by a group of eminent economists chaired by Paul McCracken, a Keynesian economist from Ohio. This report argued that, given the correct counter-inflationary policy stance, business as usual could soon be resumed, i.e. returning to the high economic growth rates of the 1960s and to full employment. Yet even in these early days, a minority report appended to the main report expressed reservations about this interpretation of events and suggested that there were deeper, structural, problems affecting the industrialized world.

As time went by, growth continued to slow and unemployment remained stubbornly high (Table 8.16). Gradually, it became quite normal to talk in terms of a 'crisis of structural adjustment', and this expression was frequently used in OECD and other governmental or intergovernmental reports. The phenomena of 'mass unemployment' and 'structural unemployment' re-emerged after a long period when it was commonly assumed that they had been laid to rest by the Keynesian revolution. Levels of unemployment in several countries were higher than in the 'Great Depression' of 1933, although they were not nearly so high in the United States (Table 8.16).

As it became clear that OPEC could not be blamed for everything and the deeper problems emerged, the search for explanations and new policies was intensively pursued. One such explanation, which found some favour temporarily in the late 1970s, was that growth had slowed down because science and technology were reaching limits, so that diminishing returns to R&D and/or lower expenditures on R&D accounted for the slow-down. After the damp squib of the McCracken Report, the OECD took this explanation seriously enough to set up a group of economists, scientists, and industrialists to prepare a report on *Science and Technology in the New Economic Context* (OECD 1982).

The group undertook a survey of 100 R&D directors and technical directors in various industries in the OECD countries. The results were striking: none of them believed that the productivity of science and technology had slowed down or that science was reaching limits to knowledge. On the contrary, almost all believed that there was never before a time when so many

TABLE 8.16. Unemployment in various countries, 1933–1993 (% of labour force)

Country	1933	1959–67 avg.	1982–92 avg.	1993
Belgium	10.6	2.4	11.3	12.1
Denmark	14.5	1.4	9.1	12.1
France	4.5[a]	0.7	9.5	11.7
Germany	14.8	1.2[b]	7.4	8.9
Ireland	n.a.	4.6	15.5	17.6
Italy	5.9	6.2	10.9	10.2
Netherlands	9.7	0.9	9.8	8.3
Spain	n.a.	2.3	19.0	22.7
UK	13.9	1.8	9.7	10.3
Austria	16.3	1.7	3.5	4.2
Finland	6.2	1.7	4.8	18.2
Norway	9.7	2.1	3.2	6.0
Sweden	7.3	1.3	2.3	8.2
Switzerland	3.5	0.2	0.7	4.5
USA	24.7	5.3	7.1	6.9
Canada	19.3	4.9	9.6	11.2
Japan	n.a.	1.5	2.5	2.5
Australia	17.4	2.2	7.8	10.9

[a] 1936.
[b] The Federal Republic for the period 1959–81.
Source: Maddison (1991); OECD, *Employment Outlook* (1993).

promising results in bio-technology, in information technology, in materials technology, and in other areas were being achieved. In the view of the scientists and technologists, there were almost unlimited horizons. The OECD group came to the conclusion, therefore, that the slow-down in industrial productivity that was now everywhere apparent must be due to a failure to utilize these new results of scientific and technological activities, not to the limits of science itself. The limits to growth were the limits of a particular set of technologies and of a particular technological and managerial regime, not limits to technology in general and certainly not to the new technologies that were forging ahead everywhere.

Obviously, these conclusions are very close to our own exposition of the need to change the institutional and social framework when a specific technological regime (in this case the mass production regime) was reaching its limits. The debate in the 1980s and 1990s increasingly turned to these problems of institutional change in relation to the extraordinarily rapid growth of the most prominent new technology—the information and communication technology (ICT)—and its potential applications everywhere in the economy.

9

The Emergence of a New Techno-economic Paradigm: The Age of Information and Communication Technology (ICT)

9.1 Introduction

In this chapter, we shall argue that we are now witnessing yet another industrial revolution in the sequence analysed in Chapters 5–8. This time the pervasive and radical nature of the wave of technical change is less controversial. The chairman of the United States Federal Reserve, Alan Greenspan, has spoken frequently of the 'new paradigm', referring specifically to computers, telecommunications, and the Internet as the source of the remarkable spurt of growth in the US economy in the 1990s. He has also warned of the 'irrational exuberance' on the New York Stock Exchange in response to the immense potential of the Internet and other new technologies. Even those who have disputed the revolutionary character of earlier waves of technical change often have little difficulty in accepting that a vast technological revolution is now taking place, based on the electronic computer, software, microelectronics, the Internet, and mobile telephones. These industries were growing in the United States in the 1990s at a very high rate and accounted for the greater part of growth in the entire economy. The dramatic nature of the technological revolution has been underlined by some of the gigantic mergers that took place in 1999 and 2000. From a very much smaller base and on a much smaller scale, bio-technology was also growing very rapidly in the closing decades of the twentieth century. In one sense, it too is a very special form of information technology and it is interacting increasingly with computer technology.

Such disagreement as remains centres on the question of whether there will be a hard or a soft landing for the United States before a longer period of widespread economic growth is unleashed in the world economy. Some leading American economists have had reservations about the 'new paradigm', believing that this expression exaggerates both the changes in the technology and even more the changes in the behaviour and management of the economy. We ourselves incline to the belief that the stock market inflation in the United States in the late 1990s was indeed based in part on irrational exuberance about the future rate of return on Internet stocks and other so-called 'high tech' stocks, as well as a more general overvaluation of financial assets. It thus had some of the features of the 1929 boom and some characteristics of the manias for canals and railways, which accompanied earlier waves of technical change already discussed (Shiller 2000).

One of the most dynamic fields of organizational and institutional innovation is certainly the financial market. The competition is ferocious: it is necessary to capture savings in all their forms by multiplying new bank products, rearranging the systems of alliances, and redefining the shape of the service. The capital market inflation is at the very centre of this drive for innovation, as it is both its cause and its consequence. Innovation requires more innovation, and the inflationary process requires more funds, and consequently further changes. The decisive change in this regard has been of course the growing privatization of national systems of social security and the reconstitution of pension, insurance, and mutual funds. These funds today own the majority of stocks in most developed countries, and this is a radical change. Furthermore, as larger and larger inflows are required in order to maintain the liquidity of this market, the process of privatization extends over borders and challenges all resistance.

The consequences of this storm are immense. Capital market inflation accelerates the process of disintermediation and weakens regulations and the effectiveness of monetary policies at the national levels, given the extreme volatility of the foreign exchange markets. Moreover, the pension funds are not strictly dependent on credit policies influencing the short-term interest rate, as they are financed from wages and salaries, not from borrowing. Consequently, their expansion diminishes the capacity of central banks to control the liquidity of the banking system (Toporowski 2000: 132). As long as this inflation is sustained through the positive prospect of gains, the failure of the scheme is not foreseeable, but its fragility is obvious in the longer term. *The Economist* magazine, which is of course very well aware of this fragility, repeatedly exhorted Greenspan to tighten credit policy throughout 1999 and 2000, and grew increasingly frustrated by his failure to respond adequately.

However, in his semi-annual report to Congress in July 2000, Greenspan explicitly disavowed any intention of targeting the stock market to counteract inflation: 'We do not and have not been targeting the stock market to stabilize the economy' (Martin 2000: 13).

It was this policy of benign neglect that caused the critics of the Fed to argue that monetary policy actually encouraged the huge inflationary distortion of asset prices. On 22 January, *The Economist* wrote in exasperation: 'if, like this newspaper, your sums tell you that shares are over-valued even on the most bullish interpretation of America's remarkable economic performance, and its future productivity prospects, then you should be worried—seriously so' ('A Tale of Two Debtors', 22 January 2000: 17).

No one can predict the future course of events in a very unstable system, as so much depends on the rate and direction of social and political change, both in the United States and in other countries, and also in the international financial institutions. Therefore, since the institutional and social changes associated with this technological revolution are still unfolding and are at a relatively early stage, this chapter is confined to an account of the emergence and formation of the new constellation of innovations, starting with the new core input of microelectronics (Section 9.2), continuing with the carrier branch, which is obviously the computer and software industry (Section 9.3) and with the new infrastructure, i.e. telecommunications and the Internet (Section 9.4), and concluding with some of the organizational innovations (Section 9.5), the cultural changes (Section 9.6), and some future problems of social change that are already apparent (Section 9.7). With such a fast-changing technology and such a rapid rate of structural change, readers should not expect to find here an up-to-date account of the latest developments in ICT. There are many other sources for such accounts. This chapter is necessarily *historical* in nature, in keeping with the main objective of the book.

9.2 The New Core Input: Chips with Everything

Integrated circuits provide the most spectacular example of price reductions of all the core inputs we have considered. The story has often been told and has become part of standard industrial history and of mythology. Although certainly not completely accurate, 'Moore's Law', first enunciated in 1965, is widely believed to have held roughly true down to the end of the century. Indeed, Bill Gates (1995/6) maintained that the law would probably hold for another twenty years. According to his account, Gordon Moore, who was the co-founder of Intel with Bob Noyce, predicted in 1965 that the capacity of a computer chip would double every year, but he revised this prediction in 1975, then suggesting that the capacity would double every two years. Gates estimates that the actual rate of doubling was about eighteen months down to 1995 (Figure 9.1).

Although not so spectacular as the integrated circuits (IC) revolution of the 1960s, the discovery and improvement of electronic components had been going on since early in the twentieth century, and had made possible

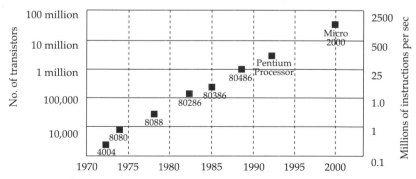

FIG 9.1. Intel microprocessor evolution, 1970–2000
Source: Gates (1996: 37).

numerous innovations in radio, radar, and television. This was especially true of the so-called *active* components—valves and transistors. It was the innovation of combining these components, at first in small but later in enormously large numbers, on one 'integrated' circuit chip that made possible the spectacular reductions in cost and improvements in performance of both electronic consumer goods and capital goods, such as computers. A few earlier innovations—in cotton spinning and weaving, in the manufacture of steel and automobiles and in the refining of oil—had reduced costs by an order of magnitude, but the microelectronic innovations reduced the cost of storing, processing, and transmitting information by several orders of magnitude. The effects of the falling cost of integrated circuits on the costs of computing are illustrated in Figure 9.2.

The earlier experimental development and manufacture of *discrete* components for electronic circuits stretched back for many decades before American firms achieved dominance in the manufacture of *integrated* circuits and electronic computers in the second half of the twentieth century. As was also the case in the electrical industry, it was mainly the research of European scientists, such as Hertz and Maxwell, that made possible the growth of the electronics industry. The interaction between scientists and engineers has

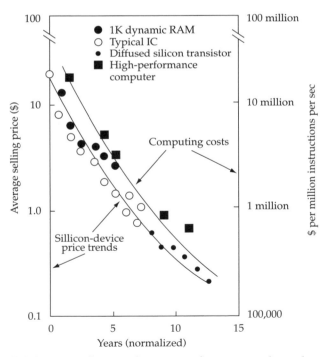

FIG 9.2. Parallel decreases illustrate how costs of computers depend on costs of semiconductors

Source: Mackintosh (1978: 53).

remained a feature of information and communication technology (ICT) so that countries with strong scientific institutions, as well as innovative engineers and entrepreneurs, have been the leaders.

The first thermionic valve was invented and patented in 1904 by Sir John Ambrose Fleming, a professor at London University, and down to the First World War the radio industry was dominated by British and German firms. The Italian inventor G. Marconi established his Wireless Telegraph Company in Britain in 1897 and first demonstrated the feasibility of ship-to-shore radio communications, as well as shore-to-shore and ship-to-ship. His firm in Britain was however closely followed by the German electrical giants, AEG and Siemens. Fleming was a consultant to the Marconi company, and outstanding German and American scientists and engineers also acted as industrial consultants. It was the American Telephone and Telegraph company (AT&T) that pioneered the use of valves as relays in the telecommunications system, having purchased the rights to the use of de Forest's triode valve, invented in 1906. However, despite the outstanding contribution of de Forest, Fessenden, Langmuir and other American inventors, it was the European radio firms that dominated the global industry down to the early 1920s. Fessenden and de Forest themselves were much less successful as entrepreneurs than as inventors (Maclaurin 1949; Freeman *et al.* 1965).

From quite early on, governments recognized the potential strategic importance of radio communications in both peace and war. The naval arms race between Britain and Germany, which has been described in Chapter 7, was one of the factors that led the Kaiser to persuade Siemens and AEG to establish a joint subsidiary for radio communications—Telefunken—in 1903. This company conducted R&D, employed consultants, and designed and installed radio stations world-wide. It disputed the priority of Marconi's patents until finally in 1912 it reached a world-wide agreement with the Marconi Company on cross-licensing and know-how. This was renewed in 1919, by which time the US government felt impelled to facilitate the buy-out of Marconi's American subsidiary and to establish a powerful unified American-owned radio company—the Radio Corporation of America (RCA). With strong encouragement from the US Navy, Owen Young of General Electric negotiated the buy-out because the US government felt, after the experience of the First World War, that it could not leave such a vital strategic and commercially important industry as radio in the hands of a foreign (though Allied) power. The new RCA negotiated cross-licensing and patent arrangements with Telefunken, British Marconi, and the French CSF, as well as with the key American companies such as AT&T and Westinghouse.

Thus, from quite early on, the nascent electronic industry was at the heart of those world-wide developments in communications technology that were even then the subject of intense government interest and regulation. This government involvement was to become even closer in the interwar period, and above all during the Second World War, when the development of oscilloscopes, radar, and gun control systems became one of the central concerns of all the combatants, especially Britain and Germany. Government-financed R&D was concentrated in Germany in a private company, Tele-funken, and in Britain in the state-owned Telecommunications Research Establishment (TRE, now RRE) and employed many thousands of scientists and engineers. Although government-financed research and design activities had also been important in the First World War for tanks, naval armaments, chemical warfare, and aircraft, this was the first technology to enjoy such massive support—which, moreover, continued in a variety of forms down to the present day. This was, of course, mainly for military equipment, culmi-nating in the 'Star Wars' programme, but it continued in many areas also for civil products and systems.

Although the American, British, and other governments certainly supported much R&D for electronic components and circuits, it was in the Bell Laboratories of AT&T that civil R&D in transistor technology[1] led to the key developments in semi-conductors and to the establishment of the US semi-conductor industry, mainly by spinoff firms from Bell Laboratories and licensees of Bell technology. The role of government continued to be important, but more in the procurement of new devices and especially of integrated circuits in large quantities, rather than in R&D itself (Golding 1972; Tilton 1971).

A report in 1963 by the consultants A. D. Little stated that:

Due to its considerable interest in semi-conductors and particularly in transistors, the government throughout the 1950s tried to stimulate the development of improved types. Around the middle of 1950 they were convinced transistors were needed for future military equipment so they accelerated the production investment. . . . The contracts for a total of thirty different types of germanium and silicon transistors were placed with about a dozen of the major semi-conductor companies . . . In many cases, this investment was matched by similar amounts of capital equipment or plant space supplied by the contracting companies. . . . Thus, a potential total capacity of over a million transistors a year was created. (Little 1963)

These numbers appear tiny today, when the integration of millions of transistors on one chip has become the norm and there is a language problem in creating the terminology to classify the increases in scale (Table 9.1).

There has seldom, if ever, been such a strong example of the cost and performance improvements that could be achieved by the scaling up of design and production, even though it was achieved in this case by miniaturization. As in the earlier examples of steel production, oil refineries, and automobiles, the combination of technical and organizational innovations with the scaling up of production proved an extraordinarily powerful method of cost reduc-tion and gave a big advantage to large firms. The conclusions of the A. D. Little

---

[1] According to some accounts, Bell hastened the announcement of its transistor discoveries in order to avoid the technology being classified and appropriated exclusively or mainly for military use.

TABLE 9.1. Integration of components per chip, 1950s–1990s

Date	Degree of integration	No. of components
1950s	Small-scale integration (SSI)	2–50
1960s	Medium-scale integration (MSI)	50–5,000
1970s	Large-scale integration (LSI)	5,000–100,000
1980s	Very large-scale integration (VLSI)	100,000–1,000,000
1990s	Ultra large-scale integration (ULSI)	>1 million

Source: Duysters (1995: 56).

Report in 1963 and the foresight of the US Department of Defense were justified by the further research on the semi-conductor industry and most notably by the work of Tilton (1971) in the USA and Golding (1972) in the UK on scale economies. Together with a series of innovations in the design and manufacture of chips, they largely explain the prolonged domination of the industry by American firms and the relative weakness of the European industry. It was only when Japanese firms were able to exploit similar economies in the large-scale production of civil electronic products that this dominance was challenged. By the late 1980s, four of the five largest producers of semi-conductors were Japanese (Table 9.2) and the American industry was

TABLE 9.2. Leading semiconductor (SC) manufacturers world-wide, 1988–1989

Rank		Company	1989 SC revenues ($m)	1989 Market share (%)
1989	1988			
1	1	NEC	4,964	8.9
2	2	Toshiba	4,889	8.8
3	3	Hitachi	3,930	7.0
4	4	Motorola	3,322	5.9
5	6	Fujitsu	2,941	5.3
6	5	Texas Instruments	2,787	5.0
7	8	Mitsubishi	2,629	4.7
8	7	Intel	2,440	4.4
9	9	Matsushita	1,871	3.4
10	10	Philips	1,690	3.0
11	11	National	1,618	2.9
12	12	SGS–Thomson	1,301	2.3
13	18	Samsung	1,284	2.3
14	15	Sharp	1,230	2.2
15	20	Siemens	1,194	2.1
16	14	Sanyo	1,132	2.0
17	17	Oki	1,125	2.0
18	13	AMD	1,082	1.9
19	16	Sony	1,077	1.9
20	19	AT&T	873	1.6

Source: Dataquest; cited in *Electronic Business*, 16 April 1990; Hobday (1991).

obliged to seek an agreement with Japan, limiting the amount of Japanese imports to the United States.

However, the US industry, US universities, and the US government still had enormous R&D capability as well as determination to wrest back their lead from Japanese competition. The development of the microprocessor by Intel in 1971–2 was one of the decisive events that transformed both the semi-conductor industry and the computer industry, since it meant that a 'computer on a chip' could be manufactured very cheaply and on a vast scale. Intel became the leading firm in the semi-conductor industry and by 1994 there were once more three US firms among the top six in world-wide sales (Table 9.3). Aided by cooperative R&D and by government support through the 'Sematech' project, the US industry had successfully fought back. Furthermore, Korean firms also successfully broke into the leading group in the 1980s and 1990s.

Thus, by the 1960s linkages between the electronics industry, the telecommunications industry and the young computer industry had already become quite strong and an interdependent constellation was emerging in ICT. In fact, the intimate relationship with the computer industry had begun as early as the 1940s and had become steadily closer in the following decades, as will be described in the Section 9.3. The computer industry and the telecommunications industry became enormous markets for the products of the microelectronic industry, and, as the interdependencies between firms in this new constellation increased, so too did both cooperation and competition. Many of the large Japanese and European multi-product firms attempted to integrate their semi-conductor operations with their other activities and to

TABLE 9.3. World-wide top ten merchant semiconductor suppliers, 1991–1994

Rank			Company	1994 total SC sales ($m)	1994 IC sales ($m)	1994 Discrete sales ($m)
1994	1993	1991				
1	1	5	Intel	9,850	9,850	—
2	2	1	NEC	8,830	7,855	975
3	3	2	Toshiba	8,250	6,614	1,636
4	4	4	Motorola	7,011	5,870	1,141
5	5	3	Hitachi	6,100	5,300	800
6	6	8	TI	5,550	5,500	50
7	7	12	Samsung	5,005	4,365	640
8	8	7	Mitsubishi	3,959	3,286	673
9	9	6	Fujitsu	3,335	2,975	360
10	10	9	Matsushita	2,925	2,145	780
			Total	60,815	53,760	7,055

Source: *Worldwide IC Industry Economic Update and Forecast*, Integrated Circuit Engineering Corporation, 1995.

gain advantages by joint R&D. IBM has been one of the largest, if not the largest, American producers of integrated circuits.

The rate of change in semi-conductors, computers, and even more in tele-communications has sometimes made integration hazardous. The manufacture of semi-conductors is still an extremely complicated and difficult process, requiring more than a hundred different steps of coating, baking, etching, etc. Appleyard *et al.*, after studying a number of firms, concluded that many of these steps

> are not well-understood and easily replicated on different equipment or in different facilities, and they impose demanding requirements for a particle-free manufacturing environment. Product innovation depends on process innovation to a much greater extent than is true of automobiles. . . . New equipment, with operating characteristics that are not well understood, often must be introduced along with a new 'recipe', also not well understood, in order to manufacture a new product. The complexity of the manufacturing process also means that isolating and identifying the causes of yield failures requires considerable time and effort. (Appleyard *et al.* 1996: 5)

This high degree of uncertainty, together with the huge costs of investment in new plant and new R&D for each generation of chips, creates formidable entry barriers. Similar considerations, although of course on a much smaller scale, apply to the costs of experimentation for the 'Application Specific Integrated Circuits' (ASICs). For this reason, microelectronics has remained a very R&D-intensive industry, with R&D often accounting for about 10 per cent of sales. The large multi-product firms, such as Siemens, Philips, Hitachi, and Matsushita, devote quite a high proportion of their total R&D budgets to microelectronics, and patents in that area can account for as much as 20 per cent of their total patents. Turbulence and uncertainty continue to rule in this still very fast-growing and changing industry.

9.3 Computers

Blaise Pascal had developed a calculating machine as early as 1642, and Charles Babbage had developed far more complex machines between the 1820s and the 1860s—an 'Analytical Engine' and a 'Difference Engine', which could be regarded as the ancestors of modern computers. However, despite the fact that Babbage received £17,000 in government grants to support his research (a large sum for those times), he never completed his machines. This was largely because the components available to him were inadequate for the task. It was only when electronic components, and above all microelectronics devices, became available that fast, cheap, and efficient machines could be produced. Before that time a variety of electro-mechanical machines were designed and used, such as the Z1 and Z2, made by Zuse, a graduate of Charlottenburg Technological High School in Berlin in the 1930s, and the Harvard–IBM Automatic Sequence Controlled Calculator (1937–44). Zuse's Z4 machine was actually used by the Henschel aircraft company for the design of aircraft wings. Zuse's research was disrupted by his own call-up, and by the call-up of his colleague, Schreyer (also a graduate of Charlottenburg THS), after they had started development work on an electronic computer. Valves had already been ordered from Telefunken when the project was cancelled and official support withdrawn. This was one more instance of the failure of the military–political leadership of Nazi Germany to understand the importance of science, even for their own narrow military–political objectives, as already noted in Chapter 8.

The British and American governments showed rather more understanding of the crucial importance of physics and mathematics, both for nuclear weapons and for computer science. The British government enlisted Alan Türing, a mathematician from Manchester University, to work at Bletchley Park on a machine called the 'Colossus', designed successfully to crack the German 'Enigma' military codes. The Colossus could fairly claim to be the first operational electronic computer outside academia. It used 1,500 valves and was one of the major British technological triumphs in the Second World War (R. V. Jones 1978). However, it was shrouded in secrecy for a long time and had rather a limited purpose, even though Türing himself as early as 1936 had written a theoretical paper entitled 'Can a Machine Think?' in which he envisaged universal computing machines able to undertake an almost infinite range of tasks. 'Colossus' itself could actually perform some tasks that were only surpassed by the much later development of parallel processing machines in the 1970s.

It was the University of Pennsylvania's 'Electronic Numerator Integrator and Computer' (ENIAC), built between 1942 and 1946, and its successors, the EDVAC and the UNIVAC in the late 1940s, that were the antecedents of what was to become the world's most successful computer industry in the United States. In this early period, IBM, the largest office equipment firm, which was already dominating tabulators and punch-cards, did not recognize the huge potential of the electronic computer. As Katz and Phillips (1982) have shown, the early enthusiasts for computers, who realized their immense potential, were from universities and the military, people who had had some experience with the early wartime design and development and had only later moved out into industry.

Von Neumann's work on computer architecture began when he first heard of the ENIAC in 1944 (McNeil 1990) and he joined the University of Pennsylvania EDSAC team, which followed ENIAC with a superior design. It was von Neumann who developed the basic concept of a computer as containing a central processor, memory devices, and input–output devices, making use of sequential programming, which has remained the paradigm or 'technological guidepost' for the computer industry for the rest of the century. It was used in the first computer introduced by Remington Rand in 1951. This was the UNIVAC 1, Eckert and Mauchly's 'Universal Automatic Computer', based on their University of Pennsylvania projects (Duysters 1995). Von Neumann and other leading mathematicians in the United States, such as Norbert Wiener, certainly envisioned very early on the huge range of potential applications for computer technology, but their enthusiasm was not at that time shared in American industry. As Katz and Phillips put it,

The general view prior to 1950 was that there was no commercial demand for computers. Thomas J. Watson Senior, with business experience dating from at least 1928, was perhaps as acquainted with both business needs and the capabilities of advanced computation devices as any business leader. He felt that the one SSEC machine which was on display at IBM's New York offices 'could solve all the scientific problems in the world, involving scientific calculations.' He saw no commercial possibilities. This view moreover persisted even though some private firms that were potential users of computers—the major life insurance companies, telecommunications providers, aircraft manufacturers and others—were reasonably informed about the emerging technology. A broad business need was not apparent. (Katz and Phillips 1982: 425)

Even though they had many shortcomings, such as the need to replace valves frequently, the large space required, and the overheating caused by numerous valves, the first electronic computers were more than a thousand times faster than the earlier electro-mechanical machines, and the later developments in microelectronics increased this speed by further orders of magnitude (Table 9.4). T. J. Watson's son, recalling these days later, said that during this period, 'IBM slept soundly' (Belden and Belden 1962: 100).

Even after producing the 650 model under the pressures of the Korean War in the early 1950s, IBM was still greatly underestimating the potential future market. Its Product Planning and Sales Department forecast that there would be no normal commercial sales of the 650, while the Applied Science Group forecast a sale of 200 machines. In the eventual outcome, over 1,800 machines were sold. However, once IBM realized that it had fallen behind UNIVAC and other firms, it did move fairly fast. This change was also associated with a change in management and with the settlement of an anti-trust suit brought by the Department of Justice against IBM over its dominant position in the punch-card market. Again, as Watson Jr put it,

Finally, we awoke and began to act. We took one of our most competent operating executives with a reputation for fearlessness and competence and put him in charge of all phases of the development of an IBM large-scale electronic computer. He and we were successful. (Belden and Belden 1962: 100).

Although IBM was successful in the 1950s and 1960s with its catch-up strategy, it remained generally a fast follower rather than a first innovator (W. D. Hoffmann 1976), and was caught 'asleep' once again when the small personal computer erupted into the market in the 1970s and 1980s. IBM had become one of the most profitable firms in the world with the success of its large mainframe business computers, the 1401 and the 360 series. Its huge success stimulated many attempts at imitation both in the USA and in Europe. Most of these efforts failed. Both RCA and General Electric had to withdraw from the market in the early 1970s after the failure of heavy investment to secure an adequate market share. IBM was successfully challenged in the market only in specialist sectors, such as process control, minicomputers, and the very largest machines. Efforts

TABLE 9.4.(*a*) Technical progress in computers, from valves to microelectronics

Measures of various characteristics	Vacuum-tube computers (valves early 1950s)	Hybrid integrated circuits IBM 360 system late 1960s
Components per cubic foot	2,000	30,000
Multiplications per second[a]	2,500	375,000
Cost ($) per 100,000 computations	$1.30	$0.02

[a] A single multiplication on mechanical or electromechanical computers took more than one second.

Source: *Fortune*, September 1966.

TABLE 9.4.(*b*) Increase in computing power over time, 1944–1981

	Model	Computational speed (arithmetic operations per second)
1944	Harvard Mark I (electromechanical)	0.4
1946	ENIAC	45
1951	UNIVAC I	270
1953	IBM 701	615
1961	IBM 7074	33,700
1963	CDC 3600	156,000
1965	IBM 360/75	1,440,000
1972	CDC Cyber 176	9,100,000
1976	Cray 1	80,000,000
1981	CDC Cyber 205	800,000,000

Source: OTA (1983).

by various European firms in France, Germany, the UK, Italy, and Sweden to compete in their national markets with some government support had only limited success.

In 1948 John Parsons had shown that all the movements and speed changes of a universal precision milling machine could be controlled by a mathematical computer, and in the early 1950s numerically controlled machine tools had been developed under a government contract at MIT Servo-mechanisms Laboratory. In the 1950s and 1960s the range of applications of computers was greatly extended. Although most computers in the 1960s were installed for office-type applications, an increasing number were installed for industrial process control systems. Many improvements in design, control, and programming followed, culminating in the MOLINS System 24 in 1969, which could be regarded as the first 'flexible manufacturing system' (FMS), combining several machine tools, together with guided vehicles and computer-aided design (CAD). The FMS, together with robotics, following Engelberger's 'Unimation'

TABLE 9.4.(*c*) Comparison of IBM 650 (1955) and Fairchild F-8 microcomputer (1970s)

	IBM 650	F-8	Remarks
Physical volume (ft^3)	270	0.01	F-8 about 30,000 times smaller
Weight (lb)	5,650	1.0	
Power consumption (W)	17,700	2.5	F-8 consumes 7,000 times less power
Memory (bits)	3K main, 100K secondary	16K ROM, 8K RAM	
CPU	2,000 vacuum tubes	20,000 transistors	650 also needed many discrete resistors and capacitors
Time for adding two numbers (μsec)	750	150	
Reliability (mean time between failures)	hours	years (3 m–10 m hours is a typical mean time between failures for a current micro-processor— more than 300 years —but the subsystems with which the microprocessor communicates—e.g. terminals, printers— may be much less reliable)	F-8 at least 10,000 times more reliable
Cost	$200,000 (1955 $)	under $1,000 with terminal	

Source: OTA (1983).

robot in the mid-1950s, made possible the diffusion of a wide variety of computer-controlled manufacturing processes over the next three decades. John Diebold (1952), in his book on the 'Automatic Factory', had envisaged many of these applications of computers but had pointed out that they could be successfully developed and used only after a prolonged period of training people with new skills, reorganizing management systems, and redesigning production processes. The development first of minicomputers by the Digital Equipment Corporation (DEC) in 1963, and later of microcomputers in the 1970s, greatly facilitated the progress of manufacturing automation together with computer graphics and work-stations incorporating specialized software and peripheral equipment.

However, it was in the service industries, in office applications, and in the home that the advent of the personal (micro)computer was to have the greatest impact. During the period of mainframe dominance, large computers were typically operated by a special department of user firms, an 'EDP' (electronic data processing department) and the major activities were fairly standard programs, such as payroll calculation, invoicing, sales records, etc. The Fordist paradigm still prevailed in the organization of large firms and EDP was fitted into it, even if sometimes rather uncomfortably. Smaller machines were used for process control in manufacturing and in medicine, as well as in design and scientific work, but computers were certainly not yet the ubiquitous feature of the industrial and office landscape that they are today. It was only the advent of the microcomputer, based on Intel's microprocessor in the 1970s, that made cheap computing universally available to every firm, large or small, to schools and colleges everywhere, and to millions of personal users (Table 9.5).

As we have already described in Section 8.6, the Fordist mass production paradigm based on oil, automobiles, and consumer durables encountered increasing social problems in the 1970s and 1980s, such as the OPEC crises of 1973 and 1979, the environmental pollution associated with fossil fuel consumption, and the increasing dissatisfaction with Fordist work-styles. The slow-down in productivity growth (Table 9.6 and Figure 8.4), the much higher levels of unemployment in this period of structural crisis, and the problems of managing inflationary pressures stimulated the acceptance of ideas such as a 'change of techno-economic paradigm' and the widespread critique of the old mass production paradigm (as for example in the MIT study *Made in America*: Dertouzos *et al.* 1989). However, it was only when computers, microelectronics, and telecommunications offered a new, technically reliable, and economically efficient mode of growth on a large scale that the new constellation could take over as the chief engine of growth. The most influential of these new developments was the advent of the personal computer and of the Internet. The stock of personal computers (PCs) reached over 100 million in 1997 in the United States, well over 50 million in the European Union, and 25 million in Japan (Table 9.5), and this scale of diffusion was possible only because of huge price reductions, and improvements in design, performance, and user-friendliness in the 1980s and 1990s.

According to most accounts, IBM was too fixated on mainframe large computers to recognize the change in the world computer market arising from the PC. By the time IBM got round (in 1980) to launching a crash development programme for its own PC, there were already several firms well established in the new market, including Atari, Apple, Commodore, and Radio Shack, and sales had already reached $1 billion. A special team was assembled outside the main IBM inhouse R&D establishment, first under Jim Lowe and later under Don Estridge, and was given one year to develop a saleable product. They succeeded, but only by (for IBM) the unusual procedure of buying in most of the parts, both hardware and software. In his iconoclastic

TABLE 9.5. National telecommunications and other indicators, various countries, 1997

Countries	GDP (US$ bn)	Population (millions)	Main lines ('000)	Lines/100 ('000)	Cellular users ('000)	PCs ('000)	Internet users ('000)
Argentina	323.2	35.7	6,750	18.9	2,013	1,400	170.0
Australia	346.3	18.4	9,350	50.7	4,893	6,700	1,600.0
Belgium	242.4	10.2	4,769	46.9	974	2,400	300.0
Brazil	688.1	164.5	15,106	10.0	4,400	4,200	1,310.0
Canada	617.6	30.3	18,460	60.8	3,420	8,200	4,500.0
Chile	77.1	14.5	2,600	17.9	410	790	2,000.0
China	917.7	1,221.6	70,310	5.8	13,233	7,500	400.0
Colombia	76.1	37.4	5,334	14.3	1,265	1,214	130.0
Denmark	169.7	5.3	3,339	62.9	1,450	1,900	300.0
Finland	119.8	5.1	2,866	55.8	2,147	1,600	1,000.0
France	1,392.9	58.6	33,700	57.5	5,817	10,200	500.0
Germany	2,102.7	82.1	45,200	55.1	8,170	21,000	2,500.0
Greece	120.9	10.6	5,328	51.0	938	470	150.0
Italy	1,145.4	56.8	25,698	45.2	11,738	6,500	585.0

TABLE 9.5. Continued.

Japan	4,192.7	125.7	60,381	48.0	38,254	25,500	8,500.0
Korea, Republic of	442.5	45.9	20,422	44.4	6,910	6,931	800.0
Malaysia	98.5	20.5	4,223	20.6	2,461	1,000	600.0
Mexico	402.8	97.6	9,264	9.5	1,745	3,600	520.0
Netherlands	360.5	15.6	8,860	56.6	1,717	4,400	900.0
Norway	153.4	4.4	2,325	52.8	1,677	950	500.0
Poland	135.6	38.6	7,510	19.4	857	1,400	800.0
Portugal	102.3	9.9	3,819	38.5	1,507	740	500.0
Russia	449.8	147.3	26,875	18.2	485	4,700	600.0
South Africa	129.1	42.3	4,646	11.0	1,600	1,800	800.0
Spain	531.3	39.1	15,854	40.5	4,338	4,800	525.0
Sweden	227.8	8.9	6,010	67.8	3,169	3,100	800.0
Taiwan	n.a.	21.7	10,862	50.1	1,492	2,570	1,500.0
UK	1,288.2	57.6	30,292	51.8	8,993	11,200	2,500.0
USA	8,079.9	268.0	170,568	64.0	55,312	109,000	40,000.0
Venezuela	87.5	22.4	2,804	12.5	1,072	850	35.0

Source: Mansell and Wehn (1998).

TABLE 9.6. Average annual growth rates of labour productivity, 1870–1980 (GDP per man-hour)

	1870–1913	1913–50	1950–60	1960–70	1970–80	1973–80
France	1.8	1.7	4.3	5.1	3.8	3.7
Germany[a]	1.9	1.2	6.6	5.2	3.6	3.2
Italy	1.2	1.8	4.3	6.3	2.5	1.7
Japan	1.8	1.4	5.7	9.6	4.3	2.6
UK	1.1	1.5	2.3	3.2	2.4	1.6
USA	2.1	2.5	2.4	2.4	1.5	0.8

[a] Federal Republic 1950–80.

Sources: Maddison (1980).

but very entertaining account, 'All IBM Stories Are True', Robert Cringely (1996) suggests that IBM made some serious strategic errors by bringing in Microsoft for the operating system, which led ultimately to that firm's dominance in the PC software market. Other accounts, however, argue that IBM could not have foreseen the fateful long-term consequences of its deal with Bill Gates,[2] head of what was then a very small software company (fifty employees). Microsoft became for a while one of the most powerful firms in the world through its near-monopoly of PC operating systems. By 2000, however, its own dominance was increasingly at risk because of anti-monopoly proceedings in the USA and the EU and the rise of new competition, notably from LINUX, an interesting non-commercial cooperative software development organization which had received some backing from IBM.

Although it succeeded in keeping a position in the world market for personal computers, IBM encountered far more serious competition in the 1980s and 1990s than ever before. It was obliged to reduce its labour force worldwide by more than 50 per cent, from 400,000 to 200,000, and suffered a drastic decline in profitability. An increasingly high proportion of IBM sales came from software and systems rather than hardware. The relative decline of large mainframe computers compared with the proliferation of PCs and workstations led to a large number of new entrants taking advantage of the drastic change in scale economies. Competition came from many sides, including Japanese firms such as NEC, Fujitsu (large machines), and Toshiba (portables), and from numerous small firms 'cloning' the main features of the PCs. It also came from software firms as the relative importance of software grew in relation to hardware. The story is somewhat cynically but amusingly told in Cringely's (1996) aptly entitled book, *Accidental Empires*. Although classified as a 'gossip columnist' for *Infoword*, Cringely was a former Stanford professor and rather well-informed. No recent book has shown more vividly the degree

---

[2] Gates himself thought that IBM had got a 'fabulous deal—a one-time fee of about $80,000 that granted the company the royalty-free right to use Microsoft's operating system forever. In other words, we practically gave the software to IBM' (Gates 1996: 54).

of turbulence and uncertainty in both software and hardware innovations in the United States, or the role of very young computer enthusiasts ('The Triumph of the Nerds'). These young enthusiasts could be compared in some respects to the creative dissenters of the Industrial Revolution. Not surprisingly, Bill Gates himself believed that IBM made a big strategic error in not accepting his proposal that IBM should buy up to 30 per cent of Microsoft stock—'so that it would share in our fortune, good or bad. We thought this might help the companies work together more amicably and productively' (Gates 1996: 63).

New developments in the 1980s for the most powerful computer systems were based on the 'transputer' and parallel processing, enabling a number of computers to combine together. The interaction between industrial R&D and university groups was again important in developing new architecture, as well as the interaction between semi-conductor firms and computer firms (Molina 1989). IBM's capability in semi-conductor technology continued to be a source of strength, although it also had to collaborate with Intel and other component firms. The rise of network computing provided new opportunities for IBM in the 1990s, and the changes in the telecommunications industry, which made this possible, are described in the following section.

9.4 Telecommunications

As with the computer industry, the forerunners of the modern telecommunication industry go back a long way, but, as with computers, the introduction first of electro-mechanical technology and then of electronics marked a decisive change in the performance of the systems. The electric telegraph of Wheatstone (UK) and Morse (USA) in the 1830s and 1840s had already provided a communications system that was of great importance for the railways, for news agencies, and for the military. Alexander Graham Bell's invention of the telephone in 1875 was not at first recognized as a revolutionary break-through in telecommunication, because the technology was at first effective only over short distances, whereas telegraphy could be used over very long distances. Western Union, the strongest telegraph company, at first thought of telephony as a small niche business and, although it was a strong competitor of Bell, using its own network of telegraph lines, it agreed to leave the telephone business to Bell in return for a percentage of Bell's rents and royalties. This followed a patent dispute in which Bell sued Western Union for infringement of the Bell patents in 1879. The Bell company agreed not to enter the telegraphy market until its basic telephony patents expired in 1894. This agreement gave Bell a near-monopoly in the telephone network in the United States which it retained for nearly a century, although at the price of accepting a fairly strict system of government regulation in order to avoid nationalization in 1913 (Duysters 1995). Most European countries had already established public ownership of their postal, telegraph and telephone services. The threat of nationalization followed Bell's aggressive acquisition of many smaller independent local telephone companies and the relocation of its stocks to the New York American Telephone and Telegraph Company in 1899 to avoid state regulation in Massachusetts.

De Forest's invention of the triode electronic valve for radio led to a drastic change in the competitive strength of telephony. As already noted, AT&T acquired the right to use the valve (tube) as a relay in the telephone system in 1907 and this enabled the telephone to replace the telegraph as the most important device for long distance as well as short distance communication. Thus began the intimate relationship between electronics and telecommunications which became ever closer during the twentieth century. The next big step was the use of the transistor in telephone exchanges. Bell and other telephone companies had attempted to use the valve in exchanges as well as in relays, because the biggest bottlenecks to productivity improvements in telephony were in transmission and in switching. As the number of subscribers grew, manual exchanges needed very large numbers of operators to make connections, but it proved impossible to use valves in the switches, because they burned out too quickly and used too much power. Consequently, the telephone networks had to rely on improvements in electro-mechanical technology between the 1920s and the 1960s.

The first electronic exchange, using transistor technology, was installed in the United States in 1960. From that time onwards computers and switching equipment were increasingly influenced by the same technological changes. The first use of *digital* technology followed in 1965 with the introduction of Pulse Code Modulation (PCM) in AT&Ts Electronic Switching System No. 1 and of Stored Programme Control (SPC), which greatly increased the speed and flexibility of the system. 'The electronics regime that drove the electronic computer market ever since it originated in the 1940s increasingly determined the rate and direction of technological progress in the telecommunications industry. This convergence of technological regimes can be seen as the start of what would be known as the overall convergence process of Information Technologies' (Duysters 1995: 83). Thus, the growing technological interdependencies of the computer and electronic industries with each other, and of both with the telecommunications industry, were already firmly established by the 1960s. The constellation of new very fast-growing industries, which had initially developed quite independently of each other in the nineteenth and early twentieth centuries, had now crystallized into a new technology system which became generally known and recognized as 'ICT'.

It is important to realize however that *technological* convergence and other close relationships between the three industries did not necessarily lead to *business* convergence. Von Tunzelmann and Soete (1987, 1988) showed that, in spite of a high degree of technological convergence, many firms in each industry in the 1980s continued to pursue their own specialized business interests and to strengthen their own core competence in that field. Analysis of patent statistics and of technology alliances by Duysters (1995) confirms this conclusion. Leading telecommunications equipment makers did take

out many patents in computers and microelectronics, and leading semi-
conductor firms took out more than half their patents in the field of
telecommunications, but there were no big changes in these proportions
between 1980 and 1993, that might demonstrate a big shift in core competence
and business specialization. Firms that did try to enter one of the other
industries (e.g. IBM into telecommunications), whether by acquisition or by
innovation, were generally not successful. However, Duysters concluded
that, in spite of the barriers to entry, such as production and marketing
know-how and skills, technological convergence would ultimately lead to
the repositioning of firms through strategic alliances and networks. Their
role in the evolution of the constellation is discussed in Section 9.5.

One other major trajectory of technical change which proceeded in parallel
in the telecommunications industry was in the carrying capacity of cables.
Originally dependent on thin copper wires, telephony systems needed greater
and greater bandwidth to carry the huge increases in traffic. At first this need
was met by the development of coaxial cables, but it was the development of
optical fibres in the 1970s that provided the orders-of-magnitude improvement
that liberated the system from bandwidth constraints (Figure 9.3). It now
became possible to deliver the huge number of signals for digital telephony,
sending vast quantities of data and images almost instantaneously over an
'ISDN' (Integrated Services Digital Network) at rapidly falling cost. An
American writer, George Gilder (1993), estimated that the 4 kHz telephone
lines to American homes and offices in the early 1990s would explode to 25
trillion Hz of fibre optics.

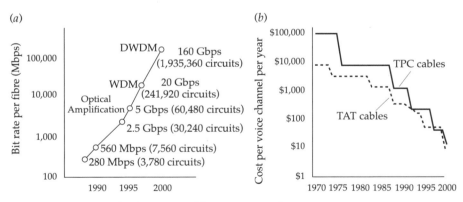

FIG 9.3. International submarine cable capacity and cost

(*a*) Capacity per fibre, 1985–2000
   Note: Circuit figures indicate the number of 64 Kbps circuits plus signalling
      overhead.
(*b*) Submarine cable cost per voice channel per year, 1970–2001
   Note: System cost is derived from total construction costs divided by the system's
      lifetime. Figures assume compression ratio of 5:1 on post-1988 systems.
Source: Mansell and Wehn (1998).

However, at the same time as *wired* communication was experiencing this technological revolution, *wireless* communication was undergoing an equally radical transformation as a result of satellite communication and cellular telephone networks. Gilder concluded that the digital computer networks of the future would function both over wires and in the air:

As for the decendants of television, the dominant traffic of the future will be store and forward transmission of digital data among millions of telecomputers. These machines will be capable of summoning or sending films or files, news stories and clips, courses and catalogues anywhere in the world. Whether offering 500 channels or thousands television will be irrelevant in a world without channels, where you can always order exactly what you want, when you want it, and where every terminal commands the communication power of a broadcast station today. (Gilder 1993: 95)

The extraordinarily rapid growth of the mobile telephone network, together with the power and performance of the handsets in 1998–2000, appeared to confirm Gilder's prophecies. He also concluded that the technical changes would drive the institutional changes and in particular that centralized broadcasting stations and/or centralized telephone systems would no longer be needed, just as in his view mainframe computers would be displaced by client–server networks and networks of personal 'wallet' computers carried by most individuals.

Whether or not this vision comes about depends of course on many social, cultural, and political changes, as well as on the technical changes, which are in many cases easier to foresee. The small size of the picture on the hand-held telephone may yet prove a major barrier to its universal acceptance, and other cultural factors may exert a powerful influence on the future evolution of the system. The social changes involve the birth of new institutions as well as the death of old ones, the rise of new forms of regulation as well as the deregulation of older services and industries. They are further discussed in Section 9.6 and in the next chapter.

The trend in the 1970s and 1980s following the breakup of the Bell system in the United States was towards privatization of the old public monopoly services and a regulation regime, which would not only permit but encourage new entrants into the world of telecommunication networks and services. This policy was based on the belief that a more competitive environment would stimulate the growth of all kinds of new information services, such as those envisaged and listed in Table 9.7, and would also lead to a more rapid reduction in charges.

Most of these services did in fact become available during the 1980s and 1990s through a combination of telephony and television, especially in the United States, where cable networks were much more rapidly introduced than in Europe. However, it was by a combination of computers and telecommunications through the Internet that the world-wide diffusion of information services made the most rapid progress. The Internet was originally introduced in the 1960s as an Advanced Research Projects Agency (ARPA)

TABLE 9.7. Information services potentially available to households as envisaged in the 1970s

Passive entertainment	People—people communications	Interactive television	Still-picture interaction	Monitoring	Telephone voice answerback	Home printer	Computer terminals (including the viewdata television set)
Radio	Telephone	Interactive educational programmes	Computer-assisted instruction	Fire alarms on-line to fire service	Stock market information	Electronic delivery of newspaper/magazines	Income tax preparation
Many television channels	Telephone answering service	Interactive television	Shopping	Burglar alarms on-line to police	Weather reports	Customized news service	Recording tax information
Pay television	Voicegram service	Quiz shows	Catalogue displays	Remote control of heating and air conditioning	Sports information	Stock market ticker	Banking
Dial-up music/sound library	Message sending service	Advertising and sales	Advertising and ordering	Remote control of cooker	Banking	Electronic mail	Domestic accounting
	Telemedical services	Television ratings	Consumer reports	Water, gas, and electricity meter reading	Medical diagnosis	Message delivery	Entertainment/sports reservations
	Psychiatric consultation	Public opinion polls	Entertainment guide	Television audience counting	Electronic voting	Text editing; report preparation	Restaurant reservations
	Local ombudsman	Audience-response television	City information			Secretarial assistance	Travel planning and reservations
	Access to elected officials	Public reaction to political speeches and issues	Obtaining travel advice and directions			Customized advertising	Computer-assisted instruction
		Television interviewers soliciting audience opinion	Tour information			Consumer guidance	Computation
		Debates on local issues	Boating/fishing information			Information retrieval	Investment comparison and analysis
		Telemedical applications	Sports reports			Obtaining transportation schedules	Investment monitoring
		Bidding for merchandise on	Weather forecasts			Obtaining travel advice/maps	Work at home
			Hobby information				Access to company files
			Book/literature reviews				Information retrieval
			Book library service				Library/literature/document searches
			Encyclopaedia				
			Politics				
			Computer dating				
			Real estate sales				

televised auctions	Games for children's entertainment	Searching for goods to buy
Betting on horse races	Gambling games (such as bingo)	Shopping information; price lists and comparisons
Gambling on other sports		Real estate searching
		Job searching
		Vocational counselling
		Obtaining insurance
		Obtaining licences
		Medicare claims
		Medical diagnosis
		Emergency medical information
		Yellow pages
		Communications directory assistance
		Dictionary/glossary/thesaurus
		Address records
		Diary, appointments, reminders
		Message sending
		Dialogues with other homes
		Christmas card/invitation lists
		Housing, health, welfare and social information
		Games (e.g. chess)
		Computer dating
		Obtaining sports partners

Source: Guy (1985: 105–7).

project, supported by the Pentagon in the United States to ensure that some decentralized communications would remain in operation even in the event of the devastation expected from nuclear warfare. As the project advanced, and as détente made this prospect less probable, the network became available to civilian users and especially to universities for electronic mail (e-mail). Its great success in this role led to its adoption by business users and to a rapid extension of the services available. Indeed, Internet service providers became the most rapidly growing and exciting sector of the economy, first in the United States but later almost everywhere. Even companies that had never yet provided any services or made any profits became the object of intense stock exchange speculation. Venture capital companies sometimes exaggerated greatly the potential of the small new companies they were promoting. This 'bubble' did however get blown up in response to a genuine proliferation of very real prospects for an immense wave of structural change. An appropriate telecommunications infrastructure for the age of ICT was at last coming into place, and this would indeed have enormous effects throughout the economy, but especially on the delivery of services of all kinds. The potential effects of the Internet on retail trade were also considerable, but its long-term future remained controversial, as the considerable costs of warehousing and delivery systems have become more apparent and consumer response less positive than often assumed.

9.5 Organizational Change: The 'Network Firm'

In the 1950s, computers were fitting in, although somewhat uncomfortably, to the old 'Fordist' organizational paradigm. They became part of the old centralized departmental, hierarchical structures of the large firms that adopted them. Few small firms could afford them. They did not yet revolutionize the *organization* of firms, for example by making information rapidly available at all levels, and it was generally assumed that large mainframe computers in specialized data processing departments would be the normal pattern. The management structure of IBM itself reflected this, although it was always a very heavy spender on R&D and on education and training.

However, the universal availability of personal computers, the introduction of local area networks (LANs), and the rapid changes in product and process design eroded this old hierarchical structure. Because of rapid, easy access to information, some layers of management became unnecessary and top-heavy. A new style of management became widespread and contrasted with the Fordist style in many respects (Table 9.8). Networking, both within the firm and in the external relations of the firm, became especially important characteristics of the new organization, although the forms of networking are extremely varied and are often exaggerated (Chesbrough and Teece 1996).

A good example of the new networking firm was Cisco Systems Inc. Founded in 1984 by a group of computer scientists from Stanford University, by 1998 it was a global leader in designing and making networking equipment

TABLE 9.8. Changes in the techno-economic paradigm

'Fordist' (Old)	ICT (New)
Energy-intensive	Information-intensive
Design and engineering in 'drawing' offices	Computer-aided designs
Sequential design and production	Concurrent engineering
Standardized	Customized
Rather stable product mix	Rapid changes in product mix
Dedicated plant and equipment	Flexible production systems
Automation	Systemation
Single firm	Networks
Hierarchical structures	Flat horizontal structures
Departmental	Integrated
Product with service	Service with products
Centralization	Distributed intelligence
Specialized skills	Multi-skilling
Government control and sometimes ownership	Government information, coordination and regulation
'Planning'	'Vision'

Source: adapted from Perez (1989).

and software for the Internet, with an annual income of over $8 billion and market capitalization of nearly $100 billion. According to *Business Week*, this firm has been a leader in transforming management practices and sells most of its own goods and services over the Internet. 'So successful has Cisco been in selling complex, expensive equipment over the Net that last year [1997] Cisco alone accounted for one third of all electronic commerce' (Byrne 1998). Of course, this commerce is itself growing at a prodigious rate, which enables Cisco to deliver technical support to its customers at a far lower cost in engineering hours. By the year 2000 it was catching up with Microsoft and GE as one of the largest firms in the world.

The network also is the glue for the internal workings of the company. It swiftly connects Cisco with its web of partners, making the constellation of suppliers, contract manufacturers, and assemblers, look like one company—Cisco—to the outside world. Via the company's intranet, outside contractors directly monitor orders from Cisco customers and ship the assembled hardware to buyers later in the day—often without Cisco even touching the box. (Byrne 1998: 57)

Again according to *Business Week*, networking has enabled Cisco to quadruple its output by outsourcing without building new plants. When an employee needs information, 'the network is also the place to go'. Most psychologists may be relieved to know that, although 'Technology aids and abets this business model . . . it does not completely displace human interaction'; the CEO has quarterly meetings with all (13,000) employees 'at a nearby convention center' and has 1½-hour birthday breakfasts with some of them. Stock options for key employees play an important role, and 'wages are less important than ownership'. Acquisitions have played a key role in Cisco's rapid growth, and critics believe that this may become a source of weakness. So far, however, few of the employees in the newly acquired companies get the sack as the acquisitions are designed specifically to capture new intellectual assets and next generation products. 'At what we pay, at $500,000 to $2 million an employee, we are not acquiring current market share. We are acquiring futures.' When Boeing and Ford told the Cisco CEO that their future networking needs were not likely to be satisfied by Cisco, the firm immediately acquired LAN switchmaker Crescendo Communications in order to satisfy the needs of its leading customers. Partnership with customers, subcontractors, and employees is the name of the game in the networking firm, according to its more enthusiastic exponents. However, the hype should not disguise the fact that real and substantial changes are indeed taking place in the ways firms are managed and conduct their external business relationships. The 'business to business' use of the Internet will probably turn out to be the most important source of productivity gains in the ICT revolution. Nor has ruthlessness disappeared from business relationships or employer–employee relationships. Insecurity of employment, temporary contracts, and part-time working have all become more prevalent, especially in the United States and the United Kingdom.

The rise of the networking firm was reflected also in the business of management consultancy. Those consultants, who continued to use the traditional media and traditional methods, were outpaced by more fleet-footed competitors who made full use of the Internet to transact their business. They were appropriately renamed 'guritos' instead of the old 'gurus'.

In his remarkable three-volume study, *The Information Age: Economy, Society and Culture*, Manuel Castells (1996, 1997, 1998) argues that in the Information Society 'the basic unit of economic organization' is no longer an entrepreneur, a family, a corporation, or the state, but a *network* composed of a variety of organizations. The 'glue' that holds the networks together is the 'spirit of information' itself—a 'cultural code' of the ephemeral, informing and enforcing 'powerful economic decisions at every moment in the life of the network'. Paying homage to Weber's analysis of the spirit of accumulation and enterprise in the rise of capitalism, Castells defines the spirit of informationalism as '[t]he culture of creative discussion accelerated to the speed of the opto-electronic circuits that process its signals. Schumpeter meets Weber in the cyberspace of the network enterprise' (Castells 1996: 199).

It is notable that Weber himself had already spoken of networks in the economy, and many economists have used the concept to characterize various features of capitalist societies, based, as they always have been, on an intense interchange between suppliers and users of materials, components, products, and ideas. How far, therefore, is Castells justified in regarding the 'network enterprise' as the defining *new* feature of informationalism and as a new stage in the development of capitalism?

In the discussion of networking among economists, there has been little disagreement on at least one major new feature of contemporary networks compared with other networks, and that is the *speed* of the technologies of communication now available—and not only the speed of processing and communicating, but also the rapid *access* to new and wider sources of information open to the participants within networks. The imaging and graphics now increasingly available within computer networks may provide a dominating framework in the representation of reality and determine the very substance of information processing for decision-making in the network firm. More than ever, the medium may become the message.

Castells has less to say about another aspect of networking, which has preoccupied economists with their focus on specialization, division of labour, and scale economies. The growing complexity of technology and science had already caused Adam Smith to stress the role of specialization in science and division of labour among scientists. Still earlier, Serra in Naples had pointed to the number of specialized skills and occupations within a city or other territory as an indicator of its sophistication and prosperity (Reinert 1997). This specialization and sub-specialization has today increased by orders of magnitude and means that any degree of 'autarchy' in the organization of 'in-house' R&D has become increasingly problematic. Networking has become more essential than ever in scientific and technical activities, as can be demonstrated by the rapid growth of collaborative research, joint ventures, consultancy, various types of licensing and know-how agreements, joint data banks, and, of course, innumerable forms of tacit informal collaboration. Hagedoorn has shown that this trend has been especially strong with respect to information technology and bio-technology (Hagedoorn 1990; Hagedoorn and Schakenraad 1992).

The advance of information and communications technology has both accelerated and facilitated the growth of networking and the economic advantages of scale economies for those firms and individuals who can accumulate specialized knowledge and have access to networks. The sub-contracting of many services hitherto performed in-house has moved in the same direction. Some economists have always thought that methodological individualism, whether of firms or consumers, was the wrong foundation for economic analysis, and they will welcome Castells's theory of the network firm. However, these changes all have to be seen in the wider context of society as a whole. (See the special issue of *Research Policy* on 'Complex Products and Systems', August 2000.)

9.6 The Institutional and Social Framework and Regime of Regulation

As Bill Gates (1996) points out in his vision of the future of the information society, this society is still in its infancy. As he shows, the potential is truly immense, whether with respect to the economy or the quality of life in relation to health and education. Yet, as with all great new technologies, the social problems of assimilation and application are also immense. This is even more true of socio-political and cultural changes than of the technology. Even in the early days of ICT, the problem of information overload had become apparent. Indeed, some observers realized as early as the 1930s that this was a serious problem even before the age of computers began. The scientist J. D. Bernal (1939), in his discussion of *The Social Function of Science*, pointed to the necessity of competent abstracting and reviewing services because of the impossibility of keeping up with the growing flood of publications and information. Even more perceptively, the poet, T. S. Eliot wrote in his 'Chorus' for 'The Rock':

> Where is the knowledge we have lost in information?
> Where is the wisdom we have lost in knowledge?

If he had lived to see the Information Society, he might have added: 'Where is the information we have lost in data?' The problems of transforming data into information and information into knowledge remain outstanding problems of the Information Society, which have not been resolved by simply calling it the Knowledge Society. In attempting to analyse the 'spirit of informationalism', Castells (1996) goes back to Max Weber's classical work on the spirit of capitalism:

No-one knows . . . whether at the end of this tremendous development, entirely new prophets will arise, or there will be a great re-birth of old ideas, or if neither, mechanized petrification, embellished with a sort of convulsive self-importance. For of the last stage of this cultural development, it might well be truly said: 'specialists without spirit, sensualists without heart, this nullity imagines that it has attained a level of civilisation never before achieved. (Castells 1996: 200, quoting from Weber's *Protestant Ethic*).

This passage recalls the debates on the future of the Internet—whether it is desirable or possible to regulate or halt the diffusion of racist propaganda or pornography, or whether the content of traffic on the Internet has its own momentum, which is beyond anyone's control. What emerges as the dominant culture of the Internet will depend as much on the 'internet service providers' (ISPs) as on the individuals who surf the net or the small firms that strive to achieve a global presence.

In the 1980s, economists such as Albert Bressand (1990) were already pointing to the ways in which networks could easily evolve into future electronic cartels. During the 1990s the wave of mergers and acquisitions heightened these fears. Whereas in the early days of ICT many economists and management consultants stressed the role of small and medium-sized enterprises (SMEs) in generating innovations and new employment opportunities, now the emphasis has shifted increasingly to the supposed advantages of the very large global firms. One of the main arguments put forward to justify the largest ever merger proposed, early in 2000, by AOL (America on Line) and the Time–Warner group of companies was that in future the large media companies must be linked to a powerful ISP. By the same token, the ISP giants would need to be linked to *content* providers. Hitherto, large media companies such as Berlusconi's European conglomerate, or Murdoch's empire, concentrated on combining various media and entertainment interests—newspapers, television, football clubs, films, etc.—under one ownership in various countries. Now such companies aspire to owning and controlling Internet access and advertising too. It is not only the sheer scale of these mergers that causes some anxiety for believers in the virtues of competition, but perhaps even more the nature of the mergers. Control over the *content* of Internet services is clearly a fundamental issue for any democratic society and for the future 'spirit of informationalism'.

M. Javary and R. Mansell (2000), in their study of 'Emerging Internet Oligopolies', conclude that 'the development of the British ISP market suggests a trend toward the emergence of an oligopolistic industry that is inconsistent with the evolution of a network "commons" which will be responsive to social values'. They point to the wave of acquisitions of small new entrants by large British and American companies, which consolidate power and control in various specialized market segments. This is a far cry from the utopian dreams of the early pioneers using the Internet, who dreamt that it would provide not only a world-wide free democratic forum for the exchange of information and ideas, but also a global market-place in which the SMEs would be able to compete on level terms. The fact that networks are everywhere forming, flourishing, and sometimes disappearing does not dispose of the question of *power* within networks. A network may seldom be a partnership of equals. Some partners are usually more equal than others, to use Orwell's satirical comment on Stalinist forms of equality. A network may be the organizational means whereby a dominant firm maintains control over its suppliers, whether of materials, components, or technology.

As in the earlier case of electrification, the Internet has indeed provided and is still providing millions of new opportunities for SMEs to enter the economy, and in some cases to prosper and make a fortune. Internet millionaires have become quite commonplace, but the trend towards concentration is very widely apparent. The risk that monopolistic corporate power will wield increasing political and cultural influence in the information society is quite evident. The information revolution did indeed weaken or destroy the *old* monopolistic power of the telecommunication utilities. As we have seen, most of these, outside the United States, were state-owned and have been broken up and privatized. Even the heavily regulated Bell private monopoly in the USA was treated in the same way. This made possible the fairly rapid development of many new services and new technologies, but renewed concentration and re-regulation is now the name of the game. Even the competition between wired (cable) systems and wireless (mobile) telephony described so eloquently by George Gilder is leading to renewed concentration. The Anglo-American Vodafone Airtouch launched a bid to merge with the German Mannesmann Corporation early in 2000, a move that rivalled the AOL merger in scale and scope. The old publicly owned state monopolies have gone, only to be replaced by new giant global multinational corporations. This has undoubtedly resulted in a substantial weakening of the power of national governments. Can they any longer control the global infrastructure?

The wave of privatization in the 1980s and 1990s and the deregulation that accompanied it were only two instances of this serious weakening of national governments, which has been a major feature of this structural crisis of adjustment. Recently, the Netherlands government published a thoughtful booklet entitled '*Governments Losing Ground: An Exploration of Administrative Consequences of Information and Communication Technology*' (Netherlands Scientific Council for Government Policy 1999: 5). This started with a proposition that is very widely accepted:

The declining ties to a particular territorial area will, it would seem, inevitably have consequences for the capacity of the national state to act, since the regulative and directive capacity of states derives to a significant extent from instruments (such as legislation and regulations) that are territorially bound. ICT can also provide impulses in more than one direction, combining both greater internationalization ('globalization') and greater emphasis on regional and local levels. In both cases, there is a declining dominance on the part of the territorial level on which national governance is based.

To some degree, this phase of deregulation is characteristic for the emergence of each new techno-economic paradigm, as we have seen in the earlier cases of electrification and motorization. The early beginnings of a new technology are necessarily confined to a few individuals and organizations, and small new firms are typically the midwives. There were hundreds of small firms making automobiles at the end of the nineteenth century, and it was by no means clear whether the future would be steam cars, electric cars, or petrol engine cars. Dominant designs, the regulation of traffic, and technical standards took decades to evolve. Even in the oil industry, as Chapter 8 has shown, small-firm competition prevailed in the early days before the speculative bubble burst and before Standard Oil ruled. It is easy to forget now that it was a long time before the giant firms grew big enough and strong enough to dominate the industry.

According to some accounts, however, the very nature of the technology determines the configuration and characteristics of the regulatory regime. The mass production technology in this view led inexorably to a centralized regulatory regime analogous to the managerial regime within the large corporations, with its hierarchical techno-structure. The ICT constellation, on the other hand, was often supposed to lend itself very easily to self-regulating networks with minimal central control. A rather utopian view of the Internet was widespread in the 1980s, even though it was first established by the Pentagon to preserve some level of communications in the event of nuclear war. This very objective of decentralized participatory communications by many individuals was thought to embody the liberal spirit and democratic values.

This contrasts with the mature period of the mass production society, when it was almost universally assumed that the role of central and local government in regulating and controlling the economy would increase. This assumption was shared by Keynesians, socialists, nationalists, militarists, and many people who could not be classified to any particular ideology. There were, of course, some very important exceptions, such as Hayek, who from the early 1940s vigorously opposed the increased role of government in the economy. In his famous book *The Road to Serfdom* (Hayek 1942), he argued that 'planning' would inexorably lead to political totalitarianism, and his arguments always commanded some respect and support, especially in the United States. However, in most countries both the mainstream trend in the economics profession and the dominant political parties favoured some type of Keynesian 'managed economy' or, as in Eastern Europe, outright central planning. Government expenditure, as a proportion of GDP, was almost everywhere much higher than before the Second World War, and this was generally assumed to be necessary, whether for military or for welfare purposes. In developing countries, it was generally assumed that the state had to play a very considerable role in efforts to organize 'catch-up' and promote industrialization, technical change, and economic growth.

Very different ideas have attended the birth-pangs of the 'Information Society' since the 1970s. In the last two decades of the twentieth century it has been quite widely assumed that taxation should be reduced and government expenditures diminished. Moreover, not only conservative and neo-liberal parties and ideologists, but also many erstwhile socialist and social democratic parties, have abandoned their belief in public ownership and central planning and embraced the philosophy of the free market. Margaret Thatcher, prime minister of Britain throughout the 1980s, was undoubtedly one of the most influential exponents of this neo-liberal ideology, even though she later lost the confidence of her own party. She was inspired directly by the ideas of Hayek, whom she greatly admired, and in one sense both the surge of neo-liberalism in Western Europe and the collapse of the centrally planned economies in Eastern Europe can be regarded as a belated vindication of his ideas. However, it remains to be seen how far the tide of deregulation and roll-back of state intervention will flow in the new information society. The weakening of government, which has occurred in the early period of the ICT revolution, has been followed by the resurgence of some tendencies to new forms of regulation and control. The last word has not yet been spoken and many possibilities are still open. No one knows what will be the last stage of cultural and political development in the information society.

We ourselves would accept the view that the characteristics of a pervasive technology do indeed influence government systems as well as corporate management systems. 'Influence', however, is not the same as determinism. The rise of totalitarian political systems and ideologies had, in our view, causes much deeper and wider than simply the prevalence of mass production; and, by the same token, computer networks, and in particular the Internet, do not inevitably or necessarily give rise to 'free' competition or democratic political institutions. The political systems in mass production societies were quite varied, as were the regulatory systems. The gas chambers and furnaces of the holocaust at Auschwitz were a macabre and horrifying example of the application of mass production philosophy as much as is the mass tourism on the Costa Brava. We have argued in Chapter 8 that the rise of nazism owed far more to mass unemployment and the complicity of some sections of big business than to the characteristics of any production system. The way in which any technological system is developed and used is the field of political conflict and ethical arguments, even though some technologies may lend themselves more easily to perverted and sinister applications. The kind of society that emerges from the ICT revolution depends on the strength and programmes of contending social groups and political forces far more than on the technologies.

This can be seen rather clearly from the current debates on taxation and the Internet. It is of course true that one aspect of the reduced power of national governments has been the loss of revenue from certain kinds of tax, especially corporate taxes and income tax. So important has this issue become that the OECD has warned of the danger of competition between governments to reduce taxes, and *The Economist* published a special feature on 'The Mystery of the Vanishing Taxpayer' in its 'Survey of Globalization and Tax' (29 January–4 February 2000: 1–20). This survey concluded that tax competition is a reality and that it could be stopped only with great difficulty. The 'Emerald' Tiger (Ireland) probably owed more to its low tax regime than anything else in its overtaking of Britain in per capita GDP. *The Economist* also considered the argument advanced by Charles Tiebout that tax competition, like other kinds of competition, is a Good Thing: 'Tax competition will put pressure on governments to provide their services efficiently, but that need not mean they have to be minimal' (p. 6).

However, *The Economist* survey does point to a major flaw in Tiebout's argument: whereas capital is mobile, most taxpayers are not, except for the most wealthy. The Internet will make more people mobile, 'rendering the rest even more wretched'. There are many forms of tax avoidance, which are facilitated by a combination of capital mobility and information technology. *The Economist* quotes American studies of tax havens which even in the 1980s showed that they accounted for 3 per cent of world GDP but 26 per cent of the assets and 31 per cent of the net profits. Murdoch's News Corporation, which earned profits of $2.3 billion in Britain since 1987, paid no UK corporation tax. It is not only corporation tax and income tax that can be increasingly avoided by fleet-footed companies and lawyers, but also sales taxes on e-commerce traded goods and services. It is true therefore that the Internet and ICT more generally lend themselves to a weakening of the tax power of governments.

To conclude that large multinational corporations (and even small ones) are the inevitable winners in the information society, and that the provision of welfare services by governments is doomed because of the nature of the new technologies, is somewhat premature. Social and political innovations, have great potential as well as technical innovations, and some could also take advantage of ICT. The Internet does make possible some forms of tax avoidance, but it also makes possible the political mobilization of groups all over the world to combat these practices and the philosophy and values that make them prevalent. As *The Economist* survey points out, 'No representation without taxation' could become an important principle in the twenty-first century. Moreover, entirely new forms of tax, which are redistributive in favour of both poor people and poor countries, are quite feasible. Luxury consumption taxes and pollution taxes can rise. Land taxes and road pricing could ease congestion and pollution problems as well as raising revenue in ways that would be harder to avoid. Finally, the provision of on-line services for health and education over the Internet could be a very powerful stimulus to the *improvement* of the welfare state. There are dangers of social exclusion with all such changes, of course, and the EU Report (European Commission 1997) on *Building the European Information Society For Us All* was right to insist that the universal service obligation must continue to provide for those who are not computer-numerate as well as for the rapidly increasing numbers who have Internet access.

Nor should the possibilities of new forms of *international* tax regimes be excluded. *The Economist* Survey points to proposals for a World Tax Organization to join the family of international organizations. The so-called 'Tobin Tax', named after the American economist who first proposed it, would offer immense possibilities for funding many of the objectives of the United Nations, including both social and environmental objectives, as well as security. According to the estimates of Robin Round (Round 2000), such a tax on speculative movements of capital could raise $150–$300 billion annually if set at a rate of 0.25 per cent. It would have the additional benefit of strengthening the position of governments and weakening the position of speculators in relation to exchange rates.

Finally, taxes on Internet traffic itself should certainly not be forgotten. When a 'Bit Tax' was first proposed by innovative economists such as Soete and Kamp (1996), it met with some strong criticism, notably from the US federal government, for rather obvious reasons; however, state governments within the United States were more sympathetic. It is quite true that there are problems of technical feasibility as well as political opposition, but these problems are not insoluble given the political will at both the national and the international level. Perez (1983) and Mansell (2000) have both quite rightly pointed to the need for bold *institutional* innovations to deal with the manifold social problems of the information society. Whether or not these can be devised and realized, in the sphere of taxation or elsewhere, is mainly a political and cultural question rather than a technical problem.

9.7 The Culture of Virtual Reality

In earlier discussion of culture and social change (Section 8.7) we have emphasized that works of art have a logic and time of their own. They may anticipate the future or recall a nostalgic vision of the past. Nevertheless, the tides of culture production are unintelligible without a consideration of the dominant modes of communication, the changing social structure, and the advent of new technologies.

Nowhere is this more apparent than in the case of the information society. The transformation of the production of works of art from the activity of a bohemian fringe of society to a major industry in its own right was one of the biggest social changes induced by the mass production paradigm. Millionaire artists, actors, sports people, and writers can now rub shoulders on almost equal terms with 'ordinary' millionaires from the worlds of commerce and industry. The entertainment industries are now a fully fledged and essential part of post-modern late capitalism. Information technology has taken this whole process a stage further and added some new dimensions.

In terms of *content*, the crucial alteration introduced in the postwar mass production period was the widespread diffusion of commercial TV. Consequently, the film industry, the epicentre of cultural production since the beginning of the century, was transmuted from a production of episodic and unique pieces, seen by large audiences in unique settings, into a production of flows of images and sounds to be seen simultaneously in private settings. The simultaneous collective experience was transmuted into a simultaneous individualized experience. The continuous flow abolishes the effort of memory and imposes the loss of historicity, mixing news, films, soaps, and contests at the same level of discourse and reducing all sounds and images to bits of *infotainment*. The great consequence of this is the fully used potential for the construction of 'fictive temporalities' and therefore the 'technological appropriation of subjectivity', generating a specific and novel type of media populism that was to become the basis for the entertainment industry (Jameson 1991: 74).

It was when the technology became available for the production of continuous flows of *infotainment* that 'postmodernism' won the day. Contrary to MacLuhan and so many other commentators, its victory did not represent the imposition of a complete universal culture: we do not live in a global village, but in 'customized cottages globally produced and locally distributed' (Castells 1996: i. 341). Each cultural artefact is locally bounded and the production of icons is still mediated by national and regional frontiers: their understanding is largely local. But icons are industrially produced and are the constitutive bits and clips of our social communication, and this is the triumph of the aesthetics of distraction.

A new world is taking shape in this end of millenium ... brought into being a new dominant social structure, the network society; a new economy, the info/global economy; and a new culture, the culture of virtual reality. (Castells 1998: iii. 336).

The social consequences of this dramatic change in culture are still to be fully understood. The growing importance of advertising, the consumption of the discourse of consumption, and the narrative of desire inscribed in publicity constitute the image as the final form of reification of the commodity: the product is identified with its brand or logo. In this critical view, advertising is the dominant form of production of signs in postmodern culture. Fashion and fast food, B-films and remakes, Warhol's pop art, parodies and kitsch, science fiction, music and video reduced to clips populate this universe of pastiche—to use Thomas Mann's concept. Categories of space have replaced categories of time, historical depth has been lost to ephemera, reality melts into thin air, and concentration has been lost to superficial trivia.

Castells notes that in this rather shallow world, drained of spiritual values, cult religions may flourish as never before. Yet, enthusiasts for the vast potential of the new media and the new technology could justifiably respond that ICT offers the possibility for *participation* in creative activities in ways undreamt of and of bringing and enhancing education in every topic to the majority of the world's population. The final outcome depends on political and social changes, which are one of the main topics in the Conclusions to this part of the book.

Conclusions to Part II: Recurrent Phenomena of the Long Waves of Capitalist Development

C.1 Introduction

In this chapter we return to some of the fundamental problems of the theory of 'reasoned history', which we raised in Part I. In Chapter 4, and in the Conclusions to Part I, we maintained that, to justify the use of the concept of 'waves' rather than simply 'stages' or 'periods' of historical evolution, it is necessary to distinguish *recurrent* phenomena in each period as well as the unique features of each technological revolution. In Chapters 5–9 we analysed some of these unique features, and in this final chapter of Part II we discuss some of the main recurrent features as they have emerged from the narrative account in this part. We also try to place these recurrent features of the changes in technology and in the economy in a wider institutional and social context, a context in which semi-autonomous political and cultural changes may sometimes predominate in determining the course of events.

We first of all distinguish some recurrent features of the successive industrial revolutions that we have analysed in Chapters 5–9, and then illustrate this recurrence with some further supporting evidence of social and political tendencies in each long wave: the growth of new large firms and the continuity of others, the incidence of strike movements, labour disputes and social unrest during various phases of the long wave, and the evolution of a new international regulatory regime in each wave.

In the Introduction to Part II, we listed several features of the successive industrial revolutions, particularly those identified by Carlota Perez (1983), which together might explain the recurrence of long waves in the economy and the social system. Foremost among these features was the periodic emergence and diffusion of a new constellation of technical and organizational innovations offering in each case exceptional super-profits of innovative entrepreneurship. These recurrent super-profits are the first feature we shall discuss in this chapter.

Both some of the sternest critics of capitalism (e.g. Marx) and some of its most ardent admirers (e.g. Hayek) have argued that one of its foremost characteristics has been its capacity to generate and to diffuse a torrent of technical innovations. Our theory has emphasized the interdependence and systemic features of these innovations, which means that they cannot simply be analysed as individual, discrete events, although, of course, micro-level agents have been essential for their inception and diffusion. In Chapter 5 we outlined the exceptionally favourable confluence of cultural, political, economic, geographical, scientific, and social circumstances in eighteenth-century Britain which gave rise to that upsurge of technical and organizational innovations known ever since as the 'Industrial Revolution'. In subsequent chapters we showed that other capitalist economies, and especially the United States, were able not only to achieve similar results but, as time went by, to outstrip Britain with new constellations of innovations.

Capitalist economies have been able to achieve these remarkable results, 'surpassing the wonders of the Ancient World', as Marx and Engels put it, by a combination of incentives and pressures affecting ultimately numerous firms and individuals. First of all, of course, a well-functioning capitalist economy offers the possibility, but by no means the certainty, of profit from successful innovation, and sometimes very large profit. This profit may be accompanied by other rewards—status, privilege, political advancement, and fame. In our account we have shown that some of the most successful entrepreneurs in each technological revolution did indeed achieve extraordinarily large profits, although they did not necessarily seek the other advantages often sought by very wealthy individuals. Fame itself they could hardly avoid, and indeed this was a very important social mechanism for the diffusion of their innovations and for efforts to surpass them. Arkwright, Wedgwood, Hudson, Brunel, the Vanderbilts, Carnegie, Krupp, Rockefeller, Rathenau, Siemens, Diesel, Ford, Gates, and Murdoch are all examples of entrepreneurs and inventors who achieved both fame and fortune through their innovations, whether technical, organizational, or both. Their innovations were very different from one another—indeed, unique—but they had in common this extraordinary profitability.

A number of long wave theorists (Mandel 1980; Goodwin 1985; Poletayev 1987) have constructed models of the behaviour of the economic system based mainly on long-term fluctuations in the aggregate rate of profit. They argued quite plausibly that a fall in the rate of profit tends to occur after a long period of prosperity and expansion, partly because of the Schumpeterian processes of erosion of innovators' profits during diffusion and partly through wider pressures from rising costs of inputs. These tendencies for the rate of profit to fall at the peak of a long boom are among the main reasons explaining the upper turning point in the long wave and the onset of a prolonged downswing in which generally lower rates of profit prevail. We provide some evidence of such a change in the most recent period in Section C.2 (Figure C.9, p. 354). The statistics are very difficult to assemble, especially for the nineteenth century, but, such as they are, they do provide some support for this interpretation. We certainly do not wish to deny the plausibility of these models, but since our emphasis is mainly on structural change, and on divergent sectoral phenomena, we stress mainly the exceptionally large 'super-profits' that were realized through the exploitation of major radical innovations. These profits appear all the more remarkable if they were made during a period of general decline in the rate of profit in the 'downswing' phase of the long wave. As Schumpeter insisted, they offered a strong signal to potential imitators.

The first distinguishing characteristic, therefore, of the long waves that we shall discuss in this chapter is the recurrent emergence and diffusion of a cluster of innovations which offered the clear-cut potential for immense profits, based on proven technical superiority to previous modes of production. Minor incremental improvements were, of course, occurring all the time, but the innovations that were at the heart of each wave that we analysed offered quite dramatic changes in productivity and profitability.

If there is substance in this theory, then we hypothesize that it might be supported not only by the examples we have cited in this second part of the book, but by other evidence on the growth of large firms associated with these exceptional innovations. The most profitable firms could plausibly be expected to grow faster than the average through an accumulation of profits and new investment. We therefore looked for such supporting evidence in the data on the changing population of the largest firms.

This information has already given rise to a debate on the so-called 'continuity' thesis. Some accounts have suggested that the population of the largest firms has been rather stable for a long time, and this would appear to contradict our theory. On the other hand, if our thesis has substance, then we would expect it to be supported by the periodic incursion of a cohort of new large firms into the top group. Section C.2 is therefore devoted to a critical discussion of the evidence for and against this 'continuity' theory.

A second case of recurrent phenomena which emerges from the account we presented in Chapters 5–9 is that of structural crises of adjustment. It seems fairly obvious that the diffusion of a constellation of major technical and organizational innovations through the economic and social system must cause profound changes in the structure, as well as in the occupation and skill profiles and management systems. Moreover, precisely because each constellation is unique, they will have very different effects in each technological revolution. The recurrent effect is a pervasive pattern of structural change, but the industries and occupations most affected will be different in each case. Obviously also, the new industries will be quite different. All this means that increased structural unemployment is likely to be a major recurrent feature of each crisis of structural adjustment, along with many changes in the conditions of employment. A mismatch of the skill profile is likely to be widespread.

The statistics of unemployment for the nineteenth century are very poor, but we argued in Chapter 5 (Section 5.10) that there is strong evidence of very serious unemployment in the 1830s and 1840s in Britain, while David Wells (1890) and other economists commented on the widespread unemployment in most industrial countries in the 1880s and especially in those that were most advanced in the use of machinery (Section 6.6). There is also, of course, abundant statistical evidence of the heavy structural unemployment in the 1920s and 1930s and again in the 1980s and 1990s (Section 8.10). Even in the 1920s boom in the United States, as Fearon (1987) and the NBER pointed out, there were sectors experiencing severe adjustment problems, such as coal, railways, and ship-building (Section 8.2).

It is hardly conceivable that structural changes of this magnitude could occur in an orderly and conflict-free manner, and it is obvious that the destruction of the livelihood of hundreds of thousands of people is bound to be a cause of acute social unrest. We have tried to show in earlier chapters that this has indeed been the case in each crisis of adjustment. Huge demonstrations and riots of unemployed workers were a widespread feature of the 1930–3 depression in both Europe and America. Even though social security legislation has lessened the hardships of the more recent period, these protests against redundancies were again a common phenomenon in the 1970s and 1980s.

There are also bound to be conflicts within the expanding industries and technologies over pay, status, and working conditions for various groups of workers and managers. We hypothesize therefore that the available statistics of strike days and the numbers of striking workers should provide evidence of the recurrent structural crises and their social consequences. Section C.3 is devoted to a discussion of the evidence on this topic. Finally, the crises of structural adjustment that we have postulated are a recurrent feature of long waves and inevitably give rise to many other social and political conflicts and debates, in addition to those which we identify in Section C.3. Such extensive changes as mechanization, electrification, motorization, and computerization give rise to entirely new requirements for industrial standards, for education and training, for tariffs and trade protection (or free trade), for safety regulations, for environmental protection, and for intellectual property rights. We postulate therefore, like Carlota Perez (1983, 1985, 2000), the periodic reconfiguration of an entire regulatory regime for each successive structural crisis of adjustment. This has not been a main theme of the book, but it has been mentioned in the framework of the windows of opportunity generated by the emergence of new techno-economic paradigms, such as the age of electrification (Chapters 6 and 7). In that context, firms and national economies could acquire new positions, surfing the wave of technical, organizational, and social innovation and adapting their national regime of regulation accordingly.

Yet, although this is not a major theme of this book, convergence and divergence are more general trends in the economic evolution of the world economy, and a brief comment is necessary. According to the OECD data investigated by Hollanders *et al.* (1999), and considering a large sample of countries, a trend of general convergence is identified from 1960 until 1973, i.e. in the upswing of the fourth Kondratiev, whereas a mixed process of convergence and divergence occurred between 1973 and 1991. If the sample is reduced just to the OECD countries, a convergence trend dominates from 1900 until 1918, as well as in the 1950–73 period, the 'golden years' after the end of the Second World War. Changes in the regulatory regime, at both the national level and the international level, have a considerable effect on the process of international 'catch-up', i.e. convergence or divergence. The new international regime is the subject of our final comment in Section C.4.

C.2 Big Business in the Long Waves[1]

Chandler and Daems (1980: 2–3) have argued that 'by 1920 big business had already become the most influential non-government institution in all advanced industrial market economies', and we would not dispute their contention. However, we do dispute some aspects of their analysis of the *composition* of the top echelon of big business. Basing our analysis on the 'Fortune' list of the largest firms in the United States and Chandler's own research on this topic, we discuss the controversial question of 'continuity' in the top echelon of large firms. From the historical analysis in Chapters 5–9 and from a variety of other sources, we endeavour to show that a cohort of new large firms has joined the list periodically, basing themselves on the new technologies and industries of each long wave. Only a minority of the largest firms were able to remain at the top through several waves. Their relative endurance, and the meteoric rise of the new contenders with each revolution, both depend on the achievement of high levels of profitability and the accumulation of both tangible and intangible capital. Efforts to achieve large market shares and high profitability clearly have profound consequences on the social conflicts over the appropriate regimes of regulation, which are discussed in the following sections.

It is employers and their organizations that have generally been in the strongest position to shape and influence the new trajectories in technology and the relevant regimes of regulation. Trade unions and other working-class organizations have usually been in the position of responding to technical and organizational changes, rather than initiating or controlling them.[2] This is not to say that any group, organization, or class has a clear idea of how a particular technology will evolve. As we tried to show in Chapters 5–9, uncertainty characterizes the evolution of any new constellation of innovations, and the ultimate outcome is not quite what anyone specifically intended in the early days. On the contrary, expectations and the balance of forces are constantly changing as a result of new developments in technology and science, as well as in the evolution of social and political systems and of culture in society more generally.

---

[1] This section is based in part on Louçã and Mendonça (1999).
[2] See Muchie (1986) for a particularly interesting doctoral thesis on the failure of attempts of workers' organizations to influence design and innovation in the early days of the revolution in Russia in the 1920s.

As we explained in the Introduction to Part II, we are concerned in this book with the evolution of recognizably capitalist economies. We have not commented on those societies in which, between 1917 and the 1990s, attempts were made to establish a different type of economic system. We believe that they too were very strongly influenced by technological and political developments in the capitalist world and by the evolution of the global economy. In fact, long wave theories were also developed within these countries, but we shall not deal with them here. Our concern has been with those economic systems that have been based predominantly on private ownership and accumulation of wealth through the profitability of enterprises. These capitalist economies have had particularly strong pressures and incentives to innovate, since the survival and growth of most enterprises depended on their profitability. We have confined our analysis mainly to the leading industrial countries, since circumstances were often very different elsewhere. It is this persistence of capitalist institutions that, in our view, explains the *recurrence* of various social phenomena, even with very different new constellations of technologies.

However, the persistence of some features of capitalist economies, such as private ownership and the imperative for firms to make profits for survival and growth, certainly does not mean that all capitalist institutions have remained unchanged. On the contrary, the pressures to earn profits, to accumulate, to invest, and to enlarge markets have themselves led inexorably to the growth of some large and very large firms. Whereas in the early nineteenth century competition between numerous small firms was characteristic of the industrial landscape, by the late nineteenth century giant firms, employing tens of thousands of people, had emerged and begun to dominate in several industries. This had already occurred in the railway industry in mid-century, and Chapter 7 has described in particular the rise of giant firms in steel and electricity. Chapter 8 concentrated on the oil and automobile industries and Chapter 9 on computers, software, microelectronics, and telecommunications. In each of these waves of technical change, entirely new firms expanded with extraordinary speed and joined the population of 'giants' that had grown up in previous waves.

Even in the eighteenth century, of course, there had been a few large firms, but these were mainly in trade (such as the East India Company) rather than industry, and in Adam Smith's time there were very few industrial firms employing as many as a hundred people. Nevertheless, as every economics student knows, Adam Smith gave severe warnings about the dangers attending any meetings of businessmen and traders in the same line of business. Conspiracies to raise and fix prices would, in his view, often follow. Classical and neoclassical economics have retained this anti-monopoly tradition, and since the 1890s much effort has gone into refining models of perfect and imperfect competition, and into devising institutions that might limit or reduce the pervasive growth of monopolistic and oligopolistic firms and practices. In the United States in particular, popular political movements have mobilized widespread support for 'trust-busting' legislation ever since the Sherman Act in 1890, and many of America's largest firms, from Standard Oil to Microsoft, have been the object of investigation and legal action to restrict their power.

While no one denies the fact of the rise of large firms in most manufacturing industries and many service activities, there are many different interpretations of this concentration process. In the 1890s Alfred Marshall had already proposed his 'trees of the forest' metaphor, in which he accepted the obvious fact of the growth of giant 'trees', but suggested that limits to their growth would mean that periodically some would die and be replaced by new, younger trees. As time went by, however, other economists pointed to the fact that some of the giant 'trees' appeared to have uncommonly deep roots and to survive for a very long time. This became known as the 'continuity' thesis, which stressed the adaptability of large firms, their financial strength, their market power, and their political influence.

The evolution of 'Big Business' will be discussed here on the basis of the statistical and appreciative analysis of the population of the 200 largest US firms in the 'Fortune' list for 1963, 1983, and 1997. Prior to that we use Chandler's data for 1917, 1930, and 1948. Although it has been accepted that these two sets of information are consistent, and although other authors have used both sources simultaneously for their work, they have important shortcomings that must be emphasized. As we move back in time, the reliability of statistical information is more doubtful; furthermore, the classification criteria have shifted through time, as a response to the very change in the structure of the main industries.

The first problem cannot be solved, although it can be lessened, as in this section, restricting as far as possible the intertemporal comparisons to those domains for which clear conjectures about trajectories can be argued. The second problem can be addressed in a more satisfactory manner, and the selected strategy here was to develop a new classification, based on the two-digit SIC, but considering complementary information about the core business of the firms. The choice of the United States must also be stressed. It was the leading country in techology throughout the period we analysed and, moreover, one with a very large market and no wars at home during that period.

This section does not consider the question of 'creative destruction' in relation to technologies. Schumpeter's (1942) use of this expression has been taken by some people to mean the 'destruction' of older technologies as well as firms. This does in fact sometimes occur, but more commonly the older technologies are transformed or complemented rather than destroyed by the newer technologies. We stressed this point in relation to electrification and electro-mechanical technology in Chapter 8, and the same point is obviously relevant in relation to electronic technology. Patel and Pavitt (1994) and Pavitt (1986), in particular, have insisted that competence in older technologies is usually still important for firms using the new ones. They have demonstrated this by analysis of the patent portfolios of large firms and argued that *multi-technology* capability is often essential for large firms today. Research by Birgitte Andersen (1998) on the accumulated trajectory of patents in the mechanical and electro-electronic industries makes the same point. She used a thirty-year weighted measure of patents in order to assess technological trajectories, and the comparison shows that mechanical inno- vations are dominant in the whole period (1890–1990). However, her research also reveals the extremely rapid rise of electronic patents in the most recent period (Figures C.1 and C.2). Even though this argument is not quite independent from the main continuity thesis, it might nevertheless be one of the factors explaining the longevity of some large firms. However, the counter-argument must also be considered—that competence in and attach- ment to an older technology may lead to some reluctance to embark on a new one. In any case, our argument here is concerned primarily with the continuity of firms, not technologies. Old and new technologies undoubt- edly co-exist, even if the population of firms that use them is changing.

We attempt to detect the major changes occurring in the twentieth century in the population of the largest firms as part of the test of the argument about

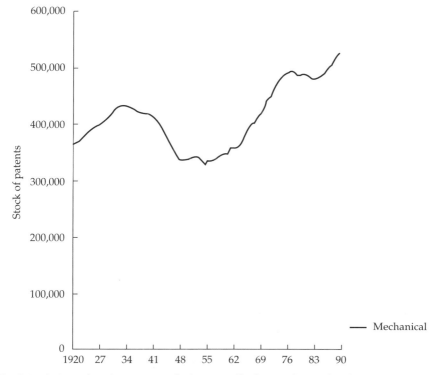

FIG C.1. Accumulated patent stocks historically for mechanical technologies
Source: B. Andersen (1998).

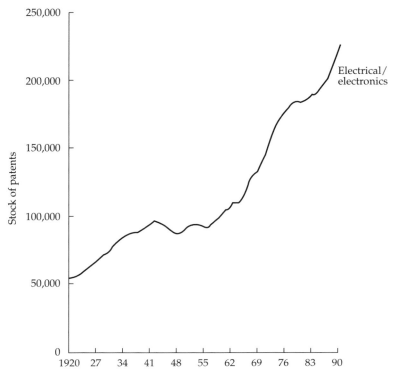

FIG C.2. Accumulated patent stocks historically for electrical/electronic technologies

Source: B. Andersen (1998).

the importance of structural change in economic history. This limited purpose is constrained by the very nature of available data: identified by a very narrow set of variables, these populations of large firms are statistically inadequate to test conjectures on degrees of monopoly or forms of competition (Stigler 1969: 338).

We now review the evidence for and against the 'continuity thesis', which emphasizes the uninterrupted dominance of the same large firms in the core industries over the whole century. We then discuss some other interpretations of the history of big business, and finally present the argument for the long wave pattern.

Based on an extended inquiry on the foundation year of the largest 500 US firms as registered by Fortune in 1994, a study by the Harris Corporation concluded that there was a 'remarkable endurance and adaptability of major firms as institutions in a world that has seen frequent, rapid, and tumultuous change' (Harris Corporation 1996: 72).

But the very inquiry conducted by the Harris Corporation actually presents mixed results. To be sure, there is a clear predominance of *old* firms: 39

per cent of the population was more than one century old; if we consider those firms founded between the 1880s and the 1920s, we get approximately 50 per cent. Yet some 16 per cent were founded after 1950, and the pattern of the emergence of new giants is clearly indicative of the new opportunities related to the ICT revolution. This evidence points to three very relevant characteristics of the giants: (1) approximately half of the larger firms were created during the third Kondratiev wave; (2) the first movers naturally created important barriers to entry; but (3) new opportunities were still open for entrants in new industries and they rapidly became part of the club.

Chandler argues persuasively that the reasons for (1) and (2) lie in the accumulation of capabilities in the framework of early oligopolistic competition and the constructed advantage of large-scale investments in physical and human capital:

By World War I the major players in the capital-intensive industrial oligopolies had established themselves. Many of these firms remained the leaders in their industries for the next half century. Some would disappear by merger, and others would drop off the list of the top 200 as new technologies brought new industrial leaders to the top. Because of continuing oligopolistic competition, ranking in terms of sales, market share, and profit within an industry rose and fell. Nevertheless the first movers, those that made the largest initial investment in capital equipment, continued during the following decades to make large scale investments in physical capital, in most cases funded by retained earnings, and to be among the nation's major employers of industrial workers. The barriers to entry became so high that few challengers entered the oligopoly. These enterprises thus became learning bases for further development of products and processes. They remained at the core of a network of suppliers, dealers, and other related firms. (Chandler 1997: 76)

And further:

By committing to the extensive long-term investment in human and organisational resources as well as physical assets, these large enterprises could exploit the complementarity between the large-scale investment in physical capital and the sustained capital formation in such intangible assets as human resources and technological knowledge. The capabilities that resulted became the core competencies of many of the international firms. These competencies enabled such firms to maintain themselves as major global players and to exploit the dramatic technological innovations in electronics, aerospace, chemicals, and pharmaceuticals associated with what might be considered a third Industrial Revolution[3] after the Second World War. (Chandler and Hikino 1997: 25).

---

[3] The expresion 'Second Industrial Revolution' is equivalent to our third and fourth Kondratiev waves, while the 'First Industrial Revolution' is equivalent to the first and second Kondratiev waves and the 'Third Industrial Revolution' is the Information Revolution. Von Tunzelmann (1995*a*: 100) designates the industrial revolutions distinguished in a similar way as 'super-cycles'.

Thus, for Chandler, this form of oligopolistic competition is at the origin of cumulative learning, leading to the construction of specific organizational capabilities, which generate high barriers against new entrants for a long period. These facilitate the persistence of high oligopolistic profits and hence fuel continued growth (Chandler 1994: 3). The oligopolistic profit is at the core of the capacity of these firms to prolong their advantage through large investment in R&D and the creation of new barriers to access.

Chandler's thesis is quite plausible as an explanation of the survival of a significant proportion of the large firms. However, Leslie Hannah came to rather different conclusions. He considered the manufacturing and mining companies of the most developed industrial nations, and compared the 100 largest ones in the 1912 and 1995 lists. The 1912 list is consistent with the results of the previously quoted research by the Harris Corporation: the average age was thirty-two years; i.e. the firms were created on average in the 1880s. But the trajectory from 1912 to 1995 suggests an outstanding conclusion: only approximately 25 per cent remained independent or grew from 1912 until 1995, and of these only about 20 per cent were still in the top 100 in 1995— i.e. 'disappearance and decline was nearly three times more likely among the giants than growth' (Hannah 1997: 18).

Hannah attributes the easy acceptance of the continuity thesis to the strong image of survivors, or to the fact that the authors treat different populations: 100 world or 500 US firms. However, he found that European firms were actually more likely to survive than American ones. The over-statement of survivors is mainly a feature of our understandably inaccurate memory: 'Who remembers today the Cudahy Packing Company?' But they were one of the giant firms of 1912.

In our own analysis, we considered only the United States and the largest population we could get from secondary sources: the 200 largest manufacturing firms, which are identified by Chandler for 1917, 1930, and 1948, and then the prolonged Fortune data for 1963, 1983, and 1997. As a consequence, we got a population of 544 firms for the whole period.

The persistence in the series is limited: only 28 firms appear in the top list for all the six years. These are the 'persistent' giants, which were founded at the turn of the century or benefited from mergers during that period (Table C.1). But if 28 firms appear in all the lists, more than half of the firms constituting our population (267) appear only once. The frequencies of presence in the top list is shown in Figure C.3. Furthermore, the 'persistent' firms are, on average, higher placed in the general ranking (i.e. their average ranking is lower), as shown in Figure C.4. The two figures draw a picture that is consistent with the continuity thesis, only under the supposition that the irregularly present firms are still part of the top, although not of the 200 top, and that there is a large dispersion in the position through history of the following firms. But the evidence does not support such an assumption. As Figure C.5 shows, 24.8 per cent of the firms are present in our list only in the pre-Second World War lists and drop out afterwards, whereas 47.8 per cent come

TABLE C.1. Persistent giants in the United States

Firm	Date of foundation/ (date of most important merger)
Alcoa	1888
Amoco	1889
BestFoods	(not known)
Bethlehem Steel	1857 (1902)
Borden	1857 (1899–1904)
Coca Cola	1886
Deere	1837 (1911–12)
Du Pont	1802 (1895–1905)
Eastman Kodak	1884 (1903)
Exxon	1870
Ford	1903
Fortune Brands	(not known)
General Electric	1892 (1901–2)
General Motors	1908
Goodyear	1898
Inland Steel	1893 (1954)
International Paper	1898
Navistar	1846 (1902)
Owen Illinois	1903 (1929)
PPG	1883
Procter and Gamble	1837
Quaker Oats	1891
R. J. R. Nabisco	1875
Sun Oil	1886 (1895–1904)
Texaco	1902
Union Carbide	1886 (1917)
Unocal	1890
USX	1901

Source: authors' own analysis.

in just after the war, and not more than 27.4 per cent are present in both prewar and postwar periods. In other words, 72.6 per cent of the firms either dominated the first period and then simply disappeared from the top, or were not in the list in that period and came in only recently. Persistence is an important phenomenon, but it is an attribute of less than one-third of the giants. There is a dramatic divide at the middle of the century, drawing a number of firms out of the list for good, and opening a window of opportunity for a number of new entrants.

Other studies confirm this result and argue that turbulence may even have increased, affecting at least one-third of the US 1950 list. Friedland (1957) studied the fifty largest US industrial firms for 1906, 1928, and 1950 and concluded that 67 per cent of the 1950 list were already present in the list for the first period, while one-third were not. Audrecht computed the time taken to

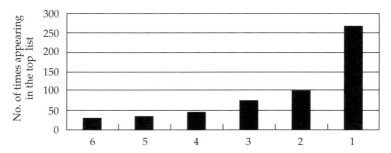

FIG C.3. The largest US firms, 1917–1997, by the frequency of their presence in the top list
Source: authors' own analysis.

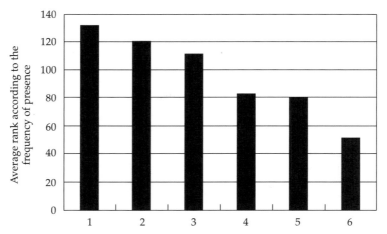

FIG C.4. The largest US firms, 1917–1997, average rank according to the frequency of their presence
Source: authors' own analysis.

replace one-third of the Fortune list (500 largest firms) and concluded that during the 1950s and 1960s it would have taken two decades, whereas in the 1970s it would have taken one decade, and in the 1980s not more than half a decade (Audrecht 1997: 50). De Geus verified that one-third of the Fortune 500 list of 1970 had already disappeared in 1983, having been bought, dismantled, or simply gone out of business (de Geus 1997).[4] Finally, Simonetti (1994: 1), in a study of the firms in the Fortune list from 1963 to 1987, found

---

[4] De Geus's information refers to a private study carried out when he was coordinator of strategic planning research at an Anglo-Dutch multinational, Royal Dutch Shell Group, planning a confidential report, 'Corporate Change: A Look at How Long-established Companies Change' (September 1993). This study was conducted under the pressure of the second energy crisis. It addressed the determinants of corporate longevity and was retrospective in nature. Planners wanted to know about, and tried to derive practical lessons from, examples of large

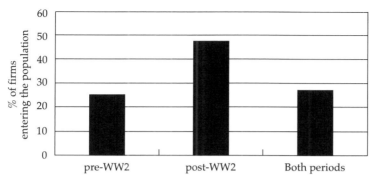

FIG C.5. The largest US firms, 1917–1997, by the percentage of firms entering the population

Source: authors' own analysis.

that takeover activity was the main source of turbulence in the list, that there were major inter-industry differences, and that the emergence of microelectronics 'had powerful destabilizing effects'.

This image of turbulence and takeovers in the highly oligopolistic and protected niche of the larger firms refutes a strong continuity thesis. Moreover, the continued emergence of new giant firms in the software and Internet industries has provided further new evidence. As we have made clear, our own explanation of this turbulence is based on the periodic rise of new constellations of industries and technologies and the consequences of their diffusion through the economic system. In each of the chapters in Part II we have given examples of major firms, emerging from obscurity or newly founded before or during a Kondratiev downswing, which grew so rapidly that they set the tone for the ensuing Kondratiev long boom. Such was the case with the electrical and steel firms established from the 1860s to the 1890s, which became the giants of the *belle epoque* before the First World War. Of course, these were not the only firms that grew enough, at least temporarily, to join the group of large firms. Others, for example, were in the production of primary commodities, of tobacco, and of metal-working machinery, all so important for the rapidly growing American economy.

A satisfactory analysis of the population of large firms must explain both the phenomena of persistence and that of change. The chemical firms were a special category of rather persistent large firms. Originally, the chemical industry had grown mainly to serve the requirements of the leading sectors of the first industrial revolution—the textile industries—for bleach and dyestuffs. Very few of these small firms were able to make the transition to heavy chemicals and electro-chemistry in the third Kondratiev wave.

companies that were older than Shell and had successfully coped with fundamental change in their business environment. As de Geus indicates, this meant going back to the past—to the early years of the Industrial Revolution and even before—and abandoning the prevailing thinking and language of management and economics (de Geus 1997: 11).

Sometimes they achieved this through amalgamation, and subsequently some of these much larger firms proved able to persist in the fourth Kondratiev wave by using their chemical know-how in the synthesis of new materials to develop and manufacture a new range of synthetic fibres, rubbers, and other materials, needed by the new mass production industries of the fourth Kondratiev. Some of them may be able to make a further transition to the new biotechnology, but it is still too early to assess this likelihood. The persistence of the largest chemical firms is clearly related to their capability in R&D and to both product and process innovations. The inhouse R&D laboratory was invented in the German chemical industry and has remained an outstanding feature of those firms that pioneered this managerial innovation, in both Europe and the United States. They are all research-intensive as well as capital-intensive firms.

However, the data set we are considering provides some confirmatory evidence, which is compatible with our own main hypothesis: new groups of firms *have* periodically entered the list of giants throughout the twentieth century based on their competence in the emerging new technologies. This has occurred with both electrification and motorization, but the ICT revolution offers the strongest confirmation.

In particular, the software industry has been populated mainly by new firms as well as by those computer firms that survived intensive competition (Chapter 9). This suggests that a concrete sociology of the diversity of agents, and not just simple assumptions on the level of information, is necessary for an explanation of technological development (Audrecht 1997: 68; Dosi 1982; Dosi *et al.* 1988).

Our argument is that there is a pattern of evolution that challenges the established firms, leading to their successful adaptation in some cases, e.g. producers of office machinery (such as IBM and NCR) and some of the chemical firms, or to their disappearance or takeover, or to the emergence of new firms from scratch. Chandler, while emphasizing the dominance of big business from the second to the third industrial revolution,[5] detects the phenomenon of new entry of ICT firms, but dubs it an exception to the path-dependent evolution.

Our argument is that this major rupture in path dependence was possible in spite of the knowledge capabilities of the major firms, in spite of the oligopolistic structure of the market, in spite of the huge advantage in capital, research facilities, and technological power of the established firms. The 'old' firms could not overcome the inertia of their previous development, and the increasing returns obtained in the general trajectory of the previous Kondratiev became limiting factors for their ability to capture the new wave of innovations.

This process of transformation took a long time, and it constitutes one of the explanations for the shape of the long wave: 'A common feature to the

---

[5] See n. 3 above.

development paths taken by major new technologies is that quite unforeseen capabilities and uses are discovered along the route' (R. Nelson 1995: 25). We emphasized in the Introduction to Part II that the (roughly) half-century pattern of long waves is attributable to these phenomena.

By 1963, at the peak of the fourth long wave, the distinctive capacity of generating and retaining larger profits in the motive and carrier branches associated with the new (ICT) techno-economic paradigm was already apparent, although industry was still dominated by the large mass and flow production firms based on mechanical and chemical processes. In 1983 and 1997 this trend was naturally reinforced, as shown in Figures C.6 and C.7. For the whole period we are considering, the history of these four sectors is presented in the Figure C.8, which shows the evolution of the weight of the firms of certain industries in the total assets of the universe. In this case 1 = 1917, and the movement is clockwise until 6 = 1997; i.e. the right-hand side of each graph shows the period 1917–48, and the left-hand side the period 1963–97.

The figure shows that: (1) the production of metal products is specifically a feature of the third long wave (the right-hand side of the diagrams); (2) the importance of oil production marks the third and the upswing of the fourth long wave; whereas (3) the chemical industry retained its weight and adapted through times; and (4) the office equipment industries emerged in the framework of the decline of the fourth wave. Furthermore, the relatively limited weight of the latter in relation to the motive and carrier branches of the previous periods of expansion clarifies why the transition from the continuing decline to the next phase of upswing is so slow and contradictory—although profitability in the new sectors is remarkably higher than in manufacturing as a whole and their applications are widespread in industry and services, the emergence of a new mode of development is far from complete.

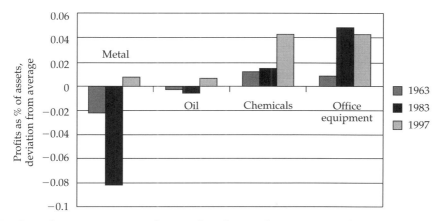

FIG C.6. The comparative evolution of profits in relation to assets for the metal, oil, chemical, and office equipment industries, 1963–1997

Source: authors' own analysis.

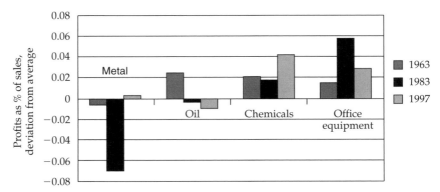

Fɪɢ C.7. The comparative evolution of profits in relation to sales for the metal, oil, chemical, and office equipment industries, 1963–1997

Source: authors' own analysis.

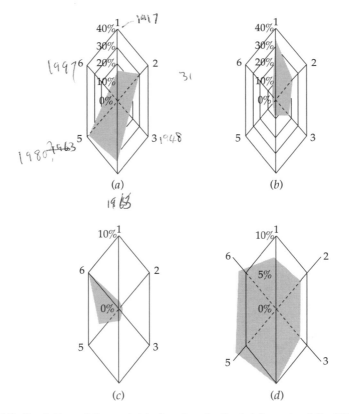

Fɪɢ C.8. Evolution of the weight of sectors in the total assets of the 200 firms (*a*) Oil, rubber (*b*) Metals and metal products (*c*) Office equipment (*d*) Chemicals, pharmaceuticals, cosmetics

Source: authors' own analysis.

Consequently, the role and fate of the computer and office equipment industries are at the core of any explanation of the general trends in development—as they are the *experimentum crucis* of the continuity thesis. Based on the persistence of some of the giants and their ability to overcome wrong strategic decisions, e.g. IBM, Chandler argues that the computer industry provides a new confirmation for his argument: 'With few exceptions the new technologies were exploited by long established large firms whose learned R&D capabilities gave them a powerful advantage over start-ups, or firms whose capabilities rested on the commercializing of less closely related technologies' (Chandler 1977: 89).

Yet some evidence indicates otherwise, as Chapter 9 has shown. IBM did indeed show great survival power, but it was a fast second, rather than a leading, innovator. Moreover, new firms have proved to be of great importance in both hardware and software. Some of the mainframe producers were *not* able to make a successful transition.

Three main conclusions emerge from this account so far. First, the continuity thesis is challenged, since evidence from the highly oligopolistic markets and from firms protected by impressive barriers to entry nevertheless suggests that change and not stasis dominated the trajectories. A significant percentage of the larger firms both emerged before the divide between the third and fourth long wave and disappeared afterwards, or were created only after that moment.

Second, the emergence of new industries based on the changes associated with the diffusion of ICT was the driving force either for the creation of new firms or for the access of old but transformed firms to the top list. Furthermore, the older surviving giants are in general those that were able to change and to explore new processes of production, new knowledge, and new markets. This dynamic was based on the accumulation of profits and, related to that, of technological competencies and organizational capabilities. In that respect, our analysis is in agreement with Chandler and his colleagues.

Whether from the standpoint of continuity theories or from our own standpoint of the periodic irruption of new firms into the top echelon, profitability is clearly of the greatest importance. Those firms that survive and continue as members of the leading group can do so only by accumulating sufficient profits to re-equip, and to conduct and finance new activities, or introduce new processes. In recent times, diversification is frequently based on expensive inhouse research and development.

Equally, the new entrants to the top echelon need profits to finance their headlong expansion at some point, even if initially they are able to expand by borrowing. During the 'bubble' expansion periods, it may sometimes seem as though the law of gravity is suspended, but sooner or later the requirement for profitable investment reasserts itself, and when the bubble bursts only the profitable survive and grow further.

The imperative need for profitability explains, on the one hand, the bitterness of some of the labour conflicts, which we shall analyse in Section C.3, and, on the other hand, the attempts of leading firms in new technology to cement their leadership through patent protection, through influencing standards, through market power, through scale economies, or through a variety of other means. This is why the evolution of a relevant *regime of regulation* discussed in Section C.4 is the arena also of intense political and social conflicts. Sometimes, attacks may be directed against the previous dominant incumbent firms, as in the assault on the 'old' monopolistic telecommunications utilities; sometimes the pressure is directed to the relaxation or abandonment of trade protection in foreign markets, and sometimes to changes in the patent regime or to taxation, or to all of these; but, in whatever specific direction policy adjustments are claimed and enforced, the objective is to improve profitability and to enlarge markets for the new constellation of technologies.

Although a precise computation of the profit rate is quite difficult with past data and even currently available data for international comparisons, it is still possible to identify the dynamics of the profit schedule in some sectors of the economy and in the aggregate national level. Available data on the most recent wave confirm several of our main points and are consistent with the swing of the last waves in the USA (Figure C.9). First, they clearly show the upswing in the postwar period: in a study for the period 1948–97 in the USA, Duménil and Levy showed that after 1948, and in particular in 1956–65, the profit rate attained a historical maximum. From the end of the Civil War, excluding from the calculation the publicly owned (transport) and public utilities, the authors concentrated on the dynamics of the private business sector and showed that this upswing gave place to a structural crisis in the 1970s. Second, in the early 1980s the profit rate had declined to half of the

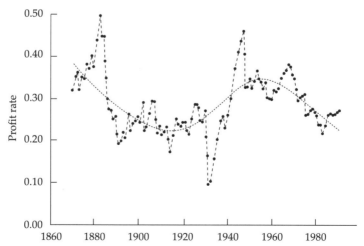

FIG C.9. The historical profile of the profit rate and its trend, USA, 1869–1989
Source: Duménil and Levy (1993: 251).

average value for the period 1956–65. Third, during the social process of adjustment in the 1970s, the 'effects of the decline of the profit rate were significantly offset by the devaluation of debt resulting from inflation and the low levels of real interest rates' (Duménil and Levy 1999: 1).

Finally, although since the mid-1980s the profit rate recovered half of the lost profitability, by 1997 it was still far short of the record values of the previous upswing. Indeed, between 1948 and 1982 the profit rate was between half and one-quarter of that rate, according to sector. And in 1997, in spite of some years of upturn, the aggregate rate had not yet recovered half of the value of 1948; in other words, the upswing still faced a mismatch and could not be generalized to the whole business economy. The fall in the productivity of capital has been mainly responsible for this behaviour, although the decrease in the share of profit also accounts for part of the effect. We have already shown the contrasting experience of the office equipment and other industries with respect to profitability during the downswing of the fourth Kondratiev.

All of this helps to explain the seductive attraction of the Internet bubble, which appeared to offer quite extraordinary profits to the most fortunate investors, and also the intensity of the conflicts over many features of the new regulating regime, such as the 'Bit Tax', the Seattle trade negotiations, and the huge takeover battles in the ICT industries.

In this section, we have examined one of the most controversial and difficult issues in the debate on long waves. The statistical data are far from satisfactory in any of the areas we have examined, but we hope that we have provided some persuasive data and arguments to justify our view that the entry and diffusion of successive new constellations of interdependent innovations has had profound effects, not only on the structure of the economy, but on the political behaviour of contending interest groups, parties, and classes, as we shall discuss further in Sections C.3 and C.4.

C.3 Strike Movements and Trade Unions in Recurrent Structural Crises

In spite of its early definition as *political economy*, since the classical period economics has never been at ease with the political and social variables that described the evolution of the system as a whole, and barriers were built in order to ignore their impact in most econometric models. Yet it is quite obvious that the production and distribution of wealth, the access to material and immaterial goods, and the power to influence, to regulate, and to determine social and technological trajectories have been and will be the subject of great conflicts. In that sense, economics must deal with these historical trends in the production, allocation, and change of power and wealth. Ricardo's work on rent exemplifies the recognition of this fundamental point in the classical tradition.

In the economics literature after the end of the great classical period, this interaction between economic variables and political and social actions, agents, and strategies was scarcely discussed. Only the institutional economists, such as Veblen, continued this debate. Supple (1963: 14) went so far as to say that, with the exception of Karl Marx and one or two individuals, 'for almost a century after 1850 there was no fresh systematic discussion of the nature of economic development'. Occasional heretics, such as Kalecki (1943), discussed the possible social and political consequences of Keynesian full employment policies with his theory of the political business cycle. Subsequently, the original agenda set by Kalecki was abandoned; yet his model of collective power and the relationships of forces in disputes over the distribution of wealth across a divided society showed insights that we need in order to understand societal changes over time. Indeed, what we have been discussing so far is precisely an interpretation of the evolution of power in modern capitalist societies. The available theories based on general equilibrium—i.e. the non-existence of social conflict—do not provide a relevant model for the understanding of political cycles, since they axiomatically reject its very existence and cannot therefore present a general explanation for the recurrence of periods of social unrest.

An insightful economic historian proposed an alternative approach. Hobsbawm had earlier suggested the hypothesis that social conflicts were somehow clustered and emerged at the end of 'long phases of development', or Kondratiev cycles (Hobsbawm 1964: 148). The four cases he indicated are the strike wave of 1847–8 at the end of the first Kondratiev cycle; the 1868–73 and 1889–93 strikes at the end of the expansion and the end of the depression of the second wave, respectively; and the wartime strikes at the turning point of the third wave (Hobsbawm 1964: 153). We will explore this hypothesis, as well as that of Kalecki, as a framework for our assessment of social conflict in the perspective of long periods of history.

Our basic hypothesis follows Hobsbawm's conjecture that there are compelling reasons for the clustering of social conflict at the two turning points of the long wave. In the long phase of the dominant expansionary trend, the workers' movement tends to build strong organizations, namely trade unions, on the basis of full employment and consequently with better chances of disputing new social gains. At the peak of this strengthening process, workers are more able to exert pressure for sharing in undistributed increases in the profits from rising productivity. However, employers try to retain these profits in order to maintain the process of accumulation in a period of growing difficulty for generating new opportunities of high profitability and of intensified competition in the 'old' activities.

Consequently, strike waves tend to cluster near the upper turning point of long waves, as was clearly the case with the 1808–20, 1868–73, 1910–12, 1968–9, and 1974–5 periods. Some of these conflicts were prolonged into the first years after the turning point, when there were still some forces not sufficiently damaged by unemployment or political repression to engage in defensive struggles or even sometimes offensive actions. Cultural and political time lags mean that traditions and behaviours, once established, may often persist in changed circumstances, as Salvati (1984) showed so clearly. A new generation of young leaders may adopt a more militant stance in industrial conflicts after a long period of full employment.

The second form of clustering is related to resistance to the adjustment process associated with the spread of a new techno-economic paradigm, which takes place before and around the lower turning point of the wave. As we have already argued, the structural crisis of adjustment at the end of each wave is attended by higher levels of structural unemployment and greater job insecurity. Those who remain in their jobs may have to adjust their expectations of remuneration and promotion. These adjustments may drastically change the daily life of the workers by requiring a renewal of skill and professional distribution as well as new forms of control and hierarchy, all of which are felt as major challenges to the previous balance of forces. The new techno-economic paradigm imposes new rhythms of mental and manual work that challenge the traditional norms of production and lead to defensive struggles. This was the case in the 1880s–1890s, the 1920s–1930s, and (in relation to ICT) the 1970s–1980s.

These conjectures may be tested against empirical evidence, such as that provided by Figure C.10, which summarizes the dynamics of strikes in five countries for the end of the second and for the third and fourth long waves. Although this figure provides valuable information, it has some shortcomings that must be pointed out. First, aggregation plays some tricks, and peculiar nationally located events may distort the picture. In spite of this, there are important elements of coherence in the strike waves across countries, and the explanation may be found in the overall political and social framework as described by the specific settings of each long wave. Second, some important countries are missing from this picture, especially Spain, a country whose social battles dominated the 1930s, a period that is particularly underestimated in Figure C.10 in view of this exclusion. Nevertheless, the graph indicates very roughly some major features of the rhythm of social movements over one century and these are summarized in Table C.2.

Although information about numbers of strikers and lost working days is scarce and frequently unreliable for the whole period we are considering, it is possible to complement it with qualitative information about the scope of social and political conflicts and insurgencies and with indirect information from other sources. This analysis demonstrates major strike waves and periods of intense conflict for those countries for which we have enough information (Table C.2). Indeed, Figure C.10 shows that there are clear patterns of strike waves: in specific political contexts, frequently dominated by international trends (e.g. the strike wave after the end of the First World War and in 1968–74). How can we explain this feature, without resorting to a conspiracy theory? We suggest that part of the explanation lies in the common dynamics of developed capitalist countries, as imposed by the diffusion of each techno-economic paradigm, including of course political as well as economic influences.

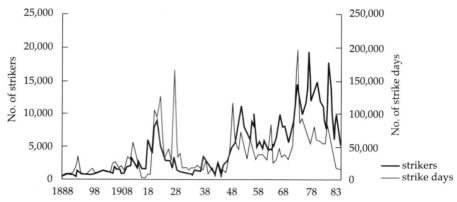

FIG C.10. Strikers and strike days for five countries (Britain, USA, France, Italy, Germany) in two long waves, 1880–1983
Source: Gattei (1989)

TABLE C.2. Major strike waves in five countries[a]

(1) Long waves[b]		(2) Major strike waves at peaks	(3) Major strike waves at troughs	(4) Peaks in numbers of strikers	(5) Peaks in strike days
I A	Expansion, 1793–1825	1808–20			
I B	Depression, 1826–47		1847–8		
II A	Expansion, 1848–73	1868–73			
II B	Depression, 1874–93		1889–93		1893
III A	Expansion, 1894–1913	1910–12			1912
III B	Depression, 1914/18–1939/45		1920–4 1936–7	1920–1, 1936	1921, 1926
IV A	Expansion, 1940/5–1974	1947–8 1968		1949, 1972	1946, 1968
IV B	Depression, 1974–...		1974–5	1975, 1979, 1982	1974, 1979, 1983

[a] Columns (4) and (5) are based on Gattei's data for five countries (UK, USA, France, Italy and Germany).
[b] A,B: dominance of expansion or depression.
Source: adapted from Gattei (1989).

This process of clustering of social conflict has been discussed by Salvati (1984) and by Screpanti (1984), who also identifies four major strike waves (1808–20, 1866–77, 1911–22, and 1967–73), all situated after a peak and early in the long period of downturn. According to his interpretation, the intensity of the class struggle increases during the expansionary phase and decreases afterwards, with the strike waves evidencing the workers' efforts to negotiate the conditions for each readjustment, but faced with the weakening of their organizations during the long downswings.

Of course, each strike wave is an individual historical event and exhibits distinguishable characteristics. The first wave, in 1808–20, was concentrated around the new centres of industrial production in Britain: Lancashire, Durham, Northumberland, Yorkshire, Nottinghamshire, and the Midlands. A very specific feature of this period was the Luddite movement (1814, 1816–17), and the whole process culminated in the 1818–20 strikes of textile workers. The strikes in the 1830s and 1840s were associated with the big Chartist demonstrations and often had a direct *political* goal. In France too the political context was important. The memory of the Revolution, the Napoleonic Wars, and the Restoration echoed in revolutionary conflicts: in 1830, in 1848, and again in the Paris Commune in 1871. The workers' movement took an active part in all these processes, as well as in Lyon in 1831, in the 1832–40 strikes, and again in 1893.

The following waves, in 1847–8 and 1866–77, were more international in character. Around the peak of the third long wave, rather militant tendencies were apparent in several countries, from a series of strikes in Berlin (1910), France (1911), and the Ruhr (1912) to the 'unofficial' strikes in Britain (1910–15) and in the USA (1911–16). But it was after the end of the war, and after the Russian Revolution of 1917, that most of the anger and delayed expectations were shown: claims for wages, employment, new legislation, reduction of the working day, and universal voting rights all came together in a period of great confrontation. In France, general strikes were called in 1919–20; in Britain, the railwaymen and steelworkers took action in 1919, and the miners in 1920, the shipbuilding workers in 1920–1, the sailors and dockers in 1922–3, and many millions of workers in the nine-day General Strike in May 1926, with the resistance of the miners continuing long after this. In Italy a movement for the occupation of factories and cities created a pre-revolutionary situation in 1920, while in Germany a strike prevented the Kapp putsch in that year. In the USA the peak of strikes occurred between 1919 and 1923 and were severely repressed. Only with the more favourable labour legislation of the New Deal was the new Congress of Industrial Organizations (CIO) able to organize big new industrial unions in automobiles, steel, and rubber (tyres) in the 1930s. Elsewhere, fascist and military governments had already crushed trade unions in Germany, Italy, Portugal, Japan, and several other countries.

Strikes in the 1930s emerged from resistance taking place after the downswing of the third wave was already largely under way. Apart from the USA, the 1936 wave centred in Spain after a number of years of conflict, leading to the proclamation of the Republic, and in France, leading to the formation of a new Popular Front government and to the Matignon agreements, which established the principle of collective bargaining, new rights for shop stewards, increases in pay, and the recognition of the right to holidays. Thus, the strike movements of the 1930s, whether in the United States, France, or Spain, again showed a close connection with political events and with attempts to create a more favourable legislative climate for the activities of working-class organizations. Following the breakup of the wartime and early postwar anti-fascist coalitions and alliances, and the outbreak of the Cold War, a new wave of conflict erupted in 1947–9, centred especially in France, Italy, and Greece. Finally, the last great wave was that of May–June 1968 in France and 1968–9 in Italy, as is clearly recognizable in Figure C.8, and had its final episodes in the strike activity around 1974.

It has not been possible in this very condensed account to do justice to the complexity and variety of labour conflicts and strike movements in various countries. We hope, however, that even this very brief and simplified presentation has been sufficient to establish two major points.

1. On both a national and an international level, there has been quite strong evidence for a much greater intensity of such conflicts during two periods: (A) around the peaks of long wave booms (1808–20, 1868–73, 1910–15, and 1968–74); and (B) during the long 'downswing' periods following these peaks, which have been designated here as 'structural crises of adjustment'. This is apparent both from the number of disputes leading to strikes and from the number of strike days.

2. Although there were specific local circumstances leading to these strikes and their varying intensity, many of them were strongly influenced by *political* events and themselves reciprocally influenced national and international politics. At the most elementary level, of course, a large number of strikes were simply about the right to organize and belong to trade unions. At a later stage, some were about the preservation of this right and of wider democratic rights in society, for example the successful 1920 strikes by German workers against the Kapp putsch (an attempt to establish military rule). Strike movements often accompanied or preceded political rebellions, as in 1905 in Russia.

However, most strikes were about 'economic' issues—pay, hours of work, conditions of work, and holidays. Many trade union leaders, as well as employers, were concerned to confine union activities to this narrower agenda, but they have never been wholly successful in this endeavour. There are obvious reasons for this, as the legal and political climate heavily influences the relative bargaining strength of the contending parties in labour disputes. From time to time rather determined efforts have been made, both by individual employers such as Ford and by governments such as fascist and military governments, to destroy unions completely. At a less acute level, there have been fairly persistent attempts to curtail union power by labour legislation limiting the right to organize, the right to picket, the conduct of strike ballots, and so forth. These attempts began in the early days of the British Industrial Revolution, as in the Combination Acts of 1799, and have periodically recurred.

Both the more serious efforts to get rid of unions altogether and the lesser efforts to curtail their activities have occurred mainly, though not entirely, during the downswing phases of the long waves. It is in these phases that employers meet with stronger competition both on the domestic and the international market. In the 'old' industries this may often be based on low wage competition, and in these industries too problems of surplus capacity and plant closures may often occur. In the 'new' industries of the rising constellations the situation is rather different, as their problem may be one of skill shortages and lack of new capacity. For a while, they may pay above-average wages and salaries and offer comparatively attractive conditions to a non-union labour force.

Thus, rather different circumstances may prevail side by side in these periods of intense structural change, with very variable levels of unionization and strike conflicts. Bitter and prolonged conflicts occur mainly in some older industries confronted with severe contraction, for example in the British coal industry in the 1920s and again in the 1980s, or in the steel and automobile industries in several countries.

However, despite the strength of feeling and bitterness often evident in such disputes, the capacity of the workers and their organizations to engage in conflict is likely to be severely undermined during the periods of structural adjustment. It is undermined on the one hand by the widespread prevalence of unemployment, and on the other hand by the heightened resistance of the employers, often reinforced by legislation and government intervention to limit union power. Whereas in the long boom period employers and governments would more often feel able and willing to make concessions on pay and would not feel disposed to endure loss of production in expanding markets, during the downswing periods they would more commonly feel that they could not possibly afford any increase in labour costs, or any other concessions to trade unions. Lockouts are quite likely to occur in these periods and were, for example, widespread in the 1830s in Britain. In 1834, in Lancashire and Yorkshire, many employers locked out workers who refused to sign a paper renouncing membership of trade unions (Cole 1941: 17).

All of this discussion demonstrates the importance of the *political* as well as the economic context in which labour disputes take place and strikes are fought out. This is most obvious of course when unions are banned and strikes illegal, but at the opposite pole, very different outcomes can occur where the legislative climate is made more favourable to unions. The most obvious example of this was the United States. For a long time, the resistance of American employers to the efforts of workers to organize had resulted in a very low level of union membership and activities. The Pinkerton

Detective Agency was used by a number of large employers to combat the formation of unions and their activities. In 1933 fewer than 8 per cent of American workers were organized, but this situation changed dramatically in the next few years as a result of the National Labour Relations Act (NLRA), passed by Congress in 1935 (Table C.3). By 1937 membership of unions had risen from 2.8 million (1933) to 7.7 million: nearly 4 million had joined the new Congress of Industrial Organizations (CIO) mass production unions. Yet, this was in a period of heavy unemployment, when union membership in many other countries was falling. In Britain, for example, the Trade Disputes Act, passed in 1927 after the General Strike, curtailed union activities, and membership fell sharply. This Act was not repealed until after the Second World War.

American employers were extremely critical of the NLRA, and in some instances continued to resist recognition of unions. In the steel industry, which had opposed unionization ever since the days of Carnegie and the Homestead strike (see Chapter 7), the smaller steel corporations (Bethlehem, Republic, Youngstown and others, known as 'Little Steel') fought bitterly against the CIO, while 'Big Steel' (Carnegie's United Steel) made a deal conceding union recognition, a pay rise, and the forty-hour week (Huberman 1940: 367). 'Little Steel' stubbornly refused to follow 'Big Steel', and the CIO strike that ensued in May 1937 was defeated by a violent campaign.

The American steel industry illustrates the point that employers themselves were not always agreed on the tactics to be followed in relation to trade unions. GM recognized the CIO early in 1937 but Ford resisted, giving way only after a sharp struggle. Generally, American employers remained hostile to the NLRA and succeeded in reversing some of its achievements by

TABLE C.3. Trade union membership in the United States, 1933–1937 (millions)

	1933	1935	1937
Organizable workers	35.0	35.0	35.0
AFL[a]	2.1	3.0	3.4
Unaffiliated unions	0.7	0.6	0.6
CIO	—	—	3.7
Total organized workers	2.8	3.6	7.7
% of workers organized	7.8	10.6	21.9

[a] The American Federation of Labor was originally mainly craft unions in the 19th century, but gradually extended its industrial membership until in the 1930s a 'Committee of Industrial Organization' made a determined effort to organize the semi-skilled and unskilled workers in the mass production industries, leading for a time to a split with the supporters of the Congress of Industrial Organizations (CIO).

Source: Huberman (1940: 359).

new legislation after the Second World War. However, in both Europe and North America, the long postwar boom period was a climate in which unions achieved widespread recognition and increased their membership. They were even recognized as 'Social Partners' in the nascent European Community, and in many countries were admitted as junior advisory participants in various government committees and organizations. This honeymoon broke down increasingly during the last part of the twentieth century, when new legislation in Britain and the United States renewed some restrictions on trade unions, while their influence elsewhere was more gradually eroded.

The case of Roosevelt's presidency in the 1930s was somewhat unusual, as the general trend during the downswing periods of the long wave has been towards rather conservative or even reactionary regimes. At the end of Chapter 6 (Section 6.8) we described the swing towards nationalist and anti-liberal parties that followed the severe recession of 1873. In Germany, Bismarck's 'Anti-Socialist Laws', passed in 1879, were intended to weaken the political representation of the German working-class movement. Protectionism became more fashionable and imperialism quite typical of the behaviour of the industrialized powers. In the downswing of the third Kondratiev, in the 1920s and 1930s, nationalistic and fascist movements were widespread in Europe and Japan. It is easy to see why such tendencies should become stronger in a period of falling prices, acute conflicts over markets, and structural unemployment. Job insecurity is clearly associated with hostility to immigrants, racism, and ethnic conflicts. This was also evident in many parts of the world during the downswing phase of the fourth Kondratiev (1970s–1990s), leading the Secretary-General of the OECD to describe the mass unemployment as 'alarming' because of its potential social consequences during the period of structural change.

The rise of the American trade unions in the 1930s, and the NLRA which facilitated it, were therefore rather atypical, as were various other features of Roosevelt's New Deal. This illustrates the point that there is no simple one-to-one correspondence between trends in the economy or technology and political events. The political subsystem is semi-autonomous and has its own dynamic and traditions.

C.4 The International Regime of Regulation

This final section deals with changes in the regulation regime, which, as Perez (1983, 1985) originally showed, is also a recurrent feature of the long wave. The changes that we have just discussed in the previous section in relation to strikes and trade unions are just one aspect of this wider regulatory regime. In this section we first of all discuss the reasons for our focus in Sections C.2 and C.3 on labour and big business, resembling in some respects the approach of the French regulation school; these authors have done more than anyone else to develop this concept (Boyer 1975, 1979, 1988; Aglietta 1976). However, our main purpose here is to raise some questions about those institutions, whose function it is to regulate international trade, investment, and financial payments: the WTO (formerly GATT), the World Bank, and the IMF.

Once industry was firmly established in Europe and North America, it was the conflict between workers and employers that moved to centre stage because of its crucial importance in determining wages, costs, and profits. So far in this chapter, we have concentrated on this source of social conflict for that reason, and because it is strongly influenced by both short-term and long-term fluctuations in economic activity.

The changing conditions of capital accumulation and the relationships between labour and capital are also at the heart of the theory of the French regulation school. Boyer and his colleagues place less emphasis on technologies than we have done in this book, but their approach has many points of affinity to our own. For example, although their periodization is slightly different, they insist that, 'contrary to the usual approach in economics', their focus is not 'on short or medium-term but on the long-run and structural change in advanced capitalist economies' (Boyer 1988: 68).

They explain that their approach, called 'Régulation' in French, is not easily translated into English, because 'the English word "regulation" is usually associated with the much narrower problem of regulation of public utilities, whilst the expression "socio-economic tuning" brings a connotation of a conscious and sophisticated adjustment mechanism. . . . For this reason, we simply use the word *régulation* in the French sense of the word' (Boyer 1988: 68).

We too have used the concept of regime of regulation in the wider sense of loose overall political and legal coordination and control, although we have placed greater emphasis specifically on the regulation of new technologies within the regime. We have briefly considered some of these specific problems of regulation of the Internet in Section 9.6, but we do not intend here to enlarge on this or any other aspects of regulation of ICT. We intend rather in this final section to concentrate on the international 'rules of the game' with respect to trade, payments, and investment.

It has become commonplace to speak of 'globalization' with reference to the most recent period of world capitalist development. However, as this second part of the book has shown, international trade, the migration of skilled people, flows of investment, and transfer of technology[6] have been characteristics of every new technology system that has diffused through the economy for the last two centuries. In this sense, 'globalization' itself is not a new phenomenon: what has changed recurrently is the regime that has sought to regulate and to some degree coordinate these movements.

---

[6] For a very good discussion of changes in regime for the transfer of technology, see Radosevich (1999).

Changes in this regime have been another of the recurrent features of the long wave. The rules of the game have to be changed periodically to accommodate not only the new technologies, but also the changes in the balance of power in international relations, in the economic strength of the various contending powers, and in the culture and ideology of the dominant social groups.

In the present change of regime, what is remarkable is the extent of liberalization of trade and of world-wide capital movements. This is true both for long-term investment, whether through multinational affiliates or otherwise, and for short-term speculative transactions. Information technology has facilitated all of these flows and, in particular, has accelerated and expanded the latter type of transaction, but it is not in itself the main reason for the changes in regime. These lie rather in the political and cultural subsystems and the hegemony of the United States in the governance of the international economic and financial institutions in the closing decades of the twentieth century.

The collapse of the Soviet-style planned economies in the 1980s and 1990s, the weakening of many attempts at planned industrialization and import substitution regimes in the developing countries, and the tide of privatization everywhere have all converged to an unprecedented degree in the hegemonic influence of one country in the world economy, world military affairs, and world politics—the United States.

Again, the dominant influence of one power is not in itself an entirely new phenomenon. Some theories of the long wave are in fact based entirely or mainly on long-term changes in the hegemony of successive different powers. For example, Modelski and Thomson (1988) suggested that changes in naval power have historically been one of the strongest influences on commercial developments and world trade, and hence on the changes in the world economy, and perhaps have been the strongest single influence on long cycles of development.

For reasons explained in Part I, our own theory of history is not based on the exclusive dominance of any one subsystem in society, whether economic, technological, scientific, cultural, political, or military–political. But we are certainly far from denying the strong influence of military power in the evolution of the social system. Indeed, as explained in Chapter 4, we explicitly rejected all those theories of the long wave that have been based on simply omitting periods of war from the statistics (especially the First and Second World Wars) as an inconvenience. For us, this is one of the major fallacies in the GDP-trend type of standard econometric analysis, and an unacceptable distortion of real historical events.

Our account, rather to the contrary, has emphasized the influence of wars, whether sometimes as a retarding factor (as with Germany in the First and Second World Wars), or sometimes as a facilitating and accelerating factor (as probably with Britain in the Napoleonic Wars and the United States in the First and Second World Wars). We would also accept with Modelski and

Thomson that the British naval supremacy in the eighteenth and nineteenth centuries was an important contributory factor to Britain's commercial and technological leadership in the world economy, as has also been the case with the United States Navy and Air Force in the twentieth century.

At the micro level, we have also reported many instances in Chapters 5–9 of the influence of military demand and military technology on the overall evolution of technological capability. Examples were block-making for the Admiralty, Henry Cort's role as contractor for the Navy, Frederick Taylor's work on special steels at Bethlehem for the US Navy, and the prolonged close relationship of Krupp with the Imperial German government and, later, the Third Reich. Finally, reverting again to the macro level of analysis, we have stressed the role of military technology in the evolution of ICT and the major influences of rearmament on the world economy in the 1930s. Thus, we have frequently reiterated the interdependence of civil and military developments at both micro and macro level.

However, in our view, the dominance of the United States in the international regulatory regime emerging with ICT cannot itself be explained exclusively in military–political terms. The technological leadership of American-based multinational corporations in ICT does owe a great deal, of course, to military R&D and procurement, and the Internet itself originated as a Pentagon ARPA project. However, the subsequent development of the Internet and of other aspects of ICT owes far more, recently, to the aggressive leadership of American firms in *civil* technology and *civil* markets.

To be sure, in the background of the international debates on the regime of regulation is always the possibility of American coercion, even though this has not always been effective, as was shown in Vietnam and Cambodia. The main sources of American dominance in the international regulatory regime now emerging lie rather in the economic, civil–political, and cultural subsystems of society, as we shall attempt to show in the example of the IMF, the WTO, and the World Bank, the principal instruments of international regulation in the global economy.

Typically, the leaders in a new wave of technology, whether Britain in the nineteenth century or the United States in the twentieth, will advocate the opening up of world markets to the new products and services, although they may at the same time try to restrict access to technological know-how, through changes in the intellectual property regime (IPR).[7] Both of these types of behaviour are fairly obvious and predictable. The need to sustain profitability, which we have discussed in Section C.2, is obviously a major factor influencing large corporations to exert political pressure on these points. The extent to which they are effective varies not only with the characteristics of the technology, but also with the balance of power in the system of international relations, and the extent to which the ideological and cul-

---

[7] For a thorough and interesting discussion, see Granstrand (1999).

tural arguments in favour of free trade and a stronger IPR carry conviction in other countries, especially those that are in a 'catch-up' situation.

In the early and mid-nineteenth century, Britain had the naval strength to enforce compliance with a fairly stable free-trade regime in many parts of the world, but it also had considerable support for the free-trade ideology. All of this was reinforced by the Gold Standard and Britain's financial strength in regulating the system of world payments in trade and capital transactions. However, during the structural crisis of adjustment in the 1870s and 1880s, this system was gravely weakened by a growing movement for protectionism in the leading catch-up countries and in the end in Britain itself.

This weakening of liberal free trade ideology was due to a resurgence of nationalism, imperialism, and colonialism, as well as to the direct political influence of agricultural and industrial interest groups seeking to retain or enlarge their markets and their profits. The conflicts that ensued led to the breakdown of the old international regulatory regime and, finally, to a huge contraction of world trade in the Great Depression and to the Second World War. The Allied victories in this war and the memories of the 1930s made possible a renewed effort to establish a new and more stable international regulatory regime in the 1940s. American dominance in most of the world economy, albeit within the framework of the Cold War with the Soviet bloc, facilitated the gradual return to a new regime of free trade and greater mobility of capital. These trends were influenced by the role of Keynes in the discussion about the design of the Bretton Woods institutions, which he intended to promote the catch-up of developing countries, and to prevent occasional balance of payments crises from leading to competitive devaluation, protectionism, and depression, as had occurred in the 1930s. Although Keynes was disappointed with the results of that discussion, he was clearly right to emphasize the dangers of uneven development.

Originally, the international regulatory institutions were intended to be part of the UN family, but disagreements among the powers led to the IMF and the World Bank being set up in Washington, under a different form of governance, amenable to much closer American influence. This Bretton Woods regime provided a fairly effective and stable regulatory framework for a quarter of a century after the Second World War during the long postwar boom.

To all outward appearances, it might seem that the American hegemony, emerging even more firmly in the 1990s, has re-established a still more stable regulatory framework for decades to come, and this is indeed the assumption of many forecasters. However, our historical analysis suggests otherwise, unless some big changes are made in this international regime. The appearance of harmony hides numerous conflicts just beneath the surface, and the instability of investment behaviour remains a fundamental problem of the system. The launch of the World Trade Organization and then its summit at Seattle in December 1999 provided abundant evidence of these problems. It was intended at this meeting to negotiate a new round of reductions in barriers to trade. The US representatives, supported by some of their allies, were anxious to use the meeting to promote easier access for the new products and services in which US firms are dominant, such as e-commerce and GM foods, but this agenda had to be abandoned because of riots in the streets of Seattle and tensions within the meeting. The official arguments in support of the American objectives went beyond the simple reductions in tariffs which were the staple diet of many previous successful trade negotiations over the last few decades within the framework of GATT, the predecessor of the WTO. So-called 'non-tariff barriers' had become steadily more important in the successive 'rounds' of trade negotiations, and the conflicts both inside and outside the Conference Hall at Seattle indicated the apprehension aroused by this trend.

For some time before the WTO Seattle meeting began, the OECD had organized discussions on an international treaty on foreign investment, whose intention would be to do away with those national laws and business procedures that restricted practices allowed in one country but not another. Each country would be obliged to grant corporations all the privileges allowed by any other country. Clearly, this could seriously undermine legislation in any country designed to protect the environment or labour and welfare legislation. The conflicts in Seattle were in part provoked by fears of this interpretation of 'globalization' as well as by other more enduring trade conflicts between the developing countries and the rich countries, as in the case of agriculture. Paul Krugman introduced 'Seattle Man' and 'Davos Man' to symbolize the conflict of ideas at the time of the 'World Economic Forum' of top business people at Davos in January 2000.

Whatever we may think of the Seattle man metaphor, this example is sufficient to show that changes in the regulatory regime, whether at national or international level, can raise the most fundamental political and ideological conflicts within and between nations. A more serious commentary on the role of the United States in the international agencies was that of Joseph Stiglitz. He started out by suggesting that the demonstrators who trashed the WTO in Seattle were not simply ignorant rioters when they demonstrated against the IMF:

They'll say the IMF doesn't really listen to the developing countries it is supposed to help. They'll say the IMF is secretive and insulated from democratic accountability. They'll say the IMF's economic 'remedies' often make things worse—turning slow-downs into recessions and recessions into depressions. And they'll have a point. I was chief economist at the World Bank from 1996 until last November during the gravest global economic crisis in a half century. I saw how the IMF in tandem with the US Treasury Department responded. And I was appalled. (www.thenewrepublic.com/041700/stiglitz)

In an outright indictment of IMF and US Treasury policy, Stiglitz went on to describe his attempts to convince top IMF economists and bureaucrats of the damage they were inflicting on the East Asian economies. He found, however, that 'changing minds at the IMF was virtually impossible':

I shouldn't have been surprised. The IMF likes to go about its business without out-siders asking too many questions. In theory the Fund supports democratic institu-tions in the nations it assists. In practice, it undermines the democratic process by imposing policies. Officially, of course, the IMF doesn't 'impose' anything. It 'negoti-ates' the conditions for receiving aid. But all the power in the negotiations is on one side—the IMF's—and the Fund rarely allows sufficient time for broad consensus-building, or even widespread consultations, with either parliaments or civil society. Sometimes, the IMF dispenses with the pretence of openness altogether and negoti-ates secret covenants. (www.thenewrepublic.com/041700/stiglitz)

Stiglitz pointed out further that, even though the World Bank was con-tributing billions of dollars to the IMF rescue packages, its voice 'was ignored almost as resolutely as the people in the affected countries'.

Even more disquieting were his comments on the calamity of Russia, which 'shared key characteristics with the calamity in East Asia—not least among them the role that IMF and Treasury policies played in abetting it'. He described the conflict between two groups of top American economists in the advice to give to Russia. One of these groups, which included Stiglitz himself and Kenneth Arrow, emphasized the importance of the institutional infrastructure. But 'The second group consisted largely of macro-economists whose faith in the market was unmatched by an appreciation of the sub-tleties of its underpinning – that is of the conditions required for it to work effectively. These economists typically had little knowledge of the history or details of the Russian economy and didn't believe they needed any.'

Stiglitz went on to describe how 'the rapid privatization urged upon Moscow by the IMF and the Treasury Department' allowed a small group of oligarchs to gain control of state assets. Through the mid-1990s the Russian economy continued to decline and the nation was beset by enormous inequality, with a large proportion of the population falling below the poverty line. These lamentable results were due, according to Stiglitz, mainly to the secrecy of the operations of the IMF. 'If the IMF had invited greater scrutiny, their folly might have become much clearer, much earlier.'

Stiglitz concluded his critique of the IMF and the US Treasury by arguing that 'some of the demonstrators are no more interested in open debate than the officials at the IMF', but 'the culture of international economic policy in the world's most powerful democracy is not democratic'.

We have quoted at length from these comments of Stiglitz, not because we wish to make proposals for specific reforms in the IMF or other institutions of the international regulatory regime, desirable though these may be, but rather to illustrate, from a uniquely authoritative and well-informed source, two of the main points we have been attempting to convey in this chapter and indeed in the book as a whole.

The first point is that the recurrent restructuring of the national and inter-national regimes of regulation is not simply a response to the diffusion of a new technology, powerful though the present information technology undoubtedly is. The evolution of the global economy depends on the interaction and co-evolution of several subsystems of society ('semi-autonomous variables'), certainly including technology and science, but also politics, economics, and culture. None of these can be ignored in a reasoned interpretation of history.

The second point is that the uneven development of the world economy, and the uneven diffusion of new technology, creates extraordinary difficulties for any regulatory regime. The British attempt to maintain an international free-trade regime at the end of the nineteenth century failed not simply because of the relative decline of British naval power and commercial supremacy, but because the entire international regulating regime in the early twentieth century could not handle the extreme inequalities and conflicts that arose, and was impotent to deal with the problems of the Great Depression of the 1930s. The present more formal institutional regime may be in danger of foundering on the same rocks. The extreme world-wide inequalities in the distribution of income have become even greater and the manifest lack of social justice within and between nations threatens the stability of the international regulatory system. The fundamentals still apply, as time goes by.

Epilogue

Throughout this book, we have maintained that economics is about the real evolution of complex societies. Assuming a realistic stance, we argued that a coherent research programme must be defined in our science by the historical nature of its subject matter, and this is why a synthetic view has been presented, discussed, and explored. We further accepted that complexity could be understood in its cognitive, organizational, and societal dimensions. But, again, our strategy has been to privilege the latter, since the problem of cognition is not our theme here, and the organizational complexity suggests too narrow an approach at the level of the economic system. Instead, we wanted to discuss the nature of its dynamics, and that was why we dealt with the co-evolution of technology and the economy, including the organizational forms it imposes.

The micro perspective suggests a limited dynamics, eventually unable to cope with the real complexity of the societies we are studying. Paul Romer (1992) gives the example of a textile factory using fifty-two different operations, all totally interchangeable. In order to establish the optimal sequence, i.e. to adapt its technology, the director of production is therefore faced with a decision problem: he has $52! \sim 10^{68}$ alternatives. This is a gigantic although innumerable dimension, which surpasses the number of seconds that eventually followed the Big Bang until the present day (10^{17}). Furthermore, combinatorics does not indicate any algorithm with which to find the optimal path—this is the very same halting problem of the Turing machines. We presume that many real-life decisions are of this nature, and that is why in this regard we follow authors such as Hayek, Simon, and Arthur who suggested that the problem of the chess player is a convenient allegory for the cognitive and decision process of the economic agents: although there are many possibilities during the game (even more than in the problem of our factory director or the number of seconds after the Big Bang), we pick a bounded area and apply our heuristics to that space of possible solutions.

But if this is so, what interests us in economics is mostly the selection of the heuristics and of the social rules for the determination of this path. This leads directly to the institutional forms of each productive order that dominated in the history of modern capitalism. In particular, we discussed the different modes of capital accumulation and technology, the culture, and the modes of social control prevailing in each epoch. We referred, although very briefly, to the international division of labour from the point of view of evolution of the frontier and leading countries in each period.

As time went by, these modes of organization of the institutionalized productive order, or modes of development, evolved and passed through dramatic changes. In order to reconcile the analysis of evolution, the cumulative and irrepeatable process of creating diversity, with a scrutiny of the social structure, which is often based on institutional continuity, we used the concept of long waves of capitalist development. This was applied to successive major examples of structural crises that marked the transition from one order to the following one. Consequently, the second part of this book discussed and identified recurrent phenomena as well as unique traits in these processes.

Institutional change, technological change, transition, and crisis: this is what real-life economics is all about. As a social science, economics is an evolutionary science, and our intended contribution in this book was to argue that technological and social innovation is the key factor for the understanding of the dynamics of long periods in leading economies. Indeed, this is the crucial problem in historical analysis: how do those economies, whose mode of development is being exhausted, recover after some time?

In the same sense, Richard Nelson argued that evolutionary theory is based on the concepts of selection and creation of variety, or novelty:

The general concept of evolutionary theory that I propose . . . involves the following elements. The focus of attention is on a variable or set of them that is changing over time and the theoretical quest is for an understanding of the dynamic process behind the observed change; a special case would be a quest for understanding the current state of a variable or a system in terms of how it got there. The theory proposes that the variable or system in question is subject to somewhat random variation or perturbation, and also that there are mechanisms that systematically winnow that variation. Much of the predictive or explanatory power of that theory rests with its specification of the systematic selection forces. It is presumed that there are strong inertial tendencies preserving what has survived the selection process. However, in many cases there are also forces that continue to introduce new variety, which is further grist for the selection mill. (Nelson 1995: 54)

With this we agree, simply adding that evolutionary economics is consequently about choice and social responsibility. The vindicated historical dimension of economic analysis only emphasizes this dimension. Unable to predict the future, economics is about our apprenticeship with the past, which matters primarily because this understanding helps us to act in the present and in the future.

Charles Dickens, in his *Tale of Two Cities* (1867), opened the book with what was to become a very often quoted passage for eras of transition such as the one we are experiencing: 'It was the best of times, it was the worst of times, it was the age of wisdom, it was the age of foolishness, it was the epoch of belief, it was the epoch of incredulity, it was the season of Light, it was the season of Darkness, it was the spring of hope, it was the winter of despair, we had everything before us, we had nothing before us . . .'

The fundamental thing is to choose.

REFERENCES

Abalkin, L. (1992). *The Scientific Heritage of N. Kondratiev and Contemporaneity: Report to the International Scientific Conference devoted to the 100th Birth Anniversary of N. Kondratiev*. Moscow: Russian Academy of Sciences, Institute of Economics.

Abramovitz, M. A. (1979). 'Rapid Growth Potential and its Realization: The Experience of Capitalist Economies in the Postwar Period'. In E. Malinvaud (ed.), *Economic Growth and Resources*, i, *The Major Issues: Proceedings of the Fifth World Congress of the IEA*. London: Macmillan, 1–51.

——(1986). 'Catching Up, Forging Ahead and Falling Behind'. *Journal of Economic History*, 46: 385–406.

——and David, P. A. (1994). *Convergence and Deferred Catch-up: Productivity Leadership and the Waning of American Exceptionalism*, CEPR Publication No. 401. Stanford: Stanford University Press.

Adelman, I. (1963). *Theories of Economic Growth and Development*. Stanford: Stanford University Press.

——(1965). 'Long Cycles: Fact or Artifact?' *American Economic Review*, 55: 444–63.

Adorno, T. (1991). *The Culture Industry: Selected Essays on Mass Culture*. London: Routledge.

Aftalion, A. (1913). *Les Crises périodiques de surproduction*. Paris: Marcel Rivière.

——(1927). 'The Theory of Economic Cycles Based on the Capitalistic Technique of Production'. *Review of Economic Statistics*, October: 165–217.

Aglietta, M. (1976). *Régulation et crise du capitalisme*. Paris: Calman-Levy (English edn.: *A Theory of Capitalist Regulation: The US Experience*. London: NLB, 1979).

Alchian, A. (1951). 'Uncertainty, Evolution and Economic Theory'. *Journal of Political Economy*, 58: 211–22.

Aldcroft, D. H. (1977). *From Versailles to Wall Street, 1919–1929*. Harmondsworth: Penguin Books.

Allen, R. (1991). *Opening Doors: The Life and Work of Joseph Schumpeter*, 2 vols. New Brunswick, NJ: Transaction Books.

Altshuler, A., Anderson, M., Jones, D. T., Roos, D., and Womack, J. (1985). *The Future of the Automobile*. London: Allen & Unwin.

Altvater, E. (1983). 'O Capitalismo em Vias de Recuperação? Sobre a Teoria da "Onda Longa" e dos "Estágios"'. *Ensaios FEE*, 3/2: 5–30.

Andersen, B. (1998). 'The Evolution of Technological Trajectories 1890–1990'. *Structural Change and Economic Dynamics*, 9: 5–34.

Andersen, E. (1994). *Evolutionary Economics: Post-Schumpeterian Contributions*. London: Pinter.

Andersen, P. (1995). 'Comment in Viewpoint: the Future', *Science*, 17 March: 1617.

Antonelli, C. (ed.) (1992). *The Economics of Information Networks*. Amsterdam: North-Holland.

Appleyard, M. M., Hatch, N. W., and Mowery, D. C. (1996). *Managing the Development and Transfer of Process Technologies in the Semi-conductor Manufacturing Industry*. Laxenburg, Austria: IIASA.

Arndt, H. W. (1944). *The Economic Lessons of the 1930s*. London: Oxford University Press.

Arnold, H. and Faurote, F. (1915). *Ford Methods and the Ford Shops*. New York: Engineering Magazine.

Arora, A. and Rosenberg, N. (1998). 'Chemicals: A US Success Story'. In A. Arora, R. Landau, and N. Rosenberg (eds.), *Chemicals and Long-term Economic Growth*. New York: John Wiley, 71–103.

Ashton, T. S. (1948). *The Industrial Revolution, 1760–1830*. Oxford: Oxford University Press.

——(1963). 'The Industrial Revolution in Great Britain'. In B Supple (ed.), *The Experience of Economic Growth*. New York: Random House, 146–59.

Atack, J. (1999). 'Comment' on Chapter 2 by C. Usselman. In N. R. Lamoreaux, D. M. G. Raff, and P. Temin (eds.), *Learning by Doing in Markets, Firms and Countries*. Chicago: NBER/University of Chicago Press, 91–101.

Audrecht, D. (1997). 'Technological Regimes, Industrial Demography and the Evolution of Industrial Structures'. *Industrial and Corporate Change*, 6/1: 49–82.

Ayres, R. U. (1989). *Technological Transformation and Long Waves*. Laxenburg, Austria: IIASA.

Baines, E. (1835). *History of the Cotton Manufacture*, quoted in Rostow (1963) and von Tunzelmann (1995*b*).

Bairoch, P. (1982). 'International Industrialization Levels from 1750 to 1980'. *Journal of European Economic History*, 11: 290–6.

Barnett, C. (1986). *The Audit of War*. Cambridge: Cambridge University Press.

Barnett, V. (1995). 'A Long Wave Goodbye: Kondrat'ev and the Conjuncture Institute, 1920–28'. *Europe-Asia Studies*, 47: 413–41.

——(1996). 'Trading Cycle for Change: S. A. Pervushin as an Economist of the Business Cycle'. *Europe-Asia Studies*, 48: 1007–25.

——(1998). *Kondratiev and the Dynamics of Economic Development: Long Cycles and Industrial Growth in Historical Context*. London: Macmillan.

Beenstock, M. (1983). *The World Economy in Transition*. London: Allen & Unwin.

Belden, T. G. and Belden, M. R. (1962). *The Lengthening Shadow: The life of Thomas J. Watson*. Boston: Little Brown.

Bellamy, E. (1888). *Utopia: Looking Backward*. New York: Modern Library, 1982.

Berck, P. (1994). 'Hard Driving and Efficiency: Iron Production in 1890'. In P. Temin (ed.), *Industrialization in North America*. For Economic History Society, Oxford: Blackwell, 575–97.

Berg, M. (1994). *The Age of Manufactures: Industry and Innovation in Work in Britain, 1700–1820*, 2nd edn. London: Routledge.

——(1998). 'Product Innovation in Core Consumer Industries in Eighteenth Century Britain', in M. Berg and K. Bruland (eds.), *Technological Revolutions in Europe*. Cheltenham: Edward Elgar, 138–61.

——and Bruland, K. (eds.) (1998). *Technological Revolutions in Europe*. Cheltenham: Edward Elgar.

Bernal, J. D. (1939). *The Social Function of Science*. London: Routledge & Kegan Paul.

——(1953). *Science and Industry in the Nineteenth Century*. London: Allen & Unwin.

Bieshaar, H. and Kleinknecht, A. (1984). 'Kondratiev Long Waves in Aggregate Output? An Econometric Test'. *Konjunkturpolitik*, 30: 279–302.

——and——(1986). 'A Reply to S. Solomou'. *Konjukturpolitik*, 32/3: 185–94.

Black, R. and Collison, D. (1992). 'Dr. Kondratieff and Mr Hyde Clarke'. *Research in the History of Economic Thought and Methodology*. 9: 35–58.

Boschma, R. A. (1999). 'The Rise of Clusters of Innovative Industries in Belgium during the Industrial Epoch'. *Research Policy*, 28: 853–73.

Bosserelle, E. (1994). *Le Cycle Kondratieff: théories et controverse*. Paris: Masson.

Bottomore, T. (1992). *Between Marginalism and Marxism: The Economic Sociology of J. A. Schumpeter*. Hemel Hempstead: Harvester Wheatsheaf.

Boyer, R. (1975). 'Modalités de la régulation d'économies capitalistes dans la longue période: quelques formalisations simples'. Mimeo, CEPREMAP, Paris.

——(1979). 'La Crise actuelle: une mise en perspective historique'. *Critique de l'économie politique*, 7–8: 3–113.

——(1988). 'Technical Change and the Theory of Regulation'. In G. Dosi, C. Freeman, R. Nelson, G. Silverberg, and L. Soete (eds.), *Technical Change and Economic Theory*. London: Pinter, 67–94.

Braudel, F. (1993). *Civilização Material, Economia e Capitalismo: Séculos XV-XVIII,* iii, *O Tempo do Mundo*. Lisbon: Teorema.

Bresciani-Turroni, C. (1917). 'Movimenti di Lunga Durata dello Sconto I dei Prezzi'. *Giornale degli Economisti e Revista di Statistica*, 55: 1–11.

Bresnahan, T. F. and Trajtenberg, M. (1995). 'General Purpose Technologies: Engines of Growth'. *Journal of Econometrics*, 65: 83–108.

Bressand, A. (1990). 'Electronic Cartels in the Making?' *Transatlantic Perspectives*, 21: 3–6.

Briggs, A. (1960). *The Age of Improvement, 1783–1867*. London: Longmans, Green.

Burns, A. and Mitchell, W. (1946). *Measuring Business Cycles: Studies in Business Cycles*. New York: NBER.

Burnside, C. (1998). 'Detrending and Business Cycle Facts: A comment'. *Journal of Monetary Economics*, 41: 513–32.

Byatt, I. (1979). *The British Electrical Industry*. Oxford: Oxford University Press.

Byrne, J. A. (1998). 'The Corporation of the Future', *Business Week*, 31 August: 56–8.

Caldwell, B. (1982). *Beyond Positivism: Economic Methodology in the Twentieth Century*. London: Unwin Hyman.

Cameron, R. (1990). 'La Révolution Industrielle manquée'. *Social Science History*, 14: 559–65.

Canova, F. (1998). 'Detrending and Business Cycle Facts'. *Journal of Monetary Economics*, 41: 475–512.

Carlyle, T. (1843). *Past and Present*. London: Chapman & Hall.

Castells, M. (1996). *The Information Age: Economy, Society and Culture*, i, *The Rise of the Network Society*. Oxford: Blackwell.

——(1997). *The Information Age: Economy, Society and Culture*, ii, *The Power of Identity*. Oxford: Blackwell.

——(1998). *The Information Age: Economy, Society and Culture*, iii, *End of Millennium*. Oxford: Blackwell.

Chadwick, R. (1958). 'The extraction process for metals'. In *Oxford History of Technology*, v, Oxford: Clarendon Press, 72–102.

Chandler, A. D. (ed.) (1965). *The Railroads: The Nation's First Big Business*. New York: Harcourt Brace.

——(1970). 'Comment'. In R. Andreano (ed.), *The New Economic History: Recent Papers on Methodology*. New York: John Wiley, 143–50.

——(1977). *The Visible Hand: The Managerial Revolution in American Business*. Cambridge, Mass.: Harvard University Press.

——(1990). *Economies of Scale and Scope: The Dynamics of Industrial Capitalism*. Cambridge, Mass.: Harvard University Press.

——(1994). 'The Competitive Performance of US Industrial Enterprises since the Second World War'. *Business History Review*, 68: 1–72.

——(1997). 'The United States: Engines of Economic Growth in the Capital Intensive and Knowledge Intensive Industries'. In A. Chandler, F. Amatori, and T. Hikino (eds.), *Big Business and the Wealth of Nations*. Cambridge: Cambridge University Press, 63–101.

Chandler, A. D. and Daems, H. (eds.) (1980). *Managerial Hierarchies: Comparative Perspectives on the Rise of the Modern Industrial Enterprise*. Cambridge, Mass.: Harvard University Press.

——and Hikino, T. (1997). 'The Large Industrial Enterprise and the Dynamics of Modern Economic Growth'. In A. Chandler, F. Amatori, and T. Hikino (eds.), *Big Business and the Wealth of Nations*. Cambridge: Cambridge University Press, 24–57.

Chapman, S. D. (1972/1992). *The Cotton Industry in the Industrial Revolution*. London: Economic History Society.

Chesbrough, H. and Teece, D. (1996). 'When is Virtual Virtuous? Organizing for Innovation'. *Harvard Business Review*, 74/(1): 65–74.

Chizov, Y. A. (1987). 'Problems of Model Estimation of Long Term Economic Oscillation'. In T. Vasko (ed.), *The Long Wave Debate: Selected Papers*. Berlin: Springer-Verlag, 5–11.

Church, R. and Wrigley, E. A. (gen. eds.) (1994). *The Industrial Revolutions*, 11 vols. Oxford: Blackwell.

Clark, J. (1986). *Revolution and Rebellion*. Cambridge: Cambridge University Press.

Clark, J. B. (1899). *The Distribution of Wealth: A Theory of Wages, Interest and Profits*. New York: Augustus M. Kelley.

Clarke, H. (1847). 'Physical Economy: A Preliminary Inquiry into the Physical Laws Governing the Periods of Famine and Panics'. *British Railway Register*, 2–15; reprinted in F. Louçã and J. Reijnders (eds.), *The Foundations of Long Wave Theory* (2 vols.). Cheltenham: Edward Elgar, i: 3–20.

Climo, T. A. and Howells, P. G. (1974). 'Cause and Counterfactuals'. *Economic History Review*, 27: 461–8.

Coats, A. W. (1980). 'The Historical Context of the "New" Economic History'. *Journal of European Economic History*, 9/1: 185–207.

Cole, G. D. H. (1941). *British Working Class Politics, 1832–1914*. London: Routledge.

Coleman, D. (1983). 'Proto-Industrialization: A Concept too Many'. *Economic History Review*, 36: 435–48.

Conrad, A. and Meyer, J. (1958). 'The Economics of Slavery in the Ante-Bellum South'. *Journal of Political Economy*, 66/2: 95–123.

——and——(1964). *The Economics of Slavery: And Other Studies in Econometric Theory*. Chicago: Aldine.

Coppock, D. J. (1963). 'The Climacteric of the 1870s'. In B. E. Supple (ed.), *The Experience of Economic Growth*. New York: Random House, 223.

Corry, A. K. (1990). 'Engineering, Methods of Manufacture and Production'. In I. McNeil (ed.), *An Encyclopaedia of the History of Technology*. London: Routledge, 388–429.

Court, W. H. B. (1965). *British Economic History, 1870–1914: Commentary and Documents*. Cambridge: Cambridge University Press.

Cowan, R. and Hulten, S. (1994). 'Accumulation Regimes and Lock-in of Technology: The Gasoline Car and the Electric Vehicle'. Mimeo, EUNETIC Conference, 6–8 October, Strasbourg.

Crafts, N. F. R. (1977). 'Industrial Revolution in England and France: Some Thoughts on the Question, "Why was England First?"' *Economic History Review*, 30: 429–41.

——(1985). *The British Economic Growth during the Industrial Revolution*. New York: Oxford University Press.

——(1989). 'The Industrial Revolution: Economic Growth in Britain, 1700–1860'. In A. Digby and C. Feinstein (eds.), *New Directions in Economic and Social History*, i. London: Macmillan, 64–75

——(1994). 'British Economic Growth, 1700–1831: A Review of the Evidence'. In J. Hoppit and E. A. Wrigley (eds.), *The Industrial Revolution in Britain*, ii. Oxford: Blackwell, 93–117.

——(1995*a*). 'Macroinventions, Economic Growth, and "Industrial Revolution" in Britain and France'. *Economic History Review*, 48: 591–8.

——(1995*b*). 'Exogenous or Endogenous Growth? The Industrial Revolution Reconsidered'. *Journal of Economic History*, 55: 745–72.

——and Harley, C. K. (1992). 'Output Growth and the Industrial Revolution'. *Economic History Review*, 45: 703–30.

Cringely, R. (1996). *Accidental Empires: How the Boys of Silicon Valley Make their Millions, Battle Foreign Competition and Still Can't Get a Date*, rev. edn. Harmondsworth: Penguin.

David, P. A. (1969). 'Transport Innovation and Economic Growth: Professor Fogel On and Off the Rails'. *Economic History Review*, 22: 506–25.

——(1971). 'Comments on Gavin Wright, Econometric Studies in History'. In M. Intriligator (ed.), *Frontiers of Quantitative Economics*. Amsterdam: North-Holland.

——(1987). 'Hero and the Herd in Technological History: Reflections on Thomas Edison and the Battle of the Systems'. CEPR, LEFR, publication no. 100, Stanford, Calif.

——(1993). 'Path-Dependence and Predictability in Dynamic Systems with Local Network Externalities: A Paradigm for Historical Economics'. In D. Foray and C. Freeman (eds.), *Technology and the Wealth of Nations: The Dynamics of Constructed Advantage*. London: Pinter, 208–31.

——(1997). 'Path Dependence, its Critics, and the Quest for Historical Economics', keynote address to the 1997 Athens EAEPE Conference. Mimeo.

Davis, L. (1966). 'Professor Fogel and the New Economic History'. *Economic History Review*, 19: 657–63.

Day, R. (1981). *The 'Crisis' and the 'Crash': Soviet Studies of the West (1917–1939)*. London: New Left Books.

Deane, P. (1948/1994). 'The Implications of Early National Income Estimates for the Measurement of Long-term Economic Growth in the United Kingdom'. In J. Hoppit and E. A. Wrigley (eds.), *The Industrial Revolution in Britain*, ii. Oxford: Blackwell, 149–84.

——(1957). 'The Output of the British Woollen Industry in the Eighteenth Century'. *Journal of Economic History*, 17: 207–23.

——(1965). *The First Industrial Revolution*. Cambridge: Cambridge University Press.

——and Cole, W. A. (1962). *British Economic Growth, 1688–1959*. Cambridge: Cambridge University Press.

de Geus, A. (1997). *The Living Company*. London: Nicholas Brealey.

Delbeke, J. (1982). *The Mechanisation of Flemish Industry, 1812–1930: The Case of Antwerp*. Louvain: Centre for Economic Studies, Catholic University of Louvain.

——(1985). 'Long Wave Research: The State of the Art, Anno 1983'. In G. Bianchi, G. Bruckmann, J. Delbeke, and T. Vasko (eds.), *Long Waves, Depression, and Innovation: Implications for National and Regional Economic Policy*, CP-85–009. Laxenburg: IIASA, 7–28.

Dertouzos, M., Lester, R., and Solow, R. (eds.) (1989). *Made in America*, Report of the MIT Commission on Industrial Productivity. Cambridge, Mass.: MIT Press.

Devine, W. (1983). 'From Shafts to Wires: Historical Perspective on Electrification'. *Journal of Economic History*, 43: 347–72.

de Tocqueville, A. (1836). *Democracy in America*. Oxford: Oxford University Press.

de Wolff, S. (1924). 'Phases of Prosperity and Depression'. In O. Jensen (ed.), *Der Lebendige Marxismus, Festgabe zum 70–en Geburtstag von Karl Kautzky*. Jena, 13–43; trans. in F. Louçã and J. Reijnders (eds.), *The Foundations of Long Wave Theory* (2 vols.). Cheltenham: Edward Elgar, i: 25–44.

Diamond, J. (1998). *Guns, Germs and Steel: A Short History of Everybody for the Last 13,000 Years*. London: Vintage.

Diebold, J. (1952). *Automation: The Advent of the Automatic Factory*. New York: van Nostrand.

Dobb, M. (1947). *Studies in Economic Development*. London: Routledge.

Domar, E. (1965). 'Comments'. *American Economic Review*, 55/2: 116–17.

Dosi, G. (1982). 'Technological Paradigms and Technological Trajectories'. *Research Policy*, 11/3: 147–62.

——Freeman, C., Nelson, R., Silverberg, G., and Soete, L. (eds.) (1988). *Technical Change and Economic Theory*. London: Pinter.

Dow, J. C. R. (1998). *The Major Recessions, 1920–1995*. Oxford: Oxford University Press.

Drucker, P. (1946). *The Concept of the Corporation*. New York: John Day.

Duijn, J. van (1977). 'The Long Wave in Economic Life'. *De Economist*, 125: 544–76.

——(1980). *Prospects of Economic Growth*. Amsterdam: Kuipers & Cajou.

——(1983). *Long Waves in Economic Life*. London: Allen & Unwin.

Duménil, G. and Levy, D. (1999). *The Economics of the Profit Rate*. Aldershot: Edward Elgar.

Dunsheath, P. (1962). *A History of Electrical Engineering*. London: Faber.

Dupriez, L. (1959). *Philosophie des conjonctures économiques*. Louvain: Institut de Recherches Économiques et Sociales de L'Université de Louvain.

Duysters, G. (1995). *The Evolution of Complex Industrial Systems: The Dynamics of Major IT Sectors*. Maastricht: UPM.

Dyke, C. (1990). 'Strange Attraction, Curious Liaison: Clio Meets Chaos'. *Philosophical Forum*, 37: 369–86.

Economist, The (2000*a*). 'The Mystery of the Vanishing Taxpayer'. In 'Survey of Globalization and Tax'. *The Economist*, 29 January–4 February: 1–20.

——(2000*b*). ' A Tale of Two Debtors', 22 January: 17.

——(2000*c*). 'The New Economy Survey.' 23 September: 1–52.

Elster, J. (1978). *Logic and Society: Contradictions and Possible Worlds*. Chichester: John Wiley.

——(1999). *Alchemies of the Mind: Rationality and Emotions*. Cambridge: Cambridge University Press.

Encyclopaedia Britannica (1898). *Encyclopaedia Britannica*, 9th edn., xiii. Edinburgh: Adam & Charles Black.

Engels, F. (1890). Letter to J. Bloch. In *Selected Correspondence of Marx and Engels*. London: Lawrence & Wishart.

Enos, J. L. (1962). *Petroleum Progress and Profits: A History of Process Innovation*. Cambridge, Mass.: MIT Press.

Epstein, R. (1987). *A History of Econometric Ideas*. Amsterdam: North-Holland.

Escudier, J. (1990). 'Long-term Movements of the Economy: Terminology and Theoretical Options'. In T. Vasko, R. Ayres, and L. Fontvieille (eds.), *Life Cycles and Long Waves*. Berlin: Springer-Verlag, 121–32.

European Commission (1997). *Building the European Information Society For Us All*, Final Policy Report of the High-Level Expert Group. Brussels: European Commission.

Eversley, D. E. C. (1994). 'The Home Market and Economic Growth in England, 1750–1780'. In J. Hoppit and E. A. Wrigley (eds.), *The Industrial Revolution in Britain*, ii. Oxford: Blackwell, 288–342.

Ewijk, C. van (1981). 'The Long Wave: A Real Phenomenon?' *De Economist*, 129: 324–72.

——(1982). 'A Spectral Analysis of the Kondratieff Cycle'. *Kyklos*, 35: 468–99.

Fabre, J. H. (1885). *The Social Life of Insects*. Avignon:

Fabre, J. (1983). 'Le Pouvoir structurant de l'électricité'. *Bulletin Histoire de L'Électricité*, June: 23–36.

Faith, N. (1990). *The World the Railways Made*. London: Bodley Head.

Fayolle, J. (1994). 'Le Répérage macroéconomique des fluctuations longues: une évaluation critique de quelques travaux modernes'. *Revue de l'OFCE*, 51: 123–68.

Fearon, P. (1987). *War, Prosperity and Depression: The American Economy 1917–1945*. Deddington: Philip Allan.

Feinstein, C. H. (1976). *National Income and Expenditure of the UK, 1855–1965*. Cambridge: Cambridge University Press.

Fellner, W. (1956). *Trends and Cycles in Economic Activity*. New York: Henry Holt.

Floud, R. C. and McCloskey, D. (eds.) (1981). *Economic History of Britain since 1700*. Cambridge: Cambridge University Press.

——and——(eds.) (1994). *The Economic History of Britain since 1700*, 2nd edn. Cambridge: Cambridge University Press.

Fogel, R. (1962). 'A Quantitative Approach to the Study of Railroads in American Economic Growth'. *Journal of Economic History*, 22: 163–97.

——(1964). *Railroads and American Economic Growth: Essays in Econometric History*. Baltimore: Johns Hopkins University Press.

——(1965). 'The Reunification of Economic History with Economic Theory'. *American Economic Journal*, 55/2: 92–8.

——(1966). 'The New Economic History: Its Findings and Methods'. *Economic History Review*, 19: 642–56.

——and Engerman, S. (1974). *Time on the Cross*, 2 vols. London: Wildwood House.

Forrester, J. (1971). *World Dynamics*. Cambridge, Mass.: Wright-Allen.

——*et al.* (1985*a*). 'Comments: Identification of Long Waves'. In G. Bianchi, G. Bruckmann, J. Delbeke, and T. Vasko (eds.), *Long Waves, Depression, and Innovation: Implications for National and Regional Economic Policy*, CP-85-009. Laxenburg: IIASA, 223–27.

——*et al.* (1985*b*). 'Comments. Theories of the Long Wave: An Integrated Approach to the Economic Long Wave'. In G. Bianchi, G. Bruckmann, J. Delbeke, and T. Vasko (eds.), *Long Waves, Depression, and Innovation: Implications for National and Regional Economic Policy*, CP-85-009. Laxenburg: IIASA, 203–10.

Fortune (1964). 'The 500 Largest US Industrial Corporations'. *Fortune*, 17 July: 179–98.

——(1984). 'The Fortune Directory of the Largest US Industrial Corporations'. *Fortune*, 30 April: 178–224.

Frank, A. G. and Fuentes, M. (1992). 'On Studying the Cycles in Social Movements'. Mimeo, Fundacion Pablo Iglesias, paper presented to the Conferencia sobre Movimientos Ciclicos y Recurrencias en Politica y Economia, Madrid, May.

Freeman, C. (1977). 'The Kondratiev Long Waves, Technical Change and Unemployment'. In *Structural Determinants of Employment*, ii. Paris: OECD, 1977, 181–96.

——(1987). *Technology Policy and Economic Performance: Lessons from Japan*. London: Pinter.

——(1991). 'Innovation, Changes of Techno-Economic Paradigm and Biological Analogies in Economics'. *Revue Économique*, 42/2: 211–32; reprinted in C. Freeman, *The Economics of Hope*. London: Pinter, 1992.

Freeman, C. (1994). 'The Economics of Technical Change'. *Cambridge Journal of Economics*, 18: 463–514.

——(1995). *History, Coevolution and Economic Growth*. Mimeo, SPRU, University of Sussex, Brighton.

——(ed.) (1996). *The Long Wave in the World Economy*, International Library of Critical Writings in Economics. Aldershot: Edward Elgar.

——and Soete, L. (eds.) (1987). *Technical Change and Full Employment*. Oxford: Blackwell.

——Harlow, C. J. E., and Fuller, J. K. (1965). 'Research and Development in Electronic Capital Goods'. *National Institute Economic Review*, 34: 40–97.

——Clark, J., and Soete, L. (1982). *Unemployment and Technical Innovation: A Study of Long Waves and Economic Development*. London: Pinter.

Frickey, E. (1942). *Economic Fluctuations in the United States: A Systematic Analysis of Long Run Trends and Business Cycles 1866–1914*. Cambridge, Mass.: Harvard University Press.

Friedland, S. (1957). 'Turnover and Growth of the Largest Industrial Firms, 1906–1950'. *Review of Economics and Statistics*, 39: 79–83.

Friedman, M. (1951). 'Comment'. In Universities–NBER Conference, New York.

——and Schwartz, A. (1963). *A Monetary History of the United States, 1867–1960*. Princeton: Princeton University Press.

Frisch, R. (1927). 'The Analysis of Statistical Time Series'. Mimeo, Oslo University.

——(1933). 'Propagation Problems and Impulse Problems in Dynamic Economics'. In K. Koch (ed.), *Economic Essays in Honour of Gustav Cassel*. London: Frank Cass, 171–205.

Galbraith, J. K. (1954). *The Great Crash*. Harmondsworth: Penguin Books.

Garvy, G. (1943). 'Kondratieff's Theory of Long Cycles'. *Review of Economic Statistics*, 25: 203–20.

Gates, B. (1995/1996). *The Way Ahead*. London: Viking (rev. edn. 1996).

Gattei, G. (1989). 'Every 25 years? Strike Waves and Long Economic Cycles'. Paper presented at the Brussels International Colloquium, 12–14 January.

Gerster, H. (1992). 'Testing Long Waves in Price and Volume Series from Sixteen Countries'. In A. Kleinknecht, E. Mandel, and I. Wallerstein (eds.), *New Findings in Long Wave Research*. New York: St Martin's Press, 120–47.

Gilboy, E. (1932). 'Demand as a Factor in the Industrial Revolution'. In A. H. Cole (ed.), *Facts and Factors in Economic History*; reprinted in R. A. Church and E. A. Wrigley (eds.), *The Industrial Revolution*, iii. Oxford: Blackwell, 1994, 342–62.

Gilder, G. (1993). 'The Death of Telephony'. In 'The Future Surveyed', *The Economist*, 11 September: 91–5.

Gilfillan, S. C. (1935). *The Sociology of Invention*. Chicago: Follet.

Gille, B. (1978). *Histoire des Techniques*. Paris: Gallinaud.

Glismann H. (1985*a*). 'Comments: Identification of Long Waves'. In G. Bianchi, G. Bruckmann, J. Delbeke, and T. Vasko (eds.), *Long Waves, Depression, and Innovation: Implications for National and Regional Economic Policy*, CP-85-009. Laxenburg: IIASA, 229–32.

——(1985*b*). 'Comments: Theory of the Long Wave'. In G. Bianchi, G. Bruckmann, J. Delbeke, and T. Vasko (eds.), *Long Waves, Depression, and Innovation: Implications for National and Regional Economic Policy*, CP-85-009. Laxenburg: IIASA, 215–21.

Golding, A. M. (1972). *The Semi-conductor Industry in Britain and the United States: A Case Study in Innovation, Growth and the Diffusion of Technology*. D.Phil. thesis, University of Sussex.

Goodwin, R. (1985). 'A Personal Perspective on Mathematical Economics'. *Banca Nazionale del Lavoro Quarterly Review*, 152: 3–13.

Goodwin, R. (1987). 'The Economy as an Evolutionary Pulsator'. In T. Vasko (ed.), *The Long Wave Debate: Selected Papers*. Berlin: Springer-Verlag, 27–34.

——(1990). *Chaotic Economic Dynamics*. Oxford: Clarendon Press.

Gordon, R. (1986). *The American Business Cycle*. Chicago: University of Chicago Press.

Gordon, R. A. (1951). *Cyclical Experience in the Inter-War Period*. New York: National Bureau of Economic Research.

Gourvish, T. R. (1980). *Railways and the British Economy, 1830–1914*. London: Macmillan.

Granovetter, M. and McGuire, P. (1998). 'The Making of an Industry: Electricity in the United States'. In M. Callon (ed.), *The Law of Markets*. Oxford: Blackwell, 147–73.

Granstrand, O. (1999). *The Economics and Management of Intellectual Property*. Cheltenham: Edward Elgar.

Graves, A. (1991). *International Competitiveness and Technological Development in the World Automobile Industry*. D. Phil. thesis, University of Sussex.

Gray, R. (1996) *The Factory Question and Industrial England, 1830–1860*. Cambridge: Cambridge University Press.

Grübler, A. (1990). *The Rise and Fall of Infrastructures*. Heidelberg: Physica Verlag.

Guy, K. (1985). 'Communications'. In L. Soete (ed.), *Electronics and Communications*. Aldershot: Gower, 90–146.

Habbakuk, H. J. (1963). 'The Historical Experience on the Basic Conditions of Economic Progress'. In B. Supple (ed.), *The Experience of Economic Growth*. New York: Random House, 111–28.

Haberler, G. (1937). *Prosperité et depression: études théoriques des cycles économiques*. Geneva: Société des Nations.

Hagedoorn, J. (1990). 'Organizational Modes of Inter-firm Cooperation and Technology Transfer'. *Technovation*, 10: 17–30.

——and Schakenraad, J. (1992). 'Leading Companies and Networks of Strategic Alliances in Information Technologies'. *Research Policy*, 21: 163–91.

Hall, P. and Preston, P. (1988). *The Carrier Wave: New Information Technology and the Geography of Innovation*. London: Unwin Hyman.

Hamilton, S. B. (1958). 'Building Materials and Techniques'. In *Oxford History of Technology*, v. Oxford: Clarendon Press, 466–99.

Hannah, L. (1983). *The Rise of the Corporate Economy*. London: Methuen.

——(1997). *Marshall's 'Trees' and the Global 'Forest': Were 'Giant Redwoods' Different?* Discussion Paper 318, Centre for Economic Performance, London School of Economics.

Hansen, A. (1941). *Fiscal Policy and Business Cycle*. New York: W. W. Norton.

——(1951). *Business Cycles and National Income*. New York: W. W. Norton.

Harris Corporation (1996). 'Founding Dates of the 1994 Fortune 500 US Companies'. *Business History Review*, 70: 69–90.

Haustein, H-D. and Neuwirth, E. (1982). 'Long Waves in World Industrial Production: Energy Consumption, Innovation, Inventions and Patents and their Identification by Spectral Analysis'. *Technological Forecasting and Social Change*, 22/1: 53–89.

Hawke, G. R. (1970). *Railways and Economic Growth in England and Wales, 1840–1870*. Oxford: Oxford University Press.

——and Higgins, J. P. P. (1981). 'Transport and Social Overhead Capital'. In R. Floud and B. McCloskey (eds.), *The Economic History of Britain since 1700*, i. Cambridge: Cambridge University Press, 227–53.

Hayek, F. (1942). *The Road to Serfdom*. Chicago: Chicago University Press.

Heinrich, T. R. (1997). *Ships for the Seven Seas: Philadelphia Shipbuilding in the Age of Industrial Capitalism*. Baltimore: Johns Hopkins University Press.

Helpman, E. (1998). *General Purpose Technologies and Economic Growth*. Cambridge, Mass.: MIT Press.

Hempel, C. (1942). 'The Function of General Laws in History'. *Journal of Philosophy*, 39(2): 35–48; reprinted in P. Gardiner, (ed.), *Theories of History*. New York: Free Press, 1959, 349–56.

Herfindahl, O. C. (1959). *Copper Costs and Prices, 1870–1957*. Baltimore: Johns Hopkins University Press.

Hills, R. L. (1994). 'Hargreaves, Arkwright and Crompton: Why Three Inventors?' In D. T. Jenkins (ed.), *The Textile Industries*. Oxford: Blackwell.

Hobday, M. (1991). 'The European Semi-conductor Industry: Resurgence and Rationalisation'. In C. Freeman, M. Sharp, and W. Walker (eds.), *Technology and the Future of Europe*. London: Pinter.

Hobsbawm, E. J. (1964). 'Economic Fluctuations and Some Social Movements since 1800'. In E. Hobsbawm (ed.), *Labouring Men*. London: Weidenfeld & Nicolson, 126–57.

——(1968). *Industry and Empire: An Economic History of Britain since 1750*. London: Weidenfeld & Nicolson.

——(1975). *The Age of Capital*. London: Weidenfeld & Nicolson.

——(1977). *The Age of Revolution, 1789–1848*. London: Abacus (first published London: Weidenfeld & Nicolson, 1962).

——(1994). 'The British Standard of Living, 1790–1850'. In J. Hoppit and E. A. Wrigley (eds.), *The Industrial Revolution in Britain*, iii. Oxford: Blackwell, 402–25.

——(1997). *On History*. London: Abacus.

Hobday, M., Rush, H., and Tidd, J. (eds.) (2000). 'Innovation in Complex Products and Systems'. *Research Policy*, Special Issue, 29: 793–1014.

Hobson, J. A. (1902). *Imperialism: A Study*. London: Nisbet.

Hodgson, G. M. (1999). *Evolution and Institutions*. Cheltenham: Elgar.

Hoffmann, W. D. (1976). 'Market Structure and Strategies of R and D Behaviour in the Data Processing Market'. *Research Policy*, 5: 334–53.

Hoffmann, W. G. (1955). *British Industry, 1700–1950*. Oxford: Blackwell.

Hollander, S. (1965). *The Sources of Increased Efficiency: A Study of Du Pont Rayon Plants*. Cambridge, Mass.: MIT Press.

Hollanders, H., Soete, L., and ter Weel, B. (1999). 'Trends in Growth Convergence and Divergence in Technological Access and Capabilities'. Mimeo, presented at a seminar in March 1999 at ISEG, Lisbon.

Homburg, H. (1978). 'Anfänge des Taylorsystems in Deutschland vor dem ersten Weltkrieg'. *Geschichte und Gesellschaft*, 4: 170–94.

'Hoover Report', (1929). *Report of the Committee on Recent Economic Changes* (Hoover Report). Washington: National Bureau of Economic Research.

Hoppit, J. and Wrigley, E. A. (eds.) (1994). *The Industrial Revolution in Britain*, ii, iii. Oxford: Blackwell/Economic History Society.

Hounshell, D. A. (1984). *From the American System to Mass Production, 1800–1932: The Development of Manufacturing Technology in the United States*. Baltimore: Johns Hopkins University Press.

Howrey, E. P. (1968). 'A Spectrum Analysis of the Long-Swing Hypothesis'. *International Economic Review*, 9: 228–52.

Huberman, L. (1940). *We, the People*. London: Gollancz.

Hudson, P. (1992). *The Industrial Revolution in Britain*. London: Edward Arnold.

Hughes, T. P. (1982). *Networks of Power Electrification in Western Society, 1800–1930*. Baltimore: Johns Hopkins University Press.

Imbert, G. (1959). *Des mouvements de longue durée Kondratieff*. Aix-en-Provence: Éditions La Pensée Universitaire.

Islam, S. (1985). 'Disequilibrium, Innovation and Periodicity in Economic Development'. In G. Bianchi, G. Bruckmann, J. Delbeke, and T. Vasko (eds.), *Long Waves, Depression, and Innovation: Implications for National and Regional Economic Policy*, CP-85-009. Laxenburg, Austria: IIASA, 68–8.

Jackson, F. (1987). *Conditionals*. Oxford: Blackwell.

Jacob, M. (1988). *The Cultural Meaning of the Scientific Revolution*. New York: McGraw-Hill.

Jameson, F. (1991). *Postmodernism or the Cultural Logic of Capitalism*. London: Verso.

Javary, M. (1999). *The Economics of Power*, D.Phil. thesis, University of Sussex.

——and Mansell, R. (2000). 'Emerging Internet Oligopolies: A Political Economy Analysis'. In W. J. Samuels and E. Millar (eds.), *Essays in Honour of H. M. Trebing*. East Lansing, Mich.: Michigan State University Press.

Jenkins, D. T. (ed.) (1994). *The Textile Industries*, viii. In R. A. Church and E. A. Wrigley (eds.), *Industrial Revolution in Britain*. Oxford: Blackwell.

Jevons, W. S. (1884). *Investigations in Currency and Finance*. London: Macmillan.

Jewkes, J., Sawers, D., and Stillerman, R. (1958/1969). *The Sources of Invention*. London: Macmillan.

Jones, D. T. (1985). 'Vehicles'. In C. Freeman (ed.), *Technological Trends and Employment*, iv, *Engineering and Vehicles*. Aldershot: Gower, 128–88.

Jones, R. V. (1978). *Most Secret War: British Scientific Intelligence, 1939–1945*. London: Hamish Hamilton.

Kadish, A. (1989). *Historians, Economists, and Economic History*. London: Routledge.

Kalecki, M. (1943). 'Political Aspects of Full Employment'. *Political Quarterly*, 14: 322–30.

Katz, B. G. and Phillips, A. (1982). 'Government, Technological Opportunities and the Emergence of the Computer Industry'. In H. Giersch (ed.), *Emerging Technologies*. Tubingen: JCB Mohr, 419–59.

Keirstead, B. S. (1948). The Theory of Economic Change. Toronto: Macmillan.

Kendrick, J. U. (1961). *Productivity Trends in the United States*. Princeton: Princeton University Press.

Kennedy, P. (1988). *The Rise and Fall of the Great Powers: Economic Change and Military Conflict from 1500 to 2000*. London: Unwin.

Keynes, J. M. (1920). *The Economic Consequences of the Peace*. London: Macmillan.

——(1921). *Treatise on Probability*, viii. In *Collected Writings of John Maynard Keynes*, 30 vols. London: Macmillan.

——(1936). *General Theory of Employment, Interest and Money*. London: Macmillan, 1973 edn.

——(1972). *Essays in Biography*, x. In *Collected Writings of John Maynard Keynes*, 30 vols. London: Macmillan.

Kindleberger, C. (1973). *The World in Depression*. New York: Oxford University Press.

Kitch, M. J. (1967). *Capitalism and the Reformation*. London: Longman.

Klein, B. H. (1977). *Dynamic Economics*. Cambridge, Mass.: Harvard University Press.

Klein, J. (1997). *Statistical Visions in Time: A History of Time Series Analysis, 1662–1938*. Cambridge: Cambridge University Press.

Kleinknecht, A. (1987a). 'Rates of Innovation and Profits in the Long Wave'. In T. Vasko (ed.), *The Long Wave Debate: Selected Papers*. Berlin: Springer-Verlag, 216–38.

——(1987b). *Innovation Patterns in Crisis and Prosperity: Schumpeterian Long Cycles Reconsidered* (preface by Tinbergen). London: Macmillan.

——(1992). 'Long Wave Research: New Results, New Departures—An Introduction'. In A. Kleinknecht, E. Mandel, and I. Wallerstein (eds.), *New Findings in Long Wave Research*. New York: St Martin's Press, 1–12.

Klimenko, L. and Menshikov, S. (1987). 'Catastrophe Theory Applied to the Analysis of Long Waves'. In T. Vasko (ed.), *The Long Wave Debate: Selected Papers*. Berlin: Springer-Verlag, 345–58.

Kocka, J. (1994). 'Capitalism and Bureaucracy in German Industrialization before 1914'. In P. K. O'Brien, *The Industrial Revolution in Europe*. Oxford: Blackwell/ Economic History Society, 3–19.

Kondratiev, N. (1923). 'Questions controversées d'économie mondiale et de crise: réponse a ceux qui nous critiquent'. In Kondratiev (1992), 493–543.

——(1924). 'Sur les concepts de statique, de dynamique et de conjoncture économique'. In Kondratiev (1992), 1–46.

——(1925). 'The Static and Dynamic View of Economics'. *Quarterly Journal of Economics*, 39: 575–83.

——(1926). 'Los Grandes Ciclos de la vida economica'. In G. Haberler (ed.), *Ensayos sobre el Ciclo Economico*, 33–54, republished in *Archiv für Sozialwissenschaft und Sozialpolitik*, 56 (1946): 573–609.

——(1926*a*). 'About the Question of the Major Cycles of the Conjuncture'. *Planovoe Khoziaistvo*, 8: 167–81.

——(1926*b*). 'Problemes de Prévision'. In Kondratiev (1992), 47–104.

——(1928*a*). 'Les Grands Cycles de la conjoncture économique'. In Kondratiev (1992), 109–68.

——(1928*b*). 'La Dynamique des prix des produits industriels et agricoles: contribuition à la théorie de la dynamique relative et de la conjoncture'. In Kondratiev (1992), 377–473.

——(1935). 'The Major Economic Cycles'. *Review of Economic Statistics*, 18: 105–15.

——(1979). 'The Major Economic Cycles'. *Review*, 11: 579–62 (first published 1925).

——(1984). *The Long Wave Debate*. St Moritz: International Moneyline.

——(1992). *Les Grands Cycles de la conjoncture*. (Louis Fontvieille edn.). Paris: Economica (includes 1923, 1924, 1926*a*,*b*, 1928*a*,*b* papers).

——(1998). *The Works of Nikolai D. Kondratiev*, ed. W. Samuels and N. Makasheva. London: Pickering & Chatto.

Kuczynski, T. (1992). 'Great Depressions as Transitional Phases within the Capitalist Mode of Production'. In A. Kleinknecht, E. Mandel, and I. Wallerstein (eds.), *New Findings in Long Wave Research*. New York: St Martin's Press, 257–75.

Kuznets, S. (1930). *Secular Movements in Production and Prices: Their Nature and Their Bearing upon Cyclical Fluctuations*. Boston: Riverside Press, 1967.

——(1940). 'Schumpeter's Business Cycles'. *American Economic Review*, 30: 257–71.

——(1955). 'Economic Growth and Income Inequality'. *American Economic Review*, 45: 1–28.

——(1957). 'Summary of Discussion and Postscript'. *Journal of Economic History*, 17: 545–53.

——(1971). *Economic Growth of Nations*. Cambridge, Mass.: Harvard University Press.

Lamoreaux, N. R., Raff, D. M. G., and Temin, P. (1999). *Learning by Doing in Markets, Firms, and Countries*. Chicago: University of Chicago Press.

Landes, D. (1965). 'Technological Change and Industrial Development in Western Europe, 1750–1914'. In *Cambridge Economic History of Europe*. Cambridge: Cambridge University Press.

——(1969). *The Unbound Prometheus: Technological and Industrial Development in Western Europe from 1750 to the Present*. Cambridge: Cambridge University Press.

——(1978). 'On Avoiding Babel'. *Journal of Economic History*, 38/1: 3–12.

——(1993). 'The Fable of the Dead Horse: or, The Industrial Revolution Revisited'. In J. Mokyr (ed.), *The British Industrial Revolution: An Economic Perspective*. Boulder, Colo.: Westview Press, 132–70.

——(1994). 'What Room for Accident in History? Explaining Big Changes by Small Events'. *Economic History Review*, 47: 637–56.

——(1995). 'Some Further Thoughts on Accident in History: A Reply to Professor Crafts'. *Economic History Review*, 48: 599–601.

Lange, O. (1941). 'Review of Schumpeter's "Business Cycles"'. *Review of Economic Statistics*, 23: 190–3.

Laski, H. J. (1944). *Faith, Reason and Civilization*. New York: Viking Press.

Laybourn, K. (1992). *A History of Trade Unionism*. Stroud: Sutton Publishers.

Lazonick, W. (1986). 'The Cotton Industry'. In B. Elbaum and W. Lazonick (eds.), *The Decline of the British Economy*. Oxford: Clarendon Press, 18–51.

——(1990). *Competitive Advantage on the Shop Floor*. Cambridge, Mass.: Harvard University Press.

Lebergott, S. (1993). *Pursuing Happiness: American Consumers in the Twentieth Century*. Princeton: Princeton University Press.

Leibenstein, H. (1957). *Economic Backwardness and Economic Growth*. New York: John Wiley.

Lenin, V. I. (1915). *Imperialism, the Highest Stage of Capitalism*. (English trans.). London: Lawrence & Wishart.

Lenoir, M. (1913). *Études sur la formation et le mouvement des prix*. Paris: Giard et Brière.

Leontief, W. (1948). 'Note on the Pluralistic Interpretation of History and the Problem of Interdisciplinary Cooperation'. *Journal of Philosophy*, 45: 617–24.

——(1963). *When Should History Be Written Backwards?* Mimeo, 1962 Lecture at the Collège de France, 1–8.

Lescure, J. (1912). 'Hausse et baisse générale des prix'. *Revue d'Économie Politique*, 26: 452–90.

Lewis, W. A. (1978). *Growth and Fluctuations, 1870–1913*. London: Allen & Unwin.

List, F. (1841). *The National System of Political Economy* (English edn., London: Longman, 1904).

Little, A. D. (1963). *Patterns and Problems of Technical Innovation in American Industry*. Washington: USGPO.

Lloyd-Jones, R. and Lewis, M. J. (1998). *British Industrial Capitalism since the Industrial Revolution*. London: UCL Press.

Lo, A. (1991). 'Long-Term Memory in Stock Market Prices'. *Econometrica*, 59: 1279–313.

Louçã, F. (1997). *Turbulence in Economics: An Evolutionary Appraisal of Cycles and Complexity in Historical Processes*. Cheltenham: Edward Elgar.

——(1999). 'Nikolai Kondratiev and the Early Consensus and Dissensions about History and Statistics'. *History of Political Economy*, 31/1: 169–205.

——(2000). 'Intriguing Pendula'. *Cambridge Journal of Economics*.

——and Mendonça, S. (1999). 'Steady Change: the 200 Largest US Manufacturing Firms in the Twentieth Century'. Working Paper No. 14/99, CISEP–ISEG, UTL, Lisbon.

——and Reijnders, J. (1999). *The Foundations of Long Wave Theory* (2 vols.), International Library of Critical Writings in Economics. Cheltenham: Edward Elgar.

Lucas, R. (1980). 'Methods and Problems in Business Cycle Theory'. *Journal of Money, Credit and Banking*, 12: 696–715.

McCloskey, D. (1978). 'The Achievements of the Cliometric School'. *Journal of Economic History*, 38/1: 13–28.

——(1985). 'The Industrial Revolution 1780–1860: A Survey'. In J. Mokyr (ed.), *The Economics of the Industrial Revolution*. London: Allen & Unwin, 53–74.

——(1991). 'History, Differential Equations, and the Problem of Narration'. *History and Theory*, 30: 21–36.

McCloskey, D. and Nansen, D. (1987). *Econometric History: Studies in Economic and Social History*. Basingstoke: Macmillan.

McCracken Report (1977). *Towards Full Employment and Price Stability*. Paris: OECD.

Machlup, F. (1951). 'Schumpeter's Economic Methodology'. In S. Harris (ed.), *Schumpeter: Social Scientist*. Cambridge, Mass.: Harvard University Press, 95–101.

Mackay, J. (1997). *Little Boss: A Life of Andrew Carnegie*. Edinburgh: Mainstream Publishing.

Mackintosh, I. M. (1978). 'Large-scale Integration: Intercontinental Aspects'. *IEEE Spectrum*, June: 53.

Maclaurin, W. R. (1949). *Invention and Innovation in the Radio Industry*. London: Macmillan.

MacLeod, C. (1988). *Inventing the Industrial Revolution: The English Patent System, 1600–1800*. Cambridge: Cambridge University Press.

Macleod, R. M. (1977). 'Education, Scientific and Technical'. In G. Sutherland (ed.), *Government and Society in Nineteenth Century Britain: Commentaries on British Parliamentary Papers*. Dublin: Irish Universities Press, 196–225.

McNeil, I. (ed.) (1990). *An Encylopaedia of the History of Technology*. London: Routledge.

Maddison, A. (1980) 'Western Economic Performance in the 1970s'. *Banco Nazionale del Lavoro Quarterly Review*, 134: 247–89.

——(1991). *Dynamic Forces in Capitalist Development: A Long-Run Comparative View*. Oxford: Oxford University Press.

Maizels, A. (1963). *Industrial Growth and World Trade*. Cambridge: Cambridge University Press.

Mandel, E. (1964). 'L'Apogée du néo-capitalisme et ses lendemains'. *Temps Modernes*, 219–20: 193–210.

——(1979). *Les Ondes longues de la conjoncture: essai d'explication marxiste*. Brussels: Société Royale d'Économie Politique de Belgique.

——(1980). *Long Waves of Capitalist Development*. Cambridge: Cambridge University Press.

——(1975). *Late Capitalism*. London: Verso.

Mandelbrot, B. (1987). 'Towards a Second Stage of Indeterminism in Science'. *Interdisciplinary Science Reviews*, 12: 117–27.

Mann, J. L. (1958). 'The Textile Industry: Machinery for Cotton, Flax, Wool'. In *A History of Technology*, iv. Oxford: Oxford University Press, 277–308.

Mansell, R. (2000). 'Knowledge and the Internet: The End of Control?' *Intermedia*, 28/2: 43–46.

——and Wehn, U. (1998). *Knowledge Societies, Information Technology for Sustainable Development*. New York: UN/OUP.

Marais, E. (1975). *The Soul of the White Ant*. Harmondsworth: Penguin.

Marchetti, C. (1988). ' Kondratiev Revisited: After One Kondratiev Cycle'. Paper presented to the International Conference on Regularities of Scientific–Technical Progress and Long-Term Tendencies of Economic Development, Novosibirsk. Mimeo, IIASA. Laxenberg.

——(1993). *Predicting Recession*. Mimeo, IIASA, Laxenberg.

Marglin, S. (1974). 'What Do Bosses Do?' *Review of Radical Political Economy*, 6: 60–112.

Marshall, A. (1890). *Principles of Economics: An Introductory Volume*. New York: Macmillan (incl. the 1898 preface).

Marshall, M. (1987). *Long Waves of Regional Development*. London: Macmillan.

Martin, M. (2000). '"Fed No Longer Targets Stock Prices", Greenspan says', *International Herald Tribune*, 26 July: 13.

Marx, K. (1867*a*). *Capital: A Critical Analysis of Capitalist Production*. London: Sonnerschein (1938 edn, London: Allen & Unwin).

——(1867*b*, 1885, and 1894). *Le Capital: Critique de l'Économie Politique*, 3 vols. Paris: Editions Sociales, 1977.

Mass, W. and Lazonick, W. (1990). 'The British Cotton Industry and International Competitive Advantage: The State of the Debates'. Columbia University Working Paper No. 90-06, New York: Department of Economics, April.

Mathias, P. (ed.) (1969). *The First Industrial Nation: An Economic History of Britain, 1700–1914*. Cambridge: Cambridge University Press; 2nd edn. London: Methuen, 1983.

Matthews, R. C. O., Feinstein, C., and Odling-Smee, J. C. (1982). *British Economic Growth 1856–1973*. Oxford: Clarendon Press.

Mazzucato, M. (1998). 'A Computational Model of Economics of Scale and Market Share Instability'. *Structural Change and Economic Dynamics*, 9: 55–83.

Mead, M. (1962). *Sex and Temperament in Primitive Societies*. New York: Dell.

Meadows, D. H., Meadows, D. L., Randers, J., and Behrens, W. W. (1972). *The Limits to Growth*. New York: Universe Books.

Menne, B. (1937). *Krupp*. London: William Hodge.

Mensch, G. (1975). *Das Technologische Patt*. Frankfurt: Umschau.

Menshikov, S. (1987). 'Structural Crisis as a Phase in Long-Term Economic Fluctuations'. In T. Vasko (ed.), *The Long Wave Debate: Selected Papers*. Berlin: Springer-Verlag, 66–75.

——and Klimenko, L. (1985). 'On Long Waves in the Economy', in G. Bianchi, G. Bruckmann, J. Delbeke, and T. Vasko (eds.), *Long Waves, Depression, and Innovation: Implications for National and Regional Economic Policy*, CP-85-009. Laxenburg: IIASA, 75–102.

Metz, R. (1987). 'Kondratieff and the Theory of Linear Filters'. In T. Vasko (ed.), *The Long Wave Debate: Selected Papers*. Berlin: Springer-Verlag, 390–404.

——(1992). 'A Re-Examination of Long Waves in Aggregate Production Series'. In A. Kleinknecht, E. Mandel, and I. Wallerstein (eds.), *New Findings in Long Wave Research*. New York: St Martin's Press, 80–119.

Meyer, J. and Conrad, A. (1957). 'Economic Theory, Statistical Inference, and Economic History'. *Journal of Economic History*, 17: 524–44

Mini, P. (1991). *Keynes, Bloomsbury and the General Theory*. London: Macmillan.

Mishina, K. (1999). 'Learning by New Experiences: Revisiting the Flying Fortress Learning Curve'. In N. R. Lamoreaux, D. M. G. Raff, and P. Temin (eds.), *Learning by Doing in Markets, Firms and Countries*. Chicago: University of Chicago Press, 145–84.

Mitchell, B. R. (1978). *European Historical Statistics*. London: Macmillan.

——(1981). *United States Historical Statistics*. Washington: USGPO.

——(1983). *American Historical Statistics*. London: Macmillan.

——(1988). *British Historical Statistics*. Cambridge: Cambridge University Press.

——and Deane, P. (1962). *Abstract of British Historical Statistics*. Cambridge: Cambridge University Press.

Mitchell, W. (1956). *Business Cycles: The Problem and its Settings*. New York: NBER (first published 1927).

Modelski, G, and Thompson, R. (1988). *Seapower in Global Politics, 1494–1993*. London: Macmillan.

Mokyr, J. (1985/1993). 'Editor's Introduction: The New Economic History and the Industrial Revolution'. In J. Mokyr (ed.), *The British Industrial Revolution: An Economic Perspective*. Boulder, Colo.: Westview Press, 1–131.

Mokyr, J. (1994a). 'Demand versus Supply in the Industrial Revolution'. In J. Hoppit and E. A. Wrigley (eds.), *The Industrial Revolution in Britain*, iii. Oxford: Blackwell, 389–418.

——(1994b). 'Technological Change, 1700–1830'. In R. Flood and D. N. McCloskey (eds.), *The Economic History of Britain since 1700*. Cambridge: Cambridge University Press.

Molina, A. H. (1989). *Transputers and Parallel Computers: Building Technological Competencies through Socio-technical Constituencies*, PICT Paper 7. Edinburgh: Research Centre for Social Services.

Morgan, M. (1990). *The History of Econometric Ideas*. Cambridge: Cambridge University Press.

Mosekilde, E. and Sterman, J. (n.d.), 'Business Cycles and Long Waves: A Behavioural Disequilibrium Perspective'. Mimeo, Aalborg University.

——Rasmussen, S., and Zebrowski, M. (1987). 'Techno-economic Succession and the Economic Long Wave'. In T. Vasko (ed.), *The Long Wave Debate: Selected Papers*. Berlin: Springer-Verlag, 257–73.

——Larsen, E., Sterman, J., and Thomsen, J. (1992). 'Nonlinear Mode–Interaction in the Macroeconomy'. *Annals of Operations Research*, 37: 185–215.

Mott, R. A. (1983). *Henry Cort, the Great Finer: Creator of Puddled Iron*. London: Metals Society in association with the Historical Metallurgy Society.

Muchie, M. (1986). 'Capitalist Technology and Socialist Development'. D.Phil. thesis, University of Sussex.

Musson, A. E. (1980). 'The Engineering Industry'. In R. Church (ed.), *The Dynamics of Victorian Business*. London: Allen & Unwin, 87–107.

——and Robinson, E. (1969). *Science and Technology in the Industrial Revolution*. Manchester: Manchester University Press.

Nakicenovic, N. and Grübler, A. (eds.) (1991). *Diffusion of Technologies and Social Behaviour*. Berlin: Springer-Verlag.

Needham, J. (1954). *Science and Civilisation in China*. Cambridge: Cambridge University Press.

Nelson, D. (1980). *Frederick W. Taylor and the Rise of Scientific Management*. Madison, Wis.: University of Wisconsin Press.

Nelson, R. (1995). 'Recent Evolutionary Theorizing about Economic Change'. *Journal of Economic Literature*, 32/1: 48–90.

——(1998). 'The Agenda for Growth Theory: A Different Point of View'. *Cambridge Journal of Economics*, 22: 497–520.

——and Winter, S. G. (1977). 'In Search of a Useful Theory of Innovation'. *Research Policy*, 6/1: 36–76.

Netherlands Scientific Council for Government Policy (1999). *Governments Losing Ground: An Exploration of Administrative Consequences of ICT*, Report to the Government No. 54, The Hague: NSCGP.

North, D. C. (1965). 'Economic History: Its Contributions to Economic Education, Research and Policy—The State of Economic History'. *American Economic Review*, 55/2: 86–91.

——(1966). *The Economic Growth of the United States, 1790–1869*. New York: W. W. Norton.

——(1978a). 'Comment'. *Journal of Economic History*, 38/1: 77–80.

——(1978b). 'Structure and Performance: The Task of Economic History'. *Journal of Economic Literature*, 16: 963–78.

——(1990). *Institutions, Institutional Change and Economic Performance*. Cambridge: Cambridge University Press.

Nye, D. E. (1990). *Electrifying America: Social Meanings of a New Technology*. Cambridge, Mass.: MIT Press.

Oakley, A. (1990). *Schumpeter's Theory of Capitalist Motion: A Critical Exposition and Reassessment*. Aldershot: Edward Elgar.

O'Brien, P. K. (1994). 'Transport and Economic Development in Europe, 1789–1914'. In P. K. O'Brien (ed.), *The Industrial Revolution in Europe*, iv. Oxford: Blackwell/ Economic History Society, 253–81.

O'Donnell, R. (1989). *Keynes' Philosophy, Economics and Politics: The Philosophical Foundations of Keynes' Thought and their Influence on his Economics and Politics*. London: Macmillan.

OECD (1977). *Towards Full Employment and Price Stability*. (McCracken Report). Paris: OECD.

——(1981). *The Measurement of Scientific and Technical Activities*. Paris: Directorate for Scientific Affairs, OECD.

——(1982). *Science and Technology in the New Economic Context*. Paris: OECD.

——(1993). *Employment Outlook*. Paris: OECD.

OTA (1983). *International Competitiveness in Electronics*, OTA-ISC-200. Washington, DC: US Congress, Office of Technology Assessment, November.

Overy, R. J. (1975). 'Cars, Roads and Economic Recovery in Germany, 1932–8'. *Economic History Review*, 28: 466–83.

Oxford History (1958). *Oxford History of Technology*, iv, v. Oxford: Oxford University Press.

Pareto, V. (1916). 'Quelques exemples d'application des méthodes d'interpolation à la statistique'. *Journal de la Société de Statistiques de Paris*, 2–21.

Parvus (1901). 'Die Handelskrisen und die Gewerkschaften'. in Parvus *et al.*, *Die Langen Wellen der Konjunktur: Beitrage zur Marxistischen Konjunktur und Krisentheorie*. Berlin: Prinkipo, 1972, 25–31.

Patel, P. and Pavitt, K. (1994). 'The Continuing, Widespread (and Neglected) Importance of Improvements in Mechanical Technologies'. *Research Policy*, 23: 533–46.

Paulinyi, A. (1989). *Industrielle Revolution vom Ursprung der modernen Technik*, Deutsches Museum. Hamburg: Rowohlt, 66, 90.

Pavitt, K. (1985). 'Technology Transfer among Industrially Advanced Countries: An Overview'. In N. Rosenberg and C. Frischtak (eds.), *International Technology Trends*. New York: Praeger.

——(1986). 'Chips and Trajectories: How Does the Semiconductor Influence the Sources and Directions of Technical Change?' In R. Macleod (ed.), *Technology and the Human Prospect*. London: Pinter, 31–54.

——(1995). 'Academic Research and Technical Change'. In J. Krige and D. Pestre (eds.), *Science in the 20th Century*. Amsterdam: Harwood Academic, 143–58.

Pearl, M. L. (1978). 'The Iron and Steel Industry'. In T. L. Williams (ed.), *History of Technology*, vi. Oxford: Clarendon Press, 462–99.

Peck, J. and Goto, A. (1981). 'Technology and Economic Growth: The Case of Japan'. *Research Policy*, 10: 222–43.

Péguy, C. (1932). *Clio*. Paris: Gallimard.

Perez, C. (1983). 'Structural Change and the Assimilation of New Technologies in the Economic and Social System'. *Futures*, 15: 357–75.

——(1985). 'Micro-electronics, Long Waves and World Structural Change'. *World Development*, 13: 441–63.

——(1988). 'New Technologies and Development'. In C. Freeman and B-A. Lundvall (eds.), *Small Countries facing the Technological Revolution*. London: Pinter, 85–97.

Perez, C. (1989). 'Technical Change, Competitive Restructuring and Institutional Reform in Developing Countries, Strategic Planning and Review', Discussion Paper No. 4. Washington: World Bank.

——(2000). 'Technological Revolutions, Paradigm Shifts and Socio-Institutional Change'. In E. Reinert (ed.), *Evolutionary Economics and Income Equality*. Aldershot: Edward Elgar.

——and Soete, L. (1988). 'Catching Up in Technology: Entry Barriers and Windows of Opportunity'. In G. Dosi *et al.* (eds.), *Technical Change and Economic Theory*. London: Pinter, 458–79.

Pietri-Tonelli, A. (1911). 'Le Onde economiche'. *Rivista Italiana di Sociologia*, 15: 220–5.

Poletayev, A. V. (1987). 'Profits and Long Waves'. Paper presented at Long Wave Workshop, Montpellier, July.

——(1992). 'Long Wave in Profit Rates in Four Countries'. In A. Kleinknecht, E. Mandel, and I. Wallerstein (eds.), *New Findings in Long Wave Research*. New York: St Martin's Press, 151–68.

Poon, A. (1993). *Tourism, Technology and Competitive Strategies*. Wallingford: Citizens' Advice Bureau.

Popper, K. (1963). *Conjectures and Refutations: In Growth of Scientific Knowledge*. London: Routledge.

Porter, G. (1973). *The Rise of Big Business, 1860–1910*. Arlington Heights, Va.: AHM Publishers.

Price, D. de Solla (1984). 'The Science–Technology Relationship'. *Research Policy*, 13/1: 3–20.

Radosevic, S. (1999). *International Technology Transfer and Catch-up in Economic Development*. Cheltenham: Edward Elgar.

Ransom, P. J. G. (1990). *The Victorian Railway and How it Evolved*. London: Heinemann.

Rasmussen, S., Mosekilde, E., and Holst, J. (1989). 'Empirical Indication of Economic Long Waves in Aggregate Production'. *European Journal of Operational Research*, 42: 279–93.

Redlich, F. (1965). '"New" and Traditional Approaches to Economic History and their Interdependence'. *Journal of Economic History*, 25: 480–95.

Reijnders, J. (1990). *Long Waves in Economic Development*. Aldershot: Edward Elgar.

——(1992). 'Between Trends and Trade Cycles: Kondratieff Long Waves Revisited'. In A. Kleinknecht, E. Mandel, and I. Wallerstein (eds.), *New Findings in Long Wave Research*. New York: St Martin's Press, 15–44.

Reinert, E. S. (1997). 'The Role of the State in Economic Growth', Working Paper No. 1997–5. Oslo: SUM University of Oslo.

Reisch, G. (1991). 'Chaos, History and Narrative'. *History and Theory*, 30: 1–20.

——(1995). 'Scientism without Tears: A Reply to Roth and Ryckman'. *History and Theory*, 34/1: 45–58.

Riden, P. J. (1980). 'The Iron Industry'. In R. Church (ed.), *The Dynamics of Victorian Business*. London: Allen & Unwin, 63–87.

Robb, A. M. (1958). 'Ship-building'. In *Oxford History of Technology*, v. Oxford: Clarendon Press, 350–91.

Romer, P. (1992). 'Two Strategies for Economic Development: Using Ideas and Producing Ideas'. *Proceedings of the World Bank Annual Conference on Development Economics*. Washington: International Bank for Reconstruction and Development, (World Bank).

Rosenberg, H. (1976). *Grosse Depression und Bismarckzeit*. Frankfurt: Ullstein Buch.

Rosenberg, N. (1963). 'Technological Change in the Machine Tool Industry'. *Journal of Economic History* 23: 414–43.

——(1969). 'Directions of Technological Change: Inducement Mechanisms and Focusing Devices'. *Economic Developments and Cultural Change*, 18: 1–24.

——(1974). 'Science, Inventions and Economic Growth'. *Economic Journal*, 100: 725–9.

——(1976). *Perspectives on Technology*. New York: Cambridge University Press.

——(1982). *Inside the Black Box: Technology and Economics*. Cambridge: Cambridge University Press.

——(1994). 'Joseph Schumpeter: Radical Economist'. In Y. Shionoya and M. Perlman (eds.), *Schumpeter in the History of Ideas*. Ann Arbor: University of Michigan Press, 41–57.

Rosier, B. and Dockès, P. (1983). *Rhythmes économiques: crises et changement social, une perspective historique*. Paris: La Découverte.

Rostow, W. W. (1948). *The British Economy of the Nineteenth Century*. Oxford: Clarendon.

——(1957). 'The Interrelation of Theory and Economic History'. *Journal of Economic History*, 17: 509–23.

——(1960). *The Stages of Economic Growth: A Non-Communist Manifesto*. Cambridge: Cambridge University Press.

——(ed.) (1963). *The Economics of Take-off into Sustained Growth*. London: Macmillan.

——(1971). 'The Strategic Role of Theory: a Commentary'. *Journal of Economic History*, 31: 76–86.

Roth, P. and Ryckman, T. (1995). 'Chaos, Clio and Scientific Illusions of Understanding'. *History and Theory*, 34/1: 30–44.

Round, R. (2000). 'Time for Tobin'. *The New Internationalist*, January–February: 19–20.

Salvati, M. (1984). 'Political Business Cycles and Long Waves in Industrial Relations: Notes on Kalecki and Phelps Brown'. In C. Freeman (ed.), *Long Waves in the World Economy*. London: Pinter, 202–24.

Samuels, W. and Makasheva, N. (eds.) (1998). *The Works of Nikolai D. Kondratiev*. London: Pickering & Chatto.

Samuelson, P. A. (1947). *Foundations of Economic Analysis*. Cambridge, Mass.: Harvard University Press.

——(1951). 'Schumpeter as a Teacher and Economic Theorist'. In S. Harris (ed.), *Schumpeter: Social Scientist*. Cambridge, Mass.: Harvard University Press, 48–53.

——(1983). *Fundamentos da Análise Económica*. São Paulo: Abril.

Saul, S. B. (1969). *The Myth of the Great Depression*, Economic History Society. London: Macmillan.

Savage, C. I. (1959). *Economic History of Transport*. London: Hutchinson.

Schabas, M. (1995). 'Parmenides and the Cliometricians'. In D. Little (ed.), *On the Reliability of Economic Models: Essays in the Philosophy of Economics*. Boston: Kluwer, 183–202.

Schubert, H. R. (1958). 'Extraction and Production of Metals: Iron and Steel'. In *A History of Technology*. Oxford: Oxford University Press.

Schumpeter, J. (1906). 'Professor Clark Verteilungstheorie'. *Zeitschrift für Volkswirtschaft, Sozialpolitik und Verwaltung*, 15: 325–33.

——(1908). *Das Wesen und der Hauptinhalt der Theortischen Nationalökonomie*. Munich and Leipzig: Duncker & Humblot.

——(1911). *Theorie der wirtschaftlichen Entwicklung*. Leipzig: Duncker & Humblot. (English trans. *Theory of Economic Development: An Inquiry Into Profits, Capital, Credit, Interest, and the Business Cycle*. Cambridge, Mass.: Harvard University Press, 1934; Spanish trans. *Teoria do Desenvolvimento Económico: Uma Investigação sobre Lucros, Capital, Crédito, Juro e o Ciclo Económico*. Sao Paulo: Abril, 1982) (referred to in the text as *TED*).

Schumpeter, J. A. (1914). *Economic Doctrines and Method: A Historical Sketch* (referred to in the text as *EDM*). New York: Oxford University Press, 1954.

——(1926). 'Gustav v. Schmoller und die Probleme von heute'. *Schmollers Jahrbuch für Gesetzgebung, Verwaltung und Voltswirtschaft*, 50: 337–88.

——(1927). 'The Explanation of the Business Cycle'. *Economica*, 7: 286–311.

——(1930). 'Mitchell's Business Cycles'. *Quarterly Journal of Economics*, 45: 150–72.

——(1933). 'The Common Sense of Econometrics'. *Econometrica*, 1/1: 5–12.

——(1935). 'The Analysis of Economic Change'. *Review of Economic Statistics*, 17/4: 2–10.

——(1936). Review of Keynes's *General Theory*. *Journal of the American Statistical Association*, 31: 791–5.

——(1937). Preface to the Japanese edition of 'Theorie der Wirtschaftlichen Entwicklung'. In Schumpeter (1951: 158–63).

——(1939). *Business Cycles: A Theoretical, Historical and Statistical Analysis of the Capitalist Process* (referred to in the text as *BC*) 2 vols. New York: McGraw-Hill.

——(1941). Introduction to the Spanish edition of *Theory of Economic Development*, in *TED*. Mexico City: Fondo de Cultura Economica, 1944: 9–15.

——(1942). *Capitalism, Socialism and Democracy* (referred to in the text as *CSD*). London: Unwin University Books, 1974.

——(1949). 'The Historical Approach to the Analysis of Business Cycles'. In Schumpeter (1951: 308–15).

——(1951). *Essays on Economic Topics of Joseph Allois Schumpeter*, ed. R. Clemence. New York: Kennikat Press.

——(1952). 'The General Economist'. In A. F. Burns (ed.), *Wesley Clair Mitchell: The Economic Scientist*, General Series (NBER) No. 53. New York: National Bureau of Economic Research, 321–40.

——(1954). *History of Economic Analysis* (referred to in the text as *HEA*). London: Routledge, 1994.

——(1990). *Diez Grandes Economistas: De Marx a Keynes* (referred to in the text as *TGE*). Madrid: Alianza Editorial.

Scitovsky, T. (1976). *The Joyless Economy: An Inquiry into Human Satisfaction and Consumer Dissatisfaction*. Oxford: Oxford University Press.

Screpanti, E. (1984). 'Long Economic Cycles and Recurring Proletarian Insurgencies'. *Review*, 7: 509–48.

Sejerstedt, F. (1998). 'An Old Production Method Mobilizes for Self-defence'. In M. Berg and K. Bruland (eds.), *Technological Revolutions in Europe: Historical Perspective*. Cheltenham: Edward Elgar, 230–41.

Shaikh, A. (1992). 'The Falling Rate of Profit as the Cause of Long Waves: Theory and Empirical Evidence'. In A. Kleinknecht, E. Mandel, and I. Wallerstein (eds.), *New Findings in Long Wave Research*. New York: St Martin's Press, 174–95.

Shiller, R. J. (2000). *Irrational Exuberance*. Princeton: Princeton University Press.

Siemens, G. (1957). *History of the House of Siemens*, 2 vols. Freiburg and Munich: Karl Alber.

Silverberg, G. (1985). 'Oral Comments'. In G. Bianchi, G. Bruckmann, J. Delbeke, and T. Vasko (eds.), *Long Waves, Depression, and Innovation: Implications for National and Regional Economic Policy*, CP-85-009. Laxenburg: IIASA, 273–5.

Simonetti, R. (1994). 'Creative Destruction among Large Firms: An Analysis of the Changes in the *Fortune* List, 1963–1987'. D.Phil. thesis, University of Sussex.

Sloan, A. (1963). *My Years with General Motors*. New York: Doubleday.

Slutsky, E. (1937). 'The Summation of Random Causes as the Source of Cyclical Processes'. *Economtrica*, 5: 105–46.

Smith, A. (1776). *The Wealth of Nations*. London: Dent, 1904.

Smith, V. (1991). 'Rational Choice: The Contrast Between Economics and Psychology'. *Journal of Political Economy*, 99: 877–97.

Soete, L. L. G. and Kamp, K. (1996). 'The "Bit Tax": The Case for Further Research'. *Science and Public Policy*, 23: 353–60.

Sohn-Rethel, A. (1978). *Economy and Class Structure of German Fascism*. London: CSE Books.

Solo, R. (1980). *Across the High Technology Threshold: The Case of Synthetic Rubber*. Norwood. Pa.: Norwood Editions.

Solomou, S. (1987). *Phases of Economic Growth 1850–1973: Kondratieff Waves and Kuznets' Swings*. Cambridge: Cambridge University Press.

Sombart, W. (1929). 'Economic Theory and Economic History'. *Economic History Review*, 2 (January): 18.

Stankiewicz, R. (2000). 'The Concept of Design Space' in J. Ziman (ed.), *Technological Innovation as an Evolutionary Process*. Cambridge: Cambridge University Press, 234–48.

Sterman, J. (1987). 'The Economic Long Wave: Theory and Evidence'. In T. Vasko (ed.), *The Long Wave Debate: Selected Papers*. Berlin: Springer-Verlag, 127–61.

——(1988). 'Non-linear Dynamics in the World Economy: The Economic Long Wave'. In P. Christiansen and R. Parmentier (eds.), *Structure, Coherence and Chaos in Dynamical Systems*. Manchester: Manchester University Press, 384–424.

Stigler, G. (1969). 'The Statistics of Monopoly and Merger'. In D. R. Kamerschen (ed.), *Readings in Microeconomics*. Chichester: John Wiley, 332–43; reprinted from *Journal of Political Economy*, February 1956.

Stolper, W. (1984). Review of *The Long Wave Debate* [by] N. Kondratiev. *Journal of Economic Literature*, 22: 1647–9.

Streissler, E. (1994). 'The Influence of German and Austrian Economics on Joseph A. Schumpeter'. In Y. Shionoya and M. Perlman (eds.), *Schumpeter in the History of Ideas*. Ann Arbor: University of Michigan Press, 13–38.

Supple, B. (1963). *The Experience of Economic Growth: Case Studies in Economic History*. New York: Random House.

Sutch, R. (1982). 'Douglass North and the New Economic History'. In R. Ransom, R. Sutch, and G. Walton (eds.), *Explorations in the New Economic History: Essays in Honor of Douglass North*. New York/London: Academic, 13–38.

Swedberg, R. (1991). *Economics and Sociology. Redefining their Boundaries: Conversations with Economists and Sociologists*. Princeton: Princeton University Press.

Tamura, S. (1986). *Reverse Engineering: A Characteristic of Japanese Industrial R&D Activities*. Tokyo: Saitama University.

Tawney, R. H. (1926). *Religion and the Rise of Capitalism*. Harmondsworth: Penguin, 1936.

Taylor, J. (1988). 'The Trouble with Cycles: A Reply to Brill'. *Review*, 11: 413–32.

Tell, F. (2000). 'Organizational Capabilities: A Study of Electrical Power Business Equipment Manufacturers, 1878–1990'. D.Phil. thesis, Linköping University.

Temin, P. (1976). *Did Monetary Factors Cause the Great Depression?* New York: W. W. Norton.

——(1997). 'The Golden Age of European Growth: A Review Essay'. *European Journal of Economic History*, 1: 127–49.

Thompson, E. P. (1963). *The Making of the English Working Class*. London: Gollancz.

——(1967). 'Time and Discipline and Industrial Capitalism'. *Past and Present*, 38: 56–97.

——(1994). 'Time, Work Discipline and Industrial Capitalism'. In J. Hoppit and E. A. Wrigley (eds.), *The Industrial Revolution in Britain*, iii. Oxford: Blackwell, 448–91.

Tilton, J. (1971). *International Diffusion of Technology: The Case of Semi-Conductors*. Washington: Brookings Institution.

Tinbergen, J. (1929). Review of de Wolff's *Het Economisch Getij*. *De Economist*, 2–31.

——(1951). 'Schumpeter and Quantitative Research in Economics'. In S. Harris (ed.), *Schumpeter: Social Scientist*. Cambridge, Mass.: Harvard University Press, 59–61.

Tobin, J. (1987). 'Irving Fisher'. In J. Eatwell, M. Milgate, and P. K. Newman (eds.), *The New Palgrave: A Dictionary of Economics*, ii. Basingstoke: Macmillan, 369–77.

Todorov, T. (1990). *A Conquista da América: A Questão do Outro*. Lisbon: Litoral.

Toporowski, J. (2000). *The End of Finance: Capital Market Inflation, Financial Derivatives and Pension Fund Capitalism*. London: Routledge.

Trotsky, L. (1921). 'Report on the World Economic Crisis and the New Tasks for the Communist International'. In L. Trotsky, *The First Five Years of the Communist International*, i. London: New Park, 226–78.

——(1923). 'A Curva do Desenvolvimento Capitalista'. In L. Trotsky and C. Leucate, *A Curva do Desenvolvimento Capitalista*. Lisbon: Delfos, 7–22.

Tugan-Baranowsky, M. (1901). *Theorie und Geschichte der Handelskrisen in England*. Jena: Fisher.

Turgenev, I. (1867/1914). *Smoke* (in Russian); English trans. London: Heinemann, 1914.

Turing, A. (1952). 'The Chemical Basis of Morphogenesis'. *Philosophical Transactions of the Royal Society of London*, 237/B641: 37–72.

Tweedale, G. (1987). *Sheffield Steel and America: A Century of Technical and Commercial Interdependence, 1830–1930*. Cambridge: Cambridge University Press.

Tylecote, A. (1992). *The Long Wave in the World Economy: The Present Crisis in Historical Perspective*. London: Routledge & Kegan Paul.

Usselman, C. (1999). 'Patents, Engineering Professionals and the Pipelines of Innovation: The Internalization of Technical Discovery by Nineteenth-century American Railroads'. In N. R. Lamoreaux, D. M. G. Raff, and P. Temin (eds.), *Learning by Doing in Markets, Firms and Countries*. Chicago: NBER, University of Chicago Press, 61–91.

Utterback, J. M. (1993). *Mastering the Dynamics of Innovation*. Boston: Harvard Business School Press.

van Gelderen, J. (1913), 'Springvloed Baschouwingen over industrielle Outwikkalieng en prijsbeweging'. *De Nieuwe Tijd*,184/5 and 6 (English trans. in C. Freeman (ed.), *The Long Wave in the World Economy*, International Library of Critical Writings in Economics, Aldershot: Elgar, 1996, 3–56).

Varga, E. (1939). *Two Systems*. London: Lawrence & Wishart.

Volti, R. (1990). 'Why Internal Combustion?' *American Heritage of Invention and Technology*, Fall: 2–47.

von Bülow, B. (1914). *Imperial Germany*. London: Cassell.

van Riemsdijk, J. T. and Brown, K. (1980). *The Pictorial History of Steam Power*. London: Octopus Books.

van Roon, G. (1984). 'Historians and Long Waves'. In C. Freeman (ed.), *Long Waves in the World Economy*. London: Pinter, 237–44.

von Tunzelmann, G. N. (1978). *Steam Power and British Industrialization to 1860*. Oxford: Oxford University Press.

——(1981). 'Technical Progress during the Industrial Revolution'. In R. C. Floud and D. N. McCloskey (eds.), *Economic History of Britain since 1700*, i. Cambridge: Cambridge University Press, 143–64.

——(1990). 'Cliometrics and Technology'. *Structural Change and Economic Dynamics*, 1/2: 291–310.

——(1995*a*). *Technology and Industrial Progress: The Foundations of Economic Growth.* Aldershot: Edward Elgar.

——(1995*b*). 'Time-saving Technical Change: The Cotton Industry in the English Industrial Revolution'. *Explorations in Economic History*, 32: 1–27.

——and Soete, L. (1987). 'Diffusion and Market Structure with Converging Technologies'. Research Memorandum, University of Limburg, Maastricht.

——(1988). 'Convergence of Firms in Information and Communication: A Test Using Patent Data'. Mimeo, SPRU, University of Sussex.

Wadsworth, A. P. and Mann, J. de L. (1931). *The Cotton Trade and Industrial Lancashire.* Manchester: Manchester University Press.

Wallerstein, I. (1979). 'Kondratieff Up or Kondratieff Down'. *Review*, 2: 663–73.

Weber, M. (1922). *The Economy and Society*, 2 vols. Tubingen; English trans. Berkeley: University of California Press, 1978.

——(1930). *The Protestant Ethic and the Spirit of Capitalism.* London.

——(1949). *The Methodology of Social Sciences.* New York: Free Press.

Webster, C. (1975). 'The Great Instauration: Science, Medicine and Reform, 1620–1660'. *Oxford Review of Education*, 2: 201–13.

Weitz, J. (1997). *Hitler's Banker.* London: Little Brown.

Wells, D. A. (1890). *Recent Economic Changes.* London: Longmans, Green.

Wells, H. G. (1895). 'The Lord of the Dynamos'. In *The Complete Short Stories of H. G. Wells.* London: J. M. Dent, 1998, 71–8.

Wilson, C. (1955). 'The Entrepreneur in the Industrial Revolution in Britain'. *Explorations in Economic History*, 7/3: 129–45.

Wilson, T. (1948). *Fluctuations in Income and Employment with Special Reference to Recent American Experience.* London: Pitman.

Wise, T. A. (1966). 'IBM's $5,000,000,000 Gamble', *Fortune*, September: 118–23.

Womack, J. T., Jones, D. T., and Roos, D. (1990). *The Machine that Changed the World.* New York: Rawson Associates.

Woodman, H. (1972). 'Economic History and Economic Theory: The New Economic History in America'. *Journal of Interdisciplinary History*, 3: 323–50.

World Bank (1992). *World Development Report.* New York: Oxford University Press.

Wright, G. (1999). 'Can a Nation Learn? American Technology as a Network Phenomenon'. In N. R. Lamoreaux, D. M. G. Raff, and P. Temin (eds.), *Learning by Doing in Markets, Firms and Countries.* Chicago: NBER, University of Chicago Press, 295–326.

Wrigley, J. (1986). 'Technical Education and Industry in the Nineteenth Century'. In B. Elbaum and W. Lazonick (eds.), *The Decline of the British Economy.* Oxford: Clarendon Press, 162–88.

Wrigley, E. A. (1994). 'The Supply of Raw Materials in the Industrial Revolution'. In J. Hoppit and E. A. Wrigley (eds.), *The Industrial Revolution in Britain*, iii. Oxford: Blackwell, 91–108.

Yergin, D. (1991) *The Prize.* New York: Simon & Schuster.

Ziman, J. (ed.) (2000). *Technological Innovation as an Evolutionary Process.* Cambridge: Cambridge University Press.

INDEX